Understanding Deviance

*A Guide to the Sociology of Crime
and Rule-Breaking*

Seventh Edition

DAVID DOWNES

PAUL ROCK

EUGENE McLAUGHLIN

OXFORD

UNIVERSITY PRESS

OXFORD
UNIVERSITY PRESS

Great Clarendon Street, Oxford, OX2 6DP,
United Kingdom

Oxford University Press is a department of the University of Oxford.
It furthers the University's objective of excellence in research, scholarship,
and education by publishing worldwide. Oxford is a registered trade mark of
Oxford University Press in the UK and in certain other countries

Published in the United States of America by Oxford University Press
198 Madison Avenue, New York, NY 10016, United States of America

British Library Cataloguing in Publication Data
Data available

ISBN 978–0–19–874734–5

Outline Contents

Contents

Preface

When the first edition of *Understanding Deviance* was published in 1982, the sociology of crime and deviance was a confusing, argumentative, and fluid sub-discipline practised by sociologists who were themselves passionate and partisan. That was a commonplace enough condition in any new field, and its successor stage was also quite predictable. The sociology of crime and deviance is now but one part of not just sociology but perhaps more significantly criminology, but what remains may still be fairly difficult to comprehend because it bears the marks of all those earlier quarrels. Many books pretending to be disinterested guides are quite partial, acting, in effect, as press-gangs for preferred theoretical perspectives. What is offered as unbiased commentary may well have commitments and purposes which cannot competently be anticipated or judged by the novice.

The formidable array of American criminology texts remains parochial. Immense as the parish is, it does not exhaust the full range of theoretically significant work that constitutes the criminological imagination. Much British work of considerable theoretical interest continues to emerge, but it has been largely ignored by American (but not by Australian, Asian, Canadian, or European) researchers. By contrast, British texts, fewer in number, continue to be deferential to the major contributions of American theorists. *Understanding Deviance* has a modest objective. It is intended to familiarize the reader with the major themes of the major theories which define the sociology of crime and deviance. We have tried to present those themes as fairly as possible, explaining their history and development, sympathetically reproducing their more important arguments, identifying core concepts, interrogating core claims, offering criticisms, and recognizing lasting strengths.

We have worked within clearly defined boundaries, our selection of theories aiming very precisely to cover the underlying thought of the *sociology* of *crime* and *deviance*. Unlike many criminology textbooks, *Understanding Deviance* consequently does not include mini reviews of police studies, penology, criminal justice process or crime prevention, or every new form of crime and deviance (green crime, cyber-crime, etc.), and we do not privilege the newer theories of penality, governance, and surveillance. It is not concerned with criminal psychology although, inevitably, it recognizes the continuing importance of social psychology. And even within those boundaries, it has not proved feasible to discuss all the specific problems and propositions currently preoccupying the criminologist. Our own parochialism is evident in our greater acquaintance with British and North American theory and research than with those from other parts of the world. And it would be *faux naïf* to claim that we have attained the impartiality we have sought. As will become apparent, the intellectual orientation of *Understanding Deviance* lies within sociology, and with the still unfolding implications of the paradigm shift wrought by symbolic interactionism in particular, but we have tried to subdue such preferences in the interests of presenting all perspectives as fairly as possible. Within these limitations, we have examined the significant frameworks of the sub-discipline, drawing on a wide range of research findings, preparing the reader for the more detailed and focused arguments which may be found in journals and research monographs.

Building on the strengths of the previous editions, this edition has been rewritten to incorporate and clarify changes in theorizing. Portions of the sociology of deviance and crime have moved during the last few years, and we have registered what has happened by way of intellectual innovation. The discipline of criminology is buoyant in many parts of the world, and in Britain especially. Strangely it appears intellectually to be in retreat in the universities of the United States where policy- and practitioner-led criminal justice studies, correctional studies, police science, and homeland security studies are in the ascendant. To a notable degree, in the United States the sociology of deviance has become detached from criminology. Notable advances seem to have been made in the revitalization of anomie and strain theory and cultural perspectives on deviance, and there have been continuing developments in control theory (and in that theory's constituent arguments about opportunities, routine activities, and the life course), and theories of crime and gender. Further changes in this edition include: discussion of cultural and public criminology, while incorporating the intense debates around the legacy of past theorizing in the field and further commentary on the implications of the dramatic social changes associated with post-modernity and the risk society. We have also included a new chapter on victimology, analysing how once marginalized and even disparaged research on the victim-offender relationship is now revitalizing criminology. At the heart of *Understanding Deviance* remains the firm belief that the study of the social production of crime, deviance, and social control should retain a central place within the ever-expanding now global criminological imagination.

David Downes, Paul Rock, and Eugene McLaughlin.
London, 2016

New to this Edition

- Rethinking the legacy and relevance of past sociological theorizing in the field of crime and deviance.
- Discussion of the significance of the emergence of cultural, public, and global criminologies.
- Further clarification of the relationship between crime, crime control, and the 'risk society'.
- Fresh assessment of the applied policy relevance of academic theorizing.
- Discussion of the twenty-first century challenges facing criminology that places the much heralded fall in crime rate across most democratic and developed societies in perspective.
- A new chapter on victimology.

1

Theoretical Contexts: The Changing Nature and Scope of the Sociology of Crime and Deviance

Introduction

Criminological thought is premised upon potent theological, moral, and cultural belief systems and multi-disciplinary scientific investigation. The scientific study of crime and deviance has undergone remarkable transformation since the late 1990s. Most notably, criminology has come to be institutionally recognized in many jurisdictions as an independent academic discipline, defining its own research objectives, accumulating a body of specialist knowledge, inventing its own intellectual histories, developing theories and concepts capable of organizing the accumulated specialist knowledge, employing a specific technical language, and utilizing research methods appropriate to its research requirements. Increasingly, researchers are happy to identify themselves as criminologists or indeed crime scientists, criminal psychologists or penologists or terrorologists. The long-term consequences of this still unfolding disciplinary shift and demarcation are not clear, but it is more than a passing fad. The rapid institutionalization of criminology as a self-contained discipline within universities has had profound consequences for the academic disciplines—criminal law, psychology, and sociology—that historically laid claim to the study of crime and deviance as one their substantive sub-fields. Criminology is now an autonomous discipline of which, in theory, they are all constituent parts. This shift requires us to re-emphasize the distinctiveness of the sociological study of crime and deviance and the sociologically grounded criminological perspectives that it sustains.

The very title of the discipline which we shall describe, the sociology of crime and deviance, is a little misleading. A singular noun and a hint of science seem to promise a unified body of knowledge and an agreed set of procedures for resolving analytic difficulties. It suggests that the curious may secure sure answers to practical, political, moral, and intellectual problems. And, of all branches of applied sociology, the demands placed on the sociology of crime and deviance are probably the most urgent. Crime and deviance are upsetting and perplexing and confront people in many settings, but, turning to sociology, enquirers are rarely given certain advice. They are more likely to encounter something akin to the Tower of Babel. They will not be offered one answer but a series of competing and contradictory visions of the nature of human beings, deviation, and the social order. Very typically, they will be informed that their questions cannot even be discussed because they are not correctly phrased: they must first reconstruct their problem so that it can be placed with others in one of a number of master theories of crime and deviance.

The sociology of crime and deviance is not one coherent discipline at all but a collection of relatively independent versions of sociology. It is a common subject, not a common approach, which has given a tenuous unity to the enterprise. At different times, scholars with different backgrounds and different purposes have argued about rule-making and rule breaking. The outcome has been an accumulation of theories which only occasionally mesh. Since crime and deviance are strategic to all ideas of morality and politics, their explanation has been championed with great fervour. After all, substantial consequences can flow from the acceptance of a particular argument. The reader will be bombarded by grand claims and criticisms, propelled towards authoritative policy solutions and definitive approaches.[1] Few scholars have attempted to reveal all the uncertainties and complexities of their stance; many have simply avoided controversy or criticism; and others are openly partisan. And the result has been that textbooks are often poor guides. After a while, the reader is prone to become giddy, defeated, or prematurely committed to one position above others.

It is only through prolonged exposure to a mass of conflicting ideas that novices can stand back and understand what has been omitted, what questions have not been asked, what evidence has not been examined, and which assertions have not been challenged. Having been thus exposed, however, they can no longer be considered novices. At the outset, they are ill-equipped to judge the merits of an apparently persuasive work.

Understanding Deviance was written to answer some of these difficulties. We have prepared it as an intellectual framework in which the various sociological theories of crime and deviance can be set and assessed. It cannot be regarded as an entirely satisfactory substitute for the reader's own analysis. Yet it can provide an intellectual guide for someone who enters the labyrinth of crime and deviance for the first time.

We shall not pretend that the diverse sociological perspectives on crime and deviance can be reduced to a fundamental harmony. Most major theories stem, either directly or indirectly, from the three great taproots of the work of Émile Durkheim, Karl Marx, and Max Weber, fundamentally distinctive approaches which for the most part resist analytical synthesis. Yet, while antinomies abound, there *are* core preoccupations and methods which lend the sociology of crime and deviance a loose working consensus. Despite their disagreements, one sociologist can still recognize and talk to another. But the consensus is rudimentary and it is sensible to acknowledge disunity

---

[1] One recent example, advocated with evangelical zeal, declares of itself that 'Cultural criminology actively seeks to dissolve conventional understandings and accepted boundaries, whether they confine specific criminological theories or the institutionalized discipline of criminology itself . . . [Our] strategy of reinvigoration is as much historical as theoretical; if we are to engage critically with the present crisis in crime and control, intellectual revivification is essential.' J. Ferrell et al., *Cultural Criminology*, 5–6.

by reviewing the divergences which mark the discipline. Accordingly, this book will undertake a survey of each of the major schools of thought, not trying to pretend that they can be easily reconciled or ranked. We shall state those schools' assumptions in a fairly bald and pure form, marshal the doubts which others have voiced, and repeat or invent the replies of the schools' champions. Instead of defending one or other strain of the discipline, we shall simply parade different alternatives so that the whole may be better appreciated and organized by the reader. The reader, in turn, would do well to suspend final judgement about the worth of particular ideas until the whole conflicting array has been examined.

The very term 'theory' is a highly contestable concept. While not wishing to depart too far from the ground staked out by Karl Popper who, in a stream of work (1934 (1959), 1963)[2] propounded the case for falsifiability as the ultimate criterion of a scientific theory, one must acknowledge the myriad difficulties involved in stipulating the grounds for testing any particular theory. Popper's definition excluded from science not only what later became known as 'Creationism' but also Marxism and psychoanalysis: all by his canons share the incapacity to state the grounds on which they could be refuted. Popper was famously driven to his search for the principle of demarcation between 'science' and 'non-science' by the experience in his own lifetime of two murderous ideologies—Nazism and Stalinism—both of which laid claim to the mantle of science. Without wishing to enter into a history of the philosophy of science, it is worth noting that falsifiability, or refutability, takes both naïve and sophisticated forms[3] and too strict an adherence to the former can block fruitful inquiry at the outset. Nevertheless, it remains—at least as yet—the ultimate criterion of what should, and what should not, be given credence as scientific knowledge, whether of crime and deviance or any other phenomena.

The Character and Sources of Ambiguity

We have observed that the sociology of crime and deviance contains not one vision but many. It is a collection of different and rather independent theories. Each theory has its own history; it tends to be supported by a long train of arguments that reach into the foundational ideas of philosophy and politics; it discloses a number of distinct opportunities for explaining and manipulating crime and deviant behaviour; and, in the main, its assertions will be put in such a discrete language that they resist immediate comparison with rival arguments. Thus one intellectual faction, radical criminology, may speak of the social harms wrought by the institutions of an inherently criminogenic capitalist society. It will call crime and deviance rebellion and conformity collusion with the system. It will point to endemic contradictions and crises culminating, perhaps, in a society rid of all crime.[4] Another faction, control theory, will depict

---

[2] K. Popper, *The Logic of Scientific Discovery and Conjectures and Refutations*.
[3] I. Lakatos, 'Falsification and the Methodology of Scientific Research Programmes'.
[4] I. Taylor et al., *The New Criminology*; I. Taylor et al. (eds.), *Critical Criminology*.

institutional restraints as indispensable to a properly conducted society. Crime and deviance become a regression to a wilder state of man (or, less commonly, woman). Conformity is there taken to be a laudable achievement.[5] Yet another faction, functionalism, portrays deviance as an unrecognized and unintended buttress of social order, and what passes for disruption actually, and ironically, supplies control. The claim is made that seemingly harmful conduct really underpins and reinforces the conventional order. Prostitution, for instance, is held to preserve marriage.[6] Organized crime defuses political dissent and undermines social inequality.[7] Heresy may be used to defend religious orthodoxy.[8] It is not certain that those theories could be reconciled or integrated. On the contrary, they are embedded in opposing metaphysical beliefs which can be neither 'proved' nor 'disproved'. One embraces an image of human beings as once perfect, corrupted by the organization of a particular phase of society. Another retains the doctrine of original sin. The third makes the sum of individual transgressions a collective virtue.[9]

Such a lack of unity should not necessarily be regarded as a failing which ought to be remedied. Indeed, it is not entirely obvious what benefit would flow from an attempt to reconcile or rank such disparate ideas. For an exploration of the diversity of intellectual positions can be instructive. Confusion is an important phenomenon in itself and its very existence can emphasize special properties of deviance. One might conjecture that deviance would actually be a rather different process if people *did* agree on its constitution and significance. But people do *not* agree, and deviation might not be susceptible to a single definition and a single explanation.

On one level, it is quite possible that all that ambiguity and uncertainty are 'integral' characteristics of deviance. Some of the phenomena of everyday life are neatly arranged and classified. Others are not. And ambiguity does seem to be a crucial facet of rule-breaking. People are frequently undecided whether a particular episode *is* truly deviant or what true deviance is: their judgement depends on context, biography, and purpose. Behaviour can provoke discomfort in those who witness it, but not such a transparent response that they display no hesitation in defining it as wrong, sinful, or harmful. Many are prepared to tolerate *some* thievery (but from institutions and not an excessive amount),[10] *some* sexual transgression (if it is discreet and does not impinge on others),[11] or *some* unruliness (if it takes place on a licensed occasion or in a proper setting).[12] Very often, there is a reluctance to identify activity as deviant until alternative explanations are exhausted. Thus, in one study, wives preferred to attribute their husbands' misbehaviour to tiredness or strain. They were initially unwilling to accept a diagnosis of mental illness.[13]

If what David Matza called 'pluralism' and 'shifting standards'[14] work on deviant behaviour to render it ambiguous and fluid no one coherent and definitive argument can

---

[5] T. Hirschi, *Causes of Delinquency*; G. Nettler, *Explaining Crime*.   [6] K. Davis, 'Prostitution'.

[7] R. Merton, *Social Theory and Social Structure*.   [8] K. Erikson, *Wayward Puritans*.

[9] B. Mandeville, *The Fable of the Bees*.   [10] J. Ditton, *Part-Time Crime*.

[11] C. Sundholm, 'The Pornographic Arcade'.   [12] S. Cavan, *Liquor License*.

[13] M. Yarrow et al., 'The Psychological Meaning of Mental Illness in the Family'.

[14] D. Matza, *Becoming Deviant*, 12.

ever completely capture it. The sociologist may have to reconcile him or herself to the fact that logical and systematic schemes are not invariably mirrored in the 'structure' of the social world.

Life seems to be a combination of contradiction, contingency, paradox, and absurdity, so much so that some have even tried to accommodate logicality and illogicality together in a 'sociology of the absurd'.[15] And, because the analysis of deviance is intellectually inexhaustible, because there is always something new to be investigated in a new way, something will always have to be left out if argument is to remain parsimonious. One conclusion could be that the analytic possibilities of the sociology of crime and deviance can only begin to be realized when they draw on an abundance of discrepant ideas which no one theory can contain. As Bittner argues, it is impossible to predict and control all its implications:

> If we consider that we must so order our practical affairs as not to run afoul of a very considerable variety of standards of judgment that are not fully compatible with each other, do not have a clear-cut hierarchy of primacy and are regarded as binding and enforceable only in the light of additional vaguely denied information; if we consider that for every maxim of conduct we can think of a situation to which it does not apply or in which it can be overruled by a superior maxim; if we consider that unmitigated adherence to principle is regarded as vice or at least folly; . . . then it is clear that all efforts to live by an internally consistent scheme of interpretation are necessarily doomed to fail.[16]

In this view, the empirical reality of crime and deviance will always be messier than the social science that attempts to grasp it. To be sure, sociologists may argue that the appearances of everyday life are deceptive and that an internally consistent scheme could be found with the proper methodology. Scientific reason might illuminate deeper principles of organization which hide beneath the muddle of ordinary thinking about crime and deviance. Yet, as we have observed, there actually appears to be little concord amongst the sociologists themselves. Each may individually be decisive, but collectively there is great indecision and, in this sense, academic disputes suggest that members of the sociological profession are just as confused as common-sense thought. Of course, it is conceivable that the claims of one school *are* valid and that deviance is actually unambiguous when it is properly interpreted. It is also conceivable that there is no single truth.

And there is another matter. Just as an addict, a dealer, a judge, a psychiatrist, a police officer, and a campaigner may share no one perspective on the use of opiates, so different researchers face deviation in numerous guises and situations. Psychiatric knowledge may be adequate enough, but it may not solve all the practical problems of policing and criminal justice.[17] It would become the sole truth only if psychiatric issues were alone important. Similarly, functionalists' problems may not be the same as those of radical criminologists. Radicals might state that the problems *should* be the same, but functionalists are unlikely to be instantly persuaded. They could retort that the

---

[15] J. Douglas, 'The Experience of the Absurd and the Problem of Social Order'.

[16] E. Bittner, 'Radicalism and the Organization of Radical Movements', 934.

[17] A. von Hirsch, *Doing Justice*.

radicals are themselves misguided. More prosaically, sociologists interested in experimental random control tests might find radical criminology less relevant than other approaches. There might be questions about *what* they should investigate but, again, those questions would take one to a wider, non-empirical consideration of what ends theory should serve. A settlement of the argument would have to take the form of a conversion that would be more metaphysical than rational. Importantly, too, theorists and theories shape their own materials. It is not as if difficulties arose simply because radical and functionalist move about the same world with different problems. In some significant measure, they seem to act as if they do not inhabit one world at all. The social world can of course answer back, and there are limits to the diversity of appearances, but believing is often seeing.

Matters are yet further complicated because the sociology of crime and deviance itself does not and cannot house all that may be said about its subject, and those who search within it alone for answers to problems may find that they have missed much of value that lies outside. There are the necessary simplifications imposed by focusing on a few variables or ideas abstracted from a larger mass, but also the simplification of relying just on criminological analysis itself. Sociology proper—and political science, economics, law, anthropology, geography, psychology, and psychiatry—also have much that is useful to say about how crime, deviance, and control arise, and the search for answers begins to acquire indefinite proportions. We also need to acknowledge that investigative journalists have produced important studies of both crime and deviance and criminal justice agencies and practices.

In short, there may be no perfect position from which crime and deviance may be surveyed as it 'really is'. Neither need there be a simple test to discover the superiority of one approach. To be sure, the members of each intellectual perspective may hold that they occupy that still centre, concluding that they alone can see what is true and real. But not all those claims can be valid, there are many centres, and it is not our intention to ally ourselves with any one position for very long.

Crime and deviance cannot constitute a single problem with a single explanation. They are so significant that they have been forced to serve a multitude of purposes. Indeed, it seems as if almost all the contrasting styles of argument which abound in the larger world have been turned on deviance at some point, and each has imposed its own distinctive gloss. Each represents a separate way of seeing such conduct and each is a separate way of *not* seeing such conduct.[18] Together, they compose a great kaleidoscope of theorems. An examination of even one small part of that kaleidoscope is illuminating, demonstrating how deviance reflects the ambitions and visions of those who probe it, laying itself open to an extraordinary range of interpretations.

Take the links between crime and politics. Some sociologists, and certainly not all, would assert that crime and deviance are political phenomena.[19] After all, they are intimately connected with the exercise of State power and the application of legal rules and

---

[18] K. Burke, *A Grammar of Motives*, pt. 1, ch. 2, 'Antinomies of Definition'.

[19] For a fuller discussion of the links between the State and different groups in the domain of political crime, see W. J. Chambliss and R. Michalowski, *State Crime in the Global Age*.

criminal sanctions.[20] But they would not agree on the consequences of that assertion. To a number, crime and deviance pose a series of questions about how best to organize the practical management of social problems. Useful knowledge is shaped by the need to formulate policy. Thus, Clarke and Cornish, Wilson, and Felson dismiss all those theories that make no explicit contribution to the business of preventing or controlling crime and deviance. Theorizing which offers no assistance to the legislator, policy-maker, and practitioner is cast as fanciful and irrelevant, mere speculation without apparent purpose, utility, or responsibility.[21] Others have joined Wilson to transform the writings on crime and deviance into a repository of practical 'what works' information and advice. A classic instance is Morris and Hawkins' *The Honest Politician's Guide to Crime Control* (1970), a compendium of useful political recipes that urges policy-makers to appreciate the unintended and undesired consequences of action. It advocates caution and modesty in the construction of crime control schemes. More minutely, there have been those who have focused on specific problems and their solution: the design of public vehicles and its effects on theft;[22] the design of public space and its effects on preventing victimization;[23] the utilization of surveillance cameras to enhance public safety and evidence gathering.[24]

But there is a different posture. Some have held that the unintended consequences of crime control are so grave and diffuse that they have moved towards a flirtation with anarchism, libertarianism, or extreme conservatism. Arguing with Herbert Spencer that rule-enforcement tends only to exacerbate social problems, they preach the politics of *laissez-faire* and *laissez-aller*. An echo of libertarianism may thus be discovered in Schur's contention that almost any official intervention with young offenders typically amplifies the phenomenon, formal regulation acting merely to confirm the deviant in an outcast status.[25] Again, Becker and Horowitz extolled the virtues of tolerance in San Francisco, describing a civilized compact between peaceable deviant groups free of undue control.[26] Szasz, too, castigated State intervention, arguing that it has no business managing the private morality of its citizens.[27]

More sceptically still, it has been concluded that the supposedly 'unintended' consequences of control are actually knowing and intended. Politicians are taken to require the presence of a criminal population. The visible petty law-breaker, it has been said, is 'manufactured' in large quantities to perform the role of scapegoat for the ills of society. The minor criminal is given great media prominence, deflecting outrage away from elite criminality.[28] It is held to follow that there is a symbiotic relationship between the State and a specially designated pool of criminals and deviants who are exploited for dramatic purposes.[29] Foucault, for example, observes that it has long been apparent

---

[20] For a particularly effective demonstration of that assertion, see the analysis of the politicization of crime control in the regulation of Israeli Arabs in A. Korn, 'Crime and Legal Control'.

[21] J. Wilson, *Thinking About Crime*.   [22] P. Mayhew et al., *Crime as Opportunity*.

[23] O. Newman, *Defensible Space*.

[24] B. C. Welsh and D. P. Farrington *Making Public Places Safer: Surveillance and Crime Prevention*.

[25] E. Schur, *Radical Non-Intervention*.   [26] H. Becker and I. Horowitz, 'The Culture of Civility'.

[27] T. Szasz, *The Manufacture of Madness*.   [28] R. Coleman and J. Sim, *State, Power, Crime*.

[29] D. Matza, *Becoming Deviant*.

that prisons generate criminality. It is not neglect or ignorance which prevents the abolition of imprisonment. On the contrary, the penal system is deliberately tended as a useful warehouse that preserves prisoners for political ends.[30]

Simon[31] has given that notion an original twist by arguing that neo-liberal governments, particularly in the United States, have taken to treating crime control through the penal sanction as a politically and administratively convenient way of disciplining problem populations and 'solving' multiple, complex, and disparate problems at a stroke, 'governing through crime' becoming the master strategy for the administration of what used to be handled separately as the policy problems of mental health, work, education, welfare, and much else.

Pursuing that vision yet further, criminals and deviants may be defined as victims, as the exploited and oppressed, and put to work in the service of social change. For instance, Thomas Mathiesen took a leading part in the Scandinavian prisoners' unions, seeking to induce changes that could not be accepted without an unspecified but profound upheaval in penal policy. Maintaining that participation in rational negotiations would only strengthen the grip of officials and domesticate the unions, he purposefully adopted a non-conciliatory posture. Formal discipline being unsupportable in an unjust society, Mathiesen countered with an apocalyptic dream of deviants belabouring their masters with their chains.[32] The political domination of analysis can thereby turn the study of crime and deviance into a combatant in class, gender, or race wars, its ideas being judged by their impact on conflict. It may even be inferred that the study of crime and deviance cannot revolve around scholarly objectivity and an orderly interchange with those theorists with whom one disagrees. Quinney[33] and Platt[34] at different times and with different emphases proclaimed that it must be surrendered to the demands of ideological struggle, promoting truths which fuel revolutionary social change. And there has been a radical twist in the skein of argument as a later generation of 'left realists', responding to crime surveys and feminism, argue for the control of predatory crime with all the commitment of the administrative criminologists they once excoriated.

Marxist historians claim that crime and deviance may be rescued from obscurity to provide a 'history from below', an unofficial commentary of the dispossessed on their own past. Rule-breaking can therefore be made to disclose the suppressed under-life of society. It documents the stirrings of the illiterate, voiceless, and dominated, outlining patterns of communal opposition to the State and its masters. Thus poachers and smugglers can be used to illustrate the hostility which attended the emergence of class society in England.[35] Attempts to enclose land were met by traditional demands based on the rights of people to use pastures, commons, and forests.[36] Efforts to mechanize agriculture or assert the supremacy of the market were stalled by resort to 'collective bargaining by riot'.[37] The very attempt to reduce poachers, smugglers, rioters, and

---

[30] M. Foucault, *Discipline and Punish.*   [31] J. Simon, *Governing Through Crime.*
[32] T. Mathiesen, *The Politics of Abolition.*   [33] R. Quinney, 'Crime Control in Capitalist Society'.
[34] A. Platt, review of *The New Criminology.*   [35] D. Hay et al., *Albion's Fatal Tree.*
[36] E. Thompson, *Whigs and Hunters.*
[37] E. Thompson, 'The Moral Economy of the English Crowd in the Eighteenth Century'.

rick-burners to 'criminals' may there be read as an aspect of a politics of naming which neutralizes the ideological content of protest.[38] Crime becomes political protest, and what is criminal may turn into a prologue to conscious and articulate resistance by the dispossessed.[39]

On occasion, crime and deviance can indeed take expressly political directions (or at least be represented as taking an expressly political direction): thus gay men and women grouped to become the Gay Liberation Front[40] and later Outrage, and prisoners adopted the tactics of student demonstrators.[41] On occasion, politics can take a deviant path: thus the interconnectedness between terrorism and organized criminal activities.[42] On occasion, however, matters are not at all clear and the criminal, deviant, and the political can merge into a definitional fog. Argument can turn on whether people are 'really' terrorists or freedom fighters, guerrillas, or criminals. There may be debate about whether a riot is 'really' a form of social or political protest or opportunistic criminality. Description becomes even more difficult because political consequences can sometimes flow from the acts of criminals who are not overtly committed to a political stance. Conversely, political motives can be claimed by those who seek justification for criminality.[43] And there are large areas of the world where States have failed, there is no legitimate government, and who or what is criminal is almost impossible to judge.[44] There are other societies where people fear the police and the security services far more than their fellow citizens.[45] All these shifts, pronouncements, and conflicts are anything but easy to analyse.

The Sources of Theoretical Diversity

It is apparent that just one segment of the sociology of crime and deviance can encompass sundry ideologies and ambitions, and part of our task must be to recount the multiple reasons as to why such diversity arose and how the separate explanations attained and retain plausibility.

First, sociology is not enclosed or sealed against arguments which exist in the wider world. It is heir to a long tradition of thinking about crime and sin, politics being but one strand of that tradition. Lawyers, psychiatrists, theologians, moralists, anthropologists, philosophers, statisticians, social reformers, historians, and psychologists have variously laid claim to the problems of crime and deviance. Each group has tried to impose its own stamp on thinking. Each has had some significant stake in the outcome. Not only will the acceptance of a particular view confirm a system of morals, law, or politics: it will also have implications for the rise and fall of creeds, policies, and

---

[38] G. Rudé, *The Crowd in History*.   [39] E. Hobsbawm, *Primitive Rebels*.
[40] L. Humphreys, *Out of the Closets*.   [41] M. Fitzgerald, *Prisoners in Revolt*.
[42] I. Shelley, *Dirty Entanglements: Corruption, Crime, And Terrorism*
[43] T. Wolfe, *Radical Chic and Mau-Mauing the Flak-Catchers*.
[44] S. Cohen, 'Crime and Politics: Spot the Difference'.
[45] S. Cohen, 'Crime and Politics: Spot the Difference'; P. Green and T. Ward *State Crime: Governments, Violence and Corruption*.

occupations.[46] Thus the right to manage the 'mad' was contested by clergymen, magistrates, and doctors. The prize was the administration of asylums.[47] Similarly, juvenile delinquents were fought over by social workers, psychiatrists, and lawyers; the prize was professional power over juvenile courts and reformatories.[48]

Second, sociology has its own disciplines, language, and techniques, but it has also fed on ideas which have been prepared by others. In this sense, it lends a special form and focus to familiar arguments, and it would be remarkable if this were not so. No thinking about social problems can be insulated against what has gone before. The reworking of old conceptions need not be conscious or deliberate: after all, few sociologists are fully versed in the history of ideas. Yet earlier thought shapes the environment in which all speculation takes place. The intellectual disputes that defined previous centuries have been handed on to acquire new shapes in the university of the twenty-first century. For example, radical criminology can trace its lineage back to such dispersed thinkers as Plato, Kant, Hegel, Rousseau, and Marx. Control theory incorporates the political philosophy of Hobbes, the psychiatry of Eysenck and Freud, and the sociology of Durkheim. Functionalists may be clustered with the biologist Cannon, the political economist Petty, the philosopher Plato, and the anthropologists Malinowski and Radcliffe-Brown. In this sense the sociology of crime and deviance is simply another way of organizing all that has passed for relevant intellectual work in the West. It gives another life to the principal ideas of some of the principal schools. Just as those schools were varied in their thinking, so the sociology of crime and deviance is varied. Just as those schools' disputes have never been conclusively settled, so the internal debates of the sociology of crime and deviance remain unresolved.

Third, those diffuse themes can set very different goals for the study of crime and deviance. We have seen that researchers may choose or be expected to contribute to crime control; undertake dispassionate analysis; provide moral commentaries; design, criticize, or close prisons; improve police effectiveness, study the past or predict the future. They may, indeed, have no great interest in crime and deviance but search for answers to analytic puzzles which have their roots elsewhere: thus Cicourel explored probation and police practices in order to illuminate some general properties of language and of social interaction;[49] Durkheim treated crime, deviance, and law as indices of social cohesion;[50] and Merton took crime and deviance to be a demonstration of the processes by which a society maintains itself.[51]

Fourth, such an interplay of projects and thoughts becomes more complicated as the minds of different sociologists work on the materials which are offered them. There is an ever-increasing body of knowledge and empirical data, and no sociologist is capable of mastering, reading, or remembering all that is produced. Every scholar will acquire a selective experience of the sociology of crime and deviance, an experience shaped by

[46] M. Foucault, *I, Pierre Rivière*.   [47] A. Scull, 'Mad-Doctors and Magistrates'.
[48] E. Lemert, *Social Action and Legal Change*.
[49] A. Cicourel, *The Social Organization of Juvenile Justice*.
[50] É. Durkheim, *The Division of Labor in Society*.   [51] R. Merton, *Social Theory and Social Structure*.

contingency, knowledge, choice, fashion, and practical objectives. S/he may consider a work important, although few of his or her colleagues may have read it. S/he may combine its arguments with those of other writings, generating a new personal synthesis. What is held to be fascinating and provocative now, in the heat of a particular research project, can be defined as irrelevant later on. The intellectual significance of a book, theory, or idea is consequently unstable: it will depend on the circumstances of those who encounter it and on its place in a sequence of thoughts. People can have very different memories of the same book and their own memories can change. Ideas therefore reflect the biographies and preoccupations of particular researchers at particular points of time.

Fifth, the sociology of crime and deviance has thereby accumulated a vast number of nuances. They are nuances which typically become exaggerated and publicized as sociologists try to make a mark on the world. Often when working in a university, sociologists are encouraged to pursue the new and the original. After all, the university is supposed to be more than a mere vehicle for transmitting received truths. Its staff are urged to submit doctoral theses before or during their period of appointment, and one of the chief criteria for the acceptance of a thesis is its originality. Promotions hinge on successful publication, and publishers are not anxious to print the simple parrottings of others' ideas. There is thus a clear imperative to be claiming to be distinctive. Sometimes, of course, sociological works are recognizably and importantly novel, but often they are not. Sociologists frequently strain after the latest intellectual turn, seeking the special emphasis that will set her or him apart as an original thinker who deserves fame and reward. That stress can foster a proliferation of crass, self-serving claims-making, and almost every published work will carry the publisher's assertion that it represents a major advance[52] or an exploration of an area hitherto scandalously neglected.[53] And the consequence is that the free market in academic thought and persons has resulted in a confusing array of efforts to achieve product differentiation. Publicly, at least, there is little merit or profit in what we might define as unobtrusive scholarship.

Sixth, the tendency towards product differentiation has inevitably been accompanied by the making of proprietorial claims. Researchers tend to acquire very real stakes in their ideas. They 'possess' them, being reluctant to share authorship or ownership, and they may strive to conserve them in a relatively pure state, guarded against adulteration. There is, after all, considerable attraction in resolutely pursuing the logic of a simplified argument. A few axioms and a few assumptions may be all the materials that a sociologist requires. They may be all that he or she can handle. Excessive complexity and a surfeit of reservations can render analysis unmanageable. Slight initial divergences can therefore culminate in radically different conclusions. Douglas once complained of this drift towards the artificial

---

[52] M. Davis, 'That's Interesting!'

[53] There is always a plethora of areas neglected and still awaiting discovery and exploration: that is a feature of all minor disciplines, but there is something of a tendency to trumpet each new piece of work as if its having been overlooked in the past is a matter of ignorance. For a not atypical claim made about one such newly-examined area, the criminology of genocide, see J. Hagan and W. Rymond-Richmond, *Darfur and the Crime of Genocide*; and A. Alvarez, *Genocidal Crimes*.

segregation of arguments. Employing the somewhat unlovely term 'simplification-ism', he observed:

> simplificationism has grown largely out of the modern scientists' self-imposed profes-sional myopia, the insistence of each specialist on seeing everything as caused by the few particular variables he happens to 'own' professionally . . . Most . . . theories are right to some degree about some part of the things they are studying, but they almost all deal with small parts—as if the parts were the whole thing—and the theories wind up being distor-tions of the vastly complex realm of human life.[54]

Seventh, the impact of the academy which both spurs and limits the growth of intel-lectual variety. Universities and disciplines enforce their own special controls and they can be taxing. Ideas will be scanned in reviews, lectures, and seminars (our own book is devoted to such a survey), it being an occupational duty of academics to recount and dissect their colleagues' work, and arguments will be examined for their logic, meth-odology, and coherence. The routine activities of academic work accordingly sustain a rough and ready process of natural selection which condemns some arguments and upholds others. Reputations have sometimes been lost irrevocably, but what passes for damning critical criteria is itself variable, enjoying a history of fashion and the popu-larity of schools. Thus, interesting developments in the social geography of crime in the mid-nineteenth century were suppressed by the end of the century, only to be revived in the 1930s[55] and again in the 1990s. What seemed to be the death of biological theo-ries of crime has proved to be only a period in which these were unfashionable. They have risen from the grave and now hold sway in a number of universities, particularly in North America.[56] Ideas fail, but so can principles of selection.

Eighth, the matter is yet further complicated by the very different traditions that are borne by the university departments and schools in which crime and deviance are studied. Processes of natural selection may be inhibited because universities are so numerous and the sociological profession is so large that antagonists need never confront one another. The advocates of a particular theory or methodology can sur-round themselves with their own circle of followers and their own network of journals and publishers. It is quite possible for one intellectual faction to create, examine, and extend its influence without much interference from outsiders. Like neighbours who prefer simply to avoid one another rather than quarrel,[57] challenges can simply be ig-nored—indeed, they may never be issued. For example, radical criminology did not dominate the sociology of crime and deviance. Many, probably most, sociologists did not entertain its assumptions. Yet radical criminology received almost no criticism. It was simply ignored by those who were not its adherents. In this fashion, phenom-enology, interactionism, structuralism, functionalism, feminism, and the other major schools such as crime science can flourish independently, constituting a number of parallel intellectual universes which need never intersect.

---

[54] J. Douglas et al., *The Nude Beach*, 51.
[55] A. Lindesmith and Y. Levin, 'English Ecology and Criminology of the Past Century'.
[56] N. Rafter, *The Criminal Brain: Understanding Biological Theories Of Crime*.
[57] M. Baumgartner, *The Moral Order of a Suburb*.

Finally, such insulation can be further reinforced by the division of intellectual labour within university departments. Students require schooling in a collection of specialist areas, universities recruit appropriate staff to service them, and there is a consequent weakening of ability to monitor and judge the works of one's colleagues in the same institution. Sociologists of religion or development may not believe themselves equipped to assess the competence and range of a colleague working on crime and deviance. There is an attendant reduction of discipline: sociologists of crime and deviance have acquired a charter to pontificate provided a publisher or media platform will broadcast it and someone somewhere will endorse it.

The Social Contexts of Differentiation

One of the chief constraints on intellectual production is the setting in which it takes place. The sociology of crime and deviance is practised in different contexts which frame what may be said and the manner of its expression. We can do no more than provide a few scattered instances of those contexts, but our illustrations should emphasize the part played by environment.

Perhaps the largest single setting is the State, and the State can dramatically affect creativity. We have claimed that the sociology of crime and deviance may be pregnant with implications for moral and political reasoning. Particular conceptions of crime and deviance can fold back on ideas of legitimacy, power, and pathology. They are capable of subverting the absolute authority of the State and may be thought to require censorship. One important example is offered by the position of criminology within the former Soviet Union. Soviet governance was ostensibly centred on Marxism which makes quite specific assertions about the character and significance of crime. Crime is held to be a defect that stems not from socialism but the larger defects of capitalism itself. It is an outcrop of the moral disorganization, inequalities, and possessive individualism of a criminogenic society based on social classes. Having become classless, it was argued, a truly Marxist society or a Marxist society in the making could not engender crime. As the director of the Moscow Institute of Criminology pronounced, 'socialism does not give birth to crime, . . . the regularities immanent in socialism do not give birth to crime'.[58] A non-Marxist sociology of crime and deviance would have located some of the sources of Soviet law-breaking in Soviet social organization,[59] but it would have upset Soviet Marxism and the claims of the Soviet Union to be a Marxist society and it was not allowed to develop. On the contrary, Soviet criminology was preoccupied with the quest for explanations which abstained from touching on the social and political order itself: crime was presented as a consequence of foreign influence (as deviance so often is—consider how AIDS is always presumed to originate somewhere else), capitalist survivals, or personal, organic, or psychological disturbance.

---

[58] I. Karpets, Director of the Moscow Institute of Criminology, quoted in W. Connor, *Deviance in Soviet Society*, 168.

[59] P. Rawlinson, 'Russian Organised Crime: A Brief History'.

In authoritarian societies, criminology is ostensibly politically neutral for very political reasons, a kind of technical instrument which abstains from questioning and criticism in the service of the State.[60]

Within societies, too, there are quite disparate contexts for the pursuit of research on crime and deviance. The discipline is so salient that it can be put to very different uses. Its practitioners may be discovered in a host of different organizations, and those organizations will shape goals and dictate intellectual styles. Institutionally, the demands of government research agencies are dissimilar to those imposed by universities. There is a clear stipulation that ideas be presented in a form useful to policy and action, that arguments be put in a fashion intelligible to the administrator, and that there should be little flirtation with the metaphysics of crime.

So defined, research tends towards a model of natural science, employing quantitative methods in practical 'what works' projects designed to evaluate policy. As we shall see, it tends characteristically to lean towards rational choice theory. Clarke and Cornish reflected of rational choice theory that its focus is 'on offenders as rational decision-makers calculating where their self-interest lies . . . '.[61] It can contribute much that is valuable, mapping events and relationships that escape others. But it is not calculated to feed a radical consciousness or explore questions simply because they are interesting. It is constrained by rules of order which need not restrain a university lecturer. People working in government agencies are not expected primarily to be original. They are required to be reliable and predictable. To be sure, agencies constantly hanker after new crime control programmes and policies—there is a perennial hunt for the obviously efficient reform. But organization is imposed by the disciplines and discourses of political rationality and practicability. Someone who worked in a British criminal justice policy planning unit declared:

> It is perhaps not a particularly difficult task to formulate the objectives of policy-oriented research. They might be stated as being to assist and contribute to the formulation and development of policy and to evaluate the effects of its implementation.[62]

Many academics *do* busy themselves with moral and political concerns, but they are not obliged to do so. Consider the scale and character of the task described in the preface to one book on the sociology of deviance:

> This book is the product of my own search for a coherent view of the relationship between persons and institutions, conducted in a context of conflicting ideas about human character and social reality. Seeking theoretical continuity, I discovered that discontinuity characterized explanations of social order and change. Reviewing these historical perspectives and issues, I found that, rather than clarifying ambiguities, deviance theories illustrate how scholarly controversies over styles of reasoning and world views produce radically different versions of social reality.[63]

---

[60] P. Solomon, *Soviet Criminologists and Criminal Policy.*
[61] R. Clarke and B. Cornish, 'Rational Choice', 2.
[62] T. Rawsthorne, 'The Objectives and Content of Policy-Oriented Research', 5.
[63] N. Davis, *Sociological Constructions of Deviance*, xi–xii.

Those rather different definitions of the academic task extend outwards to affect the network of supporting and feeding institutions that train and house sociologists of crime and deviance. There is an undoubted overlap and interplay between institutions. They are not completely insulated from one another. But there are divergent emphases which explain some of the variation in theorizing.

On the one hand, the work of the academic sociologist of crime and deviance is subordinate to rather particular demands. Quite frequently, he or she is but one sociologist amongst many, contributing to the general education of students. Her or his interests may have been subservient to the wider development of sociology itself, and their criminological expertise can become little more than yet another perspective on broad intellectual and social problems. In this sense, their attachment to crime and deviance is somewhat arbitrary. They could ask much the same questions of innumerable other areas.

On the other hand, criminologists may be discovered in special institutes or departments whose goal is not the promotion of a general theoretical competence. Globally, institutes and departments of criminology, criminal justice, police studies, penal studies, crime prevention, and counter-terrorism studies have been established with rather precise charters. Their chief aim is the production of professionals in one master discipline, criminology, or the various sub-disciplines that are themselves conceived to be multi-disciplinary in character. They are dedicated principally to the exploration of the substance of crime and crime control instead of what might be regarded as the more abstract and metatheoretical problems of sociological explanation. And they are often designed to meet the requirements of employing organizations in government and applied research. In the pursuit of these ends, they often achieve vastly more than the preparation of crime control technicians. Many institutes have attracted sociologists of distinction, yet their organization has been shaped by practical career contingencies.

The appointments secured by criminologists depend on the vagaries of the market and personal history. Someone who teaches in a criminology institute or department may have as great a dedication to theorizing as her or his colleagues in a university sociology department. The criminologist in a sociology department might have preferred a post in a specialist institute or department populated with fellow specialists. Moreover, the formal charters of institutions rarely describe the exact activities that take place: there may be many departures from official goals. Nonetheless, the difference between 'pure' and 'applied' scholarship is real enough.

There is perhaps one further source of differentiation. Universities and university departments have histories that are shaped by national, local, and intellectual influences. The study of crime and deviance has only relatively recently become a professional pursuit and its adherents have had to find a place for themselves in long-established organizations. Criminology has been grafted onto institutions whose structure defines its character and evolution. In South America, for example, many criminologists have had to associate themselves with physical anthropology: their quest has been the detection of organic sources of deviance. In continental Europe, criminology has typically been adopted by law and psychiatric departments. In the United States, it is largely identified with sociology. In Britain, criminologists are scattered amongst departments

of sociology, psychology, law, and social policy.[64] The outcome has been the introduction of complexity and greater diversity. Whilst a department or university may
be regarded by a newcomer as intellectually alien, a strange environment which one
enters without full commitment, it does force certain teaching and academic duties
on its members. Thus, sociologists of crime and deviance in a law department must
attend to a distinct syllabus and a distinct set of aims. Their students will not be versed
in sociology. Whatever their interests may be, sociologists so placed will inevitably find
that their thoughts are focused on special problems and a special body of writing, and
there is always a temptation to 'go native' and adopt local habits of thought and acquire
appropriate, local qualifications in, say, law. Theirs will still be the sociology of crime
and deviance, but it will have acquired a particular complexion.

Critique

It is clear that the sociology of crime and deviance is likely to remain a disunited enterprise and, to a great extent, such diversity cannot but be useful. However hard they may
try, particular sociologists cannot impose a single orthodoxy upon their readers. Their
arguments can always be set in the context of their competitors and critics, revealing not only their strengths but their limitations. These limitations may be very real,
greater indeed than the champions of the arguments might care to admit. Sociology
has a self-relativizing strain which can chasten people who seek immediate and unambiguous answers to moral and intellectual problems.

   Readers would do well to assume a warily disinterested approach at the beginning of
their study of crime and deviance, being simultaneously open, sceptical, and charitable
about what they encounter. It would be unwise to form premature attachments before
one knows more about the available intellectual choices. Eventually, to be sure, there
will be a need to organize one's thought and discard certain ideas but it would not be
sensible to do so without having first considered their rivals which, if only because they
persuaded some people, at some time, are unlikely to be totally lacking in merit. And
no theory can be assessed intelligently until it has been regarded with some sympathy.
Ideas can be appreciated only if there is some willingness to take their authors' assumptions and preoccupations seriously.

   We would therefore argue that the early stages of understanding crime and deviance
are most fruitful when one tries to grasp the opportunities presented by very different systems of thought, the problems which confronted their authors, and the doubts
which they may cast on favoured arguments.

   Wary disinterest is also to be commended because it is very easy to condemn and
lose what may actually be quite valuable. We shall enlarge on the methodological

----

[64] In a survey of 106 British criminologists conducted by one of the authors in 1992, it was discovered that
36 per cent (and 32 per cent of the non-respondents) were to be found in departments of law; 19 per cent
(and 18 per cent of the non-respondents) in departments of sociology; 2 per cent (and 15 per cent) in
designated research centres; and 9 per cent (and 15 per cent) in the Home Office Research and Planning
Unit: P. Rock, 'The Social Organization of British Criminology'.

problems in the next chapter. Nevertheless, it is apparent that those methods are pecu-liarly fraught. They revolve around the difficulties of knowing and describing groups which have little to gain from becoming known. The world of crime, deviance, and social control is riddled with discredited or biased information and guilty knowledge. Although research is often more flawed and slight than its authors and audience might wish, it is sometimes no mean feat to bring it to a conclusion at all. It would not do to dwell disproportionately on those flaws and neglect what has been accomplished—some critics are all too prone to dismiss the whole because of the deficiencies of a few of its parts. When ideas and information can be extracted only with great effort, it is sensible to examine work for what it may offer instead of stalking it for its failings.

Only rarely will a single study exhaust all the interesting possibilities of a problem. Few instances of crime and deviance are paraded before a researcher in their entirety, and a consequence of such restricted vision is the inevitable relativism of argument. With great good fortune, social anthropologists like the Iannis might obtain access to a family of organized criminals.[65] It would have been impossible to examine all such families or even every aspect of one single family. It would be correspondingly absurd and unhelpful to fault the Iannis for the limitations of their sampling. And it follows that such method-ological considerations invite one to treat the sociology of crime and deviance as a series of what may be little more than tenuously connected glimpses of other worlds. Much would be sacrificed by the assumption that each work must be approached as if it were defensible and complete in itself, an entity that can survive or fail only so long as it re-mains intact. It is not attractive to be intellectually indiscriminate, but neither should one forget that it is perfectly possible to treat sociology as a reservoir of different, sometimes contradictory, arguments that can be dismantled and reassembled with some freedom.

Work on youth gangs provides a useful example. Gangs have intrigued researchers (and society) for decades, and there has been a continuous stream of writing flowing from different sources, times, and geographical contexts. Yet there has been a curious and quite indefensible tendency to proceed as if all these random sightings should be treated as attempts to confront an identical problem with identical data.[66] One study has been played off against another as if only one explanation should be allowed to survive. There is no good reason to suppose that youth gangs in 1920s Chicago are the 'same' as youth gangs in contemporary Chicago or Rio de Janeiro or Johannesburg.[67] It is not necessary to try to resolve all differences between studies into simple questions of error and rectitude. It is much better to give social, geographical, intellectual, and historical context to arguments, seeing gangs, for example, as an historically-evolving and spatially and socially-embedded phenomenon open to many different questions that are themselves evolving. Even more to the point, perhaps, crime and deviance are

---

[65] F. Ianni, *A Family Business.*

[66] There were, to be sure, exceptions to this tendency to reduce all delinquents to a single mould. We shall show in Chapters 5 and 6 how, following Merton (*Social Theory and Social Structure*), Cloward and Ohlin (*Delinquency and Opportunity*) developed a typology of different forms of delinquency based on systematic variations in their response to structural opportunities and restraints. In its turn, Cloward and Ohlin's work was to be the basis of Spergel's *Racketville, Slumtown, Haulburg*, a book that pursued that theme of variation yet further by linking forms of delinquency to forms of community organization or disorganization.

[67] H. Finestone, *Victims of Change.*

historically and socially contingent, so that what was banned or stigmatized some time ago may cease to be deviant. What was not criminal or deviant in the past may be deviant now. Formally in law and informally in many parts of British and North American social life, for example, homophobia has become criminalized as a hate crime whilst gay sexuality has been decriminalized. Drunk driving was not subject to the disapproval and criminal sanctions it now receives. Texting whilst driving is illegal in the United Kingdom and in many states in the USA.

Finally, it may be argued that even sub-standard sociological studies of crime and deviance have their uses. Readers will discover that they will have to resort to second-rate reporting and theorizing because there is often no adequate alternative. Sociology may not always do its job well, but there is usually no competent competition, and bad research or analysis may always jolt useful reflection.

After all, sociological theories of crime and deviance can represent the most articulate versions of arguments that have currency in popular culture and everyday life. Almost every major common-sense explanation of crime and deviance has a modified sociological expression. In this sense, sociology is not always novel and surprising, but it does expose and scrutinize ideas that may only be dimly reviewed elsewhere. The conventions of ordinary conversation do not really allow one to inspect the weaknesses and opportunities of argument in any detail. Commonplace theorizing about crime and deviance touches on delicate moral and social matters and it is difficult, often subversive, to challenge it. It would be a fundamental breach of good manners to offer certain arguments about motives and behaviour although they can receive prolonged and sober attention in the university. Yet, many statements do require that kind of exposition if their qualities are to be assessed. Practised well, sociology should rest on canons of proof, logic, and evidence that are largely foreign to everyday 'crime talk'. It permits one to be banal, boring, naïve, or outrageous, suspending some of the inhibitions which restrict discussion outside academic life. If the sociology of crime and deviance is sometimes accused of merely repeating common-sense observations, it may be said that it can *work* on those observations in an unusual, taxing, and rather imaginative fashion. It probably represents the only important means of de-constructing commonplace explanation and gauging its worth. What emerges may not always be especially momentous, but it is usually a significant advance on the thinking that occurs elsewhere. Even the most ordinary examples of the sociology of crime and deviance will continue to be justified so long as they are more methodical, rigorous, and reflective than their alternatives. They are supported by the conscious deployment of techniques and critical procedures which are not in common use. They subject their ideas to an organized scrutiny. And they are supported by a substantial body of fieldwork and research nationally and internationally. Whatever its faults may be, the sociology of crime and deviance is a relatively orderly, disciplined, searching, transparent, and cumulative process of enquiry. Even when it is flawed, and it *is* often flawed, a confrontation with its obvious defects can force the reader to think usefully and perhaps for the first time about criticisms, contrasts, and alternatives.

But sociologists do move beyond the mere analysis and recitation of arguments. They often display a willingness to become closely involved with matters that most people shun. In this, they are unusual and perhaps a little deviant themselves. Not only may it be considered eccentric or even shocking to defend certain arguments about crime and deviance, it is also sometimes discreditable to associate with deviants without good purpose. Rape, robbery, drug dealing, drug-taking, sex work, paedophilia, violence, and corruption are some of the dangerous and morally contaminated areas of social life. People typically avoid or disclaim intimacy with such areas, and they may quite rightly be suspicious of those who do not heed taboos. There are very few who have an occupational mandate to be publicly curious and adventurous in regions where crime and deviance may be found. Yet sociologists have come to know poolroom hustlers,[68] drug-users,[69] receivers,[70] armed robbers,[71] and child molesters.[72] Not infrequently, the result has been a breaking down of barriers and an extraordinary knowledge that may be compared advantageously with the lay, political, and journalistic theorizing about crime deviance that all too frequently is lazy, speculative, based upon imagination, others' reports, and hostile encounters. As Christopher Jencks once said in a rather different context, 'In self-defense, we can only say that the magnitude of [our] errors is almost certainly less than if we had simply consulted our prejudices, which seems to be the usual alternative.'[73] At its best, sociological understanding of crime and deviance is not mere speculative argument or prejudice about dimly glimpsed others.

The judgement of theory and research should not therefore be rushed. It is a delicate process, and theory is rarely as useless and theorists as foolish as their critics would pretend. It is very easy to construct theoretical counterparts of an Aunt Sally which possesses no vitality, conviction, or endurance. More worthwhile is an intellectual approach which puts arguments and counter-arguments in their most solid form. Only in this way will the reader actually face the possibility of learning and synthesizing ideas. Few systems are so barren that something cannot be retained. By crediting other sociologists with intelligence and sensibility, the parochialism of one's own understanding might be overcome.

Accordingly, we invite readers to consider a succession of interlocking and competing ideas. By the end of this book, they should have become reasonably familiar with the basic theories, preoccupations, debates, and authors of the sociology of crime and deviance. Our discussion will be ordered historically, beginning with the Chicago School of the 1920s. Such a chronological organization seems satisfactory enough: ideas do follow one another in time and sociologists often respond to the work of their predecessors. But it should not be presumed that the sociology of crime and deviance has evolved smoothly, logically, incrementally, or as a single body of thought. Neither should it be presumed that later ideas necessarily displace those that went before. It would not do to commit what Gary Morson has called the 'chronocentric fallacy', the unfounded belief that what is argued today must necessarily be superior to what was argued before.[74] On the contrary, the temporary eclipse of a theory may have little to

---

[68] N. Polsky, *Hustlers, Beats and Others.*   [69] A. Lindesmith, *Opiate Addiction.*
[70] C. Klockars, *The Professional Fence.*   [71] W. Einstadter, 'The Social Organization of Armed Robbery'.
[72] C. McCaghy, 'Drinking and Deviance Disavowal'.
[73] In A. Heath et al. (eds.), *Understanding Social Change*, 2.
[74] G. Morson, *Narrative and Freedom: The Shadows of Time*, 235, 278–82; and P. Rock, 'Chronocentrism and British Criminology'.

do with its merit. Just as important are the effects of fashion, the desire to innovate, an impatience with the old, changing political and intellectual environments, and the turnover of generations of sociologists. Older ideas also deserve serious attention, if only because they offer a context and contrast for present concerns.

Conclusion

The sociology of crime and deviance has evolved fitfully over the decades. It has stemmed from many sources and intellectual traditions and has been intended to serve many, sometimes irreconcilable, purposes. No particular theoretical perspective can cover every facet of crime and deviance yet stay practicable and coherent, although there are always those who proclaim that one theory alone should be allowed to dominate. Neither are older, occasionally unfashionable, theories necessarily as weak as their later critics would have one believe. Our recommendation at the very opening of *Understanding Deviance* is that readers should initially approach the wealth of ideas and research findings generated by competing and complementary perspectives with an appreciative mind, willing to learn how to use theory in order to research, analyse, and critique, and, from time to time, to challenge their initial preferences and judgements.

Further Reading

M. Bosworth and C. Hoyle (eds.). *What is Criminology?*, Oxford, 2013.

E. McLaughlin and J. Muncie (eds.), *Criminological Perspectives*, London, 2013.

N. Rafter (ed.), *The Origins of Criminology*, New York, 2009.

P. Rock (ed.), *A History of British Criminology*, Oxford, 1988.

J. Tierney and M. O'Neill, *Criminology: Theory and Context*, London, 2009.

2

Sources of Knowledge about Crime and Deviance

Introduction

The sociology of crime and deviance attempts to explain a world of rule-making, rule-breaking, and rule-enforcement. That world is vast and constantly changing and little of it has been charted. Much of it is unusually difficult to observe and its very obscurity has complicated problems of exploration. Venturing into it, the researcher will continually confront dilemmas about the selection of questions and methods. Every decision to examine one possibility rather than another entails some risk and some profit and loss. The framing of such decisions is central to explanation and theory, and debate can turn endlessly around the wisdom and yield of particular choices. It is inevitable that the uses and character of evidence have been brought into dispute. Certain facts invite the acceptance of certain theories, just as certain theories propel one to search for certain facts. Any exploration of the sociology of crime and deviance must consider the ways in which deviation may be seen and how those ways affect argument.

The Elusive Quality of Crime and Deviance

We have not yet provided a formal definition of crime and deviance. That omission is deliberate and it stems from our reluctance to commit ourselves prematurely to any one position. Major theories cast crime and deviance somewhat differently and subsequent chapters will examine various possibilities in their turn. It is, however, clear that there is a basic, if unwritten, agreement between researchers that irrespective of social and cultural context, crime and deviance should be considered as banned or controlled behaviour which if discovered and exposed, is likely to generate a negative public reaction in the form of censure and sanctions, including punishment. It little matters whether the behaviour is objectively harmful or not. Crime and deviance can range from an infraction of social etiquette to the murderous actions of a State-sponsored death squad. Not all forms of deviance are criminalized and not all forms of criminality are necessarily deviant. However, those who violate, challenge, or defy the social values, norms, or beliefs of any society or social group, including deviant groups, run the risk of making their lives rather more difficult and hazardous. In many instances, the nature of the social reaction will have life-changing consequences for those individuals who are identified, classified, and stigmatized as criminal or deviant. Of course, there is abundant deviation and indeed criminality which is never discovered, censored, or sanctioned—rule-breaking defined by Edwin Lemert[1] as 'primary deviation': drug users, gamblers, and grifters will go undetected, burglars, corrupt police officers, mafia bosses, narco-terrorists, and corporate criminals may never be apprehended. But criminal and deviant pursuits can multiply the problems of ordinary existence. Only occasionally will they be publicly displayed. Whilst in cultures where homosexuality is still considered criminal, gay men and women may nevertheless decide to 'come out' and proclaim their homosexuality, or faced with a legal system which does not allow voluntary termination of pregnancy women may nevertheless decide to reveal that they have had an illegal abortion, most individuals would not choose voluntarily to advertise themselves. Instead, there is a real strain towards concealment. As Matza observed, deviation often becomes devious.

Researchers working on visible and undisguised processes have problems enough. Their work becomes more complex when subjects and events are deliberately hidden.[2] Not only is deviance generally covert and secretive, but deviants themselves are unlikely to be immediately co-operative when they are detected. After all, they have little to gain from exposure. Much rule-breaking is consequently represented to inquisitive outsiders as something else, denied when suspected and shielded behind walls or locked doors. Researchers must be exceptionally alert to its presence, defining otherwise conventional appearances as façades or deceits. They must be sceptical, assuming that all is not as it seems. Thus Ditton[3] and Henry[4] uncovered widespread deviance in settings which on the surface appeared completely normal. Ditton disclosed the existence of systematic 'fiddles' at every level of the bread industry. Henry revealed how very ordinary sites like public houses and clubs were the centres of extensive amateur receiving: they had become market-places in which stolen goods were commissioned and distributed. Farberman, too, has described how the American car industry is riddled with organized illicit practices.[5] The distribution of alcohol and cigarettes have been similarly documented as enterprises which has substantial illegalities.[6] Most occupations, it seems, provide opportunities for forbidden but unrecorded activity.[7] And, in complex organizations, deviance may become even more invisible because it may then be dispersed, fragmented, disjointed, and difficult to view in its entirety. The European Commission of the 1990s, for instance, was riddled with fraud and corruption, but middle-ranking officials charged with auditing accounts found it difficult to form anything like a comprehensive view. They saw small disconnected parts rather than the whole and, in the face of substantial opposition, it eventually required great personal persistence and enterprise by 'whistle-blowers' to piece together something

---

[1] E. Lemert, *Social Pathology*.

[2] For an illustrative discussion of the difficulties confronting criminologists interested in one area of criminal activity, see, e.g., J. Goodey, 'Human Trafficking'.

[3] J. Ditton, *Part-Time Crime*.   [4] S. Henry, *The Hidden Economy*.

[5] H. Farberman, 'A Criminogenic Market Structure'.

[6] N. Denzin, 'Crime and the American Liquor Industry'.   [7] S. Henry and G. Mars, 'Crime at Work'.

of what was afoot.[8] However, there is no evidence that anything has really changed. Even more dramatically, Newman has argued that, in the US, it is in seemingly well-integrated communities that high school mass murders are more likely to occur, and they occur because residents are prone to deny signs of trouble and assume that 'it can't happen here'.[9] It is in these senses that crime and deviance abounds but it is methodically veiled. It is only by taking a sceptical perspective on the world that its disreputable life becomes apparent. Surfaces reveal little—they certainly do not reliably point one towards self-evidently criminal or deviant populations.

Secrecy can have varied social ramifications. It can fold back on deviance itself, making research doubly complex. When rule-breaking is guarded and surrounded by devious explanations, deviants themselves may not be fully aware of the extent and nature of their own and others' activity. Many deviants are segregated from one another, unaware of who their fellows are and what they are doing. Paedophiles, for example, need take no part in organized activity. Their principal knowledge of sexual deviance may flow from the mass media, the internet, gossip, and everyday conversation. Their conception can embody that knowledge, moulding how they act, the motives they acknowledge, and their view of themselves.[10]

Criminals and deviants rarely engage in collective efforts to interpret their own behaviour. Some homosexuals did so decades ago when being gay was also held to be markedly deviant,[11] and a number of drug-takers did so in the 1960s, but many rule-breakers themselves possess no more than a fragmented and second-hand knowledge of deviance. In one important sense, that knowledge is quite adequate and authentic. It infuses and shapes the world of deviance, enabling one to explain how lines of action are formed. In another sense, it should not be confused with a developed sociological understanding because there is almost certainly much more to learn and consider. Having successfully penetrated the defences which surround rule-breaking, researchers cannot be entirely uncritical in their response to what they encounter. As Manning observed, they should not assume 'the "underdog's" narrow, often very simplistic view of large complex social segments which directly affect changes in the underdog's behavior'.[12] Penetration is not enough. Academic analysis must feed on further materials which may be beyond the subject's grasp, and the discovery of those materials is quite onerous.

Secret practices and restricted information result in most research being limited and parochial. A considerable expenditure of time and effort may give the researcher access to a deviant world. Additional expenditure might allow useful learning to take place. Months or years may have to pass before intimacy develops, a reasonable range of acts are observed, and processes are seen in anything near their completeness. What will emerge is almost inevitably a partial sighting. One might acquire some knowledge about a receiver,[13] a street gang, or an hotel for geriatric hustlers.[14] It would be quite absurd to expect to become familiar with many examples of such deviance. It would be

---

[8] P. van Buitenen, *Blowing the Whistle*.   [9] K. Newman, *Rampage: The Social Roots of School Shootings*.
[10] L. Taylor, 'The Significance and Interpretation of Replies to Motivational Questions'.
[11] L. Humphreys, *Out of the Closets*.   [12] P. Manning, 'Deviance and Dogma'.
[13] C. Klockars, *The Professional Fence*.   [14] J. Stephens, *Loners, Losers and Lovers*.

even more absurd to pretend that one had achieved an understanding of its 'essential', 'general', or 'universal' characteristics.

Even an individual subject will resist full surveillance. After all, how, can, and why should a researcher be given unfettered access to every intimate moment and thought? Why, indeed, should one trust an outsider at all? There are, Jack Katz once said, 'times and places in the subjects' lives that are beyond the ethnographer's reach'.[15] Those who study delinquent adolescents are very rarely admitted to their homes, schools, or more private moments. Those who study legislators and administrators will not be privy to every conversation and document. On the contrary, research tends to be confined to public and controlled occasions which may permit a careful preparation of appearances. Yet even those occasions can be so densely textured that researchers are still plagued by problems of what to observe, what questions to ask, what to record, and how to organize and edit their observations. It is not at all remarkable that theories and theorists come to describe phenomena quite differently. Not only do phenomena change from time to time and from setting to setting, but there are other sources of divergence that reflect the sheer variety of choices facing an observer. The 'same' process can be reduced to quite conflicting analyses, all of which may have been produced in good faith and have some validity.

For instance, early criminological research neglected policing. It was as if police work was thought to be analytically inconsequential to the criminologist, an uneventful back-cloth to the criminal process or an unproblematic response to crime that had already taken place. Then came the first wave of research on the US police in the 1950s, which stressed the dramatic and the spectacular to make the police very interesting indeed. Rank and file police officers were represented as a besieged and hostile group involved in ceaseless activity and a long succession of violent incidents.[16] There was to be a second phase of US and UK research in the 1960s and 1970s, and the police were no longer portrayed as violent or frenetic. Instead, analysis was made interesting precisely because it contrasted so markedly with that of the first wave. Policing was shown to be reactive, banal, boring, and commonplace, an occupation like any other, affected by anxieties about promotion, overtime, poor weather, monotony, and shiftwork.[17] More recently, there has been a move to depict the police as besieged *and* bored. Police officers define themselves as agents of order in the midst of disorder and disrespect, performing dull work punctuated by spurts of hedonistic and frenzied crime control activity.[18]

It is rather improbable that such shifts in emphasis can be explained solely by historical changes in the social structure and behaviour of the police, although those changes have undoubtedly taken place: the police of the 1950s also cared about avoiding unpleasant weather and getting cups of coffee; and the police of the 1960s and early 1970s had their violent moments (indeed, in 1970, Bittner defined the police role as 'a mechanism for the distribution of non-negotiably coercive force'[19]). It was

---

[15] J. Katz, 'Ethnography's Warrants', 399.

[16] W. Westley, 'Violence and the Police', and J. Skolnick, *Justice Without Trial.*

[17] M. Cain, *Society and the Policeman's Role*; P. Manning, *Police Work*; and J. Rubinstein, *City Police.*

[18] M. Punch, *Policing the Inner City*; S. Holdaway, *Inside the British Police*; and D. Smith and J. Gray, *Police and People in London.*

[19] E. Bittner, *The Functions of the Police in Modern Society*, 46.

not changes in policing alone but changes in their perception of what was interesting and reportable that led researchers to turn their gaze towards different facets of policing. There is in this sense a dialectic which will continually move a focus backwards and forwards. The first researchers of the police considered the petty, everyday features of policing analytically unimportant—there was a more absorbing story to be told. That story having become accepted and having grown familiar, a contrasting description could be given that re-emphasized the typical and mundane. And once the police had become uneventful again, there could be a third phase, with a renewed interest in violence. The sociology of the police has undergone a series of transformations but it is not always evident that each has been more truthful or comprehensive than the last.[20]

Second, sociological research is constrained by the very structure of its own field. It consists of a long train of entangling relationships. Movement through the social world is obstructed and eased in a number of ways, and it would be unwise to presume that parts of all groups are equally accessible. There *are* those who claim that obstacles are slight and that a little application will overcome them.[21] But most would acknowledge that researchers are not capable of passing effortlessly into every social situation. One cannot be at ease everywhere. There are always likely to be certain groups who resist research by certain researchers. James Carey, for example, found that his work on amphetamine users was dangerous and disturbing because his subjects were prone to erratic violence.[22] It is said that few white researchers could now undertake research in black urban communities.[23] Middle-class researchers might find it awkward to study street gangs. Male researchers working on sexual violence are not always accepted by radical feminists. Older researchers might have difficulties researching cyber-bullying environments. Many of the barriers which divide people from one another in everyday life also keep the researcher at bay. They are actually rather more formidable because researchers seek a greater intimacy and duration in their relations, and they are more demanding, asking questions and exploring secrets which are not part of polite, commonplace exchanges between strangers or acquaintances.

To be sure, most researchers do know some deviants outside the formal domain of work and research. Their life is not wholly absorbed by their work and deviants are abundant enough. They may well be deviants themselves. As one commented about his early and influential writings, 'after all, we were only talking about ourselves'. But it is inevitable that researchers are generally familiar with only a few forms of rule-breaking and there will be a temptation to focus on these. Researchers are unlikely to know arsonists, narco-terrorists, latter-day pirates, and serial killers. More common

---

[20] Punch would argue that the transformation is anything but complete; studies 'have neglected boredom and routine. However hard ethnographers try to tell us what it is really like out there, they invariably end up with rich, gripping material. . . . Researchers concentrate ineluctably on the dramatic (either in terms of hectic action or interpersonal relations) and even conspire to make tedium of interest because they describe the "easing" practices which make inactivity tolerable.' M. Punch, 'Officers and Men', 9.

[21] N. Polsky, *Hustlers, Beats and Others*.

[22] J. Carey, 'Problems of Access and Risk in Observing Drug Scenes'.

[23] J. Spiegel, 'Problems of Access to Target Populations'. But see A. Goffman, *On the Run*; M. Duneier, *Sidewalk*; and E. Liebow, *Tally's Corner*.

over the years has been an acquaintance with a restricted group of sexual deviants, soft drug-users, hustlers, youth subcultures, and progressive political radicals, who are to be found in and near the researcher's own world. Other groupings have been wilfully or inadvertently neglected[24] and unusual subjects may have to stumble or force themselves into the researcher's professional life before they receive attention.

Biographical contingency plays a part. Thus some researchers have themselves been prisoners,[25] some have suffered from mental illness, some have been jazz musicians,[26] some have even been living on the streets.[27] Because of the development of criminal justice studies within the university there is a distinctive cohort of staff who have been practitioners working with criminal and deviants.

Another, often unacknowledged problem is the sheer volatility of much crime and deviance. Research frequently entails a careful preparation of finance and time: leave may have to be requested, funds sought, plans made, and ethical approval gained. In turn, there must be some reasonable guarantee that one's research subjects will be stable and immobile enough to be there when one wants them. For example, it is much easier to study the world of fetish clubs than the solitary participant. That world is based on a network of meeting places, internet pages, and social media pages. It does not disappear or move unexpectedly. A lone fetishist may simply leave the researcher's orbit or decide not to be studied after all.

Organized and settled congregations of deviants are the most readily and intensively observed. Groups which need to maintain contact with strangers are extremely accessible. The 'fetish world' is made up in part by a host of anonymous people—the researcher is just one more visitor. Still more work is required of someone who is curious about professional crime, because the professional criminal is naturally suspicious of the stranger.[28] The most work is demanded of researchers who seek the isolated and unpredictable criminals—the 'lone wolf' bomber or the cyber-blackmailer.

There are also barriers *within* social worlds. Concentrating on one area may bar access to others. A group may not trust a person who has ingratiated himself with a rival faction. The police might not encourage a researcher who has been with a street gang for some time and vice versa. It is usually impossible to predict the inner politics of a group: only when contact has been established will the limits and hazards of research become apparent. By then it may be too late to undo any damage.

Some Methodological Strategies

We have implied that effective analysis can require the cultivation of close relations with deviant and criminal subjects. and that is especially the case when scholarly knowledge is somewhat thin. Nonetheless, there are many questions which cannot be

---

[24] There *are* exceptions. See, e.g., W. Einstadter, 'The Social Organization of Armed Robbery'.
[25] J. Irwin, *The Felon*.   [26] H. Becker, 'The Culture of a Deviant Group'.
[27] N. Anderson, *The Hobo*; P. Archard, *Vagrancy*.
[28] T. Parker and R. Allerton, *The Courage of His Convictions*.

settled by such ethnographic methods. Historical research, for instance, obviously demands very different strategies. Even when ethnography might be thought appropriate, there are many researchers who are quite content with formal interviewing or the use of indirect evidence. Yet, whatever strategy is employed, there are inherent uncertainties and risks which all researchers must confront. A number of research methods have been advanced to dispel those uncertainties and risks, and we shall review some of them in turn.

Many deviants are distinguished by their visibility. Particular styles of rule-breaking rely on acting in a particular way in public spaces. Indeed, the 'skinhead', 'Goth', or 'hoodie' identity would become meaningless if it remained private. Rather unkindly, Klapp has defined certain forms of expressive deviance which requires an audience as 'ego-screaming'. The street life associated with gangs, demonstrations, prostitutes, the homeless, and drug 'scenes' and the policing thereof, are reasonably conspicuous, and researchers can gravitate to a suitable gathering. It is often possible to join the fringes of activities, observing what goes on. The fringes themselves are generally ill-defined, few groups having a strict and enforceable criteria of membership. Sheer physical proximity can signify that one is either sympathetic or uninterested—either by approaching or distancing oneself from the area where the activity is taking place. In the absence of self-policing, certain forms of deviance may be bared to scrutiny.

Researchers have certainly moved in on the more visible and public deviant groups. Some have reported the conduct of demonstrations.[29] Stan Cohen monitored the migrations of the 'Mods' and 'Rockers' in the 1960s.[30] David Downes frequented a cafe used by local delinquents and, in time, he became accepted as a companion.[31] David Grazian used student informants to report about nightlife in Philadelphia's Center City.[32] So too, Philippe Bourgois came to know crack dealers in New York[33] and homeless heroin users in San Francisco and Philadelphia. And Sherri Cavan simply visited the bars of an American city, recording their deviant underlife.[34] There was little questioning of the presence of outsiders in a situation which could not neatly discriminate between insiders and outsiders or where strangers could not easily be expelled (although Bourgois was beaten up by the Philadelphia police who did not believe that he was the social anthropologist he claimed to be). When deviance is public, access is eased. Even the partially secluded can be laid open to observation. The more involved participants may tolerate or prepare particular identities which can be donned by observers. Voyeurism is not always wholly resented. Laud Humphreys, for instance, installed himself as a 'look-out' or 'watch queen' in 'tea rooms', American public lavatories, which allowed him to survey casual sexual encounters between homosexual men.[35]

Despite the wealth of behaviour which is publicly exhibited, it must be remembered that a lot of important activity will still remain concealed. After all, public behaviour is

---

[29] J. Halloran et al., *Demonstrations and Communications*.
[30] S. Cohen, *Folk Devils and Moral Panics*.   [31] D. Downes, *The Delinquent Solution*.
[32] D. Grazian, *On The Make: The Hustle of Urban Nightlife*.
[33] P. Bourgois, *In Search of Respect: Selling Crack in El Barrio*; P. Bourgois and J. Schonberg, *Righteous Dopefiend*.   [34] S. Cavan, *Liquor License*.
[35] L. Humphreys, *Tearoom Trade*.

usually only a small, and perhaps unimportant part of life. It is complemented by other conduct which will almost certainly be significant in the understanding of deviance. And public interchanges have their own situated character which may be quite demanding. Not only will people behave rather differently in private space, but they may also have reservations about the apparent commitments of public occasions.[36] Matza has described the 'multiple shared misunderstandings' which infuse deviant projects.[37] He argues that 'delinquents' may well have personal, unvoiced misgivings about public beliefs; and that it would be misleading to assume that they are all as zealous in their support for criminal enterprises as they appear to be. On the contrary, group activity can engender a rhetoric which may be at odds with personal beliefs. Even a small group is capable of producing such an alien reality. For instance, McCorkle and Korn provided a history of a delinquent episode in which none of the participants was really willing to go ahead, but each assumed that the others wanted a robbery to take place.[38] Only three people were involved, but their misreading of one another's intentions did lead to a robbery.

The language and conduct of public gatherings are not only coercive; they are also too standardized and anonymous to permit the expression of personal interests, although it is those interests which often influence how general understandings are translated into individual action. It would be a mistake to imagine that the slogans of a public march convey all its members' political perspectives, for instance.

Analysis therefore requires an additional mapping of private qualifications wherever that is possible. Without such a map, public language would be regarded as an accurate guide to conduct and belief, but it is not wholly accurate, and many who speak it recognize that it serves something of a rhetorical or ritual role. The behaviour and singing and chanting of football crowds must frequently be read as a series of feints and mock battles, not as aggression which will inevitably culminate in physical assault,[39] and such private qualifications may also be organized and circulated. Gang members may relate 'war' stories which give a mythic past and heroic status to themselves, but which are hugely embroidered in the telling.[40]

In an early and very influential article, Sykes and Matza discussed the 'techniques of neutralization' which delinquents employ in the explanation of conduct.[41] Claiming that would-be delinquents confront the problem of guilt, they catalogued the public formulas of mitigation and extenuation which are used to allay guilt and so ease the commission and aftermath of delinquency. It might be argued that the victim 'deserved' his or her fate or that he or she suffered no real loss. It might be argued that higher loyalties were at stake or that those who condemn action are in no moral position to judge. Reiss, too, has analysed the accounts which some adolescent gang members gave of their homosexual prostitution.[42] Not permitting themselves to take an

---

[36] J. Dollard, *Caste and Class in a Southern Town*. [37] D. Matza, *Delinquency and Drift*.

[38] R. Korn and L. McCorkle, 'Social Roles'. [39] P. Marsh et al., *The Rules of Disorder*.

[40] J. Patrick, *A Glasgow Gang Observed*; E. Schneider, *Vampires, Dragons, and Egyptian Kings: Youth Gangs in Postwar New York*; and S. Venkatesh, *Gang Leader for a Day*.

[41] G. Sykes and D. Matza, 'Techniques of Neutralization', and, for a later elaboration, S. Cohen, *States of Denial*. [42] A. Reiss, 'The Social Integration of Queers and Peers'.

'active' role, and affirming their 'real' heterosexuality, the young male prostitutes tried to acknowledge no worrying loss of sexual integrity or masculinity. In their own eyes, *they* were not gay but they cleverly exploited men who were.

It cannot be claimed that the role and functions of a sociological researcher are well understood in the wider world and, even if they were, there is no reason to suppose that trust would be any greater. Secluded deviation cannot be so effortlessly discovered. It may be furtive or disguised or so uncommon as to be unrecognizable to the naïve eye. Its practitioners may be distrustful and wary, unwilling to have dealings with a strange researcher. After all, researchers rarely praise what they see. To do so would be deemed uncritical and unsophisticated: whole schools of sociology have adopted the title 'critical' with pride.

Where there are no public groups to observe and no home territories to frequent, the researcher will be obliged to turn to alternative strategies. One device has been called 'snowballing', the collection of a sample by incremental contacts. If a researcher is able to gain the confidence of one informant, he or she may then seek a series of introductions to others in the deviant's world. Those introductions will serve as a limited reassurance to those who are suspicious. In time, a sizeable population may be met. A prime example was provided by Nancy Lee's hunt for women who had undergone abortion in America,[43] at that time (and still in many parts) an illegal procedure. Very typically, such women neither declared themselves nor courted attention from researchers. They may well have concealed their abortions from their own families. Despite their great reluctance, Lee managed to unearth a considerable number of women, being passed from one to the next in a long chain. She produced a sample of otherwise inaccessible subjects.

Chief among the limitations to snowballing are the restrictions imposed by the structure of a social network. A researcher will encounter a sample shaped by the relationships and knowledge of a particular group, and the boundaries around that group will be the boundaries of a sample. That constraint may not be especially important. We have already argued that the difficulties of research are often so impressive that every interview and meeting is an accomplishment.

What remains uncertain is the peculiar character of the group that has revealed itself. In one sense, all groups are unique and none can claim typicality. In another sense, distinctiveness *can* become a problem. Initial acquaintance is likely to be with someone in or near the researcher's circle, and the researcher may become exposed to a group whose politics, stance, or *milieux* are rather similar to his or her own. The robbers, drug-users, or thieves unearthed by snowballing may then compose a rather special network. Drug-users may be unusually articulate: and there used to be disproportionately voluminous research on the self-conscious and middle-class addict. Working-class addicts were relatively neglected. Snowballing will almost certainly generate an impression of social structure and collective behaviour. It is not and can never be designed to reach the isolated person. By extension, it invariably suggests that deviance is a collective achievement.

---

[43] N. Lee, *The Search for an Abortionist*.

Sometimes snowballing does not lead very far. Introductions are not forthcoming or prove fruitless. Sometimes, too, the researcher expresses no great desire to construct a sample. On the contrary, knowledge may be so meagre that it warrants an intensive exploration of just one subject. That exploration might be justified by the search for a biographical analysis of deviance or by the exploitation of an extraordinary opportunity. As a result, researchers have quite frequently collaborated in the writing of deviant life-histories,[44] attempting to understand the part played by rule-breaking in the life of a single person or family of people.[45] It would be an exceptional individual who consented to such documentation. Co-operation is sometimes secured when researcher and criminal/deviant establish trust after a period of prison visiting or as a result of intense interviewing. More exceptionally, volunteers are recruited by advertisement in general or special newspapers. Sometimes simple friendship can be turned into a research relationship.

A case history can never be described as a basis for substantial generalization, but the researcher may not want to produce sociological laws, or may believe that such laws are premature. In the place of generality, the criminal/deviant biography offers depth and detail. On one level, it undoubtedly yields more than brief interviews or short spates of observation. It can be conducted in a leisurely manner: questions can be asked or postponed at will; minute knowledge can be acquired; the evolution of criminal/deviant careers can be plotted, disclosures can be made which might otherwise have been withheld. Researchers of crime and deviance have accordingly returned repeatedly to the stock of criminal biographies in order to tap a source of unusually informed knowledge.[46] Biographies tend to underscore the perils of superficial classification and argument: they often present lives as more complex, intricate, and open to diverse interpretations than much conventional criminology seems to suppose.[47] One exceptional instance is Sereny's biography of Hitler's architect, Albert Speer, in which themes of guilt, knowledge, acknowledgement, and responsibility are diffusely intertwined.[48]

Observation, snowballing, and the case study are somewhat distant methods. They preserve researchers in their professional role, keeping the subject apart. But, on occasion, such distance is simply impossible to maintain: the researcher could be a deviant or a friend of deviants and research will consist merely of observing oneself and others.[49] On occasion, too, participation may be foisted on the researcher, flowing from the inescapable relationships and encounters that surround research. After all, all research is at bottom a social relation, and despite the formalities of university ethics committees, it is never easy to remain aloof and disengaged; one's sheer presence may

---

[44] E. Sutherland, *The Professional Thief*; C. Shaw, *The Jack-Roller*; W. Probyn, *Angel Face*; W. Chambliss, *Box Man*.

[45] F. Butterfield, *All God's Children: The Bosket Family and the American Tradition of Violence*.

[46] H. Becker, 'The Life History and the Scientific Mosaic'.

[47] Thus Plummer was at one time working on the life-histories of a number of sexual deviants. He argued that no conventional sexual categorization adequately describes their conduct or self-definition. Instead of 'homosexuality', for example, he preferred to talk of 'homosexualities'. See K. Plummer, *Documents of Life*.

[48] G. Sereny, *Albert Speer*.   [49] T. Shibutani, *The Derelicts of Company K*.

be read as an indication of collusion, interest, or complicity. So it is that, little by little, relations can draw the researcher in and detachment becomes insupportable.[50] Indeed, a refusal to unbend could be read as a sign of unfriendly stiffness that threatens to undermine research.

In contrast, some forms of crime and deviance make no provision for spectators. Research that entails the active collaboration of the researcher has been called 'participant-observation', and it has been employed with special frequency in the study of crime and deviance. Sometimes contingencies of biography or situation throw a researcher into such a social anthropological role. Sometimes it is a theoretical commitment which asserts that social behaviour cannot be understood until it has been personally experienced. There is an argument that researchers who lean on external accounts and objective evidence can have no good appreciation of how people act. Neither can they grasp environments and history as their subjects do. They run the very real risk of imposing a non-contextualized explanation whose links with a problem may be a little tendentious. What is represented as causal might well have had no influence on a person or a group.

Participant observation is supposed to allow the researcher to experience causes and effects in a particular social setting. Goffman argued that 'any group of persons . . . develop[s] a life of their own that becomes meaningful, reasonable, and normal once you get close to it, and . . . a good way to learn about any of these worlds is to submit oneself in the company of the members to the daily round of petty contingencies to which they are subject'.[51] It is with that knowledge that explanation can be built. As we shall see, those who employ participation as a strategy[52] are the bearers of a long tradition that may be linked in part with the University of Chicago in the 1920s. One early student of that university recalled how, in general, academic knowledge was thought to be an unreliable basis for speculation, giving no sure understanding. A sometime head of the sociology department at the university, Robert Park:

> made a great point of the difference between knowledge about something and acquaintance with the phenomena. That was one of the great thrusts in Chicago, because people had to get out and if they wanted to study opium addicts they went to the opium dens and even smoked a little opium maybe. They went out and lived with the gangs and the . . . hobos and so on.[53]

The subject of crime and deviance seems to provide an unusually attractive solution to those confronting the problems of participant-observation because participant-observers try to perform an intricate feat. They are required to reach the probably unattainable state of one who is both insider and outsider, a person who sees a social world from within yet who also stands apart and analyses it as a stranger. As an insider, the researcher will attempt to move as his or her subjects move, learning responses, definitions, and actions as they go. Their gestures will be to some extent the researcher's

---

[50] For a fictional description of such a process, see A. Lurie, *Imaginary Friends*.
[51] E. Goffman, *Asylums*, ix–x.   [52] P. Rock, *The Making of Symbolic Interactionism*, ch. 6.
[53] Interview with Leonard Cottrell, quoted in J. Carey, *Sociology and Public Affairs*, 156.

own, becoming familiar enough that they can be reproduced and described to a larger audience. As an outsider, the researcher will treat those gestures as problematic and uncertain, requiring close examination and questioning. Ideas and practices must be regarded as simultaneously natural and unnatural. Crime or deviance frequently represent an answer to that dilemma, being a satisfactory meld of the familiar and the unfamiliar, allowing the researcher to imagine that he or she is both inside and outside the worlds they create. For instance, drug-taking or sexual deviance in one's own society combines the strange and the known in a composition which excites curiosity but does not defeat understanding. There is an important affinity between the sociology of crime deviance and participant-observation, and a substantial number of studies have adopted an ethnographic style in consequence.

Nonetheless, there are often good reasons why participant-observation should not be conducted. The method may not necessarily furnish the kind of information demanded by a particular problem. There have been allegations that anthropological techniques (and especially covert techniques) pose intricate ethical problems.[54] Many researchers are indifferent to the role of meaning and experience in explanation, looking for more objective and solid variables. Others find observation difficult in certain settings. Not everyone would pass uneventfully into the world of street gangs or Hell's Angels.[55] Older researchers might find it awkward to merge with the young, women with men, whites with blacks, Arabs with Jews. Some have pulled it off. Liebow, a white male researcher, conducted a masterly anthropological study of Washington black street-corner society, and, later still, of homeless women.[56] But he was exceptional. Safer, less taxing, and ethically easier methods *can* be productive and much of the sociology of crime deviance has turned to them instead.

There is one very common strategy for reaching deviants without engaging in participant-observation. Researchers can proceed directly to a prison, mental hospital, or detention centre and the advantages of doing so are obvious. An individual who is confined and controlled is likely to be a little more amenable to interview. A meeting with a researcher might actually help to overcome the boredom of a monotonous regime. And, for the researcher, captives are neatly assembled samples requiring little pursuit. There may be considerable problems in trying to gain access to the institution itself,[57] but, in theory, prisons, hospitals, and detention centres are convenient 'warehouses'.

Interviews and studies of captive populations can be put to two major uses, and one raises rather fewer difficulties of interpretation and application than the other. The first transforms an enclosed community into a research subject in its own right. There has been a long history of work on the social organizations of prisons and asylums. Thus, Ward and Kassebaum explored a women's prison,[58] Cohen and Taylor discussed the effects of long-term imprisonment,[59] Goffman analysed the mental hospital as a 'total

---

[54] K. Erikson, 'Disguised Observation in Sociology'.   [55] H. Thompson, *Hell's Angels*.
[56] E. Liebow, *Tell Them Who I Am: The Lives of Homeless Women*.
[57] S. Cohen and L. Taylor, *Prison Secrets*.   [58] D. Ward and G. Kassebaum, *Women's Prison*.
[59] S. Cohen and L. Taylor, *Psychological Survival*.

institution,'[60] Comfort the web of relations between the inmates of San Quentin prison and their partners,[61] and Rhodes looked at the social structure of an American 'supermax' prison.[62] Their intention was to explain the social organization of very special institutions, and there was no pretence at an informed and lengthy discussion about crime and deviance outside the walls. Neither was there a very detailed analysis of what inmates did and thought before their confinement. In this first instance, institutional life was the focus.

Institutions are objects of no particular curiosity in the second use, being instead useful places where people who are of interest to the researcher may be found. Captives may well be the only accessible representatives of a certain group. There are many individuals who are not easily found in the world at large. They lack the fixed social positions and physical locations which aid discovery. Only the most unusual circumstances would bring about a profitable encounter between a researcher and a murderer or rapist. Sometimes offending is rare and haphazard and not easily monitored: an observer might have to spend many unproductive months waiting for something to turn up. Criminals and deviants are sometimes too well-protected, threatening, or secretive to be relaxed research subjects. Researchers could well feel trepidation about spending long periods of time in the unprotected company of those who are violent or disturbed.[63] If certain people are to be seen at all, it will probably be in prison or mental hospital. In effect, the researcher will entrust the business of collecting samples to the police and official agencies.

There is some risk that institutions will then become sources of distortion. An institutional setting limits enquiry about past conduct. There can be little appreciation of matters which originally escaped the subject's interest and attention. Events before incarceration cannot be observed as they unfold: they must be pieced together retrospectively. The responses of others cannot be witnessed. There are few external checks on what is said. Institutions tend to police communication, inhibiting the delivery of unguarded replies and gestures. They are certainly different from the original *milieux* or 'natural settings' that prompted the behaviour which the researcher would describe. They impose their own mark on conduct, making it difficult to detach the effects of treatment, punishment, and control from previous experience. Problems flow from the special recruitment of inmates and patients. For example, clinical reports about sex offenders, prostitutes, or drug addicts can deal only with those who presented themselves as people in need of treatment. They cannot be extended to the unexplored world of those not so designated.[64]

Basing their knowledge on a selected population, it is generally impossible for researchers to claim typicality. Few criminals and deviants at large are apprehended, and only a few of those apprehended actually enter custody. Indeed, Mack once suggested that prisoners are often no more than unusually inept criminals and that research on inmates centres on those who are particularly incompetent.[65] It is also quite possible

---

[60] E. Goffman, *Asylums*.   [61] M. Comfort, *Home Sweep*.

[62] L. Rhodes, *Total Confinement: Madness and Reason in the Maximum Security Prison*.

[63] J. Carey, 'Problems of Access and Risk in Observing Drug Scenes'.

[64] A. Lindesmith, *Opiate Addiction*; E. Hooker, 'Male Homosexuality'.

[65] J. Mack, '"Professional Crime" and Criminal Organization'.

that research on inmates will be further distorted by a reifying propensity to classify criminals and deviants by the offences for which they were incarcerated at the time. That is, those imprisoned for rape or theft will be identified for analytic purposes as rapists or thieves, as distinct from murderers or burglars. There is some evidence that such a method of official identification is misleading, that criminals and deviants are quite likely to be arrested for the acts in which they do not specialize precisely because they are inexpert at them. That is certainly the conclusion of Wright in his study of burglars and of Faupel in his study of drug users. Faupel reflected, for instance:

> Criminal addicts are disproportionately arrested for crimes that are marginal to their over-all pattern of illegal activities . . . stable heroin addicts tend to specialize . . . One of the advantages of such specialization is that valuable technical, social and intuitive skills are developed that facilitate the successful commission of these crimes. More important, these skills provide the stable addict with the ability to avoid detection and arrest.[66]

Finally, there is always the additional possibility that a researcher will be identified with the organization. Responses may be tailored appropriately, becoming ingratiating, cautious, disingenuous, or hostile.

More indiscriminate methods of rendering criminal, deviant, and other populations visible, versions of what might be described as sociological saturation coverage, may be employed. Researchers can launch what is in effect a mass attack on a substantially undifferentiated population of people. There will be little or no attempt to single out groups in advance. On the contrary, those groups will surface as the work progresses. Early instances are the self-report studies conducted by Kinsey, Porterfield,[67] Wallerstein and Wyle,[68] Nye and Short,[69] and Nettler.[70] A population most often consisting of schoolchildren will be subjected to a battery of questions about criminal incidents and its members will be required to indicate which acts, if any, they committed. One of the most sophisticated examples was Belson's massive study of London boys, a study which revealed, like many of its predecessors, that every boy interviewed had committed some act of theft.[71] The specific concern is usually with the incidence of unrecorded delinquencies in an effort to establish the 'true' rate and distribution of criminality. There are methodological difficulties with self-report studies, partly because it is accepted that adolescents are unwilling to admit to graver offences, and partly because samples of school students are likely to omit truants, the most seriously offending group.[72] A notable exception was the Youth Lifestyles Survey, which was based on interviews with just under 5,000 12–30-year-olds living in private households in England and Wales in 1998–9. In that survey, 57 per cent of men and 37 per cent of women said they had committed at least one offence in their lives, and 19 per cent said that they had committed one or more offences in the last 12 months, with 12 per cent reporting they had been formally cautioned or taken to court at some point.[73]

[66] C. Faupel, *Shooting Dope*, 140.   [67] A. Porterfield, *Youth in Trouble*.

[68] J. Wallerstein and C. Wyle, 'Our Law-Abiding Law-Breakers'.

[69] F. Nye and J. Short, 'Scaling Delinquent Behavior'.

[70] G. Nettler, 'Antisocial Sentiment and Criminality'.   [71] W. Belson, *Juvenile Theft*.

[72] M. Sullivan, *'Getting Paid': Youth Crime and Work in the Inner City*, 6.

[73] C. Flood-Page et al., *Youth Crime*.

The British Government's 'Offending, Crime and Justice Survey' which was described as 'a nationally representative, longitudinal, self-report survey which asked young people in England and Wales about their attitudes towards and experiences of offending' was launched in 2003 and completed four annual sweeps. It was on a scale and degree of complexity comparable to its sister survey, the British Crime Survey. Some 12,000 people between the ages of 10 and 65 were interviewed about their engagement in a range of illegal and legal behaviour, including drug taking and alcohol consumption, which enables the analyst to talk about trends, risks, and patterns.[74]

Cohort, criminal careers, or longitudinal studies are an extension of this second version, and they have become particularly influential in the United States, where there is an emphasis on when people embark on and then desist from offending. A sample of a generation (usually of males in the past), may be mapped over time by periodic questioning to examine not only its patterns of involvement with crime and delinquency as they unfold during the course of a life but also how those patterns intersect with other events. Measures of matters as diverse as family structure, discipline, supervision, and abuse; educational attainment and school attendance; poverty, social class, and employment; health, intelligence, drug use, and drinking; parental criminal convictions, and the like, are taken to assess their statistical connection with law-breaking. The outcome can be helpful, enabling the criminologist to learn more about the precursors and concomitants of offending behaviour; when people start to offend and when they desist; what offences are committed by whom, how often, when, and in what company; how specialized offending actually proves to be; and whether there are discernible connections between different offences within the span of a single life. The pioneering research was undertaken by Marvin Wolfgang in the 1960s,[75] and it was to be followed, amongst other studies, by the work of Wadsworth[76] and West and Farrington[77] in the United Kingdom and of Blumstein and Hsieh[78] and of Petersilia and others[79] in the United States. And most influential of all in this area, perhaps, has been the work of John Laub and Robert Sampson,[80] and we shall return to this when we discuss control theory in Chapter 9.

A third form of saturation coverage is the somewhat misleadingly named crime survey, pioneered in the United States[81] and later applied in Canada, Holland, Britain, and

---

[74] *Young People and Crime: Findings from the 2006 Offending, Crime and Justice Survey*, Home Office Statistical Bulletin 09/08, 2008; *Minority Ethnic Groups and Crime: Findings from the Crime and Justice Survey*, Home Office Online Report 33/05, 2005; *Drug Use among Vulnerable Groups of Young People: Findings from the 2003 Crime and Justice Survey*, Findings 254, 2005; and *Findings from the 2003 Offending, Crime and Justice Survey: Alcohol-Related Crime and Disorder*, Findings 261, 2005.

[75] M. Wolfgang et al., *Delinquency in a Birth Cohort*.

[76] M. Wadsworth, *Roots of Delinquency: Infancy, Adolescence and Crime*.

[77] D. West, *Delinquency: Its Roots, Careers and Prospects*; D. West and D. Farrington, *Who Becomes Delinquent?*; D. West and D. Farrington, *The Delinquent Way of Life*.

[78] A. Blumstein and P. Hsieh, *The Duration of Adult Criminal Careers*.

[79] J. Petersilia et al., *Criminal Careers of Habitual Felons*.

[80] J. Laub and R. Sampson, *Shared Beginnings, Divergent Lives: Delinquent Boys to Age 70*; and R. Sampson and J. Laub, *Crime in the Making: Pathways and Turning Points Through Life*.

[81] President's Commission on Law Enforcement and the Administration of Justice, *Crime and its Impact: An Assessment*.

elsewhere.[82] Mass surveys have been conducted of households, probing the extent of their members' experience of victimization during a particular period of time, usually a year. The original intention was to discover what were thought to be 'real' crime rates as close to the actual event as possible. Thus, the first British Crime Survey of 1981 showed that only 8 per cent of offences of vandalism known to victims were reported to the police. The rates for theft from a motor vehicle were 29 per cent, for burglary 48 per cent, for theft from the person 8 per cent, and for robbery 11 per cent.[83] Crime surveys have introduced quite dramatic changes in thinking about crime and deviance, and it was inevitable that, in time, their original goals should have been supplemented and displaced by other aims. They are rich sources of information that have not only revealed new research possibilities as interests and priorities have changed, but also affected the very agenda of the sociology of crime and deviance. Such surveys could not just continue as mere exercises in counting crimes. They were to give a new public prominence to the victim of crime;[84] raising questions about the distress of victimization and the ways in which it may be relieved;[85] directing research at the problem of the fear of crime and the measures which people take to avoid victimization;[86] and encouraging a re-emergence of the social, spatial, and demographic geography of criminal events.[87] Most recently, they are being employed by governments as measures of 'consumer' satisfaction with services delivered by the criminal justice system. The Crime Survey for England and Wales, for instance, is now annual, and it is being employed amongst other tasks to judge the efficacy of the police and prosecution service.

Crime surveys have had a revolutionary impact on the study of crime and deviance, and on radical criminology especially. As we shall argue, a revelation of the extent, intensity, and repetitive nature of working-class victimization and women led some radical criminologists to reappraise their stance towards the social and political significance and consequences of crime. They no longer discuss everyday crimes as if they were a petty and irritating diversion from more substantial political issues or as a justification for authoritarian criminal justice policies.[88] They have instead begun to take very seriously issues which were once the exclusive domain of their ideological opponents, issues focusing on the problems of police effectiveness and crime prevention.[89]

Large victim surveys are not without their defects. Being household surveys, they inevitably fail to cover a number of important, high-risk groups: the imprisoned and institutionalized, those in transit, illegal immigrants, and the homeless. They do not always embrace crimes against institutions, including the multiply-victimized small shops. Nor do they include new forms of crime such as cyber-criminality. As they were often originally conducted in the presence of other family members, they had particular difficulties in unearthing sexual abuse and domestic violence against women, although that has been remedied in later surveys with the introduction of new, more discreet, electronic equivalents to the questionnaire which require respondents merely

[82] R. Sparks et al., *Surveying Victims*.
[83] M. Hough and P. Mayhew, *The British Crime Survey*.   [84] P. Rock, *A View from the Shadows*.
[85] M. Hough and P. Mayhew, *Taking Account of Crime*.
[86] M. Maxfield, *Fear of Crime in England and Wales*.
[87] S. Smith, *Crime, Space and Society*.   [88] S. Box, *Power, Crime and Mystification*.
[89] J. Lea and J. Young, *What is to be Done about Law and Order?*

to press buttons.[90] They do not often cover children and omit the many injuries that children suffer. Those deficiencies can be and have been remedied, although often at some expense, and more tightly focused surveys are quite able to illuminate the victimization of particular groups.[91]

An under-used but recently revived approach is the comparative method of cross-cultural and historical study. Although criminology and the sociology of crime and deviance were, in a sense, born comparative—in such diverse works as John Howard's *The State of the Prisons* (1777) and Durkheim's *Le Suicide* (1897)—this approach has been singularly neglected for much of their history. The long ascendancy of positivism may in part account for this neglect. If the site of crime is to be found in the pathology of individual offenders or their families, then the comparative method is logically brought to bear only on such factors as might differentiate criminal from non-criminal within a given society at one point in time. However, part of this neglect also stemmed from the nature of the reactions *against* positivism. The symbolic interactionist stress on situated accounts, motives, and meanings reinforced a delving into the ways of life of deviant groups and agencies of control at local level. To generalize beyond the groups studied breached methodological canons for some phenomenologists.[92] At every level, from interviews to official statistics, cross-cultural study compounds problems of interpretation which are severe and laborious enough even within a single society.

Yet the past three decades have seen a growth of comparative criminology which shows little sign of slackening. Much of this work is largely descriptive and of little direct theoretical value. But increasingly the tenets of theories purporting to 'fit the facts' are being assessed in terms of trends over time and between societies rather than within single societies or at a given point in history.[93] It is Beirne and Hill's argument that 'the explanatory power of theories can be enhanced considerably if they are systematically tested under as diverse temporal and cultural conditions as possible'.[94]

One prime instance is the work of Manuel Eisner who has plotted trends in homicide rates over very long periods of time within and across societies, discovering appreciable declines in most European societies, but declines that do not march uniformly in step, leading Eisner to conclude that major structural variables must be invoked to understand change.[95] Another is Zimring's attempt to make sense of the decline in American crime rates since the mid-1990s.[96] Every major variable ventured to account for the decrease in the United States could be shown by comparative analysis of the working (or lack of working) of similar variables in other societies not to have any general explanatory power. What was held to cause shifts in the numbers of crimes

[90] P. Mayhew and C. Mirrlees-Black, *The 1992 British Crime Survey.*
[91] For crimes against shops, see British Retail Consortium, *Retail Crime Survey*
[92] R. Robertson and L. Taylor, *Deviance, Crime and Socio-Legal Control.*
[93] J. Braithwaite, *Inequality, Crime and Public Policy*, and *Crime, Shame and Reintegration.*
[94] P. Beirne and J. Hill, *Comparative Criminology*, vii.
[95] M. Eisner, 'Modernization, Self-Control and Lethal Violence. The Long-term Dynamics of European Homicide Rates in Theoretical Perspective'. And see P. Spierenburg, *A History of Murder: Personal Violence in Europe from the Middle Ages to the Present.*
[96] F. Zimring, *The Great American Crime Decline.*

applied—if it did apply—to the United States alone although those other societies (and Canada and a number of European states in particular) had undergone almost identical trends. At the very least, what was believed to apply to the United States required some re-examination and qualification.

Additional Data Sources

Crime and deviance are everywhere and leave traces everywhere. They mark those who report them, those who attempt to control them, those who gain from them, those who suffer from them, those who report or imaginatively describe them, and the contexts in which they are performed. They hold a central place in our news and popular cultures. Properly analysed, almost every environment can be interpreted as a record of the effects and responses which crime, deviance, and control produces. Gary Marx once argued that 'Traces or residue elements are separate from accidents and mistakes, and perhaps surer sources, in that for certain types of infractions they will always be present.'[97] Locks, doors, walls, surveillance cameras, ID verification, guards, police, courts, prisons, news media, popular culture, graffiti, insurance companies, tax-collectors, passport checks, credit cards, and bank vaults all embody the impact of rule-breaking. But they represent much more than simply fixed or static reactions. They provide sets of opportunities and constraints for the commission of further crime and deviance and the application of further control techniques. Indeed, Mary McIntosh described the historical evolution of crime as a competitive struggle between preventative and illegal technologies.[98]

It therefore becomes interesting to turn to other forms of evidence not only because it can lead to an appreciation of the settings and processes which manufacture criminality and deviation but also because it enlarges the sheer mass of data available. Policing, surveillance, cultural representations, common-sense assumptions, and physical structures[99] shape conduct, and researchers have worked on them all. For example, there has been innovative work on literary descriptions of crime,[100] building on the thesis that literature can be treated as a special history of ideas and ideologies of crime and control. And of course, in terms of cultural significance, crime fiction outsells all other forms of fiction. There has been a particularly intense fascination with the part played by the mass media, although it is actually very difficult to disentangle and measure the effects of crime reporting and consumption on its audiences, and debate about the matter has been acrimonious and seemingly barren.[101]

Partly because of the problems of studying audience effects, many researchers have turned their attention instead to the social construction and composition of crime

---

[97] G. Marx, 'Notes on the Discovery, Collection, and Assessment of Hidden and Dirty Data', 86.
[98] M. McIntosh, *The Organization of Crime*.
[99] Cf. J. Jacobs, *The Death and Life of Great American Cities*.
[100] D. Davis, *Homicide in American Fiction*; P. Collins, *Dickens and Crime*; S. Knight, *Crime Fiction Since 1800*.
[101] S. Livingstone, 'On the Continuing Problem of Media Effects'.

news.[102] It has been argued that news agencies are vital disseminators of second-hand knowledge about crime and deviance, furnishing a landscape of saints, evil-doers, and villains which appears to be as real as anything known to limited immediate experience.[103] People are taken to live in a universe which has been prefabricated by news reports.[104] Ericson's three-volume study of crime reporting in Toronto analyses the subtle and complicated relations between the traditional news media, sources, subjects, and events of one city.[105] Ericson has shown how the public imagery of crime is the product of negotiations between sources seeking to convey their sense of the world to reporters who are themselves policing the world for 'procedural strays' and 'irregularities', and the 'news hooks' that will organize what they can say.

Other groups and institutions have been mapped in an effort to analyse how they mould conduct. Crime and deviance are shaped in their transactions with events and people around it. Indeed, it is often practically and conceptually difficult to distinguish between deviation and its settings. Researchers, and 'labelling theorists'—phenomenologists and interactionists in particular—consequently occupied themselves with the character and workings of the social reaction to deviance. An exploration of courts,[106] prisons,[107] and police and prosecution agencies will produce oblique but powerful information about crime and deviation.

Such 'secondary' evidence has a major part to play in explanation, and it tends to be easier to compile than ethnographic data: newspapers are more tractable than burglars. Further, secondary evidence is abundant and it may be studied safely in congenial surroundings. Its producers are often more amenable than deviants themselves. Journalism, the police force, the prison service, the youth justice service, regulatory agencies, the criminal bar, and the civil service are occupations with relatively stable memberships. They are part of the everyday middle-class world of the researcher. In all these senses, they constitute a potentially more accessible research population and much research turns out not to be a study of crime and criminality at all but of criminal justice policies and practices. As a result an increasing number of researchers have little or nothing to contribute to public debates about the particularities of crime and deviance.

There are researchers who seek indices and measures which are even more remote from the sites of deviant activity. Arguing that the business of science is the exploration of 'deep' social structures, they turn to indicators which reflect the changes and states of an underlying order. Those indicators may be movements of the business cycle,[108] trends in architecture or in educational practice,[109] or signs

---

[102] M. Fishman, *Manufacturing the News*.

[103] S. Cohen and J. Young (eds.), *The Manufacture of News*.   [104] L. Wilkins, *Social Deviance*.

[105] R. Ericson et al., *Visualizing Deviance* and *Negotiating Control*.

[106] P. Carlen, *Magistrates' Justice*; M. Atkinson and P. Drew, *Order in Court*; and W. Bennett and M. Feldman, *Reconstructing Reality in the Courtroom*.

[107] M. Foucault, *Discipline and Punish*; T. and P. Morris, *Pentonville*; D. Clemmer, *The Prison Community*; and G. Sykes, *The Society of Captives*.

[108] H. Mannheim, *Social Aspects of Crime Between the Wars*; G. Rusche and O. Kirchheimer, *Punishment and Social Structure*; and J. Wells, 'Crime and Unemployment'.

[109] M. Foucault, *Discipline and Punish*.

of political crisis.[110] The organizing assumption is that crime and deviance are but a part of society and that society itself is a moving whole. Transformations of that whole will reveal themselves in many areas, present in shifting ideologies or in the political and economic system, and connections and developments can be traced at almost any point. Thus Foucault argued that there was a wholesale revolution in population management at the beginning of the nineteenth century: new disciplines were introduced into factories, workhouses, prisons, schools, and armies, embodying and echoing changing postures towards criminals themselves. Such postures, it was argued, can be appreciated by comprehending the entire revolution in practice and knowledge, new styles of handwriting and child-rearing becoming as instructive to the criminologist as the more obvious data of penal practice. Indeed, they are more instructive because they are *not* obvious.

The most common and orthodox form of indirect evidence is that contained in official statistics. There has been a long tradition of bureaucratic record-keeping in certain European societies. For example, censuses have been conducted in Britain since 1801. As a result, there has been a heavy reliance upon government-sponsored statistics as a barometer of social change. In the beginning, particularly, a new science of 'social physics' arose to respond to the opportunities presented by the new evidence.[111] It was believed that it had become possible to produce laws of social motion akin to those furnished by the natural sciences. Thus, Quetelet argued in 1869 that a competent statistician could predict within tolerable limits the numbers and characteristics of people who would be murdered and who would murder in the years to come, even though they were still alive and oblivious of what would befall them. Statistical rates were taken to be independent sources of commentary. They revealed truths which were quite superior to impressionistic and subjective evidence. That stance persisted for some time: for instance, Chevalier's history of nineteenth-century Paris contrasted the unreliable and partial accounts of novelists and journalists with what he considered to be the sound checks offered by crime rates.[112] Historians are particularly prone to defer to police and court records as indisputably sound and objective.[113]

At first glance, official statistics would seem to provide an unparalleled foundation for speculation. They are the fruits of an expenditure which no ordinary researcher could afford and are neatly tabulated for immediate analysis and use. They are compiled without any effort on the part of the researcher. In some cases, they have no rivals. Historical work, for instance, must lean heavily on official published rates.[114]

However, there have been long-established reservations about the utility of official records of crime.[115] The arguments are incompletely settled, but they take two major tacks. Apart from a brief and probably unproductive debate about whether researchers should accept classifications which have been devised for allegedly unscientific

---

[110] S. Hall et al., *Policing the Crisis*.   [111] A. Quetelet, *Essai de Physique Sociale*.

[112] L. Chevalier, *Labouring Classes and Dangerous Classes*.

[113] J. Beattie, 'Judicial Records and the Measurement of Crime in Eighteenth Century England'.

[114] T. Gurr et al., *The Politics of Crime and Conflict*.

[115] S. Box, *Deviance, Reality and Society*; and R. Hood and R. Sparks, *Key Issues in Criminology*.

purposes,[116] uncertainties hover around the problem of the 'dark figure' and the negotiated character of rates.

The 'dark figure' is that universe of incidents which may have been reported but are
not recorded by the police and the courts. Official statistics are not, and do not pretend
to be, a report of the total volume of illegal activity, whatever that might be.[117] They
are simply a measure of crimes recorded by officials. Researchers concerned with the
'real' or 'true' rates may then become preoccupied with the events that escaped the official records. Only when those events have been enumerated, it is argued, will there
be a reliable index. Researchers have accordingly devoted themselves to a cataloguing
of the processes which enhance or undermine the validity of official figures. Listed
in that catalogue are the ability and willingness of people to recognize crimes, their
willingness to report crimes, and the character of the police response to public reports.
It is acknowledged that many crimes are furtive, hidden, or technically sophisticated.
Burglaries, frauds, and embezzlement may never be identified. Even if crime *is* known
to have occurred, there may be a reluctance to notify the police: it may be thought that
the amounts involved do not warrant intervention; the police may be defined as uninterested or ineffective; the victim may be implicated (as a collaborator, or as the client
of a prostitute, perhaps); the victim may be vulnerable; there may be sympathy for the
offender; there may be little sympathy for the victim; there may be hostility towards the
police (or a fear about not showing public hostility) and accompanying prohibitions on
'grassing', 'snitching', or informing;[118] the crime may itself be condoned; or there may
be little practical utility in reporting because possessions were uninsured or uninsur-
able. The police themselves, applying their own, perhaps idiosyncratic 'counting' or
classifying rules, can declare that no crime or some other crime has been committed,
or take no further action. They may focus on particular kinds of crime, and record
them in particular ways, in the pursuit of any number of goals, including meeting performance targets to escape censure or acquire extra resources.[119] There is a long chain
of complicated decisions between the commission of a possible crime and its recording
and registration. Not surprisingly officially recorded statistics have come to be treated
with well-founded suspicion.

Certain crimes do seem to be accurately reflected in statistics. For example, the first
British Crime Survey recorded that victims notified 100 per cent of thefts of motor
vehicles to the police,[120] and that may be explained quite readily. There is a real enough
incentive to approach the police after the loss of a car because a report must be made
if an insurance claim is to be met. Homicides are heavily reported. But there are gaps
in other records of crime and deviance. Only 8 per cent of thefts from the person were

---

[116] T. Sellin, 'The Significance of Records of Crime' and 'The Basis of a Crime Index'; and A. Biderman
and A. Reiss, 'On Exploring the "Dark Figure" of Crime'.

[117] Jason Ditton has pointed out that, rather as in the light of the Heisenberg principle, the volume of
rule-breaking unearthed is, to an unmeasurable extent, a product of the diligence with which controllers
seek for it. J. Ditton, *Controlology*.

[118] R. Hood and K. Joyce, 'Three Generations'.

[119] Her Majesty's Inspectorate of Constabulary, *Crime Recording; Making the Victim Count*.

[120] M. Hough and P. Mayhew, *The British Crime Survey*.

reported. Some amounts will be considered too petty to merit action. Some thefts will be inappropriately interpreted as the mere mislaying of property. Some thefts will be of things that were gained unlawfully. Some possessions may not be missed or may not have been insured.

The emergence of crime surveys as competing sources of information has reinforced a drift towards analysing official criminal statistics as records, not so much of crimes proper, but of the number and distribution of police actions and decisions. Those figures convey little about the 'actual' volume of rule-breaking, but they are an excellent guide to how police forces are deployed and how they behave.[121]

But the matter is not simple because the official statistics are actually quite useful to the researcher, as they may mirror particular patterns of crime as they are known to victims. For instance, crime surveys of Sheffield suggested that variations between different areas' officially recorded rates of offending are matched quite closely by variations in their victimization rates.[122] Although Sheffield's police statistics may not capture the city's 'true' volume of crime, they may at least reveal the comparative pattern of dispersal of crimes.[123] If such a finding could be generalized, official statistics would provide helpful information about the geographical and social spread of crime.

A second description of crime records has emerged from phenomenology and ethnomethodology. Instead of portraying official statistics as more or less 'accurate', researchers have defined them as compressed summaries of complicated interchanges between people.[124] A statistic then ceases to be a poor measure of the worrying 'dark figure', no longer simply a self-evident trace of police action, but a condensed, shorthand expression of all the work that is undertaken when a 'suspect' is named, apprehended, charged, and prosecuted. It is a product of copious activity, and, it is argued, it will be literally meaningless until that activity is first understood. Unless one has a grasp of typical processes of plea-bargaining, for example, no significance can be attached to the classification of an offence.[125] Unless one has an understanding of police responses to calls from the public,[126] police interrogation procedures,[127] police strategies,[128] and prosecution and courtroom practices, it will remain unclear what the statistics represent. They are not the impersonal products of a mechanical process of registration. Rather, they incorporate operating assumptions and predictions which are intelligible chiefly to their producers.

A good example of the phenomenological stance is provided by Douglas'[129] (and Atkinson's)[130] criticism of Durkheim's *Le Suicide*. Durkheim depicted suicide rates as

---

[121] K. Bottomley and K. Pease, *Crime and Punishment*, for a useful summary of the official statistics of crime.

[122] A. Bottoms, R. Mawby, and M. Walker, 'A Localised Crime Survey in Contrasting Areas of a City'.

[123] R. Mawby, 'Crime and Law'.

[124] J. Kitsuse and A. Cicourel, 'A Note on the Uses of Official Statistics'.

[125] For the United Kingdom, see J. Baldwin and M. McConville, *Negotiated Justice*; and, for the United States, see M. Heumann, *Plea Bargaining: The Experiences of Prosecutors, Judges, and Defense Attorneys*.

[126] P. Waddington, *Calling the Police: The Interpretation of, and Response to, Calls for Assistance from the Public*; and A. Reiss, *The Police and the Public*.

[127] A. Cicourel, *The Social Organization of Juvenile Justice*.

[128] E. Bittner, 'The Police on Skid Row'.

[129] J. Douglas, *The Social Meanings of Suicide*.   [130] M. Atkinson, 'Societal Reactions to Suicide'.

pre-eminently objective phenomena: they were analysed as entirely accurate measures of different states of social integration in society. It was the alleged independence of such rates that Douglas challenged. Rates are not autonomous, he said; they are *constructed* by officials who confront the onerous task of deciding how problematic deaths might have occurred. Officials must operate in part with lay theories and common-sense reasoning about the nature and meaning of death. 'Suicide' is itself a classification that flows out of such theorizing, a classification which embodies assumptions about the possible meanings of loneliness, loss, grief, and social integration. In doubtful cases, for example, common-sense suggests that people who are detached and dislocated are the most likely candidates for placement as suicides.

In short, Douglas and Atkinson argued, suicide rates are compiled by officials; they encase particular hypotheses about the nature of the world. Durkheim came to the study of those rates with identical hypotheses, and applying them, demonstrated their cogency. *Le Suicide* is based on tautological reasoning. Suicide rates, and all other rates, it was said, must be decoded ('unpacked' was a word commonly used by the ethnomethodologist) before they can be put to proper analytic use.

But, in addition, crime rates may also be examined as influential phenomena in their own right. Instead of exploring their validity or construction, it is possible to discuss them as part of the setting in which crime and deviance emerge. Journalists, politicians, the police, and the public attach importance to crime rates, responding to them as vital moral facts about the state of society. Control policies will be devised to alter known trends in criminal activity. The police may be obliged to define rates as performance targets or indicators of productivity which must be defended, applauded, or carefully built up. Resources may be solicited, staff recruited, and technologies changed in answer to shifts in rates. Political debate often revolves around the impressions of success or failure conveyed by rates (although news media and popular accounts may refuse to heed or accept the rates)—the absence of significant change in the numbers of homicides and knifings in the first decade of the twenty-first century were largely ignored in debates about knife crime in London, for instance. Crime statistics are palpably significant, though the manner of their reportage may prove more consequential than the rates themselves. Katherine Beckett,[131] for example, found that public fear of crime proved far more sensitive to political and media representations of crime 'waves' than changes in actual crime rates.

Researchers now probably treat victimization surveys as the more substantial and useful sources of government information about the distribution and character of crime. Not only are the surveys interesting descriptions of patterns of victimization, but they also touch on such ancillary matters as the fear of crime, connections between postcodes and crime, and the relations between lifestyles and victimization. In Britain, the raw materials of the surveys have been deposited in the ESRC data archive in Essex University where they are accessible to research criminologists who can perform their own additional analysis upon them. Crime surveys are a significant corrective to rates of officially notified crimes, but they are not without flaws. Reverse record checks, for

---

[131] K. Beckett, *Making Crime Pay*.

instance, have established that some 10 per cent of crimes reported to the police would not be disclosed to an interviewer working on a crime survey, and we have argued that crime surveys map crimes against people, not the victimization of institutions, although there are many thefts and acts of criminal damage committed against organizations.[132] They do not count crimes committed *by* institutions. There has in the past been a severe undercounting of crimes committed against women,[133] the homeless, illegal immigrants, and ethnic minorities.[134] In time, to be sure, some of these flaws have been corrected and, indeed, recent work has concentrated quite heavily on underrepresented populations of victims.[135]

Critique

The quest for research evidence in relation to crime and deviance is burdensome: it entails an outlay of money, time, and energy. It also requires methodological skills and theoretical acumen. Except for a few instances of indirect evidence, data are actually misnamed because they are rarely *given*. They should more appropriately be called *capta*: items which are seized with difficulty. The defects and biases of particular sources cannot always therefore be automatically remedied by accumulating a huge quantity of evidence. There is too little expertise, time, money, and interest to do so. Rather, commitments must usually be made to a rather restricted group of data. Each group will preclude certain kinds of knowledge and deliver certain truths. For example, leaning upon official statistics cannot produce textured crime and deviance histories. It cannot offer much information about criminal or deviant interpretations or about how social control is handled in private. By contrast, the participant-observer is not often able to estimate the typicality of his or her group: generalizability must be sacrificed in exchange for depth.

Any decision to adopt particular methods and particular evidence reflects need, vision, and intention. *Need* is anything but uniform. The requirements of a government minister, civil servant, or criminal justice professional tend to hover around policy, planning, and implementation issues. They are concerned less with the subtle and intricate facets of crime and deviation, more with the projected size of a prison or criminal population or the short-term impact of a crime prevention project. They turn on demonstrable connections between official action and officially recorded response. The official statistics lend themselves to the satisfaction of those needs (it was for that very reason that they were compiled—the science of statistics originated in the nineteenth century in the compilation and analysis of data about the *State*). But they may sometimes be rather tangential to the purposes of other criminologists. As we have argued, they do not capture all the realities which some researchers would study. Those who dwell on crime and deviance as evolving processes tend to ignore statistics, generating their own alternative methodologies.

132 E. Smigel and H. Ross, *Crimes Against Bureaucracy.*
133 Review Symposium in the *British Journal of Criminology*, April 1984.
134 T. Jones et al., *The Islington Crime Survey.*
135 The 1988 and 1992 *British Crime Survey* rectified some of these deficiencies.

By extension, it becomes apparent that need often intersects with *vision*. It is not easy to extricate one from the other: theories prompt questions and conceptions of what is urgent. Prolonged exposure to the world made visible by statistics will, for example, suggest gaps and projects for the future, each being defined and answered by statistical means. It will increase statistical competence, put one in the company of fellow statisticians and encourage one to become a reader of statistical journals. All those choices will be at the expense of other pursuits. The cultivation of statistical capacities demands the use of time which might have been otherwise employed. Only the extraordinary polymath can now remain in mastery of very disparate skills. The participant-observer will probably become more and more innumerate as his or her observational aptitude increases. And the statistician will find phenomenological arguments ever more irrelevant, uninteresting, and unintelligible.

Forms of evidence, then, tend to be accompanied by forms of theory. Their use can never really be neutral: they lead one to perceive crime and deviance as a property of structures, groups, or individuals, as rooted in profound causes or lodged in the understandings of the people who are immediately involved in what is being described, as evolving or static, as predicted in advance in a process of hypothesis-construction or unknown before active enquiry. The relevant fact of one school of thought may then be described as trivial or ambiguous by another school.

In making sense of any theory, therefore, it is vital to ask what evidence was collected in what way, what evidence was *not* collected, and how answers might have changed had a methodology or data been different. Let us now turn to the development of theory itself.

Conclusion

There is no one, straightforward route to the amassing of information about crime, deviance, and control. Information is often hard to gather because it touches on areas which people are anxious to protect, conceal, or misrepresent, and researchers are frequently obliged to be content with less than perfect data. Data feed theory and theory guides data-collection, and readers should continually be aware of the limitations, constraints, and distortions of the research materials upon which theories are constructed. On the one hand, a critical stance is warranted, but, in such a difficult field of enquiry, too rigorous a degree of scepticism might make any research and analysis impossible.

Further Reading

I. Crow and N. Semmens, *Researching Criminology*, Buckingham, 2007.

P. Davies et al. (ed.), *Doing Criminological Research*, London, 2011.

J. Douglas (ed.), *Research on Deviance*, New York, 1972.

R. King and E. Wincup (eds.), *Doing Research on Crime and Justice*, Oxford, 2007.

L. Westmarland, *Researching Crime and Justice*, London, 2011.

3

The Chicago School

Introduction

We have chosen to present the sociology of crime and deviance chronologically, de-scribing a succession of significant intellectual episodes. Each episode may be said to have contributed a distinctive idea or set of ideas and each is independent enough to merit separate examination. But it must be recognized that some difficult assumptions underlie such an approach. Theoretical developments are not neatly insulated from one another. Neither are they arranged in neat phases. On the contrary, there is much borrowing, overlapping, and ambiguity at the boundaries. Thoughts emerge from common sources and they frequently flow into one another. Sometimes, indeed, the principal difference between theories is their use of language, similar schemes being expressed in dissimilar vocabularies.[1] And there is another, minor, problem: a history of criminology is offered no obvious beginning.

Criminology did not appear full-grown in the nineteenth century. It was instead heralded by abundant work which could properly be called a proto-criminology. Thus, the oldest form of scholarship, theology, may be understood as a prolonged attempt to make sense of moral action. Legal commentaries invariably centre it. Plays, poems, and sagas have repeatedly revolved around the conflict between good and evil. More particularly, there has been an enduring series of literary and intellectual essays de-voted to the subject of crime. This 'shadow criminology' or proto-criminology is older than the work of the universities and is almost certainly more prolific. It is composed of accounts of notorious people, sinister happenings, and awful institutions.[2] In the sixteenth century, particularly, there emerged a kind of 'low-life reporting' which purported to offer detailed information about the underworld.[3] There was a detailed description of thieves, highwaymen, thief-takers, prostitutes, and pickpockets, their social organization and careers, their techniques and argot, and their relations with victims. That reporting has continued to flourish. It contains much that is repetitive, conjectural, and fanciful. It also contains a great deal of unique material and sensible observation. Properly read, it may be recognized as an anticipation of the theorizing

---

[1] S. Cohen, Preface to *Folk Devils and Moral Panics*, 2nd edn.

[2] For general examples, see A. Hayward (ed.), *Lives of the Most Remarkable Criminals*; A. Griffiths, *The Chronicles of Newgate*; C. Gordon, *The Old Bailey and Newgate*; D. Defoe, *The True and Genuine Account of the Life and Actions of the Late Jonathan Wild*.

[3] A. Judges, *The Elizabethan Underworld*; J. McMullan, 'Aspects of Professional Crime'.

that now passes for the sociology of crime and deviance. After all, the stock of what may be said in plausible analysis is actually rather limited and many ideas are unremarkable. Rudimentary conceptions of anomie,[4] labelling theory,[5] functionalism,[6] and ecology[7] are to be discovered in writings of the seventeenth, eighteenth, and nineteenth centuries. And it is in this sense that the bulk of contemporary criminology is really little more than a reinvention or recapitulation of past explanations. On occasion, too, those shadow criminologists produced work which is still unsurpassed. The ethnography of Henry Mayhew and John Binney, for instance, is quite outstanding. It represents an excellent, graphic documentation of the crime and low life of Victorian London,[8] and its scale and detail have not really been reproduced again in England.

Shadow criminologists like Henry Mayhew, Herbert Asbury, Lucas Pike, and Tony Parker,[9] deserve much fuller incorporation into sociology. They have suffered a neglect which is unmerited but quite understandable. Sometimes their writing is superficially naïve, developed without the conventional forms of scholarship. Indeed, much of it was published before those forms were established. They worked outside universities and did not address a university audience. Their ideas display inevitable discontinuities, lacking an incremental or evolutionary character. More importantly, the authors were recruited from very diverse backgrounds and they acquired little organizational support. They were variously people of private means, journalists, playwrights, prison chaplains, magistrates, novelists, policemen, and lawyers. As they were rarely retained as professional experts on crime, their interest in criminological problems could not but be sporadic, indeed amateur, and their skills were not transmitted to a body of students or apprentices who would succeed them. After all, it is only very recently that the university syllabus has expanded to cover the projects which they initiated, and acceptance was at first difficult indeed.[10]

The University of Chicago sociology department was distinctive because it accomplished a decisive break with the haphazard, solitary, and ill-maintained studies which we have identified as proto-criminology. In it, speculation about crime and allied processes became orderly. The department's first chairman, Albion Small, transformed sociology into a permanent and co-operative enterprise. He employed people to become professional social investigators, methodically teaching what they had learned and how they had learned it to others. Modelled on the research seminar of the German university,[11] their work was a continuous, busy, and integrated attack on academic problems. James Carey observed: 'The first systematic group-related efforts to apply sociological knowledge were made in Chicago during the second and third decades

---

[4] T. Nourse, *Campania Foelix*.

[5] P. Colquhoun, *A Treatise on the Police of the Metropolis*.

[6] B. Mandeville, *The Fable of the Bees*.

[7] T. Beames, *The Rookeries of London*.

[8] H. Mayhew, *London Labour and the London Poor*, vol. 4.

[9] L. Pike, *A History of Crime in England*; and H. Asbury, *The Gangs of New York* (although an eponymous film, starring Daniel Day-Lewis, revived interest in that latter work).

[10] For a discussion of the difficulty of establishing criminology as an academic discipline in the United Kingdom, see R. Hood, 'Hermann Mannheim and Max Grünhut'.

[11] E. Shils, 'Tradition, Ecology and Institution in the History of Sociology'.

of this [twentieth] century.'[12] Everett Hughes observed that: 'in Europe various philo-sophically minded persons had written books about something called "sociology"' but 'the Department of Sociology at Chicago . . . was really the first big and lasting one in the country; thus, also the world'.[13] Leonard Broom observed: 'in Chicago, sociol-ogy was implanted in American academic life and after that nothing was the same.'[14] Albion Small himself stated that, before the founding of his department, sociology was 'more of a yearning than a substantial body of knowledge, a fixed point of view, or a rigorous method of research'.[15] If these claims are even partially warranted, it would seem that the creation of the University of Chicago provides an appropriate opening for the history of the sociology of crime and deviance. Marxism had flourished in Europe, the *Annales* group had been active in France, the Manchester and London sta-tistical societies had performed significant work, but it was in Chicago that sociology was formalized to become a body of knowledge that was routinely discussed, taught, and transmitted in an institutional setting that ensured its continuity. Thereafter, there appeared a more or less coherent sociological based criminology.

The University, the Department, and the City

> [Chicago] is a veritable Babel, in which some thirty or more tongues are spoken . . . Gunmen haunt its streets, and a murder is committed in them nearly every day in the year.[16]

The University of Chicago was an extraordinary invention. It was designed to be a nonpareil. It was taken to be the only instance of a major university being established anew.[17] Rockefeller donated 35 million dollars to found a university; William Harper, its first president, proceeded to raid other institutions by offering salaries to their staff which were virtually double those normally paid, and a number of departments were established almost simultaneously. The sociology department was itself constituted in 1892. Those processes were of great consequence for the shaping of criminologi-cal work: sociology was not a latecomer, to be resisted or dominated by entrenched disciplines as it was in the better-established universities; there was a freedom to ap-point those who were regarded as particularly able; and there was ample funding for research. Moreover, innovation was defined as the distinguishing feature of a univer-sity that was itself quite new and pioneering. Thus Leonard Cottrell recalled that '[we were] rejecting all the traditional answers and institutions that were allegedly the sta-bilizers of society'.[18] Such rejection could not but be propitious for the development of sociology. After all, the academic standing of the discipline was slight. There was no earlier generation of professional sociologists; the very respectability and tenability of the approach were disputed and the qualifications of the members of the Chicago

---

[12] J. Carey, *Sociology and Public Affairs*, 9.   [13] E. Hughes, Preface to W. Raushenbush, *Robert Park*, vii.
[14] L. Broom, Preface to R. Faris, *Chicago Sociology* 1920–1932, xi.
[15] A. Small, 'Fifty Years of Sociology in the United States', 802.
[16] Chatfield-Taylor, quoted in H. Zorbaugh, *The Gold Coast and the Slum*, 1.
[17] R. Faris, *Chicago Sociology*, 22.   [18] Quoted in J. Carey, *Sociology and Public Affairs*, 154.

department were meagre enough. Few had been able to study sociology in any formal setting. They stemmed, instead, from philosophy, biology, religion, journalism, and linguistics. One of the most distinguished Chicago sociologists, Robert Park, claimed never to have heard the word 'sociology' whilst he was a student at the University of Michigan between 1883 and 1887. Indeed, no university course was offered in sociology anywhere in America during that period.[19]

The tentative and unformed nature of American sociology revealed itself in the rather lengthy period of time that elapsed before the Chicago department came into its own. Some of the early appointments were to display little interest in the creation and dissemination of an academic sociology, treating the discipline instead as a form of applied social work. It was only later that a special working organization and array of styles emerged that could be identified as distinctive of Chicago. Those who fashioned that style were principally of the second generation.[20] As we discuss their works, it must be remembered that we are relating a history within a context set by the sociology of crime and deviance, and it is on the study of crime and deviance that we shall concentrate. Others, like Bulmer[21] and Faris,[22] would tell a different story. So manifest were the early achievements of the Chicago department that it is possible to trace their influence on approaches as diverse as Durkheimian functionalism, epidemiology, attitude research, survey methods, and much else. Our own focus will be on the social anthropological and ecological study of crime and deviance whose chief author was Robert Park, the man who was to become head of the Chicago department.

In 1915, Park published an article that was in effect to become a manifesto for urban ethnography. 'The City' described a problem, a programme, and a procedure:

> Anthropology, the science of man, has been mainly concerned up to the present with the study of primitive peoples. But civilized man is quite as interesting an object of investigation, and at the same time his life is more open to observation and study. Urban life and culture are more varied, subtle and complicated, but the fundamental motives are in both instances the same. The same patient methods of observation which anthropologists like Boas and Lowie have expended on the study of the life and manners of the North American Indians might be even more fruitfully employed in the investigation of the customs, beliefs, social practices, and general conceptions of life prevalent in Little Italy on the Lower Side in Chicago, or in recording the more sophisticated folkways of the inhabitants of Greenwich Village and the neighborhood of Washington Square, New York.[23]

Most sociology departments seem to be inattentive to the physical and social contexts in which they exist. The 'Frankfurt School', for instance, left no record of Frankfurt. Perhaps there is no 'necessary' reason why sociologists should concentrate on the environment which immediately surrounds them. But Chicago sociology was to become the sociology of Chicago itself, a detailed urban anthropological mapping of the social territories that made the city, and its particular thrust must be explained by the interplay between some peculiar phenomena and a peculiar readiness to respond.

---

[19] W. Raushenbush, *Robert Park*, 78.
[20] J. Short (ed.), *The Social Fabric of the Metropolis*, xiv.
[21] M. Bulmer, *The Chicago School*.
[22] R. Faris, *Chicago Sociology*.
[23] R. Park and E. Burgess (eds.), *The City*, 3.

The city of Chicago was an exploding mosaic of contrasting social worlds. Its growth was extraordinary, advancing as it did from a small log fort in 1833 to a substantial city by 1900: 'the newspapers show the city of Chicago amazed at itself from its very beginnings . . . The population expansion was spectacular.'[24] The bulk of that expansion was fed by immigrants from a succession of exporting countries: Ireland, Sweden, Germany, Poland, and Italy. Each group had to make a place for itself in the city. Each had to confront a series of recurring problems. Urban life resembled a phantasmagoria, a welter of shifting scenes and identities. As Park observed, 'everything is in a state of agitation—everything seems to be undergoing a change. Society is, apparently, not much more than a congeries and constellation of social atoms.'[25]

It is not unusual for burgeoning cities to attract a fascinated gaze. In its time, London was itself thought to be an extraordinary object, a new Babylon, revealing a vast kaleidoscope of new social combinations and possibilities. Victorian journalists and novelists devoted themselves to reporting the strange and remarkable events that unfolded within it. But their fascination lacked the social organization to prepare the foundation of an enduring scholarship, and it passed away. It was the Chicago sociology department that allowed curiosity to become a stable tradition. Itself influenced by the work of journalists like Lincoln Steffens and by the newspaper experience of Park, the department sought to document and analyse interesting worlds before they altered and disappeared.[26] The city was to become a laboratory in which all the nuances and interconnections of social life could be observed.[27]

The Roots of Responsiveness

As long as one continues *talking*, intellectualism remains in undisturbed possession of the field. The return to life can't come about by talking. It is an *act*; to make you return to life, I must set an example for your imitation, I must deafen you to talk, by showing you, as Bergson does, that the concepts we talk with are made for purposes of *practice* and not for purposes of insight.[28]

We do not propose to say much about the intellectual roots of sociology at Chicago. That history is intricate and complicated and cannot be easily compressed.[29] However, it is imperative to stress that the responsiveness of the Chicago School did not arise out of a simple curiosity or journalistic impulse. Neither was it an 'obvious' reaction to the extraordinary qualities of a city undergoing rapid transformation. It was the fruit of a carefully resolved philosophy of thought and action, a philosophy which emphasized the primacy of practice. Many, although not all, Chicago sociologists were wedded to two principal schools, pragmatism and formalism, and it was the fusing of those schools that produced the strain towards focused, grounded studies of observable social scenes.

---

[24] R. Faris, *Chicago Sociology*.   [25] R. Park, 'Community Organization and Juvenile Delinquency', 107.
[26] E. Hughes, 'Robert E. Park'.   [27] R. Park, 'The City as a Social Laboratory'.
[28] W. James, *A Pluralistic Universe*, 290.
[29] For a fuller account of that development, see P. Rock, *The Making of Symbolic Interactionism*.

The pragmatism of Charles Peirce, William James, and John Dewey extracted themes from German philosophy and translated them into a radical phrasing of the nature of knowledge. In brief, they maintained that knowledge resided neither in properties of the world alone nor in properties of the observer alone. Facts, it was held, are not self-evident. They are selected and interpreted by the mind that surveys them. People with different perspectives and different problems will not see exactly the same phenomena. On the contrary, they will respond to those facets of phenomena which answer particular purposes.[30] The meaning of food will not be identical for the chef, the chemist, the waiter, and the guest at a meal. It will shift in response to the peculiar dealings one has with the object. But that shift is not wholly dependent on the whim of the contemplating intelligence. The imagination is not free to create anything which it may choose to devise: it is constrained by the capacity of the world to answer back and impose itself upon thought.[31] Hence it came about that pragmatism placed effective knowledge in a transaction between the observer and the environment which he or she observed: knowledge was no longer defined as a state or as a condition but as a *process*, as action, and it was alleged that 'the problems of perception and science are straightened out when looked at from the standpoint of action, while they remain obscure and obscuring when we regard them from the standpoint of a knowledge defined in antithesis to action.'[32] Useful understanding proceeded from the activities of an engaged intellect which explored practical problems. It proceeded from experiences anchored in the world. Experience was to become elevated to a pre-eminent position: it was the guarantee of valid knowledge. Formal speculation was regarded as a pallid and misleading substitute for personal acquaintance with phenomena:

> It is the personal experience of those best qualified in our circle of knowledge to *have* experience, to tell us *what is*. Now what does *thinking about* the experience of those persons come to, compared to directly and personally feeling it as they feel it? The philosophers are dealing in shades, while those who live and feel know truth.[33]

Such extolling of experience brings copious problems in its wake. It leads to a systematic distrust of systematic reasoning, of the writings of others, and of analysis. As George Herbert Mead remarked, 'our own experience in so far as it is not reflective does not involve knowledge . . . Experiences simply are.'[34] Any attempt to distance oneself from experience and to describe it is something of a betrayal of the raw process of immediate involvement in action. It is a qualitatively different form of understanding, different from experience itself and not readily transformed back into it. Pragmatism evidently tends towards becoming self-silencing, denying the possibility of prolonged exposition and explanation. It threatens to end itself.

Robert Park was one of the major architects of the rescue of pragmatism and its transformation into a practicable sociology. He had studied under William James who had taught him that 'the real world was the experience of actual men and women and

[30] J. Dewey, 'The Reflex Arc Concept in Social Psychology'.
[31] C. Peirce quoted in C. Mills, *Sociology and Pragmatism*, 158.
[32] J. Dewey, 'Perception and Organic Action', 648.   [33] W. James, *Pragmatism*, 30.
[34] G. Mead, 'The Philosophy of John Dewey', 74.

not abbreviated and shorthand descriptions of it that we call knowledge'.[35] But he had also studied under Georg Simmel in Germany,[36] and Simmel's formal sociology provided a limited resolution to the difficulties posed by pragmatism. Formalism held that it was the task of sociology to explore the structures of social activity and that those structures could be regarded as analytically independent of the settings in which they appeared. In one sense, Simmel argued, every social occasion is unique. It will never return with an identical history, context, and membership. In another sense, it is simply part of a wider display of formal processes. For example, HM Revenue & Customs or IRS have a number of offices which are utterly distinct. No office is quite the same as any other: it houses different people with different pasts, problems, and ambitions. Yet it is also an instance of the operation of hierarchy, which is a general feature of bureaucracy, which is also general, and of routine transactions, sometimes conflict-laden, with taxpayers, which are general too. Simmel would argue that it is possible to examine hierarchy, bureaucracy, and conflict as more or less autonomous forms which manifest themselves in very diverse contents. It is those forms which can and should be analysed, not the contents themselves. Grafted onto pragmatism, formalism permitted a restricted description of an otherwise indescribable experience. It became feasible to abstract, discuss, and compare examples of social action separately from the unique settings in which they were lodged.

Together, pragmatism and formalism brought about a special phrasing of sociological work. It was argued that the business of research is to understand the social world, and the social world is itself manufactured by the practical experience of those who live in it. It is on this that sociology must concentrate, not on some alternative order generated by abstract theory. Such theory deals with a realm of 'facts' and processes which is less solid than the concrete personal knowledge of those who actually produce the behaviour that is to be explained. Thus Park argued that 'sociology is not interested in facts, not even in social facts as they are commonly understood ... Sociology wants to know how people re-act to so-called facts, to what is happening to them'.[37] And Louis Wirth argued: 'the important features of each cultural situation are not immediately evident to the observer and do not constitute objectively determinable data. They must be seen in terms of the subjective experiences and attitudes of ... individuals'.[38]

Practical experiences themselves are responses to situations and problems, and they change as those problems change. Indeed, the very task of working on a problem transforms it with characteristic repercussions on one's knowledge of it. In turn, it was said, sociology should not be devoted to the study of states but of *processes*, of things and people in change. It must be so organized that it can observe and report processes over time. It must also be so organized that it can reach those processes practically and not by speculation and logic alone. The most effective research strategy is one that requires

[35] R. Park, quoted in W. Raushenbush, *Robert Park*, 29.

[36] Anon, 'The Life Histories of W. I. Thomas and Robert E. Park'; L. Braude, '"Park and Burgess": An Appreciation'; and the Preface to R. Park, *The Crowd and the Public*.

[37] Quoted in W. Raushenbush, *Robert Park*, 112.   [38] L. Wirth, 'Culture Conflict and Misconduct', 240.

sociologists to participate personally in the world which they would analyse. Without such participation, knowledge is not experience but a far from satisfactory commentary on experience. So Park urged a student embarking on an exploration of a religious sect in Los Angeles[39] to 'think and feel Molokan'.[40]

Largely unimpressed by truths and essences which could not be delivered by experience and observation, the Chicago sociologists tended to proceed to the small social scenes which lent themselves to social anthropological research. In particular, they moved out to the territories which adjoined the university. Organized class visits were made to the ethnic communities which abounded in Chicago; 'term papers and dissertations naturally followed, and in time, research volumes'.[41] Research training itself typically consisted of a number of seminars which culminated in an instruction to leave the university for the streets. There were studies of gangs,[42] organized crime,[43] prostitution,[44] taxi-dance halls,[45] real-estate offices,[46] local newspapers,[47] the rooming house district,[48] 'hobohemia',[49] the central business district,[50] and the 'Poles',[51] 'Blacks',[52] and Jews[53] of Chicago. Collectively, 'they seem to have emerged as the most durable and widely used bases for describing the community life of the city'.[54]

Ecology

We have argued that the description of experience was tempered by Simmel's formalism. Social forms were held to be relatively abstract structures creating a kind of architecture of experience. Any situation could be described simultaneously in terms of its unique and its general properties. Those general properties were features that seemed to cut across particular events and give them a common history and a common character. Conflict, assimilation, succession, symbiosis, co-operation, and invasion are processes which appear to transform events in predictable ways. For certain purposes, it is practically irrelevant whether conflict is waged between the partners of a marriage, street gangs, or nations. It is still conflict and it manifests a number of those special qualities which are peculiar to itself.

City life and urbanization were analysed by a collection of master forms which had been borrowed from biology, and they were represented as the workings of an ecological order. Ecology is an emphasis on the patterns and organized changes which

---

[39] P. Young, *The Pilgrims of Russian Town*. [40] Quoted in R. Faris, *Chicago Sociology*, 71.
[41] Quoted in R. Faris, *Chicago Sociology*, 71. [42] F. Thrasher, *The Gang*.
[43] J. Landesco, *Organized Crime in Chicago*.
[44] W. Reckless, 'The Distribution of Commercialized Vice in the City'.
[45] P. Cressey, *The Taxi-Dance Hall*.
[46] E. Hughes, *The Growth of an Institution: The Chicago Real Estate Board*.
[47] R. Park, *The Immigrant Press and its Control*. [48] H. Zorbaugh, *The Gold Coast*.
[49] N. Anderson, *The Hobo*.
[50] E. Johnson, 'The Function of the Central Business District in the Metropolitan Community'.
[51] W. Thomas and F. Znaniecki, *The Polish Peasant in Europe and America*.
[52] S. Drake and H. Cayton, *Black Metropolis*. [53] L. Wirth, *The Ghetto*.
[54] G. Suttles, The Social Construction of Communities, 5.

are produced by different species living together in the same physical territory. The development of a biological ecology was attractive to sociologists who were searching for metaphors and principles to advance their own new and rather incoherent discipline. It proved especially attractive to those who were seeking to explain the evolution of different human groups in the geographical context of the city. Just as plants, insects, and animals translate a physical terrain into a mosaic of distinct communities, so people become separated into a network of disparate communities which form an intelligible whole. As Wirth remarked, 'whatever else men are, they are also animals, and as such they exhibit the effects of physical aggregation and of their habitat'.[55]

Biological ecology was rarely taken to be more than a convenient working description of an otherwise excessively complex process. It was acknowledged from the first that human communities are constructed on unique principles from those of animal and plant communities. People are quite capable of detaching themselves from their 'own' territories; they display rational behaviour; they can organize themselves into institutions which impose a distinct order; their works are modified by an elaborate technology; their activities are shaped by conscious planning; and they are governed by a symbolism which interprets and changes what they do.[56] Moreover, ecology was not regarded as a total explanation. It was but a 'segmental view'[57] which neglected much. With perhaps a few exceptions, the Chicago sociologists tended to refer to ecology as little more than a useful metaphor which ought not to be applied with full seriousness. Many, indeed, appear to have made a mere token bow before a theory which they largely ignored. Nevertheless, ecology offered a systematic framework for analysing the flowering of interrelated social worlds:

> The city is not merely an artefact, but an organism. Its growth is, fundamentally and as a whole, natural, i.e. uncontrolled and undesigned. The forms it tends to assume are those which represent and correspond to the functions it is called upon to perform. What have been called the 'natural areas of the city' are simply those regions whose locations, character, and functions have been determined by the same forces which have determined the character and function of the city as a whole.[58]

Of principal interest to the Chicago sociologists was the manner in which cities expand and become internally differentiated. The emergence of Chicago itself was explained by what came to be known as the zonal hypothesis, the contention that cities evolve in a series of concentric zones of activity and life. At the very centre is the business district which is typified by a small residential population and high property values. About it is the zone in transition whose population is fluid and poor, whose housing is deteriorating, and whose stability is threatened by the encroaching business district. About that zone, in turn, are areas of working-class housing, middle-class housing, and, on the fringes, suburbia. Each zone is itself composed of diverse 'natural areas' which abut on one another. They are natural because they are not entirely intended, because they

---

[55] L. Wirth, 'Human Ecology', 178.
[56] R. Park, 'The City', 4; L. Wirth, 'Human Ecology', 180.
[57] L. Wirth, 'Human Ecology', 188.
[58] R. Park, foreword to L. Wirth, *The Ghetto*, viii–ix.

represent unplanned groupings of like people, and because they manifest a rough correspondence to the territorial division of species in nature:

> In the course of time every section and quarter of the city takes on something of the character and qualities of its inhabitants. Each separate part of the city is inevitably stained with the peculiar sentiments of its population. The effect of this is to convert what was at first a mere geographical expression into a neighborhood, that is to say, a locality with sentiments, traditions, and a history of its own.[59]

Crime, Deviance, and Pathology

It was not the express ambition of the Chicago sociologists to focus on crime and deviance. Neither was criminology treated as a separate sub-discipline.[60] Deviant populations formed but one segment of the city and were, perhaps, no more engaging than any other. But there were discernible strains which encouraged the development of a sociological criminology. One was the funding and sponsorship provided by a variety of voluntary and municipal reforming organizations which sought solutions to social problems conventionally defined. Another was the sociologists' leaning towards practical intervention which had originated with Small and was retained by many of his colleagues. A third was the sheer availability of crime and deviance: graduate students, in particular, were ill-equipped to study any but the relatively visible, public, poor, and exposed neighbourhoods in the zone in transition. Other areas demanded of students an assurance, patronage, and support which were difficult to secure.

What was immediately impressive and obvious to the urban anthropologist was the massive concentration of 'pathological behaviour' in the zone in transition. Partly because of its great visibility, such behaviour appeared to be confined to a limited territorial belt. Within that belt there was a massing of all those phenomena that are conventionally identified as social problems: mental disorder, prostitution, suicide, alcoholism, infant mortality, juvenile delinquency, crime, disease, and poverty.[61] The incidence of pathology could be plotted with data collected from court records, census reports, and special surveys. 'In the zone of deterioration encircling the central business section', wrote Burgess, 'are always to be found the so-called "slums" and "bad lands", with their submerged regions of poverty, degradation and disease, and their underworld of crime and vice. Within a deteriorating area are rooming-house districts, the purgatory of "lost souls".'[62] Deviance may have been present elsewhere but it was hugely conspicuous in the transitional zone and, as Lemert remarked, the early criminologists tended to imitate Custer's men by riding to the sound of the guns.[63]

Analytically, the significance of the zone in transition was that it seemed to possess a distinctive social organization which could not be explained simply by the

---

[59] R. Park, 'The City', 6.
[60] J. Galliher, 'Chicago's Two Worlds of Deviance Research', 166.
[61] R. Faris and H. Dunham, *Mental Disorders in Urban Areas*.
[62] E. Burgess, 'The Growth of the City', 54–6.   [63] E. Lemert, *Social Pathology*.

characteristics of the populations who lived there at any one time.[64] An area with the cheapest rents, an appreciable circulation of inhabitants, and few settled institutions, it tended to be the home of the most recent generation of immigrants. National group after national group lived there. Each in its turn seemed to reproduce very much the same patterns of behaviour. Above all, it produced crime. Part of the Chicago project then turned to the explanation of how deviance arose in a particular quarter of the city.

The zone in transition was taken to be unruly. It housed people who were unaccustomed to one another, to city life, and to America. Lacking substantial resources and deserting much that had been familiar, they were required to establish a new way of life in a difficult and shifting environment. One of the prime problems they faced was the sheer array of different worlds around them. When the inner composition and external relations of those worlds appeared unstable, the whole invited the description of social disorganization. Disorganization was a facet of moral dissensus: 'the degree to which the members of a society lose their common understandings, i.e. the degree to which consensus is undermined, is the measure of a society's state of disorganization.'[65] Disorganization also characterized the fragmented, fluid, and anonymous elements of urban life: 'contacts are extended, heterogeneous groups mingle, neighborhoods disappear, and people, deprived of local and family ties, are forced to live under . . . loose, transient and impersonal relations.'[66]

That concept of disorganization is awkward and it deserves some reflection. Many sociologists avoid and criticize it because they are unhappy with the idea of social disorder. Their own orderly systems of explanation are calculated to confer a measure of coherence and pattern on what they discuss and the very idea of disorder is taken to suggest that the sociologist has somehow proved incapable of understanding what he or she saw. So it was that David Matza claimed that the Chicago School wrote of disorganization when what they were actually describing was diversity.[67] Diversity lends itself to schematic theory. Disorganization does not.

Almost any prolonged period of observation seems capable of revealing intelligible patterns in even the most chaotic situations. Indeed, Whyte asserted that reference to social disorganization merely signifies that the observer has not understood what has been seen.[68] Quite typical was the remark of another, later Chicago sociologist who stated about his ethnographic research on 'Jelly's', a bar in Chicago's South Side:

> after being around Jelly's neighborhood for a while and getting to know its people, the outside observer can begin to see that there is order in this social world . . . there is more to social life in and around Jelly's than might be suggested by a cursory inspection, informed by the stereotypes and prejudices of those not involved. Life here cannot be understood as simple 'social disorganization'.[69]

There will always remain the insuperable problem of whether the observer has recognized or imposed the patterns which have been discerned, yet the Chicago sociologists

---

[64] C. Shaw and H. McKay, *Juvenile Delinquency and Urban Areas*.
[65] L. Wirth, 'Ideological Aspects of Social Disorganization', 46.
[66] L. Wirth, 'Culture Conflict and Misconduct', 236. [67] D. Matza, *Becoming Deviant*.
[68] W. Whyte, *Street Corner Society*. [69] E. Anderson, *A Place on the Corner*, 2, 4.

who talked of disorganization did themselves go to the jungles of Hobohemia and the streets of the slums and unearthed what they described as very real social structures. Their own discovery of structure and order makes their use of the term 'disorganization' appear inappropriate and in need of redefinition. At the very least, it is clear that they used the word in an unfamiliar manner. It was not actually intended to refer to a collapse of order. On the contrary, the Chicago sociologists displayed an unusual ability to find organization in hitherto uncharted areas. In their work, 'disorganization' actually points to two distinct, but occasionally linked, properties of social life.

One such property is the reduction of social relations to a rather rudimentary condition in which mistrust, heterogeneity, and change abound. In that condition, new opportunities and combinations arise and disappear with some rapidity. Old habits are broken.[70] Life becomes unpredictable. Cohesiveness is threatened. The dependable group shrinks in size. A world so disorganized possesses a palpable order, but it is an uncomfortable order which is sensed as *comparatively* vestigial and unreliable.[71] Such a world is both more and less complicated than one conventionally defined as organized. It has its own complexities and intricacies which demand a particularly delicate analysis.[72] For its inhabitants, the negotiation of relations in uncertainty is fraught, fragile, and problematic.[73] Thus defined, disorganization is mainly a facet of *experience* and, curiously, the experience of disorganization can itself be highly organized.

On another plane, disorganization could be described as a property of the wider social structure. It would then refer to the relations *between* and not within worlds. Social differentiation, a period of rapid social change, or uneven development can exaggerate the instability of those relations, leading to strain and a breakdown of local order. In turn, particular worlds can become dislocated, thrown up out of their context and exposed. They can achieve a social and moral independence which some sociologists have chosen to emphasize.

In one sense, following this formulation, the zone in transition was wholly dependent on the city which surrounded it. In another, it could be cast as an isolated and deregulated area, an area uncontrolled by the 'master institutions' of society. Church, law, school, and commonplace morality were thought to have little sway there. A criminal area may be organized and its wider environments may be organized, but there might have been little or no articulation between them. The Chicago-trained sociologist, William Foote Whyte, described one instance, the Boston North End of the 1930s: 'Cornerville's problem is not lack of organization but failure of its own social organization to mesh with the structure of the society around it. This accounts for the development of the local political and racket organization and also for the loyalty which people bear toward their race and toward Italy.'[74]

'Disorganization' may be an unfortunate word for such a lack of social integration. The idea is perhaps better conveyed by the metaphor of a geological faultline. But it

---

[70] R. Park, 'Community Organization', 107.   [71] K. Erikson, *In the Wake of the Flood*.
[72] G. Suttles, *The Social Order of the Slum*.
[73] L. Rainwater, *Behind Ghetto Walls*; G. Suttles, 'The Defended Neighborhood', in *The Social Construction of Communities*.
[74] W. Whyte, *Street Corner Society*, 273.

is evident what was intended. Cornerville and areas like it are akin to the old thieves' quarters of the European cities. They possess a special character, at once attached and detached, a part of the city and apart from it. Neatly delimited, they seemed to justify an ethnographic response.

Integral to the conception of disorganization was the companion idea of weak social control. Those who stressed internal disorder could cite numerous obstructions to social control. Moral habits could not be properly implanted.[75] People were neither effectively curbed, nor could they curb one another. They did not know each other well, formed few commitments to the area or to its population, were confused by moral diversity,[76] were alienated from the distant authority of the State and its institutions, such as the police, and were loath to intervene in the affairs of their fellows.[77] Morality could no longer be taken for granted. It became relativistic and circumstantial, readily adapted for selfish purposes, permitting the evolution of extenuating accounts. More particularly, its influence could not extend very far. Those entitled to exercise moral claims were confined to their family and immediate neighbours, all others becoming moral strangers. Such 'amoral familialism'[78] transformed the zone in transition into an unsettled and unsafe region which abounded in potential victims. Fighting gangs might have been represented as a rudimentary effort to defend territory and impose security on the neighbourhood,[79] but they also committed violent acts of law-breaking which increased insecurity.

All these conspicuous moral and structural infirmities could become amplified. The occupants of the zone in transition had often been immigrants from Europe or the countryside (and particularly from the southern States). Their lives had been punctuated by cultural discontinuities which became especially taxing for the second generation.[80] Language, custom, and religion could fall into disuse or change significance. The children of immigrants sometimes found themselves to be marginal both to the new world of the native American and to the discarded, old world of their parents. Morally displaced, economically and politically peripheral, they might innovate new modes of social organization. Most typically they created a social order which corresponded neither to the old world nor to the new but was a shifting amalgam of both[81] ('hybridity' is the word now commonly used to describe what was intended). They also improvised new styles of behaviour and morality which could well embrace delinquency as a possible solution to the dilemmas of exclusion and impotence.[82] Those who were

---

[75] R. Park, 'Community Organization'.

[76] It is interesting that Snodgrass reports that a number of the Chicago sociologists, including Clifford Shaw, themselves experienced the moral diversity of the zone in transition as something of a revelation ('Clifford R. Shaw and Henry D. McKay: Chicago Criminologists', 4; and see L. Gelsthorpe, 'The Jack-Roller: Telling a Story?', 521).

[77] L. Wirth, 'Culture Conflict and Misconduct'.   [78] E. Banfield, *The Moral Basis of a Backward Society*.

[79] G. Suttles, *The Social Construction of Communities*. Eric Schneider has written a fascinating history of the gangs of New York City in which territoriality plays a major part. See his *Vampires, Dragons, and Egyptian Kings: Youth Gangs in Postwar New York*.

[80] W. Thomas and F. Znaniecki, *The Polish Peasant*.

[81] H. Lopota, 'The Function of Voluntary Associations'.

[82] C. Shaw, *The Natural History of a Delinquent Career*.

successful, and, more important, those who could help others to success, were well-regarded, almost becoming local heroes. The racketeer and hustler consequently attain a special importance in the neighbourhood: 'what needs to be appreciated', wrote Landesco, 'is the element of genuine popularity of the gangster, home-grown in the neighborhood gang, idealized in the morality of the neighborhood'.[83]

Local politics and local crime were intertwined in the zone in transition, supporting one another and often recruiting very much the same people.[84] Police forces in the United States are decentralized, placed under the authority of local politicians, and subject to local control.[85] It was always tempting to the police and local gangsters and politicians to come to an accommodation in the zone in transition, to support one another, and there was not much effective resistance from those who sought to oppose them. On the contrary, it was politically and administratively convenient to contain vice and deviance in an area where local resistance was weak and the social standing of the inhabitants was low.[86] There was a corresponding growth of prostitution, gambling, and illegal markets in the zone in transition. Deviant lifestyles were encouraged commercially and managerially, leading to the sifting and movement of people: 'each urban area . . . has its own moral code. A population seeks an area in which its members can be gratified with the least amount of interference.'[87] In turn, said Park:

> What lends special importance to the segregation of the poor, the vicious, the criminal, and exceptional persons generally, which is so characteristic a feature of city life, is the fact that social contagion tends to stimulate in divergent types the common temperamental differences, and to suppress characters which unite them with the normal types about them. Associations with others of their own ilk provides also not merely a stimulus, but a moral support for the traits they have in common which they would not find in a less select society.[88]

The Normal and the Pathological

It is important to emphasize that not all the sociologists practising at the University of Chicago were unanimous about the ends and methods of their discipline. Moreover, their ideas evolved over time and reflected social changes in the city itself. The crimes that were described ranged from petty delinquency to organized crime. Different features were emphasized in different studies. The explanation of criminality and deviance proposed by members of the university thus contained a number of apparent contradictions. Such inconsistency would not have exercised the Chicago sociologists very much. They were not engaged in a quest for a single theory which covered every contingency. Indeed, Louis Wirth claimed 'in the face of the imposing series of exploded

---

[83] J. Landesco, *Organized Crime in Chicago*, 169.   [84] J. Landesco, *Organized Crime in Chicago*.
[85] W. Miller, *Cops and Bobbies*.
[86] W. Reckless, 'The Distribution of Commercialized Vice'.
[87] L. Wirth, *The Ghetto*, 285–6.   [88] R. Park, 'The City', 45.

theories of criminality, prudence dictates that a new theory avoid the persistent error of claiming universal applicability'.[89]

The Chicago sociologists had no binding commitment to the discovery of any single explanation or any single *kind* of explanation. On the contrary, they awarded formal theorizing a lower priority than their own open-ended and exploratory urban anthropology that was capable of leading to unexpected results. It was as if they argued that deviance was to be found in a host of confusing and unique settings, that it was difficult to reduce its explanation to a single cause, and that it was even more difficult to explain it by pathological causes alone. In this sense, deviance was allowed to escape what has been called the 'like-causes-like fallacy'. Few sociologists or criminologists would baldly champion the assertion that bad phenomena must have bad causes. However, many do tacitly advance that argument by concentrating the search for the roots of crime in certain areas: unemployment, the slum, poverty, low intelligence, exploitative capitalism, genetic malfunction, or family breakdown. There are undoubtedly *ecological* or structural arguments associated with the Chicago School that refer to the instability and pathology of the disorganized zone in transition. But there is also the argument that crime is an unremarkable consequence of quite normal conditions.

The *ethnographic* strain in Chicago sociology emphasized moral diversity rather than discord, pathology, or disorganization. It mirrored John Dewey's 'pluralistic realism', a philosophy which pointed to the possibility that numerous, equally authentic truths can co-exist.[90] Dewey had defined truth as situated and local, part of the practical experience of people confronting particular problems. So, too, some sociologists analysed morality or culture as contingent and parochial. Society was described as a great mosaic of social worlds which housed very different forms of conduct and morality. In this sense, deviance was itself regarded as simply another form of conduct embedded in social organization. It was not merely an absence of order or an attack upon order.

Crime and delinquency were explained principally by the effects of the isolation of certain natural areas. They became a kind of surrogate social order, an alternative pattern, which replaced the workings of conventional institutions.[91] Their forms were themselves explained as a functional response to deprivation, to the social and moral structures imported by immigrants, and to the experience of growing up in the inner city. Deprived of political control and economic resources, first- and second-generation immigrants produced their own shadow politics and shadow economy. They created rackets, markets, and systems of patronage in which men of influence distributed protection and sponsorship.

In Boston's Cornerville, for instance, an area investigated by Whyte, Italian Catholics recognized an affinity between the practical organization of their community and the wider order of the Church and Heaven. The world was hierarchical, divided into big people and little people. Just as saints intercede with God on behalf of sinners, so police captains might intercede on behalf of those given a traffic ticket. Social conduct hinged

---

[89] L. Wirth, 'Culture Conflict', 229.   [90] J. Dewey, 'Realism without Monism or Dualism—II'.
[91] F. Thrasher, *The Gang*.

on networks of obligation which bound one to local people and substituted personal morality for a more impersonal subordination to law.[92] It was those networks and the reputations which were secured in them that confined the person living in the zone in transition. People *did* move away, sometimes in groups, but such movement often represented a betrayal:

> To get ahead, the Cornerville man must move either in the world of business and Republican politics or in the world of Democratic politics and the rackets. He cannot move in both worlds at once; they are so far apart that there is hardly any connection between them. If he advances in the first world, he is recognized in Cornerville only as an alien to the district. If he advances in the second world, he achieves recognition in Cornerville, but becomes a social outcast to respectable people elsewhere. The entire course of the corner boy's training in the social life of his district prepares him for a career in the rackets or in Democratic politics.[93]

Children raised in the crowded zone in transition led an intensely public life, playing with others on the street, forming into small groups which could eventually crystallize into gangs. 'Stanley', a jack-roller (or mugger of drunks), and the subject of one of the Chicago School's annotated biographies, recalled that, 'Outside, in the neighborhood, life was full of pleasure and excitement, but at home it was dull and drab and full of nagging, quarreling, and beating, and stuffy and crowded besides.'[94] Such exposure to the street placed the child under constant surveillance from others. From an early age, he (and it was almost invariably a *he* in the public domain) was awarded a communal identity and reputation. In an insecure social environment, the preservation of reputation acquired strategic importance. Responsibilities and claims revolved around one's public character. Teasing play repeatedly tested the validity, strength, and credibility of character. Not to maintain reputation meant that one could easily become dominated and exploited, a victim, in a world in which very little help could be expected from civil society.[95] It became vital to retain face by supporting and initiating joint projects in which reputations could be established or lost. Much of the early delinquency described by Thrasher consisted of a playfulness and daring: stealing fruit from stalls and stores, disrespect to authority, and playing truant. Ignored, it might progress in no discernible direction, although adult criminality was possible. Members of the group could however be prosecuted as law-breakers and, in an anticipation of the labelling theory of the 1960s, it was argued that such public identification could be fateful indeed. Identified as law-breaking, members of the group could cross a threshold and be publicly identified as delinquent. Treated simply as boyishness, the beginnings of delinquency could be channelled into organized sports and neutralized. What *is* significant is the persistence both of tradition and of structural problems in the zone in transition. Contemporary descriptions of life in the zone in transition some seventy years on echo what was written by the first generation of Chicago sociologists.[96]

---

[92] Cf. H. Gans, *The Urban Villagers*. [93] W. Whyte, *Street Corner Society*, 273–4.
[94] C. Shaw, *The Jack-Roller*, 52.
[95] E. Anderson, *Code of the Street* and J. Pitts, *Reluctant Gangsters: The Changing Face of Youth Crime*.
[96] M. Dear and J. Wolch, *Landscapes of Despair*.

William Julius Wilson describes life in Chicago's inner city as one of: 'broken families, anti-social behavior, social networks that do not extend beyond the ghetto environment, and a lack of informal social control over the behavior and activities of children and adults in the neighborhood'.[97] Ideas of conduct are passed on from generation to generation of boys living the public lives of the street: 'to a very great extent . . . traditions of delinquency are preserved and transmitted through the medium of social contact with the unsupervised play group and the more highly organized delinquent and criminal gangs'.[98]

In some measure, it became normal for young people to flirt with delinquency. Those who did not do so were unusually cloistered, marginal, or ostracized.[99] Delinquency was no longer portrayed by the Chicago sociologists as an undertaking which only pathological people could contemplate. It became commonplace, petty, and open in its implications for future experience, identity, and conduct. More particularly, it became the basis of a career which people might abandon or change unless they were under unusual constraint. Autobiographies and extended interviews were employed to grasp how crime and deviance unfolded over time, emphasis being given to the delinquent's own comprehension of significant turning-points in his life.[100] Lives were placed in the context of special meanings and distinct sub-worlds: 'If we fail to see that a gang has a moral code of its own—however immoral it may appear to the rest of us—we will not be able to understand the solidarity, the courage and the self-sacrifice of which gangsters are capable.'[101] Thus, crime and deviance research readily became an exercise in urban anthropology, a non-judgemental analysis of strange peoples and customs.

The urban anthropology of crime and deviance survived to become the core of symbolic interactionism. In part, survival was made possible in an intellectual dark time by the enthusiasm of Edwin Sutherland, once a student at the University of Chicago and eventually a professor at the University of Indiana. During the 1930s and 1940s, and in a period when the University of Chicago sociology department was in partial eclipse, Sutherland and his students (and Donald Cressey in particular) became the tenacious champions of the argument that deviance is a way of life passed from generation to generation. First advanced in 1924, his theory of differential association attempted to make systematic the thesis that crime and deviation are culturally transmitted in social groups. It was laid out as a series of numbered propositions, taking on the appearance of formal theory and intended to be a general explanation of crime.

Differential association theory holds that criminal behaviour is learned in interaction with other people, especially in intimate personal settings, in a process of communication. Learning is held to embrace techniques of committing the crime and the direction of drives, motives, attitudes, and definitions of the law. A person will become criminal if he or she is exposed to an excess of definitions favourable to the

---

[97] W. Wilson, *When Work Disappears: The World of the New Urban Poor*, xvi.
[98] C. Shaw and H. McKay, 'Male Juvenile Delinquency and Group Behavior', 260.
[99] Cf. W. Reckless et al., 'The Good Boy in a High Delinquency Area'.
[100] C. Shaw, *The Jack-Roller*; E. Sutherland, *The Professional Thief*.
[101] L. Wirth, 'Culture Conflict', 237–8.

violation of the law over definitions unfavourable to violation of the law, the process itself being described as differential association. Such differential association will be affected by variations in frequency, duration, priority, and intensity. Sutherland supposed the learning of criminal behaviour to involve all the social and psychological mechanisms at work in other learning. Finally, Sutherland claimed that, although criminal behaviour is an expression of what he called general needs and values, it is not explained by those general needs and values, because non-criminal behaviour is also an expression of those same needs and values.[102] Sutherland and his followers plotted the workings of differential association in white-collar crime[103] (a phrase invented by Sutherland himself), professional crime,[104] embezzlement,[105] and even seemingly motiveless crime. An absence of motives, it was claimed, was a powerful spur to deviation that was itself learned. Ironically, perhaps, those studies are probably now valued more for their ethnographic detail than for their development of differential association theory.

The theory of differential association insisted on the ordinariness of the processes by which deviance arose and was transmitted. It located those processes in mundane social settings which were far from pathological in nature. It argued that deviance evolves in transactions with others. It emphasized the central part played by meaning and motive in the formation of deviant projects. And its acceptance by a number of energetic scholars in the 1940s and 1950s ensured that some major part of criminology would continue to explore deviance as an embedded, shared, symbolic experience changing over time.

Few would now wish to defend the more grandly ambitious claims of differential association theory. The theory promised a kind of specious mathematical precision which could never be realized. How would it ever be possible, worthwhile, or desirable to add up, evaluate, and contrast all the competing definitions of law that one is likely to meet in one's formative years? The theory is riddled with escape clauses and qualifications that diminish its power to predict. Thus, it could always be argued that a great mass of definitions favourable to the violation of law can be outweighed by a few definitions of special intensity, priority, or duration. Unless the theory is trivialized to absurdity, it is not difficult to put forward numerous exceptions to the contention that all crime is learned in association with others. Lemert certainly discovered what appeared to be an exception in his discussion of the naïve cheque forger who had no overt criminal contacts.[106] Yet differential association theory supported a useful tradition which might otherwise have failed. It stimulated ethnographic work when such work was unfashionable, underpinning what has become, in effect, a continuous sociological history of crime. And it served as a bridge between the early work of the Chicago School and what was to become subcultural theory, a significant theory which we shall discuss in an independent chapter.

---

[102] E. Sutherland and D. Cressey, *Principles of Criminology*.
[103] E. Sutherland, *White Collar Crime*.   [104] E. Sutherland, *The Professional Thief*.
[105] D. Cressey, *Other People's Money*.
[106] E. Lemert, 'An Isolation and Closure Theory of Naive Check Forgery'.

Exported to Britain, Chicago sociology affected both the ethnographic work of the 1960s and the sociology of urban social problems. There seemed to be an affinity between the turbulent and expanding Chicago of the 1920s and the cities of England in the 1960s and 1970s. In particular, the social organization of Birmingham, Liverpool, and Sheffield was analysed with ideas that bore strong traces of the zonal hypothesis. Their inner-city areas seemed to be similar to the zone in transition of an earlier Chicago: they contained a fluid, immigrant population; they were characterized by all the conventional signs of social pathology; they were symbolically stigmatized and physically deteriorating. English theory added an English emphasis on the interplay of social classes, denying that natural areas were unplanned or spontaneous and stressing the political economy of housing policies. Much was made of the organized struggle for space and property waged between different 'housing classes' distinguished by their access to and occupation of different styles of residence.[107]

Not all the British sociologists remained at the level of the political economy of the city. Some turned to more focused studies of the politics and history of special areas, concentrating on how places became associated with high crime rates and with notorious reputations (and the two were not necessarily linked[108]). Thus it has been argued, originally by Terence Morris in his revaluation of Chicagoan concepts in his study of Croydon,[109] that accident or housing policy[110] can lead to the concentration of 'problem families' in particular areas,[111] leading to the stigmatization and criminalization of communities.[112] Not only may there be higher rates of crime and criminals in those places, but areas themselves can acquire reputations that acquire a seemingly autonomous life, affecting the treatment and attitudes of their occupants.[113] Negative definitions, restricted opportunities, and enmity may engender self-fulfilling prophecies that contribute to the perpetuation of deviance.[114] We shall return to the more recent British work when we discuss some developments in control theory.

Critique

We have not discussed many of the more specific arguments offered by Chicago sociologists of the 1920s and 1930s. For instance, Anderson's *The Hobo*, an ethnography of the itinerant worker, is an important work, but we have had to ignore it. Our intention has been to review those arguments which reveal the more important themes of Chicago sociology and, in particular, those arguments which have attracted criticism.

---

[107] J. Rex and R. Moore, *Race, Community and Conflict*.

[108] O. Gill, *Luke Street: Housing Policy, Conflict and the Creation of the Delinquent Area*.

[109] T. Morris, *The Criminal Area*.

[110] One particular consequence of British housing policy has been that planning can lead to the removal of criminal areas from the inner city. Estates later to be identified as 'problem estates' may, for instance, be placed on the borders of cities: B. Campbell, *Goliath*; D. Herbert, 'Urban Crime'; and A. Power, *Estates on the Edge*.

[111] F. Reynolds, *The Problem Housing Estate*.

[112] A. Bottoms, R. Mawby, and P. Xanthos, 'A Tale of Two Estates'.

[113] S. Damer, 'Wine Alley'.   [114] O. Gill, *Luke Street*.

Such criticism must be examined rather circumspectly. Like much other censure in sociology, it sometimes reveals more about its author's position than about ideas that were developed in Chicago itself. After all, criticism is usually advanced to promote a particular purpose, and the theories that are attacked often seem to become distorted in the process. Matza praised *The Hobo* as a major innovation which developed 'appreciative' analysis and the sympathetic interpretation of the actor's own stance. Indeed, Matza depicts *The Hobo* as the major achievement of the Chicago School. Faris, by contrast, states: '*The Hobo* achieved most of its contribution by way of informal descriptions, using informal research technique and yielding no new sociological principles.'[115] Criticism is rarely disinterested.

The exploratory and unformulated character of fieldwork has attracted criticism. Those who take to a natural-scientific model of research find the Chicago ethnographic tradition to be strangely loose, imprecise, and muddled. They argue that there is no clear investigation of hypotheses, no specification of objectives, and no means of finding that a theory is wrong. Davis remarked, for instance: 'in the naturalist's tradition, description for its own sake often superseded theoretical rationales for data analysis.'[116] Similarly, Shils observed that the Chicago School failed to 'set out to demonstrate any explicitly formulated sociological hypotheses'.[117] What these critics demand is a neat theory, a neat and articulate method, and a neat conclusion. They are frequently taxed by the Chicago sociologist's reluctance or inability to work with logico-deductive methods. 'What we shared', remembered Gusfield, 'were tacit perspectives without a great deal of concern for rigorous theoretical justifications or deductions . . . There was, and remained, a certain indifference, even disdain, for the endless efforts of sociologists to develop refined theory or methodological rigor.'[118]

In its defence, it could be argued that the imprecise character of Chicago sociology stems from the pragmatic conception of knowledge as an evolving, grounded, and open-ended process. It will be recalled that it held that hypotheses should not be too organized or explicit at the very beginning of research. On the contrary, firm expectations would only prevent the sociologist from seeing and responding to phenomena and events as they arose. Theory must not anticipate, deform, or obscure the facts. It must be allowed to emerge as research advances. In a sense, it may even be argued that the Chicago School's description of research is little more than an unusually honest account of what many sociologists actually experience in the field. Work often seems to develop in a confusing and pragmatic manner.[119] How could it be otherwise? Research almost invariably takes one into the unknown, for which one can never be fully prepared, and sociologists are generally constrained to adopt Plummer's Ad Hoc Fumbling Around or AHFA technique,[120] whatever their claims may be before or after the event. Some are in fact content to dismiss the idealistic recipes of methodologists

---

[115] R. Faris, *Chicago Sociology*, 66.　　[116] N. Davis, *Sociological Constructions of Deviance*, 53.
[117] E. Shils, *The Present State of American Sociology*, 9.
[118] J. Gusfield, preface to G. Fine (ed.), *A Second Chicago School?*, xi.
[119] P. Hammond (ed.), *Sociologists at Work*.
[120] Ad Hoc Fumbling Around: mentioned in conversation. See also his *Documents of Life*.

as 'lies'[121] which their authors mouth but cannot implement. The advocates of those recipes could well retort that it is not remarkable that the unprepared become confused, and it is indeed quite likely that there are many different worlds of research. There is no good reason to imagine that the cautious survey researcher will experience the problems of work in just the same fashion as the ethnographer. But the critics have nonetheless tended to represent Chicago sociology as if it were unnecessarily disorganized, a product of carelessness or oversight rather than a carefully resolved strategy.

Criticisms of the substantive work of the School chiefly turn on the usefulness of the ecological model. Some have pointed out that the city is clearly *not* an ecological system but that it is regulated and directed by processes unknown to the biologist and botanist.[122] Although Roderick McKenzie occasionally offered himself as a legitimate target for such an attack, we have taken pains to stress how Park, Wirth, and others expressly acknowledged the limitations of the ecological model: they too were aware that the city cannot be completely explained in such fashion. It is true, however, that their protestations may not have been enough and that they did sometimes present ecology as a system of iron laws which contradict the more indeterminate themes of ethnography.[123] And it is probably right to say that ecology actually enjoys a fluctuating importance in the works of the Chicago School. In some passages it is a central topic and means of explanation, in others it is neglected altogether.

Again, it has been alleged that persistent reference to the community and communal group imposed a misleading simplicity and distinctness on phenomena which were actually muddled and ill-defined. Suttles insists that 'natural areas' were very rarely natural. Instead of being unplanned and unanticipated, the consequence of the organic growth and differentiation of populations, the early Chicago neighbourhoods *were* planned with great deliberation. Chicago was laid out on the grid pattern and was regulated by copious statutes and ordinances (although the planned 'rationality' of the grid was confounded by the irrationality and unpredictabilty of movements in property values[124]). Moreover, the natural areas were not always internally homogeneous, frequently being inhabited by populations who shared no moral consensus and common identity. When social networks *did* emerge, they could well have been shaped by influences other than the occupation of a shared territory.[125] Indeed, Pahl observes more generally: 'Any attempt to tie particular patterns of social relationships to specific geographical milieux is a singularly fruitless exercise. Some people are of the city but not in it, whereas others are in the city but not of it'.[126]

Such a dissatisfaction with conceptions of the relations between community and territory has stemmed from, or prompted, an alternative phrasing of ideas about urban processes. Some have claimed that the mere fact that events occurred in a shared

---

[121] S. Cohen and L. Taylor, *Psychological Survival.*

[122] T. Morris, *The Criminal Area.* For an unusually full account of post-war British criminology, from the ecological approach roughly to date, see J. Tierney, *Criminology: Theory and Context.*

[123] Cf. N. Davis, *Sociological Constructions of Deviance,* 46.

[124] H. Hoyt, *One Hundred Years of Land Values in Chicago.*

[125] G. Suttles, *The Social Construction of Communities.*   [126] R. Pahl, *Whose City?,* 101; see also P-O. Wikström, 'The Social Ecology of Crime: The Role of the Environment in Crime Causation'.

physical setting could not justify the deduction that those events must be explained by that setting.[127] Instead, they have proposed that the idea of community be dissolved and replaced or complemented by other variables. In particular, classes, minority ethnic groups, and similar formations have been put forward as more significant actors in urban life.[128] It was class, for example, that dictated the allocation of housing and the uses of space.[129] Certain criminologists have consequently argued for the abandonment of social ecology and the adoption of other kinds of explanation. Their arguments are not without merit. The Chicago School did neglect the social history of the business district and the zone in transition, representing their evolution as if it were practically free of human agency:

> Their interpretation stopped abruptly at the point at which the relationship between industrial expansion and high delinquency areas could have gone beyond the depiction of the two as coincidentally adjacent to one another geographically. The interpretation was paralysed at the communal level, a level which implied that either the residents were responsible for the deteriorated area, or that communities collapsed on their own account. Instead of turning inward to find the causes of delinquency exclusively in local traditions, families, play groups and gangs, their interpretation might have turned outward to show political, economic and historical forces at work, which would have accounted for both social disorganisation and the internal conditions, including the delinquency.[130]

Suttles' answer would be that there is substance in such criticisms of the Chicago School but that *community* is nonetheless a useful idea which cannot always be reduced down to other elements: 'unfortunately, this style of research fail[s] to capture what some thought essential to communities, particularly their reputational content and the ethos of local culture.'[131] Chicago sociologists may have been deficient in their analysis of 'master institutions and contradictory systems of social relations,'[132] but their apparent deficiency does not warrant the wholesale abandonment of ecology. The idea of ecology might well have been amended, but it does analyse features of community and territory with considerable competence.

The Chicago sociologists themselves might well have been more robust in their own defence. Pragmatists especially would have maintained that 'contradictory systems of social relations', classes, and 'class struggle' are ideas which have no readily observable referents. One cannot see, touch, smell, or hear a contradictory system. It is an inference most commonly made from an abstract theoretical system. Members of the Chicago School tended to suspect such a priori schemes, arguing that they had only a superficial persuasiveness but no anchorage in an empirical world which could actually be studied. Class, society, and allied terms were handled circumspectly:

> Society is of course but the relations of individuals to one another in this form and that. And all relations are *interactions*, not fixed moulds . . . I often wonder what meaning is

---

[127] M. Alihan, *Social Ecology*.   [128] M. Davie, 'The Pattern of Urban Growth'.

[129] J. Rex and R. Moore, *Race, Community and Conflict*.

[130] J. Snodgrass, 'Clifford R. Shaw and Henry D. McKay', 10.

[131] G. Suttles, *The Social Construction of Communities*, 14.

[132] N. Davis, *Sociological Constructions of Deviance*, 49.

given to the term 'society' by those who oppose it to the *intimacies of personal intercourse*, such as those of friendship . . . We should forget 'society' and think of law, industry, religion, medicine, politics, art, education, philosophy—and think of them in the plural. For points of contact are not the same for any two persons and hence the questions which the interests and occupations pose are never twice the same.[133]

There was a preference for studying the materials of experience, materials which were lodged in people's attempts to handle specific problems in specific settings. Of course, that preference jarred with ecological themes, but it kept much abstraction at bay.

That said, there remain abundant signs that Chicagoan sociologists were all too aware of social inequalities and the pressure of economic interests in shaping the social environment. In Zorbaugh's *The Gold Coast and the Slum* (1929), page after page is taken up with the dire conditions in which slum-dwellers lived by contrast with the affluent denizens of the 'Gold Coast'. As Zorbaugh and Thrasher made all too plain, 'out of this situation arises the gang, affording the boy a social world in which he finds his only status and recognition. But it is by conforming to delinquent patterns that he achieves status in the gang. And every boy in Little Hell is a member of a gang'.[134]

Conclusion

The Chicago School represented the first, orderly, methodical, and large-scale mobilization of sociology to address an array of empirical problems, including the social problems distinctively associated with the growth of a new and vivid spectrum of cultures and styles of life in the cities of North America. Chicago sociology was a major co-operative enterprise which launched an intellectual assault on the study of the city. Part of that assault was occupied with social problems, and social problems were typically confined to particular districts. The explanation of crime and deviance centred on the peculiar conditions of the zone in transition, a turbulent area which appeared out of joint with the rest of the city. Criminality and delinquency were a local effort to restore order and opportunity to disorganization, as well as serving as its cause, and it could become the content of a stable tradition transmitted on the streets. Personal documents, anthropological fieldwork, and the analysis of census and court records were linked together to aid exploration.[135] The outcome was the production of a detailed contemporary social history of crime and deviance. It prepared the basis for some of the principal sociological perspectives that were to come. Ethnography endured to become the 'neo-Chicagoan' symbolic interactionism of the 1940s, 1950s, and beyond. The investigation of the distribution of social phenomena became sociological epidemiology: research into the connections between events in time and space. Urban studies of crime, deviance, and control, grounded in the concepts and ideas of the Chicago School, persist.

[133] J. Dewey, quoted in C. Mills, *Sociology and Pragmatism*, 426, 430.
[134] H. W. Zorbaugh, *The Gold Coast and the Slum*, 177
[135] Some kinds of evidence were inexplicably ignored. Contemporary newspapers and literary accounts, for instance, were almost never used.

Further Reading

A. Abbott, *Department and Discipline: Chicago Sociology at One Hundred*, Chicago, 1999.

G. A. Fine (ed.), *A Second Chicago School?: The Development of a Postwar American Sociology*, Chicago, 1995.

R. Lidner and A. Morris, *The Reportage of Urban Culture: Robert Park and the Chicago School*, Cambridge, 2006.

R. Park, E. Burgess, and R. McKenzie (eds.), *The City: Suggestions for the Investigation of Human Behavior in the Urban Environment*, Chicago, 1925 (reprinted 1984).

C. Shaw and H. McKay, *Juvenile Delinquency and Urban Areas: A Study of Rates of Delinquents in Relation to Differential Characteristics of Local Communities in American Cities*, Chicago, 1942.

4

Functionalism:
The Durkheimian Legacy

Introduction

In the period from the late 1930s to the late 1950s, functionalism came as near as any perspective before or since to constituting sociological orthodoxy. Since that time, it, or, rather, the variety of approaches that were so labelled, has not only fallen from grace, but has been 'every year, every Autumn term ... ritually executed for introductory teaching purposes ... the demolition of functionalism is almost an initiation rite of passage into sociological adulthood or at least adolescence'.[1] In the same vein, Percy Cohen remarked in the 1960s that 'it frequently looks as though anyone in search of theoretical acclaim has only to discover one more defect in functionalism to achieve it'.[2] Towards the end of this chapter, we shall show that those claims are premature, and that functionalism has displayed a remarkable ability to reinvigorate itself.

First, in common with most other approaches, but perhaps to an even greater extent, owing to its former domination over the field, functionalism has all too often been vulgarized by its critics. At times, a package deal is presented in which functionalism, positivism, empiricism, evolutionism, and determinism are collectively linked with a 'consensus' approach to social problems and a conservative approach to their solution. For example, in Douglas' critique of the structural-functional perspective on deviance,[3] the absurdities of such an approach are regarded as by now self-evident and the contrast is dramatically made with the 'emerging sociological perspective on deviance', which is mercifully free from such errors. (These are usually listed as the uncritical acceptance of official statistics, the permeation of a uniform value system throughout society, and a conception of deviance as pathological rather than problematic.) Without wishing to claim that functionalists have altogether avoided such formulations, we see functionalism as offering an altogether more sophisticated and subtle model of crime, deviance, and social control than emerges from such critiques. Second, crime, deviance, and social control have long been implicated with functionalism, at least since Durkheim chose to demonstrate the 'rules of sociological method' by asserting that crime had to be regarded logically as not only an inevitable but as a

---

[1] H. Martins, 'Time and Theory in Sociology', 246.   [2] P. Cohen, *Modern Social Theory*, 47.
[3] J. Douglas, 'Deviance and Order in a Pluralistic Society', ch. 14.

normal and even healthy social phenomenon. This argument put functionalism in bad odour with criminology (as distinct from sociology)—John Mays[4] could remark that, taken literally, it was a 'morally repugnant' argument. Hence, the limited forays into the analysis of crime and deviance by such American functionalists of the inter- and post-war period as Kingsley Davis, Daniel Bell, and Robert Merton, with the exception of the latter's theory of anomie, barely impinged on criminology.[5] A later revival of functionalist arguments, by Erikson and Scott, fared similarly.[6] Despite this neglect, the functionalist approach to crime and deviance continues to survive, at least in a disguised form, to raise questions of an intellectually radical kind that, as yet, no other perspective deals with at all adequately. At the very least, it can be argued, with Matza,[7] that the functionalist approach to crime has contributed significantly to the 'emerging sociological perspective on deviance' to which Douglas referred as its very antithesis.

The Sociological Background

The main tenets of functionalism seem uncontentious enough: they are that societies can, for all analytical purposes, be treated as systems whose parts (the institutions of production, education, human relations, belief, etc.) should be examined not in isolation but in terms of their interrelationships and in terms of their contribution to society in general. For example, it would be pointless to a functionalist to study family and kinship simply in terms of their forms and structures: to do so would be to fail to grasp the significance of family and kinship for other institutions and vice versa. It follows that changes in any one institution have implications for change in others, though no simple 'functional reciprocity' can be assumed: a change in the distribution of wealth may have immense implications for leisure, but a change in patterns of leisure may have negligible impact on the distribution of wealth. If this were all that functionalists contended, then it would be difficult to dispute Kingsley Davis' assertion that, far from being one school within sociology, sociology and functionalism are virtually one.[8]

Functionalists in general, as we argue below, pushed the argument further and began to detach the 'needs' of the social system from the 'needs' of the individuals who, notwithstanding analytical purposes, compose it: this is most obviously the case with Talcott Parsons.[9] Alternatively, they collapsed the 'needs' of society back onto the 'needs' of individuals, but in a somewhat circular way (this is most evident in Malinowski's 'cultural-functionalism').[10] Further, they postulated an evolutionary

---

[4] J. Mays, *Crime and the Social Structure*, 67 ff.

[5] K. Davis, 'The Sociology of Prostitution', 444–55 and 'Illegitimacy and the Social Structure', 221–33; D. Bell, *The End of Ideology*, chs. 7–9; R. Merton, *Social Theory and Social Structure*; and R. Merton and R. Nisbet (eds.), *Contemporary Social Problems*.

[6] K. Erikson, *Wayward Puritans, A New Species of Trouble* and (with R. Dentler) 'The Functions of Deviance in Groups', 98–107; R. Scott, 'A Proposed Framework for Analyzing Deviance as a Property of Social Order'.

[7] D. Matza, *Becoming Deviant*, 31–7, 53–62, 73–80.

[8] K. Davis, 'The Myth of Functional Analysis as a Special Method in Sociology and Anthropology'.

[9] See esp. T. Parsons, *The Social System*.

[10] See esp. B. Malinowski, *A Scientific Theory of Culture*.

trend, for example, from simple agrarian to complex industrial societies, with respect to which some institutions are viewed as functional and others not: this is most marked in the case of Durkheim. It should be stressed, however, that functionalist methods vary quite considerably. Different theorists by no means share the same assumptions about different problems. Malinowski, for example, viewed functional analysis as an alternative to evolutionary schemata, not as a tool for their elaboration, arguing that it is quixotic to attempt to trace the history of a society without written records. All tended, however, to conceive of society as a 'whole' (hence 'holism'), a construction that lent itself to grand and abstract theorizing that, at its worst and with its schematization way beyond any possibility of empirical validation (as in the work of Talcott Parsons' middle phase), does indeed deserve the strictures that Douglas, C. Wright Mills, and many others have heaped upon it.[11]

It is as well to begin with the problem defined as central by these theorists, lest it be thought bizarre to be so obsessed with the shortcomings of the founding fathers. Durkheim's main intellectual concern, at the turn of the century, was to analyse the possibilities of securing social cohesion in the face of rapid social and economic change in France. This problem had been central to social and political theory for much of the nineteenth century: what was novel about Durkheim's formulation was his rejection of purely economic solutions (as, in his view, Marx had proposed) and of leaving things be at all costs (as Spencer had advocated), in favour of what we might now define as a 'corporate state' solution. The division of labour had outstripped the capacity of existing institutions (such as the Churches) to promote moral regulation: yet its function was ultimately the nurturing of co-operation and the lessening of conflict by increasing resources and diminishing direct competition between people. (Its cause, by contrast, was contentiously assigned by Durkheim to increased population pressures.) The division of labour would therefore ultimately promote moral regulation on the basis of newly emergent 'occupational associations', although this could occur only if the fit between talents and occupations could be 'spontaneously' wrought, rather than 'forced': hence his preference for inherited wealth to be abolished, along with other forms of privilege which intervened between ability and assignment to roles. Sociology's task was to clarify the problems facing industrial society and, to further that end, the 'rules of sociological method' were designed to operate on lines of scientific objectivity. No topic was sacred: to emphasize that point Durkheim would frequently choose themes designed to shock; indeed, the 'sacred' became his culminating topic. In *The Elementary Forms of the Religious Life*, he analysed religion (in the form of aboriginal ritual) as the collective representation of the social: 'Society' was God. The function of religion was the celebration of the social group. How primitive man had accomplished so sophisticated a solution to the problem of social order was left unresolved.[12]

Malinowski addressed this problem much more directly, professing himself at odds with Durkheim's notion of the 'group-mind', as he put it, and also attacking the quite

---

[11] J. Douglas, 'Deviance and Order'; C. Mills, *The Sociological Imagination*, ch. 2.

[12] S. Lukes, *Émile Durkheim: His Life and Work*, is the fullest and A. Giddens' Introduction to *Émile Durkheim: Selected Writings*, the most succinct account of Durkheim's work.

separate practice of the 'hearsay' method in anthropology, whereby the anthropologist might rely only on secondary sources of information or stay long enough to write down what his informants told him about native customs and belief. Proper fieldwork involved the ethnographer's tent in the background and a prolonged period of observing what *actually* went on, as distinct from what was *said* to go on. In this context, functionalism enabled one to map social reality as it unfolded. Forms of conduct unintelligible in themselves took on meaning within the context of the patterns of reciprocity and exchange of kinship and tribe. 'Culture' could be itemized: 'it was possible to correlate one aspect of culture with another and show which is the function fulfilled by either within the scheme of culture.'[13] It should be stressed that Malinowski took pains to oppose the 'seamless web' conception of culture so often associated with functionalism. The unity of the clan is 'a social institution of great complexity'; native law is a set of ideals, 'only rarely attained in practice';[14] 'human culture is not a consistent logical scheme, but a seething mixture of conflicting principles',[15] and so on. The functionalist method of rendering culture intelligible *without* resort to an evolutionist schema was its whole point: that did not, however, imply a resistance to acknowledging the reality of change. Fletcher has stressed, in a forceful attack on the tendency to caricature functionalism as capable only of a *static* portrayal of societies, that both 'synchronic' and 'diachronic' accounts are seen as essential by Radcliffe-Brown and that both are recognized as *processes in time*.[16] This does not resolve the logical problem of how, if society 'hangs together' via mutually sustaining functional elements, change is allowed to occur.

The same problem recurs in the most ambitious conceptual attempts to map the 'functional requisites' of social order and the 'structure of social action' in the work of Parsons. Parsons' work is so little wedded to empiricism and ethnography, by contrast with Malinowski and Radcliffe-Brown, that only their underlying shared emphasis on functional relationships enables them to be bracketed together at all. Parsons' aim was to combine a 'voluntaristic theory of action' with a model of the social system that would apply to any society. Hence, he propounded his notion of the 'pattern variables', a five-fold set of 'value-orientations' to action, which matched actors' appropriate behaviour and expectations with socially structured role prescriptions. The relationships of husband and wife, doctor and patient, teacher and pupil are broadly scripted: the individuals improvise the fine detail for themselves. These broad structural constraints are theorized as varying by the type of society and in accordance with the 'functional requisites'—system 'needs' which any viable society must meet.[17] This is not the place to attempt a detailed sketch of Parsons' 'grand theory'. As critics have been keen to point out, it topples over, especially in its stress on the internalization of common values by the individual, its near-deterministic profiles of human typecasting, and

---

[13] B. Malinowski, *Crime and Custom in Savage Society*, 128.

[14] B. Malinowski, *Crime and Custom in Savage Society*, 119–20.

[15] B. Malinowski, *Crime and Custom in Savage Society*, 121.

[16] R. Fletcher, 'Evolutionary and Developmental Sociology', 42.

[17] For an analysis of the problems associated with this theme, see L. Sklair, 'The Fate of the "Functional Requisites" in Parsonian Sociology', 30–42.

near-tautologous portrayals of social systems endlessly reproducing themselves. The first and second reduce the social to the sociable[18] and nowhere convey, or allow for, the active struggle involved in, for example, simply bringing up children, even under relatively favourable conditions; the third hardly allows for the brute facts of conflict, power, and subordination.[19] Deviance is poorly dealt with, either as the product of system malintegration at the margins, or as that of inadequate socialization in childhood. What Parsons does achieve, however, is a sense of the magnitude of the accomplishment of social order, even if it is at the expense, as Wrong so eloquently put it, of an 'over-integrated' view of society and an 'over-socialized' conception of man.[20] It remains the only attempt since the classical theorists to link the processes of interaction on the face-to-face level with the institutional constellations at the macro level worthy of the undertaking itself.

It was an attempt, however, that failed. Attempts to supplant it with a superior theory, or indeed to patch it up, have preoccupied sociologists for the past sixty years. It accounts for the revival of Marxism(s), the popularity of French structuralism, the passion for symbolic interactionism, the fascination with Foucault, and, currently, with theories of globalization and post-modernity: sociology abhors a vacuum. Marxism and structuralism indeed have great affinities with Parsonian structural-functionalism: compare Hawthorne's summary of Althusser with Parsons' mode of explanation:

> modes of production . . . furnish the limits within which institutions and individuals can act and in that extremely weak sense determine that action. But . . . in any place at any time anything may be more immediately determinant, or 'dominant'.[21]

Functionalist currents also pervade symbolic interactionism. Goffman, for example, in his essay on gambling, falls back ultimately on the notion that 'Character is gambled ... We are allowed to think there is something to be won in the moments that we face so that society can face moments and defeat them.'[22] This should not surprise us: Mead, the founding father of interactionism, contributed a major essay on the functions of punishment for social structure. It begins to look as though functional analysis refuses to be struck from the sociological canon.

Before we proceed to describe the specific claims made by functionalists, it should be noted that, whilst there is a functionalist anthropology and a functionalist sociology, there is almost no recognizable, schematic functionalist criminology. Robert Merton, one of the prime functionalists, a man who had a very major impact on the sociology of crime and deviance, was reported for example to have 'had no interest in criminology and little interest in the nature of crime or its correlates. He explicitly disdained interest in prior research in the field, and he did not bother to summarize the evidence bearing on the empirical relation most important to his theory'[23] of anomie.

[18] A. Gouldner, *The Coming Crisis in Western Sociology*, 425–8.
[19] See esp. D. Lockwood, 'Some Remarks on "The Social System"', 134–46; J. Rex, *Key Problems of Sociological Theory*; and A. Gouldner, *The Coming Crisis in Western Sociology*, pt. II.
[20] D. Wrong, 'The Oversocialized Conception of Man', 183–91.
[21] G. Hawthorne, *Enlightenment and Despair*, 229.　　[22] E. Goffman, 'Where the Action Is', 237–9.
[23] M. Gottfredson and T. Hirschi, *A General Theory of Crime*, 78.

At least two general principles explain that indifference and that absence. First, it may be said that functionalism was established to analyse social systems conceived comprehensively, not any one system's minute parts. It was defined less by an interest in the empirical bits and pieces of society than with the broad formal workings of society as a whole. Like other macro theories, then, it does not preoccupy itself over much with the detail of substantive problems such as crime and deviance.

Second, from Durkheim onwards, functionalists maintained that the business of social science is with *science* and scientific knowledge which are themselves held to be quite different from, indeed antithetical to, the common-sense knowledge of everyday life. Functionalism was regarded as the scientific study of entities variously called unintended consequences, hidden processes, deep structures and 'latent functions'.[24] It was centred on the making of discoveries that were likely to confound commonplace expectations and mundane reasoning and it sometimes proceeded as if the more disconcerting its discoveries, the more powerful must be its claim to scientific standing.[25]

The two impulses were contradictory on occasion. Whilst functionalists did not choose to remain on the level of the small-scale and empirical, they *were* attracted by the possibility of showing how very surprising the workings of social systems could be. From time to time, as a result, they wrote about crime and deviance precisely because they presented the best opportunity to display the explanatory powers of scientific sociology. Commonsense could tell us that crime and deviance are palpably harmful, corrosive of social order, an evil to be eradicated at any cost. If functionalism could show that, to the contrary, crime and deviance actually *maintained* social systems, it would have been vindicated indeed. Almost all the major functionalists[26] turned to crime and deviance on at least one occasion because (it may be supposed) they could be used to illustrate the latent functions of what *seemed* incapable of having any such function. Their work resembles a series of apprentice pieces, clever demonstrations of skill before one's peers and masters and, like other apprentice pieces, it is not to be confused with the major projects and central tradition of functionalism itself.

Being peripheral and ad hoc, functionalist criminology may be represented as a somewhat piecemeal accumulation of arguments. It is not integrated, organized, or coherent and it has not been the subject of lengthy debate. Others may have criticized what it has done, but those who have been attacked have not usually turned round to amend, defend, or clarify their work. It is as if functionalists had played with criminological problems without caring about what criminologists themselves would say. In writing about functionalist criminology at all, therefore, we have been obliged to do what the functionalists did not always do themselves, reconstructing (and occasionally constructing) argument in its strongest and most consistent form—sometimes adding to the original to be cogent.

---

[24] P. Blau, *The Dynamics of Bureaucracy*, 8–9.   [25] M. Davis, 'That's Interesting!'
[26] With the exception of Talcott Parsons, who stressed the so-called *dys*functions of deviance. See his *The Social System*.

The Functions of Crime and Deviance and Control

Durkheim and Mead

Durkheim's view of the proper rules of sociological method was based on a forthright positivism: the astonishing success of the natural sciences could be matched by the social sciences, provided that similar methods were adopted. The classification of social phenomena could match the taxonomies of the natural sciences. The social world could be investigated using concepts similar to those of health and disease employed in the anatomization of living organisms. 'Normalcy' and 'pathology' could be empirically established by reference to the generality of phenomena in societies of comparable development and complexity: divergence from the average would indicate degrees of pathology. Two steps were involved in the assessment of normalcy. First, it could be empirically established if a phenomenon existed throughout the range of known societies: if it did, then its normalcy could be presumed and the sociologist was alerted to its likely functional character. Second, the contribution of the phenomenon to the 'conditions necessary for group life' had to be established. Only if both steps were accomplished could functionality be inferred and a yardstick for the assessment of pathology set up.

The illustration of these methods with reference to crime led Durkheim to make his most contentious assertion that 'crime is normal ... It is a factor in public health, an integral part of all healthy societies'.[27] Its universal character pointed to its functionality, but Durkheim could only secure his conclusion by stating the manner of the contribution that crime makes to social stability. This ensues, he argued, from the response that crime (or, by extension, deviance in general) elicits from the group or community: it serves to 'heighten collective sentiments', sharpen perceptions of moral imperatives, more tightly integrate the community against the transgressor—in short, to clarify and reinforce the norms and values of the group. A certain amount of crime is therefore functional, while too little or too much is pathological: 'There is no occasion for self-congratulation when the crime rate drops noticeably below the average level, for we may be certain that this apparent progress is associated with some social disorder'. By the same logic, 'excess [when the crime rate is unusually high] is undoubtedly morbid in nature'. The former implies that the forces of social control have become too strong, that too great a social investment is being made to eliminate it: the result is social stagnation. The latter implies that it is swamping the group's capacity to respond collectively to it and that social cohesion is gravely at risk. Commonly accepted beliefs about crime are much more likely to agree with the second rather than the first assertion and Durkheim employed all his customary eloquence to make the argument hold:[28] 'Imagine a society of saints, a perfect cloister of exemplary individuals. Crimes, properly so called, will there be unknown; but faults which appear

---

[27] É. Durkheim, *The Rules of Sociological Method*, 67.

[28] Durkheim may once again have been empirically wrong: there are a few communities where crime and deviance have no discernible presence, one being the island of Pitcairn. *The Times*, 4 July 1998.

venial to the layman will create there the same scandal that the ordinary offence does in ordinary consciousness.'[29] He would no doubt have seen what Stanley Cohen[30] has termed 'moral panics' as necessary forms of communal consciousness-raising to re-activate social controls. Such panics seem subject to eternal recurrence. As Pearson has commented: 'The terms and limits within which the problems of lawlessness are understood and acted upon are established within a form of public discourse which has been with us for generations, each succeeding generation remembering the illusive harmony of the past while foreseeing imminent social ruin in the future.'[31] To a func-tionalist, such continuities are the stuff of which social order is made.

Where Durkheim is deficient is in his analysis of precisely how all those mediations and continuities are accomplished. He failed to deliver a description of how authority works. Neither does he consider how it works repressively. As Cotterrell remarks, his more general views about the relations between condemnation, punishment, and so-cial solidarity are not 'merely unproven but dangerous.'[32]

To the functionalist, a 'crime-free society' is a contradiction in terms because to bring about the elimination of all crime and deviance would entail such a massive heightening of collective sentiment against them that currently trivial transgressions would become magnified to take their place. The attempt to eliminate them would produce a further twist in the spiral, to the point where social life logically seized up. This does not, of course, imply that Durkheim approved of all crime or all punishment; nor does it obviate debate about the most desirable 'cutting-point' at which societies should accept some crimes, but not others, as the norm. What it does insist on as an argument is the impossibility of eliminating crime, or equivalently sanctioned forms of deviance, from social life altogether.

Mead developed a complementary theme to that of Durkheim.[33] It is quite inad-equate, he argued, to account for the social organization of justice by reference to such justifications of punishment as retribution and deterrence. These would as well be served by lynch law. The ritual solemnities of the criminal law reflect rather the community's need for the criminal to be subjected to a form of punitive justice in which the re-establishment of social order is enacted in dramatic form. The two major functions fulfilled by the criminal law are the stigmatization of the offender and the reinforcement of inhibitions against law-breaking among the community at large. The hostility towards the criminal derives from his challenge to the moral boundaries with which the members of the community identify. This hostility cannot be reconciled with the desire to 'reform' or 'treat' the offender: 'It is quite impossible psychologically to hate the sin and love the sinner.' Unease in the 1970s about the grafting of rehabilita-tive measures on to the criminal justice system seemed to echo these arguments. It is not, however, entirely the case, as Phillipson suggests, that Mead and Durkheim are

---

[29] É. Durkheim, *The Rules of Sociological Method*, 66–72 and *passim*. For excellent discussions, see M. Phillipson, *Sociological Aspects of Crime*, ch. 3; and A. Cohen, *The Elasticity of Evil*.

[30] S. Cohen, *Folk Devils and Moral Panics* and Chapters 6 and 7 below.

[31] G. Pearson, *Hooligan: A History of Respectable Fears*, 229.

[32] R. Cotterrell, *Émile Durkheim: Law in a Moral Domain* 76.

[33] G. Mead, 'The Psychology of Punitive Justice'.

implicitly at one in their penal theories. Phillipson argues that, to Durkheim, in his *Moral Education*, 'the essential function of punishment is not simply retributive, nor is it to produce individual atonement, nor is it to deter the offender, but rather it is to demonstrate the inviolability of the rule broken by the offender'.[34] If the punishment *is* secondary to the reaffirmation of the rule, then the way remains open for alternative measures to the sheerly punitive.

What those alternatives might be was hinted at elsewhere in Durkheim's work.[35] In his evolutionary perspective, he saw 'repressive' justice as yielding progressively to 'restitutive' justice as society moved from 'mechanical' to 'organic' modes of social solidarity. In the former, uniformity of consciousness could accommodate deviance only by strongly punitive responses. In the latter, social order is secured by a more 'spontaneous' division of labour and restitutive justice—the minimum of reparation needed to restore harmony—becomes more apt. While Durkheim's chronology may have been partially invalidated by modern anthropology, his ideal types of justice retain their analytical force and can be seen at work in all modern criminal justice systems.[36] Indeed, the global popularity of restorative justice may prove to be a vindication of Durkheim's thesis, representing, as it does, a strong return to restitutive principles.[37]

Developments

Despite the radicalism of their tone and style, Durkheim and Mead did not go much beyond asserting, once cant and hypocrisy were swept aside, the inevitability of crime and punishment as properties of social order in at least the societies of their day (and by extension all societies based upon known principles of social organization). Tone and style aside, the American sociologists who took up the functional analysis of crime and deviance came much closer to justifying the pursuit of specific forms of deviance as positively serviceable to the social order.

> The growth of a sociological view of deviant phenomena involved, as major phases, the replacement of a correctional stance by an *appreciation* of the deviant subject, the tacit purging of a conception of pathology by new stress on human *diversity* and the erosion of a simple distinction between deviant and conventional phenomena, resulting from more intimate familiarity with the world as it is, which yielded a more sophisticated view stressing *complexity*.[38]

Appreciation carries the risk of a seeming complicity with the deviance under scrutiny, which is probably the main reason for its relatively late adoption as a method. There is no reason for appreciation to imply approval: to empathize is not necessarily to sympathize. Appreciation in this sense is a mere research tool used to enhance the study of any group.[39] However, Matza credits functionalism with playing a major

---

[34] M. Phillipson, *Sociological Aspects of Crime*, 70.   [35] S. Lukes and A. Scull, *Durkheim and the Law*.
[36] E. Lemert, *Human Deviance, Social Problems and Social Control*.
[37] J. Braithwaite, *Crime, Shame and Reintegration*.
[38] D. Matza, *Becoming Deviant*, 10, also 31–7, 53–62, 73–80.
[39] N. Fielding, *The National Front*; K. M. Blee, *Inside Organised Racism, Los Angeles*, 2013.

role in the growth of 'naturalism' in the sociology of deviance. By searching for the hidden contributions that deviant phenomena might make to the social order, 'some functional analyses sound suspiciously like the justifications of phenomena rendered by the deviant subjects who exemplify and perpetrate them'. Though this appreciation was usually 'from a distance',[40] it was still appreciation. Kingsley Davis' analysis of prostitution is remarkably similar to the more recent demands for a 'new deal' by some organized groups of sex workers in the US and some Western European countries. It is claimed, for example, that prostitution or sex work operates as a service for those unable to achieve sexual satisfaction in any other way, acting as a safety valve for potential sexual aggression. In Davis' view, this is ultimately the reason why prostitution can never be eliminated, short of abolishing the sanctity of monogamous marriage and requiring 'mutual complementariness' of sexual desire throughout society.[41] In this sense, prostitution complements the institution of the monogamous nuclear family. Both are threatened by the rise of more widespread sexual freedoms: but to push the latter too far would presumably lead to a Hobbesian state of sexual promiscuity which would chronically affect the social order. Hence, some prostitution is a good thing, an argument taken up and developed with reference to pornography some thirty years later by Polsky.[42] In a fashion analogous to prostitution, functionalists could argue that pornography canalizes into a purely commercial transaction a welter of sexual gratifications that, by comparison with adultery, for example, pose no threat to family ties.

'Appreciation' appears a mixed blessing for sociology. The injunction to empathize with the internal and subjective realities of a phenomenon is not entailed in classical functionalism. Its appeal is most obvious in the more exotic but victimless forms of deviance, such as smoking marijuana or joining a nudist colony. In cases of victimization, it carries the aura of a spiritual collaboration, although to 'appreciate' Fascism is not to condone it.[43] Matza's argument that to apprehend the world as it is involves taking that risk is best exemplified by Daniel Bell's portrayal of the racketeering in New York's dockland. Addressing the problem of why racketeering in New York should flourish long after it declined elsewhere, Bell conveys the distinctive character of the operations there as a stable organization that actually copes relatively efficiently with the unusually intricate nature of the New York dockside. That the price is graft, corruption, and exploitation does not detract from the 'beauty' of the racket, which 'provided extraordinary gain on almost no investment other than muscle-men for intimidation'.[44] As Matza comments: 'Such a truth is obviously partial, but it is necessary to begin there. Otherwise, the coherence, form, texture and even utility of deviant phenomena cannot become evident.'[45]

[40] D. Matza, *Becoming Deviant*, 32.

[41] K. Davis, 'Prostitution', 286; R. Campbell and M. O'Neill (eds.), *Sex Work Now*; R. Witzer, *Legalising Prostitution*.

[42] N. Polsky, *Hustlers, Beats and Others*.

[43] N. Fielding, *The National Front* and K. M. Blee, *Inside Organised Racism* which are appreciative but disinterested studies of fascists.

[44] D. Bell, *The End of Ideology*, 187.   [45] D. Matza, *Becoming Deviant*, 37.

Still pursuing Matza's scheme of things, in which—it should be stressed—his major aim is to chart the development of naturalism in the study of deviance, not to adjudicate on the validity or invalidity of theories, we are shown a second by-product of functionalism to be the purging of pathology. This is no small achievement, as the classical functionalism of Durkheim rested upon just such a conception. The purging is best exemplified in the work of Merton, who distinguished between manifest and latent functions to stress the ways in which social phenomena, however 'immoral' or 'unhealthy' on the surface, may actually contribute to the social order. In fact, there was nothing apart from the terminology employed that was especially new about the idea of latent function. For Durkheim, all functions were latent; he described as 'purposes' those functions that Merton called 'manifest functions'. However, in his analysis of the political machines which were a byword for corruption and graft in American life, Merton sought to establish unintended and unnoticed virtues. These reside largely in the capacity of the political machines, directed by the local Boss, to deliver actual results, against the grain of legal constraints and democratic convolutions. 'The functional deficiencies of the official structure generate an alternative (unofficial) structure to fulfil existing needs somewhat more effectively.'[46] Once learnt, this analytical model can appear to justify practically anything, a deficiency Merton sought to remedy by introducing the concept of 'dysfunction' to complement that of function. However, Davis, Bell, Merton, and others in the 1930s, 1940s, and 1950s were primarily concerned with the functions of the deviant: the dysfunctions of the conventional were merely the mirror-image that supplied a certain analytical symmetry in principle. The most deadly question, which they rarely raised, was 'At whose expense?' and its corollary, 'Functional for whom?' Their intention was not, however, to produce a functionalist theory of deviance, but to use deviance on occasion as a hard case for the exemplification of functionalist strategies.

The third achievement of functionalism, in Matza's view, was to accelerate the movement away from a view of deviance and, by extension, society as essentially simple, to an awareness of its complexity. 'Overlap' and 'irony' are terms employed to convey the processes involved. Deviant phenomena overlap with conventional: the same motives, the same organizational principles, even the same morality, can inspire deviant and conformist alike. In this sense, Al Capone, as Merton (and Capone himself) stressed, was a model capitalist entrepreneur. Racketeering was illegal, but in all other respects it conformed to the canons of good business practice. The irony employed by the functionalists was perhaps less novel than Matza implies: after all, novelists and satirists from Swift and Fielding on, dramatists as celebrated as Shakespeare and Shaw, had employed the device on these very issues to effect. Mandeville, in his *Fable of the Bees* (1714), had argued that the practice of virtue was incompatible with commercial prosperity, which can flourish only in a context of pride, greed, and emulative luxury. The use of irony in sociology, however, was decidedly novel. 'By the idea of irony, the functionalists revealed social process as *devious* and thus increasingly complex.'[47] Thus Merton: 'A cardinal American virtue, ambition, promotes a cardinal American vice,

---

[46] R. Merton, *Social Theory and Social Structure*, 73.   [47] D. Matza, *Becoming Deviant*, 77.

deviant behaviour.'[48] Thus Davis: 'If we reverse the proposition that increased sexual freedom among women of all classes reduces the role of prostitution (as Kinsey's findings suggest), we find ourselves admitting that increased prostitution may reduce the sexual irregularities of respectable women.'[49] That crime and deviance could operate as a blessing in disguise was, as Bell put it, nevertheless bought 'at a high price'—a double irony that stemmed from virtue's dependence on evil for the performance of necessary services.

In all of this, the American functionalists (Davis apart) were prone to neglect the second stage of Durkheim's methodology. Sheer persistence of a phenomenon was not sufficient to secure functionality: the ways in which it necessarily contributes to group life tended to be taken for granted. It is in this sense that Erikson's analysis of the seventeenth-century Salem witch trials, represents a return to Durkheimian orthodoxy. But it is an orthodoxy which he takes as a beginning rather than an end of enquiry:

> This [approach] raises a delicate theoretical issue. If we grant that human groups often derive benefit from deviant behaviour, can we then assume that they are organised in such a way as to promote this resource? Can we assume, in other words, that forces operate in the social structure to recruit offenders and to commit them to long periods of service in the deviant ranks? . . . Deviant forms of conduct often seem to derive nourishment from the very agencies devised to inhibit them. Indeed, the agencies built by society for preventing deviance are often so poorly equipped for the task that we might well ask why this is regarded as their 'real' function in the first place.[50]

If this is so, it may account for the surprising symmetry between the deviant and the conformist—a symmetry far more striking when scrutinized from a distance:

> A twentieth-century American is supposed to understand that larceny and other forms of commercial activity are wholly different, standing on 'opposite sides of the law'. A seventeenth-century American, on the other hand, if he lived in New England, was supposed to understand that Congregationalism and Antinomianism were as far apart as God and the Devil.[51]

His argument culminates in the linkage of the fear of deviance with the processes whereby that very thing is created: 'If deviation and conformity are so alike, it is not surprising that deviant behaviour should seem to appear in a community at exactly those points where it is most feared. Men who fear witches soon find themselves surrounded by them; men who become jealous of private property soon encounter eager thieves.'[52] And the point of this exercise in 'self-fulfilling prophecy' returns us to the most ancient antinomy of all: that good can be known only in relation to evil, its mirror image. 'In the process of defining the nature of deviation, the settlers were also defining the boundaries of their new universe.'[53]

Two subsidiary themes also occur to Erikson. He argues that the volume of deviance has more to do with the community's capacity to handle it than with the inclinations

[48] R. Merton, *Social Theory and Social Structure*, 137. [49] K. Davis, 'Prostitution', 283–4.
[50] K. Erikson, *Wayward Puritans*, 283–4. [51] K. Erikson, *Wayward Puritans*, 21.
[52] K. Erikson, *Wayward Puritans*, 22.
[53] K. Erikson, *Wayward Puritans*, 23; see also A. Miller *The Crucible*, (2003[1952]).

towards deviance among its members. Social control agencies tend to regulate rather than attempt to eliminate deviance, whatever they claim rhetorically about the 'war against crime'. Stabilization seems to be preferred to elimination partly because the control agencies demand some predictability of employment, but also because the very definitions of the problem adjust to fit the community's calibration of its control machinery. As a corollary, societies develop appropriate 'deployment patterns' to negotiate the optimum volume of deviance that they 'need' for moral boundary maintenance. Here Erikson propounds what is virtually a 'conservation of energy' theory of deviance containment. Rag-days, charivari, festivals, provide outlets for the ventilation of deviance in licensed form. Certain age-grades are extended a heightened degree of tolerance: the Amish have their 'Rumspringa' when they reach the age of 16; adolescence is a 'psycho-social moratorium'; and the young are expected to 'sow their wild oats', 'get out of hand', and generally 'raise hell' from time to time, though the tolerance is finely tuned to curb those who go 'too far'. In sum, Erikson is probing, so to speak, for a deep structure of deviance and control beneath the myriad forms they have assumed in history and from society to society. For Christie, too, crime is in infinite supply and the penal repression applied by any society reflects more about the erosion of other, more sensible ways of managing control, the relentless politics of demonizing the other, and the search to profit from the building of prisons.[54]

Functionalists from Durkheim to Erikson tend to treat social cohesion and the need for moral boundary maintenance, as their ultimate data. But why the need for boundaries at all—what does it mean to assert that societies must 'cohere'? In what remains the most comprehensive attempt to address those questions, Robert Scott draws not only on the work of the functionalists, but also on that of the philosopher of science, Thomas Kuhn, on the anthropologically based analyses of rules and meanings of Mary Douglas and on the social phenomenology of Berger and Luckmann.[55] From Kuhn, he takes the idea that people explain the world to themselves in terms of a 'paradigm', a self-contained model which is relatively immune to change, except in the form of very rare 'paradigmatic revolutions' which overturn established ways of apprehending reality and replace them by ones emergent from the new paradigm. From Mary Douglas he takes the axiom that cultures cannot explain everything, but what cannot be explained is treated as anomalous, as something that 'should not be there': 'Dirt is matter out of place' is her vivid metaphor. From Berger and Luckmann he takes the notion of 'world-openness', the absence for people of an environmental stability: thus, 'men require a symbolic framework for ordering social reality'. Social order is humanity's creation of 'world-closedness' against the void, a construction to ward off the chaos of nature; it is therefore always precarious and besieged by countless 'alternative' realities. The development of social order is made possible only by humanity's capacity to symbolize and so to habitualize actions, which by repetition and reinforcement become reified, 'real', 'social things', as Durkheim called them, with the potency of exercising constraint

---

[54] N. Christie, *A Suitable Amount of Crime*.

[55] R. Scott, 'A Proposed Framework for Analyzing Deviance'; T. Kuhn, *The Structure of Scientific Revolutions*; M. Douglas, *Purity and Danger*; P. Berger and T. Luckmann, *The Social Construction of Reality*.

over generation after generation. The legitimation of such patterns lends them moral meaning and the patina of 'naturalness'; the integration of such legitimations provides an overarching symbolic framework. Social and cultural cohesion and coherence are achieved when the group as a whole takes a particular system as *the* institutional pattern, in which 'everything makes sense'. In complex societies, many sub-universes of meaning can co-exist, but the dominant order is generally adhered to with a deep conservatism and resistance to change. Gellner assigns the term 'ironic cultures' to those forms of belief which do not ultimately challenge the dominant symbolic order, except on the surface of appearances: people may 'believe' in astrology, but they do not commonly entrust themselves to astrologers for brain surgery or bridge-building.[56]

Social order is set in a field of force which has the capacity to overwhelm it. Chaos holds the potential to confront us with things that literally should not exist if the concept of reality that is embodied in our symbolic universe is true. Yet cultures exhibit great resilience in the face of such threats to their integrity. Just as scientific paradigms can bracket away, as anomalous, events which science itself postulates ought not to exist, or which it has classified and categorized wrongly, so cultures can deploy mechanisms for smoothing out and resolving threats posed by anomalies. Deviance enters as a property of social order to serve as a category for the anomalous. Other mechanisms perform complementary functions. *Misperception* can quite genuinely occur, so that anomaly is simply not noticed. *Debunking* can flatten anomaly into the everyday. *Normalizing* can redefine it as not really what it seems, as—for example—in the anxiety to cure the deviant whose 'real' problem is something else. If recalcitrant, deviance can be coercively *controlled*. If unduly defiant and threatening, *nihilation* can occur, the 'conceptual liquidation' as 'meaningless' of the deviant's definition of reality. Finally, *change* to accommodate the deviance can occur, but Scott (following Kuhn) views this as extremely rare. In sum, deviance is not just what is left over from conformity: it is inextricably bound up with the preconditions for conformity to exist.

Critique

In a formidable summary of the strengths and weaknesses of functionalism, Percy Cohen lists three species or levels of criticism: logical, substantive, and ideological.[57] Of these, the logical criticisms are by far the most severe. First, functionalist theories are viewed as taking a teleological form which is ultimately unacceptable, despite plausible justifications for this form of argument in the human, as distinct from natural, sciences.[58] Teleology consists in the imputation of cause to beneficial consequence: for example, religion originates in the need for social cohesion. It can be argued that this presents no real problem: people have purposes and put them into effect collectively by trial and error. In other words, they have the consequences in mind as an anterior condition of behaviour. The problem here is that functionalism was created in the teeth

---

[56] E. Gellner, *Legitimation of Belief*, 191–5.   [57] P. Cohen, *Modern Social Theory*, ch. 3.
[58] E.g., A. Stinchcombe, *Constructing Social Theories*, ch. 3.

of the complexities of social life that could not be accounted for solely in terms of intended consequences. As Cohen argues:

> many, if not most, social phenomena are the product of the unintended consequences of social actions; these social actions are themselves purposive; but many of their consequences have no direct connection with these purposes. Thus, men may participate in their religion in order to achieve a state of salvation; if this widespread participation has consequences for the moral order, this may be quite unconnected with the purposes envisaged by the participants. This is not to deny that men sometimes set out to create or destroy social phenomena. . . . But whatever men do in this respect, they always unintentionally produce certain social and cultural items which, though they appear to have been devised for certain purposes, were not.[59]

The problem then becomes how to avoid a purely circular explanation, in which the grounds for the existence of the phenomenon are simply read into the alleged functions it serves. It is one thing to assert that crime can be made to serve some social end or other *once it has occurred*, for example to heighten solidarity by uniting against the paedophile. It is another step altogether to explain crime as promoted in advance by society to bring about that end. There are examples of the latter, to be sure: witch-hunting, scapegoating, and the activities of *agents provocateurs* are not least among them. In such cases it is normally particular interest groups seeking specific ends and not some emanation from the social processes of the group as a whole, that seem the more plausible causal agency.

We do have our own misgivings about Cohen's stress on the unanticipated consequences of social action. Indeed, we would argue that there must be quite substantial resort to teleology in a discipline devoted to human activity. People do have purposes and they are quite perceptive and far-sighted. They often seek what functionalists would wish to describe as unintended ends. Functionalist analyses of crime and deviance actually give us very little evidence about stated intentions; they do not busy themselves with what people *say* they are doing; although it is never very difficult to find someone, somewhere, on the social scene who is capable of putting an identifiable version of the functionalist case. After all, judges themselves state that they try to promote solidarity amongst the virtuous; drug dealers and sex workers that they are performing a social service; and organized criminals that they are exemplary entrepreneurs, mediators, and patrons.[60] No scholar is required to point them to the latent functions hiding beneath the manifest surface of things. And once the pointing occurs, functionalism becomes self-falsifying. When a description of the unintended and latent functions of action is published, it can no longer be safe to assume that the literate are innocent about the consequences of their behaviour. The result has been an odd, distorting view of social life that removes much that is purposeful and recognizable about conduct. Mary Douglas has put the argument well:

> [Functionalism] proposes an unacceptable view of human agency. . . . The argument depends on a form of sociological determinism that credits individuals with neither

---

[59] P. Cohen, *Modern Social Theory*, 49.   [60] D. Gambetta, *The Sicilian Mafia*.

initiative nor sense. It was partly for this failing that sociological functionalism has been in low repute for the last thirty years. It had no place for the subjective experience of individuals willing and choosing. To suppose that individuals are caught in the toils of a complex machinery that they do not help to make is to suppose them to be passive objects, like sheep or robots.[61]

Another vexing problem concerns testing of the theory. How could one possibly falsify a functionalist proposition? In the case of crime, for example, it may be possible to apply the normal/pathological distinction to different societies on the basis of their crime rates. The USA would undoubtedly emerge at the pathological end of any such spectrum, which indeed might point to the myriad defects which critics have long noted as built into a market society. But functionalism at this point offers an embarrassing number of solutions to the problem of accounting for those defects.[62] The high levels of criminality and deviation may be a 'warning light'; but they could also be a 'safety valve', a price to be paid for the maintenance of valued institutions, such as a relatively strong commitment to 'free enterprise'. They may be the 'functional equivalent' of what, in other societies, appear as high rates of political oppression, religious fanaticism, or mental illness. Similarly, religion has divided societies as well as united them: but this is viewed as confirming its unifying function, albeit within each subcommunity. Nothing can ever be disproved, nor can the promise of comparative analysis be fulfilled, as items can only be evaluated in their own context.

Finally, functionalism promotes holism, the tendency to analyse societies as 'wholes' or systems, which inhibits the exploration of just how a phenomenon affects different groups within it. In asking 'Functional for whom?' the bottom falls out of the functionalist case. For what is functional for one group may well be dysfunctional for another, even though this may not always be so—institutions may be functional for very large numbers. Functionalists recognize this problem, but hope to overcome it by a complicated cost-benefit analysis in which the functions and dysfunctions for various groupings are somehow totted up to produce a sociological balance sheet. Functionalism in this sense is, as Gouldner has noted, no more than sociological utilitarianism,[63] in which it is quite proper for a minority to suffer, in principle, for the social cohesion of the majority. As a *New Yorker* cartoon might put it (we do not know if one has), the victim of a mugging should be gratified that he has played his part in reactivating social solidarity. The main logical defect of such a position is that the vantage point from which such a cost-benefit analysis proceeds is inescapably value-laden.

Empirically, the grounds for opposing functionalism are mainly that little empirical work has been mounted to test its core assumptions.[64] Erikson is the main exception in the sociology of crime and deviance, but his chosen ground—seventeenth-century Puritan New England—is relatively inaccessible, set in a time remote from our own, reached only through edited accounts and thereby closed to the searching scrutiny

---

[61] M. Douglas, *How Institutions Think*, 32.
[62] For an enumeration of such functions, see A. Cohen, *Deviance and Control*, 6–11.
[63] A. Gouldner, *The Coming Crisis.*   [64] P. Rock, 'Rules, Boundaries and the Courts'.

which a test of the functionalist case would demand.[65] It is also lacking in that very complexity towards which functionalists point as the chief characteristic of modern societies. As Gellner has stressed, structurally simple and small-scale societies allow more scope for 'functionalism as a doctrine' because the problem of feedback of unintended beneficial consequences is minimized.[66] When applied to late modern societies, Erikson's assumption of constancy in the crime rate looks almost bizarre. Moreover, the effect of crime is often the reverse of that assumed in functional analysis: far from drawing together 'upright consciences', it all too often triggers off a retreat into isolationism. The community in which the 'In Cold Blood' murders occurred reportedly withdrew from any semblance of social life in the aftermath of those murders. The Bradford 'Ripper' murders had the same effect on the social life of women.[67] 'Indifference' phenomena are widely reported in the United States in the context of the seemingly intractable deterioration in inner-city victimization. On the other hand, the naming of Sir Jimmy Savile as a predatory sex offender in September 2012 did generate a powerful, shocked collective reaction that was amplified, in part, by campaigners, the mass media, and politicians anxious to use his case to impart moral and political lessons about the morally corrupt condition of England in the 1960s and 1970s. Why this scandal should have so shocked the *conscience collective*, whilst other, equally appalling crimes did not, is not at all clear. It is an issue begging for thought and research and it underscores the sad reflection that the main tenets of functionalism have not prompted anything like an adequate mass of empirical work or a viable methodology for undertaking such work in future.

Functionalists perhaps stand accused most powerfully of ignoring conflict, failing to explain change, and employing conservative ideology as a consequence. These criticisms can on the whole be discounted as misconceived or beside the point. Conflict is addressed and can be regarded as functional and, indeed, Simmel[68] and Coser[69] have produced lengthy essays arguing that a period of open conflict can resolve otherwise gnawing strains in society; that conflict promotes the social solidarity of those who are bound together to confront a common enemy; that conflict is a clear warning of the presence of social problems; and that conflict is often surprisingly orderly, a social process locked into other social processes and less disruptive than naïve spectators might suppose. Where conflict is not regarded as functional, it can be described as the outcome of 'malintegration'. Social change is no less well accounted for than persistence and, as Merton pointed out, to assert that things 'hang together' in society as an argument against reform tends as much to revolution as to preserving the status quo. Merton observed that if social structures are as integrated in functionalist analysis as its critics maintain, all change, however petty, would indeed be revolutionary because no part would remain untouched. Indeed, functionalists are the defenders of no one

---

[65] J. Goldthorpe, 'The Uses of History'.   [66] E. Gellner, 'Concepts and Society'.

[67] Truman Capote's *In Cold Blood* (1965) is the 'true crime' recreation of the notorious murder of the Clutter family in a small Kansas town in 1959. For a comparable book on the 'Yorkshire Ripper' serial murderer, see Gordon Burn's *Somebody's Husband, Somebody's Son: The Story of Peter Sutcliffe* (1984).

[68] G. Simmel, *Conflict and the Web of Group Affiliations*.

[69] L. Coser, *The Functions of Social Conflict*.

form of political or social order. They are interested in very abstract and general principles of structural organization, principles so abstract that they are intended to apply to Utopia as well as to hell. Robert Merton reflected that 'it is not at all the case that whatever is, is right, or, for that matter, that whatever is, is wrong. Rather, it is only the case that whatever is, is possible.'[70] Finally, the allegation that functionalism must be dismissed because it is conservative is itself an ideological rather than an analytical response. It assumes that conservatism is indisputably at fault and that is not an assumption that can be made on safe philosophical or empirical grounds. The merit of conservatism is a metaphysical matter. If it is found to be the case that functionalism is well-argued and solid and if the theory makes conservatism intellectually compelling, then its critics should reconsider their position on conservatism instead of using it as an argument for the rejection of functionalism.

Finally, none of the above applies to functional analysis as a method where the purposes of institutional arrangements and their effectiveness in terms of specific aims are concerned; nor are the unintended side-effects of phenomena any less central a topic if functionalism is abandoned. As a part of sociological enquiry, functional analysis remains in order. 'It is essential to evaluate the functionalist method, in the sense that it suggests to us where to look, in isolation from the functionalist doctrine, that tells us what we will find there.'[71]

Conclusion

In the seminal work of Durkheim, crime and deviance were seen as normal—as they elicit responses which clarify and reinforce fundamental norms of conduct—and therefore as functional for the very basis of social order. Crime, deviance, and control yield indices of normalcy or pathology. In the 1930s, systems-centred functionalist approaches were taken up and adapted to the analysis of American society, notably in the work of Kingsley Davis, Robert Merton, and Talcott Parsons. The limitations of functional analysis were increasingly and damagingly exposed by the conflicts that afflicted the USA in the 1960s. However, as long as it is maintained that certain institutions 'fit' other institutions more than others and some minimal congruence is suited to human association, functionalism is in principle a better guide than other approaches to many sociological questions. As soon as it is admitted, say, that modern industrial society requires some kinds of family structure, or certain types of education, rather than others, the functionalist method is also admissible. It may be that functionalists have tended to overplay their hand, but at least they appear some times to be playing the right sort of game. And it should be noticed, too, that functionalism still seems to be persuasive and pervasive enough to surface in a variety of disguises throughout sociology. There may be very few sociologists who would now advertise themselves as functionalists, but there are many who are close to being functionalist in style and thought. Christie Davies, for instance, has written extensively about the functions of

---

[70] R. Merton, *On the Shoulders of Giants*, xxv.   [71] L. Sklair, 'The Fate of the "Functional Requisites"', 40.

humour in upholding social control and social stratification and about the functions of deviance in enforcing sexual boundaries. His is a straightforward teleology that argues, for example, that 'it is clear that the strong taboos that exist against homosexuality, bestiality and transvestitism in the West are the result of attempts to establish and defend strong ethnic, religious or institutional boundaries. Where such pressures are weak or absent the taboos against these forms of sexual deviance are also weak or absent'.[72] The voice of Christie Davies in 1982 could have been that of Kingsley Davis in 1939. More recently, David Garland has revived a Durkheimian sociology of punishment which talks about the symbolic work of the penal sanction in constructing social order.[73] Punishment is, he says, a 'serious and symbolic issue in any society because it lies directly at the roots of social order, as well as having a prominent place in the psychic formation and development of individual persons. As regards the political order, punishment operates as a sign of ultimate authority and is the final materialization of that authority's force: as such it is universal and indispensable'.[74] Braithwaite, too, has revived Durkheim in his analysis of the vital part played by shame in the workings of informal social control.[75] The functionalist message is clear.

When a radical criminologist proclaims that the news media focus on the threat posed by street gangs supports the status quo by deflecting attention from the criminality of the powerful, functionalism is being advanced. When a structuralist like Mary Douglas states that the suppression of deviance promotes the integrity of cognitive orders, functionalism is being advanced. When a phenomenologist like Jack Douglas points to the symbolic interdependencies of good and evil, deviance and respectability, functionalism is being advanced.

Further Reading

D. BELL, 'Crime as an American Way of Life', *The Antioch Review*, 13:2 (1953).

K. DAVIS, 'The Sociology of Prostitution', *American Sociological Review* 2 (1937); also 'Prostitution', in R. Merton and R. Nisbet (eds.), *Contemporary Social Problems*, New York, 1961.

É. DURKHEIM, *The Rules of Sociological Method*, New York, 1964 (orig. published 1895).

A. GIDDENS, *The Constitution of Society: Outline of the Theory of Structuration*, London, 1986.

R. MERTON, *Social Theory and Social Structure*, New York, 1949 and 1957.

---

[72] C. Davies, 'Sexual Taboos and Social Boundaries', 1060. See also his 'From the Sacred Hierarchies to Flatland'.

[73] See esp. the concluding arguments that David Garland offers in his important *Punishment and Modern Society*, 282–3.

[74] D. Garland, 'Frameworks of Inquiry in the Sociology of Punishment', 11. See, too, his *Punishment and Society*.

[75] J. Braithwaite, *Crime, Shame and Reintegration*.

5

Anomie and Strain Theory

Introduction

Like functionalism, from which anomie and strain theories derive, it has become a routine conceptual folly for students to demolish before moving on to more rewarding ground. The critical onslaught has been particularly fierce in the case of Robert Merton's version of anomie theory, the turning-point being Clinard's collection of critical essays on this theme in 1964.[1] By contrast, Durkheim's original statement of anomie as a source of deviant behaviour has received more sympathetic treatment, largely because Durkheim is so central a figure in sociological history and anomie is so central a concept in his thought. That is not the same thing, of course, as continuing to take it seriously. However, both Lukes and Horton, for example, discern in Durkheim's conception of anomie a philosophical critique of capitalist society in relation to which Merton's theory of anomie is at best confused and at worst 'dehumanized'.[2] Other critics are prone to dismiss both as seriously defective: Douglas attacked the entire methodology on which Durkheim's sociology rested; Rex views Merton's central idea as 'extraordinarily over-simplified' and seeks to rescue the bulk of Durkheim's sociology from its damaging association with the former's use of anomie; in Clinard's book, Lemert, Gagnon, and others dealt a seemingly terminal series of blows at both the theoretical and empirical weaknesses of the theory. By the 1970s, Paul Rock and Mary McIntosh could refer prosaically to the 'exhaustion of the anomie tradition'.[3]

If only for its centrality to the sociological tradition of theorizing about crime and deviance, however, in the twenty-first century anomie theory deserves recovery. Among its strengths are a focus on the implications for crime and deviance of one of the defining features of free market societies, that is, the fostering of the propensity to consume *irrespective of* the material possibilities of such a course; a meta-theory which is capable of global application; and the capacity, never greatly elaborated upon since Durkheim's day, of addressing the conditions that may suffice to determine the breakdown of social order.[4] So powerful a theory cannot be disregarded. It was something of a sociological counterpart to the cosmological Big Bang, and its effects have been

---

[1] M. Clinard (ed.), *Anomie and Deviant Behavior*.

[2] S. Lukes, 'Alienation and Anomie'; J. Horton, 'The Dehumanisation of Alienation and Anomie'.

[3] J. Douglas, *The Social Meanings of Suicide*; J. Rex, *Discovering Sociology*, 234 ff.; M. Clinard, *Anomie and Deviant Behavior*; and P. Rock and M. McIntosh (eds.), *Deviance and Social Control*, xi.

[4] P. Berger and T. Luckmann, *The Social Construction of Reality*, and K. Erikson, *In The Wake of the Flood*.

both diffuse and lingering. Anomie theory was at first thought to be so compelling that it was subject to unusually sustained elaboration. After Durkheim and Merton, there followed Cloward and Ohlin, Spergel, Downes, and others working in a kind of tacit co-operation that appears only rarely in sociology. Much of the theory was never fully developed, but it has been expanded to become one of the most ambitious single attempts to explain crime and deviance. (We shall pursue the application of that attempt to deviant subcultures in the next chapter.) Anomie theory was under cultivation at a time of energetic social engineering in the United States and it was appropriated to give intellectual coherence and legitimacy to Mobilization for Youth.[5] It thereby became one of the few well-documented instances of the sociology of crime and deviance achieving a major (albeit retroactive) impact on public policy formation. Third, it may be remarked that sociologists have not yet proved able to relinquish such a pivotal part of their thought. However much they may have protested about anomie theory, it has been reincarnated again and again. It has an anonymous presence in Jock Young's essay in labelling theory, *The Drugtakers*, and appears under its own name as one of the principal themes in his account of the making of left realism in the 1980s and frames his subsequent writings on the hyper-exclusive society.[6] It is the invisible prop to the Birmingham Centre for Contemporary Cultural Studies' radical work on class, youth, and deviance in Britain. Indeed, just as Karl Mannheim was called the *bourgeois* Marxist, so Hall, Clarke, and Hebdige of Birmingham could be labelled the radical anomie theorists. Extensive echoes of the Big Bang will be discerned in any sensitive reading of the contemporary sociology of crime and deviance.

Durkheim's Theory of Anomie

There are two distinct usages of anomie in Durkheim. Lukes restates them as follows:

> In the 'Division of Labour in Society', it [anomie] characterizes the pathological state of the economy, 'this sphere of collective life which is in large part freed from the moderating action of [moral] regulation', where 'latent or active, the state of war is necessarily chronic' and 'each individual finds himself in a state of war with every other'. In 'Suicide', it is used to characterize the pathological mental state of the individual who is insufficiently regulated by society and suffers from 'the malady of infinite aspiration' . . . It is accompanied by 'weariness', 'disillusionment', 'disturbance, agitation and discontent', 'anger' and 'an irritated disgust with life'. In extreme cases this condition leads a man to commit suicide and homicide.[7]

As this passage makes clear, a shift is already under way from anomie conceived of as a constant property of industrial society, to anomie as a variable with social–psychological

---

[5] Mobilization for Youth, *A Proposal for the Prevention and Control of Delinquency by Expanding Opportunities*.

[6] J. Young, 'Left Realist Criminology'. He was to say later that 'the Mertonian notion of contradiction between culture and structure . . . has run throughout all my work, from *The Drugtakers* onwards' ('Crime and the Dialectics of Inclusion/Exclusion', 553).

[7] S. Lukes, 'Alienation and Anomie', 138–9.

implications. It is by no means the case, as Davis, for example, asserts, that this process originated with Merton's later adaptation of the concept.[8]

Durkheim's conception of anomie must be set in the context of his theory of social evolution. In his first use of the concept, it is in the transition of society from mechanical to organic solidarity that the division of labour assumes an anomic form. In the former state, the division of labour is minimal, and the term 'mechanical' is paradoxically employed to refer to the uniformity of consciousness in the simplest societies. A single normative system holds absolute sway. In the latter, it is assumed (for no society has yet attained this state) that the division of labour, though highly differentiated, has generated mediating institutions that assure social cohesion despite marked moral diversity. In the transition, however, anomie results from the rapid growth of the economy without a corresponding growth in the forces that could regulate it. 'Sheerly economic regulation is not enough . . . there should be moral regulation, moral rules which specify the rights and obligations of individuals in a given occupation in relation to those in other occupations'—'occupational groups' were somehow to be the source of this control.[9] A prerequisite is for the division of labour to assume a 'spontaneous' form, that is, individuals must be able to fill occupational positions which accord with their talents and which, therefore, they will accept as legitimate. This cannot prevail where the class system (or, presumably, any other form of stratification) inhibits the chances of large numbers of people attaining positions that fit their abilities. Such a 'forced' division of labour can only be abolished if all 'external' inequalities are ended, such as the hereditary transmission of property. It is in this sense that Taylor, Walton, and Young refer to Durkheim as a 'biological meritocrat', for he assumes an ideal correspondence is possible between 'internal' qualities and social position.[10] 'Labour is divided spontaneously only if society is constituted in such a way that social inequalities exactly express natural inequalities.'[11]

Anomie, then, is the peculiar disease of modern industrial man (and woman), for it is accepted as 'normal, a mark of moral distinction, it being everlastingly repeated that it is man's nature to be eternally dissatisfied, constantly to advance, without relief or rest, towards an indefinite goal'. Religion, State control of the economy, and occupational groups have lost their moral sway. Thus 'appetites have become freed of any limiting authority' and 'from top to bottom of the ladder, greed is aroused without knowing where to find ultimate foothold. Nothing can calm it, since its goal is far beyond all it can attain'.[12] In this analysis, class conflict and industrial crises are a symptom, not a cause, of anomie. Crucially, Marx is reviewed as reversing the true causal priority and, as a result, proffering a false resolution of the problem, a purely economic cure.

In his second usage of the concept, in *Suicide*, Durkheim elaborates on the sources of variation in the experience of anomie. In this pioneering study, the techniques of multivariate analysis are deployed for sociological ends—it can hardly be maintained that

---

[8] N. Davis, *Sociological Constructions of Deviance*, 109.
[9] A. Giddens, *Émile Durkheim: Selected Writings*, Introduction, 11.
[10] I. Taylor et al., *The New Criminology*, 81 ff.   [11] É. Durkheim, *The Division of Labor in Society*, 377.
[12] É. Durkheim, *Suicide*, 256.

Table 1 Durkheim's Typology

	Types of suicide	
	Integration	Regulation
Too strong	Altruistic	Fatalistic
Too weak	Egoistic	Anomic

Durkheim simply treated anomie as a constant and invariant property of industrialism. His argument rests on the crucial nature of the distinction between social *integration* and social *regulation*, which—largely independently of each other—are viewed as causally related to different forms of suicide (see Table 1).

With certain exceptions, the excessive strength of integration and regulation are linked with pre-industrial societies and the types of suicide characteristically prevalent, such as the honorific and the ritualistic, derive from the excessive subordination of the individual to the group. The reverse obtains in the case of industrial societies. Nevertheless, 'altruistic' suicide may still be found, for example, in military charges of 'dishonourable conduct' leading to the taking of one's own life; 'fatalistic' suicide in the acts of self-immolation by Japanese *kamikaze* pilots in World War Two, and in cases of 'suicide terrorism' that define twenty-first century Islamist terrorism.[13]

The egoistic form of suicide was seen by Durkheim as the product of excessive individuation, or the 'cult of the individual', which he saw as the moral counterpart of a specialized division of labour. It was exemplified by the higher suicide rate among Protestants as compared with Catholics; among the unmarried compared with the married; and among the childless as compared with parents. The force of the thesis was most strikingly displayed by the explanation Durkheim gave of the lower rates that obtained at times of political crisis compared with periods of political stability, as in France in 1830, 1848, and 1870. 'Great social disturbances', he argued, 'and great popular wars, rouse collective sentiments, stimulate partisan spirit and patriotism and, concentrating activity towards a single end, at least temporarily, cause a stronger integration of society.'[14] Suicide, therefore, varies inversely with the degree of integration of society.[15]

Economic crises produced the contrary effect: a sharp increase in the suicide rate. This, argued Durkheim, is *not* due to the sudden loss of livelihood or amenities, for an increase in prosperity produces the same result as a decline. Also, suicide rates were at their lowest in the poorest regions of Europe, such as Calabria. (These also were the most Catholic, but Durkheim was not equipped statistically to avoid confounding possibilities of this sort.) To account for this phenomenon Durkheim invoked the concept of anomic suicide, that which flows from the disturbance such crises create in the regulatory aspect of social activity. Subject to deregulation in such crises, people's aspirations overshoot socially contrived limits and fix on the unattainable. Durkheim spent a great deal of time accounting for people's inherent capacity to adopt this course *unless*

[13] W. Laqueur, 'Life as a Weapon'.   [14] É. Durkheim, *Suicide*, 208.
[15] A striking confirmation of this aspect of Durkheim's theory is provided by P. O'Malley, 'War and Suicide'.

they are curbed by social regulation. In striving to convey the character of anomie, Durkheim was driven to his most rabbinical purple passages: 'To pursue a goal which is by definition unobtainable is to condemn oneself to a state of perpetual unhappiness.'[16] It occurs because 'nothing appears in man's organic nor in his psychological constitution which sets a limit to such tendencies', i.e. the 'quantity of well-being, comfort or luxury legitimately to be craved by a human being'. 'It is not human nature which can assign the variable limits necessary to our needs. They are thus unlimited so far as they depend on the individual alone.' If human nature does not set limits, individuals must receive regulation from without, from 'an authority which they respect, to which they will yield spontaneously': and that can only be provided by society. Hence, economic disasters and sudden surges in prosperity alike disrupt the capacity of society to exercise this influence and—for a time—all regulation is lacking. 'Consequently, there is no restraint upon aspirations. . . . At the very moment when traditional rules have lost their authority, the richer prize offered these appetites stimulates them and makes them more impatient of control. The state of de-regulation of anomie is further heightened by passions being less disciplined, precisely when they need more discipline.' The causal flow is from the prior fracturing of social regulation, to the adoption of unattainable goals, to suicide.

It is essential, in Durkheim's view, to avoid confounding that type of suicide stemming from the 'malady of infinite aspirations' with that resulting from the weakening of the social bond, in which the individual is 'detached from life because, seeing no goal to which he may attach himself, he feels himself useless and purposeless'. The two types also display distinctive psychological states at the point of suicide and affect different groups in society. Egoistic suicide is associated with lassitude, weariness, goallessness, and has its principal victims among those in intellectual careers, the world of thought; anomie is associated with irritation, self-disgust, normlessness, and draws its recruits from the industrial and commercial world in which anomie is endemic and 'chronic'.

Despite Durkheim's eloquence, his attempts to differentiate egoism and anomie— and integration and regulation—strike many observers as overdone.[17] Indeed, beside the main point: that is, the tendency for industrialism to lead to what Weber termed the 'disenchantment of the world', with all that that implies by way of existential doubts and insecurities. A separate issue is: is a state of normlessness conceivable? This is, after all, an extremity beyond anarchy which is, properly conceived, the relatively simple notion—by comparison with anomie—of a society without government. A society without norms seems, on the face of it, a contradiction in terms. (There is also the problem of how, once deregulated, norms are reconstituted.) In general, cases where such extremes are approached empirically are infrequent, appearing in the very young and the very old; there are very few even among those designated as mentally ill. The feral child, the senile dement, the psychopath are our only approximations to the anomic in everyday terms. There are, however, a few good descriptions of societies and communities that come close to Durkheim's conception of the anomic. Thus, Rainwater's *Behind*

---

[16] É. Durkheim, *Suicide*, 248 ff. for this and subsequent quotations.
[17] S. Lukes, 'Alienation and Anomie', 139, n. 14.

Ghetto Walls[18] depicted the mistrustful, nasty, alienated, and fragmented world of the Pruitt-Igoe housing development in St. Louis, Missouri. So suspicious and isolated had the tenants of the estate become that there was no longer anything approaching a viable social life. Neighbour preyed on neighbour. People were reluctant to leave their homes for fear of others breaking in. They were loath to ask one another to keep an eye on their apartments because everyone was a potential predator. In time, the municipal authority concluded that existence in Pruitt-Igoe was so intolerable that the apartment blocks would have to be physically destroyed by dynamite. Other examples have been given by the neo-Durkheimian Kai Erikson, who described the impact of such diverse disasters as the pollution of a river upon a fishing community; fraud and default upon a group of poor Haitians whose savings were stolen; the Hiroshima bomb; and the near-catastrophe of the Three Mile Island nuclear plant.[19] His most extensive study, *Everything in its Path*,[20] narrates the devastation caused by the collapse of a dam in the mining community of Buffalo Creek, West Virginia, in 1972. As 132 million gallons of mud rushed down the creek, it carried away houses, people, roads, and possessions. Many were killed and a once-orderly chain of communities was radically disrupted. Neat settlements were replaced by a haphazard trailer camp that incorporated no substantial social and spatial organization. There was an accompanying loss of moral regulation, a decline in co-operativeness, a pervading sense of meaninglessness, and a lack of purpose. People retreated inwardly, ceasing to busy themselves with one another. Rates of alcohol abuse and illegitimate births soared.

Other societies could also be described as anomic. One was that of New Guinea which, in the path of the American attack on the Japanese in the Pacific in the Second World War, had seen the sudden and inexplicable arrival of military aeroplanes carrying strange, powerful men and vast treasures and had then seen the aeroplanes just as inexplicably depart again, never to return. The old economic and religious rationalities seemed to make no more sense. It was better to pray and wait for the strangers to return with their wonderful cargoes. In effect, the emergence of the 'cargo cults' signified a major loss of meaning and purpose.[21]

Another anomic society was the Ik of Northern Uganda, as documented by Turnbull.[22] These 'mountain people' were subjected to a sudden deregulation born of economic catastrophe, when their traditional hunting grounds were designated a national park. Though Turnbull does not invoke Durkheim, he lists a mixture of Ik characteristics reminiscent of both egoism and anomie: 'acrimony, envy and suspicion' even among (illegal) hunting parties; 'excessive individualism, coupled with solitude and boredom'; 'lassitude and inertia'. Children over the age of three, and the old or disabled, were abandoned or robbed: 'without killing, it is difficult to get closer to disposal than by taking the food out of an old person's mouth, and this was primarily an adjacent-generation occupation, as were tripping and pushing off balance. Moreover, I confess they never expressed any intent to kill; it was all good, clean fun.'[23] The extremities

---

[18] L. Rainwater, *Behind Ghetto Walls*.
[19] K. Erikson, *A New Species of Trouble*.
[20] K. Erikson, *In the Wake of the Flood*.
[21] P. Worsley, *The Trumpet Shall Sound*.
[22] C. Turnbull, *The Mountain People*.
[23] C. Turnbull, *The Mountain People*, 252.

of hunger and dispossession, such as the industrial West has not experienced outside the concentration camps (since even in prison regular food and shelter are to be had), lead Turnbull away from moral censure. Like Durkheim, he is concerned to stress the similarities between the anomic and the lives that we lead (overdrawn as some of these are by Turnbull: leaving children to the bush is hardly the same as sending them to summer camp[24]). But he notes the extent to which, in a context of plenty unknown to the Ik, we countenance suffering at home and starvation abroad. However, in other respects, Durkheim's analysis does not fit the Ik. They did not lack a goal (as in egoism), for their goal was survival; nor did they 'aspire infinitely' (as in anomie), for they aspired very specifically towards such mundane goals as food and water. Yet, in key respects, Durkheim offers more of a vocabulary for the understanding and prediction of the Ik than other classical theorists. And though the Ik cannot be said to represent pure anomie (in which, presumably, no rules of conduct can obtain, and people resemble dements) they come sufficiently close for credence to be granted the proposition that 'sudden deregulation' may bring social disaster. However, as other peoples in the region of the Ik had prospered through relocation, this is not necessarily the case. The irony is that the best-documented example of this 'disease' of modern industrial man should be a pre-industrial people. As Turnbull stresses in perhaps too melodramatic a way, however, the parallels are all too close. Surely there are echoes of the Ik in the crime-ridden estates and neighbourhoods of America, France, and Britain,[25] where attempts to establish community policing and similar initiatives fail because the concept of community has no meaning. One such divided and fearful London estate was graphically described by Sampson:

> [An] important feature was the multi-dimensional nature of residents' fears. Their lives were blighted by social conflicts and tensions. Some of these conflicts reflected divisions between gender, race, and age while others were about divergent life-styles, divisions between the employed and the unemployed, disparate values and the use of space on the estate. These differences engendered significant resistances to care watches, improved neighbouring and more effective social control between neighbours and their children. The fear of being attacked was found to be widespread, and for women this was a fear of sexual attack. The interviews with burglary victims showed that fears about burglary were also fears of being personally harmed. Living in run-down high density housing contributed to these 'fears'. Isolation seemed to be another source of anxiety.[26]

Indeed, anomic disorder is beginning to preoccupy many sociologists of crime and deviance. They may not use the word 'anomie' explicitly, but that is what their analysis conveys. Much of the world appears to them to be veering towards a disorganization and disequilibrium in which the State and formal social control, community, and informal social control, can no longer be taken for granted. One of the most graphic examples has been provided by Mike Davis in his description of Los Angeles as a moral

---

[24] C. Turnbull, *The Mountain People*, 234.
[25] N. Davies, *Dark Heart*; B. Campbell, *Goliath: Britain's Dangerous Places*; F. Reynolds, *The Problem Housing Estate*.
[26] A. Sampson, *Lessons from a Victim Support Crime Prevention Project*, 32–3.

topography emerging immediately from the hellscape worlds of *Blade Runner* and *Mad Max*. Davis argues that public, comprehensive, regulation has collapsed in Los Angeles. The rich buy private safety in their own defended enclaves. The poor are exposed only to perfunctory policing which keeps them under token control but offers no security. The outcome is that, in the poorest areas, beyond the fortified core in which the rich live and work, may be found 'the halo of barrios and ghettos [where there] is now a free-fire zone where crack dealers and street gangs settle their scores with shotguns and Uzis . . . . Both cops and gang members already talk with chilling matter-of-factness about the inevitability of some manner of urban guerilla warfare'.[27]

What Davis claimed for Los Angeles has been extrapolated to anomic nation states. 'Institutional anomie' certainly seemed to be an appropriate term when it was applied in the context of human rights abuses by Raquel Aldana-Pindell to describe states veering on illegitimacy because social elites enjoyed impunity from legal control, and judges and police were corrupt, brutal, and partial.[28] It may be extrapolated to whole societies. Some have alleged that disintegrating economies, dysfunctional governments, unenforceable frontiers, uncontrolled population movement, and the globalization of crime have combined to render the State inoperative as the effective maker and enforcer of law. Governments will no longer be able to impose their will within or across their own borders. There will no longer be the assurance that the sovereign nation state can provide security or law and order. Corruption will be endemic. In short, there has arisen in many parts of the world an 'appalling expression of . . . the obliteration of any distinction between political dispute and criminal violence'.[29] War itself will cease to be a relatively disciplined process conducted between the identifiable armies of discrete states who wield a monopoly of violence. Rather, it will be replaced by what van Creveld has called a ubiquitous 'low-intensity conflict' that inflicts a previously unsurpassed level of violence on civilians and armed forces alike.[30] Kaplan writes about the increasing lawlessness of several African states, the emergence of criminal anarchy as a strategic danger, the pursuit of war as an end in itself, the 'privatization of violence', and the breakdown of armies and police forces as accountable bureaucracies. His future is bleak indeed: there will be a 'rundown, crowded planet of skinhead Cossacks and *juju* warriors, influenced by the worst refuse of Western pop culture and ancient tribal hatreds, and battling over scraps of over-used earth in guerilla conflicts that ripple across countries and intersect in no discernible pattern'.[31] And there is evidence enough to sustain his Hobbesian argument. When the police are massively corrupt (as they appear to be in Russia and Mexico); when the police routinely sexually assault women complainants as they do in India; when criminal warlords assume control in Kosovo and Somalia; when the Chinese People's Liberation Army smuggles contraband on an immense scale; when Latin America is governed by narco-states; and

---

[27] M. Davis, 'Beyond Blade Runner', 6, 721.

[28] R. Aldana-Pindell, 'In Vindication of Justiciable Victims' Rights to Truth and Justice for State-Sponsored Crimes', 1466–7.

[29] S. Cohen, 'Crime and Politics', 19.   [30] M. van Creveld, *The Transformation of War*, 58, 192.

[31] R. Kaplan, 'The Coming Anarchy', 62–3.

when the governing systems of States ranging from Greece to Indonesia are defined as kleptocracies;[32] it is not difficult to acknowledge the anomic disarray to which Stan Cohen pointed when he wondered whether it was possible any longer to distinguish clearly between 'crime' and 'politics'.

Merton's Theory of Anomie

Merton took the conception of anomie as a starting point for fresh theorizing, rather than as an end-product to be embellished.[33] The very different context in which he was writing, the America of the immediate post-Depression years, provides the main clue to that decision. For Merton, the key feature of his society of the 1930s was the contrast between the 'American Dream' and the enduring reality of harsh economic inequality. The difference between that society and the France of the 1890s, in which Durkheim had written, lay chiefly in the Dream and not the inequality. In Europe, centuries of inequality were institutionalized in the complexities and subtleties of a feudalistic class society that re-formed rather than changed in any dramatic way. Despite the French Revolution of 1789, hereditary privilege and status still counted. In contrast, as the floods of immigrants to the New World testified, America still held out the promise of an open society of opportunities. In America, no hereditary aristocracy held even vestigial sway. There was Old Money and New Money, but in the end it was simply money that counted. Hence there was the 'American Dream', open to all, given hard work and the opportunity to realize one's talents.

In this context, Merton argued, the condition of anomie which Durkheim had regarded as exceptional, as visited upon people in boom and slump but as otherwise held at bay by social regulation, becomes routine, a built-in and unintended[34] feature of the social world. In this respect, he came closer to Durkheim's first Hobbesian depiction of anomie as endemic in industrial capitalism.[35] But the *source* of anomie for Merton was not the asymmetry between talent and reward; it lay rather in the lack of symmetry between the culture and the social structure. The 'culture' of the USA was taken to be, at bottom, the American Dream; but the social structure, however rapidly and widely it spawned and spread prosperity, could not yield limitless opportunities for all. Only a minority could enjoy the reality of super-abundance. As a process, however, 'Americanization' pivoted on the hope that ultimately everyone could attain levels of prosperity unknown by all but the tiny aristocratic and bourgeois élites of old Europe. 'Infinite aspirations', far from being released only under the shock of economic disturbance, were the very seam of the cultural fabric of the American way of life. Such a phenomenon was unprecedented, since only in America were the conditions of advanced

---

[32] J-F. Bayart et al., *The Criminalization of the State in Africa*; K. Hirschfeld, *Gangster States: Organized Crime, Kleptocracy and Political Collapse*, 2015.

[33] R. Merton, 'Social Structure and Anomie'.

[34] R. Merton, 'The Emergence of a Sociological Concept', 10.

[35] Durkheim also regarded the state of anomie as 'chronic' in the 'sphere of trade and industry' in his analysis in *Suicide*; see esp. 254–8.

Table 2 Merton's Typology

	Culturally prescribed goal	Institutionally available means
Conformity	acceptance	acceptance
Deviant adaptations:		
Innovation	acceptance	rejection
Ritualism	rejection	acceptance
Retreatism	rejection	rejection
Rebellion	replacement	replacement

industrial society combined with a distinctive ideology of classless egalitarian democracy, an ideology which has proved remarkably resilient even amongst the poor and the unsuccessful in the United States.[36] For this reason, Merton regarded his theory as applicable only to America. The basic argument on which it was based, however, i.e. the consequences of disjunction between goals, and the means of goal attainment, could be applied to any social context where the same type of disparity arose.

The pursuit of infinite aspirations was not seen by Merton as an innate human tendency that emerged whenever social regulation was weakened. It was, rather, the product of a particular culture that needed incessant nurturing if it was to persist and develop. A key feature of Merton's theory is his sensitivity to the dramatic growth of advertising in the inter-war period. A necessary adjunct to the growth of mass production and mass distribution was mass consumption. In this respect, Merton is—as Gouldner has noted—at one with Marx.[37] The fostering of the propensity to consume, with its creation of wants and dissatisfactions, is basic to economic growth in 'free market' economies. American ideology supplied the cultural counterpart of economic accumulation: fluid social mobility, the capacity to make it from Log Cabin to White House, was transmitted as a core value by the churches, the schools, and the mass media. The 'success' goal was sacred, failure profane: but in a society founded on the repudiation of monarchy and aristocracy, success came to be symbolized by sheer material gain (a future predicted with some assurance by de Tocqueville a century earlier). 'Money-success' was coined by Merton as *the* core value of American society, a 'cultural goal' extolled above all others, and one to be analysed for the sake of simplicity in what would otherwise be an excessively complicated theory.[38]

For Durkheim, deregulation led to infinite aspirations; for Merton, infinite aspirations led to deregulation. The result, for both, was the same: high rates of deviation. The 'strain to anomie' crystallized in Merton's view in four types of deviance, differentiated by their combination of either acceptance or rejection of the goal and the means for realizing the goal (see Table 2).

---

[36] K. Newman, *Chutes and Ladders: Navigating the Low-Wage Labor Market.*
[37] Gouldner's Foreword to I. Taylor et al., *The New Criminology*, x–xi.
[38] R. Merton, 'The Emergence of a Sociological Concept', 30.

Despite the formidable strain to anomie, the majority of the population adhered, in Merton's view, to conformity. The mass of middle America remained small-town Puritans, wedded to cautious advancement, but with an eye to the main chance. Their conformity ensured some social stability. For those unable to hold the socio-cultural tensions in balance, however, four 'deviant adaptations' were available. The first of these, 'innovation', basically involved the adoption of illegitimate means to the attainment of the cultural goal, 'money-success'. Crime, as Bell was later to put it, was a 'queer ladder of social mobility' in American life. Racketeering was the deviant response to the small-town Puritans' recipe for conformity, Prohibition, but any chicanery in politics or worldly affairs would exemplify deviant innovation just as well. Its mirror-image, 'ritualism', entailed the elimination of the goal and an obsessive attachment to the institutional means: here Merton is attempting to capture the ultra-conservative response to social tension, the celebration of sticking to the rules, of 'being in a rut', of staying put, that characterizes much of respectable lower- and middle-class life. 'Retreatism' involves the rejection of both goals *and* means, by dropping out of conventional society and yet not consciously striving to construct one afresh: the 'tramp', the 'hobo', the drug-taker are his key examples. Finally, 'rebellion' is seen as the rare attempt to resolve the tensions by not only rejecting both aspects of the status quo, but also actively seeking to replace them by alternative goals and means. Merton illustrated his thesis with a wealth of symbolic reference to key cultural myths. Empirically, his central conclusion was that, owing to the more intense and widespread experience of the disparity between the goal and the means at the bottom of the social hierarchy, deviance is inversely related to social status. Again, Durkheim had argued the reverse, for in his view, the social pressure exerted by the layers above them acts to limit the aspirations of the lower orders: 'those who have only empty space above them are almost inevitably lost in it.'[39] And John Hagan would later concur, arguing that those at the summit of business corporations can experience a kind of giddy lack of restraint which releases them to deviate.[40] By contrast, Merton writes:

> Of those located in the lower reaches of the social structure, the culture makes incompatible demands . . . In this setting, a cardinal American virtue—'ambition'—promotes a cardinal American vice—'deviant behaviour' . . . Within this context, Al Capone represents the triumph of amoral intelligence over morally prescribed 'failure' when the channels of vertical mobility are closed or narrowed in a society which places a high premium on economic affluence and social ascent for *all* its members.[41]

Merton's brief statement of anomie theory was first published in 1938, and revised and somewhat expanded versions were included in the four editions through which his major textbook has passed since then. For almost half that period, it received almost uncritical acceptance; since the early 1960s, it has been over-critically rejected. Before going on to the criticisms that have real substance, it is useful to look at those which appear misplaced. The first of these is that Mertonian anomie theory presumes a simple

---

[39] É. Durkheim, *Suicide*, 257.   [40] J. Hagan, *The Disreputable Pleasures*.
[41] R. Merton, *Social Theory and Social Structure*, 145–6.

consensus about the primacy of 'money-success' as a cultural goal. It is necessary to point out that sharing a goal does not imply simple consensus: the sharing of goals can generate the most bitter conflict. Anomie theory does not collapse when confronted with the realities of class and value conflict (and, indeed, Merton's ideas had roots in a Marxist analysis of the contradictions of class society), as class divisions and value conflicts may be framed in terms of inequalities of access to material wealth which all (to varying extents) desire. In his analysis of class and class conflict in Britain, for example, Westergaard documented the division of life-chances that persisted along class lines, in terms of wealth, income, health, educational achievement, mobility, and even access to welfare. He cited as an aggravating feature of class conflict the very 'revolution in rising expectations' which has often been equated with the 'withering away' of class: such expectations tend to surpass the material possibilities of their fulfilment, and promote what Marshall termed 'mild economic anomie'.[42] The fostering of consumerism means that all come to share the aspirations once appropriate only to the élite: 'the luxuries of today become the necessities of tomorrow.' Indeed, in a number of recent pieces of writing, it has been argued that, in a 'media-saturated world', the idealization of 'celebrities' and the wealth they accrue has amplified the gulf between young people and what they conceive to be a desirable and, perhaps, even attainable style of life. In what has been called a 'rampant consumer marketplace',[43] there is an aspiration to a life-style which is quite out of gear with the life-chances of the urban poor, and the result is a kind of giddying acceleration of anomie, a blend of the Durkheimian and Mertonian strains, in which regulation is further eroded. This process is entirely in accord with that of Merton's theory: though it is clear that class loyalties may profoundly modify the strain to anomie, they hardly negate it, especially when working-class communities have been fragmented by de-industrialization.

A second such criticism is that, as Merton himself, applying Occam's razor, had recognized, in a diverse and complex society, 'money-success' is not the only goal; it competes with a myriad of other goals for a claim on energy and time; or it is itself mainly a *means* to quite different goals, such as family support and well-being. To pursue a variety of goals is not, however, to transcend the goal of 'money-success',[44] which is at its most potent when legitimized by 'higher' things: the 'family' is as important to the 'Godfather' as to the early settlers. It may well be that it is successfully resisted by a minority of active 'rebels'; but so all-pervasive is the cash-nexus that such 'rebellion' is rare, and may well be replaced by an equally exclusive 'cultural goal', such as membership of a religious 'elect' or of a 'party' élite that are in themselves anomie-promoting. The abolition of private property did not abolish, but rather heightened, the attractiveness of the perquisites of high office in State socialist societies. Merton's own defence

---

[42] T. Marshall, *Sociology at the Crossroads*; J. Westergaard, 'The Withering Away of Class'.

[43] S. Winlow and S. Hall, *Violent Night: Urban Leisure and Contemporary Culture*, 12; J. Young, *The Vertigo of Late Modernity*.

[44] It is worth commenting, too, that the quest for money and money-success have their own special criminogenic features. Money, as Simmel and Engdahl pointed out, has a capacity to liberate people from the control of institutions and social groups; it is anonymous; and it promotes a species of individualism. O. Engdahl, 'The Role of Money in Economic Crime'.

would be that to consider all the goals pursued by Americans would have unnecessarily complicated analysis.

A third, vivid criticism is that Merton's theory is both ahistorical and lacking in critical perspective. Laurie Taylor compares Merton's image of society to that of a giant fruit-machine,[45] whose pay-outs are rigged, but which most players delude themselves into perceiving as fair. The deviants are those who try to rig the machine to *their* advantage; who play it blindly and obsessively; who ignore its existence; or who smash it up and seek a better model. Nowhere, however, says Taylor, does Merton tell us who is taking the profits, and who put the machine there in the first place. This telling criticism applies more to Merton's exposition of his theory than to the validity of the theory itself, for it would strengthen the theory rather than the reverse if it were to be prefaced by a history of American capitalist exploitation, and a synopsis of who owns what.

Anomie and After

Merton would never have described himself as a criminologist or sociologist of deviance: his interest lay elsewhere, in formal theorizing and in the sociology of science and knowledge. Although his account of anomie was to be so very central to the analysis of deviance, it was also oddly brief and uncherished. Anomie was discussed in two essays which were never lengthy or expansive enough to develop more than a few of its possibilities. There was to be very little reply to many of the criticisms subsequently levelled at his thesis. It would not have been difficult to form a response or adapt his theory, but ideas were left in limbo.

In a sympathetic but critical reappraisal of Merton's theory by one of his students,[46] Albert Cohen noted that its author had laid it out in a surprisingly insulated fashion, not only from the allied work in the sociology of crime and deviance in the 1920s and 1930s, but also from his own contributions to general sociology: reference group theory and role theory.[47] Reference group theory has alerted us to the limited social worlds in which people invest their energies and the generally limited horizons which mark them out. We typically compare ourselves, not with the upper echelons or the supremely successful, but with the peer groups of our own age, sex, and approximate social position. Among others, Runciman has demonstrated this effect for a variety of groups in Britain: manual workers tend to compare themselves with other manual workers, rather than with dukes.[48] Role theory is concerned with the kinds of people it is possible to be in a society and with how roles are allocated and taken on; but, again, we are mostly preoccupied with roles that are accessible to us, and not with those beyond our reach. Knowing this, asks Cohen, how could Merton propound so individualistic a

[45] L. Taylor, *Deviance and Society*, 148.
[46] Merton said, 'Cohen went on to extend and deepen the paradigm by showing how social interaction among those subjected to structurally induced pressures leads to patterned collective responses and the emergence of a delinquent subculture' ('The Emergence of a Sociological Concept', 9).
[47] A. Cohen, 'The Sociology of the Deviant Act', 5–14.
[48] W. Runciman, *Relative Deprivation and Social Justice*.

theory as anomie, as if people exercise choice in a kind of social vacuum, save for their sense of strain born of a heightened awareness of success-goals? Had Merton combined these different aspects of his own theorizing, he would surely have made a more realistic thesis. As it stands, anomie theory is static, individualistic, mechanistic, and focused on 'initial states and deviant outcomes rather than on processes whereby acts and complex structures of action are built, elaborated and transformed'.[49] People do not jump from conformity to deviance without, typically, 'a tentative, groping, advancing, backtracking, sounding-out process' going on. Cohen's own seminal contribution to meeting this difficulty, whilst retaining the strengths of the goals–means formulation, was the concept of subcultural process.[50] It is in the development of different versions of subcultures of deviance that anomie theory has persisted most influentially. Merton was himself later to acknowledge that a neglect of differential association had been a defect in his work. He had, he wrote candidly, 'simply failed to "seize the opportunity" of consolidating the two strands of sociological thought'.[51]

Otherwise, anomie as an explicit concept has been little more than marginal in the development of post-war theories of social problems and almost totally absent from theories of social structure. Parsons[52] and Rex used it to mean imperfect understanding.[53] Empirically, despite many attempts, it did not lend itself to survey work or field methods of observation.[54] Becker parodied the theory in guying students who failed to find it on visits to car factories.[55] Like phlogiston in eighteenth-century physics, it increasingly appeared to be an artefact of an outmoded view of the social universe. The few serious attempts to measure its incidence have not established support for the theory in any direct sense. Stinchcombe found the strongest pressures for 'rebellion' lay among middle-class boys in high school, whose commitment to success goals was most marked and whose failure to achieve the most resented.[56] This finding has implications for any theory which invokes anomie and/or subcultural variants as an explanation for middle-class delinquency, but undermined confidence in Merton's overall theoretical emphasis on high rates of deviance among the lower classes. Mizruchi complicated the model further by suggesting that middle-class anomie ('boundlessness') differed fundamentally from working-class anomie ('bondlessness').[57] Srole's 'anomie scale' employed questions designed to elicit the extent to which people felt at home in the world, but items such as 'little can be accomplished in a society which is seen as basically unpredictable and lacking order' appeared more as tests of political orthodoxy than existential unease.[58] Such over-schematic tests were so reliant on ambiguous indicators and almost infinitely elastic and subjective measures of 'deviance' that the theory faded from serious consideration.

---

[49] A. Cohen, 'The Sociology of the Deviant Act', 9.   [50] See Chapter 6.
[51] R. Merton, 'The Emergence of a Sociological Concept', 39.
[52] T. Parsons, *The Social System*, 39.   [53] J. Rex, *Key Problems*, 177.
[54] See the formidable inventory compiled by S. Cole and H. Zuckermann in Clinard, *Anomie and Deviant Behavior*, 243–83.
[55] H. Becker, 'Labelling Theory Reconsidered', 50.   [56] A. Stinchcombe, *Rebellion in a High School*.
[57] F. Mizruchi, *Success and Opportunity*.
[58] See the comments by Merton in Clinard, *Anomie and Deviant Behavior*, 227–8.

Yet the questions raised most profoundly by anomie theory recur in various guises, not least as the central strand in 'left realism',[59] and also as the underlying concern in theories of crime, modernization, and development. In their analysis of a collection of studies of cross-national criminal trends, Heiland and Shelley examined 'the complementary and sometimes contradictory concepts of civilization and modernization'[60] in relation to the development of crime and social control. Their inference from the work of Norbert Elias[61] is that:

> in the pre-modern age sanctions controlled individual actions by external controls. But with the development of civilization, controls are slowly shifted inwards. . . . If Elias's hypothesis is correct that interpersonal relations change with the civilization of society, then so should the nature of interpersonal violence and crime. Important indicators of this process of civilization would be a decline in violent crime and an increase in self-inflicted harm (i.e. drugs) on individuals.[62]

In Garland's summary:

> . . . typically, the civilizing process in culture involves a tightening and a differentiation of the controls imposed by society upon individuals, a refinement of conduct, and an increased level of psychological inhibition as the standards of proper conduct become ever more demanding. . . . It is the specific and fragile outcome of an evolutionary process which was socially determined though by no means inexorable, and which may at any time be reversed if wars, revolutions, or catastrophes undermine the forms of social organization and interdependence upon which it depends.[63]

These changes of sensibility, first evident amongst the court aristocracies in Europe and later assumed by the rising bourgeoisie, were to become far more widely diffused in the course of the twentieth century. They are seen, most importantly by Spierenburg,[64] to entail a shift from brutal and degrading to less punitive and more restrained forms of punishment. Yet, as Garland notes,[65] the thesis is prone to over-interpret rhetoric, as if only that which is written exists, and to underplay the force of political, economic, and institutional change. One must look for 'corroborating evidence drawn from other fields of enquiry and spheres of social life'. On that basis, some support for the thesis can be found in the widespread evidence for a 'long-term and very substantial decline in levels of violent crime in English society from the thirteenth to the twentieth centuries'.[66] Gurr[67] both documents and explains this decline in terms of the 'growing sensitization to violence' and 'the development of increased internal and external

---

[59] See below, 276 *et seq.*
[60] H.-G. Heiland and L. Shelly, 'Civilization, Modernization and the Development of Crime and Control', 7.
[61] N. Elias, *The Civilising Process* (*Vol. 2*): *State Formation and Civilization*, and 'Violence and Civilization: The State Monopoly of Physical Violence and its Infringement'.
[62] H.-G. Heiland and L. Shelley, 'Civilization, Modernization and the Development of Crime and Control', 3–4.
[63] D. Garland, *Punishment and Modern Society*, 217–18.
[64] P. Spierenburg, *The Spectacle of Suffering*, 217–18.   [65] D. Garland, *Punishment and Society*, 229–30.
[66] D. Garland, *Punishment and Society*, 230.
[67] T. Gurr, 'Historical Trends in Violent Crime'; and Gurr et al., *The Politics of Crime and Conflict.*

controls on aggressive behaviour'. Stone, Thomas, Beattie, and Gatrell[68] also provide a wealth of supportive theory and evidence for the overall trend. There seems little doubt that, whatever the reasons, violence and aggression in civil society were massively and progressively reined in over the period from the late medieval to the mid-twentieth century.

The very strength of this evidence, however, serves to magnify the problem of how one might account for trends *since* the mid-twentieth century in terms of this theory. For if, as Elias contends, psychic configurations have been restructured and profound cultural transformations have enveloped whole societies, the rise in rates of violent crime since the 1950s becomes truly anomalous. One can only sustain the theory by assuming with McClintock[69] that the 'growing sensitization to violence' widened the net to include minor assaults which would previously have gone unreported and un-recorded (in which case, it seems that trends in official crime rates are to be accepted when they suit the thesis but rejected when they do not); or we must presume a greatly increased propensity to violence amongst a minority somehow untouched by the 'civi-lizing process'. The latter argument has much in common with theories of the 'new underclass' (see Chapter 6).

A second problem with the thesis is its incapacity to account not simply for wars, revolutions, and catastrophes, viewing these phenomena as setbacks to the civilizing process rather than as problems which it does not address, but also for the capacity of the *most highly civilized* societies to degenerate into what can only be called geno-cidal abattoirs. As George Steiner[70] has observed, to the Jews, 'the house of civilization proved no shelter'. These questions remain unanswered by any sociologist (although some, like Bauman,[71] have made the attempt), but they present particular difficulties for a thesis pivoting on a conception of civilization which does not, as in Durkheim's idea of anomie, allow for the sudden collapse of hard-won moral regulation.

'Modernization' theories of crime stress the disruptive impact of industrialization and urbanization on traditional ways of life. Their proponents seek to link the uneven development of different dimensions of modernization with trends in crime and its control (see, for example, Shelley; Clinard, and Abbott[72]). Heiland and Shelley argue:

> Modernization is a continually developing process of structural differentiation, combined with an increase in the complexity of the norms of social organization. . . . It has been graphically shown that modernization does not always lead to more contentment and

---

[68] L. Stone, *The Family, Sex and Marriage in England*; K. Thomas, *Man and the Natural World*; J. Beattie, 'Violence and Society in Early Modern England'; V. Gatrell, 'The Decline of Theft and Violence in Victorian and Edwardian England'.

[69] F. McClintock, *Crimes of Violence*. Certainly the rise of feminism in the late 1960s and early 1970s was accompanied by an increasing awareness of the problems posed by violence against women and children, particularly in the domestic sphere. What had previously been treated by many as a private matter, not to be brought into the open or managed as a problem for criminal justice, came, in time, to be redefined as a criminal phenomenon that could neither be ignored nor resolved by informal methods of dispute resolution.

[70] G. Steiner, *Language and Silence: Essays and Notes 1958–1966*, 175.

[71] Z. Bauman, *Modernity and the Holocaust*, esp. 212–13.

[72] L. Shelley, *Crime and Modernization*; M. Clinard and D. Abbott, *Crime in Developing Countries: A Comparative Perspective*.

harmony. Rather, enhanced social tensions, conflicts and social disharmony are the results of social differentiation, the growing number of life choices, and the relative deprivation that accompanies the modernization process . . . With modernization, a shift occurs in the relationship among forms of criminal behavior. Violent offenses become less important as property offenses achieve pre-eminence . . . As modernization proceeds, inequality still exists, . . . the crime pattern begins to change from crimes typical of poverty to crimes common to the affluent society. Many property crimes are not caused by societal or individual crises such as unemployment or illness, but by wealth and the abundance of goods.[73]

Empirical support for the theory can be found in such studies as that of Schichor,[74] who explored the relationship between patterns and trends of crime and various socio-economic factors in forty-four countries: 'Modernization is negatively associated with violent crime (homicide) and positively associated with property crime (larceny).' Economic development increases the availability of material possessions and their cultural priority. As he observes, however, property crimes are also more likely to be reported and recorded in more modern societies, due to the making of insurance claims. Regression analysis also masks the immense variation between countries within each category: for instance, the much higher levels of violence in the United States of America than in Switzerland or Japan.

Overall, theories of civilization, modernization, and crime cover much the same ground as anomie theories, but avoid, presumably deliberately, strong emphasis on the damage wrought by the pursuit of 'infinite aspirations' which links Durkheim and Merton. The analytical need to integrate the 'civilizing process' with that of 'modernization' leads Heiland and Shelley to loose rule-of-thumb judgements, such as 'Japan appears to be a developed society which has succeeded in both developing and civilizing'[75] and 'it would be presumptuous to suggest that the tendency towards civilization is absent in the USA' but high rates of violent crime and punishment do show 'how difficult it is to maintain the standards of a civilized society'.[76]

Similar problems arise in the global resort to evolutionist concepts in the work of Clinard and Abbott on crime in developing countries.[77] Rapid urbanization and uneven industrialization in developing countries are seen as the key causal preconditions for soaring rates of crime and delinquency. In what has come to be regarded, rather dismissively, as the 'orthodox criminological perspective' on crime in developing countries,[78] Clinard and Abbott proposed a neo-Durkheimian perspective based on the mismatch between rapid change and social regulation. It is an optimistic model hinged on the assumption that once developing countries 'catch up' with the developed, crime and delinquency rates will level off, at least in their violent form. Sumner is scathingly critical of this 'fundamental misconception' of modernization in the developing world as a 'delayed replay of nineteenth-century European development with its extensive

---

[73] H.-G. Heiland and L. Shelley, 'Civilization, Modernization and the Development of Crime and Control'.
[74] D. Schichor, 'Crime Patterns and Socio-economic Development: A Cross-National Analysis'.
[75] H.-G. Heiland and L. Shelley, 'Civilization, Modernization and the Development of Crime and Control', 18.
[76] H.-G. Heiland and L. Shelley, 'Civilization, Modernization and the Development of Crime and Control', 10.
[77] M. Clinard and D. Abbott, *Crime in Developing Countries: A Comparative Perspective*.
[78] C. Sumner (ed.), *Crime, Justice and Underdevelopment*, ch. 1.

urbanization and industrialization . . . held up (mainly) by the deep sleep of "custom" or the rigid ties of "tradition".[79]

It is all too evident that no such exact parallelism exists. The global expansion of nineteenth-century Western capitalism was relatively unfettered, whilst the modernization of late twentieth-century developing countries is massively distorted by capitalist penetration and direction. 'Modernization' theory only sees crime as a result of 'development' and the criminal law as crime's necessary counterpoint. What it does not see is all the criminal law and crime that went into the very making of 'underdevelopment'.[80] Sumner is, however, too sweeping in his condemnation of Clinard and Abbott's 'social reformism'. In Hong Kong, for example, anti-corruption measures and economic development made some impact on rates of violent crime.[81] In short, there are huge variations to be mapped and, while some of the studies we have cited have made an impressive beginning, the dismissal of anomie theories, or stripping them down to their critical elements in the pursuit of somewhat bland notions of 'modernization' and development, seem premature.

A major exception to the above is the 'institutional-anomie theory' of Steven Messner and Richard Rosenfeld.[82] In an important development of Merton's theory, they 'assign a critical role to structural dynamics and, more specifically, to the balance among major social institutions (e.g. the economy, the family, the polity) . . . According to institutional-anomie theory, the form of institutional structure that is particularly conducive to high levels of crime is one in which the economy dominates the institutional balance of power'.[83] The over-powerful economic institutions weaken the capacity of the non-economic, in particular the family and the school, to socialize the young and exert informal controls effectively. In a key study they utilize Esping-Andersen's concept of the 'decommodification of labour' (1990) to measure the degree to which this, in societies that make the political choice to intervene into the market, to guarantee citizens adequate levels of welfare, militates against high crime rates. 'Our basic hypothesis is that homicide rates and decommodification vary inversely: the higher the level of political protection from the vicissitudes of the market, the lower the national homicide rate.'[84]

'The results support our basic hypothesis. Controlling for a wide range of other structural characteristics of nations, the decommodification measure exhibits a strong negative effect on homicide rates.'[85] Their study thus 'lends credibility' to the larger theoretical framework of anomie theory, and does so in ways which link with other findings and a large sample of nations. It also explicitly links with the long-standing tradition of Social Democracy, and its foundational belief that a mixed economy and generous social security provision along with inclusive citizenship offers the best basis for stable prosperity. As Messner and Rosenfeld point out, however, that 'balance of

[79] C. Sumner (ed.), *Crime, Justice and Underdevelopment*, 22.

[80] C. Sumner (ed.), *Crime, Justice and Underdevelopment*, 35.

[81] H. Traver, 'Crime Trends', 22.   [82] S. Messner and R. Rosenfeld, *Crime and the American Dream*.

[83] S. Messner and R. Rosenfeld, 'Political Restraint of the Market and Levels of Criminal Homicide', 1396.

[84] S. Messner and R. Rosenfeld, 'Political Restraint of the Market and Levels of Criminal Homicide', 1394.

[85] S. Messner and R. Rosenfeld, 'Political Restraint of the Market and Levels of Criminal Homicide', 1407.

institutional power' is now threatened, as never before in the post-war era, by the para-doxical aftermath of the Cold War, in which a capitalist triumphalism threatens the welfare and citizenship gains that the 'spectre of communism' helped to bring into being. The commitment to welfare and inclusionary strategies has now been empiri-cally linked cross-nationally with protections against high rates of homicide and the resort to higher levels of imprisonment.[86] Too marked a reduction in welfare spending and a resort to punitiveness would, in all likelihood, incur unwanted consequences on both fronts.

The Crisis of Social Capital

Over the past decade or so, concerns about the pace and direction of social and eco-nomic change have increasingly taken the form of anxieties about a decline in social capital. In one sense, this is simply the latest phase in the long-standing preoccupation with the loss of, or retreat from, 'community', the spectre that has haunted sociology—rather more than the fear of revolution—since its early nineteenth-century formation. The adoption of the term 'social capital', notably by Pierre Bourdieu, James Coleman, and Robert Putnam,[87] has nonetheless reinvigorated and reshaped those concerns. 'Community' had come to have a rather folksy and quaint set of connotations on the one hand, or had been devalued by its endless invocation by politicians, on the other. It had also been lent a disciplinary dimension in community crime prevention pro-grammes[88] and in the communitarianism of Etzioni, which relies, inter alia, on the exclusion of deviants who threaten family and group cohesion. 'Social capital', unlike 'community', connotes the importance of social networks as a whole rather than purely neighbourhood-based relations.

Social capital requires more than just a network of ties, however. Bourdieu notes that social capital also involves 'transforming contingent relations, such as those of neighbourhood, the workplace or even kinship, into relationships that are at once nec-essary and elective, implying durable obligations subjectively felt (feelings of gratitude, respect, friendship, etc.)'.[89] Thus, network ties must also be of a particular type—trust-ing and positive.[90]

In a society denuded of social capital, people can literally take nothing for granted. Such a society would be scarcely worthy of the name, would—in short—be little more than a state of anomie.

Social capital has, as a concept, strong Durkheimian roots. In his celebrated critique of Herbert Spencer, the Victorian progenitor of 'New Right' politics, Durkheim might well have had Margaret Thatcher and Ronald Reagan in his sights, particularly for the

---

[86] Lacey, *The Prisoners' Dilemma*; D. Downes and K. Hansen, 'Welfare and Imprisonment in Comparative Perspective'.

[87] P. Bourdieu, 'Forms of Capital'; J. Coleman, 'Social Capital in the Creation of Human Capital; R. Putnam, 'Bowling Alone: The Collapse and Revival of American Community* (2000).

[88] S. Cohen, *Visions of Social Control*. [89] Bourdieu, P., 'Forms of Capital', 249–50.

[90] P. Paxton, 'Is Social Capital Declining in the United States? A Multiple Indicator Assessment', 92.

Thatcherite statement that 'There is no such thing as "society": there are only individuals and their families.' As Durkheim wrote in *The Division of Labor in Society*:

> But it is not only outside of contractual relations, it is in the play of those relations themselves that social action makes itself felt. For everything in the contract is not contractual. . . . The greater part of our relations with others is of a contractual nature. If, then, it were necessary each time to begin the struggles anew, to again go through the conferences necessary to establish firmly all the conditions of agreement for the present and the future, we would be put to rout. For all these reasons, if we were linked only by the terms of our contracts, as they are agreed upon, only a precarious solidarity would result. . . . In sum, a contract is not sufficient unto itself, but is possible only thanks to a regulation of the contract which is originally social.[91]

Social capital is much the same, therefore, as Durkheim's notion of the non-contractual elements of contract—the active ingredient that makes societies both tick and hang together. Shorn of social capital, not only are people adrift in a state of anomie, they are also, for that very reason, more prey to authoritarian remedies born of desperation. If social capital falls too far short of some theoretical minimum, democracy in America, or anywhere else, is on the line.

Hence the urgency with which the issue is addressed in Robert Putnam's *Bowling Alone* (2000) and Richard Sennett's *The Corrosion of Character* (1998). Putnam documents the withdrawal of Americans from group and community life at every level—from the family to voting, from bowling to having friends round to dinner, from voluntary work to attending PTAs, from churchgoing to trade union membership. Four main reasons are explored empirically. Television and the computer keep people at home and apart even there, due to multiple sets per household. Residential 'sprawl' keeps people 'driving alone' as commuters for three hours a day, draining them of time and energy for joint social activities. 'Dual career' families experience pressures of time, necessarily putting their jobs first, otherwise they would lose them, and therefore everything else second. Most of all, each successive generation after the Second World War—the social capital high-spot—has increasingly withdrawn from social life. As to why this should be so, Putnam cites changing values—basically, getting ahead has become much more highly valued than getting together. Making good is far more intensively pursued than doing good. Paxton[92] has challenged some empirical aspects of the (earlier) Putnam thesis, notably the stable rates of group membership over the four decades 1950–90. Putnam's (later) data transcend nominal membership as too weak a measure of association, citing dramatic falls in active involvement, as shown in leadership role-taking, actual attendances at meetings and time spent, as more relevant to testing the issue of a disturbing collapse in social capital.[93]

Does it really matter? Putnam argues that it does, because States with high social capital do better economically, in the human capital terms of health and education, democratically in terms of tolerance and freedom from persecution, and socially in

---

[91] É. Durkheim, *The Division of Labor in Society*, 211–15.
[92] P. Paxton, 'Is Social Capital Declining in the United States?'
[93] R. Putnam, *Bowling Alone: The Collapse and Revival of American Community*, 59–62.

terms of lower rates of crime and disorder. Can the decline be reversed and social capital revived? He ends on an upbeat note, claiming that it happened before—in the 'Progressive' era of 1900–15 following the extreme inequalities of the 'Gilded Age' of the late nineteenth century—and therefore can happen again. However, his slender chapter on the prospects for the revival of American community is by far the weakest in the book, pinning hope on the encouragement of extracurricular activities in high schools, and the like. That his remedies are so dwarfed by the scale of the crisis they are meant to resolve reflects weaknesses in his analysis of the structural sources of the collapse of social capital in the USA. He does not engage with the post-1970s rise of globalization and the changed political economy, which has allowed de-industrialization to be the harbinger of new insecurities, inequalities, and disinvestments in social capital. Nowhere does he mention the huge rise in imprisonment in the USA, yet arguably the greatest single perverse side-effect of dwindling social capital is its replacement by *penal* capital. Despite the severe limitations of equating more punishment with less crime, *some* effect is to be expected from so extensive a form of mass imprisonment as that experienced in the USA over the past three decades, in which two million adults, some 2 per cent of the male labour force, half of them black and one-fifth Hispanic, are locked away, and a further two million are under the disciplinary constraints of probation and parole. Scaled to factor in the most 'at risk' populations, some downtown neighbourhoods are virtually bereft of young males. Without invoking that harsh reality, Putnam is unable to confront or account for the coincidence of declining social capital and falling rates of crime. For a democratic society, America is now perilously close to re-imposing a segregative regime of penal exclusion combined with punitive surveillance on its most discriminated against minority groups.[94] 'Governing through crime'[95] entails increasing claims to legitimacy by 'punitive populism'[96] surveillance, and exclusion, a symbolic politics replacing those of inclusion and solidarity. This trend remains most developed in the USA, with Britain a 'Trojan Horse' intermediate between American exceptionalism and the stronger traditions of inclusive solidarity in France, Italy, and the non-Hispanic countries of Western Europe.

Whilst documenting in masterly detail some of the major trends involved in this debacle of democracy, Putnam arguably mistakes symptoms for cause in certain instances as, for example, seeing 'dual career' families as inevitably contributing to declining social capital. They could equally well be seen as enriching social capital, or as needing more sympathetic arrangements if the emancipation of 'captive wives'[97] to pursue working careers was not to be at the expense of their family lives. Putnam oddly neglects the new individualism as a likely explanation linking all four 'causes'. He pays too little regard to the New Deal of Roosevelt and the 'Great Society' experiments of the Kennedy era, which succeeded in tempering American individualism on the grounds of equality of opportunity. The post-1970 era of globalization and de-industrialization

[94] L. Wacquant, 'Deadly Symbiosis: When Ghetto and Prison Meet and Mesh'.
[95] J. Simon, 'Governing Through Crime'.
[96] A. Bottoms, 'The Philosophy and Politics of Punishment and Sentencing'.
[97] H. Gavron, *The Captive Wife*.

legitimized a more *macho* form of individualism than at any time since the 'Gilded Age', and not only in the USA. In the UK, current trends in policing can be related to the decline of more indirect (and arguably more effective) sources of social control. There has been a marked decrease in employment in a range of occupations providing 'natural surveillance' and other low level controls as part of their primary function. In part, this has been a consequence of the development and spread of new labour-saving technologies such as self-purchasing ticket machines and automatic barriers, CCTV, and automated access control. The spread and impact of such technologies were underpinned and encouraged by neo-liberal public policies which sought to maximize profit, often through reductions in labour costs via 'downsizing'.[98]

The huge rise in private, commercial security, often of an aggressive, 'in your face' character, and lacking any primary social role, has been at the expense not so much of the public police as of the diverse occupations of roundsmen, park-keepers, public transport conductors, and guards, etc., whose primary roles carried an incidental but vital 'secondary' component of social capital. The loss of social capital does not, however, figure on the economic capital balance sheet, at least in the short term. In the longer term, however, the loss of trust has profoundly adverse economic consequences, as neoconservatives such as Francis Fukuyama[99] are now acknowledging, a century after Durkheim spelt them out with exemplary force.

To John Hagan, in contrast to Putnam, the resurgence of inequality is pivotal. 'The central point is that the concentration of poverty plays a key role in intensifying the linkages between weak labor force attachment and crime. The result is a dramatic deprivation of all kinds of capital, from physical and financial to social and cultural.'[100] Crime and delinquent subcultures are a form of *re*-capitalization in the wake of the huge capital disinvestments in previously prosperous industries and the communities they sustained. The most abundant evidence for that equation can be found in the illicit drug economies that have flourished in the most economically and socially deprived areas. Several key studies, both ethnographic[101] and quantitative[102] draw out the links between structural changes and community-level consequences that make for depleted social capital and burgeoning crime, links which take on a more florid cast with regard to ethnic minorities of colour. It is not simply that low social capital deprives those it disadvantages (especially young men) of job opportunities and exposes them to heightened risks of criminal 'embeddedness' as a result. It is also that high social capital protects those it advantages from the criminal labelling for youthful misdeeds which in lower-class areas would spare them no stigmata. 'Deviance service industries', for drugs, vice, gambling, and 'protection', become yet more central to local economies

[98] T. Jones and T. Newburn, 'The Transformation of Policing? Understanding Current Trends in Policing Systems', 140–1.

[99] F. Fukuyama, *Trust*.   [100] J. Hagan, *Crime and Disrepute*, 76.

[101] M. Sullivan, '*Getting Paid': Youth Crime and Work in the Inner City*; E. Anderson, *Streetwise*; and J. Moore, *Going Down to the Barrio: Homeboys and Homegirls in Change*.

[102] R. Sampson, 'Race and Criminal Violence: A Demographically Disaggregated Analysis of Urban Homicide' (1985), 'Effects of Inequality, Heterogeneity, and Urbanization on Intergroup Victimization' (1986); S. Messner and R. Rosenfeld, *Crime and the American Dream*.

depleted of social capital just as changes in the macro-economy entail the shedding of yet more mainstream jobs. In Britain, Robert McAuley[103] has documented how one such 'ghost town' offered local youth little more than a crime-drugs nexus for economic survival.

Richard Sennett explores these themes afresh in his *The Corrosion of Character: The Personal Consequences of Work in the New Capitalism*. He argues that the 'new capitalism' generates work of a quite different character to that of the 'old'—not only more insecure and short-term but more mystifying and fragmented. Power has been reconstituted rather than democratically constrained. Political economy now 'consists of three elements: discontinuous reinvention of institutions; flexible specialisation of production; and concentration without centralisation of power'.[104] All are lauded as integral to success in the globalized market-place. All entail a 'loss of narrative' on which to base not only identity but also trust, loyalty, and commitment. Not surprisingly, social capital—the commitment to community and shared ways of resolving conflict—is gravely weakened by these conditions. Freedom is not enhanced by this shift and older forms of resistance to exploitation are continually eroded.

How valid is Sennett's analysis? His sources are few, but deeply mined. Rico, the son of a caretaker whom Sennett interviewed and got to know three decades earlier, and who—unlike his father—had become a 'success', had nevertheless been drained of any sense of meaningful relation to work in the process of several job changes to further his chances. Rose ventured into advertising in middle age from her own business of running a bar, yet returned after a year baffled and defeated: 'I lost my nerve.' A group of former IBM employees, victims of the seismic downsizing after the company's defeat at the hands of Bill Gates' Microsoft, go through phases of blaming the Jewish Chief Executive and cheap Asian labour before settling on their own lack of entrepreneurship as the cause of their job losses. Sennett uses these sources creatively and self-validatingly in his analysis, much as Max Weber used the key figure of Benjamin Franklin to authenticate his thesis on the Protestant Ethic and the Spirit of Capitalism.

The case is immensely persuasive but also problematic. The best of the 'old' capitalist order, its coherent career-building for the middle class and its stable and worthy employment for the working class, is compared with the worst of the 'new'—the amoral and blame-free culture of the advertising world, for example. But what became of David Riesman's 'other-directed' conformists of *The Lonely Crowd* (1950) or the bureaucratic time-servers of William H. Whyte's *The Organization Man* (1956)? Not much sense of character or narrative drive there, either: so what has changed? Arguably, what Sennett has done is take on the task that C. Wright Mills[105] urged on his fellow sociologists over fifty years ago: to answer the question 'What kinds of character will come to predominate in our social structure?' The answer seems to be a set of super-predators on top (not the delinquents of DeIullio but the CEOs of Enron, World.com, Arthur Andersen, Lehman Bros, and Volkswagen) and a vast array of

---

[103] R. McAuley, 'The Enemy Within: Economic Marginalisation and the Impact of Crime on Young Adults'.
[104] R. Sennett, *The Corrosion of Character: The Personal Consequences of Work in the New Capitalism*, 47.
[105] C. Wright Mills, *The Sociological Imagination*.

what Durkheim termed 'disaggregated individuals' for the rest. What has changed is the trained incapacity to resist.

There is, in all of these 'big pictures' of social change, a tendency to reify and stereotype. Just as Herbert Gans challenged Whyte's picture of conforming suburban man in his detailed study of diversity *The Levittowners* (1967), so Sennett may be hugely over-generalizing and over-interpreting from a very few sources and accounts. Yet in one sense Sennett may be letting the 'new' order down too lightly. Some years on and hindsight shows the force of his arguments to have even more to them than he allows. Lack of trust and the abandonment of blame can undermine the very basis for what keeps the market buoyant—investment. Without a modicum of trust in financial systems and services, why invest at all, especially over the very long term, as the personal pensions schemes crisis, and the banking crisis in 2008–9,[106] have shown? Durkheim was right—capitalism and its attendant utilitarian philosophies depend on the 'non-contractual elements in contract' after all.

There is one further point to be factored in. The road to anomie in Western Social Democracies has been cleared of a significant road-block—the spectre of Communism no longer haunts the world. It was that threat which galvanized capitalism to adopt the mixed economy, the 'Welfare State', the right to unionize and the full panoply of Social Democratic alternatives to the extremes of capitalism or communism. With the spectre removed since 1989, there are already signs of significant shifts away from Social Democracy to neo-liberal models of political economy. The implications for crime and its control are, from the anomie perspective, clear. It is a race between crime control through a resort to penal capital[107] or by the recovery of Social Democracy.

Towards an Anomic Culture?

Richard Sennett[108] takes his analysis a stage further, seeing a new kind of character as needed to flourish in the fragmented society that has ensued from economic growth in the context of de-industrialization and the dominance of the electronically powered, global institutions of corporate financial 'service' industries: 'a self oriented to the short term, focused on potential ability, willing to abandon past experience . . . an unusual sort of human being. Most people are not like this . . . '[109] While 'the new economy is still only a small part of the whole economy'[110] and should *not* be regarded as the inevitable future, its influence is becoming all-pervasive—in welfare, education, and health care as well as its core location in the hi-tech conglomerates of 3,000 or more employees. Walmart, with 1.4 million employees, and revenues of $284 billion, some 2 per cent of US GDP, is its symbolic avatar.

---

[106] G. Tett, *Fool's Gold*.

[107] N. Christie, *Crime Control as Industry: Towards Gulags Western Style*; D. Garland, *Mass Imprisonment: Social Causes and Consequences*.

[108] R. Sennett, *The Culture of the New Capitalism*.   [109] R. Sennett, *The Culture of the New Capitalism*, 5.

[110] R. Sennett, *The Culture of the New Capitalism*, 10.

Culture cannot long be immune to such fundamental changes in social and economic structures. In the realm of production and employment, the rise of what might be termed 'hit and run' capitalism in the 1980s devalued long-term growth in favour of short-term gains. The leveraged buyout, transcending management, became the ideal. Stable, lasting careers became subject to delayering, casualization, and non-linear sequencing. Rampant inequality brought in its wake what Jock Young has termed 'a veritable chaos of reward',[111] huge gains for those at the pinnacle of the new hierarchies of wealth and power, derisory and uncertain earnings for those at the base of the 'lo-tech' service industries.[112]

The replacement of stable bureaucracies by 'fluid' post-modern organizations, staffed by the graduates of the new business schools, jettisons two key components of social and personal cohesion: deferred gratification and long-term strategic thinking. Other consequent social deficits are low commitment to the institution; low trust in the top echelons; and poor institutional knowledge, much of which inhered in low-status workers. Talent in the form of experience and expertise developed over time is replaced by talent measured by indicators of 'potential', such as flexibility and presentational skills: the surface 'knowledge' of the consultancy, not the practical and long-honed skills of the craftsman and the professional. Three new 'sources of uselessness' now render job-holding even more precarious: (1) the export of skilled work to low-wage economies; (2) 'true' automation, where microelectronics and computers have pushed mechanization to levels where very large numbers of skilled workers become expendable (while these outcomes were long predicted for manual workers, what was *not* predicted was the extent to which this process affects routine white collar as much as manual work); and (3) the expansion and extension of ageing, now pervading the culture to such an extent that even 30-year-olds in certain jobs feel 'over the hill'. The result for the middle class and middle-aged is a generation of Willy Lomans, who at least found tragic expression in Arthur Miller's classic *Death of a Salesman* (1949), whose predicament is now far more prevalent. There is no working-class equivalent, unless it is Alan Bleasdale's *The Boys from the Blackstuff*, the British television series of the 1980s that had an all too timely revival in the autumn of 2010.

Despite such a catalogue of economic casualties and social costs, as long as the system keeps on delivering greater prosperity, the show stays on the road, even if that road is increasingly pot-holed, congested, and destructive of the environment. Momentum is sustained by new forms of what Marx termed commodity fetishism. Rising levels of consumption are no longer driven by the prime modern phenomena of built-in obsolescence[113] and the 'motor of fashion'. To them can now be added 'branding', based on the increased technological capacity to 'gold-plate' products, Sennett's term for a basic standard object being superficially differentiated 'so that the surface is what counts': add-ons to any goods or services which inflate price for minimal production cost.[114]

---

[111] J. Young, *The Exclusive Society*, 152.

[112] B. Ehrenreich, *Nickel and Dimed: Undercover in Low-wage USA*; P. Toynbee, *Hard Work: Life in Low-Pay Britain*; L. Tirado *Hand to Mouth*.

[113] V. Packard, *The Hidden Persuaders*.   [114] R. Sennett, *The Culture of the New Capitalism*, 144.

A key example is business class travel by train or plane, which makes no difference at all to travel time but offers a bit more space to the passenger. A second innovation is the exploitation of 'potency', or the selling of unrealizable potential. Consuming potency is at its height in the iPod, a store of music which vastly exceeds any possibility of playback: in that instance, differentiation and accumulation are combined with the appeal of miniaturization. The SUV stuck in traffic is the emblem of unrealizable potency in its starkest form. Though Sennett does not invoke the parallels, the innovations of ceaseless 'choice' and unrealizable fulfilment are all too redolent of the pressures towards states of anomie.

The political realm now shows every sign of succumbing to the new capitalism. Political parties 'gold-plate' their differences but increasingly share common ground in offering a far narrower range of choices: a neo-liberal economy with a decreasing commitment to public sector welfare, and an increasing resort to the 'market' for future delivery of health, education, criminal justice, and income maintenance policies. Unrealizable potency inheres in the vast investment in armaments, which dwarfs that of foreign aid, and penal policies that aim to eliminate not only crime but all 'anti-social behaviour'. Moreover, an enfeebled culture flows from the new capitalism, a culture which veers towards the anomic and away from sustained relationships. Anomic culture may be a contradiction in terms, but the paradox may become all too real unless counter-movements to such trends can be generated.

In many respects, anomie theory, at least in its Durkheimian form, seems vindicated by the events of the past few years, during which the deregulation of the banks and financial markets allowed investment banking to spiral out of control to the point where, in 2008–9, a financial meltdown brought economic growth to a halt and some countries, such as Greece, to the verge of economic collapse. The British contribution to this debacle of neo-liberal economics has been downplayed by successive governments, but the 'Big Bang' in 1986 inaugurated forms of deregulation which gave the City of London a competitive edge over Wall Street, greatly strengthening its role as a world financial centre. Wall Street followed suit, with the last defences of the 1933 Glass-Steagall Act—devised to prevent a recurrence of the 1929 Great Crash by separating retail from investment banking—being scrapped in 1999. However, two likely outcomes of this dramatic exposure of the follies of leaving 'the market' to regulate 'itself', have yet to materialize. First, the resumption of Social Democratic forms of political economy, which intervened in the market for social ends and which protected key sectors of retail banking and housing finance from the search for profits at all costs, has not as yet occurred. Indeed, except in the USA, where President Obama's election signalled criticism of the excesses of the Bush era in widening inequalities, more conservative administrations have been electorally successful. Secondly, the crime rates of both Britain and the USA have declined rather than risen over the past 15 years—though the rates of more serious violence have bucked this trend.[115] It may well be that,

---

[115] See for detailed analysis, R. Reiner, *Law and Order: An Honest Citizen's Guide to Crime and Control*; 'Citizenship, Crime, Criminalization: Marshalling a Social Democratic Perspective'.

just as ingenious forms of 'securitization' masked the dangers of a looming loss of faith in credit markets[116] so 'securitization' in the form of burgeoning types of crime prevention have driven property crime rates down whilst the 'causes of crime' proliferate. Anomie theory nevertheless implies that, unless the commitment to a more socially just society can be revived, the underlying trend is a resumption of rising rates of crime in the near future.

Critique

'These facts', Durkheim stated characteristically, in a crucial passage in *Suicide*,[117] 'are susceptible of only one interpretation'. Durkheim's passion for facts, his demand that 'social facts' should be 'treated as things', is the basis for his particular form of sociological positivism. But even the most sympathetic reader of *Suicide* cannot fail to be struck by Durkheim's boldness in bending 'the facts' to suit his theory. 'Crises' are classified as such on several occasions to suit the suicide rate, rather than being allowed to stand as anomalies. For example, the unification of Italy is treated as an economic, not as a political, event, primarily—one suspects—because it coincided with a rise rather than a decline in the suicide rate. Certain elections which produced, in Durkheim's view, a change in the suicide rate comparable in scale and intensity to the major crises of 1830, 1848, and 1870 lead him to comment, 'Mild as they are, mere election crises sometimes have the same result (as crises of war and revolution)'.[118]

We have already pointed to Douglas' argument that Durkheim's whole approach (and, by extension, that of positivism in general) was based on a methodological fallacy.[119] The flaw can be illustrated by Durkheim's treatment of the different suicide rates of Protestants and Catholics, of fundamental importance for his concept of egoism. Durkheim asserted that *both* groups strongly opposed suicide on theological grounds and therefore the differences between the two groups' rates of suicide could not be accounted for in terms of their belief structures. Rather, it was the Protestant emphasis on free enquiry that attenuated the social bond and promoted greater strain towards egoistic suicide among Protestants. Douglas criticizes Durkheim for not going beyond sheer assertion on so crucial a point, since the particular form of Catholic doctrine concerning suicide, which entails eternal damnation, is far more emphatic than Protestant doctrine. The point for Douglas, however, is not simply that Durkheim was wrong on a specific point, however crucial; it is that his method of reliance on official rates eliminated the possibility of eliciting such meanings from individuals.

Differences in the official rates of suicide were taken by Durkheim to be social facts *sui generis*. Douglas asserts by contrast that they are prone to all the weaknesses inherent in official statistics and are most prone to distortion in just those respects where differences in the rates are most crucial, as in the case of Protestants and Catholics, or at times of crisis. Against this view, Durkheim tried to guard himself against the charge

---

[116] G. Tett, *Fool's Gold.*   [117] É. Durkheim, *Suicide*, 208.   [118] É. Durkheim, *Suicide*, 204.
[119] J. Douglas, *The Social Meanings of Suicide*; and also in A. Giddens (ed.), *The Sociology of Suicide*.

that many of the variations he noted were administrative artefacts, as may be caused, for example, at points of revolutionary change by the disruption of the administrative machinery for the registration of suicides. Were this the case, Durkheim argued on several occasions, the rates would be affected only in the areas where disruption was located, whereas in reality the variations were far more widespread. Douglas, however, is most concerned to stress the ways in which officials are themselves influenced by the social meanings of suicide. For example, the view that certain social situations, such as social isolation, may promote suicide, may influence coroners in returning such a verdict in otherwise ambiguous cases. Researchers then proceed to establish isolation as a 'cause' of suicide, and the theory appears confirmed. Social meanings also pervade the presentation of death in everyday life: Durkheim's confidence in the suicide statistics is summed up in his phrase 'a corpse is a corpse', but if, for example, some groups rather than others, for doctrinal and/or social reasons, have a strong interest in concealing or disguising suicides, the official rates may compound this practice. Durkheim himself allowed for the passive as well as the active suicide—the person who fails to stop himself or herself falling as distinct from jumping—but arguably failed to follow this insight through to a radical enough extent. In his table of suicides as classified by manner of death, such processes as drowning, leaping from a high place, and self-strangulation by hanging, outnumber poisonings and other forms of self-inflicted destruction less amenable to ready classification as suicide.[120] Douglas' alternative approach, the close scrutiny of suicide notes and allied correspondence, was expressly ruled out by Durkheim as unrepresentative. This exclusive reliance on official rates was assumed by Durkheim to be valid because of the regularity and stability of such rates. But if errors fit stable patterns and are routinely reproduced, this assumption is invalid. The fallacy is to presume that official rates and indices are somehow constructed independently of social meanings.

This criticism was employed with even greater force against the assumption of Merton that the lower class were pressurized into higher rates of deviance than the middle and upper classes. 'Anomie theory stands accused of predicting far too little bourgeois criminality and too much proletarian criminality.'[121] This time it is the acceptance of the official rates of crime and delinquency, rather than that of suicide, which is seen as unwarranted. In Box's view, by accepting a simple inverse relationship between deviance and social status, Merton reduces anomie theory to that of 'relative deprivation'.[122] The entire house of cards collapses once this prop is removed and the theories which base themselves upon it can be seen as mystifications blurring our view of 'deviance, reality, and society'. Such a perspective is reproduced in police practices, which focus far more on public working-class than on private elite criminality. These practices naturally lead to official statistics which lend credence to the theory, and so, in a self-confirmatory circle, a politically innocuous conception of deviance is propagated.

---

[120] É. Durkheim, *Suicide*, 291.   [121] I. Taylor et al., *The New Criminology*, 107.

[122] S. Box, *Deviance, Reality and Society*, 105–6. Box bases his case on the much more random distribution of criminality to be inferred from 'self-report' studies. For a critique of such studies, see A. Reiss, 'Inappropriate Theories and Inadequate Methods as Policy Plagues: Self-Reported Delinquency and the Law', 21–2. Reiss argues *inter alia* that police practices are largely *reactive*, and therefore have little probable impact on crime rates.

Lindesmith and Gagnon note the severe limitations of both Merton's theory of anomie and one of its variants, the 'double failure' hypothesis of Cloward and Ohlin, in accounting for the social character of addiction.[123] Merton had typified addicts, along with vagrants, inebriates, and psychotics, as retreatists, i.e. 'as non-productive liabilities' and as 'asocialized persons who are *in* society but not *of* it', who have both 'relinquished culturally prescribed goals and abandoned the quest for success'.[124] Even if it is conceded that not all anomie produces deviance and not all deviance flows from anomie, Lindesmith and Gagnon argue that the theory fails to specify clearly *which* forms of addiction may flow from anomie; or to confront the reverse proposition, that addiction may lead to anomie; or to square with the specialized social skills that addicts must develop if they are to survive the control measures against them, and finance a highly expensive habit; or to convey the complexity of the social worlds constructed by the diverse groups so readily tagged 'asocial'. The application of anomie theory to a specific form of deviance raises, in short, the most fundamental doubts about its capacity to either explain or enhance our understanding of the origins, consequences, and processes of development of deviance in general.

In the same volume, Lemert argues that the theory 'strains credulity' for reasons that go beyond the purely logical or empirical. First, the very terms so confidently used by Merton to sustain his theory are highly problematic: 'social structure' and 'culture' are at best abstractions that are exceptionally difficult to differentiate in terms of data, at worst reifications that derive from the fallacy of misplaced concreteness. 'Inescapable circularity lies in the use of "culture" as a summary to describe modal tendencies in the behaviour of human beings and, at the same time, as a term of designating the causes of the modal tendencies.'[125] The same term, 'culture', tends to be applied across the board to the small-scale, relatively unified society (such as Tikopia) and to the highly differentiated agglomeration of often diverse sub-societies, such as the USA.

> It is theoretically conceivable that there are or have been societies in which values learned in childhood, taught as a pattern, and reinforced by structured controls, serve to predict the bulk of the everyday behaviour of members and to account for prevailing conformity to norms. However, it is easier to describe the model than to discover societies which make a good fit with the model.[126]

Lemert prefers a model of a pluralistic society, in which different groups and associations negotiate compromises and reach contingent accommodations that derive, if at all, only at several removes from a consensus over some ultimate values.

> One objection to Merton's view of choice and action by individuals is that it simplifies something enormously complex. Instead of seeing the individual as a relatively free agent making adaptations pointed toward a consistent value order, it is far more realistic to visualise him as 'captured' . . . by the claims of various groups to which he has given his allegiance [familial, occupational, religious, ethnic, and political ties are what Lemert has

---

[123] A. Lindesmith and J. Gagnon, 'Anomie and Drug Addiction'.
[124] R. Merton, *Social Theory and Social Structure*, 142–4.
[125] E. Lemert, 'Social Structure, Social Control and Deviation', 60.
[126] E. Lemert, 'Social Structure, Social Control and Deviation', 63–4.

in mind, *inter alia*]. It is in the fact that these claims are continually being preemptively asserted through group action at the expense of other claims, frequently in direct conflict, that *we find the main source of 'pressures' on individuals in modern society*, rather than in 'cultural emphasis on goals'.[127]

It is possible to refine Merton's conception to take account of Lemert's quite distinct model of social structure and culture: but only at the cost of reducing the intensity of the 'strain' induced by the goals–means discrepancy to far milder levels than he proposed.

Second, Merton's theory neglects altogether the implications of social control for the shaping of deviant behaviour. Lemert's critique takes two major forms: one, the need to allow theoretically for the promotion of 'active' as well as 'passive' social control; and two, the need to differentiate between 'primary' and 'secondary' deviation. 'Active social control' refers to the growing organizational tendency in complex industrial societies with a high rate of technologically induced growth to regulate activity in purely instrumental ways. For example, the regulation of pollution, industrial safety, traffic, and commercial and financial transactions is only negligibly concerned with the imputation of stigmas and moral evaluations and is primarily designed to enforce minimum standards of compliance that do not signally interfere with production and profits. Innovation, far from emerging as a 'deviant or non-conforming response of structurally disadvantaged individuals':

> . . . has become organised or institutionalised in our society . . . Nowhere is the contingent nature of deviation made more apparent than in the action of government regulatory agencies with adjudicative and punitive powers in situations where they are confronted by consequences of technological and organisational change. Large areas of action to do with business, finance, health, labor, housing, utilities, safety and welfare are subject to control through administrative rules discontinuous in origin and form from the culturally derived norms which impressed Merton and others seeming to favor a conception of passive social control.[128]

In other words, an increasing proportion of control activity is 'active' and cannot be seen to flow in any simple or direct fashion from 'the norms' that are presumed to inhere in patterns of childhood socialization.

'Passive social control', however, still operates in the sphere of the 'sacred': and it is in this respect still potent in the operation of the criminal justice system. Moral character and 'status degradation' remain part of the armoury that produces 'secondary deviation', i.e. 'how deviant acts are symbolically attached to persons and the effective consequences of such attachment for subsequent deviation on the part of the person'.[129] In such secondary deviation, 'the original "causes" of the (primary) deviation recede and give way to the central importance of the disapproving, degradational, and isolating reactions of society'.[130] Lemert holds this to be 'pragmatically the more pertinent' a

---

[127] E. Lemert, 'Social Structure, Social Control and Deviation', 68.
[128] E. Lemert, 'Social Structure, Social Control and Deviation', 89–91.
[129] E. Lemert, 'Social Structure, Social Control and Deviation', 82.
[130] E. Lemert, 'Social Structure, Social Control and Deviation', 81; see also Chapter 7 on interactionism.

research problem, and one to which anomie theory has as yet contributed nothing. To put it crudely, it may be that the majority of people 'steal', but only a minority become processed as 'thieves': anomie theory alerts us to possible reasons for the former, but precludes analysis of the processes underlying the latter proposition.

In a more structurally inclined critique of Merton, Gouldner makes the point that more follows from the malintegration of goals and means than appears in even the revised statements of the theory:

> The allocation of the means to succeed and, with this, of position in the class system, is in appreciable part a function of the institution of private property and its hereditary or testamentary transmission. Thus the distribution of anomic responses is a function of this institution. But it does not follow that those on the top of the class system are less anomic, if by this is meant that they have more of a genuine belief in and devotion to their culture's moral values. Indeed, there is reason to predict that their genuine commitment to these moral values is undermined by the very institution from which they derive their advantages. For this institution makes it possible for them to sever the connections between gratification and conformity to cultural values . . . In short, the spoiler of the society's morality is . . . 'vested interest', the right to do something for nothing.[131]

To this critical catalogue, we would wish to add only four more problems. First, although he later attempted to plug the gap,[132] Merton ignored the reverse situation to the malintegration of goals and means that occurs when results *exceed* expectations. The 'anomie of success' is again more prevalent at the top than the bottom of the system, and applies whether the success is 'earned' or not. The overnight 'star', the unexpected 'bestseller', the 'pools winner', are arguably candidates for anomie just as much as the relative failures (though data exist which cast doubt on this response for one group of pools winners in Britain).[133] There is, argues Hagan, the problem of too much 'social capital': 'The trust that derives from successfully being embedded in powerful occupations and corporate networks can be a source of freedom and, therefore, power to commit large-scale white-collar crimes.'[134]

A second problem is the difficulty of conceptualizing the chronology of anomie and deviance. Once formulated, deviant adaptations exist in the world as social institutions possessing some degree of stability and continuity. They may be encountered before any exposure to the 'strain to anomie' has occurred. However, if the 'solution' is embraced before the 'problem' is encountered, as described, for example, in Whyte's depiction of neighbourhood rackets in an Italian–American slum, then the experience of anomie is pre-empted.[135] It becomes a purely structural property without subjective counterpart. The problem of investigating anomie empirically may therefore elude available methodologies, since the only indicators of anomie that remain are its presenting symptoms, such as high rates of crime and delinquency.[136] The

---

[131] A. Gouldner, *The Coming Crisis*, 325.
[132] R. Merton, in M. Clinard, *Anomie and Deviant Behavior*, 219–22.
[133] S. Smith and P. Razzell, *The Pools Winners*.   [134] J. Hagan, *Crime and Disrepute*.
[135] W. Whyte, *Street Corner Society*.
[136] Merton and Srole distinguished *anomie* as a systemic property from *anomia* as a psychological state. This differentiation does not resolve the problem as we see it here.

circularity is well demonstrated in Lander's study of Baltimore, in which the best predictors of delinquency could not be adequately disentangled from the best predictors of anomie. Third, there is the problem raised by Albert Cohen and Arthur Stinchcombe. Anomie seems to be conceived as the outcome of a yawning gap between aspiration and the prospect of final achievement. It is presumably most grievous in its effects on ambitious but disadvantaged young people who cast ahead to augur their life-chances. But it appears that people actually tend not to project their lives very far ahead. Indeed, Stinchcombe argued that adolescents plan only a little into the future.[137] Expectations and motives are frequently confined to limited periods of time, shifting with each significant turning-point in the life cycle. Experiences, perspectives, projects, and acquaintances interact and evolve continuously and ambition and explanations of failure are significant parts of that phased growth. They are not usually set but emergent, they are often short-term, and anomic disjunction itself may not be as profound as Merton claimed. To be sure, there are groups whose deprivation is so great that their frustration can never be modulated. It is unclear if anomie theory is intended to refer chiefly to them or to others whose lives are rather too complicated to be captured so simply. Lastly, there is the problem posed by the stable institutionalization of deviance in the routine activities of central organizations of State and business. Bauman, in his analysis of the holocaust, and Punch, in his work on corporate misconduct,[138] have shown how very difficult it can be to distinguish it from conformity or claim that it is a consequence of relative deprivation or deregulation.

Conclusion

It may well be the case, as Douglas argues, that Durkheim's methodology is flawed, but that does not invalidate the general support for his theory that can be drawn from a revised view of the official statistics. Douglas' alternative method 'for determining and analysing the communicative actions which can be observed and replicated in real-world cases of suicide' remains obscure, beyond the examination of suicide notes and the like. Indeed, it was the limitations of such methods that led Durkheim to focus on the rates as alone capable of providing sufficient evidence for analysis. The two methods are, in certain respects, quite compatible. As Atkinson's work testifies, however, there are perhaps intractable problems involved in a reliance on the rates alone.[139] While empirical support for Durkheim's theory remains mixed, it is still a formidable source for theory and research.

Merton's application of the concept draws both its strengths and its weaknesses from his Americanization of anomie. The weaknesses stem from too facile an acceptance of the apparent implications of the official rates of deviance, and too standardized a view of the prevalence of the American Dream. But 'Americanization'

---

[137] A. Stinchcombe, *Rebellion in a High School.*
[138] M. Punch, *Dirty Business: Exploring Corporate Misconduct.*   [139] M. Atkinson, *Discovering Suicide.*

remains a real phenomenon, as generations of immigrants from diverse cultures were and are subject to a relatively unbridled ideology of egalitarian consumerism. The content and consequence of these processes have been, if anything, too little researched and explored. Jules Henry echoed Merton and elaborated on the theme of 'money-success' in writing: 'In contemporary America children must be trained to *insatiable* consumption of *impulsive* choice and *infinite* variety.'[140] The relationship between saturation advertising and relative deprivation remains relatively unknown, but such evidence as we have gives point to Merton's thesis. Nor is the imputed effect confined to the USA: all consumer societies have experienced rising rates of crime and delinquency in the context of growing affluence; and anomie theory remains one of the most plausible attempts to account for this seeming paradox.[141] In the most systematic review of the evidence to date, Braithwaite concluded that it supported 'a strong *prima facie* case . . . that reducing inequalities of wealth and power will reduce crime.'[142]

Lemert may be right in proposing the general inadequacy of anomie theory in any simple sense to convey the processes involved in deviance and control. His own critique, however, fails to differentiate between social change resulting from innovation that falls *within* the realm of institutional means, and social change resulting from innovation which does not. An example of the latter is the extent to which the 'informal economy' is producing considerable distortions in taxation and consumption by comparison with the 'formal economy.'[143] Lemert seems in this and other respects to miss the point of Merton's analysis. Even planned social change can disrupt lives for the worse. For example, the unemployment that can result from technological obsolescence falls unevenly on the population, and for those adversely affected, the goals–means equation is arguably subject to sharp deterioration. It remains an empirical question as to whether that promotes higher rates of crime and deviance, of whatever kind. In sum, though substantial revision is in order, there is a great deal of unexplored mileage in anomie theory, whichever version we prefer.

[140] J. Henry, *Culture Against Man*, 70.

[141] Experience in England and Wales may offer a test of sorts between these versions of anomie theory. Ten years after the end of the Second World War, crime rates were actually lower than in 1945. After their single sharp rise, of 15 per cent in 1950–1, they fell back below their 1945 level. After 1955, they began their almost uninterrupted climb of 5–6 per cent annually. Durkheim's theory (which was admittedly of suicide rather than crime, but which is conventionally applied to both) does not fit very well with so sharp a rise in crime rates in the middle of the Korean war—in which Britain was fully engaged—and while a tough regulatory framework, the culture of rationing, was still largely in place. Merton's theory fits the trends far better: people put up with post-war austerity in the glow of victory and post-war reconstruction. But by 1950, when their patience wore thin, the austerity was prolonged by a far-distant war. Aspirations shot ahead of reality. With the election of the Conservatives in 1951 and the Korean armistice, rationing finally ended and, for a few years at least, reality outpaced aspirations. By the mid-1950s, the 'never-had-it-so-good' society was born, and aspirations began to soar, if not infinitely, then at least indefinitely. Unlike all other European parties of the Left, Labour have been dogged ever since by the aura of delivering the Good but not the goods.

[142] J. Braithwaite, *Inequality, Crime and Public Policy*.

[143] R. Neuwirth, *Stealth of Nations: The Global Rise of the Informal Economy*; S. Witt, *How Music Got Free*.

Further Reading

R. AGNEW, *Pressured to Crime*, Oxford, 2010.

É. DURKHEIM, *Suicide*, London, 2006 (1897).

R. MERTON, *Social Theory and Social Structure*, New York, 1949 and 1957.

S. MESSNER and R. Rosenfeld, *Crime and the American Dream*, Belmont, Cal., 1993 (5th edn, 2012).

J. YOUNG, *The Vertigo of Late Modernity*, London, 2007.

6

Culture and Subculture

Introduction

Attempts to explain and understand crime and deviance, in particular youth offending, in terms of adherence to distinctive cultural patterns became commonplace in the 1960s and 1970s, although at first it was considered somewhat novel even to link the two concepts. It was also considered scientific, in so far as sociologists, with respectful nods in the direction of anthropology, sought to divide up the population in relation to their parent class cultures, varieties of subcultures, and burgeoning counter-cultures, each with their distinctive norms, values, and beliefs, each with a clear-cut relationship to the others, all invested with a degree of clarity which consigned any lingering doubts about the reality of all this cultural attribution to the margin. It is all too easy, in retrospect, to see this body of work as a somewhat mechanical attempt to pin down the unpinnable: cultures as they are lived. But there were real gains none the less, not least establishing the proposition that the most apparently senseless and meaningless forms of aggressive delinquency could be rendered intelligible and rational by taking account of their authors' 'definitions of the situation' and by conceiving of delinquency as a solution, rather than as a problem, to dilemmas that they faced.

We shall argue that there was an excessively schematic quality about the subcultural theories of delinquency of this period. It was held that society, whether American, as in the work of Albert Cohen, Cloward and Ohlin, and Miller, or British, as in the work of Mays, Downes, and Hargreaves, could be clearly layered and categorized into classes, sectors, age-groups, and sex-roles.[1] Overall, especially in Cohen's influential work, there loomed in stable ascendancy the 'dominant' culture: White Anglo-Saxon Protestant culture, the ascetic, achievement-orientated, highly competitive, middle-class way of life. Everyone was pulled to this centre of cultural gravity: none could escape its clutches, though in line with the model underlying Merton's theory of anomie, those most embroiled in the system's contradictions could kick against it in various ways. Deviant subcultures could be originated as a reaction against it; once they came into being, they became a form of constraint in themselves. Delinquents acted out delinquent subcultures: the real analytical problem was to theorize why such deviant solutions could be generated in the first place. The sociologist, in short, was the

---

[1] A. Cohen, *Delinquent Boys*; R. Cloward and L. Ohlin, *Delinquency and Opportunity*; W. Miller, 'Lower Class Culture as a Generating Milieu of Gang Delinquency', 5–19; J. Mays, *Growing Up in the City*; D. Downes, *The Delinquent Solution*; D. Hargreaves, *Social Relations in a Secondary School*.

dispassionate observer and analyst of deviant behaviour, albeit one who credited that behaviour with a version of rationality, collective problem-solving, and group process.

The break with these variations on the 'delinquent subculture' theme came with the work of Matza.[2] It was a partial break only, for—as we shall see—Matza retained certain features of these theories in his own work. But he helped to open up, along with the exponents of labelling theory, a Pandora's box whose contents—the emphasis on free will, the argument that all prior theorizing had 'over-predicted' delinquency, the rejection of the attempt to differentiate deviants from non-deviants as a fruitful mode of enquiry—swamped the neat boundaries between subcultures which was the hallmark of existing approaches. By no means all of this was incompatible with the theories under attack. For example, the focus of labelling theory on such variables as police bias against gang compared with non-gang boys rather neatly complemented them.[3] Even so, the later phase of work in the cultural and subcultural vein shifted in the 1970s to markedly different theories and methods.

After 1967, subcultural theory languished. For five years or so no substantive work appeared which derived from its central tenets or which developed its major propositions. Its similarities with anomie theory subtly became more obvious. The critical exposure of the defects of anomie theory was extended to subcultural theory. Both rested on the assumption that deviant behaviour originated in socially induced 'strain' or 'pressure'. Underlying that 'strain' was the image of society as basically stable and consensual, though flawed by remediable inequalities of opportunity. Such an image was unattractive both to the labelling theorists, who favoured a more pluralistic model of society as a mosaic of disparate social worlds; and to the more radically inclined sociologists of deviance who sought to base their theories on the central assumption of class struggle. It was not until 1972 that a perspective emerged that was capable of accommodating such diverse strands. Phil Cohen's analysis of working-class youth cultures in East London emphasized the latter approach to such effect that it became the basis for the substantial work on deviance and control by the Birmingham Centre for Contemporary Cultural Studies (CCCS).[4] Their work concentrated in general on the interplay between class conflict, youthful rebellion and media representations and did not entail first-hand ethnographies. Paul Willis' work at the CCCS was somewhat exceptional. He engaged with the complexities of fieldwork, not in the traditional manner of the theorist out to prove or refute a theory, but in the mode that Jules Henry has termed 'passionate ethnography'.[5] He attempted (with rare success) to describe and analyse the subjective unfolding of 'contradictions and problems' as they are 'lived through to particular outcomes'.[6] The result was a series of re-creations of 'cultures' (Willis significantly did not use the term subculture at all, preferring the term 'subordinate cultures') which could hardly have been accomplished if Willis had been preoccupied by formal theory-testing. His work has, nonetheless, a real significance for theories of culture and subculture.

[2] D. Matza, *Delinquency and Drift.*
[3] I. Piliavin and S. Briar, 'Police Encounters with Juveniles', 206–14; also C. Werthman and I. Piliavin, 'Gang Members and the Police'.
[4] P. Cohen, 'Working Class Youth Cultures in East London'.   [5] J. Henry, *Culture Against Man,* 3.
[6] P. Willis, *Profane Culture,* 1. See also his *Learning to Labour.*

In the 1970s a flood of work appeared in Britain which took as its axis the need to 'capture' cultural meanings, but to contextualize their source in the larger social structure, usually in terms of its contradictions. The works of Murdock, Pearson, Corrigan, Cohen and Robins, Hebdige, Brake, and Pryce shared this broad perspective. Important exceptions such as Parker, Gill, and Marsh, draw more comprehensively from labelling theory and earlier sociological and subcultural approaches while achieving considerable observational records.[7] Exceptional, too, are the studies that retain the Chicago ethnographer's interest in the social organization and transmission of belief and knowledge in an urban environment. Overall, the priority accorded formal theory-testing receded in the face of an unprecedented enthusiasm for more extensive explorations of diverse social worlds.[8] The materials gathered in the process enhanced the possibilities for cultural and subcultural theories to develop in a less constricted way than in the past. There is a tendency now for theories to be couched in terms of 'cultural capital' rather than subcultural terms. The proliferation of recent cultural ethnographies analysed by Muncie[9] raise the question of whether the possibilities exist, in a rapidly changing multicultural networked society, for evanescent mediatized cultures and subcultures to crystallize long enough for adequate delineation and signification.

Theoretical Perspectives

Strain theories constitute the first truly systematic use of the concepts of culture and subculture. This occurs in the explanation of delinquency in the work of Albert Cohen. The problem, as he stated it, was that previous theories had made only a limited and largely circular use of such concepts. To say that delinquency was 'part of' a culture, or was 'culturally transmitted', did not take one very far. What was needed was a theory of the *origins* of such culture. Again, the delinquency previously theorized about had been mainly of the acquisitive kind, akin to adult forms of theft and robbery. Yet the more puzzling forms of delinquency were primarily expressive in character. Violence, vandalism, joy-riding: these kinds of activity were simply not addressed by existing theories (though he made little reference to the work of Thrasher in this respect). Cohen argued that an adequate theory should address itself to both the character and social distribution of the most serious forms of delinquency; and

[7] G. Murdock and R. McCron, 'Youth and Class; The Career of a Confusion'; G. Pearson, '"Paki-Bashing" in a North East Lancashire Cotton Town'; P. Corrigan, *Schooling the Smash Street Kids*; P. Cohen and D. Robins, *Knuckle Sandwich: Growing up in the Working Class City*; R. Hebdige, *Subculture: The Meaning of Style*; M. Brake, *The Sociology of Youth Culture and Youth Subcultures*; K. Pryce, *Endless Pressure: A Study of West Indian Lifestyles in Bristol*; H. Parker, *The View From the Boys*; O. Gill, *Luke Street*; P. Marsh et al., *The Rules of Disorder*.

[8] This has not been so in the case of traditional criminology, and somewhat less so in the USA. D. West, *Present Conduct and Future Delinquency*; D. West and D. Farrington, *Who Becomes Delinquent?* and *The Delinquent Way of Life*; also M. Hindelang, 'The Social versus Solitary Nature of Delinquent Involvements', 167–75; and D. Elliott and H. Voss, *Delinquency and Dropouts*.

[9] J. Muncie, *Youth and Crime: A Critical Introduction*.

it should also employ the concept of culture in ways which specify the functions it performs and the problems it solves, for the groups whose behaviour it allegedly influences so strongly.

This conception of culture is characteristically functionalist. Culture enables people to solve the problems created *for* them by the social structure. Culture consists of 'traditional ways of solving problems' or of 'learned problem solutions' which are transmitted through the processes of childhood socialization. Cohen was concerned to address the problem of why, if such a strong basis for conformity is provided by cultures, there should be any possibility of innovation. The answer he supplies is reminiscent of Merton's anomie theory and consists of accepting that, at some points in the social system, normative conflict is possible. Structure and culture make incompatible demands and it is at these points of pressure that subcultures have evolved to 'solve' the problems that arise. Subcultures typically borrow elements from the larger culture and rework them into distinctive forms. Such elements (violence and hedonism, for example) are available to all: but not everyone is a bearer of a subculture which gives them unusual predominance. 'The crucial condition for the emergence of new cultural forms is the existence, *in effective interaction with one another, of a number of actors with similar problems of adjustment*.'[10] Cohen vividly conveyed the scope for distinctive subcultures to emerge as solutions to problems posed for different groups. 'Each age, sex, racial and ethnic category, each occupation, economic stratum and social class consists of people who have been equipped by their society with frames of reference and confronted by their society with situations that are not equally characteristic of other roles.'[11] The task was to theorize 'the role of the social structure and the immediate social milieu in determining the creation and selection of solutions' in a manner applicable to gang delinquency.[12]

The main plank of Cohen's own theory was his characterization of gang delinquency and his assumption that it amounted to a 'way of life' in deprived metropolitan and inner-urban neighbourhoods. This pattern of delinquency could be summarized as displaying the following six characteristics: (1) non-utilitarianism: even in the case of thefts, economic rationality seemed rarely to prevail, since goods would be stolen 'for kicks' and given away, discarded, or destroyed, rather than consumed or sold for profit; (2) malice: a thread of destructiveness ran through the delinquency which seemed quite distinct from damage wrought as a by-product of sheer skylarking (for example, the apparently wanton vandalism that accompanied some break-ins); (3) negativism: much delinquent behaviour seemed not simply at odds with respectable values, but their inversion; (4) short-run hedonism: the cult of instant gratification 'reached its finest flower' in the delinquent gang; (5) versatility: the gang's activities ran the gamut of theft, vandalism, aggression, and general hell-raising (by contrast, the delinquency of girls seemed more aligned with sex-role expectations, as manifested in such offences as shoplifting clothes and cosmetics); (6) group autonomy: gang loyalty came first, all other allegiances were subordinated to it.

---

[10] A. Cohen, *Delinquent Boys*, 59.   [11] A. Cohen, *Delinquent Boys*, 54.
[12] A. Cohen, *Delinquent Boys*, 55.

This profile of the delinquent subculture did not aim to be an exhaustive catalogue of all delinquency, but an inventory of the most serious forms that group delinquency took. It should also be stressed that Cohen was accentuating tendencies which occasionally became 'reality', rather than a set of everyday activities. Criticisms of the theory which caricature it for conjuring up an image of incessant warfare between youth and the adult world often ignore its 'ideal-typical' character.

The explanation of such delinquency was sought by Cohen in terms of the initial conformity of youth to the established cultural order. In the case of subordinate groups in a society stratified along lines of social class, the very process of adhering to the values of the dominant culture makes for the creation of problems rather than their resolution. The rationale for the apparently motiveless and meaningless behaviour of delinquent gangs is to be found in the problems faced by the sector of society apparently most involved: lower-class, male, urban adolescents. For Cohen, they commonly experience great tension and strain in handling the paradoxical many-are-called-but-few-are-chosen nature of democratic schooling. Schools exist to *make* children care about social status and academic achievement, but on terms which effectively deny them to all but a minority of the working class. Faced with a common 'problem of adjustment' caused by school failure, the rejected evolve the delinquent gang solution as a means both to acquire status in a more accessible form and to hit back at the system that has branded them as failures. The gang takes the rules of respectable society and turns them upside down: the D stream's revenge. The theory is neatly tailored to account for the much lower rates of such delinquency among the middle class (they are far more likely to attain success by the conventional route); girls (they value marriage to an occupationally successful male far more highly than 'making it' in career terms themselves—a proposition that in turn would predict relatively more female delinquency as that tradition weakens); and in non-urban areas (schools hold less sway as the route to honoured crafts and trades). It seemed to fit the facts extremely well: to aid in both explaining and understanding the group character of most delinquency and to go beyond previous theories whilst retaining their more valuable insights.

The theory quickly stimulated variants of much the same model and a plethora of attempts at empirical testing. The most sympathetic work to that of Cohen was Cloward and Ohlin's study, dedicated, significantly, to Robert Merton, the father of the American version of *anomie* theory, and to Edwin Sutherland, the Chicagoan father of differential association theory.[13] They proposed a similar structurally generated model of delinquency causation as Cohen, but argued that he had seriously underrated the degree of *specialization* that existed and overrated the role of the school as the crucible of delinquency. They discerned three types of delinquent subculture arising in different types of neighbourhood: criminal (gangs pursuing quite utilitarian forms of robbery and theft); conflict (fighting gangs); and retreatist (drug-using gangs). The major source of variation was the presence or absence of stable recruitment into adult criminal enterprises in the local community: where such patterns existed, the criminal gang would predominate; where not, the conflict gang would do so. Boys failing to

---

[13] R. Cloward and L. Ohlin, *Delinquency and Opportunity*.

succeed either legally or illegally in any context would slough off this 'double failure' by resorting to drug-using and 'hustling'. The root cause of the original emergence of delinquent subcultures was not so much the school—largely an irrelevance to the downtown street-corner youth—as the economic pursuit of 'money-success' earlier emphasized by Merton in his anomie theory and reinstated by Cloward and Ohlin as the prime source of embittered frustration in the metropolitan slums. In some of the ghetto areas, youth unemployment reached the level of 40 to 50 per cent and, although Cloward and Ohlin did not see ethnicity as a significant causal variable, their approach does make some sense of the 'fact that homicide is the leading cause of death among young black males in the USA'.[14]

Empirical studies based on testing these two theories became a major factor of criminology in the late 1950s to mid-1960s. The main conclusions to emerge from the most meticulous of these projects, that of Short and Strodtbeck in Chicago,[15] inclined towards Cohen's more generalized characterization of gang delinquency, but rejected his emphasis on the oppositional character of the subcultural values that supported it. Situational elements were acknowledged: the precipitating motive for gang fights supplied by the fact that threats to the leader's status loomed larger at street level than in theory; the part played by sheer contingency in dragging large numbers of otherwise only marginally delinquent youth into the fray; and the disconcerting ability to accommodate apparently quite contradictory 'value systems' shown by gang boys, who gave more support than non-gang boys to values favourable to delinquency without significantly disaffiliating from the values of conventional society. A major problem in all of this was the sheer difficulty of testing more than a few facets of the theories in other than a somewhat mechanical fashion: but the data pointed to the inescapable conclusion that delinquency was far more autonomous and contingent than earlier theories had allowed.

The work of David Matza made rather more impact by achieving a partial critical break with the underlying assumptions of strain theory and by proposing an alternative theory of delinquency. His theory is nowhere presented as a coherent whole, but is to be assembled, albeit with some inconsistencies, from several sources.[16] He roundly condemns strain theorists (along with virtually all prior work) for 'over-predicting' delinquency, for accounting for far more of it than exists. At the same time, he retains some of strain theory's central features, notably the stress on group process and—in his assertion that 'preparation' and a sense of 'desperation' are preludes to delinquency in certain areas—he conjures up an implication of strain akin to the earlier subcultural theorists. Matza's major achievement is to build his theory around the axiom that delinquency is *willed* behaviour and is in general 'intermittent' and 'mundane' as well as subject to a sharp diminution with the onset of adulthood. The idea that delinquency flowed from a deeply held commitment to a set of oppositional values embodied in

[14] V. Fuchs, *Who Shall Live? Health, Economics and Social Choice*, 40.

[15] J. Short and F. Strodtbeck, *Group Process and Gang Delinquency*.

[16] David Matza's work on delinquency and deviance emerged chronologically as follows: with G. Sykes, 'Techniques of Neutralization', 1957; 'Subterranean Traditions of Youth', 1961; with G. Sykes, 'Delinquency and Subterreanean Values', 1961; *Delinquency and Drift*, 1964; *Becoming Deviant*, 1969.

delinquent subcultures could not account for these patterns. Instead, he proposed that a state of drift typically precedes delinquency. Drift entails a loosening of controls from which delinquency is only *one* possible outcome. 'The delinquent transiently exists in a limbo between convention and crime . . . postponing commitment, evading decision.'[17] Delinquency, however, does not occur in a vacuum. It is facilitated by a 'subculture of delinquency' comprising a set of precepts that both release the delinquent from the constraints of law and custom and caricature commonly held values rather than representing an inversion of them. 'Techniques of neutralization' solve the problem of moral scruples: 'I didn't mean to do it', 'They had it coming to them', 'Everybody does it', 'Nobody got hurt', and 'I only did it for my friends' are commonly held justifications for deviance rather than the peculiar preserve of offenders. Similarly, delinquency is rendered attractive, not by adherence to a bizarre morality unique to young offenders, but by their exaggerated valuation of widely circulating 'subterranean' values: the pursuit of excitement, the disdain for routine work, and the equation of toughness and masculinity. This combination encourages males in the 'limbo' of adolescence to manufacture excitement by law-breaking. The process of drift helps account for the episodic and generally 'mundane' character of delinquency. The closeness of the delinquent's values to those of conventional society helps account for the relative ease with which maturation out of delinquency is accomplished with the onset of adulthood and more structured role-playing in work and family life. Unfortunately, in setting out to remedy theories which he saw as 'over-predicting' delinquency, Matza over-corrects to the point at which his own theory *under-predicts* both its scale and, in particular, its more violent forms. In his discussion of violence, Matza employs the idea of 'desperation', but the theme is left relatively unexplicated. 'The drifter is not less a problem than the compulsive or committed delinquent even though he is far less likely to become an adult criminal. Though his tenure is short, his replacements are legion.'[18] It is as if, in crucial respects, Matza is addressing a different problem to the earlier theorists, who focused on the 'committed' rather than the 'mundane' delinquent. The notions of 'compulsive' and 'committed' delinquency retain the links with positivism that Matza had been concerned to repudiate.

Matza actually devoted rather little space to the examination of evidence about rates and styles of delinquency, and the picture must be more variegated than his somewhat over-generalized and blanket argument suggests. How could it not be? There *are* places where a delinquent subculture in its most determined form appears to exist. Simon's and Burns' graphic description of life on the 'corners' of West Baltimore in the 1990s talks of the disorganized and predatory life of drug-users and sellers for whom much conventional morality has no apparent relevance.[19] And what we know from cohort studies does not wholly support his imagery of the drifting and episodic rule-breaker. For example, almost all the British youths in West and Farrington's and Belson's self-report studies had engaged in crime. To be sure, much of that criminality was petty enough, but there was violence too. By the time they are 28, some 30 per cent of men

---

[17] D. Matza, *Delinquency and Drift*, 28.   [18] D. Matza, *Delinquency and Drift*, 30.
[19] D. Simon and E. Burns, *The Corner: A Year in the Life of an Inner-City Neighborhood*.

in England and Wales have appeared before the courts.[20] Whilst most of those who offend are not serious or committed rule-breakers (conforming to Matza's description of 'episodic delinquents') there is a small minority of some 6 per cent who *do* offend repeatedly and, it has been estimated, are responsible for about two-thirds of the total number of offences.[21] 'Drift' is not very helpful in accounting for them. Again, delinquents do not always 'age out' of offending, as criminologists put it. Instead, the quantitative analysis of cohorts of recorded offenders, with all its limitations, suggests that statistically defined groupings behave very differently over time.[22] There are marked variations in the ways in which they start and cease to put themselves at risk of arrest and conviction (although that is not a feature that the cohort analysts consider as attentively as they should). More important, because it is a self-report study, a substantial survey of 10,000 people in England and Wales induced that some 60 per cent of active offenders were younger than 25 and 'many desisters' had relatively short criminal careers,[23] but 40 per cent of offenders were nevertheless over 25. And the qualitative analysis of offending, including unrecorded crime, suggests that behaviour may simply change from the more hazardous and exposed forms of offending to ones that are more circumspect. The work of Janet Foster, discussed below, shows that delinquents do not necessarily cease to break rules altogether on achieving maturity, but may instead start to break rules more *discreetly*. They may come off the streets, where they are the highly visible perpetrators of public-order and status offences, to enter the less visible world of the informal economy. In short, the scale or duration of crime and delinquency in the West should not be underestimated. Nor should some features of the lesser styles of offending be confused with the whole.

More recently, Elijah Anderson[24] has managed to move us somewhat further forward and out of this impasse in a masterly ethnographic account of black life in Philadelphia. There is a spectrum, he argues, of adherence to law. At one pole, there are predominantly religious families, often with a father in place, lawfully employed, aspiring towards a secure and law-abiding existence and struggling to exercise control over their children. Most of the people in his study awarded them moral authority although many claimed that their way of life was not actually practicable for them. At the other pole were those who achieved conspicuous monetary success through crime—principally drug dealing. The streets are hazardous for those growing up in black inner-city Philadelphia: they are marked by the ever-present threat of violence, robbery, and exploitation. A measure of security can be purchased only by acquiring

[20] *Home Office Statistical Bulletin*, 7/85.

[21] M. Wolfgang et al., *Delinquency in a Birth Cohort*; and D. West and D. Farrington, *Who Becomes Delinquent?*

[22] M. Ezell and L. Cohen, *Desisting from Crime: Continuity and Change in Long-term Crime Patterns of Serious Chronic Offenders*. The work is a statistically sophisticated secondary review and original analysis of patterns of youth offending. What it does fail to examine, however, is the utility of conviction data as a measure of criminality. After all, only 3 per cent of crimes in England and Wales result in conviction, and the vast bulk of offending passes with any record.

[23] T. Budd and C. Sharp, *Offending in England and Wales: First Results from the 2003 Crime and Justice Survey*, 8.

[24] E. Anderson, *Code of the Street: Decency, Violence, and the Moral Life of the Inner City*.

a reputation for physical prowess and attachment to a group of other young people who will defend or avenge one. It is dangerous to be unattached. Boys, especially, must work to gain entrance to those territorially-based groups and they do so by proving themselves as tough and streetwise. The dilemma for the sons of the conforming and aspiring families is that they are at risk if they venture out into the streets: they must either be imprisoned at home (as were Harriett Wilson's heavily chaperoned children[25]) or acquire some of the streets' colouring. They can become, in effect, the inhabitants of the two remotely-linked worlds of the law-abiding family and the law-violating street group; speaking two languages and appearing to subscribe to two cultures. They confront recurrent difficulties of traversing the boundaries and negotiating the contradictions between them. In this sense, the mother's cry 'he was always a good boy' may have considerable validity, but his goodness had necessarily to be contingent. For girls it was different. One of their chief difficulties was that they were obliged often to try to achieve social and economic success by attaching themselves to sexually predatory men who passed as financially secure, but were not, or who professed to be faithful and supportive, but were not.

One virtue of subcultural theories was that they seemed to lend themselves well to comparative work. The causes of delinquency that they specified were not just to be found in the USA. To varying degrees, they exist in all industrial, urban societies with democratic political institutions. For example, the murder rate for Britain is startlingly lower than that for the USA. This may be partly explained by the differential availability of hand guns (although Switzerland, with its citizen Army and widespread dispersal of guns, has the lowest rate of all[26]). With the possible exceptions of Glasgow and some groups of football supporters,[27] the violent fighting gang has not emerged as a phenomenon in Britain, though this is an increasingly contested issue. Three main structural and cultural differences may help explain this variation, all of which can in turn be related to the apparently stronger class allegiances that exist in Britain as compared with the USA. First, there used to be a much more moderate adherence in Britain to the theme of individual success or failure; second, there was a relative absence of minority group loyalties based on ethnicity that cut across class allegiances to any significant extent; and third, post-war 'affluence' was combined with relatively full and stable employment.

These points of difference have lost much of their force over the past two decades and there have been corresponding changes in crime and delinquency that may be partly attributed to this development. Officially recorded 'acquisitive crimes' rose in England and Wales by 40 per cent between 1987 and 1991 and 'acquisitive crimes' measured by crime surveys rose by 28 per cent,[28] only to start falling again from the mid-1990s.[29] Indeed, Simon Field of the Home Office Research and Planning Unit traced a

---

[25] See Chapter 9.   [26] M. Clinard, *Cities with Little Crime*.

[27] D. Robins, *We Hate Humans*; J. Patrick, *A Glasgow Gang Observed*.

[28] P. Mayhew and N. Maung, *Research Findings No. 2*, Home Office Research and Statistics Department, 4.

[29] The fall in officially recorded crime began in 1992 in England and Wales and continued thereafter. The fall in crime registered by the British Crime Survey began later, in 1995 and also continued thereafter, suggesting that the discrepancy was due in some measure to changes in police recording behaviour.

larger negative correlation between the volume of crimes against property and general patterns of consumption during much the same period: 'When people are increasing their spending very little—or even reducing it,' he wrote, 'property crime tends to grow relatively quickly, whereas during years when people are rapidly increasing their expenditure, property crime tends to grow less rapidly or even fall.'[30] To be sure, the interpretation of such official records does require caution. Much of the comparatively high rate of reported property crime in England and Wales could until quite recently be explained by a greater propensity to *report* rather than by a greater propensity to offend.[31]

Class identity as a variable which diminished the strain to anomie loomed large in Downes' observations of delinquency among a small number of adolescent boys in East London in the early 1960s and recurs in similar respects in Wilmott's study in Bethnal Green at much the same time.[32] 'Status frustration', 'alienation', and 'delinquent subculture' were concepts that did not seem to fit descriptions of boys involved intermittently in offences of the fighting/joy-riding/theft/vandalism variety. Typically, they were not members of structured delinquent gangs, with a marked sense of territory, leadership, hierarchy, and membership. Delinquency was a *fact* of life, but not a *way* of life. Educationally, their talk of school implied dissociation from its values rather than embitterment at academic failure. Occupationally, aspirations and expectations were pitched realistically low, consistent with their experience of a succession of 'dead-end' jobs. Early marriage and 'settling down' were already in view. In a negative sense, though, the theories could be regarded as validated since the conditions they held to be essential for the emergence of gang delinquency were largely absent. In a study carried out within a school in a comparable inner-city area, Hargreaves found that C and D stream boys engaged in behaviour analogous to that described by Albert Cohen, but of a milder 'delinquescent' character. Copying, cheating, messing, and rowdyism were the converse of the 'pupil' ideal, but in general fell short of full-blown delinquency.[33]

Elias and Scotson, in an oddly neglected book written at much the same period, unite Downes' theme of delinquency as a hedonistic response to the anomic strains of dull English life with Hargreaves' theme of delinquency as oppositional and diacritical. The delinquents whom they studied were 'outsiders', younger members of the loosely structured and discredited Estate which adjoined the more cohesive, established and virtuous Village of 'Winston Parva'. Their delinquency was rowdiness in cinemas and clubs, sexual misbehaviour, and public drinking. It was construed as part of the structured opposition between organized respectability and its symbiotic counterpart, organized disreputability. Elias and Scotson argued that the respectability of the Village *generated* the deviance of the Estate as part of the 'peculiar guerilla warfare waged almost incessantly between established sections . . . and socially produced outsider groups, in this case outsider groups of the younger generation'.[34]

[30] S. Field, *Trends in Crime and their Interpretation*, 5.
[31] P. Mayhew, *Residential Burglary: A Comparison of the United States, Canada and England and Wales*.
[32] D. Downes, *The Delinquent Solution*; P. Wilmott, *Adolescent Boys in East London*.
[33] D. Hargreaves, *Social Relations in a Secondary School*.
[34] N. Elias and J. Scotson, *The Established and the Outsiders*, 112.

The question that remains in the British context is to account for delinquency at all, given the rough correspondence that seemed to obtain between aspirations and expectations (although it must be noted that American ethnographic work also points to just such a correspondence in certain inner-city areas, with just the consequences that Downes and Hargreaves discerned[35]). It is at this point that Matza's theory seems to have most to offer. The most frequent reason quoted by the boys for their delinquency was boredom, a word that takes on additional meaning when used with reference to leisure—the one domain in which they have the opportunity to express their character through action. Because their fatalism about school and work is so entrenched, leisure assumes immense significance, not least when the expectation of action is met with the reality of 'nothing going on'. It is out of their response to this impasse that not only much delinquency, but also the successive styles of youth culture have emerged, particularly since the post-war employment boom for young workers led commercial interests to develop the lucrative 'teenage market'. Even so, for working-class adolescents in particular, leisure is too often a counterpart of work: a dreary 'caff', nowhere to go, too little cash for the 'good times'. In this context, delinquency is a repertoire of possibilities for the display of toughness, daring, and panache. The streets, soccer matches, the law itself provide the setting and raw material for action: delinquency is 'something happening'. The meanings and forms are immensely varied—from 'weird ideas' that emerge from hanging about 'doing nothing', to clashes between groups contriving different expressive styles, to more ambitious criminal or anti-social enterprises. 'One has to strip all the hub caps off every car in a parking ground, one has to wait until the last possible moment before dropping an object from a bridge onto the railway line, one has to paint a slogan on the opposite wall of the underground train tunnel.'[36] There are by now at least three linkages between delinquency and excitement. Delinquency is the means to buying excitement: the Round House boys bought the good times (pubs, girls, motors, pot) with the proceeds of the theft of car radios;[37] delinquency is the raw material of excitement (Matza's and Cusson's view[38]); and delinquency is a by-product of the pursuit of actions that are exciting in themselves (smashing milk bottles is Corrigan's example).[39] There seems no particular reason to regard these as self-cancelling alternatives: at different times and places, one option may be preferred to another. Indeed, Light and his colleagues, studying 100 young English car thieves, claimed that careers in 'taking without consent' typically started in the hedonism of stealing and fast driving but progressed in time to theft for gain, cars being stolen so that they could be sold whole or in parts.[40] There is similar evidence from Sullivan's American ethnographic work.[41] Many deviants change their offending over time as they become less agile and strong. Eventually perhaps, they will slow down so much that they will neither be able

---

[35] M. Sullivan, *'Getting Paid': Youth Crime and Work in the Inner City*, 116.
[36] S. Cohen, 'Directions for Research on Adolescent Group Violence and Vandalism', 337.
[37] H. Parker, *The View From the Boys.*   [38] M. Cusson, *Why Delinquency?*
[39] P. Corrigan, *Schooling the Smash Street Kids.*
[40] R. Light, C. Nee, and H. Ingham, *Car Theft: The Offender's Perspective.*
[41] M. Sullivan, *'Getting Paid': Youth Crime and Work in the Inner City*, 117.

to enjoy the physical exploit of crime nor keep up so well with their younger, more agile confederates.[42]

An affinity with strain theory is that excitement tends to be the 'taken-for-granted' goal of young male adolescents. Strain theorists tend to assume that this is only so in leisure because other valued goals have been denied them in school and at work. With the rise of forms of deviance among relatively privileged youth groups in the 1960s, such as drug-use among middle-class hippies and student 'violence', these theories lost some of their force. Labelling theory assumed greater plausibility.

Labelling theorists[43] do not particularly address themselves to the 'causes' of delinquency, since they are far more concerned to develop a missing dimension in previous theorizing: the impact of social reactions to deviance. The tradition from which labelling theory emerged, symbolic interactionism, supplied a number of insights which could only enrich analysis.

Becker, Lemert, Cicourel, and other theorists in the labelling tradition, broadly conceived, were the first to approach the social reaction to deviant behaviour as a *variable*, not a constant. They argued that the relationships that developed between deviants and social controllers are in themselves important influences that help to shape and transform deviant phenomena.[44] Dramatic analogies played a major part in the models of deviance and control that flowed from this perspective: the process of *becoming* deviant was conceived in terms of the gradual construction of a role and an identity that mirrored the conventional career. The early emphasis was on the amplificatory potential of social control for deviance: the agencies of the State could create far more deviance than would otherwise exist by criminalizing morally disturbing activities (for instance, certain forms of drug use); by mobilizing bias and unduly heavy penalties against groups low in power and status; by attributing quite spurious and stigmatizing features to deviant groups and so on. As Young stressed, the media in particular could be singled out as promoting stereotypical images of the deviant, which are then contrasted with a picture of 'normality' that is over-typical.[45] The result is to polarize society into a conforming majority and a deviant minority, a dynamic process that helps create a self-fulfilling prophecy, since those to whom deviance is attributed become both objectively and subjectively more at risk: they are subjected to forms of exclusion (from jobs, housing, recreation)[46] that worsen their situation and they are under pressure to collude with the majority view that they are 'essentially' deviant.[47]

British researchers have contributed strongly to this perspective. In Stan Cohen's study of the 'moral panic' induced by the Mods and Rockers conflicts in the mid-1960s we have a repository of the nuances of social control of at least one moment in British social history.[48] Loose stylistic associations were metaphorically transformed by the media into tightly knit gangs. Ideal-typical 'folk-devils' were created: the youth who offered to pay

---

[42] N. Shover, *Aging Criminals*.   [43] See Chapter 7.

[44] For references, see Chapter 7. For a comprehensive analysis of their work, see R. Ericson, *Criminal Reactions*.   [45] J. Young, 'Mass Media, Drugs and Deviance', 241.

[46] G. Marx, *Under Cover*, 126–7.   [47] D. Matza, *Becoming Deviant*, 179.

[48] S. Cohen, *Folk Devils and Moral Panics*. For a review of the concept of moral panic and its evolution, see the symposium in the *British Journal of Criminology*, 49:1, January 2009.

his fine by cheque was parodied as a symbol of youthful affluence, defiance, and indifference to authority. His actual inability to pay attracted less publicity. Even non-events
were news: towns 'held their breath' for invasions that did not materialize. Cohen argues
that the sensationalistic treatment of the initial events sensitized far more adolescents
on the fringes of the Mods and Rockers scene to a novel form of action than would have
been the case with more modest and realistic reportage. That emphasis on the impact of
the outsider's uncomprehending gaze has been revived to great effect recently by Katz
and his colleagues who claimed that 'gangs' (in America) are all too often a lazy and
misleading description imposed by criminologists who have failed systematically to consider the implications of their arguments. It is all too easy, they claimed, to invoke the
idea of gangs when more complicated and nebulous processes are at work.[49]

Work in this perspective carried out in the 1970s tended to ally it with class conflict
and culture conflict theories,[50] or with functional approaches.[51] All stress the inadequacy
of labelling theory alone to account for the phenomena concerned, but see it (as Becker
originally did) as addressing an essential dimension missing from previous theorizing.
Thus, Gill is concerned to trace the emergence of 'Luke Street' as a delinquency area from
the initial policy which allocated a cluster of larger than average, publicly owned houses
in one small neighbourhood to families already classified as 'problems'. These families
faced considerable difficulties owing to their large size, low incomes, and high levels of
unemployment. Adverse labelling impinged on the lives of the relatively large number of
adolescents who came of age together in this context in various cumulative ways. Coming
from the 'worst' area of Liverpool, they found even 'dead end' employment withheld; episodes of street delinquency were given wide press coverage which reinforced the stereotype; local youth clubs banned them; they felt they were subject to unusually fierce police
harassment. Gross exclusion fuelled a sense of local territoriality which in one episode,
on Bonfire Night, escalated into a running battle with the police. It is improbable that any
wider youth culture had very much to do with Luke Street delinquency.

For all its concern to avoid it, Gill's study still conveys a sense of determinism. It
is as if the fate of Luke Street was sealed the moment the Housing Authority decided
to allocate a critical mass of the housing to large, poor, families. The press, the police,
and the authorities in general closed the trap progressively over time. Lashing out was
the boys' only resource, apart from passively sinking into apathy. In another Liverpool
study of a contrasting form of delinquency 'on the move', the systematic pilfering of
car radios, Parker perhaps demonstrates most plainly the problems of applying the
concepts of 'culture' and 'subculture' to the explanation of delinquency.[52] This emerges
most of all because of the strengths of his observational work. The boys' 'conversation
culture' is depicted with immense sensitivity and skill. The rapport that Parker established allowed him to sustain his role for three years. He observed both major and
minor changes in the boys' views of themselves and the world. Yet no clear-cut picture
of their 'culture' emerges because their 'culture' is not clear-cut. Parker's methods are

[49] J. Katz and C. Jackson-Jacobs, 'The Criminologists' Gang'.
[50] S. Hall et al., *Policing the Crisis*; O. Gill, *Luke Street*.   [51] P. Marsh et al., *The Rules of Disorder*.
[52] H. Parker, *The View from the Boys*.

those of interactionism. He is alert to the qualities of improvisation, negotiation, and the genuine 'emergence' of new ways of defining the situation and moving on to different ways of handling it. But the boys' autonomy was bounded by the rules of the larger society and eventually they acceded to that power, after a calculated appraisal of the risks which was worthy of Bentham. Theoretically, the study shows affinities with strain theory (the 'good times' must be wrung from a penny-pinching society); with labelling theory (the subjective shift from a sense of apartness to a sense of alienation results from first-hand experience of the police and the courts); with control theory (the 'streetwise' involvement in trouble from early childhood and the eventual decision that the costs outweigh the benefits); and conflict theories (the 'iron cage' which ultimately clamps down on their horizons and life chances). It is because the nuances of meaning are so well conveyed that 'capturing' their culture seems a scholastic irrelevance.

Nevertheless, certain themes recur in different studies of boys engaged in alternative forms of trouble that seem to reaffirm the reality of subculture. In their study of soccer hooliganism, Marsh and his colleagues argue that such behaviour is basically a ritualized form of aggression ('aggro') which would only contingently escalate into real violence were it not for the disruption of group-controlled processes by outside agencies, particularly the police. In a particularly shrewd assessment of the dynamics of such hooliganism, they explain the fans' apparently 'schizoid' accounts of their behaviour in terms of a 'conspiracy'. Fans claim that those they oppose 'get their heads kicked in': but miraculously the boys so kicked are 'all right—usually anyway'.[53]

> In conspiring to construct a reality which seems to be at variance with their tacit knowledge of orderly and rule-governed action, fans are engaged in the active creation of excitement. For fans, regularity and safety are things to be avoided . . . What the soccer terraces offer is a chance to escape from the dreariness of the weekday world of work or school to something which is adventurous and stimulating. But in order to achieve the contrast it is necessary to construe, at least on one level, the soccer terraces as radically different from the weekday world.[54]

The media collude with the conspiracy. The police play a more complicated role, since the fans script them in to defuse a situation without loss of face to themselves. Should the police either over- or under-react, by implication, things go awry. This chimes extremely well with Matza's notion of delinquency as the 'manufacture of excitement'. In the case of soccer hooliganism, however, the delinquency is mainly a matter of rule-governed symbolization and fantasy. As Armstrong (1998) stresses in his anthropological account of 'the Blades', Sheffield United's self-styled hooligan following, the naming is taken from the club's and city's links with steel manufacturing, not the use of knives, which they see as the resort of cowards. In key respects, he agrees with Marsh's analysis: 'hooligan dramas are contextual, negotiated and improvised. . . For most people in Britain now there is no epic of poverty or war, for life is relatively safe. . . Modern-day consumer lifestyle increasingly lacks any sense of danger or ordeal and the problem then becomes one of transcending monotony'.[55] The 'risk society' is no longer

---

[53] P. Marsh et al., *The Rules of Disorder*, 82.   [54] P. Marsh et al., *The Rules of Disorder*, 97.
[55] G. Armstrong, *Football Hooligans: Knowing the Score*, 233, 296.

risqué and hooliganism somewhat redresses the balance, creating a ritualized and there-fore largely *non*-violent context for the display of the still-valued masculine attributes of daring, prowess, and panache. Interestingly, Tuchman[56] has shown how medieval warfare had many of the same qualities. The last thing many soldiers and mercenaries wanted was to be hurt or killed, the first priorities were loot and the establishment of character. Much military manoeuvring consequently actually took the form of armies wheeling about trying to avoid one another.

In like manner, and in a close-grained ethnography of youth groups and cultural styles in Hastings, a south coast British town, Shane Blackman (1995) showed how violent masculinity is far more contained and symbolic, erupting only rarely in actual combat.

> The mods' promenade of male solidarity was more significantly related to territo-rial responses as a youth cultural style than an expression of social class resistance. Their 'tough behaviour' did not in any sense become an anti-intellectualism: the mod boys pursued fighting and gaining qualifications with equal rigour. In school it was their potential for violence rather than the reality which formed the basis of their authority . . . [57]

For those averse to physical combat, the adrenalin rush can be sought in other scenes and leisure, if not leisurely, pursuits. Andrew Wilson[58] explored the experience of en-gagement with and disengagement from the Northern Soul scene of the 1970s. Two decades later, interviews with former followers of that scene testified to its long reach into middle age. The heady cocktail of music, dance, drugs, and what Shover termed 'life as party' did not, for the substantial majority, impinge on their life chances. They went on to become wage or salary earners and raised families. But the 'scene' remained their pivotal site of intense experience, group life, and heightened interaction. For a minority, that was too good to lose: they contrive to stay involved with the shifting scene well into their forties. For a minority of a minority, it was more fateful: already mired in problematic family backgrounds, the 'scene' was their route to crime, custody, and, in some cases, early death. What emerges is that, if this rare follow-through is any guide, involvement in youthful subcultures is immensely varied in its character and aftermath, neither all too ephemeral nor—for all except a very few—tragically consequential.

Culture conflict theories are based on the idea that the clash of conduct norms has a central role to play in the explanation of crime. Such a view was presented in suc-cinct form by Thorsten Sellin: 'If the conduct norms of a group are, with reference to a given life situation, inconsistent, or if two groups possess inconsistent norms, we may assume that the members of these various groups will individually reflect such group attitudes.'[59]

---

[56] B. Tuchman, *A Distant Mirror: The Calamitous Fourteenth Century.*
[57] S. Blackman, *Youth: Positions and Oppositions,* 254.
[58] A. Wilson, *Northern Soul: Music, Drugs and Subcultural Identity.*
[59] T. Sellin, 'Culture Conflict and Crime', in M. Wolfgang et al. (eds.), *The Sociology of Crime and Delinquency,* 228.

The most obvious conflicts of conduct norms arose in the process of migration to the USA of people from an immense variety of cultural backgrounds. As the process of acculturation developed, criminological interest shifted towards the cultural conflicts that arose from social structural sources and away from the issue of disparate geographical origins. The model could be adapted to explain aggressive delinquency by invoking the sheer magnitude of the cultural differences between the middle and working classes (without implying any necessary built-in antagonism, as do class conflict theories; and without implying that working-class adolescents are significantly influenced by middle-class culture, as do (some) strain theorists). They share with control theorists a definition of the dominant society as unable to gain any effective purchase on the 'hearts and minds' of the working class. They hold that working-class culture is profoundly lodged (in Miller's words) in a 'generations-old shaking-down process' born of industrialization and urbanization. As yet it is little affected by the changes and reforms which are so often heralded as the promoters of classlessness,[60] such as the 'Welfare State', the 'affluent society', and other alleged diversions from a distinctive class consciousness.

Miller's theory (in many ways the inheritance of Thrasher's portrait of the gang) simply argues that lower-class group delinquency, far from representing a 'counter-culture', is the direct, intensified expression of the dominant culture pattern of the lower-class community: 'a long-established, distinctively patterned tradition with an integrity of its own'. This culture comprises six 'focal concerns' to whose polarities each individual can, in principle, orient himself (or, rarely, herself) somewhat idiosyncratically. They are: trouble (the tension between law-abiding and law-violating behaviour); toughness (masculinity–effeminacy); smartness (sharp-wittedness–dull-wittedness); excitement (activity–passivity); fate (luck–being unlucky); autonomy (independence–dependency). For Miller, engagement with these 'concerns' tends to involve lower-class adolescents in a head-on clash with a dominant society whose legal code is underwritten by middle-class values. The delinquent gang intensifies such commitment, since its members are likely to be socialized in female-based households where little reliance is placed on the stability and earning power of the male. The gang helps resolve sex-role problems by providing a vehicle for the pursuit of masculine status and reassurance. Miller claims much empirical support for this theory, notably the high proportion of aggressive acts in street-corner groups that are intra-group, verbally expressive of his focal 'concerns' alone and rarely directed against middle-class or even adult targets: signs that ambivalence about status in those terms is negligible. Most delinquency is non-violent. Theft accounts for a far higher proportion than any kind of assault: such delinquency is, however, rare in itself. Violence, when it does occur, is a response to perceived insults and/or rejection by specific others, not a random outpouring of 'senseless' aggression. It is a source of group cohesion and an affirmation of group values, rather than a springboard for hostility against 'society', the 'adult world', or 'middle-class values'.

---

[60] W. Miller, 'Lower Class Culture' and in M. Wolfgang et al. (eds.), *The Sociology of Crime and Delinquency*, 267–76; and (with others) 'Aggression in a Boys' Street-corner Group'.

A similar type of explanation is afforded by Oscar Lewis' concept of the culture of poverty. Generated by the experience of poverty, this culture takes much the same form whatever the national or structural context.[61] Whether it is studied in Buenos Aires, Glasgow, or New York, the same combination of values is observed: it includes, *inter alia*, a refusal, amounting to inability, to defer gratification; a stress on *machismo* or the primacy accorded the sexual prowess of the male; and a profound fatalism about the possibility of influencing events. Violence, particularly as an outcome of the impugning of masculinity and honour, finds fertile soil in such values. Adherence to this culture alone would vitiate any prospect of betterment.

There are several counterparts of these theories. Indeed, the theme of masculine consciousness as a legitimation of crime and delinquency is a recurrent one from the work of the Chicago School onwards. The ideas of John Mays in Liverpool are akin to those of Miller. John McVicar describes 'crude machismatic values' as central to his boyhood. He claims that it was not material gain but prowess which attracted him to the delinquent subculture.[62] Similarly Paul Willis discerns, throughout the culture of motorbike boys, a concern with the elaboration of masculine imagery, an imagery that 'owed nothing to the conventional notion of the healthy masculine life. . . Valued tenets of this code. . . such as impudence before authority, domination of women, humiliation of the weaker, aggression towards the different, would be abhorrent to traditional proponents of honour and labelled criminal by agents of social control'.[63] In early rock and roll, they found a musical form that corresponded perfectly to their self-image. The motorbike was culturally appropriated rather than just mechanically used. Phillipe Bourgois[64] employed the theme to explain domestic violence in New York City, arguing that *Latino* men resented being overshadowed by socially and economically more successful *Latina* women and resorted to violence crudely to reassert their superiority and keep women in their proper place. And, in his analysis of murder in Australia, Ken Polk[65] claimed that insult, respect, and face were key dimensions of a violent culture of honour amongst lower-class males.

It follows that what may be true is that male sensitivities about shame and the preservation of respect are particularly acute where the greatest humiliations are experienced, that those humiliations tend to be found amongst the poorest and most devalued strata of men, and that the more unequal a society becomes, the greater are the hurts and degradations that are undergone. Wilkinson and Pickett put it that:

---

[61] O. Lewis, *Five Families: Mexican Case Studies in the Culture of Poverty*; also *The Children of Sanchez* and *La Vida: A Puerto Rican Family in the Culture of Poverty*. In his introduction to *La Vida*, he made it plain that poverty and the 'culture of poverty' are not mutually inclusive terms. For example, the Jews of Eastern Europe were very poor, but their literacy and religion insulated them from the culture of poverty. However, despite some disclaimers on both parts, the culture of poverty corresponds closely with Liebow's observations of one group of the urban poor in the USA (E. Liebow, *Tally's Corner: Negro Street-corner Men in Washington, D.C.*). For a discussion, see C. Valentine, *Culture and Poverty*. For a criminological statement of much the same position, see M. Wolfgang and F. Ferracutti, *The Subculture of Violence*.

[62] J. Mays, *Growing Up in the City*; J. McVicar, *McVicar by Himself*.

[63] P. Willis, *Profane Culture*, 29–30. There is an affinity between Willis' stress on the creativity of subordinate cultures and Karl Mannheim's distinction between 'ideology' as expressing superordinate class interest and 'utopias' as emanating only from the dispossessed (K. Mannheim, *Ideology and Utopia*).

[64] P. Bourgois, 'In Search of Masculinity'.   [65] K. Polk, *When Men Kill: Scenarios of Masculine Violence*.

Reckless, even violent behaviour comes from young men at the bottom of society, deprived of all markers of status, who must struggle to maintain face and what little status they have, often reacting explosively when it is threatened . . . Increased inequality ups the stakes in the competition for status: status matters even more.[66]

Interestingly, it was Elias' argument[67] that honour has largely been displaced by shame in the West that allowed him and others, such as Leyton,[68] to explain the decreasing rates of homicide over the last 200 years.

There are naturally a host of criticisms that have been directed against the conception of working-class male culture propounded by Miller and others. Some have held that it is highly dubious to attribute the toughness and defiance of authority found among the 'roughest' communities to the working class in general. However, it must be remembered that part of that criticism may flow from a misreading of Miller. Miller had written about 'lower-class culture' and, in American speech and possibly in American sociology, the lower class is *not* the same as the working class, but a small, *lumpenproletarian*, chiefly black, segment of it.

There is also an element of tautology in reading behaviour culturally. Nevertheless, scientifically unsatisfying as they may be, these approaches do 'resonate' with some aspects of the more serious forms of violence in a way that the more abstract Mertonian theories do not. *Class conflict* theories basically apply much the same set of ideas to the explanation of crime and delinquency as do other theorists; but they do so within a broad Marxian framework which takes it as an axiom that class conflict is inevitable in capitalist societies and that the dynamics of such conflict must be related to issues of deviance and control. This does not necessarily mean that delinquency is simply 'decoded' as a symptom of class warfare; or that delinquents are seen as fighting 'the system', albeit in a regressive way. But it does mean that connections are sought between the structural 'contradictions' of capitalist societies and the forms assumed by deviance and control.

The concept of subculture, for example, has been applied by Phil Cohen to innovations in youth culture.[69] Those innovations are seen to emerge where the contradictions of capitalist political economy work their chief effects—in working-class neighbourhoods. Post-war changes in housing, transport, and technology have, despite some gains in affluence, served to fragment working-class communities. The costs of the faltering of the machinery of prosperity in the 1970s and 1980s fell quite disproportionately on working-class youth and on immigrant minorities. The inability of the 'parent' working-class generation to cope with these problems means that they were refracted, already freighted with associations of class defeat, onto the young. Their response to the resultant family tensions, fragmented community, and economic insecurity was necessarily symbolic. It was to create a succession of subcultural styles which 'express and resolve, albeit "magically", the contradictions which remain hidden or unresolved in the parent culture'. Thus, for example, the Mod style could be

---

[66] R. Wilkinson and K. Pickett, *The Spirit Level: Why More Equal Societies Almost Always Do Better*, 314.
[67] N. Elias, *The Civilizing Process*.   [68] E. Leyton, *Men of Blood: Murder in Modern England*.
[69] P. Cohen, 'Working Class Youth Cultures in East London'.

interpreted as an 'attempt to realize, *but in an imaginary relation*, the conditions of existence of the socially mobile white-collar worker. While their argot and ritual forms stressed many of the values of their parent [i.e. working-class] culture, their dress and music reflected the hedonistic image of the affluent consumer'.[70] The skinhead style was an attempt to recover and assert the traits associated with hard manual labour under threat from technological change. And if there is a certain uniform pattern to the rise and fall of successive youth subcultures this is because 'revolts into style'[71] can only ever retranscribe and not resolve in any structural sense, the set of contradictions that gives rise to them.

Stuart Hall and his colleagues have applied much the same model to the issue of youth subcultures in general and to middle-class expressive movements in particular, since the war.[72] The rise of the hippy 'counter-culture' is attributed to the growing incompatibility between the traditional puritan ethic and the new-found affluence and consumerism of the expanding middle class. The breakdown of traditional middle-class constraints began from *within* the dominant class. It was then transformed and pushed to expressive lengths, in both the hippy and student protest movements. So lodged, it was perceived as a threat to social order. The authors are aware of the pitfalls of giving too ideological a reading to youthful styles, since 'disaffiliation' is frequently short-lived and some phenomena are so ephemeral that it strains credulity to invest them with much symbolic significance. While that awareness is only parenthetic and class conflict approaches are as likely to 'over-predict' as strain and culture conflict theories, there are some safeguards in the ethnographic work which the Birmingham School has evolved.

In his study of 'how working-class kids get working class jobs', Willis tackled a subject that is almost worn out by the sociological repetition of the observation that schooling is perceived by such youths as a massive irrelevancy. His work gained a wealth of insight by combining interviews and observations of a small group of boys in a typical comprehensive school during their last year at school and first year in work. What they revealed above all was their clear sense of their limited life-chances in the industrial division of labour and the implications of that sense for their resistance to schooling. Their own hidden curriculum was a timetable of 'skiving', 'dossing', and 'having a laff', all forms of escape from the tedium of the everyday round. Their culture stressed the perennial themes of 'symbolic and physical violence, rough presence and the pressures of a certain kind of masculinity'.[73] 'Sexism' and 'racism' were part of the price to be paid for the accomplishment of a form of masculine self-image which rendered the prospect of routine manual work palatable and which sets off the alternative major grouping in the school, the 'ear'oles' who were destined for superior skilled manual or technical jobs, as cowed conformists. Willis undercut the moral condemnation of their culture by making the profound point that only such a willed appropriation of labouring saved a liberal society from forced labour.

[70] P. Cohen, 'Working Class Youth Cultures in East London', 23–4.
[71] G. Melly, *Revolt Into Style*.
[72] S. Hall et al. (eds.), *Resistance through Ritual*.
[73] P. Willis, *Learning to Labour*, 36. The colloquialisms roughly translate as work-dodging, cat-napping, and fooling about.

Willis uses the terms 'culture' and 'counter-culture' in a far more 'dialectical' sense than occurs even in the work of most other class conflict theorists. His main concern is to convey the 'profane creativity' of subordinate cultures as the 'only route for radical cultural change'.[74] By implication, earlier approaches define cultures as 'simply layers of padding between human beings and unpleasantness'.[75] The active appropriation and reworking of cultural items junked by capitalist commodity fetishism can provide the materials for at least temporary challenges to the cultural dominance of the bourgeoisie. Willis' analysis of the cultures of motorbike boys and hippies and Hebdige's of Punks, share a view of profane culture as a refusal to be silenced by superior cultural forces.[76] In his study of the school counter-culture and shop-floor cultures, Willis goes further. He acknowledges that 'it would be wrong to impute to "the lads" individually any critique or analytic motive', yet 'their collective culture shows both a responsiveness to the uniqueness of human labour power and in its own way constitutes an attempt to defeat a certain ideological definition of it'.[77] Though he fights shy of using the term 'alienation'[78] he is in effect applying Marx's original use of that term to the realm of cultural production. Capitalism ultimately determines the conditions whereby the limited 'penetrations' the lads collectively make into the mysteries of bourgeois ideology become a weapon for their own willed subordination. They in no sense colluded, or merely collided, with bourgeois ideology. They fashioned their own independent critique of the system—the higher values placed on manual labour in particular—the logic of which was their eventual entrapment in labouring. The system won, though a certain autonomy at the cultural level was salvaged.

Corrigan adds a historical dimension to the seeming paradox that the long struggle to win the right to schooling for working-class children is so largely wasted on the supposed beneficiaries. We should not be too surprised about the result, he argues, in view of the fact that what has been won is the right to a form of schooling originally *imposed on* the working class (the term used by Forster was 'gentling the masses') in a struggle that robbed them of their own emergent educational institutions. Corrigan also proposed a different interpretation of Matza's idea that much street delinquency is the 'manufacture of excitement' in a context of 'nothing going on'. The elaboration of 'weird ideas' as a feature of apparently 'doing nothing' involves frequent rule-breaking. But the 'rules are not broken *specifically because they are rules*; rules are broken for the most part as a by-product of the flow of activity engaged in by the boys'.[79] His work compares well with Jack Katz's phenomenology of street crime in America and Cusson's later analysis of delinquent motives in Canada. To Katz, violent crime has its own hedonistic and sensual aesthetics centred on excitement. Skinheads, for instance, take violence to have 'a seductively glorious. . . significance. . . .Being in this world of experience is not simply a matter of detailing posture and using violence to raise the specter of terror. It is also a contingent sensual involvement'.[80] So too with Cusson's subjects. The pursuit of crime, he argued, seems to be linked with four broad sets of

---

[74] P. Willis, *Profane Culture*, 1.   [75] P. Willis, *Learning to Labour*, 52.
[76] R. Hebdige, *Subculture: The Meaning of Style.*   [77] P. Willis, *Learning to Labour*, 132.
[78] P. Willis, *Learning to Labour*, 143, n. 22.   [79] P. Corrigan, *Schooling the Smash Street Kids*, 140.
[80] J. Katz, *Seductions of Crime*, 128, 139.

goals: those related to action (which include playfulness and excitement), appropriation, aggression, and domination. Action itself 'is the commission of crime to expend energy and to get the sensation of living intensely'.[81] But in all cases, the class context both limits and subverts autonomy.

The most recent development along these lines, the work of 'cultural criminologists', addresses these themes afresh. Hayward argues that 'hyper consumerism. . . is contributing to the crime problem in ways that are new and qualitatively different from those expressed in classical strain theory . . . '.[82] The over-reliance is on consumption rather than production for, in particular, young people's very sense of identity promotes expectations of claims to key symbolic goods. The market increasingly swamps all competing values with its own credo of force-feeding 'hedonic consumerism'. This chimes well with Elizabeth Burney's[83] and Simon Hallsworth's[84] studies of youths engaging in street robbery, not for survival, or even profit, but for the cash to buy the latest fashion accessories with the most prized logos, vital for 'street cred'. Symbols of criminality and deviance are fed into marketing, even mainstream advertising, which trade on defiant images of violence, pillage, and drug dealing.[85] Moreover, hemmed in by the 'hyper-banalization' of over-regulation, excluded from ever greater swathes of public and private space (from shopping malls to schools), the most comprehensively demonized youth are goaded into manufacturing excitement by conjuring up 'carnivals of crime'.[86] These analyses, whatever their claims, do not logically break with strain theories and allied approaches, but seek to relate them anew to the changed social and economic conditions of late modernity.

Other British studies are centred on the subcultural reproduction of crime and deviance, but they are based on a very different foundation of theory, being more redolent of the Chicago School in their emphasis on the embedded and normal character of rule-breaking in urban settings. Deviation is not necessarily taken to be a spirited or half-spirited gesture of refusal, frustration, or anger at capitalism and its structured deprivations. It is, instead, part of the fabric of everyday life, transmitted uneventfully as a tradition in certain working-class communities (although, it must be said that tradition is not without its problems for victims and others living nearby). Bottoms, Mawby, and Xanthos wrote about how in one Sheffield working-class estate:

> criminality was intimately interwoven with the social life of the estate. Dominant features of the social life of the estate . . . were the typically long tenancies; the fact that many had grown up on the estate and absorbed its way of life; and the closely interlocking family networks, especially in south-east Gardenia. Where, as in the south-east of the estate, there is a particularly high proportion of 'rough' families, this group of social features produces a distinctive way of life which is obviously related to the mainstream working-class culture, yet which differs somewhat from it: in short a *subculture* . . . [One] feature of the subculture

---

[81] M. Cusson, *Why Delinquency?*, 32.

[82] K. Hayward, *City Limits: Crime, Consumer Culture, and the Urban Experience*, 86; S. Hall and S. Winlow, *Criminal Identities and Consumer Culture*.

[83] E. Burney, *Putting Street Crime in its Place*.   [84] S. Hallsworth, *Street Crime*.

[85] See also S. Blackman, *Chilling Out*.

[86] M. Presdee, *Cultural Criminology and the Carnival of Crime*.

was that criminality was in some circumstances tolerated—so many or most members of the subculture (including women) were occasional offenders; some were career criminals, consistently seeking out opportunities for . . . material gains through criminal activities; and all accepted that some activities (such as dad 'fixing' the electric meter or mum buying a carpet 'very cheaply' off someone in a pub) were part of the normal pattern of life.[87]

Ethnographic studies have illuminated the processes buttressing such a 'normal pattern of life'. Walklate and Evans'[88] study of a stable, high crime area in Salford in the north of England, demonstrated how criminality imposed organization on social relations and where insiders claimed that they felt protected, and less fearful, because they knew local offenders and did not suffer from their predations. Consider too Janet Foster's *Villains*, a book that began life as a study of a commonplace south-east London neighbourhood, a neighbourhood not taken to be especially notorious for its criminality. Foster came eventually to focus on '"street-wise" teenagers. . . [who] were not professional criminals but mundane and petty offenders, who graduated from a highly visible and public juvenile street life to the private, institutionalized exploitation of black economy outlets as adults'.[89] One of her chief conclusions was how very mundane, orderly, and conventional those teenagers' delinquency could be. It fitted into the structure of local life. Members of each generation seemed to progress quite smoothly from public, expressive rule-breaking to a more secure, inconspicuous, and lucrative participation in the informal economy. Members of each generation were ambivalent about the deviance of people younger than themselves, not only condoning their delinquencies (after all, they said, they had done very much the same when they were young) but also subjecting them to mild criticism (it was not as if those activities were really laudable). Ambivalence was framed by something of a working consensus about the limits of tolerable rule-breaking (gross violence, for instance, was considered to be quite impermissible) and delinquency was confined and regulated informally in consequence.

Dick Hobbs pursued a like theme by exploring the connections between the individualistic, entrepreneurial world of the working class in the informal economy of the East End of London.[90] Hobbs' subjects were forever ' "duckin' and divin', wheelin' and dealin"' beyond and around the borders of legality, searching for the good deal, the market opportunity, and the clever score. Theirs was also a shadow criminal tradition of some antiquity, a tradition that mirrored the East End's long-standing provision of personal services and goods to the City of London further to the west and it was not imbued with a marked spirit of resistance, refusal, or frustration. Indeed, it was not perhaps so very different from that of the cony catchers or confidence tricksters and thieves of Elizabethan and Jacobean London. Ben Jonson would certainly have recognized the rueful, wily, instrumental, witty people moving through Dick Hobbs' pages.

---

[87] A. Bottoms, R. Mawby, and P. Xanthos, 'A Tale of Two Estates', in D. Downes (ed.), *Crime and the City*, 57.
[88] S. Walklate and K. Evans, *Zero Tolerance or Community Tolerance*.
[89] J. Foster, *Villains: Crime and Community in the Inner City*, 2.
[90] D. Hobbs, *Doing the Business*; see also D. Hobbs, *Lush Life: Constructing Organised Crime in the UK*.

Crime and the Labour Market: The 'New Underclass' Thesis and After

The 1980s in Britain and the USA proved to be a decade of the 'New Right' which climaxed in the collapse of the State socialist regimes of the USSR and Eastern Europe. A domestic version of that collapse in Britain was the defeat of organized labour and the substantial diminution of the power of left-wing local authorities. The return to a 'free-market' economy gave impetus to the already strong trend of what has been called a 'jobless growth' born of the new information technologies. Unemployment, particularly male unemployment, grew in Britain from some 5 per cent in 1979 to 14 per cent in 1983. For women it rose less sharply, from 3 to just under 6 per cent, reflecting the steady rise in women's participation in the labour force compared with that of men, especially in part-time work.[91] Long-term unemployment among men emerged as a central feature of this trend. In the worst-hit areas, unemployment rates among young males reached between 80 and 90 per cent.

In terms of subcultural theories of crime and delinquency, this was a recipe for anomie, and so it proved, although unevenly in time and space. In the worst afflicted neighbourhoods a 'crisis of masculinity'[92] was discerned, in which working-class youths with no apparent hope of gaining manhood in the traditional breadwinner role sought fulfilment in the manufacture of excitement. Forms of delinquency were evolved which transcended the intermittent and the mundane: 'steaming' brought the force of numbers to bear for robbery and theft in crowds and shops; 'hotting' meant bravura displays of racing stolen cars around local estates; and 'ram-raiding' entailed smashing stolen vehicles into shops or even houses as a method of gaining forcible entry. Official crime rates doubled over the 1979 to 1992 period, most dramatically rising by 40 per cent in the three years between 1989 and 1992, although the findings of victim surveys of households would halve that rate of increase, only to mirror a fall from the latter half of the 1990s onwards. More surprising was that public anxiety mounted with the rise but failed to decline in its wake, most plausibly because the fear of crime came to be fuelled as a major component of the 'war' against crime and anti-social behaviour waged intensively by the New Labour Governments 1997–2010.[93]

The most convincing analysis of the link between unemployment and crime, particularly property crime, has been supplied by Wells and Dickinson. Allowing for a time lag between movements in the business cycle and changes in the crime rate, they demonstrated with great success that there is a decline in property crime during years of economic recovery and a rise during recession.[94] More surprisingly, perhaps, although on grounds quite consistent with their beliefs about individual moral responsibility, successive Conservative Governments resisted the view that crime and unemployment trends were connected. Lack of personal morality, inadequate discipline in the

[91] J. Hills, *The Future of Welfare: A Guide to the Debate*, 32–3.
[92] B. Campbell, *Goliath: Britain's Dangerous Places*.
[93] See esp. R. Reiner, *Law and Order: An Honest Citizen's Guide to Crime and Control*.
[94] J. Wells, 'Crime and Unemployment'; and D. Dickinson, *Crime and Unemployment*.

home and school, and increased opportunity were officially cited as the reasons for the growth of crime. A more pronounced theory about how these attributes derive from a new 'underclass' born of welfare dependency was proposed by Murray[95] in the USA. Wilson[96] retorted that the roots of the 'underclass' are to be discovered in economic inequalities, most markedly amongst the black populations of the inner cities. In England, Dennis and Erdos, arguing from within 'ethical socialism', contested the 'underclass' thesis and contended that rising lawlessness was explicable only in terms of the decline of the traditional family: the 'anomie of fatherlessness' rather than of unemployment.[97] They put this question: 'Which exponent of the view that unemployment in itself is a principal cause of contemporary crime levels would be prepared to maintain. . . that if the rate of unemployment were to fall to the level of the 1960s, the crime rate would fall to the level of the 1960s?'[98] Ironically, if Crime Survey data are to be believed, it has now fallen to the level of 1981.

In this welter of assertion and counter-assertion, the exclusivity of the focus on employment or on single parenthood is the most striking trait. In an outstanding attempt to rethink the complex issues and evidence involved, Elliott Currie[99] argued that false antitheses bedevilled analysis. First, economic trends and inequalities affect not only employment opportunities but also destabilize communities and families. Second, under-employment may be little better than unemployment as a source of livelihood sufficient to support a family and to experience an active sense of citizenship. Dennis and Erdos would undoubtedly reply that in the inter-war period high rates of unemployment left community and family frameworks relatively unimpaired. Any job was welcomed as better than none. However, although rates of crime were indeed far lower in that period than now, they did double in the 1920s and 1930s. As Currie remarked, the crime rate would have arguably been higher in the USA but for the public-works job-creation schemes of the 'New Deal', a factor forgotten by those who look back on the 1930s as a proof that economic depression and crime need not be linked. Moreover, a basic component of anomie theory, the long revolution of rising expectations, interacts with the changing meaning of joblessness in the late twentieth century to produce a new moral calculus. In the 1930s, however scarring the experience of unemployment, the shared hope was that jobs were being withheld and would reappear when times and governments changed.[100] The communal sense of outrage was well-conveyed by one of the most celebrated banners of the 1930s hunger marches: 'Jarrow—the town that was murdered'. In the wake of automation, the prospect of 'jobless growth' seemed to deny even that hope. As Lea and Young argued, 'The first Industrial Revolution involved the exploitation of labour by capital. The second Industrial Revolution involves the emancipation of capital from labour.'[101] Rising aspirations of consumption combined with

[95] C. Murray, *Losing Ground: American Social Policy, 1950–80.*
[96] W. Wilson, *The Truly Disadvantaged: The Inner City, The Underclass and Public Policy.*
[97] N. Dennis and G. Erdos, *Families without Fatherhood*, 102.
[98] N. Dennis and G. Erdos, *Families without Fatherhood*, 88.
[99] E. Currie, *Confronting Crime: An American Challenge.*
[100] H. Mannheim, *Social Aspects of Crime between the Wars.*
[101] J. Lea and J. Young, *What is to be Done about Law and Order?*

falling expectations of productive employment lead to a particularly corrosive sense of exclusion.[102] Young's striking metaphor for this intensification of cultural inclusion and structural exclusion is 'bulimic culture', a process of force-fed ingestion followed by compulsive expulsion.[103]

The fate of Detroit over the past three decades shows the scale and complexity of the problems involved. Fine argued:

> The declining economy had its effect on the quality of life in the city . . . Detroit as of 1987 had the second highest infant mortality rate in the nation, about 65 per cent of its families were single parent households . . . Violent crime was of special concern to Detroiters, the per capita homicide rate being 3 times higher in 1987 than in 1967 and higher than that of any other city . . . Were the Detroit of the late 1980s to return to the conditions prevailing in the city of 1967 . . . it would be hailed as a remarkable and happy achievement. And yet it was in 1967, not 1987, that Detroit experienced its great riot. How is one to explain this seeming anomaly?

Fine's answer is that, despite some positive changes (the emergence of a black leadership in city government and an integrated police force), the mood of Detroit blacks was:

> one of despair rather than hope . . . The rioting of 1967 was born of hope, not of despair, the hope that improvement would follow the disorder in the streets . . . the 'inescapable reality', wrote Barbara Stanton, was that there was 'far more destruction and violence in Detroit in 1987 than in 1967 . . . It is as if the riot had never ended, but goes on in slow motion. Instead of a single stupendous explosion, there is a steady, relentless corrosion.'[104]

The evidence in Britain and the USA tends to support Currie's re-analysis of trends in crime and unemployment. Rising youth unemployment in the early 1980s was followed by the spread of 'hard' drug use in the most deprived areas in Britain. In a key English study of one area of Merseyside, a 'new to crime' group was identified as extensively involved in much higher rates of property crime to finance their drug use.[105] Rates of opioid use correlated strongly with rates of unemployment. Pearson[106] portrayed the life of heroin users as a way of filling the void created by joblessness. Important American studies have examined how the quality of work and under-employment vie with unemployment as progenitors of crime. In a rare study utilizing both variables,[107] unemployment was found to be most strongly associated with high juvenile (14–17) arrest rates, but under-employment (as measured by poor pay and hours) with high young-adult (18–24) arrest rates. Against the view that arrest rates reflect police numbers rather than criminal activity,[108] one study based on victim survey data found that

---

[102] It is interesting that, in an ethnographic study of American young men, McLeod found that blacks were less delinquent, in part, because they perceived themselves to be on a rising curve of prosperity, whilst whites were more delinquent because they thought themselves to be in decline as a group. J. MacLeod, *Ain't No Makin' It*.

[103] J. Young, *The Exclusive Society*.   [104] S. Fine, *Violence in the Modern City*, 459, 461, 462–3.

[105] H. Parker, K. Batx, and R. Newcombe, *Living with Heroin*.

[106] G. Pearson, *The New Heroin Users*.

[107] E. Allan and D. Steffensmeier, 'Youth, Underemployment and Property Crime: Differential Effects of Job Availability and Job Quality on Juvenile and Young Adult Arrest Rates'.

[108] R. Carr-Hill and N. Stern, *Crime, the Police and Criminal Statistics*.

the probability of victimization from burglary and theft increased significantly with the rate of local unemployment.[109] The exigencies of street life have been found sharply to increase the engagement of dropout and homeless youth in property crime.[110] Impressive ethnographic work in three contrasting Brooklyn neighbourhoods established the links between access to primary labour-market jobs and relatively petty and short-lived delinquency, on the one hand, and restriction to secondary labour-market job networks and more serious offending, on the other.[111] In the later 1990s and 2000s, as unemployment declined again in the UK and the USA and there was a move to mass imprisonment in the USA that accelerated the formally-recorded drop in unemployment, crime rates themselves began again to fall. Much was attributed to changes in policing and in fashions of drug use, but it is tempting simply to assume that employment is an antidote to youthful crime.

On the other hand, as Wilkinson has argued, crime reductions could prove all too ephemeral if extremes of inequality persist or increase:

> In the developed world, as much as half the variation in population health, in homicide rates and in social cohesion appear to be due to income inequality alone. . . . Nor is this picture based on an unrealistic contrast between the levels of inequality common in modern societies and some unreachable level of total equality. Rather, the picture reflects the importance of the relatively small differences in inequality between US states or between the developed market democracies.[112]

The work of McAuley[113] on a bleak Midlands estate shows how the crime-drugs nexus fills the vacuum created by de-industrialization. And Winlow's study[114] of the changing criminal opportunity structures of north-east England show the rise of entrepreneurial alongside surviving craft and traditional petty crime, with masculinity traded in 'bouncing' not ship-building.

Hobbs et al. present a consummate analysis of how changes in political economy connect with apparently disparate trends in violence and disorder on the streets. In the wake of de-industrialization, local authorities in the worst affected cities and towns received little help from central government in making good the loss of industrial revenue. As the day-time economy based on production foundered, they were encouraged to exploit the night-time economy based on consumption. The twin trends of 'marketization' and 'de-regulation', begun by the Tory Governments of the 1980s and 1990s, came to be further pursued into the twenty-first century by New Labour.

> Following a decade of rapid expansion within its leisure infrastructure . . . Manchester City Centre now attracts crowds of up to 100,000 people on Friday and Saturday evenings. A liberal estimate is that approximately thirty to forty [police] officers are engaged on

[109] R. Sampson and J. Woolredge, 'Linking the Micro and Macro Levels of Lifestyle—Routine Activity and Opportunity Models of Predatory Victimization'.

[110] J. Hagan and B. McCarthy, 'Streetlife and Delinquency'.

[111] R. McGahey, 'Economic Conditions, Neighborhood Organization and Urban Crime', in A. Reiss and M. Tonry (eds.), *Communities and Crime*; M. Sullivan, *'Getting Paid': Youth Crime and Work in the Inner City*.

[112] R. Wilkinson, *Mind the Gap: Hierarchies, Health and Human Evolution*, 64.

[113] R. McAuley, 'The Enemy Within: Economic Marginalisation and the Impact of Crime on Young Adults'.   [114] S. Winlow, *Badfellas: Crime, Tradition and New Masculinities*.

public order duties at these times, whilst the crowds are simultaneously controlled by an estimated 1,000 bouncers working per night. Similar comparisons can be drawn in towns and cities throughout the UK . . . This 'honey-pot' effect facilitates the creation of social environments in which aggressive hedonism and disorder become the norm. In such ways, the market-led destruction of diversity serves to fuel the gradual atrophy of 'democrati-cally accessible' night-time public space . . . *In the night-time economy, locations that are 'bad' for crime and disorder are invariably 'good' for business.*[115]

The night-time economy, far from being a panoply of diverse recreational services, has seen traditional pubs, cafés, and restaurants driven out by novel, often vast, super-pubs and clubs and fast-food outlets whose profits derive from a cult of quick-fire 'vertical' drinking of sedulously-marketed alcohol. Currently, in the UK, concern about drink-fuelled disorder centres around the legalization of 24-hour opening times. However, the key move towards opening up the night-time frontier to a licensing free-for-all had already taken place.[116]

Since then, licensing has been transferred to local authorities, themselves complicit in weakening constraints against whatever expansion the 'market' will bear. Predicting more violence and disorder from this point is '. . . hardly a matter of "rocket science". . . When the activity levels of an intoxicated night-time consumer base increase, . . . more crime and disorder will be generated in the streets and public places of our night-time leisure zones'.[117]

As cities also compete for the marketing of corporate conferences and tourism, such rising violence and disorder will be met by tougher policing and more punitive sen-tencing. Yet as the above analysis makes clear, the police may be hopelessly swamped at peak times and the deficit in democratic policing is met by the stopgap of the growing numbers of bouncers, without whom clubs and pubs in the key leisure zones simply cannot function, let alone gain and renew licences to trade. While Hobbs et al. are keen to avoid scapegoating bouncers for their often marked associations with illicit drug dealing, organized crime, and 'protection', and while bouncers are increasingly subject to modes of professionalized training, and certification, their growth as a form of quasi- but unaccountable policing cedes an important aspect of the Weberian defi-nition of the rule of law in modern societies: the State's monopolization of legitimate violence. Although many clubs and bouncers operate to regulate rather than propagate deviance,[118] their ambience is still contrived to stimulate a transgressive aura, with displays of 'face', 'respect', and the more *macho* masculine profiles a recipe for descents into violence. This makes the process of deregulating the night-time economy an all too costly drain on social capital, as well as a route to a late modern version of Hogarth's Gin Lane, and it may now be nearing the limits of what seemed at one point to be an inexorable logic of growth. One of the authors of *Bouncers*, Phil Hadfield,[119] remained behind in the night-time economy to document how drinking establishments were to

---

[115] D. Hobbs et al., *Bouncers: Violence and Governance in the Night-time Economy*, 43, 247–8.

[116] D. Hobbs et al., *Bouncers: Violence and Governance in the Night-time Economy*, 248–9, italics added.

[117] D. Hobbs et al., *Bouncers: Violence and Governance in the Night-time Economy*, 41.

[118] See on this point in particular, D. Silverstone, *Night Clubbing*.

[119] P. Hadfield, *Bar Wars: Contesting the Night in Contemporary British Cities*.

be designed and managed not only to maximize the sale of alcohol but also to regulate drinking behaviour; how the police and informed outsiders came in time to argue that such concentrations were not conducive to public order and how they began to contest licensing applications. His conclusions are mildly pessimistic, the police and councils being out-gunned by those who champion deregulation, but it is noteworthy that challenges are now being presented.

Some of these new studies have revived, extended, and strengthened the 'blocked opportunities' approach associated most distinctively with the subcultural theory of Cloward and Ohlin. It should be stressed that they are not theories linking crime to sheer deprivation or working-class culture or, indeed, to an 'underclass'. They view the most serious and pervasive forms of crime and delinquency as the consequence of a combination of complex experiences born of relative deprivation in a highly competitive, increasingly fragmented social order (and see Karmen for an analysis of the variable impact of economic and employment factors on criminality, and on murder in particular, in the highly differentiated population of New York City[120]). Those most at risk of becoming what Cohen and Robins (1978)[121] termed 'careering delinquents' are the politically and economically marginalized youths most disaffected from the core institutions of family, school, work and the standard forms of leisure. As a number of projects have shown, however, they are far from unreachable, and one of the key interventions may have been the growth in further and higher education which has had cultural, economic, and regulatory implications for young people who might once have been deemed at risk.[122] What remains elusive is the political will to fund basic community resources to which they will demonstrably respond. Yet the same tendencies to anomie which strain theorists argue underlie their delinquency also furnish the motives for social polarization, the pursuit of wealth, and the 'crimes of the powerful'.

Street Gangs

Over four decades ago, in a critique of the applicability of portrayals of the 'structured' American delinquent gang to the British context, it was nevertheless argued that the more that context changed to share key features of American society, the more gang formations in Britain could be expected to evolve more closely to American patterns. The strain to anomie in British society was seen as constrained by strong class-based communal identity. The question raised over the past decade in particular is how far that process of convergence has already occurred.

There is little doubt that major economic changes have occurred in the UK which have accelerated the shift to a 'neo-liberal' economy that bears a closer resemblance to that of the USA than to European Social Democracies. Not least, the outright privatization of public services; health and educational expansion funded through private finance deals; the prioritization of the interests of corporate finance over the needs

---

[120] A. Karmen, *The New York Murder Mystery*.   [121] P. Cohen and D. Robins, *Knuckle Sandwich*.
[122] A. Karmen, *The New York Murder Mystery*, ch. 6 and, more generally, Chapter 12 in this book.

of manufacturing industry; and the growth of a winner/loser celebrity culture amidst growing inequality combined to promote individualism and erode social solidarity. That said, substantial differences remain: the National Health Service and the British Broadcasting Corporation being the strongest institutional defences against the rampant market forces that dominate health care and the mass media in the USA. But both the NHS and the BBC are now assailed by calls for their greater exposure to market forces which may be difficult to resist.

The strongest proponent of the case for a corresponding change in gang formations in Britain is John Pitts:[123]

> Things have changed, and despite a steady decline in adult and youth crime in Britain in the past 15 years, in certain parts of our towns and cities and among certain social groups, life has become far more dangerous for children and young people. And the immediate reason for this is the proliferation of violent youth gangs and the culture that they ferment.[124]

His study of the scale and character of youth gang membership, one-third of whom are estimated to be 'reluctant gangsters'[125] in three high-crime London boroughs echoes much of the analysis of gang delinquency in metropolitan America by Cloward and Ohlin in the late 1950s and early 60s. De-industrialization, the social polarization of public housing and the salience of illicit drug-dealing as an often illusory but potent means to quick cash returns far beyond minimum-waged work are the chief background components of this step-change in youth crime. On the worst-hit estates, where postcode loyalties transcend all others, most adolescents are recruited into the local gang due to their fear of reprisals against themselves or their families if they resist, rather than by any active embrace of gang values. Escape by moving up socially or out physically hits the reefs of blocked opportunities at every level. The waiting lists for social housing—since all else is unaffordable—number over a million. The very colleges and training courses that might spell opportunity may be located in rival gang territory and hence are out of bounds. This level of social exclusion goes far beyond that usually associated with the concept and amounts to cumulative entrapment. For those most adversely affected, 'joining' the gang thus becomes the only 'rational choice' for survival.

Hallsworth and Silverstone[126] take issue with Pitts' analysis for its over-reliance on the change in gang formations as the prime cause of the upsurge in weapon-related lethal violence among young males. Drawing on research projects in several of the metropolitan centres worst hit by gun crime, they see the gang shift as a complicating factor, plagued by definitional vagaries, rather than the main event. They see two principal phenomena as implicated in the trend. First, the more professional, older criminals, involved in the burgeoning illicit drugs trade, tend to avoid using guns themselves but—in classic mode—deploy younger, less skilled criminal labour to

---

[123] J. Pitts, *Reluctant Gangsters: The Changing Face of Youth Crime*; see also H. Sergeant *Among the Hoods: Exposing the Truth About Britain's Gangs*.

[124] J. Pitts, *Reluctant Gangsters: The Changing Face of Youth Crime*, 4.

[125] J. Pitts, *Reluctant Gangsters: The Changing Face of Youth Crime*, 101.

[126] S. Hallsworth and D. Silverstone, '"That's Life Innit": A British Perspective on Guns, Crime and Social Order'.

supply the firepower. Second, and more involved in the kind of seemingly pointless carnage that fuels public outrage, are those who see themselves as 'on road'—a term which covers a host of options in makeshift lives. The lack of any viable career or status in conventional terms leads them to place a hugely disproportionate stress on eliciting 'respect' in even casual encounters, the absence or withholding of which can lead to ballistic and at times fatal responses. 'What makes this social order so destructive is that it is socially destructive in significant ways. The violence within it is *anomic* as opposed to *ritualized*, making it difficult to predict and thus control. . . "On road" is not a place where instrumental reason prospers and pragmatic resolutions occur. It is an intense hothouse of emotions that find expression in deeply internalized anger and rage felt by these unstable young men.'[127]

Much of the gist of these analyses is shared by the authors of the most exhaustive British study of youth gangs to date in one of England's largest cities.[128] They accept the emergence of gang formations, over a slightly longer period, but document the critical significance of how gangs are defined and membership ascribed, not only by the gangs themselves but also by the police and other agencies, such as the school, which wield power over their lives. The police now devote substantial resources to monitoring youth gangs and basing operations on intelligence systems culled from inventories of gang members and associates. 'The police employed similar strategies to rival gangs when evaluating whether somebody was a gang member, most often based on being seen in the company of known gang members.'[129] The processes of the classic theories of adverse labelling are intensified and amplified in graphic form in such examples as boys, especially black males, being excluded from school, within months of crucial examinations, due to being defined as gang members even when they study hard and have no arrests or convictions against them, simply on the strength of other family members having gang associations. Indeed, guilt by association is fast becoming a part of the landscape in and around the 'set spaces' known as gang territory. Joint enterprise convictions can lead to years of imprisonment simply by dint of 'being there', even if no part at all was played in an offence. Not surprisingly, distrust of and alienation from authority in general and the police in particular abound as a result. Exclusion and marginalization diminish life chances even further, heightening the risks of being drawn to crime in self-fulfilling prophecy mode. Under-reporting is the norm, as residence in such places leads people to be wary of reprisals for any hint of co-operation with the police, indeed to be 'highly fearful' in general, leading to the proverbial 'wall of silence' that plagues criminal justice investigation and prosecution in the wake of lethal violence.

In a summary of the state of play in British gang studies, Marian Fitzgerald[130] makes the point that the US gang situation has hardly remained static over the past half century.

---

[127] S. Hallsworth and D. Silverstone, ' "That's Life Innit": A British Perspective on Guns, Crime and Social Order', 1720.

[128] R. Ralphs, J. Medina, and J. Aldridge, 'Who Needs Enemies With Friends Like These?'

[129] R. Ralphs, J. Medina, and J. Aldridge, 'Who Needs Enemies With Friends Like These?, 8.

[130] M. Fitzgerald, ' "Gangs"–a UK Perspective'.

Gang researchers—including the people who are officially responsible for counting gangs in the USA—have for nearly 20 years been referring to the emergence of a 'new generation' of youth gangs. Hybrid or 'modern' gangs . . . lack the trappings of the old style gang, are less hierarchical, less formal (e.g. with regard to initiation rites, symbols etc) more diverse in their membership and no longer exclusively found in traditional gang heartlands.[131]

Even so, the long-held, clear distinctions between the British and the American gang have markedly diminished over the past two decades. In the context of de-industrialization, the 'crisis in masculinity'[132] due to changes in the labour market, and with the rise of the drug economy, gang formations have become more prevalent—though the strictures of Hallsworth and others against too facile an acceptance of the gang stereotype are important *caveats*. Moreover, ethnicity, in a multitude of 'post-code' configurations, has become a factor in disproportionate levels of gang-related lethal conflict, notably in London.

In sum, whatever divides current researchers in their conclusions about the reality or otherwise of gang formations, they concur on the social location and likely causes of persistent male youth violence phenomena: the same old combination of severe economic inequality, social exclusion, educational under-achievement, and neighbourhood polarization now combine with chronic under-employment and a thriving illicit economy of drug dealing to make street crime a commitment on which it is all too easy to embark and from which it is all too difficult to desist. That some nevertheless manage to is a sign that closure is never complete.

Critique

The promise of subcultural theory was that it would be better than any other at 'fitting the facts' of the problem it was designed to explain. Those 'facts' clustered around one central assumption: that the most serious forms of youth offending are to be found in a highly localized form in one sector of the social system, that of the male, lower-class, urban adolescent. A basic problem from the outset was that the prevalence of youth offending was far from general, even in this sector. The problems allegedly encountered by members of this category plainly led only a small minority to serious offending and only a minority of that minority to serious *gang*-related offending. Yet the other options open to such boys, the 'college' (upwardly mobile) and the 'corner-boy' (respectable, working-class) 'adaptations', were never successfully differentiated causally from the delinquent option. The question 'Why should similarly situated youths sometimes choose offending and sometimes the alternatives?' was left open, so that subcultural theory became all too vulnerable to David Matza's criticism that it 'over-predicted' offending by accounting for far more than actually existed. Later subcultural theories of the Marxist school are open to the same criticism: though Matza's own approach, with its characterization of most offending as 'mundane' and 'periodic', veers towards the opposite fault of 'under-prediction'.

---

[131] M. Fitzgerald, '"Gangs"–a UK Perspective', 19.   [132] B. Campbell, *Goliath: Britain's Dangerous Places*.

A related problem in the assessment of the theory revolves around its dependence on the official criminal statistics. Numerous self-report studies threw serious doubt on the subcultural theories' identification of the more serious forms of offending with lower-working-class, male, urban adolescents. The more sophisticated studies, such as that by Martin Gold, narrowed the differentials between male–female and lower class–middle class to something approaching unity.[133] Moreover, throughout the 1960s, forms of social deviance such as drug-use and even instrumental violence became associated with just those groups that were theoretically most immune to offending: the middle-class 'college boys'. It began to look as if subcultural theories were addressing a non-problem and were incapable of addressing emergent ones.

A third difficulty was that the theories had always relied heavily on analytic imputation. Subcultures were alleged to arise in situations of socially structured 'strain' or, in the Marxist version, in situations where the 'contradictions of capitalism' were experienced most intensively. This search for correspondences between 'problems' and 'solutions' could lead all too easily to the circularity of explanation already familiar to students of the 'social disorganization' and 'functionalist' schools. The saving grace of earlier subcultural theories had been an insistence on evidence that adherents to a subculture should be aware, however dimly, of the problems to which it was a response and the values around which it was held to cohere. In later subcultural theories, this safeguard has been eclipsed all too frequently by the methodology of 'decoding' subcultural style into what are assumed to be its immanent properties.

Attempts to solve the problem of analytical imputation—that is, to establish whether or not the distinctive meaning systems of the various subcultures are in reality those imputed to them—have taken successively complicated forms. In David Maurer's classic early work, subculture was inferred from the distinctive linguistic vocabulary used by pickpockets and sneak thieves.[134] The homology between language and practices was complete. A self-enclosed, relatively unchanging, and antique way of life was depicted. Such unity was never established in the more variegated instances of expressive delinquency.[135] Early subcultural theorists sought to link distinctive sets of norms, values, and beliefs to allegedly distinctive types of delinquent subculture. The work of Cloward and Ohlin is a prime example. In such work, the relationship between the parent culture and deviant subcultures was essentially static. The only source of change was the apparently growing instability of the inner city. Hence, it was appropriate to attempt to 'trap' subcultural norms by standard techniques of interview and survey methods. Labelling theory introduced a fresh source of change, the nature of the social reaction. A certain dynamism was lent to the somewhat static conception of subculture, but the gain was limited. Social reaction could reinforce subcultural cohesion, as in Young's depiction of the impact of police harassment on drug users.[136] Such work tended to complement earlier approaches, though the preferred method

---

[133] For a comprehensive review of such studies, see S. Box, *Deviance, Reality and Society*; and M. Gold, *Delinquent Behavior in an American City*.

[134] D. Maurer, *Whiz Mob: A Correlation of the Technical Argot of Pick-pockets with their Behavior Pattern*.

[135] Though Willis establishes a considerable symmetry in the relations between lifestyles and musical forms in his studies of 'profane cultures'.   [136] J. Young, 'The Role of the Police as Amplifiers of Deviancy'.

of the labelling theorists, participant observation, could enrich available accounts of cultural meanings. Sources of change in delinquency still seemed inadequately explained by such methods, however. This failing was most pronounced in the analysis of what Hebdige has termed the 'spectacular subcultures' of adolescence that periodically emerged in Britain as apparent symbols of youthful defiance: Teds, Mods, Rockers, Skinheads, Punks. The introduction of a fresh dynamic, developments in class conflict in post-war Britain, promised a means of accounting at several removes for the shape such subcultures took. New methods were employed, in particular semiotics, to capture the nuances of each successive style as a *mélange* of signs, or *bricolage*, as Lévi-Strauss would call it: but the problems of imputation have become, in the process, more rather than less evident.

In a searching critique of the work of the 'new' subcultural theorists, Stan Cohen addresses the problem of imputation at three levels of analysis: structure, culture, and biography.[137] At the level of structure, the main innovation has been an appeal to history. In the work of such theorists as Phil Cohen, Corrigan, and Pearson, working-class delinquency is placed in the context of class struggle. This perspective enables the theorist to analyse both continuity and change afresh. The daily toll of routine delinquency (which may be termed the 'unspectacular' subcultures) can be related to the reproduction of order by repressive means: in Gouldner's terms, 'normalized repression'. The innovations or 'spectacular subcultures' can be related to crucial 'moments' or 'conjunctures' in the class struggle. For example, the Skinhead style emerged in the attempt to retrieve traditional symbols of working-class cohesion devalued by post-war 'affluence'. The problem, however, is that such an approach assists 'an over facile drift to historicism. . . In each case the connections sound plausible. But in each case, a single and one-directional historical trend is picked out—commercialization, repression, bourgeoisification, destruction of community, erosion of leisure values—and then projected onto a present which (often by the same sociologists' own admission) is more complicated, contradictory or ambiguous'.[138]

At the level of culture, these new approaches:

> are massive exercises of decoding, reading, deciphering and interrogating. These phenomena *must* be saying something to us—if only we could know exactly *what*. So the whole assembly of cultural artefacts, down to the punks' last safety pin, have been scrutinised, taken apart, contextualised and re-contextualised. The conceptual tools of Marxism, structuralism and semiotics, a Left Bank pantheon of Genet, Lévi-Strauss, Barthes and Althusser have been wheeled in to aid this hunt for the hidden code.[139]

The dominant themes of *resistance* (to subordination) through *ritual* (symbolic displays of various kinds) typically confront the awkward problem of intra-group or minority-group victimization by the notion of 'misrecognition'. The real enemy (the bosses, the State, or the dominant class) remains unscathed. The essentially 'subversive' nature of the subcultures can be inferred from their styles. As Hebdige put it: 'These "humble objects" (bikes, clothes, make-up) can be magically appropriated: "stolen" by

---

[137] In the Introduction to the revised edition of his *Folk Devils and Moral Panics*.
[138] S. Cohen, *Folk Devils and Moral Panics*, viii–ix.   [139] S. Cohen, *Folk Devils and Moral Panics*, ix.

subordinate groups and made to carry "secret" meanings which express, in code, a form of resistance to the order which guarantees their continued subordination.'[140] This may, as Stan Cohen puts it, be 'an imaginative way of reading the style; but how can we be sure that it is also not imaginary?'[141] Ultimately, this approach finesses the problem of intent. Symbols may mean what they appear to mean; they may, by exaggeration or parody, be taken to mean the opposite, as Hebdige claims they should in the case of the Punks' wearing of the swastika emblem; or they may represent a latent intentionality. '"Literary ethnography"... is substituted for direct empirical observation as a means of obtaining evidence for theory', leading to the 'central problem' that he 'over-emphasizes the political significance of style.'[142] At this point, the method comes close to producing a cultural Freudianism.[143]

At the level of biography, much the same problems recur, in a fashion akin to earlier subcultural theory. With delinquency as with other phenomena, many are called but few are chosen or self-elected. The subcultural activists are greatly outnumbered by the conforming majority, despite their common exposure to similar pressures. No fresh insights are offered as to which variables might intervene to differentiate the two. In this respect, there is continuity with, but no significant improvement on, earlier cultural approaches: that delinquent and troublesome youth cultures signify 'a reaction (with more or less degrees of commitment, consciousness and symbolic weight) to growing up in a class society'.[144]

A final criticism of subcultural theory in general applies with particular force to the exponents of the various class conflict approaches. It may be termed 'differential magnification', the tuning of the analytical lens to an almost exclusive degree on the 'subordinate cultures', with a corresponding neglect of the 'dominant' or 'subaltern' cultures. In these works, the worlds of teachers, social workers, policemen, prison officers, employers, and even academics are treated with the very disregard for ambiguity, complexity, and resistances to ideology that would be (rightly) impugned if applied to working-class or delinquent cultures. This massive over-simplification is at times justified in terms of structuralist method: whatever they think they are doing, those in authority are doomed to support the system. Such an assumption can only be supported on a historicist basis. The limitations of this position could be overcome by extending to these groups the forms of research reserved as yet for 'subordinate cultures'. The idea that upper- and middle-class cultures comprise merely 'stultification, reification and pretence'[145] merits

---

[140] D. Hebdige, *Subculture: The Meaning of Style*, 18.   [141] S. Cohen, *Folk Devils and Moral Panics*, xv.

[142] S. Blackman, *Youth: Positions and Oppositions*, 4–5.

[143] As, e.g., in Hebdige's assertion that 'Everytime the boot went in, a contradiction was concealed, glossed over or made to "disappear"' (*Subculture*, 60). The drift to a facile idealism recalls Zilboorg's Freudian explanation of why pickpockets plied their trade at public hangings. 'This was their revenge for their own vicarious execution.' As Maurer notes, Barrington, the famous eighteenth-century thief, gave a sounder explanation: 'Everybody's eyes were on one person and all were looking up' (D. Maurer, *Whiz Mob*, 14–16). In this case, however, a clear-cut purpose was involved: thieving as a trade. Expressive 'spectacular subcultures' do not lend themselves so readily to instrumental accounts, so that Hebdige's approach is correspondingly more defensible and in general his methods lend themselves to a more rigorous use of evidence than the above might imply.   [144] S. Cohen, *Folk Devils and Moral Panics*, xxv.

[145] P. Willis, *Profane Culture*, 5.

sceptical examination. Indeed, there has been throughout an unfortunate neglect of the taxing methodological problems involved in exploring, describing, and analysing entities so complicated and intangible as 'culture' and 'subculture'. It is as if culture were regarded as a self-evident body of monochromatic beliefs laid out as propositions that any intelligent observer could read. Little heed has been given to the situated, heterogeneous, and fluid nature of belief; to its ambiguities, anomalies, and contradictions; and to the sheer difficulty of pinning it down and arranging it as a 'system'. On the contrary, subcultural theorists have embarked on their work without any but the most token of nods at the sociology of knowledge, cultural anthropology, and the like.

Causal explanation and interpretative approaches have both been addressed, though the focus has been almost invariably limited to juvenile delinquency and adolescent trouble-making.[146] Criticisms of the factual basis for much theorizing in this vein have in their turn been subjected to substantial attack, not least for their tendency to overstate the impact of selective forms of policing on the construction of delinquency.[147] Certain basic assumptions have resisted invalidation.[148] Above all, perhaps, the logic of subcultural theories predicted with some success, albeit imprecisely, such developments as the emergence of a street crime culture among black youth and the appeal of extreme authoritarianism among the most disadvantaged white adolescents.[149] It may well be that such predictions are eminently possible without the aid of subcultural theory. But they at least afford support for the view that such theories have barely explored strengths as well as demonstrably glaring weaknesses. Finally, despite the obvious dangers of overstretched antennae, the work of the 'Cultural Studies' School has reanimated the possibilities of making 'culture' more than a synopsis of the very problems it is employed to explain.

Indeed, culture has been resuscitated in the emergence of what, in a novel turn, is now called 'cultural criminology', a blend of symbolic interactionism, phenomenology, the work of the Chicago School and the CCCS, and radical criminology. Criminology has a habit of forgetting its past and then reinventing itself, and in this, its latest guise, it celebrates as new a culturally-framed description of such phenomena as street-racing, graffiti, and 'masculine fantasy and the internet'. It is set, as some of its predecessors were, in juxtaposition to a somewhat demonized and over-simplified representation of competing work as positivistic (not recognizing that many other diverse strands of criminology also take an interpretive stance). Ferrell and his colleagues declare, for instance, that 'cultural criminological writing and research tends [sic] to look and feel different from the "normal science" of positivist criminology. . . .in choosing any mode of analysis or representation, cultural criminologists remain conscious of pluralities of meaning and possibilities of alternative perception'.[150] It emphasizes, as did its

[146] An exception is K. Plummer, *Sexual Stigma: An Interactionist Account.*

[147] A. Reiss, Jun., 'Inappropriate Theories and Inadequate Methods as Policy Plagues'; and R. Mawby (ed.), *Policing the City.*

[148] M. Brake, *The Sociology of Youth.* Brake demonstrates that there is greater agreement over views of the self, other groups, and society, within as compared to between the youthful subcultures of Skinheads and Hippies.   [149] D. Downes, *The Delinquent Solution*; S. Cohen, 'Directions for Research'.

[150] J. Ferrell et al., 'Fragments of a Manifesto', 6; see also Young, J, *The Criminological Imagination*, Cambridge, 2011.

predecessors and contemporaries, the biographical and the lived reality of subordinate groups. It rehearses familiar themes of political economic crisis. It traces elements of ideas current elsewhere in theoretical sociology—ontological insecurity, globalization, post-modernism, the commodification of leisure, the ever-growing stress on consumption, the lack of biographical continuity over time (described as broken narratives), the so-called fracturing of community, and much else. It celebrates crime and deviance as forms of transgressive excitement and, in so doing, it tends rather to forget the victim who may well *not* celebrate what is done and whose cultural work is not taken to be worth inspection.[151] And it also tends to follow members of the CCCS in its portrayal of those who respond to deviants as cardboard figures without depth or complexity. Criticizing the work of Ferrell on graffiti-artists, O'Brien remarks, for example, that 'in marked contrast to the multidimensional and sympathetic interpretation of the graffiti writers' activities, assertions and arguments, anti-graffiti campaigners and "average persons" amount to one-dimensional ciphers of a one-dimensional culture'.[152] Cultural criminology evidently extends the right to create and inhabit webs of meaning to some but not to others.

It may be that what *is* actually new about cultural criminology is that it locates analysis in what is called a 'media-saturated world' and adds to it the special inflection lent by Jack Katz in his interpretations of the seductive excitement of the criminal exploit. Essays in the *genre* focus on stylized transgression and subversion as a form of cultural resistance to oppression, especially in what Brotherton has called 'hyper-ghettoized America.'[153] Typical of its world view is the following:

> As identities and meanings become more fluid and contested, populations become more transient, and citizens become more wary of face-to-face interaction, traditional forms of collectivism, sociality and communality appear to fragment and disintegrate. New media technologies provide a means of achieving a sense of identity, belonging and community in this climate of uncertainty.[154]

Despite perhaps not being quite as novel a departure as some of its proponents pretend, and despite ignoring some of the reality-check qualifications that victimology might have introduced, the cultural (re)turn is nevertheless a welcome return to an engagement with the complexities of the lived reality of crime and deviance. It performs a useful service in tracing the many forms of deviance with its attendant motives and accounts, reminding us once more of the importance of the phenomenological aspects—will, exploit, performance, and existential meaning—of transgression.

Ferrell et al. elaborate on these themes, and victims are brought into the frame. 'Liquid ethnography' is celebrated as the capacity to capture the fleeting climactic event, equated with the 'decisive moment' in the photography of Cartier-Bresson. '*Verstehen* criminology' is pitted against positivism as the more authentic criminology. Feyerabend is invoked to make the case against formulaic accounts of scientific 'progress'. While there is much to be said for these approaches, the critique of positivism is

---

[151] D. Downes, review of K. Hayward, *City Limits.*
[152] M. O'Brien, 'What is *Cultural* About Cultural Criminology?', 603.
[153] D. Brotherton, 'Subversive Subcultures', np.   [154] C. Geer, 'Crime, Media and Community', 117.

overdone, despite the cultural criminologists' justified criticisms of the methodological and intellectual constraints on imaginative research ventures posed by funding councils. Not all quantitative research is as crass as the examples they claim, and it would be a dumbed-down criminology that ignored such painstaking work as that of Hood on capital punishment, Pease on repeat victimization, and Sherman and Strang [155] on restorative justice, to name just a few from a host of 'positivist' examples. It is worth remembering that Weber criticized positivism as inadequate rather than wrong. It is doubtful if he would have embraced Feyerabend's *credo* of 'anything goes'.

Conclusion

Ethnographies of diverse and deviant or criminal cultures had been a major approach by the 'Chicago School', but it was Albert Cohen's 1955 analysis of 'subculture' in relation to gang delinquency which broke new ground. Approaching subculture as a 'way of life' evolved to resolve problems facing lower-class youth in a highly competitive society, the concept became a method for inferring a situated rationality from conduct usually dismissed as motiveless, meaningless, and purely destructive. His book provoked an onrush of work, by Cloward and Ohlin, and David Matza in particular, challenging Cohen's theory but retaining much of his analytic framework. Subcultural research flourished for a time both in the USA and cross-nationally, was revivified in Britain in the 1970s and, despite being reworked, displays a discernible continuity between current work and that of the 1950s and 1960s. What is noticeable when one reads contemporary research on criminal cultures, subcultures, and gangs in their youthful manifestations is how the original studies are either not fully acknowledged or are caricatured.

Further Reading

D. C. BROTHERTON, *Youth Street Gangs*, New York, 2015.

R. CLOWARD and L. Ohlin, *Delinquency and Opportunity: A Theory of Delinquent Gangs*, New York, 1960.

A. COHEN, *Delinquent Boys: The Culture of the Gang*, Glencoe, Ill., 1955.

S. HALL et al., *Resistance Through Rituals*, London, 2006.

D. MATZA, *Delinquency and Drift*, New York, 1964.

[155] L. Sherman and H. Strang, *Restorative Justice: The Evidence*.

7

Symbolic Interactionism

Introduction

The Chicago School dominated North American criminology for some two decades. Its students were to set the agenda for the evolution of American sociology, and the sociology of crime and control in particular, and it was an agenda which remained virtually unchallenged until the appearance of structural-functionalism at Harvard in the late 1930s. As work proceeded and scholars dispersed, the various strains of Chicago sociology tended to undergo separate development. Ethnography became associated with one wing, eventually to be described as symbolic interactionism by Herbert Blumer in 1937.[1] The connection and continuity have been real enough for some to call interactionists 'neo-Chicagoans'[2] and others to call them a second Chicago School.[3]

Interactionists were to be overshadowed during the 1940s and 1950s, the period of rampant functionalism.[4] We did note that Edwin Sutherland, his colleagues, and his students did continue to pursue a heavily modified version of symbolic interactionism, differential association, by writing about embezzlement,[5] drug addiction,[6] professional crime,[7] the crimes of business corporations,[8] and deviant motivation.[9] Another Chicagoan, Everett Hughes, wrote about matters that were of some interest to sociologists of deviance and, in particular, about the moral division of labour into clean and dirty work, with its accompanying stocks of innocent and guilty knowledge about the world.[10] Frank Tannenbaum, a sociologist who had been imprisoned for his involvement in the radical politics of the 1930s, produced a celebrated analysis of the 'dramatization of evil': 'the process of making the criminal', he said, 'is a process of tagging, defining, identifying, segregating, describing, emphasizing, making conscious and self-conscious; it becomes a way of stimulating, suggesting, emphasizing, and evoking the very traits that are complained of'.[11] One man, Edwin Lemert, himself not a Chicagoan, and not writing in interactionist style, was to be recognized later as a vital forerunner of the interactionist sociology of deviance.

---

[1] H. Blumer, *Symbolic Interactionism*. [2] D. Matza, *Becoming Deviant*.
[3] G. Fine, *A Second Chicago School? The Development of a Postwar American Sociology*.
[4] Cf. K. Davis, 'The Myth of Functional Analysis'. [5] D. Cressey, *Other People's Money*.
[6] A. Lindesmith, *Opiate Addiction*. [7] E. Sutherland, *The Professional Thief*.
[8] E. Sutherland, *White Collar Crime*.
[9] D. Cressey, 'Role Theory, Differential Association and Compulsive Crimes'.
[10] E. Hughes, 'Good People and Dirty Work'. [11] F. Tannenbaum, *Crime and the Community*, 20.

He borrowed from symbolic interactionism to construct a general theory of social pathology.[12] But all this work, later to feed into what was to be called 'labelling theory', seems to have been identified at the time as rather peripheral to the main body of American sociological writing.

It is not at all clear why the Chicago School should have been eclipsed.[13] Nor is it clear why its heir, symbolic interactionism, should have come to prominence in the criminology of the 1960s. Symbolic interactionists claimed that they were a little bemused themselves and Howard Becker, the man held chiefly responsible for the renaissance, expressed surprise at his own influence.[14] The possibilities of the functionalist and anomie models had certainly not been exhausted. Indeed, they had never been fully exploited in criminology. In contrast, it cannot be alleged that the Chicago School had practised a kind of withdrawal and return. There had been no willing retreat. Neither had there been any lack of work on deviance. Re-adoption may have to be explained by what seems to be the inevitable half-life of sociological fashions: there is an ingrained impatience with the old which condemns every set of ideas to a limited vitality. It may also have to be explained by the great expansion of higher education which took place in the 1960s, an expansion which disrupted routine and introduced large numbers of young, marginal academics to teaching and research. It may have been connected with what were thought to be some of the distinctive qualities of the decade: the flowering of expressive deviance, the novel sense of openness, and a toying with what Horowitz called the politics of experience.[15] There was indeed something of an affinity between the particular social world known to many young sociologists of the time and the particular kind of writing they practised. Interactionism was held to be an existential sociology which seemed remarkably well equipped to capture the new *demi-monde*. Thus Alvin Gouldner, not a warm friend of symbolic interactionism, argued:

> This group of Chicagoans finds itself at home in the world of hip, Norman Mailer, drug addicts, jazz musicians, cab drivers, prostitutes, night people, drifters, grifters and skidders, the cool cats and their kicks. To be fully appreciated this stream of work cannot be seen solely in terms of the categories conventionally employed in sociological analysis. It has also to be seen from the viewpoint of the literary critic as a style or genre and particularly as a species of naturalistic romanticism.[16]

Although interactionism was actively pursued long before the emergence of the low life of the 1960s and participation in that life was no prerequisite to becoming an interactionist, a number of interactionists have apparently accepted a history of themselves as crypto-deviants.[17] They certainly did not vociferously reject the biographies which were constructed for them. Consider what Stan Cohen and Laurie Taylor said about themselves at the time: we 'took notes about our own "normal" deviance; smoking dope with our students, organising anti-Vietnam war demonstrations, watching

---

[12] E. Lemert, *Social Pathology*.

[13] A. Reiss and M. Tonry, Preface to *Communities and Crime*.

[14] J. Debro, 'Dialogue with Howard S. Becker'.   [15] I. Horowitz, 'The Politics of Drugs', 165.

[16] A. Gouldner, 'Anti-Minotaur: The Myth of a Value-Free Sociology', 209.

[17] S. Cohen, 'Criminology and the Sociology of Deviance in Britain'; I. Taylor and L. Taylor (eds.), *Politics and Deviance*; N. Polsky, *Hustlers, Beats and Others*; J. Weis, 'Dialogue with Matza'.

porno movies'.[18] Consider, too, Jock Young's observation that 'We were all moved by the times: the possibility of social change, the worlds of diversity that the new bohemia promised, the youthful colonization of leisure and the rejection of austerity and discipline in a world seemingly in fast-forward, all of which made the choice of being on the side of progress well nigh inevitable'.[19]

Interactionism did suddenly seem to loom large in the 1960s and 1970s. Sections of certain works were to be described as 'catechisms' for the sociology of deviance.[20] One book in particular, Becker's *Outsiders*, was to become one of the two most frequently cited of all American criminological writings in the period between 1945 and 1972.[21]

Symbolic interactionists take part of their job to be a formal description of the little social worlds that constitute a society. Schools, gangs, families, pubs, and hospitals are not unlike the natural areas of the Chicago School. They are bounded social situations, created by people who experience them as sets of changing resources, opportunities, contexts, and constraints. Any social situation will be a blend of activity, history, and material props which achieves its definition and coherence from shared symbols, symbols themselves being described in part as embedded in social relations and consisting of a past experience of, and an imagination of projected action towards, an object.[22] Some features of those worlds will be familiar and general and others will not, and it is never easy to say in advance what one will discover. Indeed, interactionists would say that understanding is always emergent, that an explorer can never properly know what he or she is exploring until it has been explored. It requires a particularly patient, cautious, and attentive methodology to chart such a delicate and complicated process as social life, and it is all too easy prematurely to impose an alien explanatory scheme that obscures vision, ignores problems, and pre-empts solutions. Gusfield remarked, 'What stands out for me is the intensive focus on the empirical world; on seeing and understanding behavior in its particular and situated forms. Data that do not stay close to the events, actions, or texts being studied are always suspect'.[23] Above all, interactionists held that analysis must grasp the meaning that animates and shapes social activity. Significant meaning is that employed by the social actors themselves, not by the sociologist, because it is that meaning which structures behaviour. Interactionism is consequently designed to take the observer and audience as far as is practicable inside the actors' own perspectives on selves, acts, and environments. Howard Becker, the most influential of all the interactionist sociologists of deviance, reflected: 'The so-called "labelling theory" revolution should never have been required. It was not an intellectual or scientific revolution. . . .[It merely] directs us to understand how the situation looks to the actors in it, to find out what they think is going on so that we will understand what goes into the making of their activity'.[24] Interactionists thus tend to practise a social anthropology of participant-observation, an anthropology which marries surveillance

[18] S. Cohen and L.Taylor, *Escape Attempts*, 2.

[19] J. Young, 'Moral Panic: Its Origins in Resistance, Ressentiment and the Translation of Fantasy into Reality', 8.

[20] G. Pearson, *The Deviant Imagination*, 52.   [21] M. Wolfgang et al., *Evaluating Criminology*.

[22] G. Mead, *Mind, Self and Society*.

[23] J. Gusfield, preface to G. Fine (ed.), *A Second Chicago School?*

[24] H. Becker, *Tricks of the Trade*, 53.

to an involvement in the affairs of a social world. The resulting reports cannot but be limited, dwelling on small clusters of events, but their yield can be especially rich.

Symbolic Interactionism

There is a modest compatibility between interactionism and crime and deviance which stems from the propensity of rule-breakers to gather in the small, bounded social worlds which interactionist ethnography can map. Heroin-users, thieves, and prostitutes may set themselves apart, seeking out those who share common problems, experiences, and solutions. Together, they can create a series of groupings whose peculiarities can stimulate the sensitivities that are indispensable to interactionism.

We have already argued that ethnography requires sociologists to reconcile the two contradictory states of participation and observation. They must so distance themselves that they can define commonplace actions and utterances as problematic, yet their knowledge must be intimate enough to permit a reasonable interpretation of the inner meanings of those selfsame actions and utterances. Deviant phenomena can take the form of people doing extraordinary things in an ordinary and familiar world, or vice versa, and they lend themselves particularly well to participant-observation. Theft, drug-taking, and prostitution are a useful blend of the common and the uncommon which permits the sociologist to be both sensitized and appreciative.

Deviance itself is defined as a product of the ideas or meanings which people form of themselves and one another. Social action, it is argued, cannot be a response to people as they 'really' are and in every detail. How is one to know people in that way? After all, encounters are often brief and much is unknown, concealed, irrelevant, or ambiguous. People are constrained to react to a filtered, adapted, and limited conception of themselves, each other, and the situations in which they meet. Activities must therefore necessarily be grounded in working, practicable definitions which are situated and negotiable. Central to such conceptions are the names and symbols upon which definitions are built: as names change, so do actions. Anselm Strauss once reflected that 'any particular object can be named, and thus located, in countless ways. The naming sets it within a context of quite differently related classes. The nature or essence of an object does not reside mysteriously within the object itself but is dependent on how it is defined by the namer'.[25] Criminologists and sociologists simply extrapolated this observation to rule-breaking phenomena and, for a while, the naming associated with deviance was held to be so important to its interactionist analysis that the entire approach was generally, if misleadingly, termed 'labelling theory'. The remarks of Becker, Kitsuse, and Erikson are frequently cited:

> Social groups create deviance by making the rules whose infraction constitutes deviance and by applying those rules to particular people and labeling them as outsiders. From this point of view, deviance is *not* a quality of the act the person commits, but rather a consequence of the application by others of rules and sanctions to an 'offender'. The deviant is one to whom that label has successfully been applied; deviant behavior is behavior that people so label.[26]

---

[25] A. Strauss, *Mirrors and Masks: The Search for Identity*, 20.   [26] H. Becker, *Outsiders*, 9.

I propose to shift the focus of theory and research from the forms of deviant behavior to the processes by which persons come to be defined as deviant by others. Such a shift requires that the sociologist view as problematic what he generally assumes as given—namely, that certain forms of behavior are per se deviant and are so defined by the 'conventional or conforming members of a group'.[27]

The critical variable in the study of deviance . . . is the social audience rather than the individual actor, since it is the audience which eventually determines whether or not an episode of behavior or any class of episodes is labeled deviant.[28]

All three remarks emphasize that the sociologist should concentrate on the work wrought by naming. Deviance is held to be a kind of description used in the conversations that order social life; conversations themselves have distinct and analysable qualities; and it is those qualities which organize some of the character of deviance. It should be noted that interactionists do not take conversation to be confined entirely to relations with others. Their discussion of deviance hinges on a larger conception of names, selves, and conversations, and it is useful to turn to that conception before their more focused analysis becomes clear.

Chief amongst the problematic objects confronting an observer is the self. Unlike the phenomenologists, interactionists maintain that people lack a sure knowledge of what they are and what they can accomplish. New problems and settings pose new tasks and it is not always certain that one is equal to them. It is not even certain that one can always repeat past achievements. Indeed, one tends to experience oneself as a somewhat erratic and opaque entity that can let oneself down, surprise, and embarrass oneself. Every situation has the capacity to establish, educate, and redefine the self.

Any action requires an appraisal of one's capacities and of the action's implications for oneself. There are certain things one can or cannot do; certain things which might seem incongruous with past performances, or which humiliate or elevate the self. It follows that a continual monitoring and assessment of the self are indispensable. A mind must ceaselessly attempt to make sense of itself just as it makes sense of other objects in its environment. Only then will it be able to form conjectures about what it appears to be, what a situation will permit it to do, and how it may work back on the situation to shape it to its will. In all this activity, it is evident that there is a vital division within consciousness. One phase or aspect of reasoning becomes a surveying subject, an 'I', the other becomes a surveyed object, a 'me'. Activity may then be likened to a kind of intellectual acrobatics in which mind becomes contorted in an effort endlessly to view itself.

Those internal gyrations of the self would be virtually impossible without language. Words have a power to fold back on the speaker with a special force: people cannot see themselves, but they can hear themselves speak and it may well be that their hearing is not too dissimilar to the hearing of others. Speaking, they can become their own stimulus: they are able to act and then react to themselves. In this fashion, speech makes possible a sense of self-estrangement, an opening-up of the 'I' and the 'me',

---

[27] J. Kitsuse, 'Societal Reaction to Deviant Behavior', 19–20.

[28] K. Erikson, 'Notes on the Sociology of Deviance', 11.

which allows one to become his or her own audience. Words have an additional power, in that they are relatively anonymous, accessible to anyone. Describing oneself, one is required to employ terms which are universal and universalizable, transforming private experience into a public matter, and making the unique general and social. As one uses words, so very particular circumstances receive a common classification. Further, that public currency of speech is also used by those about one. It becomes possible to imagine through such a currency some of the responses which others might make to one's action and projected self.

An imagination of others' replies is the prerequisite of social action. It distinguishes the mere emission of actions from concerted and co-operative behaviour. Imagination permits the construction of the 'significant gesture', a gesture which is at the very core of all sociability. A person who acts is rarely heedless of the effects of what he or she does. Whether action is benevolent or malevolent, it is normally intended to achieve some response from other people. In turn, it must be tailored to the anticipated reply which others might make. Anticipation in its turn requires one to take the role of another, to envisage how he or she views what one does and predicts one's intentions. It forces one to mould one's gestures so that their significance is properly and efficiently conveyed.

The work of composing a significant gesture is yet further complicated. It entails rehearsing one's own reply to the other's reply, conceiving the other's answering response and so on. It also entails a running interpretation of the complementary activities which the other does. Imaginations thus become intertwined, mingled in a common social undertaking. The private and subjective are locked into a wider structure. It does not follow that one's interpretation of the other is 'correct'. Indeed, there is no sure method of establishing the inner meaning of one's own and another's acts. But all joint behaviour rests on a series of working conjectures and definitions.

Interactionists thereby hold that life is patterned by symbolic indications. People continuously interpret themselves, their settings, and their partners. They must make sense of the past, make plans, and infer intentions. Indications are predominantly linguistic, although gestures, expression, clothing, and context also convey meaning. Language permits the identification and stabilization of social affairs. It allows one to assume persistence and similarity so that responses become available. It is the common medium which integrates public activity.

It is in this sense that the self has been compared to a dialogue within consciousness. The 'I' and the 'me' talk to one another, stimulating one another, interpreting one another, and relying on words for their understanding. The process of recognizing and negotiating deviance is itself thus importantly merged with the inner moral world of the self. Decisions about future conduct turn on readings of the meaning of action, the acceptability of deviant identity, the significance of particular acts, and the possible responses of others. They revolve around the character and significance of potential selves and they are all transacted within the self. An early and important article by Becker traced some of the stages of one such private conversation.[29] It discussed the

---

[29] H. Becker, 'Marihuana Use and Social Control'.

manner in which the marijuana user came to terms with known and likely definitions of drugs. When the article was written, marijuana was thought to be a dangerous
substance with moral implications for its consumer. The prospective user was obliged
to consider what kind of person he or she might become should he or she start using
the drug. Plans were moulded by an acceptance, rejection, or redefinition of the possible stigmas associated with use. Management of the problem had little to do with the
social control emanating from direct confrontations with other people, the police, or
courts. But it did centre on the social control embedded in the meanings of deviation
and the self.

The experience of oneself as free to deviate, then, depends in part on access to appropriate names and explanations.[30] Doing something is eased by sympathetic description. When acts and states can be reassessed as worthy or innocuous, or when
they can be presented as not 'really' deviant, it is a little easier to accept them. We
have already described how, arguing that deviation requires a mastery of guilt, Sykes
and Matza listed the techniques of neutralization which offer more or less honourable
motives for dishonourable acts.[31] An appeal to higher loyalties or the denial of injury
can exculpate the deviant and permit a drift into rule-breaking (Arendt once recalled
how Dostoevsky said in his diaries 'that in Siberia, among scores of murderers, rapists
and burglars, he never met a single man who would admit that he had done wrong'[32]).
An invocation of impossible constraint is yet another technique of accounting. Thus
women sometimes claim that they had no choice but to offend because of the coercion
exercised by their male partners.[33] And, again, the very absence of an apparent motive
can itself become a motive, liberating the offender from personal responsibility for his
or her conduct.[34]

All that concerns possibly hidden transactions within consciousness. Deviance can
become qualitatively transformed when it ceases to be the subject of purely private
contemplation. One is then required to rehearse and provide an account to those who
may be curious, offended, perturbed, or charged with the enforcement of rules. The
account must not only satisfy oneself but also manage the responses of the suspicious
outsider. Strategies are routinely employed to contend with the problems which deviance brings in its train. Amongst them is penitence and the acknowledgement of
fault[35]—not all deviation is magnified when it is confronted by accusation or sanction,[36] it may decline and the rule-breaker can feel shame or fear. And there are the alternative strategies of denying blameworthiness, representing deviance as some other
phenomenon, or deflecting attention away from treacherous signs.[37] Quite commonly,
problems are solved by retreating to the company of those who are similarly beset,

---

[30] Cf. C. Mills, 'Situated Actions and Vocabularies of Motive'; M. Scott and S. Lyman, 'Accounts, Deviance
and Social Order'.
[31] G. Sykes and D. Matza, 'Techniques of Neutralization'.
[32] H. Arendt, *Eichman in Jerusalem*, 52.   [33] S. Jones, 'Partners in Crime', 160.
[34] Cf. D. Cressey, 'Role Theory'; L. Taylor, 'The Significance and Interpretation of Replies to Motivational
Questions'.
[35] M. Cameron, *The Booster and the Snitch*.   [36] H. Parker, *The View From the Boys*.
[37] F. Davis, 'Deviance Disavowal'; E. Goffman, *Stigma*.

those people who may give support and may not demand such a strenuous control over the presentation of self. When deviance is co-operative, dependent on joint activity or on a division of labour, it is especially likely that errant sub-worlds will emerge.[38] In those sub-worlds, pretences may be partially abandoned, unwelcome relationships avoided,[39] skills learned, and supportive interpretations acquired.[40] Deviant subcultures represent limited answers to the difficulties of living in a hostile, critical, and discouraging world. Over time, they can come to offer a modest refuge, providing new meanings to overcome the opprobrium which deviance may attract. Such subcultures have come to be the special province of the interactionists, and research is replete with ethnographies of small deviant circles.

In the main, it is the *public* meanings and structures of deviation which interactionists choose to study. Not only does interactionism deny the sociologist much of a capacity to reach the inaccessible processes which make up subjective experience;[41] it also asserts that recognized deviance is the proper topic for a sociology that focuses on the *social* organization of behaviour. Deviance enters social life when it receives a response, and interactionists may be a little indifferent to first causes. In the analysis of mental illness, for example, there are those, like Thomas Scheff, who argue that the origins of such illness are diffuse, numerous, and often untraceable. The important sociological problem is not the explanation of those origins but the fashion in which mental illness becomes identified and shaped in public interaction.[42] Similarly, Lemert observed that rule-breaking is commonplace in everyday life. Sociology should not focus on the multiplicity of petty, undistinguished, and unacknowledged breaches, on what he called 'primary deviation'. It should analyse the forms that breaches take when there is some reaction from others. Deviance then intrudes into the public arena to become a socially consequential event.[43] In a supporting illustration, Becker returned to the social anthropologist, Malinowski, and his description of a Trobriand Islander who had committed incest.[44] The incest was tacitly condoned as long as it was not heeded but then denunciation made it inescapably public. Advertisement transformed what had been a tolerated private act, impelling the Islander to face an untenable situation and kill himself.[45]

It is quite important to note that a concentration on public response does not entail the claim that there is no deviation without labelling by others. Considerable confusion has arisen from the critic's belief that interactionism treats public labelling as a fundamental prerequisite of deviance. Indeed, some critics have maintained that 'hidden' or 'secret' deviance poses insuperable problems for the interactionist.[46]

We have shown that interactionism does indeed recognize the way in which people can answer and adapt to their own private descriptions of self without any intervention

---

[38] M. Leznoff and W. Westley, 'The Homosexual Community'.   [39] D. Tanner, *The Lesbian Couple*.

[40] A. Lindesmith, *Opiate Addiction*; E. Schur, *Narcotic Addiction in Britain and America*; K. Plummer, *Sexual Stigma*.

[41] H. Becker, 'The Self and Adult Socialization'.   [42] T. Scheff, *Being Mentally Ill*.

[43] E. Lemert, *Social Pathology*.   [44] H. Becker, *Outsiders*.

[45] B. Malinowski, *Crime and Custom*.

[46] J. Gibbs, 'Conceptions of Deviant Behavior'.

from outsiders and that it has demonstrated that the consequences of such self-labelling are real enough. Indeed, an influential study has argued that what affects whether prisoners re-offend or not is the character of the narratives of the self that they can construct and project into the future. One who has reformed through religion, 'self-realization', a new understanding of the consequences of crime and the like may then base his or her life on a new 'me' as a person now 'straight'.[47] But interactionists do attach uncommon significance to the public recognition of deviance. When rule-breaking receives a reaction from the outside world, its meaning must be bargained, defended, ended, or disguised. It must be altered to cope with novel, often painful restraints. The deviant may have to contend with the imputation of sinister intentions, the awarding of an unpleasant identity and social placement with pariahs. There is a significant difference between the experience of one who has 'merely' stolen and one who is validated as a thief. Stealing might not hitherto have been incorporated into core definitions of the self. It might have been construed as a lapse or atypical adventure, an act that was rather peripheral to the kind of person that one really is. Public definition can translate it into a 'master status' or pivotal feature of the offender's personality. It will affect the manner in which he or she is treated by others. The thief may become obliged to reconsider who he or she is and what he or she might do in time to come. There is, Lemert argues, the possibility of a symbolic reorganization of the self: 'When a person begins to employ his deviant behavior or a role based upon it as a means of defense, attack, or adjustment to the overt and covert problems created by the consequent societal reaction to him, his deviation is secondary.'[48]

Secondary Deviation

Secondary deviation can occur in any of the transactions which centre on the overt deviance of a person. It may arise in informal relations. Indeed, official intervention by the police and other agents being relatively uncommon, it is the informal response which is most frequently encountered. Quite crucial will be the general and local assumptions which people apply to detected deviation. It is evident that much rule-breaking is tolerated providing secondary rules are themselves observed. There is theft and pilfering at work. There is lying in everyday life. Sexual transgressions occur. It is not every instance of such rule-breaking that becomes condemned or reported to law enforcement agencies. Some is condoned, some falls outside the aegis of law, and some is thought insufficiently problematic to merit action. It is equally evident that what is intolerable in one group can be approved in another. For instance, what is proper in a bar is not always proper in a lecture theatre. Deviation is defined by its situation, by its perpetrators, and by its audience. In the course of a day, a person will pass through innumerable settings and the rules of one will not necessarily be the rules of another. The conventional order of a family does not apply to relations between strangers in the street or to the organization of a workplace (and we shall see that that has important

[47] S. Maruna, *Making Good*; and, for an extension of the theme, S. Maruna and R. Immarigeon (eds.), *After Crime and Punishment*.   [48] E. Lemert, *Social Pathology*, 76.

ramifications for differential rates of male and female offending). More dramatically, there may be quite marked discontinuities between worlds, discontinuities which turn 'normal' order upside down. For instance, Barbara Heyl has described how the madam of an American brothel educated novice prostitutes by attempting to insulate them from the universe of 'squares': she attempted to inculcate a systematic inversion of strategic sexual and social conceptions about men, money, and intercourse.[49]

It is not then the simple presence of deviance but its quality, scale, and location which typically shape a reply. Very often, deviation can be 'normalized' and accommodated[50] inside the fabric of accepted life. It is only when it is unusually inexplicable, disordering, harmful, or threatening that a critical reaction can take place. Crisis occurs when others cannot or will not cope. Its precipitation hinges on prevailing ideas about propriety and harm, the social organization of the audience, and the appreciation of possible remedies.

Some groups are tightly organized, others have a loose order, and others little apparent order at all. For instance, the army is regulated by elaborate, interconnecting, and precise rules of conduct. It assigns special personnel—military police and advocates—to the business of administering order and judging disputes. By contrast, a group of youths who 'hang out' on a street corner inhabit a rather simpler world: it *is* rule-governed, but its rules are often implicit, ad hoc, negotiable, and unenforced. Remedies are also coloured by social ideology. There is an appreciable difference between the punishments inflicted, say, by an army, a street-corner group, and a therapeutic community and each punishment will mirror something of the symbolic universe of those who impose it. For example, a Quaker body might use discipline to underscore the importance of forgiveness and tolerance.[51] An army might use it to emphasize the need for subordination. Yet, even so, connections are rarely simple and uniform. Quakers *do* expel members and call upon the police. The army and para-military organizations *can* exercise clemency, recognize religious objections to certain practices,[52] and make use of psychiatry.

The interplay between social control, social organization, deviance, and identity is neatly illustrated by Scheff's *Being Mentally Ill* (1966). It was Scheff's contention that mental illness is a social role. Initially a disconcerting and anomalous breach of an unnamed, unnameable, 'residual' rule, mental illness is given form by lay and professional stereotypes of madness. There are abundant labels and definitions which describe the character and behaviour of the mad and they are available to those who witness strange conduct. They are also available to those who have otherwise inexplicable and disturbing experiences. Labels may not be applied immediately. They may not be accepted without qualification when they are applied: there is often some scope for negotiation.[53] But labels do embody general and seemingly objective ideas. They make sense of problems, suggesting ways or scripts by which one can and should go mad and subsequently seek help. In particular, they inform psychiatric practice, providing a basis for diagnosis and treatment. Scheff would argue that much psychiatry is devoted to

---

[49] B. Heyl, *The Madam as Entrepreneur.*   [50] S. Cavan, *Liquor License.*

[51] R. Dentler and K. Erikson, 'The Functions of Deviance in Groups'.

[52] Even members of the German special police battalions charged with the murder of Jews in occupied Europe were allowed to exempt themselves if their conscience militated against it. C. Browning, *Ordinary Men: Reserve Police Battalion 101 and the Final Solution in Poland.*

[53] T. Scheff, 'Negotiating Reality: Notes on Power in the Assessment of Responsibility'.

the 'apostolic mission' of persuading people to accept one of a limited number of mad roles. Patients are encouraged to comply with therapeutic authority, gain insight, and accept an appropriate definition of themselves. It is a paradox that those who reject diagnoses may be taken only to confirm the lack of insight of the patient and the astuteness of the diagnostician.[54] It little matters whether psychiatric analyses are 'correct' or not: the social consequences of analysis would remain the same. The sociological import of labelling is that certain versions of mad behaviour are rewarded. People learn to be mad, confirming the validity and utility of the original stereotypes.

Social Control

Partly because of its consequentiality, formal social control has been subjected to extensive analysis by the interactionists. It was interactionism that enlarged the task and complexity of criminology by insisting on the creative role played by outsiders in the production of deviance. So it was that Howard Becker reflected that ' "deviance" includes both a possible infraction of a law or rule and a process of acting in some fashion against whoever might be thought to have committed the infraction'.[55] Scheff and others demonstrated that it was difficult to explain the social organization of deviance by referring to properties of the offender alone. They argue that deviance is identified, answered, and formed by those who deal with rule-breakers. The character of the response given by bailiffs,[56] the police,[57] psychiatrists,[58] magistrates,[59] and doctors[60] will provide the materials for the deviant's own significant gestures. At the very least, the deviant will be obliged to construct his or her actions around the probable reaction that they will elicit.

The violation and enforcement of rules are contingent upon place, time, and character. Certain rules are not enforceable, because it seems, they are expressly designed not to *be* enforced.[61] And law officers are not automata. They are also responsive to setting and organization, behaving rather differently in the inner city, the office, and the suburb.[62] When offences are comparatively mild (and the definition of mildness is itself contingent), much may hinge on the demeanour and response of the deviant. Whilst compliance and deference might bring about a decision not to charge a person, surliness and tardiness can hasten action.[63] Choongh would argue that in many cases the police make it a practice to use the law simply as a resource to discipline and confirm the subordination of particular populations, and the 'dross' above all, and thereby uphold a moral order on the streets.[64] All this will be negotiated in a moving context of plans and relations. Police officers might, for example, be just about to come off their shift, they might seek overtime work, they might be under scrutiny for poor performance or for excessive zeal.[65]

---

[54] E. Goffman, 'The Moral Career of the Mental Patient'; D. Rosenhan, 'On Being Sane in Insane Places'.

[55] H. Becker, *Tricks of the Trade*, 119.   [56] P. Rock, *Making People Pay*.

[57] D. Bordua (ed.), *The Police*.   [58] E. Goffman, *Asylums*.

[59] R. Emerson, *Judging Delinquents*; P. Carlen, *Magistrates' Justice*.

[60] E. Freidson, *Profession of Medicine*.   [61] R. Baldwin, 'Why Rules Don't Work'.

[62] E. Bittner, 'The Police on Skid Row'; A. Stinchcombe, 'Institutions of Privacy in the Determination of Police Administrative Practice'.

[63] C. Werthman and I. Piliavin, 'Gang Members and the Police'; J. Wilson, *Varieties of Police Behavior*.

[64] S. Choongh, *Policing as Social Discipline*.   [65] J. Rubinstein, *City Police*.

The agencies' intentions and capacities will be central. Certain enforcement institutions are geared to regulating occupations or industries and their prime objective is not to punish but to transform behaviour. The Oxford Centre for Socio-Legal Studies produced a spate of studies of those who employ such 'compliance-based strategies'. Hawkins, for instance, examined the control of the industrial pollution of rivers and canals;[66] and Hutter has written about environmental health officers.[67] The business of the environmental health officer is not to make moral pronouncements or punish those who produce contaminated food. It is to stop contamination and unhygienic practices. Yet, when people resist seemingly reasonable attempts to make them comply, they may well come to be treated as if they were conventional deviants. In all those studies of otherwise neutral, 'compliance-based' enforcement, may be found the construction of distinct pariah roles conferred on those who persistently, flagrantly, and disrespectfully ignore compliance strategies by disobeying enforcement officers. A dispassionate process will then give way to moral outrage at the deviance of those who disobey rules and rule-enforcers.

The work of the Centre also pointed to the manner in which the wealthy, well-informed, and powerful are able to make creative use of the law's provision of resources for its own avoidance. It is the business of tax lawyers and accountants continually to discover gaps, anomalies, and inconsistencies that permit their clients to escape compliance.[68]

Other institutions lack the power or means to manage deviants as outsiders. After all, enforcement is an expensive and laborious process when it is waged against those who have no wish to comply. Those institutions will then create identities which are expressly designed to ease their work. Being perhaps unable to control hostile and alienated people, they may instead emphasize the normality and conventionality of those whom they may privately define as abnormal. In the case of the mass collection of small commercial debts, for example, enforcement procedures are designed principally to persuade most defaulters that they are fundamentally honest, albeit forgetful, people. Were enforcement to antagonize them, the routine collection of small debts would become impossibly expensive, time-consuming, and inefficient.[69] For rather different reasons, it was the policy of a home for unwed mothers to convince its clients that pregnancy was a misadventure which should not be blamed on them. The mothers were innocents, not sexually experienced women who used contraceptives.[70] In both instances, the regulation of deviance contributed roles that protected the self of the rule-breaker. In the latter instance, the proffered role confirmed the woman's virtue and her lack of any need to take future precautions, permitting future unintended pregnancies and a further drift into deviation.

There is thus a tendency to treat rules as *resources* rather than as binding instructions. It is a tendency that creates considerable flexibility in the organization of relations between deviants and agents of control. Rule-breakers may be co-opted as allies or informants,[71] they may become part of a game-like and well-regulated exchange,[72]

---

[66] K. Hawkins, *Environment and Enforcement*.

[67] B. Hutter, *The Reasonable Arm of the Law?*

[68] D. McBarnet, 'Whiter than White Collar Crime'.

[69] P. Rock, *Making People Pay*.

[70] P. Rains, *Becoming an Unwed Mother*.

[71] G. Marx, 'The New Police Undercover Work'.

[72] H. Sacks, 'Notes on Police Assessment of Moral Character'.

they may be effectively ignored, or they may be pursued with great vigour. Typically, for instance, it is so difficult to obtain information about activities that have no willing complainant that the police have to offer a licence to insiders.[73] Drug suppliers may trade information for lesser penalties or immunity from prosecution.[74] And relations may also change over time: shifts in personnel, policy, or politics can introduce pressures to abandon old strategies or adopt novel ones. In one celebrated instance, the appointment of a new chief constable led to a blitz on homosexual importuning. What had been neglected became a target for energetic prosecution.[75]

More minutely, there is a great scope for injecting variety *within* relationships. Thus, in one study, Paul Willis observed that there was no uniform suppression of drug use in an English town. On the contrary, users and members of the local drugs squad appeared to enjoy a symbiotic relationship: the police arresting those whose offences were relatively flagrant and substantial and the users themselves reporting 'pushers' whose behaviour was held to be exploitative and bullying. Most consumers were allowed to proceed undisturbed, co-existing quite amiably with the police.[76]

The orderly production of deviance and deviants therefore hinges on a complicated and fluid set of interchanges. It cannot be distilled down into a series of mechanical and predictable processes. Interactionism is accordingly somewhat reluctant to rely on schematic descriptions of social control. Instead, it turns sociology towards the detailed analysis of specific events. General themes *do* dominate that analysis, but they are not held to have the character of iron laws. On the contrary, outcomes are treated as uncertain and possibly surprising.

Scott's *The Making of Blind Men* (1969) is an important demonstration of the intricate and largely unexpected forms that social control can take. It stresses the interdependence of control and deviation, arguing that at the time of his study the blind were manufactured in the United States by the special agencies which cared for them. Organizations had to achieve a limited success, displaying their capacity to train blind people for work and activity in the world of the sighted. Not every blind person could be educated. Only a few were eligible as candidates for transformation into the acceptably functioning blind. It is those few who were heavily recruited by the voluntary agencies for redemption. They were the 'blind children who can be educated and the blind adults who can be employed. The system largely screens out the elderly, the unemployable, the uneducable, and the multiply-handicapped—in other words, the vast bulk of the blindness population.'[77]

Blindness is rarely a total loss of vision. Many of those in the charge of American blindness agencies could see a little, but they were methodically encouraged to play the blind role, relinquishing any use of their residual sight and adopting the methods of the utterly sightless. They were required to learn incapacity, conforming to embedded institutional definitions of blindness. In this fashion, skills and senses are surrendered, being replaced by an orderly incompetence:

[73] J. Skolnick, *Justice Without Trial.*   [74] B. Cox et al., *The Fall of Scotland Yard.*
[75] *Police Review*, 3 August 1963.   [76] P. Willis, *Profane Culture.*
[77] R. Scott, *The Making of Blind Men.*

The disability of blindness is a learned social role. The various attitudes and patterns of behavior that characterize people who are blind are not inherent in their condition but, rather, are acquired through ordinary processes of social learning. Thus, there is nothing inherent in the condition of blindness that requires a person to be docile, dependent, melancholy, or helpless; nor is there anything about it that should lead him to become independent or assertive. Blind men are made and by the same processes of socialization that have made us all.[78]

The awarding of deviant identity cannot then be portrayed as an elementary reflex action on the part of the State or powerful institutions. To be sure, the State does have considerable power to describe its subjects. It is a power which sometimes allows the subject little scope for negotiation or rebuttal. In many transactions, the authoritative expert on control or treatment can impose his or her will on the deviant. Yet the definitions offered vary and they may have remarkable consequences. Becoming deviant is not always a straightforward process of amplification. The rule-breaker may be coaxed into any one of a number of roles, immorality being ascribed only when an agency or witness holds to ideas of free will, when the offender was thought to know what he or she was doing and when he or she could have done otherwise.[79] Equally available are penitent, sick, or probationary roles.[80]

We have used the language of role and role-playing and there is some little confusion in the suggestion that the world is neatly scripted and organized for dramatic purposes. As Goffman observed, 'all the world is not a stage—certainly the theater isn't entirely'.[81] Roles are adapted and created in use, breaking down their stereotyped character and replacing it by innovation.[82] Deviant roles themselves resist precise classification. So it was that interactionists began increasingly to write of homosexualities instead of homosexuality, stressing the wealth and diversity of sexual deviation.[83] It would be misleading to argue that the business of deviating consists merely of stepping into an arranged part. Interactionism casts deviance as a process which may continue over a lifetime, which has no necessary end, which is anything but inexorable, and which may be built around false starts, diversions, and returns. The trajectory of a deviant career cannot always be predicted. However constrained they may seem to be, people can choose not to err further. Phillipson has likened the process to a long corridor with numerous doors: one is not compelled to travel the entire length but may leave at almost any stage.[84] Indeed, one might go further, pointing to the ways in which deviant careers are likely to become chaotic and *disorderly*,[85] 'careering'[86] rather than organized, because of the marked instability of the deviant's world, an instability wrought by cycles of boom and bust in drug dealing,[87] for example, by the unexpected

---

[78] R. Scott, *The Making of Blind Men*, 14.

[79] P. McHugh, 'A Common-Sense Conception of Deviance'.

[80] J. Gusfield, 'Moral Passage'.　　　[81] E. Goffman, *Frame Analysis*, 1.

[82] R. Turner, 'Role-Taking: Process versus Conformity'.

[83] K. Plummer (ed.), *Modern Homosexualities: Fragments of Lesbian and Gay Experience*, esp. ch. 1.

[84] M. Phillipson, *Sociological Aspects of Crime and Delinquency*.

[85] J. Katz, *Seductions of Crime*. For a contrary argument, see J. Stander, D. Farrington, G. Hill, and P. Altham, 'Markov Chain Analysis and Specialization in Criminal Careers'.

[86] D. Robins, *Tarnished Vision*.

[87] C. Faupel, *Shooting Dope: Career Patterns of Hard-Core Heroin Users*.

arrest or experience of violence and compounded by a lack of firm structures and controls.[88]

Luckenbill and Best argue:

> Riding escalators between floors may be an effective metaphor for respectable organizational careers, but it fails to capture the character of deviant careers. A more appropriate image is a walk in the woods. Here, some people take the pathways marked by their predecessors, while others strike out on their own. Some walk slowly, exploring before moving further, but others run, caught up in the action. Some have a destination in mind and proceed purposively; others view the trip and enjoy it for its own sake. Even those intent on reaching a destination may stray from the path; they may try to shortcut or they may lose sight of familiar landmarks, get lost and find it necessary to backtrack. Without a rigid organizational structure, deviant careers can develop in many different ways.[89]

Becoming deviant is itself described dialectically by interactionists as a series of phases which tend to supersede one another, each phase reworking the significance and causal impact of what has gone before. In turn, each phase is held to be causally important in its own right. It is not enough to describe the initial conditions of rule-breaking (be they social disorganization, conflict, or defective personality), it is also necessary to appreciate the evolving character of the deviant career as it emerges in time. Thus Lindesmith and others have been somewhat scathing about psychiatric analyses which presume that traits diagnosed in treatment were somehow invariant dimensions of personality. They insist, instead, that those traits may have arisen in the treatment or control of deviation itself. Drug addicts, for instance, may not have been passive or inadequate when they made their first moves towards deviation. Becker accordingly stressed the need to employ a model of 'sequential causation' which can comprehend the developing, staggered, and changing qualities of deviation. It is a model whose construction requires an expenditure of time and patience, and research is probably at its most fruitful when it monitors or reconstructs events as they unfold. In this sense, interactionism reveals its Chicago lineage by defining research as emergent and exploratory.

Deviancy Amplification and Moral Panic

Interactionism and labelling theory were given a new, dramatic, and possibly somewhat awkward emphasis in the British sociology of deviance of the 1960s and beyond. Deviance amplification and moral panic were to become the distinctive big idea of the era. The origins of the idea were a little odd. Independently of and simultaneously with the emergence of 'labelling' theory in the USA, a social statistician, Leslie Wilkins, had drawn certain inferences about the effects of the distribution of phenomena in social space.[90] He had observed that deviants were statistically uncommon, a peculiar claim unless it was intended to refer to *assumptions* about the frequency of rule-breaking. Wilkins proceeded to argue

---

[88] P. Reuter, *Disorganized Crime*.

[89] D. Luckenbill and J. Best, 'Careers in Deviance and Respectability: The Analogy's Limitation', 201.

[90] L. Wilkins, *Social Deviance*.

that there was a tendency for deviants to become structurally isolated from the majority. This was also an argument that *might* be said to hold about popular *assumptions*. He concluded that information about such an isolated minority was necessarily transmitted over a distance to the majority: it was second-hand and, being mediated by the press, radio, and television, it was liable to distortion. The effect was 'deviancy amplification', a process which resembles the workings of a cybernetic system with inaccurate feedback loops. Amplification occurs when the majority or its agents react to a deforming representation of the deviant minority, creating a new situation, problems, identity, and context for deviation. The answering replies of deviants are again distorted, generating a new response and a new reply. Incorporated by Stan Cohen[91] and Jock Young,[92] amplification theory explained the dialectical progression of deviant processes: action producing reaction in a spiralling chain of ever more alienating gestures.[93] Some slight initial difference in dress, expression, or conduct can lead to a sequence of events which magnifies, exaggerates, and creates deviance. Thus Teddy Boys were given a demonic cast in the England of the 1950s, coming to stand for much that was corrupt and evil.[94] Amplification theory seems to be most telling when it is applied to symbolic or expressive deviation, deviation that is publicly proclaimed and designed to invite a public response; its uses elsewhere are less certain. It is not clear how such amplification cycles start and end,[95] nor is it clear why particular cycles amplify and others serve to reduce visible deviation.[96] At stake, it may be supposed, are not only the problems of recruitment confronted by deviant groups that have become ever more estranged from the mundane world, but also the difficulties faced by those who remain, difficulties of increasing censure, sanction, and isolation. Becoming and staying deviant can become simply too costly. But deviance amplification and moral panic injected a novel, dynamic, and political emphasis into analysis which pointed to process, signification, and the workings of control as the prime constituents of individual and collective deviant careers.

Another important advance has recently been made by Randall Collins, a student of Erving Goffman, who has written persuasively and in detail about the choreographed interplay between aggressor and victim in violent transactions. His focus is neither on the psychology or physiology of the victim or offender nor on the broader features of the social structures which they inhabit. Alcohol may be linked to violence, he argues, but alcohol typically makes would-be violent people incompetent in the use of force and most drunk people are not violent. Similarly, masculinity may be associated with violence, but most males most of the time are not violent. Neither alcohol nor the performance of gender can explain the actual forms and progression of violence. Something else is at work. Like Goffman and Georg Simmel before him, he attends instead to the micro-dynamics of particular situations, analysing step by step how violent transactions unfold. Violence is actually difficult to accomplish: most people—even soldiers and police who are professionally engaged to deploy force—are reluctant to attack others. A mixture of tension and fear holds them back. It is a 'forward panic'

---

[91] S. Cohen, *Folk Devils and Moral Panics.*   [92] J. Young, *The Drugtakers.*
[93] J. Young, 'Moral Panic'.   [94] P. Rock and S. Cohen, 'The Teddy Boy'.
[95] P. Jenkins, 'Failure to Launch: Why Do Some Social Issues Fail to Detonate Moral Panics'.
[96] J. Ditton, *Controlology.*

that can overcome that mix, and it may be enabled in part by the manifest weakness of
the potential victim, in part by an egging-on by spectators: 'the tension of the struggle
[can] turn[] into the hot rush and vicious overkill of forward panic'.[97] Collins has analysed how victims themselves can enter into what he calls interaction ritual chains of
'emotional entrainment' whereby they become progressively swept up in one another's
actions and reactions to be dominated, steered, and incapacitated by violent offenders.
Looking, say, at episodes of domestic violence or crowd disturbance, he narrates how,
little by little, people may come collaboratively and almost collusively to assume the
roles and identities of victim and offender.

Critique

As the interactionist sociology of deviance came to the fore, so criticism itself mounted. In
part, there was a response from those whose work had been overshadowed. In part, there
was a reaction from those who had exploited developments within interactionism, pursued
them beyond the limits of interactionist analysis and returned to interactionism with their
new arguments. As Plummer remarked in 1979, 'In just ten years, labelling theory has
moved from being the radical critic of established orthodoxies to being the harbinger of
new orthodoxies to be criticized'.[98] The history of interactionism has followed the conventional pattern of much sociology: the extraordinary has become ordinary and then banal.

Attacks have typically been coloured by the parent perspectives of the critic.
What one takes to be a conservative stance[99] is thought by another to be radical.
Interactionism is defined as overly empiricist by one[100] and insufficiently empiricist
by another.[101] Debates about sociology are inordinately complex because they entail a
series of interminable questions about the position of the questioners.

The first and most obvious objection to interactionism challenges its scientific standing. Science is held to characterize disciplines which are articulate, precise, and reasoned
in their methods. Above all, it is held that sociology should proceed by logically scan-
ning problems, formulating hypotheses, and rigorously applying them. Interactionism
is heir to the assumptions and practices of the Chicago School and it is as resistant
to an orderly logico-deductive methodology. It patently fails to conform to the strict
model of scientific procedure.[102] It is hesitant about elaborate planning and exposition,
arguing that such work blinds one to the possibility of learning in the field. Thus, Laud
Humphreys observed 'hypotheses should develop *out* of . . . ethnographic work, rather
than provide restrictions and distortions from its inception'.[103] Interactionists would
preserve their openness to the social world, being educated as they pursue research.

Hostile critics find this deliberate lack of preparation unsatisfactory. They portray
interactionism as ambiguous, ill-resolved, and evasive. They are particularly distressed

---

[97] R. Collins, *Violence: A Micro-Sociological Theory*, 135.
[98] K. Plummer, 'Misunderstanding Labelling Perspectives', 85.
[99] A. Platt, review of *The New Criminology*.   [100] I. Taylor et al., *The New Criminology*.
[101] W. Gove (ed.), *The Labelling of Deviance*.
[102] J. Huber, 'Symbolic Interaction as a Pragmatic Perspective'.
[103] L. Humphries, *Tearoom Trade*, 22.

by its refusal to offer conjectures that might sustain or refute its fundamental propositions. Adopting a falsificationist philosophy of science,[104] they remark that interactionism is not scientific because it is a closed system which resists refutation. There
is merit in the observation: symbolic interactionism has woven such a subtle system
of indeterminate ideas that the rejection of one can always be explained by invoking
another. Its proponents would retort that science should respect the qualities of the
materials which it explores: ambiguity, contradictoriness, and openness distinguish the
social world and it would be foolish to impose schemes that block them out. To pretend otherwise could lead, in Rorty's words, to the kind of ahistorical scientific method
that would be employed by one who 'knows in advance what results he or she desires
and has no need to adjust his or her ends'.[105] There are many occasions when the perspectives and methods of interactionism are peculiarly appropriate, particularly, Katz
argues, where new, complex, hitherto unexplored, or especially vivid phenomena are
emerging.[106] But interactionism is reduced a little in the process. It may well be that
sociology cannot be otherwise, that efforts to make it conform to a simplified version
of the natural sciences do violence to enquiry and that society cannot be distilled into
clear formulas. It may well be that sociology can never be stereotypically scientific. Yet
the appeal of interactionism must retreat towards the sheer persuasiveness of its imagery of people and it is evident that not all *are* persuaded.

More telling is the phenomenological assertion that interactionism fails even in its
core task. If interactionists resist the codification and formalization of their approach, it
is because they say that they wish faithfully to reflect central properties of social order,
to capture the authentic workings of symbolic processes. To be sure, they recognize that
those workings are not 'naturally' reproduced by sociology, that sociology is a distorting
activity that answers special purposes and employs a special language. But there is assumed to be correspondence between the structure of social life and the structure of its
reports. Some phenomenologists have argued that that correspondence is less than sure.
They claim that there is a problematic gulf between the interactionist vocabulary of 'role',
'deviance', and 'process' and the actual procedures by which people organize their affairs. Cicourel, for instance, questioned whether one does, in fact, order one's life by role
analysis.[107] If one does not, it becomes uncertain what status the word 'role' is supposed
to occupy. Roles are sociological inventions, not features of the social world itself. People
presumably turn to different practices and ideas when they behave and Cicourel would
have the sociologist inspect *them* rather than the suspect conception of role itself. We
have observed that roles are not discussed as if they were binding instructions to people.
We have also observed that roles are imprecise, fluid, and negotiated. Nevertheless, roles
appear to be the sociologist's invention, not the role-player's. Similarly, Phillipson and
Roche have argued that the rules which are broken when 'deviance' takes place are those
devised by sociologists, not those of people in everyday life.[108] Deviance is *not* a label

[104] K. Popper, *Conjectures and Refutations*.   [105] R. Rorty, *Objectivity, Relativism and Truth*, 68.
[106] J. Katz, 'Ethnography's Warrants'.
[107] A. Cicourel, 'Interpretative Procedures and Normative Rules in the Negotiation of Status and Role'.
[108] M. Phillipson and M. Roche, 'Phenomenology, Sociology and the Study of Deviance'.

that people bestow on one another very freely. One may be identified as a 'slag', a 'punk', a 'thief', or a 'liar' instead.

There may be some formal similarity in the consequences of such acts of identification. But the overarching term 'deviance' is more generally a sociological artefact; it is not just a natural phenomenon which the sociologist discovers in an undisturbed state. Interactionists are relatively unprepared to define that term too precisely—to do so would compound the error which the phenomenologists have already emphasized. *Deviance* is tacitly taken instead to be what has been called a 'sensitizing concept': 'Hundreds of our concepts—like culture, institutions, social structure, mores and personality—are not definitive concepts but are sensitizing in nature. They lack precise reference and have no bench marks which allow a clean-cut identification of a specific instance and of its content. Instead, they rest on a general sense of what is relevant.'[109]

Little intellectual capital has been sunk in the interactionist's sensitizing concept of deviance. The concept maps out a vague idea and propels sociologists towards it. It does not inform them about what exactly they will find there. *Deviance* has become instead a loose working idea whose details have been progressively supplied by studies of concrete events. The conception is built up 'crescively'[110] and gradually, including the consideration of marginal and perhaps even absurd cases. It has at various times been treated as including, for example, dwarfs, giants, stutterers, prostitutes, strippers, and thieves. Whether those disparate figures do share a list of common properties which exclude all ambiguous or difficult cases is not discussed. Perhaps it is not thought to be important. More significant, it seems, is the utility of an *approach* that employs the term and ideas of deviance.

Quite different criticisms have flowed from radical criminology and its sympathizers, those whom 'left realists' might call 'left idealists'. We shall discuss below how radical criminologists seek to place the analysis of specific and general events in the context of a particular master vision of society. It is a vision which borrows heavily from Marxism and the sociology of conflict. Every individual phenomenon is thought to acquire its significance from a larger framework of political economy and from its contribution to that framework. Radical criminologists dwell on the structures and transformations of capitalism, relating crime and its control to the larger organization of capitalism itself. Sociological theory is also given meaning by that organization, regarded as a political process in its own right. It is alleged that criminological ideas should be assessed as agents in a wider struggle for power and authority. They are not simply dispassionate commentaries which can be examined for their logicality, coherence, and appropriateness.

Thus defined, the business of criminology is very unlike the interactionist project. It is concerned with a critical mapping of the major systems of power and their interconnections with the State, its enforcement apparatus and modes of governance. Interactionism does touch on power and it has offered histories of law-making and control. But it also refrains from translating such work into a schematic, political

---

[109] H. Blumer, 'What is Wrong with Social Theory?', 148.
[110] A. Rose, Preface to *Human Behavior and Social Processes*.

theory of society, into what post-modernist critics would call foundational narratives. On the contrary, the interactionists hold that the sociologist is offered only a series of partial glimpses which may lack overall unity. They argue, for instance, that delinquent groups change from time to time, situation to situation, and place to place and the intensive study of a delinquent group cannot provide the truth about all delinquents. It certainly does not furnish information about the innermost workings of capitalism.

Interactionists and radical criminologists have melded many of their ideas,[111] but there does remain an irreconcilable gulf between them. In particular, there is no agreement about the character or very existence of social structure. Whilst radical criminologists hold to a view of structure that supports strong political recommendations, many interactionists would doubt that there is a self-evident structure that can be investigated by any actual defensible empirical means.

Interactionism has also been subjected to more minute criticisms—a response to the central importance which some have awarded to labelling. Studies of police and judicial reaction have been taken to argue that there would be no deviance without formal intervention. Further, it has been said that the theory portrays deviant careers as a steady progression into ever-increasing alienation. Gouldner stated, for example, that interactionism has 'the paradoxical consequence of inviting us to view the deviant as a passive nonentity who is responsible neither for his suffering nor its alleviation—who is more "sinned against than sinning".[112] Ronald Akers, too, observed: 'One sometimes gets the impression from reading this literature that people go about minding their own business and then—"wham"—bad society comes along and slaps them with a stigmatized label.'[113] There are certainly instances which could support such a criticism.[114] On occasion, deviants are presented as if they were the innocent, passive targets of signification; but those strains are not necessary or widespread. We have remarked that deviation can take place without the manifest interference of others. We have also remarked that the effects of labelling are not at all determinate: they are contingent and variable, having no predictable outcome in individual cases. Criticisms of the species offered by Gouldner really reflect a response to only one narrow and perhaps over-simplified version of interactionism.

A more robust, and sometimes puzzling attack on symbolic interactionism and labelling theory has been mounted by Colin Sumner, who argued in *The Sociology of Deviance: An Obituary* (1994) and elsewhere[115] that the theory has evolved from being a liberal and tolerant response to borderline infractions to an understanding, particularly in the work of Austin Turk,[116] of the necessity of focusing on 'political resistance and revolt'.[117] That new appreciation, said Sumner, was to be the nemesis of interactionist criminology. Deviance could no longer be represented as part of a project to enforce coherent values. If capitalism strenuously controls the dissident, the different, and the disadvantaged, Sumner argued, there should be a theory appropriate to the

[111] R. Scott, *Why Sociology Does Not Apply.*   [112] A. Gouldner, 'The Sociologist as Partisan', 38.
[113] R. Akers, 'Problems in the Sociology of Deviance', 463.
[114] T. Scheff (ed.), *Mental Illness and Social Processes.*
[115] Introduction to C. Sumner (ed.), *The Blackwell Companion to Criminology.*
[116] A. Turk, *Criminality and Legal Order.*
[117] C. Sumner, *The Sociology of Deviance: An Obituary*, 246.

theme, a new fusion of the ideas of Durkheim and Marxism in the concept of 'censure', a ban embodying the ideology and power of the State.

From a distance, it is a little difficult to understand why Sumner should have been so adamant that invoking ideas about censure and the State repression of serious deviation must mark the demise of symbolic interactionism; and why, indeed, he should have felt obliged to write its 'obituary' at all. Symbolic interactionism has not only succeeded in analysing serious crime[118] and, indeed, the State in the past (although its preferred methodology of participant-observation makes it a little disinclined to do so because the State is something of a massive abstraction), but there are no principles within the theory to preclude such analysis. Of course, that work has had to be performed in a manner compatible with interactionism, leading to distinctively interactionist portraits of crime and the State;[119] but why should that have been otherwise? Moreover, interactionism has been found by some to be perfectly complementary to larger theories of the State and it has entered the writings of Marxists and others who have examined the impact of power on particular social settings.[120]

It is, of course, true that macro-structural analyses of the State are not the chosen domain of interactionism, but it is curious that Sumner seems to have felt himself impelled to argue that there must be only one sovereign model of crime and control that can brook no rivals. Our own contention would be, first, that the politics of symbolic interactionism are not unambiguous (sometimes they are marked, sometimes they are not, and when they *are* marked they can take quite different guises);[121] second, that there is more than enough room for competing theories to co-exist within a division of intellectual labour; third, that the chosen terrain of interactionism is far from exhausted (why should not interactionists continue to study what Sumner dismisses as borderline cases if they wish to do so?); and, last, that the insight (if it *is* an insight) that the State can be oppressive and protective of class interests has no plausible bearing on the validity or appeal of the labelling approach (that insight has only a tangential relevance to the approach's own work).

The most vigorous, direct, and revealing exchange of ideas about one of the principal strands of the symbolic interactionist sociology of deviance was launched in *The American Journal of Sociology* in May 2002 when Loic Wacquant published a review symposium[122] that castigated books by Elijah Anderson[123] (which explored how young African-American men managed to live on the streets of Philadelphia), Mitchell Duneier[124] (which discussed the trade in second-hand books and magazines developed by homeless men on the streets of Greenwich Village in Manhattan), and Katherine Newman[125] (which explored the ways in which men and women coped with living in and around the fast food industry and a minimum wages economy). In it are laid bare

---

[118] L. Athens, *Violent Criminal Acts and Actors*; and J. Katz, *Seductions of Crime*.
[119] P. Rock, *A View from the Shadows* and *Helping Victims of Crime*.
[120] Prime examples are S. Hall et al., *Policing the Crisis* and J. Ferrell, *Crimes of Style*.
[121] They are libertarian interactionists like Schur; conservative interactionists like Klapp; and socialist interactionists like Smith. Most have no clear political markings at all.
[122] L. Wacquant, 'Scrutinizing the Street: Poverty, Morality, and the Pitfalls of Urban Ethnography'.
[123] E. Anderson, *Code of the Street: Decency, Violence, and the Moral Life of the Inner City*.
[124] M. Duneier, *Sidewalk*.   [125] K. Newman, *No Shame in my Game*.

some major fissures between the micro-sociological and macro-sociological, between a sociological emphasis on the meanings attached by subjects to their social world and on the larger, 'objective' conditions of that world identified by the scholar; between sociology as tentative, grounded exploration and sociology as theory-building. The general tenor of the critique is most pithily conveyed by the observation that there:

> is the deeply problematic relationship between theory and observation . . . Together these three books illustrate well the perennial pitfalls of ethnography as embedded social research when it is carried out under the banner of raw empiricism. It can get so *close* to its subjects that it ends up parroting their point of view without linking it to the broader system of material and symbolic relations that give it meaning and significance, reducing sociological analysis to the collection and assembly of folk notions and vocabularies of motive' (p. 1523, emphasis in the original.)

Wacquant attacked the ethnographers liberally and on a broad front, castigating them for an appreciative stance which he claimed had eulogized, beautified (p. 1478), sanctified, and bowdlerized the condition of the poor, translating them into what he called '*paragons of morality*' (emphasis in original, p. 1469); being 'blind' in the telling of what he called '*neo-romantic tales*' (emphasis in original, p. 1471) to 'issues of class power and [a] stubborn disregard for the deep and multisided involvement . . . of the state in producing the social dereliction and human wretchedness they . . . portray' (p. 1470). There is, he says, an 'unwarranted empiricist disjunction of ethnography from theory' (p. 1470).

Let us concentrate on the criticisms levelled specifically at Duneier and Anderson, the two sociologists who have contributed more directly to the sociology of crime and deviance, because those criticisms and the ripostes which were made reveal something of the standing and relations of symbolic interactionism within the larger body of sociological criminology.

Duneier, Wacquant says, 'does not discuss the structural forces—the desocialization of labor, the erosion of the patriarchal household, the retrenchment of the welfare state, the criminalization of the urban poor, the conflation of blackness and dangerousness in public space . . .' (p. 1480). Anderson is accused of 'reifying' 'cultural orientations into groups' (p. 1487); confusing the values of respectable 'decency' and the disreputable 'street' with what Wacquant claims are the structural locations of different groups (p. 1489); taking sides with the one group against the other in his analysis of how people make out in adversity; failing to link the de-industralization of the city with the behaviour he described on the street; and failing to trace the 'genesis of the "code of the street"' as historically sedimented and class-ethnically inflected masculine ways of thinking, feeling, and acting in urban public space . . .' (p. 1492).

Duneier's reply was to challenge Wacquant's allegation by allegation, claiming that his review had been highly selective in its use of illustrations and copyings from *Sidewalk,* that Duneier had depicted his subject 'warts and all', checked what he said methodically, and 'devot[ing] four *whole* chapters to documenting various "deviant and unflattering behaviors," including the excessive drug use Wacquant is otherwise able to note . . .'[126](p. 1556). Above all, Duneier argues:

---

[126] M. Duneier, 'What Kind of Combat Sport Is Sociology?'.

[A] key component of his argument falls apart in the light of overwhelming evidence that *Sidewalk* does *not* turn the vendors into saints: it presents them in such complexity that there is no division between 'good' poor people and 'bad' poor people, legal and illegal, or any such false dichotomy. Rather, the book consistently argues that within the same individuals one often finds struggles to live moral lives and tendencies that would undermine social order, and that many of the same people cycle in and out of vending, scavenging, and panhandling, drug use, alcoholism, and criminal behavior. . . . The people who work on Sixth Avenue . . . have lived their lives in interaction with a variety of political, economic, and historical conditions, including housing segregation, spatially concentrated poverty, deindustrialization, and Jim Crow.[127] (pp. 1562, 1565)

Anderson, too, quarrels with Wacquant's reading of *Code of the Street*:

[he] fails to engage the main thrust of the book: As a result of the breakdown or weaknesses of civil law in the most distressed inner-city communities, a survival strategy with implications for local public order has emerged—a 'code of the street' that relies on 'street justice,' whose transactions involve a currency of reputation, respect, retribution, and retaliation. Because civil law has been so compromised and eroded locally, people often rely on themselves and their reputations for protection, a situation that leads to high rates of urban violence.[128] (p. 1534)

Wacquant's 'distortions', Anderson continues:

derive in part from his peculiar view of the role of social theory in ethnographic work. His view demands that the ethnographer begin with a rigid commitment to a theory. The ethnographer must then subordinate the cultural complexity he or she finds in the field to that theory . . . Should the subjects and their behavior fail to correspond to the suppositions made by that theory, the subjects are dismissed as hapless 'victims of false consciousness,' and a 'true' consciousness is inserted for them in the analysis. An ethnographic work that fails to reflect this conception is judged deficient. Thus one proceeds from preconceptions to demonstrate the correctness of the theory in order to fit the subjects to its orthodoxy. Only this approach will do. . . . there is no real conception of an autonomous, situational, micro-sociological level of analysis.[129] (p. 1535)

And that, perhaps, is the very nub of argument, the divide which separates symbolic interactionist and allied approaches from structural sociology. It is not a divide that is likely ever to be bridged, because the protagonists give such very different answers to fundamental questions of method, analysis, interpretation, and the character of authoritative evidence.

Conclusion

Symbolic interactionism evolved out of the work of the Chicago School, receiving its name—perhaps not accidentally—just as the School began to be eclipsed by the functionalism of Harvard and Columbia Universities. It too was grounded in a social

---

[127] M. Duneier, 'What Kind of Combat Sport Is Sociology?'.
[128] E. Anderson, 'The Ideologically Driven Critique'.
[129] E. Anderson, 'The Ideologically Driven Critique'.

anthropology which explored the linguistic conventions and practical actions of people 'doing things together' in small social worlds. Significance was attached to how selves, motives, and conduct were named, because important controls and guides for action are built into how we categorize and view the objects around us. Criminal and deviant acts and actors were also taken to be phenomena that take shape in language, and the interactionists traced the manner in which they could be transformed as their private and public designations changed.

Symbolic interactionism held sway over the sociology of crime and deviance in the 1960s and early 1970s. Antipathetic to systematic theorizing and insistent on empirical research, it emphasized the active discovery of knowledge in the research setting. Some interactionists have correspondingly denied that they possess a 'theory' at all. Instead, they insisted that theirs was a perspective which enabled them to venture out into society to observe people, in Becker's phrase, 'doing things together'.[130] One of the prime contributions made by interactionism is its compilation of detailed information about criminal and deviant practices and the social reaction to those practices. Its practitioners are not content to speculate about how crime or deviance is transacted; and crime and deviance have as a result been presented as a series of highly complicated processes without a single, fixed structure. Interactionists do not claim to manufacture grand theory. They do not answer all the pressing social problems which bedevil people. They proceed more modestly and slowly. As Plummer suggested, 'symbolic interactionism is only one theory that need be used within the labelling perspective, but it has an affinity with the study of marginality and deviance and it is a useful corrective to grander, more general theories. It has a useful role to play.'[131]

Further Reading

H. BECKER, (ed.), *The Other Side: Perspectives on Deviance*, New York 1964.

H. BLUMER, *Symbolic Interactionism; Perspective and Method*, Englewood Cliffs, NJ, 1969.

S. COHEN, *Folk Devils and Moral Panic*, London, 1972, (3rd edn, 2011).

P. ROCK, *The Making of Symbolic Interactionism*, London, 1978.

E. RUBINGTON and M. Weinberg (eds.), *Deviance: The Interactionist Perspective*, New York 2007.

[130] H. Becker, 'Labelling Theory Reconsidered'.
[131] K. Plummer, 'Misunderstanding Labelling Perspectives', 119.

8

Phenomenology

Introduction

Phenomenology came out of a great mass of debates about the character, scope, and certainty of knowledge. Those debates have only a remote bearing on our theme and we shall not explore them in any detail. It is enough to recall that, although there have always been some misgivings about our ability to make sense of the world, a severe doubt became central to the writings of particular English empiricists and German philosophers at the beginning of the nineteenth century. The claim was made that observation and the methods of science provided no foundation for iron laws of nature and science. It was even argued that observed objects are not necessarily what they seem.

Let us reconstruct one version of that argument. It was stated that observation is manifestly constrained. It is affected by the physical capacities of the body and brain, by assumptions about the patterning of things and by memories of past connections. One does not usually see confusion but order and it is difficult to determine how that order arose and whether it flows from the things in themselves or from how we see them. At the very least, perspectives are shaped by a rank inability to attend to more than a limited range of sensations at any one time and in any one place. Order may inhere in the world, but things cannot be grasped without the active workings of consciousness. In particular, appearances are structured by the present and future purposes of the observer, by experience, and by stocks of knowledge.

Let us consider those points in turn. It is clear that what is known hinges on practical objectives. A desert is simply not the same thing to oil prospectors, readers of *Dune* and *The Seven Pillars of Wisdom*, ecologists, botanists, painters, Bedouin, and tourists. It is not even the same thing to an oil prospector over time. It is a *phenomenon*, a phenomenon being 'that which appears to be the case, that which is given in perception or in consciousness, for the perceiving and conscious subject'.[1] Phenomena are those organized experiences which are available to us as we explore the world with our senses and imagination. They are utterly distinct from what are called *noumena*—what are assumed to be the undeformed, unchanging, and absolute essences of things. It was held by the phenomenologists to follow that the world can never be understood immediately and as it 'really' is. Indeed, it is possible to conclude only that the true nature of a thing is unascertainable. Like the people in Plato's cave, the people whose back is turned to the sun

---

[1] M. Phillipson and M. Roche, 'Phenomenology, Sociology and the Study of Deviance', 126.

and who see only shadows, we can only guess what that true nature might be. To pretend otherwise would require, in Rorty's words, 'a God's-eye standpoint–one which has somehow broken out of our language and beliefs and tested them against something known without their aid. But we have no idea what it would be like to be at that standpoint.'[2]

Phenomenology explicitly addresses the possibilities of phenomena. It consists of a series of answers to the problems posed by the sheer inaccessibility of sure knowledge about things as they 'really' are. In response to an apparently inescapable uncertainty, some of its authors proposed that philosophy should turn away from the quixotic search for an impeccable truth about the external world because one can never know something which is uncontaminated by its own investigation. All that remain are phenomena and the processes which give them birth. Phenomenology accordingly tended to redefine the proper business of philosophy as a descriptive analysis of how things are grasped by consciousness. It directed attention at a relatively certain area whose limits are the limits of effective knowledge itself. It no longer enquired whether knowledge was correct, but how it came into being. By extension and with a little irony, a number of phenomenologists could proceed to argue that almost all knowledge becomes correct for all imaginable purposes. After all, there is no accessible deeper, higher, or more fundamental truth with which it may be compared and revealed as false.

Phenomenology was for a while to become a flourishing intellectual enterprise and, like any such enterprise, it acquired its own peculiar conflicts and ambiguities. Not only does it encompass what might be described as rather marginal and inconsistent themes,[3] it is not always clear what unites those who call themselves phenomenologists. There are profound contradictions between the ideas of Hegel, Heidegger, Scheler, and Schutz. Indeed, a number of phenomenologists would not agree with our description of their fundamental position.

Happily, what passes for phenomenological sociology is only a partial rendering of the opportunities offered by the school. No criminology has yet been grounded in the writings of Husserl, Jaspers, and Merleau-Ponty, and many complexities were never imported to affect the analysis of deviance. Some disharmony does undoubtedly remain and it *has* been taken into criminology. Moreover, the exponents of different versions have not even been entirely faithful to their own principles. Phenomenological criminology does not offer an integrated logic and methodology. Rather, it forms a loose and sometimes inconsistent collection of observations.

Phenomenology and Sociology

Outcrops of phenomenology are scattered throughout sociology, but their distribution and character are a little capricious. The very resort to phenomenology suggests that some sociologists had identified social meaning as a subject or problem. Such an

[2] R. Rorty, *Objectivity, Relativism and Truth*, 6.
[3] An instance is the debate about whether significant differences exist between phenomenology and symbolic interactionism. G. Mead, *The Philosophy of the Act*, esp. 360; D. Miller, *George Herbert Mead*; B. Meltzer et al., *Symbolic Interactionism*; J. Douglas (ed.), *Understanding Everyday Life*, chs. 1, 11, and 12.

identification is more likely to be made when there is a deliberate attempt to comprehend the social organization of thought: the sociologies of religion, ideology, knowledge, science, and literature being obvious candidates. Phenomenology is manifestly
better suited to the study of religion than the study of the State. But the connection
between topic and interpretation is not at all straightforward. Not every sociologist
of religion would find phenomenology persuasive, although he or she may have to
contend with its arguments. And it could be argued that the sociology of the State
would be enhanced by an injection of phenomenology[4] (after all, phenomenologists
can claim that *every* topic is a problem in the explanation of consciousness). The State,
it would be maintained, is not independent of the imagination. As Berger asserted,
'the "stuff" out of which society and all its formations are made is human meanings
externalized in human activity. The great societal hypostases (such as "the family", "the
economy", "the state" and so forth) [should be] reduced by sociological analysis to the
human activity that is their only underlying substance'.[5] Thus conceived, the 'State' is
an aspect of consciousness and it is to the exploration of consciousness that the phenomenologist would go.

The appropriateness of phenomenology does not then seem to reside in the subject,
but in the sociologist's knowledge and sense of what is fitting. Deviance itself is not
taken by all sociologists to be so infused with problems of meaning that it must be
submitted to phenomenological analysis: it may be thought that meaning is unimportant, or that it is 'objective' enough to forestall the demands of phenomenology.[6]
Indeed, the very definition of deviation as a process rooted in symbolism and consciousness appears typically to stem from a prior commitment to phenomenology or
the symbolic interactionism with which is closely allied. Most criminologists lacked
that commitment, and criminology was pursued for decades before it experimented
with phenomenology. The phenomenological experiment was rather short-lived and
was confined to a peculiar, slender version of the doctrine which had been exported to
America in the 1930s, remained unnoticed for some while and was rediscovered and
put to use in the California of the late 1950s and early 1960s.[7] What we are treating as
the phenomenological sociology of deviance and crime was principally the work of
Cicourel, Douglas, Bittner, Sudnow, and a few others. Reimported into Europe, it was
also developed by Atkinson, Phillipson, Coulter, and Drew. It is that joint work which
we shall describe.

Our description of phenomenology will be simplified and limited. It is confined to
a few arguments which are at the centre of the imported version accepted by criminology. It is designed to explore the practical knowledge which people have of their social
world, knowledge which is awarded a paramount significance. Society is not taken to
be something apart from practical consciousness. Rather, it is represented as an object

---

[4] Works which point to the kind of analysis that might ensue include M. Edelman, *Politics as Symbolic Action*; W. Lippmann, *Public Opinion*; J. Douglas, *American Social Order*; P. Manning, *The Narc's Game*.

[5] P. Berger, *The Social Reality of Religion*, 18.

[6] Cf. L. McDonald, *The Sociology of Law and Order*, 18.

[7] One of the very first references to phenomenology made by those who would later affect the sociology of deviance is to be found in A. Cicourel and J. Kitsuse, *The Educational Decision-makers*, 11.

or process which wells up from the workings of common-sense. It cannot be analysed or considered until it is experienced. Experienced, it becomes a phenomenon. It must be examined as a facet of thought.

The sociological phenomenologist is particularly concerned about the nature and ownership of the experiences which make society available to consciousness. Those experiences are not entirely and always his or her own. Approaching phenomena outside the social domain, phenomena, say, in the so-called natural world, the philosopher need reflect only on his own responses and the responses of some imaginary and typical other introduced to generalize his observations. But approaching social materials, it is apparent that reflection is directed at the responses and reflections of others. Those others may not share the phenomenologist's sensibilities. They are independent of his or her will. In this sense, sociological phenomenology is a reaction to others' reactions, a consciousness of others' consciousness, a knowledge of others' knowledge. Alfred Schutz emphasized its character by distinguishing between constructs of the first and second degrees, arguing that social phenomena are chiefly shaped by constructs of the first degree:

> [The social scientist's] observational field, the social world, is not essentially structureless. It has a particular meaning and relevance structure for the human beings living, thinking and acting therein. They have preselected and preinterpreted this world by a series of common-sense constructs of the reality of daily life and it is these thought objects which determine their behaviour, define the goal of their actions, the means available for attaining them. . . . The thought objects constructed by the social scientist refer to and are founded upon the thought objects constructed by the common-sense thoughts of man living his everyday life among his fellow-men. Thus, the constructs used by the social scientist are, so to speak, constructs of the second degree, namely constructs of the constructs made by the actors on the social scene.[8]

Social reality must be real for someone somewhere—its reality must be publicly endorsed and publicly visible, a reality which receives life only in the activities of people in the everyday world. It is those activities which create and animate social phenomena, not the analysis of the phenomenological observer. The description offered by the phenomenologist is in this sense secondary and removed, and phenomenology itself is actually a rather pallid facsimile of reality devised for special purposes unrelated to most practical action. Social reality appears when people decipher their environment; put forward proposals and interpretations; respond to their own and others' constructions; modify, accept, or reject what is about them and thereby build a world for themselves. In this manner, description, describing, and described are much the same. What gives them authenticity and solidity, making them properly social, is recognition and ratification by others. The phenomena of society—including all the social facts associated with deviance, crime, and control—emerge when they are endorsed in public response. In Peter Berger's words, they are sustained in conversation.

The phenomenological project is almost wholly taken up with discussing the construction and application of measures to enter and reproduce that critical subjective experience of others. In practice these measures tend to consist of an amalgam of

---

[8] A. Schutz, 'Common-sense and Scientific Interpretation of Human Action', 5–6.

introspective, functionalist, literary, and observational techniques. Particularly important is introspection, defined by the phenomenologist as the phenomenological or eidetic reduction. Mind is turned back on itself, examining its own processes and replies to the world. Read as a practical demonstration of method, much phenomenological writing then becomes an exploration of how its author imagines he or she understands his or her reactions to his or her surroundings. It is represented as a distillation, a stripping-away of the inessential and the murky, which reveals the formal rules and procedures of the conscious mind. The only mind nakedly before the phenomenologist is his or her own. Others are opaque, impatient, and fleetingly present. Given no other viable work material, the practices of people in the social world are almost inevitably portrayed for pragmatic purposes as identical to the phenomenologist's own. Phenomenological analysis tends to be a projection or working extension of the private world of the sociologist, and its authority rests in large measure on an appeal to plausibility and to a community of experience. It is as if the author had added a rhetorical preface which not only asserted that things could not possibly be otherwise, but also called upon the reader's own sensibility and knowledge of the world to confirm everything that is said. Such a preface is supported by the implicit functionalism of much phenomenology. Many of the more general treatises tend to assemble a list of rules and qualities which are supposed to be indispensable to a viable existence in society. It is not that the phenomenologist can prove or observe the presence of all the phenomena described. But it can be argued that these phenomena *must* be so ordered if people are to live with one another. One instance is Berger's claim that social order is an over-arching canopy of objectified, seemingly solid beliefs which keep madness at bay.[9] Without that canopy, Berger seems to say, how could anyone survive? Another is Schutz's observation that one must make certain assumptions before any social conduct emerges. Those assumptions are identified by Schutz as 'pragmatically motivated basic constructions', constructions which are brought into being so that action can go forward. They include the belief that people tend to exchange perspectives when they exchange positions ('the idealization of the interchangeability of standpoints'); the belief that people interpret the world in much the same way despite their diverse personal histories ('the idealization of the congruence of relevance systems'); and the synthesizing belief that 'the life-world which is accepted as given by me is also accepted by you, indeed, by us, fundamentally by everyone'.[10] Schutz could never offer an indisputable demonstration of these propositions. He *could* argue that it is difficult to imagine or plan a social world constituted in any other fashion.

Schutz did not often obey his own injunction to move beyond introspection to a properly described and close observation of behaviour. But a number of phenomenologists did become empirical in their approach. Variously referring to themselves as ethnomethodologists, existential sociologists, and sociologists of everyday life, they relied less obviously upon introspection. They undertook detailed examinations of how conversation unwinds, believing that social worlds are manufactured in talk.[11]

⁹ P. Berger and T. Luckmann, *The Social Construction of Reality.*
¹⁰ A. Schutz, *The Structures of the Life-World*, 61.   ¹¹ M. Atkinson and P. Drew, *Order in Court.*

They have staged frightening or disconcerting encounters which were designed to make subjects and themselves newly aware of rules that were previously taken for granted.[12] They have improved new methods for alienating people from themselves, forcing a self-consciousness and a production of accounts which had hitherto been un-demanded.[13] One such method was what was called 'glossing', whereby subjects were asked to explain what they had said or done in activity recorded in videotape or inter-view transcript, and were then asked to give explanations of their explanations, giving accounts of accounts, as interrogation relentlessly mined meanings and rules of behav-iour. All this work is directed to the same ends as those of the phenomenologists of the eidetic reduction: there is a quest for knowledge about interpretative practices that are so familiar and understated that they are normally beyond the reach of the conscious mind as it works in busy, everyday life. After all, because we are rarely able to 'stop and think', the ethnomethodologists and conversation analysts conceived their task to be devising ways of prompting people to take time out and stand back and consider what they were doing.

Phenomenology, Crime, Deviance, and Control

Phenomenologists tended to be preoccupied with the rule-like ways in which con-sciousness worked. Theirs was an interest in the very general and formal properties of behaviour rather than with the particulars of any concrete setting in which that be-haviour took place. Few phenomenologists have therefore attached themselves perma-nently to one substantive area. Reluctant to become sociologists of education, politics, or development, they moved from site to site. Aaron Cicourel, for example, pursued his investigations across a very broad front, including the linguistics of Ladino, or Judaeo-Spanish; the demographics of Argentina;[14] the philosophical assumptions of different forms of sociological methodology;[15] and testing,[16] ranking, and grading in American high schools.[17] Indeed, there was a strain which encouraged the recogni-tion of two distinct kinds of rule, variously defined as 'deep' and 'surface' or 'syntactic' and 'semantic'. Deep rules regulate the construction of phenomena: they permit one to constitute 'teachers', 'students', and 'lessons', enabling those social phenomena to emerge, receive definition, and remain stable. It is not at all self-evident at first how to become a teacher, and novices have to learn the rules to perform the role. Surface rules are directed at the understanding and manipulation of intact phenomena, enabling a teacher and students—once they have been constituted, as it were—to embark on a lesson. In the main, phenomenology was thought to be taken up with an analysis of deep rules, and the phenomenology of deviance itself was accordingly concerned with

[12] H. Garfinkel, *Studies in Ethnomethodology*.
[13] R. Hill and K. Crittenden, *Proceedings of the Purdue Symposium on Ethnomethodology*.
[14] A. Cicourel, *Theory and Method in a Study of Argentine Fertility*.
[15] A. Cicourel, *Method And Measurement In Sociology*.
[16] A. Cicourel et al., *Language Use and School Performance*.
[17] A. Cicourel and J. Kitsuse, *The Educational Decision-Makers*.

how deviant phenomena were constructed. That manufacturing process was held to be substantially similar to any other: the peculiar facts of crime and deviance were not so peculiar that they demand specialized attention. It was in this sense that Phillipson argued:

> [we should] turn away from constitutive and arbitrary judgements of public rule breaking as deviance towards the concept of rule itself and the dialectical tension that ruling is, a subject surely more central to the fundamental practice of sociology where men and socio-logical speakers are conceived as rule-makers and followers. What is now the sociology of deviance might then be pushed to the margins of sociological discourse as a museum piece to be preserved perhaps as that antediluvian activity which sought to show oddities, curiosities, peccadilloes and villains as central to sociological reason.[18]

Such indifference to matters of the surface prevented the emergence of a dedicated phenomenological criminology. Nonetheless, curiosity about the conditions of rules and rule-observance did produce a limited affinity between criminology and phenom-enological sociology. At some point in their careers, many phenomenologists flirted with the sociology of deviance because that was what was then on offer in courses deal-ing with interpretative sociology. An important generation of American West Coast sociologists passed their apprenticeship in symbolic interactionism before the redis-covery of Alfred Schutz in the 1960s. Interactionist work on symbolism, meaning, and rules fostered a sensitivity to qualitative analysis which could then sometimes evolve into phenomenology.

Empirically and methodologically, the investigation of rules can lead the investi-gator to those marginal and strange situations where the constitution of social life seems particularly stark. Phenomenological sociologists were especially interested in what they called the common-sense reasoning of everyday life.[19] Precisely because it *is* common-sense, it is prone to appear natural, familiar, and unproblematic. It is liable to be approached with what Schutz called the 'natural attitude', an attitude which does not question or disbelieve what is seen or thought and which thereby obscures the more important and interesting aspects of how people construct actions. Schutz rec-ommended the suspension of the natural attitude by treating the ordinary as if it were extraordinary and by regarding mundane phenomena with an anthropological naïvety that refuses to take the world for granted. One difficulty is that any suspension of the natural attitude is precarious and difficult. It is almost impossible to cease believing in the objectivity, solidity, and permanence of the social world around one. Disbelief may have to be forcibly secured by jolting one's trust in appearances. So it was that Harold Garfinkel invited his students to haggle over prices in supermarkets and to behave at home as if members of their own family were complete strangers.[20] Creating 'trouble' in such 'breaching experiments' was thought to be a method of disrupting normal ap-pearances and flouting normal expectations. In the shocked and newly questioning

---

[18] M. Phillipson, 'Thinking Out of Deviance', 5–6.

[19] The collection of essays in J. Douglas (ed.), *Understanding Everyday Life*.

[20] It is said that Garfinkel himself was not amused when his own students tried breaching experiments on him.

reactions of its audience it might lay bare that which is usually so silently presupposed that it is unnoticed.[21] It was as if people could sometimes affirm the existence of rules only when they were not obeyed: it is so conventional to wear clothes that public nudity forces one to assert what should be done; it is so normal to face one's audience in a conversation that turning one's back on another forces a realization of the practical rules of proper behaviour; and so it goes on.

Trouble is also a form of mild deviance. The deviant, like the blind, may be endowed with a special vision. They are offered unusual perspectives on social phenomena. They are beset by questions which little affect others, questions about the character and presentation of the normal. How, that is, does one identify and apply those often indistinct and elusive rules of conduct which can make one appear commonplace? How do the stigmatized conceal their stigmata?[22] How can people defined as 'mentally ill' behave as if they are not? How can a gay person pass as straight, or a hit man or suicide bomber as an ordinary member of a crowd?[23] It may well be that they are more conscious of the prerequisites of competent performance than most of us. It was for that reason that Harold Garfinkel went to a hermaphrodite to learn about sexual meanings.[24] He maintained that marginality imposes a heightened awareness of conventional social arrangements. Agnes, the hermaphrodite he consulted, had something of a sensitivity to phenomenological issues. She seemed to have suspended her natural attitude. It could not be argued that Garfinkel was a criminologist, yet he sought out deviant occasions because they nursed the sensibilities which Schutz and Husserl had praised.

Deviance can be even more intimately implicated in the phenomenological conception of rules. It was held that the social world is constituted by rules of description and classification, that classification is a process whose formal properties can work back on the world in their own right, and that an understanding of the power of classification can disclose the forms which society will assume. It was in that sense that Mary Douglas observed that a 'heavy social load . . . is carried by apparently innocent-looking taxonomic systems'.[25] We have already illustrated the character of that load in our discussion of functionalism: functionalism, structuralism, and phenomenology are indistinguishable at points. But the topic is important enough to warrant some repetition and amplification.

We have said that phenomenological sociology argued that society can be analysed only as a set of experiences, that experiences are ordered by consciousness, and that order is built on a vital framework of sense-making—of editing, categorization, and sifting. Phenomenology could then argue that social order is a fragile human accomplishment achieved only in the face of potential meaninglessness. If the universe is not intrinsically significant but has meaning bestowed upon it by people, any system or set of phenomena may be regarded as an area of organization sometimes arbitrarily carved out of disorganization. Society itself can be defined as sense surrounded by

---

[21] H. Garfinkel, *Studies in Ethnomethodology*, ch. 2.
[22] E. Goffman; *Stigma: Notes on the Management of Spoiled Identity.*
[23] R. Collins, *Violence.*   [24] H. Garfinkel, *Studies in Ethnomethodology*, ch. 5.
[25] M. Douglas, Preface to *Rules and Meanings*, 11.

things which make no sense, and any one society is itself but one of a number which crowd upon each other and the order of one may be the disorder of another.

Any classification system must recognize its own. The integrity, clarity, and coherence of society must be defended against threats to meaning—indeed, against the very collapse of meaning. Minor instances of such collapse have been documented: societies can seem to lose corporate identity and purpose.[26] But some phenomenologists would claim more, saying that death, nightmare, and madness present glimpses of the unreason that lurks at the boundaries of society:

> Society is the guardian of order and meaning not only objectively in its institutional structures, but subjectively as well, in its structuring of individual consciousness. It is for this reason that radical separation from the social world or anomy, constitutes such a powerful threat to the individual . . . He becomes anomic in the sense of becoming worldless . . . The socially established nomos may thus be understood, perhaps in its most important aspect, as a shield against terror. The ultimate danger of . . . separation is the danger of meaninglessness. This danger is the nightmare *par excellence*, in which the individual is submerged in a world of disorder, senselessness and madness. Reality and identity are malignantly transformed into meaningless figures of horror.[27]

Those who appear to deny or defy important separations and definitions within society may then do more than merely break a rule. They may be thought to challenge the very legitimacy and structure of sense to become agents or instances of chaos. Homosexuality or mental health problems, for example, can thereby become laden with a significance which bears on the entire project of maintaining social order. Describing that project of sense-making as a programme, Berger observed that serious deviance 'provokes not only moral guilt but the terror of madness . . . The so-called "homosexual panic" may serve as an excellent illustration of the terror unleashed by the denial of the programme.'[28]

Some forms of deviance may thereby be treated as a symbolic refutation of organization, an affirmation of meaninglessness, which demands control and suppression. Its forms may be interpreted as phenomena which borrow from the particular fears and order of a society, so that, when threats to sense are countered, they typically take the shape imposed by the sense that is under assault. Kai Erikson's *Wayward Puritans* (1966) described very precisely such a symbiotic relation between ideas, ideology, and deviance. He asserted that the crime waves of the early Massachusetts Bay Colony mirrored central disturbances in the society's classification scheme: Quakers, witches, and Antinomians were the deviant unreason of one small seventeenth-century community because they negated core beliefs that were thought by elites to be under threat.[29] They would not be so now. Again, Shoham claimed that the Nazi stereotype of the Jew was a simple antithesis of the Teutonic Superman.[30] The image of the Jew owed less to the character of Jewry than to the structure of Nazi cosmology. It is in this fashion that a system of belief

---

[26] K. Erikson, *In the Wake of the Flood* and *A New Species of Trouble*; and T. Shibutani, *The Derelicts of Company K.*

[27] P. Berger, *The Social Reality of Religion*, 30, 31, 32.

[28] P. Berger, *The Social Reality of Religion*, 33, 34.

[29] K. Erikson, *Wayward Puritans*, 7–8.

[30] S. Shoham, *The Mark of Cain*, 7–8.

manufactures its own deviants. People 'covenant implicitly to breed a host of imaginary powers, all dangerous, to watch over their morality and to punish defectors'.[31]

When eruptions from without are identified as dangerous, it becomes evident that danger, its forms, and its magnitude will be affected by the character of the frontiers which have been breached. All societies are defined or imagined in some way, but they are not identically marked-off from what is about them. Mary Douglas would argue that they may be ranked by the emphasis which they place upon their boundaries. Those which stress their apartness will generate a distinct kind of explanation for deviance. Deviants will then more commonly be presented as outsiders to the virtuous group, evil itself not being produced by the group but by a dangerous environment without. The threats presented by BSE, terrorism, and organized crime tend characteristically to be located symbolically and geographically outside the system. For example, AIDS was often thought to have been brought in by the stranger or foreigner, not by members of the community itself.[32] The weakly bounded, however, tend to lodge the origins of deviance in their own community, looking to their fellow beings as a source of danger.[33]

Deviance is sometimes more than a simple threat of disorganization. It can also take the guise of an orderly and solid enough antithesis to familiar morality. Part of the fascination of strangers is that they are outsiders who not only confirm our own identity but also offer glimpses of a tantalizing freedom because they are not bound by our rules. Societies are defined by what they are not and we can only know what we are by identifying things that negate us. We have already said that Jack Douglas argued that good and evil, God and Satan, morality and immorality are inseparable twins. Meaning and social organization would be impossible without the continuous juxtaposition of their contrasts. Communists drew symbolic sustenance from capitalists and capitalists from communists, victims and enemies drawing symbolic sustenance from one another.[34] Indeed, the contradictions of politics often seem staged to dramatize rectitude and confirm organization. The far left and the far right *need* one another. Moderates require extremists. The manner in which they portray one another may depend as much on the dialectics of the political process and the ideology of the definer as on any 'real' or 'independent' properties of the defined. They create one another. And that work of creation is never a fixed or stable activity. As a society changes and its moral frontiers move, so its companion forms of deviance will also shift. Davis maintained, for example, that pornography will always be discovered *just* outside the boundaries of conventional sexuality and that it changes with every alteration of convention.[35]

Internally, the defence of social order rests upon the preservation of neat distinctions between the classes and phenomena which constitute a society. Those things and processes that are recognized as separate and detached must retain their separation. Confusion would erode social organization and the chief instruments of confusion are ambiguity and anomaly. Following Mary Douglas and Peter Berger, Scott states that 'no

---

[31] M. Douglas, *Implicit Meanings*, p. xiv.
[32] P. Farmer, *Aids and Accusation: Haiti and the Geography of Blame*.
[33] M. Douglas, *Natural Symbols*.   [34] I. Buruma, 'The Joys and Perils of Victimhood'.
[35] M. Davis, *Smut*.

social order can survive unless it develops mechanisms for protecting the symbolic universe against the threats that chaos and anomaly present to it . . . The property of deviance is conferred on things that are perceived as being anomalous from the perspective of a symbolic universe.'[36] It was Scott's contention that danger emanates from those who seem responsible for blurring and disrupting the outlines of categories. The hermaphrodite is neither male nor female, but a disturbing exception.[37] So, too, witches, homosexuals, and those with mental health problems wreak damage on the socially constructed world. They cannot be contained, but threaten to expose the fragility of conventional meanings. Significantly, those who straddle categories may then sometimes be awarded non-human or superhuman qualities. Witches were once thought able to assume the shapes of beasts. The very violent and rapists are often described as 'beasts' or 'animals'.[38] Outlaws in medieval England were treated in law as wolves to be killed with impunity.[39] The 'mad' were thought to be possessed. They were described as the inhabitants not only of the ruled world of human beings, but also of the chaotic world of unruled nature. It was their conceptual unruliness which chiefly required discipline, and they could variously be avoided, interpreted as innocuous, destroyed, or labelled as dangerous.[40] Perhaps the very starkest example of the man who straddled boundaries was Oedipus, the parricide and incestuous lover of his own mother, who was so abominably unnatural that he brought a plague on Thebes and had to be banned or killed before the pestilence abated. All classification systems must engender anomalies because none can be exhaustive. It is intrinsic to organization that it produces the unmanageable cases that subvert it.

Turning to those who are to be found in such areas of anomaly and ambiguity, some phenomenologists have argued that certain instances of deviance may themselves be described as a response to the apparent disorderliness of everyday life. Deviants may experience the social world as absurd and morally unstable. There are many settings which seem to be governed by no consistent rules and where any conduct is forced to become the breach of some precept or principle of order.[41] Joseph Heller's *Catch 22* is a vivid literary example of such a contradictory system.

Moreover, in a pluralist society, there are many settings that are condemned by those who may don the trappings of an absolute morality. Disinclined to subscribe to a single, absolute, and unequivocal truth and well before the so-called post-modernist turn, the more libertarian phenomenologists of deviance were prone to describe society (and particularly society in the United States) as a welter of competing and contradictory worlds which constituted no unified whole and whose cultures were inextricably bound to local context.[42] Deviance is evidence of a moral diversity which others would repress in the name of an oppressive uniformity.

---

[36] R. Scott, 'A Proposed Framework for Analyzing Deviance', 22.

[37] R. Edgerton, 'Pokot Intersexuality'; and Y. Teh, *The Mak Nyahs*. Yik Koon Teh analyses in some detail the conceptual, civil, and religious problems posed for transsexuals and for civic and religious authorities in Malaysia, a predominantly Muslim society.

[38] K. Soothill and S. Walby, *Sex Crime in the News*.

[39] *Fleta.*   [40] M. Douglas, *Purity and Danger*.

[41] J. Douglas, 'The Experience of the Absurd and the Problem of Social Order'; and D. Hargreaves, *Deviance in the Classroom*.

[42] J. Douglas, *American Social Order: Social Rules in a Pluralistic Society*.

Much of this phenomenological analysis lodges the roots of deviance in the formal properties of classification. It is not so much the contents of a scheme, but its structure, which creates deviation, the cleavages, links, and limits of systems being important in their own right. The very existence of internal differentiation can work characteristic effects upon deviance. Mary Douglas argued that 'sets of rules are metaphorically connected with one another, allowing meaning to leak from one context to another along the formal similarities that they show'.[43] Such leakage is admirably exemplified by the influence exerted by hierarchy. Phenomena tend to be ranked, ranking in a legitimated social order tends to be a moral matter, and matters clustered around the various ranks tend to borrow their moral meanings. In particular, stratification by social class or ethnicity can be so dominant that it absorbs other major systems of classification. Classes or ethnic groups can become morally meaningful categories which colour the artefacts and conduct of those who are assigned to them.[44] Troy Duster asserted that opiate addiction carried little stigma when it was widely dispersed amongst the different classes of nineteenth-century America. It was only when middle-class addiction was confined in discreet private clinics and the poor and discreditable user could be seen queuing for supplies that drug use became publicly identified with the disreputable and was held to be disreputable itself.[45] Similarly, Provine argued that the racial stratification in the United States of the users of different drugs, and of cocaine and crack cocaine in particular, has long affected the moral meanings and the penalties attached to use. Crack cocaine use is subject to much graver punishment because, she said, it is associated with African-American consumers.[46]

Much of the work we have reviewed so far is ambitious, devoted to the resolution of big questions about cosmology and the fabric of the social universe. It is representative of one tradition of phenomenology associated with the New School for Social Research in New York and the anthropology of Mary Douglas. In the main, criminologists have either ignored its arguments or regarded them as somewhat tangential to the central problems of their discipline. It has now, in the early 2000s, tended to forget that they existed. Criminology is probably the poorer for that neglectfulness. If it does still recognize phenomenology, it is a different tradition that receives acknowledgement. That tradition, based largely on work conducted in California in the 1960s and 1970s, preserved an emphasis upon the futility of a quest for absolute and fixed truth. It focused on the phenomena which have been constituted by consciousness. However, the contexts and phenomena which it describes are superficially rather distinct. The criminologically acknowledged phenomenologists have concentrated instead upon small, observable settings. Their work dwelt on interchanges between probation officers and delinquents and between prostitutes and their clients, on the physical design of abortion clinics, on the structure of homosexual encounters, on the work of the courtroom, and on the social order of nude beaches. It would appear to be a more humble, exact,

---

[43] M. Douglas, *Rules and Meanings*, 13.

[44] J. Douglas, 'Deviance and Respectability', in J. Douglas (ed.), *Deviance and Respectability*, 6–7.

[45] T. Duster, *The Legislation of Morality*.

[46] D. Provine, *Unequal under Law: Race in the War on Drugs*.

and empirical enterprise. Yet, in one important sense, its goals and ideas are quite consistent with the grander analysis. Both are firmly anchored in phenomenology. Both explore the constitution and operation of rules. Both display some indifference about the specific phenomena that rules produce. A juvenile delinquent and a cosmos are equally the artefacts of interpretative practices.

What made the second tradition especially significant to criminology was its commentary upon the manufacture of official criminal statistics. We have argued that those statistics have always served as an important resource for theorization and inference. It had long been understood that they were atypical of the larger 'real' population of criminals and criminal incidents. It was recognized by Thorsten Sellin and others that there *was* a worrying dark figure which had to be ascertained in some fashion. Different stages *had* been mapped in the flow of decisions that make up the criminal justice system, leading to what some call 'attrition'. But the statistics themselves were defined as somehow independent of theory, acting as a reasonably objective and precise check on speculation. The phenomenological excursion into the social construction of crime rates was unexceptional phenomenology but it proved to be momentous to criminology. Rates were to be newly treated as *phenomena*, produced, as all phenomena are, by the interpretative work and social organization of actors on the social scene. Crime rates were to be treated as no different, say, from the rates of academic success and failure manufactured by schools.[47] However, what was relatively unremarkable in spheres such as educational sociology could become the catalyst of considerable debate and revision in criminology. The solid facts of crime seemed to melt into a rather fluid and unreliable subjectivity.

In a pivotal article, Kitsuse and Cicourel (who had previously written about educational success and failure) were to argue, 'In modern societies where bureaucratically organized agencies are increasingly invested with social control functions, the activities of such agencies are centrally important "sources and contexts" which generate as well as maintain definitions of deviance and produce populations of deviants.'[48] Theories and hypotheses employing crime statistics were to become redefined as constructs of the second degree. Rates were seen not as the raw, objective, and unprocessed indices which Émile Durkheim, Louis Chevalier, and later criminologists had supposed them to be. On the contrary, they were themselves condensed interpretations of the world, interpretations made by the others who processed deviance and crime, and theorizing based on them were interpretations of interpretations. They were embedded in background information, structures of activity, and contexts of meaning which tended to remain unanalysed. They compressed numerous decisions, preoccupations, and practices. As Jack Douglas put it, 'Once we follow . . . "disembodied numbers" back to their sources to see how they were arrived at and what, therefore, they actually represent, we find that they are based on the most subjective of all possible forms of activity.'[49] Thus the categories of 'juvenile delinquent' and 'thief' do not emerge quite spontaneously

---

[47] A. Cicourel and J. Kitsuse, *The Educational Decision-Makers*.

[48] J. Kitsuse and A. Cicourel, 'A Note on the Uses of Official Statistics', 139.

[49] J. Douglas, 'Understanding Everyday Life', in J. Douglas (ed.), *Understanding Everyday Life*.

and immediately from the doings of everyday life. They reflect the application of very practical assumptions about troublesome behaviour, rules of classification, and the assignment of people to different classes. They turn on assumptions about the meanings of past conduct and predictions about conduct in the future. Clustered together, slotted into categories made available by the criminal law and the practical work of the police and courts, given a numerical form, those terms are more or less unintelligible unless those who use the statistics take into account the manner in which they were put together: 'Sociologists have been slow to recognize the basic empirical issues that problems involving language and meaning pose for all research.'[50]

Borrowing from the sociologist of knowledge, Karl Mannheim,[51] ethnomethodologists[52] adopted the word 'indexical' to refer to the dependence of meaning on its social environment. They said that the social world was 'awesomely indexical'. It followed that all utterances and signs were to be understood as indices which point to and stand for the wider and fuller situations in which they arose.[53] Suicide rates, for instance, incorporate the lay and scientific reasoning of those officials who determine the cause and character of death. They reflect shorthand definitions of typical motives, circumstances, and courses of action.[54] Similarly, judicial statistics record the routine practices and conceptions of the courtroom. The staff of busy courts tend to standardize their tasks, establishing patterns of co-operation, a division of labour, and sets of stereotyped operations. Those operations, in turn, can be performed only when the work material is itself stereotyped and standardized. Cases must be predictable, simple, and repetitious, enabling the ordinary activity of the court to go on without obstruction. They will become 'normal cases',[55] those unambiguous and elementary scenes which can be efficiently processed by the existing organization of the court. In those jurisdictions which rely heavily on plea-bargaining and 'negotiated justice',[56] there will be a systematic strain towards the discovery and reproduction of such normal cases. Defendants or incidents which are anomalous may be subject to an unusual pressure to undergo redefinition. In all this, phenomenologists are concerned to investigate 'the processes by which persons come to be defined, classified and recorded in the categories of the agency's statistics'.[57] Their concern stemmed largely from a wider interest in the social production of knowledge. Only rarely was it confined merely to the problems of those who compiled and consumed statistics. Their concern was also part of a more general campaign against the procedures and claims of 'orthodox' sociology. Phenomenology and ethnomethodology, in particular, tended to be championed as a rival to sociology and its methods rather than as a complement or source of correction.[58]

[50] A. Cicourel, *The Social Organization of Juvenile Justice*, 331.

[51] K. Mannheim, 'On the Interpretation of "Weltanschauung"'.

[52] 'Ethnomethodology' is the study of the common-sense practices or methodologies which ordinary people employ to make sense of the everyday world.

[53] A. Cicourel, *Method and Measurement in Sociology*.

[54] J. Douglas, *The Social Meanings of Suicide*; M. Atkinson, *Discovering Suicide*.

[55] D. Sudnow, 'Normal Crimes: Sociological Features of the Penal Code'.

[56] J. Baldwin and M. McConville, *Negotiated Justice*.

[57] A. Cicourel and J. Kitsuse, *The Educational Decision-makers*, 9.

[58] Cf. W. Sharrock, 'Ethnomethodology and British Sociology'.

It would be rather misleading to portray the phenomenology of deviance as a sociological perspective that focuses solely on official social control. Jack Douglas, Jack Katz,
Peter Manning, and others have been especially active in charting deviant worlds and
their writing is occasionally indistinguishable from that symbolic interactionism.[59]
(Indeed, it must be remembered that titles like 'interactionist', 'phenomenologist', and
'qualitative sociologist' are often lightly worn. They do not necessarily signify a strong
and abiding allegiance to one solitary theory.)

Critique

Perhaps the most telling criticism of phenomenological work on deviance proceeds
from phenomenology itself. We have related how importance is attached to understanding, reproducing, and analysing constructs of the first degree. The phenomenologist sought to learn how his or her subjects made sense of themselves and their world,
replicating their own procedures and assumptions. It is apparent that utter fidelity can
never be attained: any piece of written analysis will change and distort its object. Indeed,
the business of analysis is largely unfamiliar in everyday life—the very idea of the 'natural attitude' is founded on that belief. There is seldom time to 'stop and think': thinking
does require the interruption of stopping, it usually occurs after the event and, when
it does occur, it is rarely trained on phenomenological questions. Sociological analysis
embodies practices, ideas, and objectives that are necessarily different from those of
the natural attitude. Phenomenology must deform its subject if it is to advance at all.

What phenomenologists do is to advocate the use of one or more tests of adequacy
which might help to undo some of the deformations imposed by their own sociology
or philosophy. One such test is the provision of an effective scheme of translation which
could eventually permit the subject to recognize himself or herself in any description
that has been offered. It is a test that is seldom applied[60] and its results could not but be
uncertain. Translation transforms meaning: what is recognizable might not be phenomenology and what is phenomenology might not be recognizable. The subject is unlikely
ever to have pondered about the constitution of his or her consciousness in the intense
manner of the phenomenologist. What the subject would be offered could thus be 'correct', but still almost wholly foreign. The subject could as readily be converted by a description as recognize himself or herself in it. After all, descriptions can work on people
and change them. A prime example is that of the controversy surrounding the idea of
'multiple personalities' and 'recovered memory'.[61] Whilst some maintain that intensive
therapy can disclose buried memories of abuse, including memories of satanic abuse,
others hold simply that such therapy is part of a collusive project in which patients are

---

[59] Cf. J. Douglas (ed.), *Research on Deviance*.

[60] The major example was conducted not by a phenomenologist but by a Marxist anthropologist,
Paul Willis, in *Learning to Labour*. Willis presented his subjects with the somewhat abstract and abstruse
commentary which he had constructed to explain their conduct. They flatly refused to accept it as a proper or
appropriate analysis.

[61] I. Hacking, *Rewriting the Soul*.

guided towards fabricating false pasts and false selves.[62] In all this, the gap between constructs of the first and second degree remains unbridged, but the phenomenological sensitivity remains to trouble those who examine their own and others' accounts.

Cicourel, for example, turned on the sociology of deviance and enquired what was intended by central phrases that had never been properly amplified or explained: 'Recent advances recognizing the problem of how members of a group come to be labelled as "deviant", "strange", "odd" and the like, have not explicated terms like "societal reaction" and "the point of view of the actor", while also ignoring the practical reasoning integral to how members and researchers know what they claim to know'.[63] Applied liberally and turned on his own work, such observations are likely to lead to the demise of much of what passes for the phenomenology of crime and deviance itself. The use of words like 'rules', 'deviance', 'natural attitude', 'indexicality', and 'social order' is as vulnerable to the accusation that they are unexplicated. After all, the experience of everyday life does not embrace many of the ideas lodged in phenomenology. Any investigation of the basis of that experience is calculated only to move one from deviance to an analysis of quite different phenomena and problems. In practice, that move has taken place. Phillipson, Cicourel, and others deserted deviance for the more fundamental problems of deep rules. It is as if they tended to represent deviation as a clumsy idea that belongs neither to phenomenology nor to lay experience.

External criticism of ethnomethodology and the phenomenology of deviance has been somewhat scarce. Criminology itself tends to remain an eclectic discipline which subordinates an activity called 'theorizing' to practical ends, theory sometimes being taken to be an encumbrance which is independent of policy, methodology, and serious problems. Theory which muddles and complicates analysis is a distraction. 'Reflexive' theory which urges the theorists to study themselves as they theorize is held to be especially burdensome. Having noted the mass of phenomenological observations about the significance of data, the conventional criminologist might just about encourage people to be cautious in their interpretation of official criminal statistics. But that is all. Phenomenology is not represented as particularly salient to the resolution of critical criminological problems. In the division of intellectual labour, the pursuit of phenomenology is assigned to others. It is 'bracketed away' as an interesting, irrelevant, and possibly rather fanciful enterprise. Some sociologists, indeed, dismissed ethnomethodology altogether as a piece of Californian silliness that would pass:[64]

> The 1960s were indeed a revolutionary and romantic period, for well known reasons, at least on the major campuses and in California. If one wanted to project or translate its distinctive mood, the cult of subjectivity, the rejection of external structures, into the language and *problematik* of sociology, then one should quite naturally end up with something just like Ethnomethodology. So this movement would be the manner in which subjective, 'Californian' mood enters the otherwise sober, scientistic, sociological segments of the groves of academe.[65]

---

[62] M. Pendergast, *Victims of Memory*; and R. Ofshe and E. Watters, *Making Monsters*.
[63] A. Cicourel, *The Social Organization of Juvenile Justice*, 331.
[64] And, of course, their prediction proved accurate enough.
[65] E. Gellner, 'Ethnomethodology', 435.

Other sociologists described phenomenology and ethnomethodology as substantial projects, but joined with Gellner and the criminologists to define them as not quite pertinent to their work. Lynn McDonald introduced her study of crime rates by asserting:

> What the phenomenologists do is change the level of inquiry. It is not just that they do their research in a different way, but they ask different sorts of questions—*how* social control agencies work, *how* officials and the public interact, as opposed to who becomes a client of such an agency in the first place and *why* . . . Questions as to why certain societies have high crime rates and full prisons and others do not, cannot be addressed with phenomenology and this is the sort of question I wished to entertain.[66]

It is apparent that the major critical drift is to present phenomenology as marginal to 'real' issues in the 'real' world. McDonald actually advanced her own argument by turning to Lenin. She did acknowledge that Lenin 'came on strong',[67] but did not seem to disapprove of his statement that 'ideals of causality, necessity, law, etc. are a reflection in the human mind of laws of nature, of the real world'.[68] Neither does she dissent from Lenin's belief that 'the mastery of nature manifested in human practice is a result of an objectively correct reflection within the human head of the phenomena and processes of nature and is proof of the fact that this reflection . . . is objective, absolute, eternal truth'.[69] Radical criminologists echoed Lenin implicitly or explicitly, repeating his accusation that phenomenology perversely refuses to appreciate the real character of the setting in which it was lodged. The sometime radical, Richard Quinney, thus attacked 'the epistemological assumption of a social constructionist thought [phenomenology] . . . that observations are based on our mental *constructions*, rather than on the raw apprehension of the physical world'.[70] And Ian Taylor, Paul Walton, and Jock Young would also have wished to restore an absolutist conception of the social order, a conception which deferred only to one essential and true description of society:

> In essence the ethnomethodological critique of sociology . . . is that our shorthand concepts like alienation, class, deviance, etc. are either meaningless or if they do have meaning, they are no more meaningful than the generalization made by members . . . Our final assessment of ethnomethodology's contribution to the study of deviance is that in 'bracketing' away the question of social reality, it does not allow of any description of *the social totality* we assert to be productive of deviance.[71]

Allied to this argument about the absoluteness of reality is a companion criticism of the absurdity of reflexive analysis. It will be recalled that phenomenologists urge sociologists to examine their own practices as they examine the practices of their subjects. They proposed that methodology and theory should bend back on themselves, becoming their own topics. The radical and absolutist tend to maintain that interpretative analysis is foolish and that an interpretative analysis of interpretative analysis is doubly

---

[66] L. McDonald, *The Sociology of Law and Order*, 18.
[67] L. McDonald, *The Sociology of Law and Order*, 279.
[68] V. Lenin, *Materialism and Empirio-criticism*, 15.
[69] V. Lenin, *Materialism and Empirio-criticism*, 190.
[70] R. Quinney, 'Crime Control in Capitalist Society', 184.
[71] I. Taylor et al., *The New Criminology*, 199, 208.

foolish. Borrowing from attacks on the sociology of knowledge, they raise the spectre of an infinite regress of reflexivity. The observing observer would have to be observed by another who would be observed by yet others in an endless chain. The inconvenience, pathos, and folly of such a regress are thought to be potent reasons for avoiding reflexivity and interpretative work altogether.[72]

The phenomenological reply might well ask its own questions about the status of conceptions of 'social reality', 'social totality', 'the real world', and the like. The critics of phenomenology do not always seem prepared to trust ordinary people or one another with a reliable sense of the real.[73] Ernest Gellner, Richard Quinney, and others berated ethnomethodology for its subjectivism, but they themselves manifestly failed to agree on what is objective and real. Phenomenologists themselves would not accept Quinney's or Gellner's description of reality. It appears that social reality may not really be quite so objective or self-evident after all. It is contingent, in part, on description, describer, purpose, experience, time, and place—the reality of one is the fantasy of another. And that is the starting point of phenomenological analysis. The phenomenologists may well be right: ideas about social reality are constructed like any other: they are mediated and Richard Quinney and others like him have not offered any formulae for grasping the physical world immediately and as it 'really' is. Further, those who uphold the dignity of sociology by avoiding the absurd have not refuted arguments for reflexivity. They have merely said that they were disagreeable. A priori, there is no reason why sociology and, indeed, social life itself, should not be a little absurd.

Our own reservations about the phenomenology and ethnomethodology of deviance centre on one core problem. Ernest Gellner put the matter well when he wrote about the 'scandal of undemonstrated privacy'.[74] We have said that in an important fashion the inner subjectivity of the phenomenologist's mind is held to be a model for all practical analytic purposes. It is to be mined by the phenomenologist for ideas about ideas. What emerges as a result of that mining has a plausibility for many. It can awake a shock of recognition. Indeed, much of it seems convincing to us. But it is patently *not* accepted by all. The Freudian, Jungian, Adlerian, Marxist, and the interactionist have not been persuaded; their reasoning is neither the science nor the common-sense of Schutz's life world; and in that difference lies the need for a more powerful demonstration of the phenomenological sensibility. As Queen Elizabeth I was once said to have remarked, 'We have no window into men's souls.' The appeal to plausibility, self-evidence, or functionality is obviously insufficient.

There are other, lesser problems allied to the first. Some ethnomethodologists and phenomenologists are blandly indifferent to questions about the scope and validity of their work. Their indifference has been compounded by their conception of indexicality which insists on the situationally embedded character of all phenomena. If utterances and processes can only attain significance in context, it is argued, they cannot be

---

[72] B. Hindess, *The Use of Official Statistics in Sociology*.

[73] For an example, see E. Gellner, *Postmodernism, Reason and Religion*.

[74] E. Gellner, 'Ethnomethodology', 431.

examined as if they were ever context-free, general, or abstract.[75] There is an ingrained resistance to the asking of questions about the nature, typicality, distribution, and incidence of processes and phenomena described by phenomenological sociology. It is a resistance that is quite understandable. Perhaps the phenomenologists are justified in their tacit assertion that there is no answer to the problem of generalization.[76] But their resistance seems to be contradicted by other arguments that are offered *as if* they were universal. It has not been alleged, for instance, that examples of phenomenological or ethnomethodological analysis should be treated as temporally, spatially, or socially limited. Sudnow's courtroom seems somehow to be presented as an archetype for all courts anywhere; Agnes appears to have a mandate to describe the character of all American (and perhaps all human) sexuality, and abortion clinics are implicitly claimed to resemble the one studied by Ball.[77] If that is a misconstruction, a misreading of the phenomenologist's intentions, there are no cautionary words to advise one to the contrary.[78]

The outcome has been that much phenomenological analysis has been left in a limbo from which it cannot easily be retrieved. It really is important to know whether Agnes' perspective is unique (and *how* it is unique), whether Sudnow's courtroom is typical (and of what) and what uniqueness and typicality themselves are. We are given no help in reaching an answer. Neither has the pivotal idea of 'context', the idea that limits generalization, been made very clear. Contexts are not at all self-evident: they are contingent, shifting, and biographical, of indefinite scope and uncertain meaning. How is one to identify those problematic things called contexts and establish their effects? In short, it is difficult to know quite how phenomenological analysis should be assessed and what it is intended to accomplish. As a result of that difficulty, perhaps, phenomenological sociology fell on a sword of its own making and disappeared.

The unfortunate outcome of this has been that generations of criminology students have no knowledge of the phenomenological period. They have instead simply, often without due acknowledgement, been taught some of its arguments, under the rubric of 'post-modernism' or, borrowing from Berger's *Social Construction of Reality*, 'social constructionism' consigned the intellectual core to an unacknowledged oblivion.

Conclusion

Phenomenology was a brief but highly active and fruitful episode in the history of the sociology of deviance. It was brought to bear on two principal areas. There were, on the one hand, broad, structural questions about the dramatized interplay between

---

[75] Of course, there are major exceptions to the phenomenologists' insistence on the awesome indexicality of everything. The work of Merleau-Ponty is an important instance.

[76] One of the authors was once told a story about a prominent ethnomethodologist who refused to examine a PhD dissertation about his work on the ground that it could not be laid out as a system in a thesis.

[77] D. Ball, 'An Abortion Clinic Ethnography'.

[78] Some of the issues arising from this problem are considered in a volume of essays edited by C. Ragin and H. Becker, *What is a Case?: Exploring the Foundations of Social Inquiry*.

conceptions of good and evil and of the manner in which ambiguities, contradictions, and anomalies in systems of categorization give rise to aberrant cases regulated as deviant phenomena. And there were, on the other, questions about how people go about the business of identifying, classifying, managing, and reporting criminal and deviant events in everyday life. The 'facts' of crime, deviance, and control could no longer be regarded as independent of human agency but were, to the contrary, deeply implicated in interpretative practices.

Further Reading

A. Cicourel, *The Social Organization of Juvenile Justice*, New York, 1968.

J. Douglas, *The Social Meanings of Suicide*, Princeton, 1967.

S. Gallagher and D. Zahavi (eds.) *The Phenomenological Mind*, London, 2012.

J. Katz, *Seductions of Crime*, New York, 1990.

J. Wender, *Policing and the Poetics of Everyday Life*, University of Illinois Press, 2009.

9

Control Theories

Introduction

Control theories have a formidable pedigree. They can be traced back through Durkheim to Hobbes and to Aristotle: 'It is in the nature of men not to be satisfied . . . The fact is that the greatest crimes are caused by excess and not by necessity.'[1] The curbing of desires, not the equalization of property, was the appropriate remedy. Hobbes asked: 'Why do men obey the rules of society?' He himself answered in terms of 'fear . . . It is the only thing, when there is appearance of profit or pleasure by breaking the laws, that makes men keep them.'[2] Similarly, Durkheim wrote in *Suicide*: 'It is not human nature which can assign the variable limits necessary to our needs. They are thus unlimited so far as they depend on the individual alone. Irrespective of any external regulatory force, our capacity for feeling is in itself an insatiable and bottomless abyss.'[3] Bentham and the utilitarians followed Montesquieu in seeking to base social and legal controls on the principle of rational calculation. The 'felicific calculus' presumed the human capacity to align actions with whatever course would maximize pleasure and minimize pain, a premise which opposed overly severe, as well as too lenient, penalties for infraction.[4] In short, control theories are rooted in fertile and popular philosophical soil: householders who lock their doors at night are articulating one aspect of such theories, the belief that *opportunity* in itself is a cause of crime.

How, then, do we account for the fact that, until very recently, control theories have been virtually discounted in sociological theorizing on deviance and control? Even in more orthodox criminological work, they have been accorded a rather marginal role. The most plausible explanation would turn to the sheer obviousness of control theories. Science at large and sociology in particular, has a tendency to interest itself in the unexpected. One of the principal contemporary control theorists, Ron Clarke, lamented: 'Despite its improved theory and its growing record of success, [it] still meets with indifference or hostility from criminologists.'[5] Many sociologists, Karl Marx and Émile Durkheim amongst them, proclaim that science should busy itself with the unintended

---

[1] Aristotle, *Politics*, quoted in L. McDonald, *The Sociology of Law and Order*, ch. 2.
[2] Hobbes, *Leviathan*, 195; also the discussion in T. Hirschi, *Causes of Delinquency*, 4–6.
[3] É. Durkheim, *Suicide*, 247.   [4] L. McDonald, *The Sociology of Law and Order*, ch. 2.
[5] R. Clarke, 'Situational Crime Prevention, Criminology and Social Values', 109.

and latent consequences of social action. They hold to the belief that consequential discoveries are those which lay people cannot make for lack of skill. It is a mark of science that it confounds common-sense,[6] and control theories are not likely to do this. On the contrary, they confirm it. In doing so, they lose some of their sociological appeal. They are simply too obvious. Pursuing control theory, some would argue on like grounds, can rob criminology of its intellectual interest and turn the criminologist himself or herself into a hack. Haggerty asserted, for example, that 'rather than attending to questions of social causation or individual pathology, situational criminology [one of the synonyms for control theory] concentrates on reducing crime through loss prevention, target hardening and enhanced visibility. Many criminologists have resisted calls to focus on measures like fence height, lock strength or surveillance capacity, perceiving them as belonging to the domain of security consultants more than research criminologists'.[7]

In criminology, the neglect of control theory may also have been due to the unpopularity in liberal sociological circles of work which appears to lend practical and ideological support to deterrence and detection. Far more congenial are ideas which debunk control strategies. Unpopular too has been the work of the Gluecks,[8] whose attempts to predict delinquency in the 1930s, 1940s, and 1950s became associated with the sociological equivalent of Original Sin—a stress on the pathological, the individualistic, and the psychological (although they were later to be resuscitated by two currently acclaimed criminologists, Sampson and Laub[9]). The three variables which they came to employ in their predictive studies—mother's affection for the child, mother's supervision of the child, and family cohesion—have now resurfaced in modified forms in the work of Hirschi, Wilson,[10] and Carr and Napolitano.[11] Although the methodological and theoretical problems of the Gluecks' work perhaps led to the neglect of such variables in the 1960s, their centrality to the revived forms of control theory cannot be denied. Some criminologists remained interested in this approach even in the days of the ascendancy of strain and labelling theories—Reckless, for example, elaborated the notion of 'self-concept' as an 'insulating factor' in delinquency.[12] Such work was largely ignored, however, in the sociological reaction against the more psychoanalytical and family-centred explanations of delinquency, which in the post-war period were viewed as the somewhat dated products of the 1920s and 1930s. That period also produced the main sociological version of control theory: Shaw and McKay's concept of 'social disorganization', as the principal cause of high rates of crime and delinquency—a theory that Albert Cohen temporarily eclipsed with his argument that the absence of controls cannot explain the presence of stable and recurring deviant phenomena.[13]

---

[6] M. Davis, 'That's Interesting!'   [7] K. Haggerty, 'Displaced Expertise', 218.

[8] Chiefly in S. and E. Glueck, *Unravelling Juvenile Delinquency*.

[9] R. Sampson and J. Laub, *Crime in the Making*.

[10] T. Hirschi, *Causes of Delinquency*; and H. Wilson and G. Herbert, *Parents and Children in the Inner City*.

[11] P. Carr and L. Napolitano, 'What Moms Supply: What Distinguishes Delinquent and Non-Delinquent Girls in Three High Crime Philadelphia Neighborhoods'.

[12] W. Reckless et al., 'Self-Concept as an Insulator against Delinquency'; and W. Reckless, *The Crime Problem*.   [13] Ch. 3 and A. Cohen, *Delinquent Boys*, 33.

The undertow of dissatisfaction with the strain theorists' tendency to place virtually the whole weight of explanation on the sheer intensity of deviant motivation led to several attempts to give some emphasis at least to control variables. Sykes and Matza argued that delinquents commonly adhered to much the same set of values as everybody else. Deviants differed chiefly in their invocation of 'techniques of neutralization' which freed them from guilt and shame and which temporarily neutralized the social bond to enable them to engage in delinquent activities. Sykes and Matza acknowledged, however, that these rationalizations hardly accounted for the attractiveness of delinquency in the first place. In accounting for that,[14] their theorizing overlapped far more with strain theories than they were prone to acknowledge at the time. Jackson Toby, a trenchant critic of the Gluecks for their 'theoretical blindness',[15] proposed a more sociological version of control theory by asserting that delinquents were chiefly to be distinguished from non-delinquents by their minimal 'stake in conformity'. In this approach, the common impetus to deviate interacts with varying commitments to conformity stemming from family as well as school and work experiences and opportunities.[16] A more sophisticated version of this argument was presented by Briar and Piliavin, who added the notion of 'situational inducements' as a fresh motivational slant.[17] The combination of variations in the inner commitment to conform and the external opportunities to deviate was already furnishing an alternative, however rudimentary, to the by now over-elaborate 'motivation' offered by the strain theorists.

Though few explicit links were fashioned, the work of Homans and Blau[18] in sociological theory provided a model for the analysis of the individual in society that corresponded in its essentials with the work of control theorists in criminology. In 'social exchange' theories, a sociological version of Economic Man is approximated. It is held that human behaviour is best explained by the individual gratifications that 'exchange' provides and moral values are themselves emergent from on-going exchanges. One of Homans' key examples is drawn from the famous Westinghouse Electrical Company study, in which informal group norms emerged to restrict production to levels set by the workers and not the management: deviants (rate-busters) were sanctioned to enforce group conformity. The pay-off for the group as a whole was perceived to be superior to that which would accrue from outright individualism. More generally, social behaviour is seen as grounded in quite tangible forms of exchange which provide the bases for rational choice. Accordingly, men (and women) should be 'brought back in' to social theories in a far fuller sense than was imaginable in the Parsonian 'social system'. In this respect, Homans in particular is close to Simmel and the symbolic interactionists.[19] He and Blau differ from interactionists chiefly in their relative indifference to meanings and interpretations: Homans' view of people is more attuned to the behaviourism of Skinner than to the interactionism of Mead. To Gouldner, his 'is

[14] Ch. 6.
[15] J. Toby, 'An Evaluation of Early Identification and Intensive Treatment Programs for Pre-Delinquents'.
[16] J. Toby, 'Social Disorganization and Stake in Conformity'.
[17] S. Briar and I. Piliavin, 'Delinquency, Situational Inducements and Commitment to Conformity', 35–45.
[18] G. Homans, 'Social Behavior as Exchange', 597–606; P. Blau, *Exchange and Power in Social Life*.
[19] G. Homans, *The Human Group* and 'Bringing Men Back In', 809–18.

the most unabashedly individualistic utilitarianism in modern sociology'.[20] People do what they do to maximize pay-off, whether it takes the form of material well-being, status, or affection. The approach is somewhat unforthcoming on how people choose *between* different pay-offs. Also, as Heath points out, 'Skinnerian man is based on the common pigeon. He is not a forward-looking maximiser endowed with sophisticated reasoning powers but a practical creature who learns from experience, avoiding what has proved painful in the past and seeking out what has proved rewarding.'[21] The implications for crime and its control are not as stark as this might imply, but the scope for applying exchange theory to these phenomena has often suffered critically from guilt by association: it is assumed that any truck with Skinner, pigeons, and control must be bad for any criminological theory. The more recent forms of control theory may have been keen to avoid such imputation,[22] but the affinity between control theory and theories of rational choice remains strong and we shall return to it below.

Sociological Control Theories of Deviance

Hirschi states that the common property of control theories at their simplest level is their assumption that 'delinquent acts result when an individual's bond to society is weak or broken'.[23] But what are the elements of the social bond? He specifies four elements: attachment, commitment, involvement, and belief.

'Attachment' to others is viewed as prior to caring about their opinions and wishes. It is therefore a variable superior to the 'internalization of norms' since 'to violate a norm is to act contrary to the wishes and expectations of other people. If a person does not care about the wishes and expectations of other people, that is, if he is insensitive to the opinions of others, then he is to that extent not bound by the norms. He is free to deviate'.[24]

'Commitment' signifies that:

the person invests time, energy, himself, in a certain line of activity, say, getting an education, building up a business, acquiring a reputation for virtue. When or whenever he considers deviant behaviour, he must consider the costs of this deviant behaviour, the risk he runs of losing the investment he has made in conventional behaviour . . . Most people, simply by the process of living in an organised society, acquire goods, reputations, prospects that they do not want to risk losing. These accumulations are society's insurance that they will abide by the rules.[25]

'Involvement' is the behavioural counterpart of commitment: 'A person may be simply too busy doing conventional things to find time to engage in deviant behaviour . . . To the extent to which he is engrossed in conventional activities, he cannot even think about deviant acts, let alone act out his inclinations.'[26] Finally, the assumption that

---

[20] A. Gouldner, *The Coming Crisis*, 140.   [21] A. Heath, *Rational Choice and Social Exchange*, 171.
[22] The opening section of H. Wilson, 'Parental Supervision: A Neglected Aspect of Delinquency'.
[23] T. Hirschi, *Causes of Delinquency*, 16.   [24] T. Hirschi, *Causes of Delinquency*, 18.
[25] T. Hirschi, *Causes of Delinquency*, 20–1.   [26] T. Hirschi, *Causes of Delinquency*, 22.

delinquents and non-delinquents alike share a common value-system is not the same as insisting that their 'belief' in the rules derived from it attains a common intensity. 'We assume that there is variation in the extent to which people believe they should obey the rules of society and that the less a person believes he should obey the rules, the more likely he is to violate them.'[27]

These four variables interact to produce an ideal-typical portrait of a non-delinquent who is strongly attached to conventional others, strongly committed to conventional activities, heavily involved in them, and imbued with a strong belief in the need to obey the rules. The delinquent is relatively free from such controls and hence more at risk of deviation. Such deviation is not, however, automatic or determined: it is simply no longer ruled out as a possibility. It is certainly significant that those who offend whilst on bail tend disproportionately to have no fixed address and to be unemployed,[28] both indicators of the controls exerted by commitment and involvement. And, for the same reasons, it is also significant that leaving or not attending school are strongly linked to delinquency.[29]

As Hirschi acknowledged, the most disconcerting question remains: 'Yes, but why do they do it?' He accepts the force of Cohen and Short's criticism of control theories that they explain delinquency in the absence of effective controls and accordingly imply 'that the impulse to delinquency is an inherent characteristic of young people and does not itself need to be explained; it is something that erupts when the lid—i.e. internalised cultural restraints or external authority—is off'.[30] Hirschi's reaction is to accept that this is indeed the case and that while certain motivations of a situational character are consistent with control theory, they are 'by no means deducible from it . . . The question "Why do they do it?" is simply not the question the theory is designed to answer. The question is, "Why don't we do it?"'.[31] An earlier piece of work written by Kornhauser is even more dismissive of the motivational issue: 'The question is not whether control theory can account for the motivation of delinquency, but whether it is necessary to specify the motivation of delinquency in order to explain its occurrence.'[32] The problem of motivation is resolved by its redefinition as a non-problem.

The strength of Hirschi's work, however, is empirical rather than theoretical. Much of *The Causes of Delinquency* is taken up with testing a variety of propositions derived from subcultural theory (in both its 'strain' and 'cultural deviance' forms)[33] and finding them wanting. For example, he shows social class to be related only very weakly to delinquency. Adherence to the 'values' most commonly cited as 'working-class' (such as 'smartness' and 'fatalism') is in Hirschi's data most remarkable for its lack of relation to class. Control variables correlate with delinquency quite closely and consistently. For example, parental supervision was measured by the extent to which parent(s) knew

[27] T. Hirschi, *Causes of Delinquency*, 26.
[28] P. Morgan and P. Henderson, *Remand Decisions and Offending on Bail*, 48.
[29] K. Hansen, 'Time to Educate the Criminals?'
[30] A. Cohen and J. Short, Jun., 'Juvenile Delinquency', 106.
[31] T. Hirschi, *Causes of Delinquency*, 34.
[32] R. Kornhauser, *Social Sources of Delinquency: An Appraisal of Analytic Models*, 154.
[33] See Chapter 6.

where and in what company boys were, when away from home. The results for non-delinquents ranged from none reporting 'low' to 63 per cent 'high' supervision; for relatively serious delinquents, 55 per cent reported 'low' and only 12 per cent 'high' supervision, results which are corroborated by Wilson's English study.[34] 'Intimacy of communication' and 'affectional identification' with parents showed similarly strong links with delinquency: the less strong the child's reported bond with his family, the greater his involvement in delinquency. Findings on links with the school and teachers showed the same trend. Hirschi's data were based on a large-scale self-report survey of over four thousand children aged 12 to 17, sampled from a predominantly urban-industrial area and the population surveyed seems about as representative of American society as possible. Although the self-report technique is open to question (as indeed are official criminal statistics), the results were the first substantial sign that the most attractive approaches theoretically were the weakest empirically and vice versa.

A study by Steven Box[35] went some way towards redressing the more glaring theo-retical deficiencies of control theory, whilst retaining its basic tenets. First, he sought to align control theory with labelling theory; second, he furnished a theory of delin-quency congruent with control theory but sensitive to the issue of motivation. The need for the alignment with labelling theory stems from Box's attempt to explain how and why social class and ethnicity have such weak relations with delinquency in self-report studies and such strong links in official statistics. The answer he proffers is that the first capture 'primary' and the second 'secondary' deviations.[36] By the processes of official intervention, at every stage of which the more powerful members of society are relatively advantaged, the raw data of primary deviation are filtered, screened, and ne-gotiated to produce predominantly lower-status and Black populations of 'secondary' deviants—the probationers, prisoners, and ex-cons who come to represent collectively the 'crime problem'. Labelling processes interact with control variables to make matters worse for those defined as deviant: such bonds as they already had with conventional society are attenuated even further. Their exposure to the risks of fresh deviations is correspondingly heightened. At each stage of the spiral, a greater feat of self-redefini-tion is needed if the deviant is to conform.

Motivation looms larger for Box than for earlier control theorists. 'Whether or not an individual with the option to deviate decides to, depends to some extent on what he makes of the issue of *secrecy, skills, supply, social,* and *symbolic support.*'[37] The first re-lates to chances of concealment; the second to the knowledge required for deviance; the third to the necessary equipment; the fourth to the support of associates and the fifth to that drawn from the wider culture. A pot-smoking campus party scores highly on all points, at least in the 2000s: in 1950, it would have been almost impossible, in England at least, to secure the vital ingredient. These elements, however, are little more than those termed by Briar and Piliavin 'situational inducements': they do little to suggest why some individuals and not others, would choose to take up this particular option.

---

[34] T. Hirschi, *Causes of Delinquency*, 89, Table 18; and H. Wilson, 'Parental Supervision'.
[35] S. Box, *Deviance, Reality and Society*.   [36] See Chapter 7.
[37] S. Box, *Deviance, Reality and Society*, 150.

Box makes more extensive attempts to develop a theory of the will to delinquency in discussing the work of Cohen and Matza.[38] Cohen, he argues, portrays the delinquent as both frustrated by and resentful of, the experience of school failure. But his eventual theory stresses status frustration at the expense of sheer resentment, since the former implies at least some prior internalization of middle-class norms, while the latter implies only that boys cannot be indifferent to the imputation of failure. The former leads to 'reaction formation', the denial of a (real) attachment by the ostentatious display of rule-breaking. The latter leads to behaviour which seeks to assert independent standards. Cohen employs a logic which forces him to accept the first, but not the second, route to delinquency, yet it is the latter which in Box's view is far more in line with social reality. The weight of the evidence on this point is against Cohen, though it might be remarked in passing that the delinquent subculture, as he conceived it, has a dual functionality: the restoration of status and the collective provision of social means to hit back at the source of imputed failure. Phenomenologically, it seems eminently possible to be frustrated in terms of social status *and* resentful about being induced to care about status in the first place.

A similar criticism is made of Matza's attempt to depict the delinquent as both aiming at restoring 'the mood of humanism' *and* rationalizing his delinquency away as the result of being 'pushed around'. These, says Box, are incompatible: either you are restoring the mood of humanism and mean it, or you genuinely feel pushed around and 'objectified'. Box prefers to treat the second technique as a purely situated account in the context of arrest. Again, the logic of strain theory is pitted against that of control theory. In strain theory, to which Matza partially adheres, delinquents care about breaking the law: hence they invoke 'techniques of neutralization' to justify their deviations ('I was pushed', etc.). To control theorists, no such commitment to the rules exists in the first place, hence 'I was pushed' is a sheer *ex post facto* excuse which offenders hope will evoke leniency. There is no way of settling this issue here, particularly as the negligible amount of empirical evidence is indecisive, but again it could be added that the appeal of Matza's 'techniques' lies in their dual functionality: they both express an existential state of mind and assist in self-exculpation.

Wilson's study of socially deprived families in inner Birmingham produced findings which are strikingly in line with the tenets of control theory. An index of 'chaperonage'[39] was developed to measure the degree of protection given to their children by parents to ensure their safety. Scores were allocated to parents on such items as fetching children from school, allowing them to roam the streets, and whether or not there were rules for coming in at night. Though the numbers involved were very small (fifty-six families in all) the selected families shared certain characteristics, including: intact family status, having five or more children, and residing in old housing in a deprived inner-city area. Within this group, the 'chaperonage' variable sharply distinguished delinquents from non-delinquents, whereas other factors, such as the 'happiness' of the

---

[38] S. Box, *Deviance, Reality and Society*, 106–9 and 122–33.
[39] First employed by J. and E. Newson, *Seven Years Old in the Home Environment*.

home atmosphere, did not. 'Chaperonage' was related to 'strict' rather than 'permissive' standards of morality: '"strict" parents insist on a degree of tidiness and cleanliness in the home, they tend to discourage or punish genital play, children looking at each other when undressed, or giggling over the toilet and parents tend to avoid undressing in the children's presence'.[40]

> The families who exercised chaperonage and who tend to adhere to traditional standards of strictness are motivated in many different ways, but they share the belief that the deprived neighbourhood and its inhabitants are bad and that their children need protection against this badness. . . . These parents were driven into applying child-rearing measures which under more normal conditions in a friendly and known neighbourhood they would not be likely to apply. They kept their children indoors or under close supervision in the back yard; they accompanied them to and from school; they forbade them to play with undesirable youngsters in the streets. If the boys played out their mothers knew where to find them. These measures are applied at great cost to themselves.[41]

In a further study Wilson extends the support for this conclusion, but she is careful to state that:

> the essential point of our findings is the very close association of lax parenting methods with severe social handicap. Lax parenting methods are often the result of chronic stress, situations arising from frequent or prolonged spells of unemployment, physical or mental disabilities among members of the family and an often permanent condition of poverty. . . . If these factors are ignored and parental laxness is seen instead as an 'attitude' which by education or by punitive measures can be shifted, then our findings are being misinterpreted. It is the position of the most disadvantaged groups in society and not the individual, which needs improvement in the first place'.[42]

In such an analysis, a control theory of delinquency is combined with a strong sense of structural context. It has received consistent empirical support[43] in, for example, the attempt by an American group of criminologists and others to provide recipes for the explanation and prevention of criminal violence. Amalgamating ideas flowing from the Chicago School, anomie theory, and control theory, they argue that violence is most likely to occur in communities marked by social heterogeneity, by rapid change (both economic decline and 'gentrification'), by the growth of an illegal market in drugs, and a more general ensuing social disorganization. Those communities can no longer exert informal controls over their members, in particular their younger members. Parents are unable to distinguish local youths from outsiders, 'to question each others' children, to participate in voluntary organizations and friendship networks and to watch neighborhood common areas . . . Many "old heads"—community elders who took responsibility for local youth—have left urban communities'.[44]

---

[40] H. Wilson and G. Herbert, *Parents and Children*, 176.
[41] H. Wilson and G. Herbert, *Parents and Children*, 177.
[42] H. Wilson, 'Parental Supervision', 233–4.
[43] C. Flood-Page et al., *Youth Crime*, 32–3; and H. Juby and D. Farrington, 'Disentangling the Link between Disrupted Families and Delinquency'.
[44] National Research Council, *Understanding and Preventing Violence*, 15.

What offers a limited redoubt against delinquency in such areas of the United States, as in Wilson's Birmingham and virtually in Wilson's words, is an intact, two-parent family continuing to exercise discipline over its children:

> Two parents, together with the extended network of cousins, aunts, uncles . . . can form a durable team, a viable supportive group engaged to fight in a committed manner the problems confronting inner-city teenagers, including drugs, crime, pregnancy and lack of social mobility. This unit, when it does endure, tends to be equipped with a survivor's mentality. It has weathered a good many storms. . . . The parents are known in the community as 'strict'; they impose curfews and tight supervision, demanding to know their children's whereabouts at all times. Determined that their offspring will not become casualties . . . they scrutinize their children's associates, rejecting those who seem to be 'no good' and encouraging others who seem on their way to 'amount to something'.[45]

Nevertheless, when reading all this, perhaps one should heed Hagan and McCarthy's warning that the family can itself on occasion be a site of abuse which young people may be only too eager to leave.[46] Far from protecting its own, it may expose them to hazard. Indeed, in the 1980s, the Ministry of the Solicitor General of Canada proposed a campaign to restore missing children to their homes, but it reversed its decision on discovering some of the reasons why the children had left. Even when the family *does* exercise benign control, its capacity to do so tends to decline quite rapidly when children reach their middle teens and acquire a substantial degree of independence from parental scrutiny and discipline.[47]

Control theories have attracted a considerable following. Such textbooks as those by Nettler and Hagan[48] argued that they provide the most promising foundation for criminological theory. Hagan, Simpson, and Gillis have proceeded to explore the impressive potential of control theory for the explanation of gender differences in criminality; their work is discussed in Chapter 11. Again, Hagan, in conjunction with McCarthy, examined how the children of large working-class families 'are more likely to take to the streets and that streetlife itself increases serious delinquency',[49] an erosion of family controls being exacerbated by the structured strains of living on city streets.

In the USA, versions of control theory have become bound up with studies of what is called 'the life course', the sequence of biographical events which seem to be linked with the onset, desistance from, and cessation of offending.[50] The high flowering of that version of control theory was presaged in Sampson and Laub's *Crime in the Making* of 1993 and then realized in Laub and Sampson's *Shared Beginnings, Divergent Lives* of 2003. Both works examined the role of delinquency in the lives of men studied over decades, paying particular attention to the manner in which the social bonds of family, friends, employment, and military service work as controls that mediate influences emanating from the wider social structure. Marriage, the onset of work, and military

---

[45] E. Anderson, *Streetwise*, 123.   [46] J. Hagan and B. McCarthy, *Mean Streets*, 58.
[47] D. Riley and M. Shaw, *Parental Supervision and Juvenile Delinquency*.
[48] G. Nettler, *Explaining Crime*; J. Hagan, *The Disreputable Pleasures*.
[49] J. Hagan and B. McCarthy, 'Street-life and Delinquency', 555.
[50] J. Laub and R. Sampson, 'Understanding Desistance from Crime'.

service may act as critical turning points which induce discontinuities in a life history; create new sets of social relations, dependencies, and responsibilities; introduce new disciplines into social life; and invite stock-taking and reflection. Conversely, involvement with the criminal justice system and imprisonment may interrupt or undermine participation in stabilizing social environments; stigmatize the offender and prevent re-entry into the 'straight' world; encourage cynicism about criminal justice through a close acquaintance with its game-like and seedier features; and introduce the offender to other law-breakers who help to amplify deviance through differential association (for an exploration of much the same theme employing a different theoretical framework, see Western[51]). And, throughout, and following Matza, Katz, and others, Laub and Sampson represent the process not as a grim and ineluctable progression into criminality, but as a sequence of events and actions which is influenced always by the capacity of people to interpret and choose how they will respond. The part played by human agency and contingency is repeatedly underscored, leading them to observe how impossible it is to predict future criminality from present circumstances.

In common with almost all criminology, there are contradictory political and policy strains in control theory. Whilst some, such as Laub and Sampson, take certain forms of punishment, and incarceration in particular, to interfere with desistance, others represent its appeal as the implicit links it shares with the perhaps temporary demise of rehabilitation and the call for a return to sentences based upon untrammelled 'due process'—based upon 'harm done', i.e. retributivism. On the one hand, imprisonment has been portrayed as a damaging rupture in vital social and family relations and an erosion of the offenders' prospects of entry into the world of conventional work. On the other hand, Patricia Morgan[52] argued that delinquency was fostered by the fashion for permissiveness in family life, education, and crime control; a vogue bolstered by labelling theory. In her view, adolescents had too much, not too little, freedom to act out their fantasies. And, in even sterner vein, James Q. Wilson argued that incapacitation alone provides a guarantee against criminality: he called for unrepentant incarceration of offenders as a costly but sure means of combating crime.[53]

Miscellaneous Social Control Theories

'Control' is a term of such common currency in criminology and the sociology of deviance that it is essential to distinguish between three separate usages. First, there are control theories, discussed above, which take control variables, of different kinds, to be the most significant causes or preconditions of deviance. Second, there is control as a substantive phenomenon in its own right, i.e. the sanctions that are brought to bear against deviancy. Third, there is that aspect of all theories of deviance that deals with

---

[51] For an exploration of much the same theme employing a different theoretical framework, see B. Western, *Punishment and Inequality in America.*   [52] P. Morgan, *Delinquent Fantasies.*

[53] J. Wilson, *Thinking About Crime*; see also C. Murray, *Does Prison Work?* A Home Office study questions the feasibility of this approach: S. Brody and R. Tarling, *Taking Offenders Out of Circulation.*

control, either implicitly or explicitly. In strain theories, for example, that aspect is largely unexplored, but a generally neutral set of control responses to deviance tends to be assumed. In labelling theories, controls that are differentially and often maladroitly applied are paradoxically viewed as a major source of deviation ('secondary' deviation). In some culturally framed theories, which site the causes of deviance in 'culture conflict' (Sellin) or 'cultural diversity' (Miller, Mays, Oscar Lewis), the strength of the controls exerted by the dominant (generally middle-class) culture are seen as weakened by the offenders' adherence to an exaggerated form of alternative culture ('lower-class culture', 'the culture of poverty', and so on); in Sutherland's theory of 'differential association', variation in exposure to such alternative cultures is viewed as sufficient to explain different rates of deviance.[54] The concept of 'social disorganization' of Shaw and McKay also rests on the premise that lax controls generate deviance. Durkheim's theory of anomie alone discerns greater attenuation of controls at the top, rather than the bottom, of the social hierarchy.[55] In general, however, it would be inappropriate to call the third set of theories 'control theories', since the weakness or absence of controls is caused by adherence to alternative cultures or subcultures, rather than (as in control theories properly so described) by contingent or random events that serve to deregulate individual families or careers, or that exist as a built-in feature of certain *milieux*.

In the realm of psychological theories of deviance, however, virtually all approaches arguably rest on the efficacy of psychodynamic controls. Various explanations are proffered by different schools of psychology and psychoanalysis for their strength or weakness. While it is an over-generalization to see the control variable as predominant in all psychological theories,[56] there are certain instances where it is unequivocally so. Perhaps the archetypal example is Eysenck's theory of crime and personality and its social psychological variant, Trasler's explanation of criminality in terms of 'inadequate socialization'[57] (see Rafter[58] for a general introduction to these ideas). The main premise of Eysenck's theory is that extroverts are more resistant to conditioning (a crucial element of social learning) than introverts and that logically it is to be inferred that, in all contexts save a criminal sub-society, extroverts will tend to be more amenable to criminality than introverts. It is also argued that neuroticism interacts with extroversion to heighten the likelihood that inhibiting responses will be overwhelmed by excitation. Trasler argued that, in addition, the techniques of child socialization employed by lower-class families were less efficient than those used by the middle class in the reinforcement of inhibition. The typical delinquent on this basis would be the lower-class, neurotic extrovert, though it should be added that even on unrepresentative populations, such as prisoners and institutional youths, these propositions have not,

---

[54] T. Sellin, *Culture Conflict and Crime*; W. Miller, 'Lower Class Culture'; J. Mays, *Growing Up in the City*; O. Lewis, *The Children of Sanchez*, xi–xxxi; E. Sutherland, *Principles of Criminology*, first published in 1924 and since 1955 extensively revised by D. Cressey.

[55] J. Hagan, *The Disreputable Pleasures*, and M. Punch, *Dirty Business*.

[56] As A. Cohen implies in his trenchant critique 'Seven Limitations of Psychodynamic Control Theories', in his *Deviance and Control*, 59–62.

[57] H. Eysenck, 'Crime and Personality'; G. Trasler, *The Explanation of Criminality*.

[58] N. Rafter, *The Criminal Brain*.

in general, been confirmed. Cochrane[59] listed some twenty tests of Eysenck's theory which, in all cases but one, falsified rather than verified the central point of his theory concerning extroversion. It remains a classic instance of a control theory, however, not least for Eysenck's proposal that 'conscience is a conditioned reflex'.

It may nonetheless be the case that certain social contexts do indeed produce neuroticism in more extroverted children. Harriett Wilson quotes one telling example: 'Some permissive mothers have quiet, withdrawn children who give little cause for friction and if parental demands are minimal, conflicts rarely arise. Others reported much trouble, which they linked with explanations of their temperament: "He's got a terrible temper, if you cross him he throws things—you've got to get round him." "If he can't have his own way, he shouts and kicks the furniture—in the finish I give him his own way—I have to".'[60] It may well be that, in the contexts of poverty and over-crowding, the more extroverted children are socialized into neuroticism, not so much because that is an innate condition, more because—faced with intolerable physical constraint—they cannot withdraw into protective apathy as do their more introverted siblings. Again, Oliver James suggests that mothers living in conditions of hardship induced by the severe economic policies of the 1980s might well have become clinically depressed, withdrawing into themselves and responding erratically and sometimes punitively to their children. Those children—and boys especially—could develop in their turn a heightened, almost exaggerated wariness and sensitivity to the reactions of others, sometimes responding violently to perceived threat.[61] In these instances, however, the social context appears to be the most salient causal variable.

Psychological control theories of the kind developed first by Eysenck have more recently been resuscitated in a new guise. The reborn idea of economic or utilitarian man (or woman) lent itself to a psychology of crime that Clarke and Cornish described as radical behaviourism sympathetic to rational choice theory.[62]

Consider Wilson and Herrnstein's *Crime and Human Nature*.[63] Any theory of crime, they contend, is usually no more than an instance of a more general theory of behaviour and it should be able to explain the forces that control individual behaviour. Crime is held to be a preferred choice determined by its consequences, that is, by the pleasures and pains that are likely to flow from particular decisions. More particularly, decisions to offend are defined as the outcome of an interaction between innate drives and secondary reinforcers of behaviour, the biological and the cultural and social conditioning supplies the links between the two.[64] Whilst the rewards of crime to the offender may be tangible and immediate, the losses tend not only to be more remote but also more indefinite and delay and uncertainty in apprehension and punishment enhance criminality.

Consider, too, a very similar work, Gottfredson and Hirschi's *A General Theory of Crime*, published in 1990. Crime, they argue, stems from low self-control: it provides

---

[59] R. Cochrane, 'Crime and Personality: Theory and Evidence', 19–22; and H. Eysenck, 'Crime and Personality Reconsidered', 23–4.   [60] H. Wilson and G. Herbert, *Parents and Children*, 177.

[61] O. James, *Juvenile Violence in a Winner-Loser Culture*.

[62] R. Clarke and D. Cornish, 'Modeling Offenders' Decisions: A Framework for Research and Policy', 155.

[63] J. Wilson and R. Herrnstein, *Crime and Human Nature*.

[64] B. Lahey and T. Moffitt (eds.), *Causes of Conduct Disorder and Juvenile Delinquency*.

an immediate, easy, and simple gratification of desires that is attractive to those who cannot or will not defer enjoyment. It requires little skill or planning. It can be intrinsically pleasurable because it involves the exercise of stealth, agility, deception, or power. It demands a lack of sympathy for the victim. But it does not provide medium- or long-term benefits equivalent to those that may flow from more orthodox careers. In short, it is, they say, likely to be committed by those who are 'impulsive, insensitive, physical . . . Risk-taking, short-sighted and non-verbal'.[65]

Low self-control, in turn, is associated with a lack of discipline, training, or nurturing and those are properties vested in a number of institutions, including schools, friendship groups, and the family and its child-rearing practices. Successful socialization hinges on someone caring enough for a child to monitor his or her behaviour, identifying deviance when it occurs and punishing that deviance in a consistent and appropriate manner.

Yet another variant of control theory, manifest most strongly in feminist theory, arises from emulating Travis Hirschi and turning a conventional criminological observation on its head. It used to be argued that women were not of great interest to the criminologist because they committed so little crime, the quintessential stuff of criminology.[66] Feminist criminologists and others adopting a control perspective retorted that that was precisely what made women so important analytically, asking how it was that women offended so rarely. Differential control was held to be key. It was held that controls are applied quite differently in private and public space. As we shall argue in Chapter 11, the domestic sphere is held by Hagan,[67] Carlen,[68] and others characteristically to be a feminine preserve in which emotionally-based disciplines are imposed: the consequences of a young woman transgressing are likely to be exposure to the more effective and private sanctions of shaming and the withdrawal of affection practised in the home. The public sphere is held to be a male preserve and the less effective formal disciplines exercised there are more likely to propel young men into the workings of the criminal justice system and hence towards criminalization. One further fillip to that model was offered by Hagan and McCarthy in 1998: delinquency, they argued, is likely to be amplified when young people voluntarily or involuntarily leave their home, live a precarious and vulnerable existence in the public space of the streets and not only suffer greater victimization but also commit a greater volume of crime and become exposed to considerably aggravated risks of becoming processed as criminals. 'Consistently', they claim, 'hunger causes theft of food; problems of hunger and shelter lead to serious theft; and problems of shelter and unemployment produce prostitution.'[69] Pat Carlen extended that notion to women adrift on the streets, arguing too that their homelessness exacerbates risk, vulnerability, and exposure to formal agencies of control.[70]

---

[65] M. Gottfredson and T. Hirschi, *A General Theory of Crime*, 90.
[66] M. Innes, *Understanding Social Control*, 54.
[67] J. Hagan, J. Simpson, and A. Gillis, 'The Sexual Stratification of Social Control'.
[68] P. Carlen, *Women, Crime and Poverty*.
[69] J. Hagan and B. McCarthy, *Mean Streets*, 184; and see T. Newburn and P. Rock, 'Urban Homelessness, Crime and Victimisation in England'.   [70] P. Carlen, *Jigsaw: A Political Criminology of Youth Homelessness*.

'Anti-Sociological' Control Theories

One particularly influential anti-sociological variant of control theory lends itself to the application of technologies of crime control which chimes with the lay theories of crime that stress the inadequacy of preventative measures. That variant is 'situational crime prevention'

The case for this form of control theory is succinctly made by Ron Clarke:

> Criminological theories have been little concerned with the situational determinants of crime. Instead, the main object of these theories (whether biological, psychological, or sociological in orientation) has been to show how some people are born with, or come to acquire, a 'disposition' to behave in a consistently criminal manner. This 'dispositional' bias of theory has been identified as a defining characteristic of 'positivist' criminology, but it is also to be found in 'interactionist' or deviancy theories of crime developed in response to the perceived inadequacies of positivism. . . . In fact . . . a dispositional bias is presented throughout the social sciences.[71]

The immediate stress of situational control theories, by contrast, is on the purely technical, cost–benefit-ratio aspects of crime: the opportunities for crime available in the environment and the risks attached to criminal activity. Both variables are—in his view—more amenable to change than those policy recommendations that flow from 'dispositional' theories, which lead people to suggest 'methods of preventive intervention precisely where it is most difficult to achieve any effects, i.e. in the relation to the psychological events or the social and economic conditions that are supposed to generate criminal dispositions'.[72] The argument is significant not only because of its content but also because of its provenance. Ron Clarke was Head of the Home Office Research and Planning Unit in the 1980s and he was able to influence the making of policy and the funding and direction of criminological research in England and Wales. When he declared that policy-relevant research should focus on containment, deterrent sentencing, police effectiveness, and crime prevention, his ideas were unusually consequential.[73] One outcome was the establishment of the Home Office Crime Prevention Unit in 1983 and the commissioning of a series of research reports on small practical campaigns to modify crime.[74]

Situational theories are not limited to purely technical and mechanistic manipulations of the environment; they are consonant with a model of offenders as capable of rational choices and decisions. Indeed, the representation of criminals as reasoning people implicated in chains of decisions lent itself remarkably well to research conducted within and for the government. Much control theory may be found in and around the boundaries of official action. Two of its principal authors, Ron Clarke and Derek Cornish, observed, 'both [of us] spent their early careers in the British government's criminological research department. This made [us] acutely aware of the need for criminology to be useful in solving policy and practical problems and explains

---

[71] R. Clarke, 'Situational Crime Prevention', 136.   [72] R. Clarke, 'Situational Crime Prevention', 137.
[73] R. Clarke and D. Cornish, *Crime Control in Britain*, 41.
[74] D. Cornish and R. Clarke, *The Reasoning Criminal*, 1.

why the rational choice perspective was explicitly developed to assist policy thinking.[75] Rational criminals confronting critical choices are fairly readily susceptible to intelligent control strategies. Moreover, the presumption of rationality had a common-sense appeal: that is how most people, including politicians and officials, would care to explain their own and others' behaviour. It lent itself to neat, demonstrable experiments in crime prevention. Clarke lists some examples: the virtual elimination of airline hijackings in the 1970s by baggage screening; the elimination of robberies of bus drivers in America by the introduction of exact fare systems; and the virtual elimination of graffiti on New York City subway cars by systematic and prompt graffiti removal.[76]

Rational choice theory is now itself in the ascendancy in a number of areas of social science and it has come to play an increasingly important role in the arguments of control theory itself. Some part of that ascendancy may be explained by the intellectual dominance and apparent successes of behavioural economics and the corresponding authority which economic models of behaviour exert over psychology, sociology, political science, and criminology. One particularly important early paper was Gary Becker's 'Crime and Punishment: An Economic Approach',[77] published in 1968, which attempted to assess the consequences of the balance between expenditure on control and punishment on the one hand and social losses from offending on the other.[78] Becker adopted the economist's assumption that people will offend if the utility of doing so exceeds the utility of not doing so. Crime was not a matter of motivation, he argued, but of costs and benefits weighed by one contemplating whether to break the law (although, presumably, that weighing was itself influenced by a motive to seek gain). Just as economic man maximizes utility, so, Clarke and Cornish argue, criminal man chooses crime 'because of the benefits it brings to the offender. This holds in all cases of crime, with the possible exception of some crimes committed as a result of serious mental illness'.[79] That simple economist's calculus was subsequently to be extended and complicated by the inclusion of a larger cast of actors conceived continually to be making decisions about the rewards and penalties of committing crime, reporting crime, and enforcing the law. It was never utterly rational but based on imperfect information, improvisation, and experience. Its use came to be described by Clarke and Cornish as staggered over time, organized by scripts which chart decisions in sequence, breaking down complex acts into 'aggregations of simpler elements',[80] from preparation, through target selection, entry to the setting, commission of the act, and escape to aftermath. The calculus seemed to have support in 'the evidence of ethnographic studies of delinquency[81] [which] strongly suggest that people are usually aware of consciously choosing to commit offences'.[82] It is, they said, most powerfully

---

[75] R. Clarke and D. Cornish, 'Rational Choice', 14.

[76] R. Clarke (ed.), *Situational Crime Prevention: Successful Case Studies*.

[77] G. Becker, 'Crime and Punishment: An Economic Approach'.

[78] For a more general and critical discussion of that trend, see F. Fukuyama, *State Building*, 61 ff.

[79] R. Clarke and D. Cornish, 'Rational Choice', 2.

[80] D. Cornish and R. Clarke, 'Analyzing Organized Crimes', 20.

[81] The reference is to H. Parker, *The View from the Boys*.

[82] R. Clarke, 'Situational Crime Prevention', 138.

exemplified by organized crime and, however non-rational or irrational some other forms of criminal behaviour might appear to be, in that one domain, at least, it was held incontestably to apply there.[83]

In short, control theory is in line with theories of social learning and rational choice; and it has no difficulty, unlike dispositional theories, in accepting that 'the bulk of crime—vandalism, auto-crime, shoplifting, theft by employees—is committed by people who would not ordinarily be thought of as criminal at all'.[84] Far from narrowing the scope of criminological hypotheses, it enriches its possibilities: 'First, explanation is focused more directly on the criminal event; second, the need to develop explanations for separate categories of crime is made explicit; and, third, the individuals' current circumstances and the immediate features of the setting are given considerably more explanatory significance than in "dispositional" theories.'[85]

Nevertheless, the 'zero sum' cast of situational crime prevention (SCP) theory, whereby the situational is magnified at the expense of the dispositional, including much social control theory, is ultimately a self-inflicted limitation. Studies of traffic control, reducing fare evasion, and graffiti 'show that proponents of SCP have, curiously, tended to understate the importance of situations . . . Instead of emphasizing the contrast between changing situations and changing people, it is necessary to study how persons, behaviour and the social and physical environment interact . . . It (then) becomes clear that persons develop and change in response to their experience in particular situations, so that changes in situations can produce more persistent changes in people'.[86] What Clarke terms 'standing decisions' can become, in effect and over time, changed norms and values. As Smith adds,[87] 'it does not follow that it (SCP) is necessarily the best method, or the most practicable'.

Measures for crime prevention have two linked emphases: reducing the physical opportunities for offending and increasing the risk of an offender being caught. The first embraces such examples as the replacement of vulnerable coin-boxes with stronger ones, which virtually eliminated theft from telephone kiosks; and the dramatic fall in the Birmingham suicide rate when supplies of non-toxic (North Sea) gas were installed in people's homes.[88] Several well-researched instances of specific successes in crime prevention can be adduced to bear this approach out. There is Laycock's demonstration

---

[83] Cornish and Clarke observe 'Whatever the merits of . . . criticisms for other offenses . . . they carry little weight in respect of organized crime. This is rational crime par excellence . . . ': 'Analyzing Organized Crimes', 1.

[84] R. Clarke, 'Situational Crime Prevention', 137.   [85] R. Clarke, 'Situational Crime Prevention', 139.

[86] D. Smith, 'Changing Situations and Changing People', 171–2.

[87] D. Smith, 'Changing Situations and Changing People', 172.

[88] Sainsbury ('The Epidemiology of Suicide') has questioned the inference that trends in the detoxification of gas supplies to domestic consumers in England account for the sharp decline in the suicide rate between 1963 and 1975. He notes the similarity between rates of suicide in a number of towns in England and Wales and provinces in Holland, despite dissimilar phasing of the detoxification process. Clarke and Mayhew ('The British Gas Suicide Story and its Criminological Implications' and 'Crime As Opportunity A Note On Domestic Gas Suicide In Britain And The Netherlands') rebut this criticism by reference to the inadequacy of the data for Holland and their inconclusive nature for England and Wales, owing to the small number of towns sampled ('The British Gas Suicide Story and its Criminological Implications', 130). The balance of evidence now seems to favour control theory on this issue, whose significance as a test of displacement makes it a priority for further research.

that acceptance of the advice of police officers on target-hardening led to a decline in burglaries from pharmacies;[89] and that property-marking schemes reduced residential burglary in an experimental site in Wales. Possibly the most phenomenological application of this approach has been the attempt made by Bennett, Wright, and others to reconstruct the environment as potential predators see it. They conducted extensive interviews with burglars, using videotapes of residential housing and venturing on tours with an accompanying commentary from experienced criminals, to establish how surroundings are interpreted. It has become clear that signs of occupation, the presence of dogs, surveillance by neighbours, and ease of access are critically important in the decision to break in to a house.[90] In contrast, the activities of the police and technical controls such as alarms and locks are relatively inconsequential.

The result has been an increasingly meticulous mapping of the visual controls built into space. It is as if the built environment could be transformed by control theory into a bundle of observed offending opportunities. One clever demonstration of those links between design and crime may be found in a study of burglary in schools. Hope contrasted two different styles of school building in Britain—the large, modern, and sprawling schools which were often set in spacious grounds and the small, old, and compact schools with only a modest amount of space around them. Between 1977 and 1978, the average number of burglaries in his sample was 7.9 for the large and sprawling and 2.2 for the small and compact schools. Having explored rival explanations, it was his conclusion that the differences in burglary rates could be attributed to features of design: the small schools were less accessible to predators and afforded 'greater opportunities for surveillance by the public and by school caretakers'.[91]

The second prong of the preventative approach builds on the assumption that there is 'a good deal of unrealized potential for making use of the surveillance role of employees who come into regular and frequent contact with the public in a semi-official capacity'.[92] Control theory has translated the physical environment into a terrain patrolled, watched, and guarded by numerous official and unofficial custodians. Doorstaff, car-park attendants, caretakers, ticket-collectors, park keepers, and community support officers,[93] and the like have been shown to make a considerable impact on specific crime rates. For example, on double-decker buses without conductors, the areas of least supervision attracted the most damage: drivers could monitor behaviour on the lower deck but not on the upper and 'there was about 20 times as much damage on the upper as on the lower deck'.[94]

An allied example is that of the municipal housing estates[95] in England and Wales whose structure and administration became ever more frequently examined for their impact on deviance and conformity. During the 1960s, a drive for economy and rationalization removed administrative and maintenance work from the estates and centralized it in main offices. Repairs and caretaking tasks were undertaken by mobile

[89] G. Laycock, *Reducing Burglary*.

[90] T. Bennett and R. Wright, *Burglars on Burglary*.

[91] T. Hope, *Burglary in Schools*.

[92] R. Clarke, 'Situational Crime Prevention', 142.

[93] T. Jones and T. Newburn, 'Urban Change and Policing: Mass Private Property Re-considered'.

[94] P. Mayhew et al., *Crime as Opportunity*, 26.

[95] What would be called 'projects' in North America.

teams. Latterly, however and partly as a result of the movement towards centralization, a number of housing estates became identified as something of a social problem. To the Department of the Environment, they were the 'hard-to-let' estates. To the Home Office they were a new kind of criminogenic area. The beginnings of a political response could be seen in the estate-improvement schemes run by the National Association for the Care and Resettlement of Offenders and the Department of the Environment's Priority Estates Projects, schemes encouraging a return to decentralized maintenance, lettings, and administration. In the process of devolution it was discovered just how much informal social control could be exercised by local caretaking staff. Resident caretakers play 'a key role in helping to reduce vandalism, patrolling public areas and supervising the cleaning of them and dealing at first hand with tenants' problems'.[96]

Architecturally, Oscar Newman's study, *Defensible Space* (1972), has been the most discussed, if not the best-attested, theory to be centred on the passive controls that can be mobilized by improvements in housing design. His work attracted a great deal of attention because he claimed to have demonstrated the link between high-rise public-sector housing and increased rates of crime and delinquency. Jane Jacobs had laid its foundation in her classic lament for the rapidly disappearing intimacy and diversity of city life,[97] a lament which chronicled the progressive extinction of the street as the urban form most in harmony with human scale. The street had originally evolved as an arena for diverse activities and safe associations, particularly for children at play and was enhanced by passers-by, the presence of traders and news-vendors, and ease of natural surveillance from houses and shops.[98] The high-rise housing complex has planned these features of urban concourse away. As a result, social processes have been squeezed out by built forms. It was Newman who then proceeded to describe how areas of space of an 'indefensible' character have been created, consisting of deserted through-ways and underpasses, unobservable lifts and stairwells. Entrances to buildings are used by so many people that it is no longer certain who has a right to pass through them and who has not, who is safe and who is not. In particular, there has been a proliferation of 'confused' and anonymous areas which belong to no one and are cared for by no one. It has become impossible to decide who has a reasonable claim to be present in a tract of land or a building, and people are unable to establish practical or symbolic boundaries around territory which is their own or to exercise informal social control within them. The result has been a great increase in rates of crime. Ironically, inner-city building that was planned to pack the maximum number of people into the minimum permissible amount of space, in part to prevent the suburban drift of workers essential to the political economy of the city, has accentuated problems which hasten that very process.

Subsequent criticisms have dented Newman's authority somewhat,[99] although the criticisms themselves are not without flaw. In Britain, especially, the argument has

---

[96] Department of the Environment, *Reducing Vandalism on Public Housing Estates*.

[97] J. Jacobs, *The Death and Life of Great American Cities*.

[98] See the work of M. Duneier in *Sidewalk*, a study that leans heavily on the arguments of Jane Jacobs and which unearths complex webs of informal control practised by homeless entrepreneurs on the streets of New York. [99] A. Bottoms, 'Review of *Defensible Space*'

been put that Newman neglected the social effects of communal reputation on the behaviour of those who lived in crime-ridden neighbourhoods: people who are part of a morally stigmatized area are alleged to experience discrimination, impaired life-chances, and unsupportive neighbours (a criticism that is not universally borne out). There has been the charge that Newman was insensitive to the effects of different policing strategies: the high crime-rates of the problem estates, it is said, reveal police assumptions and policies as much as real variations in behaviour (although later work disclosed how such estates seem to be *under-policed*[100]). It has been argued that Newman ignored housing allocation policies: a community's characteristics reflect letting and transfer decisions. It has been suggested that he made the unsupported assumption that criminals do not belong to an area, but are outsiders against whom space can successfully be defended (an assumption found most wanting in studies of certain high crime estates or projects in the United Kingdom[101] and United States[102]). Hillier and others have taken further issue with Newman's assumption that a sense of territoriality is a widespread or fundamental human drive. People, they say, may not invariably wish to have a symbolic stake in space.[103] But Newman's work was original, stimulating, and politically timely and it did succeed in drawing together a number of strands usually considered in isolation from each other by urban planners, criminologists, and environmentalists. Moreover, although it focused on the control aspects of the environment, his theory implicitly raised questions of a more symbolic character. There is an extensive programme of questions which is beginning to be asked about the features which enhance the social sense of 'belonging' to a neighbourhood and make for a feeling of involvement rather than indifference, a sense which is now described collectively as communal 'efficacy'.[104] The argument runs that 'the differential ability of neighborhoods to realize the common values of residents and maintain effective social control is a major source of neighborhood variation in violence'.[105] They continue: 'Together, three dimensions of neighborhood stratification—concentrated disadvantage, immigration concentration, and residential stability—explained 70 per cent of the neighborhood variation in collective efficacy'.[106] In this respect, the work combines both situational and sociological control variables.

Perhaps the most direct application of Newman's concept of 'defensible space' has been Alice Coleman's *Utopia on Trial* which is based on a survey of 4,099 blocks of flats, listing those design features which seem to correlate with such measurable signs of disorder as graffiti, litter, vandalism, and the number of children in care.[107] The assumption has been that it is poor physical design that causes social breakdown by estranging members of a community from one another, by letting marauders in, and by preventing

---

[100] F. Reynolds, *The Problem Housing Estate.*

[101] A. Sampson, *Lessons from a Victim Support Crime Prevention Project.*

[102] L. Rainwater, *Behind Ghetto Walls.*   [103] B. Hillier, 'In Defence of Space'.

[104] R. Sampson, J. Morenoff, and T. Gannon-Rowley, 'Assessing "Neighborhood Effects": Social Processes and New Directions in Research'.

[105] R. Sampson, S. Raudenbush, and F. Earls, 'Neighborhoods and Violent Crime: A Multilevel Study of Collective Efficacy'.

[106] R. Sampson, S. Raudenbush, and F. Earls, 'Neighborhoods and Violent Crime: A Multilevel Study of Collective Efficacy', 923.   [107] A. Coleman, *Utopia on Trial.*

an effective response. Crime itself is believed to flow from the uncontrolled circulation of strangers along the walkways of poorly planned estates; from the residents' loss of a sense of territoriality; from an abundance of escape routes for predators; and from inadequate opportunities for surveillance. It can be reduced by redesigning or eliminating portions of estates so that entrances can be controlled, the movement of strangers restricted, spatial ambiguity reduced, and monitoring improved. In newly created small, private, and enclosed areas of residence, outsiders may imagine that they are more conspicuous and insiders that they have a greater stake in territory. Coleman has given an insistent emphasis to the importance of design, tending to devalue social and symbolic variables and she has attracted the ire of critics who defend social explanation and critics who do not. The most strident has again been Bill Hillier, who maintained roundly that 'her method of quantification of malaise is flawed, her correlations largely illusory and her attempt to test for social factors desultory'.[108] Hillier objects that many of Coleman's correlations between malaise indicators and design may actually be explained by the effects of increasing population density in flats. Design features and signs of malaise are both likely to vary with the size of blocks. Others have repeated the criticisms that were first directed at Newman, arguing that Coleman neglects the influence of stigma, social organization, and formal social control. Perhaps the point has been made most succinctly by the National Research Council: 'Crime and violence arise from interactions between the social environment and the physical environment, which cannot be controlled entirely through manipulations of the physical environment.'[109] Yet in the work of Newman, Poyner,[110] Coleman, and others there does remain a provocative line of reasoning whose potential is far from exhausted.

Situational crime prevention, defensible space, and other facets of control theory point to the growing role of informal and formal surveillance in the regulation of everyday life. Especially significant was the concept of 'broken windows', that was mooted first by Jane Jacobs and then became celebrated in an essay published by Wilson and Kelling in 1982.[111] Broken windows, graffiti, and malicious damage were held to be the visible and obvious signs of a neighbourhood in decay, a neighbourhood which was open to depredation and about which no one effectively cared. They seemed to be linked in the public mind with disorder, crime, and the fear of crime. By extension, Wilson and Kelling surmised, broken windows signified that social control itself had been eroded: 'Families move out, unattached adults move in. Teenagers gather in front of the corner store. The merchant asks them to move; they refuse. Fights occur. Litter accumulates.'[112] In short, broken windows were to be regarded as a phase in a natural history of communal disintegration.

Wilson and Kelling came to exercise an appreciable influence over the reformation of policing in a number of American cities. 'Incivilities', beggars, 'squeegeeing', graffiti,

---

[108] B. Hillier, 'City of Alice's Dreams'.

[109] National Research Council, *Understanding and Preventing Violence*, 148.

[110] B. Poyner, *Design Against Crime*, and B. Poyner, P. Helson, and B. Webb, *Layout of Residential Areas and its Influence on Crime*.

[111] J. Wilson and G. Kelling, 'The Police and Neighbourhood Safety'.

[112] J. Wilson and G. Kelling, 'The Police and Neighbourhood Safety'.

and the like had formerly been dismissed as 'not real police work' and certainly not as important a part of the police mandate as confronting 'serious crime'. The new argument now came to assert that intervening in the cycle of communal deterioration by joining local residents and police together in campaigns to discourage panhandling, litter, and public drinking could reverse decline and bring about a reinvigoration of informal social control. Successes claimed have included the decline in the rates of crime that seem to have been associated with the reclamation of the New York subway system, the practice of so-called 'zero-tolerance' policing in American cities, and with neighbourhood improvement schemes in New York City[113] and Baltimore.[114]

Yet the most rigorous empirical test of the thesis to date rebuts the core assumption that signs of disorder precipitate a vicious spiral of increasing rates of crime and social deterioration. Sampson and Raudenbush (1999) criticize the whole argument as tautological, mistaking symptoms for causes. Using an ingenious method of videotaping some 23,000 street 'segments' or face blocks in Chicago, they constructed scales of physical and social disorder for 196 neighbourhoods. These variables were then analysed with other data sets from census, police, and interviews with residents to assess the significance of 'broken windows' against that of 'collective efficacy' (a version of social capital) and 'structural constraints' (especially concentrated poverty) in explaining lower rates of crime.

> Contrary to the 'broken windows' theory, the relationship between public disorder and crime is spurious, except perhaps for robbery . . . Put differently, the active ingredients in crime seem to be structural disadvantage and attenuated collective efficacy more so than disorder. Attacking public disorder through tough police tactics may thus be a politically popular but perhaps analytically weak strategy to reduce crime, mainly because such a strategy leaves the common origins of both, but especially the last, untouched.[115]

Again, an attempt to understand the decline in New York's homicide rate hit upon the marked incursion of new immigrant groups with a strong motivation to succeed and intact families as the most plausible explanation, not changes in policing style.[116] And a more comprehensive, comparative analysis of the likely causes of the drop in the American crime rate failed to find any convincing explanation at all.[117]

Routine Activity Theory

Another, more recent extension of pragmatic theories of control and opportunity into the domain of everyday life has been supplied by the 'routine activity theory' of Cohen and Felson. They argue, as Clarke and others also argued, that the focus of attention should shift from the criminal to the ordinary circumstances of offending. They prefer

---

[113] W. Bratton (with P. Knobler), *Turnaround: How America's Top Cop Reversed the Crime Epidemic.*
[114] G. Kelling and C. Coles, *Fixing Broken Windows.*
[115] R. Sampson and S. Raudenbush, 'Systematic Social Observation of Public Spaces', 603, 638.
[116] A. Karmen, *The New York Murder Mystery: The True Story Behind the Crime Crash of the 1990s.*
[117] F. Zimring, *The Great American Crime Decline.*

to understand those ordinary circumstances with the aid of simple models of rational choice rather than more complicated descriptions of human motive and interpretation.[118] Echoing Hirschi, they hold that the big question is not why people commit crime but why everyone does not do so.[119] Like other control theorists, they offer an imagery of innate human susceptibility to temptation, original sin, and the perils of idleness. Criminology, their argument continues, should assume that people will offend if they are sufficiently provoked or enticed to do so, that they will not offend if they are prevented from doing so and that any pattern of offending must consequently be analysed as a product of the way in which temptations and controls are woven into the fabric of society. Unlike situational crime prevention theorists, they tend to be macrosociological, concentrating on what Clarke calls 'broad social trends',[120] but the two approaches are perfectly compatible.

The principal contentions of routine activity theory are, first, that the probability of offending will be affected by the manner in which 'likely offenders', 'suitable targets', and 'capable guardians' converge in space and time[121] and, second, that those factors will reflect the commonplace structures of social life. Together, they constitute what Felson was to call a 'crime chemistry'[122] or 'ecosystem'[123] which shapes and galvanizes crime.

For instance, an increase in the volume of cars is liable not only to expand the quantity of 'suitable targets' but also to make it easier for likely or motivated offenders to travel widely and anonymously, conceal stolen goods, and make a rapid departure. Moreover, such increased car ownership will act to spread housing more thinly in space, reduce population density, and lessen the numbers of capable guardians who might witness and report suspicious phenomena.

Again, changes in family structure can bring about a growth in the number of single people living alone, a proliferation of households containing property, and a consequent reduction in the population of capable guardians. After all, single people are more likely to leave their homes unattended and they cannot but be less competent as custodians. In this manner, offering example after example, Cohen and Felson document how mundane social change can influence opportunities for offending. Later, and underscoring further the links between their ideas, Felson and Clarke[124] were to produce a list of propositions about crime and opportunity: opportunities, they say, play a role in causing all crime; crime opportunities are highly specific (they differ between bank robbery, mugging, and burglary); all crime opportunities are concentrated in time and space; crime opportunities depend on everyday movements and activity; one crime produces opportunities for another (burglary may lead to selling stolen goods); some products offer more tempting crime opportunities; social and technological changes produce new crime opportunities; reducing opportunities can curb criminal

---

[118] R. Clarke and M. Felson (eds.), *Routine Activity and Rational Choice*.
[119] M. Felson, *Crime and Everyday Life*, 15.
[120] R. Clarke, 'Situational Prevention, Criminology and Social Values', 1.
[121] L. Cohen and M. Felson, 'Social Change and Crime Rate Trends'.
[122] M. Felson, *Crime and Nature*.
[123] M. Felson, *The Ecosystem for Organized Crime*.
[124] M. Felson and R. Clarke, *Opportunity Makes the Thief*.

motivation; and reducing opportunities does not normally displace crime. Thus, to take one example, organized crime is affected by opportunities for the sale of illegal goods and services; and by the guardianship of what Felson called 'place managers' who control what happens in public space where those sales may occur.[125] Newman and Clarke now argue that the principles of opportunity theory can be used to combat terrorism.[126] For then there is no difference between terrorism and other forms of crime. Lawrence Sherman's idea of 'hot spots' has also emphasized how crimes tend to take place only at certain times and in certain places, and he argues that police resources and other control strategies should concentrate there and then rather than be diffusely targeted.[127]

The Surveillance State and the Widening Web of Control

The explicit shift to using control theory to build better mouse traps and surveillance systems has alarmed some criminologists, who started to stress the darker side of control theory by focusing on the increasing and, to them, alarming capacity of the networked state to govern. Of particular importance in their work has been Foucault's conception of the carceral society,[128] a society in which an apparently ubiquitous surveillance is enforced by a welter of direct and indirect means.

Underlying Foucault's metaphor is another core image: that of Bentham's panopticon, a projected design for a prison that would have worked on revolutionary principles had it been built when it was conceived in the late eighteenth century.[129] Plans for the panopticon envisaged a vast, circular building with cells housing prisoners about its rim and a dimly-lit central tower with inspectors at its centre. The very architecture of the prison gave dominion to authority. From their central tower, only a few inspectors would have been required to monitor multitudes of inmates. And those inmates could never have known with certainty when they *were* being monitored or by whom: their cells would have been illuminated, but the tower would not and its obscurity would have made it difficult to establish not only whether observers were actually in place at any time but whether they were watching any particular cell. In the panopticon, the 'gaze' was to be sovereign: prisoners were seen but they could not see.[130] Control would have been economic, efficient, and omnipresent: there was no need for arms, violence, or coercion because inmates would have become individualized, isolated, and constrained to police themselves. Power so perfected, Foucault maintained, rendered its practical use unnecessary.

---

[125] A. Edwards and M. Levi, 'Researching the Organization of Serious Crimes', 374–5;

[126] G. R. Newman and R. Clarke, *Policing Terrorism: An Executive Guide.*

[127] L. Sherman, P. Gartin, and M. Buerger, 'Hot Spots of Predatory Crime: Routine Activities and the Criminology of Place'; L. Sherman and D. Weisburd, 'General Deterrent Effects of Police Patrol in Crime "Hot Spots": A Randomized, Controlled Trial'.

[128] M. Foucault, *Discipline and Punish.*   [129] J. Semple, *Bentham's Prison.*

[130] C. Gordon (ed.), *Power/Knowledge*, 154–5.

Liberally transposed to contemporary society, that metaphor suggested that controls were continually being driven, dispersed,[131] and extended[132] by technological change towards a growing dependence on surveillance, electronically generated information,[133] and calculations of risk. There was, in Stan Cohen's phrase, 'a deeper penetration of social control into the social body'.[134]

Populations and territories, it is held, are now under general, often remote surveillance by closed-circuit television, helicopter, satellite, drones, and the collation of globally networked electronic ID traces generated by phone calls and email communication, banking transactions, payments, driving licences, travel cards, and the like.[135] This has of course been intensified as a result of the massive increase in resourcing for the intelligence agencies in the current phase of the war on terror. By 2013, it has been estimated, that up to 5.9 million CCTV cameras had been installed in the United Kingdom, including 750,000 in 'sensitive locations'[136] operating with uncertain success. The broad result has been the fashioning of new 'scanscapes'[137] of control and new mechanisms of indirect regulation and self-policing, including police officers wearing cameras in order to collect evidence and to protect themselves from allegations of misbehaviour. Surveillance, argues Graham, has added layer upon layer to urban terrain: 'Each layer has its own finer and finer mosaic of socio-spatial grids; its own embedded assumptions and criteria for allocating and withdrawing services or access; its own systems for specifying and normalizing boundary enforcement through electronically defining the "acceptable" presence of individuals in different urban "cellular" space-times'.[138] Very general, categorical assessments of risk, it has been argued, are beginning to supersede a system of control and justice that had been distinctively individualistic. And those assessments and controls are increasingly being driven by technologies which are less and less centred on moral or indeed legal judgement and more on 'operational efficiency'.[139]

Two intellectual influences are perceived to be at work in this new vision of control.[140] First is the analysis of what is thought to be the partial retreat of a now 'hollowed-out' neo-liberal State and its formal agencies of control into core activities concentrated on regulating especially troublesome groups and spaces. The State has become less and less able to guarantee the safety of all its citizens (although it is also said to be redrafting the boundary between those who are recognized as citizens and those who are not, between insiders and outsiders, the protected and the unprotected). Those who can afford to buy additional safety in the form of SUVs, walls, gates, alarms, surveillance systems, and private security guards will do so. Those who cannot will

---

[131] S. Cohen, 'The Punitive City'.
[132] N. Fraser, 'Foucault on Modern Power'.
[133] D. Lyon, *The Electronic Eye*.
[134] S. Cohen, 'The Punitive City', 356.
[135] D. Lyon, *Surveillance After Snowden*; J. Angwin, *Dragnet Nation: A Quest for Privacy, Security, and Freedom in a World of Relentless Surveillance*.
[136] The British Security Industry Authority.
[137] The phrase is that of M. Davis in 'Beyond Blade Runner'.
[138] S. Graham, 'Surveillant Simulation and the City', 26–7; see also S. Graham, *Cities Under Siege: The New Military Urbanism*.
[139] M. Lianos and M. Douglas, 'Dangerization and the End of Deviance', 270.
[140] P. O'Malley, 'Risk, Power and Crime Prevention'.

be left with relatively vestigial defences against crime,[141] although it is clear that such patterning will vary from area to area and country to country. The product is a new urban landscape in which the wealthy can afford to live in 'security bubbles' and travel within 'security corridors' set in the midst of insecure space. In Houston, Texas, for instance, an extensive network of safe underground streets is being developed to protect office workers from the dangers above.[142] The most imaginative and apocalyptic description of that new topography is the Los Angeles of Mike Davis, a socially and spatially segregated city in which fortress-homes surrounded by gates, fences, moats, and alarms separate the urban rich from the urban poor, in which the private areas of the wealthy cannot be reached by the public transport of the poor and in which the poor, the underclass, and the homeless are confined to dangerous areas and free-fire zones. Another, more mundane example is Shearing and Stenning's vivid description of Disney World as a private domain ingeniously engineered to exercise discreet, diffuse control over its visitors from their very first entrance to their final exit.[143]

The second influence is a growing criminological emphasis on the importance of 'risk' and its origin can be linked with the work of Ulrich Beck.[144] Beck proposed that risks are phenomena mediated by people's dependence on social institutions. Populations are differentially affected by risk: some are relatively exposed, some are not, and the foundation is prepared for a new system of stratification organized around hierarchies of vulnerability. Beck did not write explicitly about crime and victimization, but his conception of social groupings defined by risk has proved attractive to the criminologist.[145] Feeley and Simon, in particular, contend that in America the State's focus is beginning to shift away from the control of individuals to the actuarial identification,[146] classification, and management of social aggregates deemed to be dangerous or problematic. The idea of crime and its control, it is argued, has become a general source of methods and metaphors for dealing with an array of different social problems that used once to be the province of separate agencies providing educational, welfare, and health services—the phrase employed being 'governing through crime'.[147] And crime itself is said no longer to be discussed professionally in a moralizing and individualizing discourse but in probabilistic statements. Crime control becomes risk-management: it is no longer thought to be feasible to eliminate crime: simple management will do. Less is expected of the criminal sanction: rearranging the distribution of offenders in the community and incapacitating them in prison are beginning to replace rehabilitation as a goal.[148] And there is also what is in effect a new privatization of culpability based on what O'Malley calls a rejection of the social foundations of offending and a devolution of responsibility for crime prevention onto the victim and potential victim,[149] an extension of what some feminists used to call 'victim-blaming'.

---

[141] A. Bottoms and P. Wiles, 'Crime and Insecurity in the City'.

[142] S. Graham and S. Marvin, *Telecommunications and the City*, 223.

[143] C. Shearing and P. Stenning, 'From the Panopticon to Disney World'.

[144] U. Beck, *Risk Society*.   [145] J. Simon, 'The Emergence of a Risk Society'.

[146] J. Simon, 'The Ideological Effects of Actuarial Practices'.

[147] J Simon, *Governing Through Crime: How the War on Crime Transformed American Democracy and Created a Culture of Fear*.   [148] M. Feeley and J. Simon, 'The New Penology'.

[149] P. O'Malley, 'Risk, Power and Crime Prevention', 264, 266.

Critique

Control theorists are quite open about the most telling criticism of their approach: 'I have frequently heard the statement "it's an absence of something explanation" used as an apparently damning criticism of a sociological theory. While the origins of this view are unknown to me, the fact that such a statement appears to have some claim to plausibility suggests one of the sources of uneasiness in the face of a control theory.'[150] Earlier, Hirschi asserted: 'The primary virtue of control theory is not that it relies on conditions that make delinquency possible while other theories rely on conditions that make delinquency necessary. On the contrary, with respect to their logical framework, these theories are superior to control theory and, if they were as adequate empirically as control theory, we should not hesitate to advocate their adoption in preference to control theory.'[151] As these passages make clear, there is a tendency to overdraw the differences between what are presented as the empirically sound but modest claims of control theory and the empirically unsound but more pretentious alternatives.[152] Leaving aside for the moment the question of whether or not such theories do indeed 'make delinquency necessary', the chief point at issue is how far these theories are addressing the same problem as control theory. In one respect, there is agreement: all theories attempt to explain the occurrence and social distribution of crime and deviance, much as that might vary according to the indicators used. In other respects, there is substantial divergence, for the equally important aim of alternative sociological theories is to account for the *character* of crime and deviance, one principal aspect of which is to attempt to construct models of motivation which correspond with its typical forms. It is hardly adequate for control theorists to assert that 'we would all be criminal/deviant, if we dared'. How criminal/deviant and criminal/deviant in what ways? Shorn of any meaning, for control theory deprives it of such an attribute, crime and deviance are presumably pursued for the sheer gratification of appetites—acquisitive, aggressive, and sexual. If this is indeed the case, then we are certainly wasting our time in pursuit of some Weberian ideal of *verstehen*. But it is also difficult to account for the very phenomena that theorists of other persuasions set out to explain: why crime and deviance are so often non-utilitarian; why aggression is so frequently ritualized and non-violent in its outcome; why sexual gratification takes such complex forms. In short, control theorists make far too little of both crime and deviance and conformity: as Kornhauser put it, why bother with motivation?

---

[150] T. Hirschi, *Causes of Delinquency*, 32–3, n. 44.   [151] T. Hirschi, *Causes of Delinquency*, 29.

[152] Since control theorists make so much of the strength of their case empirically, it is worth noting that in certain respects Hirschi's data strain credulity—a pleasant change from theories producing that effect. His definition of serious delinquency is weak in the extreme: any two or more of six offences—theft of under $2; theft of $2 to $50; theft of over $50; joy-riding; 'banging up something that doesn't belong to you'; and, not counting fights with a brother or sister, the beating up or hurting of anyone on purpose. How is it that over 50 per cent of Hirschi's Californian sample of white boys are non-delinquent by these standards throughout adolescence? Presumably they put their own interpretation on minor vandalism and fighting, in which case we need to know what implicit standards they are employing. This, needless to say, is the major problem with self-report studies of this kind. (Another reason may be that school drop-outs did not fill in the questionnaire.) T. Hirschi, *Causes of Delinquency*, 54 ff.

Small wonder, then, that control theorists dismiss as of negligible impact the role that norms and values play in social behaviour. These are viewed as almost entirely dependent on attachments to those whose opinions we value. Weaken or remove those attachments and we feel free to deviate. It may well be that Parsons' assumption that, once adequately internalized, norms and values are with us for life is hopelessly over-blown; that it constitutes, in Dennis Wrong's memorable phrase, an 'over-socialized conception of man'. Nor would we wish to dissent from the view that norms and values are fluid, negotiable, and subject to constant revision. But to link adherence to norms and values so strongly to personal attachments, whether to families or to institutions, is to go too far towards a purely 'other-directed' and 'under-socialized' view of man. Norms may be shed and values revalued, but that can take place in the context of strong attachments, as well as in their absence. Rates of deviation may rise after marital break-up: but most divorcees remarry. School failures may resent the school (as Box suggests), but it has not yet been established that they do so without reference to an alternative set of norms and values. On the other hand, delinquents may be attached to their peers as a kind of quasi-family, and one wonders what to make of the idea of attachment there. In sum, norms and values cannot as easily be reduced to attachments as control theorists contend.

Situational control theorists are also well aware of the weak link in their arguments. Clarke argues that 'the specificity of the influences upon different criminal behaviours gives much less credence to the "displacement" hypothesis; the idea that reducing opportunities merely results in crime being displaced to some other time or place has been the major argument against situational crime prevention'.[153] He argues that 'displacement' is least likely in cases of 'opportunistic' crime, most likely in cases of professional crime. Even for the bulk of offences that arguably lie in between these extremes, he cites success in specific cases (such as kiosk design and vandalism, or the West German installation of compulsory steering locks and theft of cars) and refers elsewhere to a review by the Dutch Ministry of Justice of fifty-five situational prevention projects. No evidence of displacement was found in twenty-two of the projects and only partial displacement in the remainder.[154]

The issue of displacement exercised Pat Mayhew and her colleagues, who remarked that 'advocates of "situational prevention" . . . encounter particular difficulties in dealing with the criticism that the effectiveness of opportunity-reducing measures is undermined by displacing offenders' activities to other times, places, targets, or types of crime'.[155] It seemed, for instance, that older vehicles were stolen when modern cars were fitted with steering-column locks and that there was an increase in street robberies after the police had acted against muggings in the New York subway system.[156] Examining data on trends in the theft of cars, motorcycles, and bicycles in West Germany, England, and the Netherlands between 1980 and 1986, it was concluded that the introduction of

[153] R. Clarke, *Situational Crime Prevention*, 138.
[154] R. Clarke, 'Situational Prevention, Criminology and Social Values'.
[155] P. Mayhew, R. Clarke, and D. Elliott, 'Motorcycle Theft, Helmet Legislation and Displacement', 1.
[156] J. Chaiken, M. Lawless, and K. Stevenson, *Impact of Police Activity on Crime: Robberies on the New York City Subway System*.

laws making the wearing of motorcycle helmets compulsory *had* brought about a decline in the theft of motorcycles. In West Germany, for example, the numbers of thefts fell from some 150,000 a year in 1980 to 54,000 in 1986.[157] It seemed to have become much more difficult for the casual, opportunistic thief to steal a motorcycle unless the potential thief had planned the crime by taking a helmet with him or her. Moreover, the drop in motorcycle theft was not matched by a commensurate increase in car theft, there being no effective crime displacement. In another article, Pat Mayhew returned to the same data to observe that the increase in bicycle thefts from 360,000 to 410,000 between 1980 and 1981 in West Germany was 'much greater than would have been predicted by displacement'.[158] She concluded that displacement was not evident in this case but, elsewhere, an international crime survey did suggest that there were puzzling signs of displacement from car thefts to bicycle thefts: 'these results appear to suggest that when there are plenty of bicycles around, some thieves will make do with two wheels instead of four'.[159] The contradictory results could have been a mere statistical artefact, they run counter to the general grain of findings that displacement effects are rare,[160] and, like all such confusing statistical computations, elucidation does require complementary research on the offenders' own behaviour and logic-in-use. As we shall argue, much situational theory, having deliberately eschewed ideas of disposition and motivation, can sometimes be markedly at a loss to explain its findings. It tends to be a one-dimensional criminology, unable to theorize motive and meaning not only, as Trasler,[161] a telling critic, argued in relation to *expressive* delinquency but also with regard to crime and deviance in general.

Again, apart from the non-toxic gas example quoted above, there is also some doubt that gun control would do much to lower levels of violent crime in the USA—though one would welcome its implementation.[162] As Clinard has pointed out, guns are present in most homes in Switzerland, owing to the system of citizen defence, yet the rate of crimes of violence is very low.[163] The vast differences in rates of criminal violence between the USA and Switzerland can hardly be accounted for in terms of the availability of firearms alone: presumably socio-cultural differences play a more considerable causal role (although those differences are sometimes more elusive and difficult to trace than might be supposed[164]). Indeed, unpublished secondary analysis conducted by Mayhew on a recent international crime survey suggests that, even if the influence of guns *were* eliminated, the United States would still have appreciably higher rates of homicide and serious violence than almost every other country.

---

[157] P. Mayhew, R. Clarke, and D. Elliott, 'Motorcycle Theft, Helmet Legislation and Displacement'.

[158] P. Mayhew, 'Displacement and Vehicle Theft', 235.

[159] P. Mayhew, 'Displacement and Vehicle Theft', 236.

[160] P. Goldblatt and C. Lewis (eds.), *Reducing Offending*, 28.

[161] G. Trasler, 'Situational Crime Control and Rational Choice: A Critique'.

[162] J. B. Jacobs, *Can Gun Control Work?*

[163] M. Clinard, Cities *with Little Crime: The Case of Switzerland*, 114–15.

[164] Michael Bellesiles argued, for instance, that, contrary to the more mythologized accounts of the history of the place of the gun in American life, few Americans owned guns until the Civil War, most were averse to using those guns, and were incompetent when they did use them. It was only later that the legend of the intrepid and well-armed frontiersman began to emerge. See his *Arming America: The Origins of a National Gun Culture.*

Control theorists would doubtless reply that it is easier to control firearms than to 'Helvetianize' America and it would be absurd to deny that certain control measures demonstrably deter certain offences at what Matza has termed the 'invitational edge'. However, as David Smith points out, ' . . . judgments about what can and cannot be changed are highly contestable . . . (They) may too easily emerge from cultural biases, rather than analysis. For most British people, gun control would "obviously" be the most effective and efficient method of reducing homicide in the United States, but for most Americans it is equally "obvious" that such a policy could not be implemented. This example starkly illustrates the limits of (J. Q.) Wilson's robust pragmatism.'[165] Situational crime prevention theory simply cannot cope with the paradox that, in the USA, gun control is ruled out for 'cultural' reasons while drug prohibition, which is hugely invasive of personal liberty, is deemed perfectly feasible.

There are also dangers that situational crime control may prove counter-productive in unanticipated ways. First, as Clarke acknowledges, there is the danger that it acts *repressively*, excluding particular groups defined as risks from private or semi-public space and subjecting the population as a whole to surveillance techniques which constrict freedom of movement, privacy, or action. Clearly, circumstances alter cases and few airline passengers now resent screening for weapons or explosives, and there have not been many complaints about the spread of CCTV in Britain. Similar-sounding arguments can be advanced for fingerprinting or DNA-banking the entire population. (Clarke, however, would dismiss most of those anxieties, claiming as a utilitarian that the strategy's benefits tend to outweigh its inconveniences and that: 'Many situational prevention measures are entirely unobtrusive or can even improve the quality of life.'[166])

Second, situational prevention may operate *regressively*, as the bill for monitoring and securing shops, public buildings, and transport systems is heaped on the consumer regardless of ability to pay. Third, it may deflect attention from attempts to engineer those difficult social and economic changes that control theorists regard as too remote for contemplation, such as the reduction of inequality. And yet, as riots demonstrate, increased security does not prevent looting and torching of shops. The 'technological fix' is double-edged; it may ease the crime problem in certain specific respects, but also blunt our awareness of the need to examine the more fundamental causes of high rates of crime. Housing built on the cost–benefit principle, without regard to the human factor, cannot be rescued by cost–benefit crime control.

One of the most pressing problems of control theory stems from its propensity to combine assumptions about the rationality of behaviour with the measurement and comparison of objective behavioural indicators, leaving a black box in between. It is as if a sensible criminologist sitting in an office or library knows everything about how people conduct their affairs, how they go about stealing, burgling, surveying, interpreting, and controlling. It is assumed that we are quite familiar with the routine practices of residents, caretakers, and others as they go about such tasks as looking

---

[165] D. Smith, 'Changing Situations and Changing People', 155.
[166] R. Clarke, 'Situational Prevention, Criminology and Social Values', 106.

out of their windows and making sense of the social scene. It also seems to be assumed that the simplicities of rational choice theory afford us a 'good enough' understanding of the way in which would-be predators decipher their environment and formulate plans, being deterred or seduced by signs, obstructions, and opportunities. It is the environment which is sovereign in rational choice theory and those who move about in it are reduced to ciphers. There is almost no warrant for taking it that those assumptions are adequate. Control theorists have done little to observe ordinary behaviour, they have no evidence that it is as they describe and their analyses and inferences are correspondingly suspect. Supposition and the easy assumptions of rational choice theory have been allowed to replace observation. To be sure, their supposition is often intelligent enough, but people are prone to do untoward and surprising things and supposition is not enough. Not everyone—and certainly not the delinquent—is risk-aversive. Quite the contrary. People can find risk attractive or even seductive[167] and, as we argued in Chapter 6, criminals and deviants are reported to be attracted especially to what Matza called the 'manufacture of excitement', to making things happen in a dull, disenchanted world, to getting an 'adrenalin buzz', or a sense of the consequential and the thrilling.[168] Others may act in the spirit of what Matza described as a mood of fatalism. Neal Shover, in his foreword to Richard Wright and Scott Decker's ethnography of armed robbers, reflected that 'Street-level robbers typically make decisions in contexts of hedonism and desperation in which the likely consequences of their acts are neither weighed carefully nor taken seriously'.[169] His comments were to be echoed by a later study of street robbers in England and Wales, also conducted by Richard Wright and others,[170] a group of offenders who seemed to be driven by a sense of edgy excitement, and of life as play and showy performance infused by a short-term hedonism and pleasure in fighting. There are cultural dimensions to the assessment of risk which lead to conclusions that may be far from obvious to the observer, people attaching what seems to be excessive importance to slight risk, little importance to great risk.[171] Indeed, 'cultural criminology' has taken to emphasizing the seductions of the liminal and transgressive qualities of what they call 'edgework'. Those who succumb to the more extreme of such seductions are said to be 'neither dangerously "out of control" nor possessed of some self-destructive "death wish". Instead, they push themselves to "the edge", and engage there in "edgework", in search of "the adrenalin rush", authentic identity, and existential certainty; they lose control to take control'.[172]

The 'low self-control' theory of Gottfredson and Hirschi counters all such niceties of motivational analysis with the presumption that crime and criminality are overwhelmingly the outcomes of the inability to defer gratification. Whilst low self-control is not to be equated with criminality, it is *the* universal and necessary, if not sufficient cause

---

[167] A. Giddens, *Modernity and Self-Identity*, 132.

[168] R. Ericson and A. Doyle, *Uncertain Business*, esp. 10.

[169] Foreword to R. Wright and S. Decker, *Armed Robbers in Action*, x.

[170] R. Wright, F. Brookman, and T. Bennett, 'The Foreground Dynamics of Street Robbery in Britian'.

[171] M. Douglas, *Risk Acceptability According to the Social Sciences*. (J. Ferrell, K. Hayward, and J. Young, *Cultural Criminology*, 72).   [172] J. Ferrell et al., *Cultural Criminology*, 72.

of crime. The major problem for so all-encompassing a theory is how to account for the decline in rates of criminality with the onset of adulthood. The maturation out of delinquency was seen by Matza in particular as presenting insurmountable problems for strain and subcultural theories. Yet those theories did attempt to deal with the problem by arguing that the sources of strain—such as the search for status, manhood, and 'respect'—are at least attenuated by job-holding, marriage, and parenthood. Gottfredson and Hirschi are scathingly dismissive of such tenets, on both theoretical and empirical grounds.[173] Other studies of desistance have weighed the evidence somewhat differently. For example, Maruna[174] states: 'Substantial research confirms that desistance from crime is at least weakly correlated with stable employment . . . , getting married, . . . completing education . . . , and becoming a parent.' Weak correlations are belittled by Gottfredson and Hirschi, but they are the pointers to more effective prevention which in recombination can produce more substantial effects, as the 'What Works' literature stresses.

Given their investment in this single, stable variable of low self-control, in effect a 'slob' theory of crime, Gottfredson and Hirschi acknowledge the importance of 'ageing out of delinquency' as in especial need of explanation. A stable factor should, *ceteris paribus*, produce stable outcomes: continuingly high rates of crime throughout the life cycle. But it is the onset of adulthood, not just old age, which is associated with declining offending. There are two ways of handling this problem. The first is to argue that offending does not so much decline with age as change its form, from the predominantly expressive and public to the largely instrumental and private.[175] But Gottfredson and Hirschi show no inclination to this view, and indeed reject the instrumental/expressive polarity as meaningless.[176] The second is to analyse what it is about 'maturation' which outweighs low self-control. This is precisely what they do not do: what stands in need of explanation is treated flatly as self-explanatory: 'Crime declines with age. Spontaneous desistance is just that, changes in behavior that cannot be explained and changes that occur regardless of what else happens.'[177] This is particularly lacking in explanation of how young adult offenders, facing the full force of economic realities, somehow raise their levels of self-control to desist from crime. At the minimum, consumer capitalism is a sophisticated set of devices for *lowering* levels of self-control with the attainment of the age of majority: quite how every incentive to consume anything from fast food to fast sex via fast credit or fast crime suddenly proves so resistible flies in the face of the logic of low self-control theory.

O'Malley takes that argument considerably further by giving the connections between risk and crime a history. Risky behaviour by the emerging working class, he argues, was actively discouraged in the new disciplines imposed by industrial capitalism in the nineteenth century. What was coaxed instead was financial prudence, self-control, punctuality, and the restraint of appetite as a compliant workforce began to form

---

[173] M. Gottfredson and T. Hirschi, *A General Theory of Crime*, 138–9.
[174] S. Maruna, *Making Good: How Ex-Convicts Reform and Rebuild their Lives*, 30, n. 6.
[175] J. Foster, *Villains: Crime and Community in the Inner City*.
[176] M. Gottfredson and T. Hirschi, *A General Theory of Crime*, 22.
[177] M. Gottfredson and T. Hirschi, *A General Theory of Crime*, 136.

in and around the new institutions of production and consumption. Sobriety, thrift, and self-regulation were policed by an array of novel voluntary and State associations. But, he contends, much of that has now been jettisoned and risk-taking has been actively promoted: entrepreneurs and financiers have been rewarded for gambling in what, in retrospect, some have taken to calling a casino economy; and consumers have been coaxed into borrowing, consuming, and living in what now may appear to be a reckless manner.[178] Deviance and criminality are but the dark side of such energetic risk-courting.[179]

Sometimes control theorists are quite candid about the problem of the black box. Tilley, for instance, noting that the installation of CCTV cameras in car parks did seem to reduce crime, was moved to argue about one scheme that the 'data does not allow us to clarify the mechanism through which car crime has been reduced, beyond saying that usage changes and natural human surveillance does not seem to have played a part. Thus, we do not know what it is about the CCTV set-up which has led to the reduction in car crime'.[180]

One of the central tasks of criminology is to replace wild or informed guesses about conduct with more reliable charts of the social world. A beginning has been made with Walsh,[181] Bennett and Wright's interviews with burglars and robbers, and Short and Ditton's interviews with offenders on probation or undertaking community service.[182] Short and Ditton concluded that the responses of offenders to CCTV were so varied that they seemed to display no discernible pattern, although the willingness to commit public disorder offences did seem to be affected and some offenders actually welcomed the intensification of surveillance. Norris and Armstrong watched the watchers in the control room at the heart of a network of CCTV surveillance and found not only that they were not particularly adept at identifying deviant or potentially deviant conduct, but that they were as much interested in following the movements of attractive women or observing couples making love[183] as in acting the detective. A similar study by Norris and McCahill[184] described how some watchers were as much interested in reading newspapers, dozing, or talking on their mobile phones as in monitoring the screens. Together with Goold,[185] Norris and McCahill commented on the poor liaison between civilian watchers, security guards, and police despatchers. And there were technical shortcomings as well. In the beginning, many opportunities to survey crime electronically were marred by grainy pictures, or by video cameras that were not loaded or defective. For example, the IRA bomb that was left outside the Carlton Club in London in June 1990, injuring twenty-one people, was covered by cameras that were not switched on. Matters may be changing:

---

[178] P. O'Malley, *Crime and Risk*.   [179] J. Hagan, *Crime and Disrepute*.

[180] N. Tilley, *Understanding Car Parks, Crime and CCTV: Evaluation Lessons from Safer Cities*, 13. A more recent evaluation of the impact of CCTV reported substantial and largely unexplainable variations in rates of offending. M. Gill et al., *The Impact of CCTV*.

[181] D. Walsh, *Break-Ins* and *Heavy Business*.   [182] E. Short and J. Ditton, 'Seen and Now Heard'.

[183] C. Norris and G. Armstrong, *The Maximum Surveillance Society*.

[184] C. Norris and M. McCahill, 'CCTV: Beyond Penal Modernism?'

[185] B. Goold, *CCTV and Policing: Public Area Surveillance and Police Practices in Britain*.

one interesting instance where controls did seem effective was the use of CCTV cameras in police stations where suspects seemed to feel a little safer and the police better protected against charges of improper conduct.[186] Another success, admittedly after the event, was the identification of those engaged in both the suicide bombing attacks and attempted attacks on London's public transport system in London in July 2005.[187] Another tack has been taken by Shapland and Vagg who studied the informal social surveillance and control practised by people in everyday life, recounting, for example, how villagers would step outside their front doors and clatter their dustbins to advertise to suspicious strangers that someone was about and watching them.[188] Again, Dowd has undertaken secondary analysis on the social composition of witnesses and bystanders, discovering, perhaps unremarkably, that they are very similar to victims and offenders in specific cases.[189] Much offending, after all, is the result of similar people milling together in the same place at the same time. Knife wounds, for instance, are often inflicted on young men by other young men often in the presence of groups of other young men. But that work is only a beginning and quite an edifice has been built on a foundation of unsubstantiated surmise about the invasion and defence of territory, the creation and loss of attachments, and mutual surveillance.

Control theorists might reply that they do not wish to rule out the search for patterns of motivation that help us to understand deviance: they merely argue that no theories so far advanced actually work. Situational controls need not rule out the search for dispositional causes: they do, however, help us cope with the crime problem we face here and now. At the very least, both aspects of control theory point to a dimension that is missing from existing theories and which needs to be included.

Conclusion

Control theories are of two major types. Social control theories stem from the work of Durkheim and the concept of the social bond as the irreducible component of social systems. However, unlike theorists in the functionalist and anomie tradition, social control theorists focus on variations in social bonding as *the* major source of deviance, rather than as a prelude to other, more important causes of crime, such as structured inequality. Situational control theories place the main weight of explanation on variations in opportunities to commit crime and on the defensibility of targets. It derives from Bentham's conception of offending in relation to cost/benefit analyses on the part of offenders exercising rational choice. Both approaches pay little attention to issues of meaning and motivation, which they tend to see as irrelevant to a practical understanding of the aetiology of crime causation as a failure of crime prevention.

---

[186] T. Newburn and S. Hayman, *Policing, Surveillance and Social Control*.
[187] <http://news.bbc.co.uk/1/hi/uk/4676577.stm>.   [188] J. Shapland and J. Vagg, *Policing by the Public*.
[189] L. Dowd, 'Witnessing of Incidents and Intervention: Informal Social Control in Action'.

Further Reading

C. L. BRITT and Michael Gottfredson, *Control Theories of Crime and Delinquency*, New Brunswick, 2003.

S. COHEN, *Visions of Social Control*, Cambridge, 1985.

M. FELSON, *Crime and Everyday Life*, Thousand Oaks, Calif., 1994.

M. FELSON and R. Clarke, *Opportunity Makes the Thief: Practical Theory for Crime Prevention*, London, 1998.

D. LYON, *Surveillance After Snowden*, Cambridge, 2015.

10

Radical Criminology

Introduction

At the time of its emergence in the early 1970s the very phrase 'radical criminology' seemed a contradiction in terms. There had, after all, been a concerted attempt to differentiate 'criminology' (which was associated with government and 'positivism') from the 'sociology of crime and deviance' (which espoused a more 'radical' definition of the subject and a preference for methods, in particular that of participant observation, which were of reputedly marginal scientific status).[1] To reintroduce the term 'criminology' seemed to fly in the face of much that had been gained over the previous decade. To yoke it to the term 'radical' (or 'new', 'critical', or Marxist) seemed both perverse and over-ambitious. The directive in the phrase, however, was clear: to break with the seeming limitations of the 'sociology of crime and deviance' without a regress to conventional administrative criminology.[2]

What had led, in so short a time, to so signal a break in the ranks of those who had collectively opposed administrative criminology? In criminology, as in sociology and the humanities more generally, the answer must lie at least partly in the context of the times. In the USA and more mutedly in Britain, the late 1960s produced a significant minority of students 'radicalized' by the Vietnam war, racial conflict, and a host of more minor issues, such as those surrounding new forms of drug use. A fierce impatience was expressed with the gradualism of liberal, Social Democratic politics. Both the American 'War on Poverty' and the Labour Government in Britain were seen as failing crucially to correct structural inequalities of class, status, and power. At this point, the longer-standing project of the New Left, to dissociate Marxism from the 'State socialist' regime of the USSR and to regenerate it as a critical force, bore fruit. May 1968 came to symbolize the possibility of revolutionary change in affluent, Western societies. A variety of neo-Marxist philosophers reinterpreted Marxist theory to attempt to account for the crises that arose, the inability of capitalism to resolve them, and the inevitability of new and more devastating conflicts.

---

[1] S. Cohen, Introduction to *Images of Deviance*; M. Phillipson, *Sociological Aspects of Crime and Delinquency*; S. Cohen, 'Criminology and the Sociology of Deviance in Britain'.

[2] The operative image of administrative criminology was of activity almost exclusively geared to the more precise measurement, prediction, and control of criminality without regard to wider social and economic contexts and by quantitative methods. The reality was naturally more diverse.

Against the appeal of Gramsci, Habermas, and Althusser[3] the work of even such gifted interpreters of deviance as Matza, Lemert, and Becker seemed tame and that of Merton and Albert Cohen positively antediluvian. Whereas the latter offered tentative 'processual' models for an enhanced understanding of 'becoming deviant', or theories aimed at explaining lower-class forms of delinquency, the former seemed to provide a basis for grasping the 'total inter-connectedness'[4] of crime and capitalist society. The appeal of the application of Marxist theory and method to criminology was also increased by the growing visibility of what came to be termed 'crimes of the powerful'. None of the theories in vogue in the 1950s and 1960s addressed white-collar crime and the crimes of corporations and the State at all satisfactorily. To adapt Sutherland's dictum about the limitations of psychoanalytical theories of crime, it seemed absurd to regard Investors Overseas Services or Barings Bank as suffering from 'status-frustration', or the corporations involved in the 'Great Electrical Conspiracy' as victims of 'secondary deviation' or undue stigmatization.[5] The problem is neatly summarized by Taylor, Walton, and Young's criticism of earlier theories as predicting too little upper-class and too much lower-class criminality.[6] Such theories could not be readily adapted to resolve their shortcomings: a new paradigm was called for. The adequacy of the Marxist criminology that emerged as an alternative to other perspectives forms the subject of this chapter.

The New Criminology

The most vigorous attempt to supplant existing approaches by a neo-Marxist alternative occurs in the work of Taylor, Walton, and Young. In *The New Criminology*, a comprehensive appraisal of the full range of theoretical approaches in criminology is made. The main criterion by which such approaches are evaluated and, in general, found wanting, is their capacity to provide what the authors term, in the book's subtitle, a fully 'social theory of deviance'.[7] Their own model for a fully social theory is Marxism, but it is the Marx of the *Economic and Philosophical Manuscripts of 1844*, as well as of *Capital*, which they commend: Marx the dialectician rather than the determinist, Marx the action theorist as much as the analyst of political economy, who was concerned with alienation and consciousness as much as modes of production.[8] To establish the

---

[3] The work of Antonio Gramsci and Jurgen Habermas has no direct connection with criminological issues, but had by the late 1960s an immense significance for the New Left. Major themes from their work are closely integrated in S. Hall et al., *Policing the Crisis*, which also deploys some conceptions from Althusser. The structuralist Marxism of Althusser had elsewhere been viewed as incompatible with the study of crime, deviance, and allied concerns. P. Hirst, 'Marx and Engels on Law, Crime and Morality'.

[4] I. Taylor et al., *The New Criminology*, 278.

[5] C. Raw et al., *Do You Sincerely Want to be Rich: Bernard Cornfeld and IOS: An International Swindle*; and G. Tyler, 'The Great Electrical Conspiracy'.

[6] I. Taylor et al., *The New Criminology*, 107.   [7] I. Taylor et al., *The New Criminology*, 281–2.

[8] This brought them quickly into dispute with Hirst, whose Althusserian Marxism stressed the latter and largely excluded the former concerns. Hirst, 'Marx and Engels' and the reply by Taylor and Walton in I. Taylor et al., *Critical Criminology*, chs. 8 and 9.

new criminology as superior to the old involved a ground-clearing critique, a critique which forms the bulk of the 1973 book and which is concerned to salvage certain elements from prior theorizing for integration into an improved Marxist criminology.

In nine chapters, issue is taken with eight major approaches and their variants and a synthesis of their most useful insights is attempted in the ninth. In the first chapter, the philosophical bases for liberal criminology are located in the work of Hobbes, Locke, Bentham, and the utilitarian tradition. This 'classical criminology' and its neo-classical variants are viewed as incapable of reconciling forms of inequality rooted in property relations and the extension of rationality (as distinct from responsibility), to those who offend against the law.[9]

In Chapter 2 the 'appeal' of positivism is viewed as residing in its claim to be capable of accounting for criminality in neutral, scientific terms which situate pathology in the individual offender and deflect attention from the social context of unequal social relations which basically frame the offence. The third chapter is perhaps the most crucial, for in it they challenge the conventional image of Durkheim as a functionalist who argued that crime is both inevitable and necessary if society, *any* society, is to survive. They argue instead that Durkheim restricted his view of the functionality of deviance to societies that fell short of true 'organic' solidarity. On this reading of Durkheim, the proposition that 'crime is normal' need not inhibit the pursuit of a 'crime-free' society.[10]

The next five chapters deal critically with ecological and anomie theories; labelling theory; what are termed American naturalism and phenomenology; Marx and Engels' own view of crime and the lone attempt of Bonger to apply formal materialism to its study; and to the conflict theories of Turk and Quinney.[11] All are found wanting in terms of their potential as a basis for a 'fully social' theory of deviance, either because they dehumanize the deviant, or fail to furnish an adequate context of political economy, or both. Ecological theory is valued for its move away from individualistic accounts, but placed far too great an emphasis on purely urban processes, such as the emergence of 'natural' delinquency areas, divorcing these from the play of economic forces. Anomie theory—and its subcultural variants—related crime and deviance to the social structure, but reduced the deviants themselves to purely reactive or adaptive and therefore not creative, people. Labelling theory made a crucial break with positivism by treating deviance and control dialectically, as variable and dynamic processes implicated one with the other, but ultimately merely transposed one over-simple model for another: control leading to deviance not the reverse. Images of deviance remained flawed as a result, since deviant motivation was reduced to passive resistance to

---

[9] 'The "solution" in social contract to the problem of inequality . . . is an evasion and is best seen in Locke. He makes a distinction between those numbers of the poor who have chosen depravity and those who, because of their unfortunate circumstances, were unable to live a "rational" life. Thus, crime is *either* an irrational choice (a product of the passions) *or* it may be the result of factors militating against the free exercise of rational choice. In neither respect can it be fully rational action in the sense that conforming action is invariably seen to be. These two alternative views of criminal motivation have dominated criminology (surviving the attack of positivism) ever since.' I. Taylor et al., *The New Criminology*, 6–7.

[10] See Chapter 4.

[11] References here are primarily to W. Bonger, *Criminality and Economic Conditions*; A. Turk, *Criminality and the Legal Order*; and R. Quinney, *The Social Reality of Crime*.

or acquiescence in the superordinates' definitions of reality: in Gouldner's phrase, the deviant is regarded as 'man-on-his-back' rather than 'man-fighting-back'.[12] American naturalism attempted to restore a more humanistic model of deviance, but 'appreciation' as a method merely gave unwarranted primacy to the deviants' own view, thus abdicating the sociological task of mediating the relations between that view and those from other vantage points. Phenomenology moved even further away from a concern with the social context to a preoccupation with individual perceptions of deviance and control. Even Marx and Engels, in the occasional passages where they focused on crime, were prone to a determinism at odds with the role accorded creativity and consciousness elsewhere in Marx's work, a mechanistic lapse mistaken for a truly Marxist approach to crime by Bonger and other formal Marxists. Finally, non-Marxist radical criminologists, in particular Turk and Quinney, whilst attempting to relate crime to the structural sources of conflict in advanced societies, confused authority relations with power relations, obscuring their actual foundation in class conflict.

In all these approaches, partial gains are offset by significant flaws that are rooted in their inadequate epistemologies. The last chapter of the book attempts to synthesize the gains and eliminate the flaws by recovering them for a fully Marxist model of deviance and control. It is axiomatic that capitalism is criminogenic, as are all societies based on exploitation and oppression. The only form of society which in principle holds out any possibility of being crime-free is one embodying the principles of 'socialist diversity'. 'Socialism' entails an absence of material differences and a willed commitment to equality. It removes the rationale for crimes against property, the bulk of offences in any capitalist society. 'Diversity' entails a commitment to the toleration of minority beliefs and activities which many formally socialist States proscribe, such as drug use, sexual deviance, and gambling. To do otherwise than to work for the demise of capitalism and the transformation of society to one of socialist diversity, is to implicate oneself in correctionalism, i.e. the coercive use of the criminal sanction to 'correct' behaviour on a personal basis when its roots lie, on one level, in social structural inequalities of wealth and power and, on another, in the ideological mystifications that mask those inequalities. In their introduction to their later edited work, *Critical Criminology* (1975), these themes are recapitulated, but not greatly elaborated, save for the argument by Young that working-class control over policing should be greatly extended.

Policing the Crisis

In the 1970s, the Centre for Contemporary Cultural Studies at Birmingham University became, under the aegis of its Director, Stuart Hall, of some consequence in the sociology of deviance and control. While its members' interests were diverse and embraced the fields of industrial relations, the media, and race relations, the unifying feature of

---

[12] A. Gouldner, 'The Sociologist as Partisan'. This article formed the basis for much of the critique by the 'new' criminologists of what Gouldner termed the 'zookeepers of deviance', that is, the work of Howard Becker and the symbolic interactionists. See Chapter 7.

their work was the reproduction of order in capitalist Britain, a theme which they came increasingly to research and theorize in the context of youthful deviance and adult control. This theme had been dealt with by the media and by some sociologists as a product of 'intergenerational conflict', a mode of explanation which the CCCS rejected at the outset as misleading. The CCCS held that, in a class society, youthful deviance is most profoundly lodged in the refusal to accept, and the struggle against, relations with 'authorities' which administer, on the State's behalf, institutions based on a rule-bound set of interests which are ultimately those of a capitalist ruling class. Youth is a crucial point of vulnerability for the reproduction of order, for if capitalism allows the members of its subordinate working class a 'moment of truth', it is at the point of entry into the occupational order. Willis is especially preoccupied with the manner whereby that structural problem is culturally resolved by 'the boys' themselves.[13] Phil Cohen supplied the School with a method for bringing class struggle far more centrally into focus in the analysis of youthful subcultures than earlier, non-Marxist theorists had envisaged.[14] However, these studies took no more than marginal note of societal reactions to deviance and of the details of the manifestations, both social and economic, of the 'contradictions of capitalism' to which subcultures were allegedly a symbolic response. In *Policing the Crisis*, Stuart Hall and his colleagues make a most ambitious attempt to integrate these various levels and aspects of analysis around the phenomenon of 'mugging'.

Policing the Crisis is by no means the complete expression of the kind of 'critical' criminology urged by Taylor, Walton, and Young, for it deals only fleetingly with the third and the sixth 'formal requirement' of their 'fully social theory': the 'actual act' and the 'outcome of the social reaction on deviants' further actions'. On the remaining five such requirements, however, it attempts an exhaustive analysis and still provides the most sophisticated basis so far[15] by which we might assess the claim that critical criminology is superior to alternative approaches.[16]

The book is divided into four parts, each dealing with a major aspect of 'Mugging, the State and Law and Order', as the subtitle puts it. Part I deals with the rise of a generalized concern about 'mugging' in England in the early 1970s. Part II follows the particular case which led to three youths from Handsworth, Birmingham, receiving sentences of ten and twenty years' imprisonment for their commission of one such offence. Part III sets both the pattern of offences and the official and societal reactions to

---

[13] P. Willis, *Learning to Labour*. See Chapter 6.

[14] P. Cohen, 'Working Class Youth Cultures'; see Chapter 6.

[15] Another interesting and unusual example of analysis that comes close to being a 'fully social theory', is M. Davis, *City of Quartz*. *City of Quartz* is not an explicit piece of radical criminology. Rather it might be called a historically based political economy of the city of Los Angeles which narrates how that city emerged within the labour and industrial markets of the United States, how its social ecology reflected a geographical separation between the physically defended rich and the undefended poor, how policing was devised to protect the one from the other, and how crime, deviance, and gang activity emerged amongst the Blacks and Hispanics as a defensive response; see also M. Davies, *Planet of Slums*.

[16] The formal scope of a fully social theory, presented in *The New Criminology*, was held to require coverage of: (1) the wider origins of the deviant act; (2) immediate origins of the deviant act; (3) the actual act; (4) the immediate origins of social reaction; (5) the wider origins of social reaction; (6) the outcome of the social reaction on the deviant's further action; and (7) the nature of the deviant process as a whole. Taylor et al., 270–8.

which they appeared to give rise within the context of the 'crisis of hegemony' (or ideological legitimation) afflicting the British State in that period; and Part IV links these aspects together in the depiction of a 'politics of mugging'. It connects street crime, among black youth in particular, to what are seen to be the fundamental contradictions of political economy in Britain. It is these which promote the real crisis; 'mugging' is both product and palliative, rather than the source, of intensifying class conflict.

The study opens with a painstaking examination of the 'facts' which were held to justify the importation from the USA of a term—'mugging'—by which to describe crimes of robbery with violence long extant in England. It came to signify a trend which in turn came to justify the creation of 'anti-mugging' squads, or their equivalent, by the transport and ordinary police forces; and in turn to justify sentences far exceeding existing norms for a period in which the length of sentences of imprisonment had been rising anyway. It was widely alleged, by press, police, and judiciary alike, that the ever-rising crime rate was a product of the 'permissive' society, coupled with too lenient a pattern of sentencing; that certain aspects of street crime *were* novel and that these features had been the subject of rising public anxiety. Hall and his colleagues argued, with considerable evidence, that only the label, not the crime, was new. Different crimes were conflated to give the impression, particularly in the crucial 1972–3 period, of a sharp and unprecedented rise in street crimes of violence. In some instances, even pickpocketing, by definition a crime of stealthy non-violence, was added to the 'mugging' total. They are able to show that the link between the rise in crime and lenient sentencing had no basis even in official facts, since the 1965–72 period saw a *lower* rise in the crime rate than the 1955–65 period, though sentencing in the 1960s was far tougher than in the 1950s; there was no change in the rate of acquittals; and even in the specific case of robberies with violence, there was no uniform or steeper trend in either London or the provinces in 1972–5 than in 1955–65. The much-quoted rise of 129 per cent in 'muggings' in London over the 1968–72 period was derived from figures clouded in ambiguity. Most surprising of all, 'we have never had any figures at all concerning the scale and rate of increase, of provincial muggings'.[17]

This unpacking of the moral panic about 'mugging' is the foundation for all that follows, for it enables the authors to ask: 'If the reaction to mugging cannot be explained by a straightforward reference to the (official) statistics, how *can* it be explained?'[18] Their answer is:

> When the official reaction to a person, group of persons or series of events is *out of all proportion* to the actual threat offered, when 'experts', in the form of police chiefs, the judiciary, politicians and editors *perceive* the threat in all but identical terms . . ., when the media . . . stress 'sudden and dramatic' increases . . . and 'novelty', above and beyond that which a sober, realistic appraisal could sustain, then we believe it is appropriate to speak of the beginnings of a *moral panic*.[19]

---

[17] S. Hall et al., *Policing the Crisis*, 16. But see M. Pratt, *Mugging as a Social Problem*; E. McLaughlin, 'Hitting the Panic Button Policing/"Mugging"/Media/Crisis'.

[18] S. Hall et al., *Policing the Crisis*, 16.

[19] S. Hall et al., *Policing the Crisis*. The term was originated earlier by Stan Cohen in *Folk Devils and Moral Panics*.

A 'referential context' is built up in which the 'meaning of mugging' is taken to be the growing social malaise of the inner city, a symbol of urban violence long associated with America (to which frequent allusions are made) but now increasingly evident in Britain. The crucial novelty is not the rise in crimes of violence, but the involvement of black youths and white victims. The orchestration of an authoritarian consensus by police, media, and judiciary now assumes a *vox populi* role, in which the media represent the judiciary as speaking *for* the public and the judiciary can quote the media as 'evidence' of the strength of public opinion. They interact to produce 'an effective ideological and control closure around the issue'.[20] At which point the news media, without any recourse to conspiracy or dragooning, operate as an 'ideological State apparatus'.

The second stage of the analysis concerns the particular response elicited by the case of Paul Storey and two accomplices who 'mugged' an elderly man in Handsworth and whose sentences were for twenty and ten years' imprisonment respectively. The case made for saturation media coverage, in part because the boys returned to inflict further injuries on the victim two hours after the original attack. The age and defence-less character of the victim, the small sum of money stolen, combined with the second assault, were picked up as features of the menace of mugging. In addition, however, Storey was half West Indian and one of his accomplices was of Cypriot background: the link with 'race' was reinforced. The local press treatment of the case is analysed in detail and while much was made of the associations between deviance and urban decay, lost neighbourhood and family cohesion, and poor recreational facilities, the structural background remained absent from even feature articles. The national press probed no deeper and the 'liberal' papers, such as the *Guardian*, are defined as largely silent on the issues involved. Letters to the press were analysed, as were anonymous and abusive letters to the Storey family. Certain 'root-concepts' emerge from all sources which can be read as 'English ideologies of crime'. 'Englishness' equals a belief in the necessity for work to be undertaken as a source of livelihood. By contrast, crime is parasitic. Certain key symbols recur: the family, the need for discipline, respectability, and decency: the police and the law are seen as the guarantors of these core values, to which the working class adhere as fiercely as others. Detestation of crime transcends and ultimately unites classes in the face of class differences in other respects. The 'black mugger' is thus the perfect 'folk devil', a scapegoat for all the social anxieties produced by the change to an affluent, but destabilized, society.[21] Unable to generate a political solution to these problems, the working-class response is that of corporate, defensive class consciousness, a regress to *exclusion* and *typification* of a surrogate enemy; that of the lower middle class is to react with moral indignation. Against the full force of English common-sense and traditionalism, liberalism wilts and runs for cover.

If crime is one of the few symbolic sources of unity in an increasingly divided and embittered class society—if, moreover, the traditional armoury of consensus (power, deference, fatalism, and external enemies) is exhausted, diminishing, or absent—then it follows that the State, faced with a 'crisis of hegemony', will need little incentive to use the 'war against crime' as a source of authoritarian re-legitimation. The management

---

[20] S. Hall et al., *Policing the Crisis*, 76.   [21] S. Hall et al., *Policing the Crisis*, 159 ff.

of consensus had, in this view, only recently become of truly critical significance for the British ruling class. It may well be that Britain's economic decline, relative to its competitors, can be traced to 1870 and beyond: but it was only in the 1960s, 1970s, and 1980s that the international context had been so transformed that the decline was beyond dispute. The breakdown of the machinery of prosperity coincided with the loss of empire, a conjuncture that left only one serious candidate for bearing the costs: the working class. Yet the working class had been incorporated into political society and would 'pragmatically accept' the status quo only as long as certain conditions hold. As the economic crisis deepened, hegemony became increasingly difficult to sustain. The Heath–Wilson years of the 1960s and 1970s revealed the bankruptcy of Social Democratic reformism in the face of stubborn working-class resistance to a change in the rules of the game that had evolved over the previous century. Important concessions had been wrung from the ruling class—most notably the extension of the rule of law to all groups, the guarantee of certain union immunities and rights, and universal suffrage; a host of others, such as universal education, the Welfare State, and an increasingly mixed economy, were administered by a massive increase in the numbers of bureaucratic State employees, who stood in a 'subaltern' relation to the hegemonic class. By the late 1960s it was evident that the inter-class truce grounded in full employment, free collective bargaining, and rising wages could not be sustained. Working-class resistance to the erosion of first one and then the other led most dramatically to the three-day week, the miners' flying pickets, and the fall of the Heath Government, a sequence which coincided with a fresh 'wave' of immigration from Kenyan Asians and alarm about the numbers of immigrants still 'flooding into' the country as dependants of those already here. 'All four themes (political and economic crisis, ideological struggle and race) must be understood as unrolling within an organic conjuncture whose parameters are over-determined by two factors: the rapid deterioration in Britain's economic condition; and the maintenance of a political form of "that exceptional state" which gradually emerged in 1968–72 and which now appears . . . to be permanently installed.'[22] The latter reference is to the increasing readiness to arm the police in the light of terrorist attacks connected with Ulster; an upsurge in armed robbery and hijackings; and to erosions of civil liberties in the process of criminal justice, such as the attempt to install control units in two prisons. The State's main concern was to define the crisis away, or to set the terms in which it was discussed apart from that of class relations. The crisis was thus defined as a crisis of legitimate authority, prevented from 'doing its job' by deviants: criminals, industrial dissidents (the then Prime Minister, Harold Wilson's, 'small group of politically motivated men'), scroungers, or political deviants. Images of deviance became commonplace in the realm of industrial relations. Enough confusion was created to lead the working class to 'misrecognize' their enemy: the crisis was deflected onto youth, crime, and race, and away from class relations onto authority relations.

Finally, the 'politics of mugging' emerged: policing the blacks (the poor and the unemployed) amounted to policing the crisis.[23] There was a reality to young black crime,

---

[22] S. Hall et al., *Policing the Crisis*, 307.   [23] S. Hall et al., *Policing the Crisis*, 332.

increasingly so in the wake of unemployment which bit most deeply on the black la-bour force—'a super-exploited sub-proletariat'.[24] Hustling, a semi-criminal mélange of 'informal dealing, rackets, semi-legal practices and small-time crime'[25] emerged to meet 'sheer, material needs'[26] in part to service the black community's leisure in a con-text where blacks could less feasibly aspire to a common class identity with whites. The young, second-generation blacks experienced both exploitation and expendability, but increasingly refused to accept the 'reserve army of labour' role assigned to them under capitalism. Yet the refusal to carry out 'white man's shit-work' entailed a wagelessness that was a forcing-ground for hustling. 'Crime is one perfectly predictable and quite comprehensible consequence of this process.'[27]

Gangster Capitalism

In America, as in Britain, radical criminology moved from a 'radical liberal' stance in the late 1960s to a more thorough commitment to a Marxist position in the 1970s. The American-based Marxist criminologists were more concerned with a relatively uncomplicated application of Marx's most central concepts to the analysis of crime and crime control, by comparison with the British theorists' attempts to draw more fully on 'critical' neo-Marxists such as Habermas and Gramsci. This may reflect what was seen as a more obvious and uncomplicated set of relations between American crime and American capitalism. The shift is well drawn out by Klockars, who juxtaposes passages written by Chambliss and the English *emigré*, Platt, in the 1960s which, on re-publication in the 1970s, had been revised in a Marxist direction: for example, by the substitution of terms like 'ruling class' for the apparently vaguer and more pluralist 'the social order'.[28] There is also, especially in the work of Chambliss and Quinney, a link with the tradition of American populism and its traditional desire to expose the threat to the integrity of community by the graft and corruption of Big Business, Big Government, Big Unions, and (a theme which did not find inclusion in the work of C. Wright Mills, its most celebrated exponent) Big Crime.[29]

In *On The Take* (1978), Chambliss found the perfect vehicle for an expression of these concerns: the character and social composition of racketeering in Seattle. The book's subtitle, 'From Petty Crooks to Presidents', summarizes its major finding: the 'hidden hand' in organized crime in America is not 'the Mafia', but leading representa-tives of the city's ruling class. A diagram which at first glance resembles a high school chart of civic worthiness, with its listing of financiers, businessmen, politicians, and law-enforcement officers, is headed 'Seattle's Crime Network'.[30] The evidence for this profile is gathered from several years' participant observation in Seattle, beginning with Chambliss 'hanging around' bars in which gambling, drug, and vice connections might be made. After several months' involvement in card schools, Chambliss found

---

[24] S. Hall et al., *Policing the Crisis*, 375.   [25] S. Hall et al., *Policing the Crisis*, 351.
[26] S. Hall et al., *Policing the Crisis*, 360.   [27] S. Hall et al., *Policing the Crisis*, 390.
[28] C. Klockars, 'The Contemporary Crises of Marxist Criminology', *Criminology*, 487 ff.
[29] C. Mills, *The Power Élite*.   [30] W. Chambliss, *On the Take*, 74.

several contacts with inside knowledge who were willing to talk. It was from these informants, motivated in part by grievance or substantial experience of victimization, that he pieced together the links between the front-line operators and the more shadowy entrepreneurs who ultimately controlled the crime networks: key personnel in the police force, the legal profession, business, local government, and the public prosecutor's office. Meyer Lansky was named as the main link with 'a national crime network, the structure and organization of the network in Seattle'.[31] Both Nixon and Johnson as Presidents had substantial dealings with men 'whose business profits derived at least in part from illegal business'.[32] In conclusion, 'crime is not a by-product of an otherwise effectively working political economy: it is a main product of that political economy. . . . The logic of capitalism is a logic within which the emergence of crime networks is inevitable'.[33] Despite variations, 'such networks are also pervasive in Europe and Scandinavia'.[34] A visit to Poland confirmed that here, too, corruption and profiteering of a systemic kind flourished. 'Does this weaken the argument that it is the structural characteristics of capitalist democracies . . . that create and sustain crime networks? Not at all . . . The kind of "socialism" that was extant in the Soviet Union and eastern Europe shares with western capitalism many essential features: a rigid class system, the use of money for exchange and the alienation of workers from the product of their labour, to mention only a few'.[35] He concluded with the hope that decriminalizing gambling and drug dependence would mitigate the hold of the rackets on the trade in these illicit goods and services.

Tony Platt was concerned to make much the same connection in almost identical terms with the phenomenon of 'street crime': 'They [US Government-sponsored Crime Surveys] supported the conclusion that "street" crime is not simply a *by-product* of the capitalist mode of production. . . . Rather, it is shown to be a phenomenon *endemic* to capitalism at its highest stage of development'.[36] Far from seeking to ignore it, glorify it, or minimize it, the Left should recognize that official agencies 'grossly underestimate' such crimes.[37] The victim surveys tapped an incidence of street crimes, theft, car theft, burglary, rape, assault, and armed robbery, almost four times as great as the rate reported to the police. 'Police brutality, corruption and incompetence' account for much of the difference, particularly as far as working-class and black minorities are concerned. Moreover, such crimes are 'primarily an *intra-class* and *intra-racial* phenomenon. . . . The highest incidence of violent and property crime is among the poor and unemployed, specifically the super-exploited sectors of the working-class, young men and single or separated women'.[38] The death-rate for black males by homicide was over eight times that for white males: the starkest illustration of the extent to which the costs of crime are regressive in their effects. However, crime is by no means restricted to the poor: the better-off were shown by self-report studies to engage in crime as frequently as, if less seriously than, the most disadvantaged. Much the same

[31] W. Chambliss, *On the Take*, 151. [32] W. Chambliss, *On the Take*, 158.
[33] W. Chambliss, *On the Take*, 16, 181. [34] W. Chambliss, *On the Take*, 185.
[35] W. Chambliss, *On the Take*, 185. [36] A. Platt, ' "Street Crime"—A View from the Left', 29.
[37] A. Platt, ' "Street Crime"—A View from the Left', 27.
[38] A. Platt, ' "Street Crime"—A View from the Left', 29.

situation prevailed in the England of the nineteenth century 'at the peak of industrial capitalism'.[39] The conditions under which crime could assume a semi-political character were destroyed by capitalism: 'social banditry' was purged as a form of crime by the new technologies of control and superseded as a means of rebellion by the rise of the political organization of the working-class movement. What remained was predatory 'street' crime that offered no hope of a political solution for the:

> super-exploited sectors of the working class. Monopoly capitalism emiserates increasingly larger portions of the working class and 'proletarianizes' the lower strata of the bourgeoisie, degrades workers' skills and competency in the quest for higher productivity and organizes family and community life on the basis of its most effective exploitability. It consequently makes antagonism rather than reciprocity the norm of social relationships.[40]

A latter-day American new criminology, a blend of the ideas of Taylor, Walton, and Young, Marxist functionalism, and the Birmingham School, a blend which refers quite characteristically neither to Taylor, Walton, and Young, nor the CCCS, is Jeffrey Reiman's *The Rich Get Richer and the Poor Get Prison* (1990). Reiman claims that the American criminal justice system methodically created a misleading imagery of the criminal as young, black, working-class, and male, an imagery that filters out the middle-class and the white collar criminal by differential treatment.[41] The American criminal justice system, argues Reiman, *generates* and reproduces crime by criminalizing drug use, maintaining recidivist-producing prisons,[42] neglecting to address issues of social and economic inequality, stigmatizing offenders so that re-entry to the conventional world is blocked, and the like. The somewhat teleological conclusion to be drawn was that:

> The goal of our criminal justice system is not to reduce crime or to achieve justice but to project to the American public a visible image of the threat of crime. To do this, it must maintain the existence of a sizeable or growing population of criminals. To do this, it must fail in the struggle to reduce crime . . . the practices of the criminal justice system keep before the public the *real* threat of crime and the *distorted* image that crime is primarily the work of the poor. The value of this *to those in positions of power* is that it deflects the discontent and potential hostility of middle America away from the classes above them and toward the class below them.[43]

Ideological Mystification

A continuing source of inspiration for Marxist criminologists has undoubtedly been the longer-standing project of socialist historians to recover what has come to be termed 'history from below'. From the work of Hobsbawm, Thompson, and Rudé, on

---

[39] A. Platt, ' "Street Crime"—A View from the Left', 30.

[40] A. Platt, ' "Street Crime"—A View from the Left', 31.

[41] Exactly the same point was made by Chapman in his *Sociology and the Stereotype of the Criminal*, a book ignored by Reiman.

[42] Exactly the same point was made by Foucault in *Discipline and Punish*, although Reiman does not refer to the work.

[43] J. Reiman, *The Rich Get Richer and the Poor Get Prison*, 2, 4.

social banditry, machine-breaking, and the London mob, to the detailed documentation of working-class history by the Ruskin History Workshop, the attempt has been made to rescue the lives of people consigned by orthodox scholarship to the margins of history from what Thompson has aptly termed 'the enormous condescension of posterity'.[44] However, although any deliberate policy of exclusion has been disclaimed by Hay in a potent volume of essays on crime in the eighteenth century, the focus of such work has been almost entirely on those forms of deviance which seem to embody substantial elements of political resistance to ruling-class or State power, rather than more predatory victimization.[45] Perhaps because those who are often cast as latter-day 'Luddites' and 'wreckers' can, through the labour movement, speak quite forcefully for themselves, there are relatively few attempts to apply this approach at all directly to equivalent contemporary forms of crime. Pearson has sought to explain violence against ethnic minorities in part by using much the same framework: racist attacks in an economically blighted Northern town are related to the resentment felt against immigrants taking jobs and apparently making good in a context of rising unemployment.[46] As we have seen, the work of Phil Cohen, Stuart Hall, and his colleagues is informed by a similar approach.

A historical approach has also been employed in the analysis of relations between social control and the political economy of the capitalism that emerged from the Industrial Revolution. Scull has viewed the nineteenth-century asylum- and prison-building programmes as functional for the iron discipline that employers enforced in the period of maximum capitalist growth: by comparison, the stagnant capitalist economies of the 1970s and 1980s sought to offload their institutional charges for cut-price 'community care'.[47] Ignatieff has explored the religious mediations between forms of prison discipline and the symbolic order of capitalist political economy.[48] In a series of works, Foucault employed a 'structuralist' method along similar lines: capitalist industrialism employed a logic which its agencies applied to ruthless effect in one institutional sphere after another—the asylum, the prison, the clinic, the school, and the factory.[49] Charles Dickens had conveyed the same insight with more poetic force, but he believed in the power of the human heart to reform such organized cruelty. Needless to say, the work of Foucault holds no such illusions.

Unlike Scull, Mathiesen and Fitzgerald saw the prison as a functional and continuing necessity for capitalist society.[50] Evidence for the use of the prison as an instrument of class oppression was inferred from the relative over-use of the prison for lower-class populations and its under-use in connection with 'crimes of the powerful'. Even in the courts, allegedly the most neutral and disinterested forum for the promulgation of the rule of law, class bias was seen to persist: Carlen[51] analysed modes of courtroom

---

[44] E. Hobsbawm, *Bandits*; E. Thompson, *Whigs and Hunters: The Origin of the Black Act*; G. Rudé, *The Crowd in History*; R. Samuel (ed.), *Ruskin College, History Workshop Pamphlets*.

[45] D. Hay et al. (eds.), *Albion's Fatal Tree: Crime and Society in Eighteenth Century England*, 14.

[46] G. Pearson, ' "Paki-Bashing" in a North East Lancashire Cotton Town'.

[47] A. Scull, *Decarceration*.   [48] M. Ignatieff, *A Just Measure of Pain*.

[49] M. Foucault, *Discipline and Punish*; also *Madness and Civilization* and *The Birth of the Clinic*.

[50] T. Mathiesen, *The Politics of Abolition*; M. FitzGerald, *Prisoners in Revolt* and (with J. Sim) *British Prisons*.

[51] P. Carlen, *Magistrates' Justice*.

interaction as functioning to bestow a sense of impotence and inferiority on the largely working-class defendants and to buttress the superiority of the overwhelmingly middle- or upper-class lawyers and judiciary. The very language of the courtroom polarizes defendants and prosecution along class lines; and Griffith has documented the unified class character of the judiciary, both in terms of its social composition and its ideology.[52]

The 'crimes of the powerful' and their relative immunity from prosecution and penal sanction, with all due allowance for the occasional exemplary sentence, was a potent theme for the emergent Marxist criminology, though it is by no means the case that they pioneered its study—that honour must go to Edwin Sutherland.[53] Given what it brings empirically to radical criminology's framing of capitalism as criminogenic and institutionally corrupt, this important topic remains central to the work of a group of contemporary radical criminologists.[54] Frank Pearce provided a largely historical study of violations of the anti-trust laws in America and a critique of the Mafia myth. Prior to Chambliss, but drawing on the work of Albini,[55] he argued that organized crime in America is far more subservient to the imperatives of Big Business, to which it stands in a 'servant' class relation (as, for example, in strike-breaking), than contemporary analyses allow. In a somewhat different vein, Colin Sumner attempted to integrate the emphasis on labelling of the interactionists with the stress on class conflict of the Marxists by means of a focus on criminal sanctions or 'censure' as the ultimate means by which class rule is secured and symbolically expressed through ideology.[56] In sum, in a relatively short period of time, Marxist criminology sought to redefine and extend the purposes and boundaries of the field.[57]

We now turn to the question of how far those processes are themselves adequately grounded.

Determination

If all that was being asserted by radical criminologists were series of propositions to the effect that capitalism and crime were arguably interconnected, that crime tends to assume a distinctive form under capitalism, and so on, then there could be little to object to in adopting such premises as a basis for further analysis and research. The problems that plagued the earlier structural approaches would still need to be surmounted—that of reification of 'structure', for example and the adoption of somewhat deterministic models of criminality—but all approaches linking crime to the social structure share these pitfalls. Indeed, it was only with the advent of an interactionist approach that they were teased out. But the advocates of a Marxist perspective tend to assert far more

---

[52] J. Griffith, *The Politics of the Judiciary.*   [53] E. Sutherland, *White Collar Crime.*

[54] W. J, Chambliss et al., *State Crime in the Global Age*; J. Minkes and L. Minkes, *Corporate and White-Collar Crime*; S. Tombs and D. Whyte (eds.), *Unmasking the Crimes of the Powerful.*

[55] J. Albini, *The American Mafia: Genesis of a Legend.*

[56] C. Sumner, 'Marxism and Deviancy Theory' and *Reading Ideologies: An Investigation into the Marxist Theory of Ideology and Law.*   [57] P. Hillyard et al., *Beyond Criminology: Taking Harm Seriously.*

than this. The 'new' criminologists, for example, assert the 'total interconnectedness' between crime and capitalism. Class conflict is viewed as *the*, rather than simply one form of, group conflict in advanced industrial societies. As a result, it is regarded as a cardinal error to argue for a modified capitalism and a modified crime problem: for if the former is eliminated, the possibility exists for the elimination of crime as well (or, at least, the bulk of crime which is attributable to social, rather than psychological or biological factors).

The first and most obvious criticism is that the search for a 'total interconnectedness' leads to a revival of the more doctrinal versions of functionalism, in which deviance is viewed as an expression of, or resistance to, capitalist exploitation. Correspondingly, censure,[58] and control are viewed as functional for the maintenance of bourgeois hegemony.[59] For example, Young argued that:

> when the State of California spends $73 million in 1968 on marijuana control, when more is spent on Social Security prosecutions than has ever been obtained illegally from the State, when supposedly scarce police resources are utilized in the persecution of gays and when legislation denies women the right to choose whether to give birth or not—all this seeming ruling-class irrationality contributes enormously to the maintenance of bourgeois institutions.[60]

It is far from clear how such 'irrationality' does in practice contribute to bourgeois hegemony: the processes whereby this aim is accomplished are not examined. If certain offences are decriminalized, it can equally plausibly be argued that the purpose is to secure bourgeois domination by 'repressive tolerance'.[61] This form of circular argument is endemic in the search for 'total interconnectedness'.

Underlying this mode of analysis is a 'new' form of determinism and essentialism. Determinism is shifted from the socio-cultural context to the realm of political economy. Essentialism inheres in that:

> other-worldly realm of real processes which must not be confused with mundane appearance, everyday belief and social phenomena. It cannot be understood by entering the lifeworld of those who actually experience those processes. The consciousness of essential truth is distinct from the false consciousness of ordinary people . . . Radical criminology . . . rejects a dependence on empiricism and *Verstehen* . . . After all, empiricism merely investigates the sensory world, a world which is not metaphysically authentic. *Verstehen*, too, simply reproduces false consciousness and is incapable of explaining what is real.[62]

It would be idle to pretend that 'false consciousness' does not, in some form or other, constitute both a major problem for sociology and its chief justification. If perfect social

---

[58] A prime example of the radical functionalism of 'censure' is provided by one of Colin Sumner's students who, in his analysis of corruption, argues, 'The logic is that if the dominant class decides to censure corruption, at the expense of jeopardizing its entrenched interests, then it must have a specific target to achieve, a pressing problem to solve, a hegemonic function to perform . . . Its aim may be to combat corruption to dispel public discontent, to reclaim its declining legitimacy, to discipline its black sheep, to isolate political rivals or to eliminate class enemies.' (T. Wing Lo, *Corruption and Politics in Hong Kong and China*, 4.)

[59] D. Downes and P. Rock (eds.), *Deviant Interpretations: Problems in Criminological Theory*, 12–13.

[60] J. Young, Foreword to F. Pearce, *Crimes of the Powerful*, 18.   [61] H. Marcuse, *One-Dimensional Man*.

[62] P. Rock, in D. Downes and P. Rock (eds.), *Deviant Interpretations*, 75–6.

knowledge could be assumed to exist, then sociology (and Marxism) would be super-fluous. However, there is a marked difference between the assumption that knowledge is inadequate or partial and that it is 'false': the one assumes at least a relative openness to fresh information and insights; the other a pre-structured 'falsity' which can be cor-rected only by a total transformation of consciousness itself. Sociology is, in general, wedded to the former, with its corresponding 'hard-core' commitment to some form of 'falsificationism'; Marxism, in general, eludes or rejects that criterion.

This point is germane to consideration of the second issue, the Marxian theory of class conflict as a necessary outcome of capitalist structure. If Marx was correct in identifying the central properties of capitalism, then class conflict will inevitably grow as the crises of capitalism, born of its contradictions, intensify. It might be thought that Marx's clear specification of a particular evolutionary sequence *could* be tested, partic-ularly as—since 1917—societies based upon a communist alternative were constructed (and are now being reconstructed with an uncertain future). Marxism is particularly replete, however, with subsidiary clauses, which protect its theoretical hard core from critical attack. If the proletariat have not been progressively 'emiserated' under capital-ism, that is because their affluence has been secured at the expense of the Third World. If proletariat and bourgeoisie have not as yet been polarized, then that is because, as Marx predicted, the bourgeoisie have exploited to the full the capacities of their tech-nologies to buy time and buy off opposition, with further dollops of prosperity. Yet that prosperity remains precariously based and, as the proletariat presses home its strategic advantages, it can be sustained only at the cost of successive crises and hidden forms of exploitation, e.g. of migrant labour. Plausible as these arguments may be, their elabora-tion lends force to Popper's critique of Marxism as non-scientific because unfalsifiable; and the concentration on capitalism entails a corresponding analytical impoverish-ment in dealing with conflict, deviance, and control in the former State socialist or communist societies. Even when, those societies collapsed quite spectacularly, one by one after 1989, there are still some radical criminologists who do not seem to act fully on what they see:

> Despite current rhetorics and feelings against a certain kind of communism and indeed against the very mention of the word socialism in some countries, this is not a time for socialistic capitulation on questions of theory. The theoretical work done by socialists within sociology of crime and law, however much it may be dubbed 'neo-Marxist' or 'marxisant', remains the most vibrant and explanatory available.[63]

This limitation does not extend to alternative theories of conflict, including class con-flict, which stem from the sociology of Max Weber.[64] The major difference between Marx and Weber lies in their fundamental assumption about the development of capi-talism: for Marx, capitalism rests upon a particular mode of exploitation; for Weber, it rests upon a particular form of rationality. These are not mutually exclusive ideas in principle, but in their philosophical development they become so. For Marx, class

---

[63] C. Sumner, introduction to T. Wing Lo, *Corruption and Politics in Hong Kong and China* x.
[64] F. Parkin, *Marxism and Class Theory: A Bourgeois Critique*.

domination culminates in the revolutionary transcendence of capitalism and the opportunity to construct, after a transitional 'dictatorship of the proletariat', a classless,
free, and equal communism. For Weber, rationality generates bureaucratic authority,
which can be harnessed, with immense difficulty, only by the retention of 'charismatic'
authority in the framework of constitutional democracy. In a sense, both have been
invalidated by history: Marx failed to predict the logic of the Russian Revolution and
its ironic aftermath (capitalism being perhaps the highest state of communism); Weber
the rise of Hitler and Fascism, the yoking together of charisma and bureaucratic authority.[65] Ultimately, however, if a choice between the two *has* to be made (and many
would argue that neither provide a satisfactory framework for explaining these phenomena), Weber at least provides the conceptual vocabulary with which to make sense
of such developments, whereas, in our view, Marx does not. The sociology of Weber
can handle the growth of State powers, the rise of bureaucracy, the 'routinization of
charisma', the myriad forms assumed by conflict between classes, racial groups, the
sexes, religions; Marxian sociology collapses these into endless variations of the class
struggle. The appeal of Marxism is clear: it portends the 'good' society, whereas, in
Parkin's phrase, Weber (and Social Democracy) can promise at best the 'not-so-bad'
society. But at least the possibilities for the improvement of the latter can be prescribed
with some precision: the former still resides in the realm of pure theoreticity.

The principal gap in Marxism concerns the lack of any political theory of liberty
in socialist societies. No general sequence has been offered concerning 'how power
should be distributed; how conflicting interests should be represented and resolved,
how abuses to socialist legality should be checked.' The most developed institutional
mode of resolving such problems, parliamentary democracy, is especially anathema
to Marxists, Marx himself having dismissed it as 'parliamentary cretinism'. As Parkin
points out, the rejection of Marxism by the working class is not so very odd, since its
members 'might reasonably wonder why, if all known versions of Marxist society are
so seriously flawed and their revolutions always betrayed, the result next time should
be any different'. There is no need to invoke 'false consciousness' or the tortuous workings of 'ideological State apparatuses' to account for their reluctance to engage in revolutionary praxis.[66]

The strengths and weaknesses of Marxist analysis are well exemplified in *Policing the
Crisis*. Theoretically, the advance made by this book was the attempt to integrate Stan
Cohen's interactionist insight concerning 'moral panics' with the Marxian insight into
the nature of the 'crisis' wrought by capitalism in Britain in the early 1970s. The intention was to ratchet up the explanatory power of the concept of moral panic through
politicization. Empirically, however, this integration is not accomplished. The reality of
the 'moral panic' is most skilfully analysed and conveyed:[67] but the grounds for asserting that the official reaction sought to promulgate such a panic for larger ideological

---

[65] R. Aron, 'Max Weber and Power Politics', 99.

[66] F. Parkin, *Marxism and Class Theory*, 178, 199, and ch. 9, *passim*.

[67] Not all commentators would agree with this view. See, e.g., C. Sumner, 'Race, Crime and Hegemony'.
One strand in the analysis of Hall et al., the adoption of tougher forms of policing that are more resistant to
democratic controls, is forcefully developed by Hall in *Drifting into a Law and Order Society*.

and political ends are not established. This is not to say that they could not be established, for even if they are unlikely to issue forth from the mouths of the 'master institutions' themselves, they might be inferred from the demonstration that 'crises' and 'panics' are correlated. But this kind of evidence is not advanced: and, indeed, perhaps could not be advanced, without firmer criteria for the identification of 'crises'. Was there a similar panic in 1925–6? Or 1929–30? Or 1966–7? Or, indeed, 1979–80, the winter of strike action affecting hitherto 'sacred' areas of institutional life, such as—with supreme irony—cancer wards and grave-digging?

There is also a central inconsistency in the analysis: young black second-generation men are exonerated from any undue contribution to the rise in crime, but are simultaneously identified as a 'super-exploited sub-proletariat' whose increasing contribution to crime is defined as 'inevitable'. On inspection, that inconsistency *can* be resolved, but the main grounds for its resolution in *Policing the Crisis* seem far less defensible in the light of critical analyses of its statistical basis. Ironically, the attempt by Hall et al. to be more precise in their definition of a 'moral panic' than was usually the case opened up that terrain for reappraisal. Locally, Pratt has shown that the Metropolitan Police kept records of events called 'muggings' in their area, drawing on McClintock's categories of robbery and that those events did both increase at the end of the 1960s and also shift in location from the classic sites of skullduggery—towpaths, tunnels, and commons—to far less avoidable high streets.[68] More significantly, Waddington has shown that there was a real and continuous national rise in muggings before the 'moral panic' allegedly arose. There may have been a slight decline in the *rate* of increase, but there was no decline in the propensity of street crime to grow steadily and uninterruptedly: 'the only valid conclusion to be drawn from the figures presented by Hall et al. . . . is the opposite one to that drawn by the authors themselves. It is that crime during the period immediately preceding the onset of concern about "mugging" was indeed increasing and doing so by increasing increments.' Moreover, 'the lack of any criteria of proportionality allows no distinction to be drawn in general between a "sober, realistic appraisal" of a problem and a "moral panic".'[69] Reviewing evidence about the experience of crime in the inner city some years later, the left realist criminologists Jones, McLean, and Young were prompted to observe that fears about mugging are not panicky but sober and sensible: 'people's perceptions of crime are not based on moral panic'.[70] Suggestive as the work of Hall and his colleagues remains, one may conclude that, both statistically and conceptually, their interpretation of the social history of mugging is flawed.

Even if one does accept the statistical argument of *Policing the Crisis*, the official reaction can be indicted for a premature rather than a faulty analysis of the situation, which renders the lengthy sentences intelligible in terms of lay sociology, if indefensible in terms of humane legality. Similarly, the media and judiciary are assailed for their frequent invocation of the American comparison as a prefiguration of the inner-city future: yet the authors themselves make much the same comparison, albeit in more sociologically

---

[68] M. Pratt, *Mugging as a Social Problem*.   [69] P. Waddington, 'Mugging as a Moral Panic', 252.
[70] T. Jones, B. Maclean, and J. Young, *The Islington Crime Survey*, 35.

acceptable terms, though the nub of the analysis is the same. This seems to extend to sociology a 'benefit of clergy' denied to those engaged in formal social control. In sum, the prior commitment to a particular version of class struggle 'over-determines' (for the phrase is acceptable in intellectual, if not in empirical terms) the analytical outcome.

In the work of Platt and Chambliss there is above all a conviction that American capitalism is capitalism, that American crime is crime, and that elsewhere may be found less of much the same thing. Platt sees American capitalism as its 'highest' form, though no grounds are given for this assumption. Giddens could equally plausibly make quite the reverse assumption in his study of the 'advanced societies'.[71] In general, however, the main limitation of their work is that no intermediary or distinctive forms of political economy are worthy of analysis save for capitalism and socialism. Social Democracy is lesser capitalism, State socialism is failed socialism.

The symmetry between crime, control, and capitalism is questioned by comparative work. For example, Hagan and Leon, in a study of juvenile justice in Canada, could find no basis for the links implied by Platt to exist between the reform of the juvenile justice system and capitalist interests in the child labour market in the USA.[72] Clinard, in his study of crime in Switzerland, *Cities with Little Crime* (1978), found a surprisingly low rate of working-class criminality in a supremely capitalist society. The marked variations in crime that obtain in widely differing societies of a formally capitalist type seem scarcely addressed by this approach. And if the net is broadened to include the history of the former State socialist societies, the yield drops even lower. In short, important as it is to seek the connections between crime and capitalism, it does not improve matters to make the fit, in Cicourel's phrase, 'by fiat'.

Finally, we might return to an inspirational source for the 'new' criminology: Gouldner's insistence that criminology should encompass 'man-fighting-back' rather than 'man-on-his-back'. This theme has been embroidered into a rich symbolic tapestry of deviant 'resistance', 'struggle', 'creativity', and the like.[73] It has been argued that the crime rate can be interpreted as an index of 'the credibility of a propertied society at particular stages of its development—the extent to which the distribution of property is latently accepted or rejected amongst certain sections of the working population'.[74] It is difficult to reconcile this political reading of deviance with actual patterns of criminal victimization, which are overwhelmingly intra-group rather than inter-group. Such a reading also obscures the extent to which deviance is only at several removes a problem for the State. It primarily affects local communities, whatever their class composition. Crime and its control in effect operate as a regressive tax on the more powerless and vulnerable sections of society. Much evidence suggests that working-class communities desire more, rather than less, policing and are less critical of police work than middle-class groups.[75] To sustain the case for crime as a 'misrecognition' of

---

[71] A. Giddens, *The Class Structure of the Advanced Societies*, Preface.

[72] A. Platt, *The Child Savers: The Invention of Delinquency*; J. Hagan and J. Leon, 'Rediscovering Delinquency: Social History, Political Ideology and the Rule of Law'.

[73] See Chapter 6.   [74] I. Taylor et al., *Critical Criminology*, 42.

[75] R. Sparks et al., *Surveying Victims*, 187–8.

the 'real mechanisms'[76] of subordination involves the risk of reducing crime to a 'very bad case indeed of false consciousness'.[77]

In counter-criticism, some Marxist scholarship is not so tied to apriorism as the preceding critique implies. Two outstanding examples of rigorous research, by contrasting methods, would be Thompson's social historical studies and Willis' ethnographic work. Thompson describes his method in *Whigs and Hunters* as resembling 'a parachutist coming down in unknown territory: at first knowing only a few yards of land around me and gradually extending my explorations in each direction. Perhaps three-quarters of this book is based on manuscript sources. One source led me to the next; but also, one problem led to another'.[78] In his already classic defence of the rule of law, he remarks that the Whig oligarchy employed the law:

> very much as a modern structural Marxist should expect it to do. But this is not the same thing as to say that the rulers had need of law, in order to oppress the ruled, while those who were ruled had need of none . . . . Most men have a strong sense of justice, at least with regard to their own interests. If the law is evidently partial and unjust, then it will mask nothing, legitimate nothing, contribute nothing to any class's hegemony . . . We reach then not a simple conclusion (law = class power) but a complex and contradictory one. On the one hand, it is true that the law did mediate existent class relations to the advantage of the rulers ... On the other hand, the law mediated these class relations through legal forms, which imposed, again and again, inhibitions upon the actions of the rulers.

His own conclusion is that to dispense with the restrictions of bourgeois legalism, in favour of Utopian projections, 'is to throw away a whole inheritance of struggle *about* law and within the forms of law, whose continuity can never be fractured without bringing men and women into immediate danger'.[79]

Left Realism

In the 1980s, some radical criminologists themselves found their older, rather aprioristic position untenable. Perhaps in response to external critics and certainly in response to a series of changing circumstances, there was a revolution within radical criminology itself. Building on the structure created by Taylor, Walton, and Young and members of the CCCS, but also reacting against it, there emerged a new form of pragmatism which is not very different from the older, administrative criminology that was deserted in the early 1970s. Jock Young and, to a lesser extent, Richard Kinsey, John Lea, Roger Matthews, and Geoffrey Pearson, were to be the architects of what Young called 'left realism', a realism that inserted itself between what was defined as the overreaction of 'law and order politics' and the gross insensitivity to criminal victimization of the left in Britain. It is an approach which has had analytic and political promise;

[76] P. Cohen and D. Robins, *Knuckle Sandwich*, 113.   [77] S. Cohen, Introduction to *Folk Devils*, p. xi.
[78] E. Thompson, *Whigs and Hunters*, 16; see ch. 6 for references to Paul Willis.
[79] E. Thompson, *Whigs and Hunters*, 261–7, *passim*.

between the astructural lay and professional criminologies of the right and the wilfully myopic and 'impossibilist'[80] political analysis of the left. Jock Young reflected:

> ... those of the right frequently attempt to suggest that levels of crime have no relationship to ... changes in work and leisure but are rooted in the supposedly autonomous area of child rearing, drug use or a world of free-floating moral values. On the other hand, those on the left repeatedly attempt to suggest that changes in imprisonment, patterns of social control, the emerging actuarialism, etc. are political or managerial decisions unrelated to the problem of crime.[81]

Left realism has diverse social and intellectual roots. One influence must have been the sheer tedium which inventive minds experienced in emphasizing again and again arguments about the class-bound nature of crime, the forgotten importance of political economy, and criminology's scandalous neglect of Marx, Engels, and Pashukanis. As publishers appreciated the academic and commercial appeal of radical criminology, as the Academic Press established its radical *Law, State and Society* series, Macmillan its *Critical Criminology* series, Penguin published books sponsored by the Socialist Society, and Martin Robertson its largely radical *Law in Society* series, it became less and less plausible to contend that critical themes were ignored and that administrative criminology exercised intellectual hegemony. On the contrary, criminology was awash with critical argument. To some of its advocates radical criminology began to seem increasingly scholastic, established, and ritualistic. There were diminishing marginal returns in calling for a socialist analysis of crime. The old new criminology, Matthews and Young concluded, 'was never able to offer a competing alternative. Its critique was essentially negative and reactive'. Moreover, it was a critique that had its affiliations with a position rapidly being discredited by revelations of the terror exercised in the name of Marxism in Europe.[82]

Second, with the election of left wing local government administrations in Britain, a number of radical criminologists discovered that there were new contexts and opportunities for practical engagement. Some local authorities, a few inner-city councils and the now defunct Metropolitan Authorities in particular, had begun to espouse a politics with a marked affinity to the politics of critical criminology. They were in noisy opposition to the national Conservative 'New Right' Government elected first in 1979 and then re-elected three times. Many of those councils were composed of people who had had some confrontation with radical thought in University and Polytechnic, who were often themselves a new species of radical intellectual activist, and who sought intellectual support from a wider network of the left. In Merseyside, Manchester, the Greater London Council, Islington, and Camden Councils, a new shadow criminology developed around Police Monitoring Groups, lesbian and gay rights, and the discriminatory experiences of black communities. In turn, Jock Young, John Lea, and Richard Kinsey among others received administrative and financial patronage from the new radical councils. Their words and ideas acquired a new political consequence.

---

[80] J. Young, foreword to R. Swaaningen, *Critical Criminology: Visions from Europe*.
[81] J. Young, 'From Inclusive to Exclusive Society', 64–5.
[82] R. Swaaningen, *Critical Criminology: Visions from Europe*, 6.

Third and less importantly, the 'left realists' who taught probation officers, social workers, and others became bowed down under the repeated retort of 'it's all right for you to talk'.[83] Nellis observed that, for those students, the issue of ' "what can be done?," was a question they had to ask themselves every day of their working lives'.[84] A faith in the redemption of socialist diversity after the revolution was no guide to action now. The new criminology was obliged to become a little more practical.[85]

Fourth, the rise of feminism in the 1970s generated a critical attack on critical criminology. In 1977 Carol Smart published *Women, Crime and Criminology*. In the name of radical criminology, she reproached radical criminology for ignoring the politics of gender, for forgetting the extensive victimization of women, and for celebrating what seemed to be patriarchal oppression. Feminists researched rape, sexual abuse, and battering. They were to be radical champions of the *victim*—there had been little enough radical talk of victims before. Previous descriptions had been piecemeal and unreflective. Some had dwelt on mental illness, prostitution, homosexuality, and drug-taking—all forms of deviance without immediate and visible victims. Some had refrained from discussing victimization altogether, as if deviance occurred in a void. Some had rather grandly presumed that victims were impersonal organizations or members of the property-owning classes and therefore politically peripheral or, indeed, blameworthy. There had been little attention paid to the ordinary, abundant suffering and cruelties which crime inflicts on the powerless and vulnerable. The criminal had been romanticized and the victim liquidated. The rediscovery of the female victim had momentous consequences:

> Studies of domestic violence, rape and sexual harassment have been central to the feminist case since the mid-sixties. Feminist victimology was to create enormous theoretical problems for the radical paradigm in criminology . . . Radical criminology had tended to focus on crimes of the powerful and on the way in which vulnerable groups in society are criminalized. All very worthy stuff, but the traditional concern of criminology—crimes occurring within and between the working class—was a conceptual no-go area. This was part of a general tendency in radical thought to idealize their historical subject (in this case the working class) and to play down intra-group conflict, blemishes and social disorganization. But the power of the feminist case resulted in a sort of cognitive schizophrenia amongst radicals.[86]

Left realism, then, had one beginning in a stress on the female victim and the acknowledgement that it was difficult for radicals to find anything politically, morally, or intellectually commendable to say about her condition or her assailant. As will be discussed in Chapter 12, it had another beginning in the American, Canadian, and British national and local victimization surveys of the 1970s and 1980s. Survey after survey demystified crime. It became increasingly evident that it was not the bourgeoisie but the proletariat who were the chief victims of crime, that they were less capable

---

[83] S. Cohen, 'It's All Right for You to Talk: Political and Sociological Manifestoes for Social Work Action'.

[84] M. Nellis, review of R. Reiner and M. Cross (eds.), *Beyond Law and Order*, 348.

[85] R. Matthews and J. Young, 'Reflections on Realism', 7.

[86] T. Jones, B. Maclean, and J. Young, *The Islington Crime Survey*, 2–3.

of coping with crime when they *were* victimized,[87] and that crime was a major problem in their lives—a problem that threatened to subvert community and destroy happiness. In trenchant manner, the far from radical criminologists, Gottfredson and Hirschi, proclaimed that 'crime is an ill-conceived mechanism for the redistribution of wealth or for the extraction of revenge on one's oppressors . . . it is implausible to argue or believe that the pain of inequality may be alleviated by assaulting, robbing or stealing from similarly situated people'.[88] John Lea and Jock Young conceded:

> There was a schizophrenia about crime on the left where crimes against women and immigrant groups were quite rightly an object of concern, but other types of crime were regarded as being of little interest or somehow excusable. Part of this mistake stems . . . from the belief that property offences are directed solely against the bourgeoisie and that violence against the person is carried out by amateur Robin Hoods in the course of their righteous attempts to redistribute wealth. All of this is, alas, untrue.[89]

Indeed, chapters of the major manifesto for left realism, Lea and Young's *What is to be Done About Law and Order?*, were themselves stolen on two separate occasions. Radical criminology had had a brutal confrontation with the facts of victimization.

Left realism set itself a number of tasks. The first and most important was a programme of empirical enquiry. There were new facts of crime, deviance, victimization, and social control to be discovered and, newly financed, the radical criminologist intended to discover them. The British Crime Surveys of 1982 and 1984 were held to be insufficiently attentive to the victimization of women and ethnic minorities and the Islington Crime Survey was one answer. It disclosed the enormous weight of suffering which crime inflicts on people, especially, for instance, older black women living in the inner city. (Thus, 30.7 per cent of older black women lived in households that had been burgled during the previous year; and 49.2 per cent of black women between 25 and 44 had been assaulted.) In turn, crime and crime control became identified as pressing problems for the critical criminologist. They were no longer to be dismissed as insubstantial distractions or ideological mystifications. Crime was redefined as painful and the police and crime prevention as necessary. The second task was to rewrite radical criminology without radical censorship. The left realists do not as readily discredit others whose politics they do not share and they are correspondingly catholic in their range of sources and arguments. They also became less fearful of taboo topics. For example, *What is to be Done About Law and Order?* discusses the manner in which crime takes place *within* the working class. Following an earlier book, *Policing the Riots*,[90] it also recognizes the heavy participation of young British blacks in crime, a recognition which encouraged other radicals to accuse its authors

---

[87] Mawby who, on the basis of a re-analysis of the 1988 British Crime Survey, was to conclude that 'the evidence . . . points unequivocally to crime having most impact on the most vulnerable members of the community: the poor, council tenants, blacks, women, the divorced and those living alone or in one-parent families'. Quoted in T. Newburn, 'The Long-Term Impact of Criminal Victimization', 33.

[88] M. Gottfredson and T. Hirschi, *A General Theory of Crime*, 152.

[89] J. Lea and J. Young, *What is to be Done about Law and Order?*, 262.

[90] D. Cowell, T. Jones, and J. Young (eds.), *Policing the Riots*.

of racism.[91] Having identified the significance of young black men's involvement in crime, they could proceed to an analysis of the interplay between racist policing, victims, and young, marginalized black males in areas of high unemployment.

The argument runs that effective policing is reactive, not proactive, dependent on the willing co-operation of witnesses and victims. Yet there are particular forms of crime in the inner city that inhibit a reactive stance. Street crime, for instance, is not easy to detect, being anonymous, committed by strangers, and difficult to report. As unemployment and political marginality increased the alienation of certain groups in the inner city, so their co-operativeness receded and the police received less and less voluntary information. The police response was to deploy para-military policing strategies which inevitably were perceived as harassment by the young men living their lives on the street. These strategies only increased marginality and animated a spiral of confrontation and defiance. Criminalization and criminality thereby amplified and co-operation declined further.

Crime surveys and particularly the local crime surveys conducted by left realists, encouraged the next turn in radical criminology. They were taken to be the foundation of a new propensity to intervene, to formulate policy and crime prevention strategies. John Lea remarked that 'the research techniques at our disposal in the development of crime prevention policy have progressed in leaps and bounds during the last decade. The importation of the victim survey gave us a qualitatively new type of data on which to base policy formation.'[92] Crime surveys had thereby not only illuminated new areas of the world, justifying a new political stance towards the nature of social problems under capitalism; they had also become a guide to practical action. Crime had 'been taken seriously'.[93] Where once radical criminologists would have disparaged surveys as positivist and action as correctionalist, they now embarked on a programme of policy-making as vigorous as that of any government department. The dominant model with which they worked was that of a parallelogram of forces that bears an imprint of the earlier 'fully social theory' of the new criminology, a parallelogram composed of the State, society, and the offender, but which was fuller still because it now made provision for the victim.

Effective analysis and intervention flowed from a new synthesis of the twin intellectual antecedents of anomie theory, which supplies a vision of the relations between crime, motive, and structured inequality (as labelling theory had not) and labelling theory, which focuses on the existential consequences of control (in a way that anomie theory had not[94]). They are held to depend on incorporating all the interactions between the State, victim, offender, and society. Special emphasis has been given to 'society', that is, to the community and its informal social controls and resilience. Much of what is recommended is little different from the ideas of situational crime prevention.[95] Left realists have advocated improved street lighting to reduce crime

---

[91] J. Lowman and B. MacLean, introduction to *Realist Criminology: Crime Control and Policing in the 1990s*, 6.   [92] J. Lea, 'Towards Social Prevention', 4.

[93] I. Taylor, 'Left Realist Criminology and the Free Market Experiment in Britain', 97.

[94] J. Young, 'Left Realist Criminology'.

[95] P. Brantingham and F. Faust, 'A Conceptual Model of Crime Prevention'.

and the fear of crime,[96] better street design to foil kerb-crawlers,[97] housing estate improvements, and better-co-ordinated neighbourhood policing. They would use crime surveys to establish more effective police priorities. They would found hostels, youth clubs, drop-in centres, and clinics in areas of high crime rates.[98] From time to time, however, their radicalism takes them beyond the conventional reformism of government. They felt able to argue that, where necessary, crimes could be displaced from the most vulnerable and poorest sections of society to areas occupied by the more wealthy members. That is certainly not what the officials of any existing department of State would propose and, in such remaining differences, the 'leftness' of the new left realist criminologists may still just about be recognized.

Within radical politics, left realism was a new beginning to the criminology of the left and it displayed a marked openness to evidence and criticism. Like the older radical criminology before it, it had a political agenda; but, unlike the older criminology, it had few political anathemas. In its evolution it became more and more a practical administrative criminology of the left,[99] taking the problems of victimization seriously but giving a modestly radical inflection to their solution, awarding prominence to politically preferred victims and seeking to influence the police response to their needs.[100]

Within mainstream criminology, the *applied* version of left realism started to look very much like any other digest of orthodox theory, not an intellectual revolution at all but a return to convention. Indeed, one of the present authors described it as the criminology that has come in from the cold.[101] Empirically, it has the local crime surveys to its credit, but it is now difficult to discern quite what distinguishes it from a combination of anomie, interactionist, and subcultural theories with a covert superaddition of social and situational control theories.

Theoretically, however, left realism has more recently taken on a new direction and a new vitality with the publication of two books written by two of the troika who had authored the original radical manifesto, *The New Criminology* of 1973. Just as *The New Criminology* refracted the big sociological ideas of the early 1970s, so those two books resonate theoretical themes current in sociology at large at the end of the twentieth century. Ian Taylor's *Crime in Context* and Jock Young's *The Exclusive Society*, both published in 1999, talk about the common problem of crime in late modernity and come close to the 'fully social theory of crime' which they had promised in 1973.

Taylor lists a series of social transitions in the political economy of society and the fashion in which they press down on poverty, class, gender, race, and the family to affect the national and transnational contexts of crime. Socialism as a utopian alternative to capitalism, pronounced Taylor, 'is dead, not least because of the collapse of the

---

[96] K. Painter, *Crime Prevention and Public Lighting with Special Focus on Women and Elderly People* and *Lighting and Crime Prevention for Public Safety.*

[97] R. Matthews, *Policing Prostitution: A Multi-Agency Approach.*

[98] R. Matthews, 'Replacing "Broken Windows": Crime, Incivilities and Urban Change'.

[99] G. Pavlich, 'Critical Genres and Radical Criminology in Britain', esp.151.

[100] D. Downes and T. Ward, *Democratic Policing.*

[101] P. Rock, foreword to J. Lowman and B. MacLean (eds.), *Realist Criminology: Crime Control and Policing in the 1990s.*

only existing experiment with that form of societal organization, the Soviet Union.'[102] However, a seemingly triumphant capitalism is continually beset by a series of interlocking crises in unemployment and job insecurity; material poverty and social inequality; social uncertainties and a fear of a demonized Other; problems of social inclusion and exclusion that manifest themselves, for instance, in a renewed nationalistic xenophobia and the racialization of crime; crises of masculinity and what Taylor called the 'gender order', linked to a sense of dispossession and loss of power by newly insecure, largely proletarian men; ensuing crises in authority, power, and relations within the family; and related crises of poverty in childhood and in the transition to adulthood. This amounts to a powerful formula for the generation of delinquency amongst the poor and, with the emergence of a transnational capitalism, for a globalization of organized and institutional crime amongst the rich.

Young is also interested in social transformations, in particular, the causes and consequences of vast increases of crime in the West. Late modern capitalist society, Young maintains, has become mapped socially, politically, economically, and geographically into an inner core which is economically flourishing; a 'cordon sanitaire' that serves as a buffer about that core; and a rim of outer regions, populated by a threatening, marginalized, and regulated underclass. Crime is no longer defined as abnormal, the property of a pathological minority who can be restored therapeutically to the security of a moral community at one with itself, but *normal*, the actions of a significant, obdurate group of Others who are stigmatized and ostracized from protected spaces in a world newly insecure, fractured, and preoccupied with problems of risk and danger. The whole is blanketed by the blandishments of a consumer society that motivate members of the underclass strongly to desire the goods and services that large groups take properly to be their own. Such an order, Young claims, is inherently fragile, punctuated by outbreaks of implosive rioting, on the one hand and, on the other, the 'slow rioting of crime' that combine to rebound on the people and property of the nether regions, making miserable conditions worse.

Both descriptions are graphic. They synthesize masses of ideas into a coherent analytic model. But it is moot whether they should be taken to refer to a state of affairs that is itself transitional or one that will endure and become ever more grave over time. Unemployment rates decline as well as rise—and they were *falling* at the end of the twentieth and beginning of the twenty-first century—although the nature of work itself is changing and insecurities have undoubtedly appeared to mount. So too with crime. Crime rates have been falling, not rising, in the West, although they are falling from high levels. When and how unemployment-linked crime will rise again is not clear and some of the gloomiest assumptions made by Taylor and Young may have begun to date, though the likely scale of cuts to public sector employment resulting from the election of a radical right Conservative government will test that thesis either to reaffirmation or destruction.

Other matters are rarely as monochromatic as Taylor and Young claim. For instance, in some respects late modern societies are markedly less exclusionary than those of high modernity. Those with mental health problems or learning difficulties may be

---

[102] I. Taylor, *Crime in Context*, 3.

adversely affected by decarceration and some by transcarceration, but wherever possible individuals are no longer consigned to highly regimented mental health units and are 'treated' in the community. Mainstream secondary schooling is now comprehensive, however flawed that may be by residues and revivals of the older, much more exclusionary division of grammar and secondary modern schools. Higher education is no longer the preserve of the 'top' 5 per cent and so on. Also, however strident they may be, the more overt forms of racism have not really become politically consequential in the UK context. Again, the current fashion for restorative justice in Canada, Australia, and the United Kingdom underscores contradictory trends towards *inclusionary* models of control that sit oddly with a drive to exclude. In France and Germany, too, there are strong emphases on 'solidarity' as well as on exclusion in criminal justice practice. It remains uncertain how crime, deviance, and control and, with them, the radical or critical criminology that tries to capture them, will evolve. What is sure is that the greater part of radical criminology has now been absorbed into the theoretical mainstream.[103]

It should be added that not all radical criminologists have taken the 'realist' route. There are those who still disavow any connection with what might loosely be called mainstream administrative criminology and its works and lamenting the passing of the radical moment. Hillyard and his colleagues, for instance, rather inelegantly enjoined 'orthodox, contemporary criminologists [to] reflect upon the morality of "keeping their snouts in the State's trough", as opposed to actively disengaging from the supporting huddle around the trough . . . '.[104] Like comments have been made by Pearce who talked about the need for a commitment '*not* to take the claims of the powerful at face value . . . ' and about how 'notable and depressing . . . ' and 'how unusual is this commitment' in academic criminology. 'There is now', he said, 'a whole generation of academics . . . many of whom lack any basic training in Marxist concepts or modes of analysis.'[105] Theirs is a radical criminology which looks back to Poulantzas[106] to portray the academy as a medium for the construction of bourgeois ideology; intellectuals as the servants of capitalism; and criminology itself as a State lackey. They would return to the Schwendingers[107] and others to reject bourgeois definitions of crime and insert in their place the evils of racism, imperialism, and capitalism as proper objects of study.

Critique

Steve Hall et al.[108] provide one of the most sweeping critique of previous waves of radical as well as liberal criminology. They build on concepts derived from Lacan and Zizek to argue that capitalist consumer culture has, over the past few decades,

---

[103] K. Stenson and N. Brearley, 'Left Realism in Criminology and the Return to Consensus Theory'.

[104] P. Hillyard et al., 'Leaving a "Stain Upon the Silence"', 383; see also R. Coleman and J. Sim, *State, Power, Crime*; W. J. Chambliss et al., *State Crime in the Global Age*.

[105] F. Pearce, foreword to S. Tombs and D. Whyte (eds.), *Unmasking the Crimes of the Powerful*, xi, xii.

[106] N. Poulantzas, *Classes in Contemporary Capitalism*.

[107] H. and J. Schwendinger, 'Defenders of Order or Guardians of Human Rights'.

[108] S. Hall et al., *Criminal Identities and Consumer Culture*; see also S. Winlow et al., *Riots and Political Protest: Notes from the Post-Political Present*.

intensified its hold over the great majority to fragment and marginalize all competing cultures, especially those promoting Social Democracy and working-class solidarity. Their image of consumer culture is far more potent and destructive than simply being that of the dominant class overlaid on those of subordinate classes, or as the goal of material prosperity which is unattainable by the majority. It is essentially seen as a void, an extreme form of narcissistic self-worship which is far more self-centred and solipsistic than even the ultra-competitiveness of a 'dog eat dog', winner/loser culture. The self becomes totally defined by hedonistic consumerism, masquerading under the hyper-macho posture of 'cool', motivated solely by the urge to acquire the symbolic trophies signifying success—the most sought after cars, clothes, drugs, property—which justifies their pursuit of predatory crime and instrumental violence.

Virtually all previous theorizing is deemed either irrelevant or too limited to begin to encompass the analysis of the apogee of consumer capitalism, embodied in the 'greed is good' ethic of Wall Street and the City of London. It is beyond even 'greed is good', as that ethic had some form of justifying *credo*, however flawed, that wealth 'trickled down', albeit unevenly, to promote greater prosperity for all. The narcissistic extreme of consumer culture is its own justification. 'Techniques of neutralization' are redundant, as there is no guilt or shame to neutralize. Either 'everybody does it' or, if they don't, they are simply losers to be viewed with contempt. Theories of labelling prematurely shifted the focus onto a side issue: elements of authoritarianism in Social Democracies. Left idealism promoted the fallacy that crime is displaced revolutionary resistance. Both deflected attention from the main event: the rise of criminal identity forged by and lived through consumer culture. Only Mertonian anomie theory came anywhere near the truth.

What is the basis for this scathing denunciation of virtually the entire field? First, there is the reality of the cataclysmic shift from a mixed, Social Democratic political economy to a market-led, neo-liberal form in which corporate capitalism has come to rely utterly on what Marx termed commodity fetishism—the pursuit of material property becomes the overriding basis for symbolic identity and social distinction. Consumption replaces production as the key to status: the bonus-ridden banker whose wealth is, as Adair Turner put it, based on a welter of transactions that are 'socially useless' is honoured by governments and politicians and the Murdoch-led media as the icons of popular culture—far more than manufacturers and engineers. Much of this is common ground with the views of Richard Sennett, Robert Putnam, John Gray, and other analysts of the 'false dawn' of global capitalism—but they would not share the assumption that narcissism has entrapped the great majority or blanked out alternative sources of identity.

The second source for their analysis is a set of interviews conducted with chronic repeat offenders from the de-industrialized heartlands of North East England's white working class. These are remarkable for the ruthless and self-serving explanations they offer for their offending careers, largely of unspectacular mediocrity in crime terms but with a vicious utter disregard for their victims. Their accounts have no resonance with theories of 'relative deprivation'—they do not feel unfairly deprived; with adverse labelling—they do not feel unfairly or unjustly labelled; or with class oppression—they do not feel or acknowledge being oppressed. They are motivated principally by an overriding equation of self-worth with the acquisition of material wealth, valued more for its symbolism than any use value, which they could not possibly attain by any other means than crime.

The interview data are powerful testimony to self-serving amorality and ruthless predation which a resilient working-class culture would once have reined in if not forestalled more or less completely. But the leap from this ethnographic basis to the theoretical explanation in terms of narcissistic motivation shaped by 'turbo-consumer capitalism' is asserted rather than drawn out of the case studies. Any combination of Marx and Freud, the great unfalsifiables in Popper's lexicon, especially as filtered through the work of Lacan and Zizek, becomes massively vulnerable to over-prediction and metaphysics. It is a kind of criminology on steroids. That said, this is one of the few books to take on the awesome implications for crime and control of a global market economy unrestrained by the 'spectre of communism' and run by financial corporate matrices seemingly beyond not just national but international governance.

Conclusion

Radical criminology, despite a lineage based on Marx's theories of capitalism and class conflict, emerged surprisingly late as a major perspective on criminal and deviant behaviour, and had disappeared when it might have come into its own. Part of the upsurge of neo-Marxist theorizing in the late 1960s and early 1970s, it was more a British than an American development, drawing on the thinking of Gramsci, Habermas, and Marcuse, thinking which stemmed from different strands of European Marxism. Its genesis as the 'new criminology' was later to be termed 'left idealism' by one of its authors, Jock Young, who in the 1980s revised the approach to become the more Social Democratic left realism. More recently, as was noted above, this has produced a hyper-realist analysis of the predatory, entrepreneurial 'badfellas' produced by turbo-charged gangster capitalism, for example, drug dealers, enforcers, human traffickers, arms dealers, money launderers, warlords, and terrorists. The work of the CCCS, led by Stuart Hall, owed much to the thinking of the 'New Left' in Britain and shifted an intellectual gear towards identifying an emergent authoritarian State form. This idea has been developed in recent work on 'states of exception'. The key CCCS publication, *Policing the Crisis*, has also formed the basis for the development of a critical race perspective in criminology. In the United States, the roots of radical criminology are more firmly grounded in populism, anarchism, and libertarianism. Exposing the elite crimes (and impunity) of the powerful, in all their guises (corporate crime, State crime, eco-crime), remains a central concern for US-based radical criminologists. All such approaches claim allegiance to a distinctive 'critical' criminology, though the 'left realist' approach converges in most respects with the earlier anomie, subcultural, and labelling perspectives. From its inception, radical criminology has also championed a 'replacement discourse' that will not just move beyond and/or dissolve the category of 'crime' but de-invent 'criminology'. This replacement discourse is also intended to provide intellectual liberation.

However, despite advocacy of 'abolitionism', 'censure', 'social justice', 'social harm', 'zemiology', and the ever-present reference to 'human rights', it has not, as yet, been able to generate a convincing alternative to 'criminology', which continues to replenish itself.

Further Reading

I. TAYLOR, P. Walton, and J. Young,*The New Criminology: For a Social Theory of Deviance*, London, 1973.

S. HALL et al., *Policing the Crisis: Mugging, the State and Law and Order*, London, 2013.

P. HILLYARD and C. Pantazis. *Beyond Criminology: Taking Harm Seriously*, London, 2004.

J. LEA and J. Young, *What Is To Be Done about Law and Order?*, London, 1993.

I. TAYLOR, *Crime in Context*, London, 1999.

11

Feminist Criminology

Introduction

One of the most notable developments in theorizing about crime and deviance has been the emergence of what has been termed 'feminist criminology'. This is a diverse body of work united by the critical view that the understanding of the criminality of women and the role of gender in theories of crime, deviance, control, and victimization in general have been ill-served by criminology. So successful has that development been that, by the early 1990s, it was possible to claim that 'it is now no longer true that women's issues are being ignored, for there are whole shelves of work on women as victims of male violence, women offenders and women police officers. The more extreme examples of sexism found in criminological theory have been discredited—at least in the eyes of those who read feminist works'.[1]

Despite earlier statements in both Britain and the USA which anticipated much of the force of the feminist critique,[2] the emergence of feminist criminology is generally assigned to the publication of Carol Smart's *Women, Crime and Criminology* in 1977.[3] Though not without its critics among female criminologists[4] and received sceptically by some male sociologists of crime and deviance,[5] the work of those to the fore in feminist criminology has tended to reaffirm rather than challenge Smart's fundamental analysis. It is worth looking in some detail at her critique of the field as a template for feminist criminology in the past three decades.

The basis for Smart's critique is that, not only is there a paucity of material on female criminality, but also what does exist:

> shares an entirely uncritical attitude towards sexual stereotypes of women and girls. From Lombroso and Ferrero (1895) to Cowie, Cowie and Slater (1968) and from W. I. Thomas (1923) to Konopka (1966) the same attitudes and presuppositions reappeared, confirming the biologically determined inferior status of women not only in conventional society but also in the 'world' of crime and delinquency. [Despite rare exceptions], the majority of these studies refer to women in terms of their biological impulses and hormonal balance or in terms of their domesticity, maternal instinct and passivity.[6]

[1] M. Valverde, 'Feminist Perspectives in Criminology', 241.

[2] F. Heidensohn, 'The Deviance of Women: A Critique and an Enquiry'; M. Chesney-Lind, 'The Judicial Enforcement of the Female Sex Role'; D. Klein, 'The Etiology of Female Crime: A Review of the Literature'.

[3] L. Gelsthorpe and A. Morris, 'Feminism and Criminology in Britain', 221.

[4] A. Campbell, *Girl Delinquents*, ch. 7.   [5] P. Rock, review of C. Smart, '*Women, Crime and Criminology*'

[6] C. Smart, *Women, Crime and Criminology*, xiii–xiv.

The neglect of female criminality by the predominantly male criminological profession had several undesirable consequences. First, the 'arrested development' of the subject as regards female offenders left it ossified at the positivist stage of development. Women offenders alone are subject to a form of intellectual atavism aping the Lombrosian theory of crime: theorizing female deviance is a throwback to the earliest stage of criminological evolution. Second, policies and attitudes towards female criminality mirrored such determinisms. 'In advanced industrial societies, there tends to be an a priori assumption that women are irrational, compulsive and slightly neurotic. Criminological theories have reflected this predominant paradigm.'[7] Adolescent girls face much higher risks of institutionalization than boys for non-criminal forms of sexual 'deviance'. Such regimes as the 'new' Holloway prison confirmed the biological determinist view, with therapy but no vocational training for women prisoners.[8] The 'sick' role-model 'is a consequence of the failure of criminological theorists to explicate or treat as topics for analysis the understandings which they share with those engaged in formulating penal policy'.[9] Thirdly, unreconstructed notions about women's 'nature' have lent undue prominence to 'sexual deviance' as the focus of inquiry appropriate to the study of female criminality. 'Double standards' become institutionalized across the board in theory, research, law, treatment, and control. Prostitution is more studied than rape, as an example of female pathology—despite the male clientele—while rape, when it is studied at all, leans heavily towards the imputation of victim precipitation,[10] or on the need to protect the accused against false conviction. Though Smart overlooks his work, Heidensohn has pointed out[11] that even so relatively sophisticated a theorist as Albert Cohen assumed that 'female delinquency is relatively specialized. It consists overwhelmingly of sexual delinquency or of involvement in situations that are likely to 'spill over' into overt sexuality'.[12] To paraphrase Gouldner, patriarchally inclined criminologists have portrayed the female deviant as 'woman-on-her-back, rather than woman-fighting-back'.

In their concern to expose the defects of both classical and contemporary studies of female criminality, feminist criminologists have been energized as much by the belief that the task has been unduly neglected by their male colleagues and predecessors, as by the view that such work has exerted a malign effect on policy and control. Since the work of Matza,[13] zapping the positivists has become almost a spectator sport in the sociology of crime and deviance, as indeed in sociology in general, encouraging forms of intellectual laziness[14] which have invited counter-attack by more sophisticated defenders of positivism.[15] In contrast, the perceived resilience of the Lombrosian underground in the realm of female deviance and control has provoked every sign of close and attentive reading of key sources by feminist criminologists such as Smart and Heidensohn. Tedious as it may be to the jaded palate, the defects of criminological

[7] C. Smart, *Women, Crime and Criminology*, 111.
[8] P. Rock, *Reconstructing a Women's Prison*; and 'Holloway'.
[9] C. Smart, *Women, Crime and Criminology*, xiii–xiv.
[10] M. Amir, *Patterns in Forcible Rape*.   [11] F. Heidensohn, *Women and Crime*.
[12] A. K. Cohen, *Delinquent Boys*, 144.   [13] D. Matza, *Delinquency and Drift*.
[14] N. Walker, *Behaviour and Misbehaviour: Explanations and Non-explanations*.
[15] P. S. Cohen, 'Is Positivism Dead?'.

positivism have to be exposed once again, though this time with a female rather than a male subject as the target for concern. The work of Lombroso and Ferrero is not,[16] in their view, an antique intellectual curio, but a living body of thought, setting an agenda that is still operative: the subordination of women to the view that female crime is biological destiny, a view long since dispelled in the case of men.

The durability of the Lombrosian legacy in relation to female criminality is not simply due to its neglect as a topic, but inheres in the long-standing prescriptions about the female role and the 'essence' of the nature of women. Lombroso and Ferrero accounted for their finding fewer signs of degeneration among female, by comparison with male, offenders by resorting to the view that 'as all women are relatively "primitive", the criminals amongst them would not be highly visible and would be less degenerate than their male counterparts'.[17] Citing their belief that the greater conservatism of women must be sought 'in the immobility of the ovule compared with the zoosperm', Smart links their justification for the view that 'the born female criminal was perceived to have all the criminal qualities of the male plus all the worst characteristics of women, namely cunning, spite and deceitfulness'[18] with the confusions between sex and gender and the attribution of masculine traits to female offenders, later to recur in the work of Pollak and others. The work of Cyril Burt[19] escapes her net, but he tended to this view, referring to posturing as 'masculine hobbledehoys'[20] as typical of female delinquents. The early theorists, indeed, gave more coverage to female delinquency than those writing after the Second World War: pictures of 'Girl Aged 18–11/12' are included as well as those of such oddly immortalized boy delinquents as 'B.I. (15–7/12)'.[21] The combination of the 'worst of both sexes' led to attributions of a third abnormality in this conception of the born female criminal: the lack of maternal instinct. In this respect, Lombroso and Ferrero reproduced in scientistic form the set of common-sense beliefs about female criminality which is exemplified in the apparently greater popular detestation of Myra Hindley, the accomplice of Ian Brady in the notorious 'Moors Murders' of several children, compared to Brady himself. The majority of female offenders are not, however, so depicted: Lombroso and Ferrero viewed them as inferior criminals to the male, inadequate and more easily caught. In this respect, Pollak[22] was later to take the opposite view, whilst sharing their tendency to essentialize both female nature and female criminality.

The work of Pollak so perfectly encapsulates every feminist heresy that it might be said that, if it did not exist, it would have been necessary to invent it. Pollak's main empirical contention is that rates of female crime are much the same as those of male crime, but appear far lower because of under-reporting, lower detection, and greater leniency in prosecution and sentencing. None of these assertions is particularly outrageous and some self-report studies can be found to lend some credence to at least the basis of the first assertion, that the disparity between 'real' and official rates of crime

---

[16] C. Lombroso and W. Ferrero, *The Female Offender*.
[18] C. Smart, *Women, Crime and Criminology*, 33.
[20] C. Burt, *The Young Delinquent*, 217.
[22] O. Pollak, *The Criminality of Women*.

[17] C. Smart, *Women, Crime and Criminology*, 32.
[19] C. Burt, *The Young Delinquent*.
[21] C. Burt, *The Young Delinquent*, 214 and frontis.

is quite marked for first offences[23] and reduces the sex differential in general to two to one rather than several to one in respect of boys and girls. However, it was the manner of exposition and the nature of the theories he advanced that strained the credulity of successive generations of criminologists, though Heidensohn points out that some orthodox texts dealt quite respectfully with Pollak. First, Pollak sought evidence of greater female criminality, mainly in domestic and employment spheres, using highly problematic sources and ignoring the potential for 'masked' male criminality in these selfsame contexts. Second, he imputed to women the time-worn catalogue of vices, such as cunning, deviousness, and deceit, as a way of accounting for the putative 'concealment' of their crimes. Third, although giving cultural factors some weight, he located the ultimate source of legendary female deceitfulness in the woman's capacity to simulate sexual arousal. 'Thus rather than considering the implications of the sexual politics which produce a situation in which many women endure intercourse when they are neither aroused nor acquiescent, Pollak takes the existence of a passive engagement in sexual activity as a basis of assumptions about women's ambiguous attitude towards honesty and deceit.'[24] Fourth, credence is lent to the 'chivalry' hypothesis, the claim that police and courts deal leniently with women offenders, being both self-deceiving and deceived about the essentially passive nature of women—a myth nurtured to justify women's inferior social status. 'However, in spite of an apparent recognition of the darker side of chivalry and the possibility of scapegoating the "fallen" woman, Pollak neglects to incorporate these elements into his study.'[25] While Lombroso and Ferrero were at least working in sympathy with the grain of their time—a period that also saw the rise of eugenics and the widespread acceptance of social Darwinism[26]—Pollak's study bore no resemblance to the then burgeoning sociological theories of crime and delinquency. As Sutherland and Cressey pointed out in a dismissive reference to Pollak's work,[27] the latter had made an earlier foray into the realm of hidden criminality among the aged.

A more formidable figure in the pantheon of unfeminist criminologists is that of W. I. Thomas, author of such key interactionist insights as, 'What men define as real is real in its consequences'. Applying that dictum to his study of female delinquency, *The Unadjusted Girl* (1923), feminist criminologists have found it to be depressingly accurate. For what Thomas defined as real was that the 'source of female criminality, which he believed to be mainly sexual, was the breakdown of the traditional restraints on women who formerly would not have thought of working outside the home or marrying outside the ethnic or community group. . . . Because they have been most repressed, therefore, Thomas argued that women are more likely to become "maladjusted" when social sanctions are removed'.[28] On this basis, Thomas favoured the earliest possible intervention by welfare agencies into the lives of 'pre-delinquent' girls and resistance to further moves away from existing social relations. The more enduring legacy of his work is to be found in the impetus it gave to the focus on treating individual

---

[23] M. Gold, *Delinquent Behavior in an American City*.
[24] C. Smart, *Women, Crime and Criminology*, 84.   [25] O. Pollak, *The Criminality of Women*, 50.
[26] R. Hofstadter, *Social Darwinism in American Thought*; D. J. Kevles, *In the Name of Eugenics: Genetics and the Uses of Human Heredity*.   [27] E. Sutherland and D. Cressey, *Principles of Criminology*, 110, 112.
[28] C. Smart, *Women, Crime and Criminology*, 41–2.

maladjustment so characteristic of social work agencies and the shying away from any analysis of the structurally wrought constraints on improvements in women's social and economic situation. More damningly, Thomas is seen as the most authoritative link in the chain of criminologists lending their voice to the resistance to female emancipation, on the grounds that it would inevitably entail an increase in female deviance. This issue was later to become explicit in the work of Adler.[29]

Contemporary studies of female criminality are divided into those that carry on the classical tradition of Lombroso and Ferrero, Thomas, and Pollak, with no fundamental change to the terms of reference they set; and work in the field of role theory which takes the social differentiation of gender roles as the point of departure for analysis, thus breaking with the biological and psychological determinism of the classical tradition. Smart sees marked continuity between the Lombrosian tradition and the study by Cowie, Cowie, and Slater[30] which takes an institutionalized sample of girls as representative of delinquents; takes sex roles to be constitutionally predetermined; and reduces social and cultural factors to 'channels' for abnormal biological states. Chromosomes, rather than culture, are seen as the root of the problem. The work of Thomas is influential in the study by Konopka,[31] with its emphasis on liberal treatment strategies as the most appropriate response to female delinquency: although sympathetic to the problems posed by poverty and unequal opportunities for women, these are viewed as secondary to personal maladjustment. Both fail to distinguish the biological variable of sex from the socially constructed and culturally fluid character of gender.

It was this crucial distinction that opened fresh possibilities within criminology, as well as sociology in general. From the late 1960s, a veritable flood of sociological work which had its philosophical, historical, and aesthetic counterparts, challenged taken-for-granted axioms about the nature, status, and role of women in contemporary society and sought with varying success to mount a feminist critique and alternative mode of study to covertly male chauvinist orthodoxy. Though characteristically lagging a decade behind, early work in this vein in criminology mapped out an agenda for the analysis of female criminality in terms of 'such factors as differential socialisation, differential illegitimate opportunity structures and differential social reaction'.[32] Although focusing on such neglected topics as the extent to which the greater conformity of women may be attributable to quite distinct methods of socialization and supervision during childhood and the generally subordinate character of their participation in crime as reflecting their role and status in the social structure in general, Smart argues that work until the mid-1970s still lacked the capacity to 'situate the discussion of sex roles within a structural explanation of the social origins of those roles'.[33] Nor did it address the motivation of those women who did engage in crime. She concluded by arguing that the time for a feminist criminology was ripe, but no precise shape could be given to its character. There was the clear risk of ghettoization on the

[29] F. Adler, *Sisters in Crime*.   [30] J. Cowie, V. Cowie, and E. Slater, *Delinquency in Girls*.
[31] G. Konopka, *The Adolescent Girl in Conflict*.
[32] F. Heidensohn, *Women and Crime*; D. Hoffman-Bustamente, 'The Nature of Female Criminality'; K. Rosenhan, 'Female Deviance and the Female Sex Role'.
[33] C. Smart, *Women, Crime and Criminology*, 89.

one hand, tokenism on the other. Recognizing that a 'critique alone cannot constitute a new theoretical approach',[34] further research was needed before the goal of a 'women's perspective' could be achieved on such questions as typical patterns of offending, the 'leniency' hypothesis, the treatment of female deviants, and the role of gender in the framing and execution of laws.

In a paper on feminism and criminology in Britain, Gelsthorpe and Morris[35] took stock of what had been achieved in the decade following the publication of Smart's critique. Though much had been accomplished to redress the balance and undo the neglect of gender in the study of crime, deviance, and control, they assert that 'a feminist criminology cannot exist'. As in sociology in general, 'just as we had to talk of "feminisms", we have to talk of feminist criminologies, or, better still, feminist perspectives within criminology'.[36] Shared concerns are the opposition to positivism, stereotypical images of women, the use of methodologies sympathetic to such concerns, and the analytical centrality of gender and the subordination of women. In both sociology and criminology, however, the active pursuit of such concerns is far from transforming the subject; and the study of female criminality and its control, as well as the issue of gender in more general theories, faces constant problems of marginalization, incorporation, and tokenism.

Gelsthorpe and Morris, following Heidensohn,[37] regard existing theories as distorted by the almost unrelieved focus on the criminality of males and the invisibility or, at best, marginality of women and girls to the field. Nor can the situation be remedied by 'inserting' women into theories already formed on so patriarchal a basis: 'These critiques demonstrated that theories of criminality developed from and validated on men had limited relevance for explaining women's crime'.[38] Using this view, this book should be titled 'Understanding Male Deviance' and has indeed been criticized by Heidensohn for neglecting gender in the assessment of the validity of the various theories.[39] They acknowledge, in criticism of a purely gender-based view, that criminological theories have neglected other variables: crimes of the powerful, ethnicity, and other 'blind spots'. Second, emptying such theories of sexism does not render them valid; third, 'masculinity' has been subject to stereotyping; fourth, variables mediating the significance of gender, such as class and race, tend to be ignored by feminist criminologists; and fifth, sources of sexism tend to be analysed one-dimensionally, emanating from some global notion of men, or from the capitalist mode of production. The study of victimization constitutes the sole area in which gender has transformed research,[40] though even here the focus is on women's oppression and their fear of crime, rather than their subordination to male domination as the source of that fear.[41]

---

[34] C. Smart, *Women, Crime and Criminology*, 183.

[35] L. Gelsthorpe and A. Morris, 'Feminism and Criminology in Britain'.

[36] L. Gelsthorpe and A. Morris, 'Feminism and Criminology in Britain', 225.

[37] F. Heidensohn, *Women and Crime*.

[38] L. Gelsthorpe and A. Morris, 'Feminism and Criminology in Britain', 226.

[39] F. Heidensohn, 'Women and Crime: Questions for Criminology'.

[40] R. Matthews and J. Young (eds.), *Confronting Crime*; T. Jones, B. Maclean, and J. Young, *The Islington Crime Survey*.

[41] E. Stanko, 'Typical Violence, Normal Precaution: Men, Women and Interpersonal Violence in England, Wales, Scotland and the USA'.

Substantive achievements may, however, be more impressive than this self-appraisal from a feminist perspective might allow. Four substantive areas where significant work has been accomplished are; the 'female emancipation leads to crime' debate; the invalidation of the 'leniency' hypothesis; the emergence-from-within control theory of a gender-based theory of both male and female delinquency; and the raising to greater prominence of the female victim in political and academic analysis, a matter perhaps more properly reserved for victimology than criminology, which we shall return to in the next chapter.

Offending Behaviour

That females commit markedly fewer crimes than males, of a generally less serious character, and are less likely to persist after a first conviction is a criminological fact.[42] Research has suggested that women have a lower threshold of shame and guilt than men and are less prone to 'deviance disavowal' as a result.[43] Barbara Wootton wrote, in short, that 'if men behaved like women, the courts would be idle and the prisons empty'.[44] Two sets of theories have addressed this difference quite explicitly. Subcultural theories have assumed that females pursue less criminogenic and more attainable goals than men, namely relationships and family life, and are therefore insulated from the social sources of delinquency, the main exception being the strain to sexual deviance. Control theories specify with some precision the far more intensive and extensive informal social controls that are brought to bear on girls rather than boys, which constitute powerful inhibitors against criminality. In so far as greater equality operates to weaken or alter either or both sets of conditions, to that extent, it can be argued, females will converge with males in their exposure to criminogenic influences. The assertion that such a consequence has already flowed from the activities of the Women's Liberation movement in all its forms, or that such a consequence will necessarily occur in the future should emancipation be actualized more tangibly than is currently the case, is strongly contested by feminist criminologists. In the context of the crude ideological battles that have been fought around the issue of the 'maternal deprivation' of delinquent children by working mothers,[45] it is not surprising that such a proposition should be fiercely challenged. For the 'female emancipation leads to more female crime' thesis offers a new guise for the same old double standard: the Angel in the House must not—for the sake of the social order—be allowed to 'fall'.

The thesis that the 'fall from grace' has already begun and that both the extent and character of female crime have converged quite significantly with those of males, has been argued by Adler[46] and Simon.[47] In a rigorous review of the available evidence,

---

[42] Ministry of Justice, *Statistics on Women and the Criminal Justice System 2014*.

[43] R. Morris, 'Female Delinquency and Relational Problems' and 'Attitudes Towards Delinquency by Delinquents, Non-Delinquents and their Friends'.

[44] B. Wootton, *Social Science and Social Pathology*.

[45] P. Morgan, *Child Care: Sense and Fable*; M. Rutter, *Maternal Deprivation Reassessed*.

[46] F. Adler, *Sisters in Crime*.

[47] R. Simon, *Women and Crime*; F. Adler and R. Simon (eds.), *The Criminology of Deviant Women*.

Box concluded that when trends in crime are properly related to social and economic indicators of liberation on the one hand and economic marginalization on the other, it is the latter which best accounts for the modest convergence in property crime rates between the sexes. No change in rates of violent crimes was evident on that basis between 1951 and 1979. The 'new violent' female offender was a myth.[48] Even the convergence in convictions for property crime can be seen as the effect of changes in arrest and prosecution practice resulting from perceived changes in the criminality of women: though, on that basis, one would have expected as great, or greater, a rise in female rates of violent crime. If it is indeed the economic marginalization of women which best accounts for property crime convergence, then female emancipation in its most basic form has not occurred at all—a view which most feminist sociologists hold. In that respect the debate remains open. It should be emphasized, however, that the 'emancipation causes more female crime' view assumes that structured inequalities are held constant, when the preconditions for its attainment make such an assumption improbable. Some support for that view can be culled from one of the few studies of female as well as male youth cultural styles:

> The only real challenge to the mod boys' patriarchal power came from the new wave girls. Most importantly, the girls showed that they could see through the mod boys' public face rituals of exaggeration . . . They were the only group of pupils who successfully opposed and countered the ritualistic patriarchal behaviour of the mods . . . The new wave girls, through their spoken interactions and written communications, reverse the symbolic order of language; they demonstrate the denial of speech and then set about reclaiming the right to speak, define and know.[49]

Leniency as a Mode of Control

The view that women and girls are treated more leniently, for reasons of 'chivalry' or self-deception, so commonsensically proposed by Pollak but quite widely shared, has been rebutted and in significant respects even reversed by a number of studies over the past twenty years.[50] In the most authoritative study of sentencing, Farrington and Morris[51] found that the lighter sentences passed on women offenders in a Cambridge court were accounted for by the nature of their offences and their previous convictions. Similar findings explained the greater proportion of females cautioned by the police.[52] In a review of the evidence, Heidensohn[53] finds much support for the view that women are doubly punished when their rule-breaking is compounded by perceived role-breaking.

[48] S. Box, *Power, Crime and Mystification*, ch. 5; F. Heidensohn, *Women and Crime*.

[49] S. Blackman, *Youth: Positions and Oppositions*, 254–5.

[50] Although, ironically, some feminists would cede to certain women charged with offences of violence against men a special exemption based on the idea of the 'slow burn'—the gradual accumulation of fear that can infuse an abusive relationship and justify a reformulation of provocative behaviour by men and reasonable violence by men. S. Westervelt, *Shifting the Blame*.

[51] D. Farrington and A. Morris, 'Sex, Sentencing and Reconvictions'.

[52] C. Fisher and R. Mawby, 'Juvenile Delinquency and Police Discretion in an Inner City Area'; S. Landau and G. Nathan, 'Juveniles and the Police'.   [53] F. Heidensohn, *Women and Crime*, chs. 4 and 5.

Carlen's interviews with Scottish sheriffs[54] elicited views consonant with a dual morality that justifies imprisonment more readily for women offenders who have 'failed' as mothers. The Cambridge study found that divorced or separated women, or those from 'deviant' family backgrounds, were more likely to receive severe sentences. This holds open the possibility that women who conform to the conventional female role do benefit from judicial discretion, for which some support exists in American research[55] (Eaton[56] has found, however, that family and employment factors of mitigation are deployed similarly for males and females alike). But it is in the realms of 'protective' custody for non-criminal behaviour that dual morality looms largest: girls are far more likely than boys to be 'taken into care' for a range of misconduct which may include truancy as well as sexual waywardness.[57] Leniency is also more apparent in cases of domestic violence for men who victimize their female partners, where non-prosecution is the norm;[58] and in cases of corporate or white-collar crime, which women are rarely given the occupational opportunities to commit, but where non-prosecution tends to be the norm. In these major respects, women—by comparison with men—are 'under-protected and over-controlled'.[59] Prostitution is perhaps the single most notorious instance of 'double standards', with a long history of vilification by statute and stereotype. 'Common prostitutes' are 'fallen' women: men, whether prostitutes or clients, escape both forms of censure.[60] Moreover, despite the strong economic incentives for women to become prostitutes in the context of job discrimination, motivation is usually ascribed to psychogenic causes.

Gender, Crime, Deviance, and Social Control

In two notable studies, Hagan, Simpson, and Gillis[61] have directly addressed the relations between gender, crime, and social control, using a synthesis of control and conflict theories of deviance. Their first study, based on data gathered in 1976 from a mixed-sex sample of several hundred Toronto high school adolescents, tested and explored the theory that the self-reported rates of delinquency both within and between males and females would be linked to differentials in socialization and informal social control. 'There is a sexually stratified inverse relationship between structurally differentiated processes of social control such that women are more frequently the instruments and

[54] P. Carlen, *Women's Imprisonment.*

[55] I. Nagel, 'Sex Differences in the Processing of Criminal Defendants'.

[56] M. Eaton, 'Mitigating Circumstances: Familiar Rhetoric'; 'Documenting the Defendant: Placing Women in Social Inquiry Report'; *Justice for Women?*   [57] M. Casburn, *Girls Will be Girls.*

[58] R. Dobash and R. Dobash, *Violence Against Wives: A Case Against Patriarchy*; 'The Nature and Antecedents of Violent Events'; S. Edwards, *Female Sexuality and the Law*; 'Police Attitudes and Dispositions in Domestic Disputes: The London Study'. Such a trend may be in reverse. An 'automatic charging' policy is becoming urged with greater frequency precisely in response to the privatization and softening of controls in cases of domestic violence. L. Sherman and R. Berk, *The Minneapolis Domestic Violence Experiment.*

[59] D. Downes and T. Ward, *Democratic Policing*, 17.   [60] M. Sumner, *Prostitution and Images of Women.*

[61] J. Hagan, J. Simpson, and A. Gillis, 'The Sexual Stratification of Social Control'; 'The Class Structure of Gender and Delinquency: Toward a Power-Control Theory of Common Delinquent Behaviour'.

objects of informal social controls.'[62] Segregative formal control is seen as emerging with industrialization, with the site for informal social control increasingly confined to the private realm of the home,[63] from which men were increasingly absent and to which women became more and more frequently sequestered. Men became subject to formal social control, whilst women did not. The exclusion of women from the 'rat race' and their lower crime rate are thus jointly rooted in family-based patterns of informal social control. It was stressed that informal social control is not synonymous with less, but probably more, control; and that exposure to formal and informal controls are inversely related. Also, even 'career' women tend to inherit the responsibility for the care and control of children, so that inter-generationally transmitted gender roles flow from the earliest experiences.

The data bore out the hypotheses that subjecting girls to a dense array of informal social controls, primarily mediated maternally, would ensure greater compliance; while young males are freed to pursue more active forms of risk-taking, with the consequence that they are more at risk of encountering the world of formal control. Males more than females defined risk-taking positively; defined delinquency more positively; and engaged in delinquency more frequently and seriously. The control variables also produced the predicted relationships within gender groups. On this basis, Hagan, Simpson, and Gillis conclude that, accurate as Dennis Wrong's critique of functionalist sociology may be with regard to men, women *are*, in effect, over-socialized.

A key omission in the study was the interaction between sexual and social stratification, which is rectified in their second study,[64] carried out in 1979 on a similar sample in Toronto. Drawing more fully on a neo-Marxian class analysis than is usually the case, they differentiate four groups in the stratification order: employers and managers and employed and unemployed workers. The power variable was therefore entered into the frame as well as control variables. Class was found to be unrelated to the common forms of delinquency measured, with the predicted exception that the children of employers were reportedly the most delinquent, being highest on power and least fettered by both formal and informal controls. Introducing gender revealed a decrease in the relationship between gender and common forms of delinquency with each step down the class structure.[65] In sum, as Bonger asserted in 1916, just under a century ago, differences in the way of life between the sexes are at their height in the upper reaches of society,[66] at their minimum in the lower working class. Among children of parents excluded from the labour market, delinquency approached unity by gender once parental controls are taken into account.

---

[62]　J. Hagan, J. Simpson, and A. Gillis, 'The Sexual Stratification of Social Control', 25.

[63]　Strong historical support for that argument has subsequently been provided by Malcolm Feeley. See 'The Decline of Women in the Criminal Process: A Comparative History' and 'The Vanishing Female: The Decline of Women in the Criminal Process, 1687–1912'.

[64]　J. Hagan, A. Gillis, and J. Simpson, 'The Class Structure of Gender and Delinquency'.

[65]　J. Hagan, A. Gillis, and J. Simpson, 'The Class Structure of Gender and Delinquency', 1151.

[66]　Well caught in Flaubert's parody: '*Young gentleman*: Always sowing wild oats; he is expected to do so. Astonishment when he doesn't. *Young lady*: Utter these words with diffidence. All young ladies are pale, frail and always pure. Prohibit, for their good, every kind of reading, all visits to museums, theatres and especially to the monkey house at the zoo.' (J. Barzun, tr., *Flaubert's Dictionary of Accepted Ideas*, 84).

It is stressed that the most serious forms of delinquency are not adequately covered by the early research design, based on Hirschi's self-report questionnaire;[67] but such forms of delinquency are so uncommon that adequate sampling across all social groups would be scarcely feasible with current resources. However impressive the analysis and suggestive the data may be, we remain somewhat sceptical about too great a reliance on the self-report technique, applied to in-school populations and lacking detailed specification of community type. Reiss and Rhodes established over forty years ago that community type was a key variable in delinquency rates:[68] working-class delinquency rates tended to increase with the degree of class homogeneity. What such work should stimulate is a redressing of the balance in respects other than gender alone and by methods other than self-reported delinquency alone: in particular, the filling of the gap in ethnographies of 'employer class' crime and delinquency.

In a number of studies, Pat Carlen advanced the analysis of the links between forms of female crime and social regulation by pointing to the ways in which the lives of criminal women in Britain seem significantly to have been associated with early ruptures in domestic social control.[69] Female offenders, she claims, stem from amongst the poorest and the least powerful of all social groups. They are disproportionately lower-class women and many were abandoned by their families in childhood. Such women are disproportionately likely to have been placed in institutional care, free from family bonds and the customary restraints of gender. They have shrugged off what she calls the 'gender deal', the array of quasi-contractual understandings that routinely control the boundaries and character of femininity in a patriarchal society. As women with radically impaired life-chances, they have also shrugged off the 'class deal', the understandings about effort and reward that bind men and women to the conventional labour market. Doubly free, they can deviate in ways denied to the traditionally fettered woman.

Of late, work is beginning to suggest that the trend towards the erosion of gender difference has advanced in ways that are particularly consequential for delinquency, control, and gender relations. In particular, Hagan and his colleagues conjecture that the decline of male work and the rise of female work have brought about a transformation in patterns and models of domestic control. There has, they argue, been a move away from patriarchal dominance:

> women . . . have become agents of change in the gender schemas that surround work and the family. As these gender schemas are diminished or discarded in families where mothers have gained occupational power . . . adolescent males may benefit less from this [process of] capitalization and still remain at greater risk of involvement in delinquency. The implication is that the male subculture of delinquency is a residue of the former hegemony of a patriarchal power structure. In this sense, male subcultural delinquency may be a vestigial social trait, making male subcultural delinquents the social dinosaurs of a passing, more patriarchal era.[70]

[67] T. Hirschi, *Causes of Delinquency*, ch. 9.
[68] A. Reiss and A. Rhodes, 'The Distribution of Juvenile Delinquency in the Social and Class Structure'.
[69] P. Carlen and A. Worrall, *Gender, Crime and Justice* and P. Carlen, *Women, Crime and Poverty*.
[70] J. Hagan et al., 'Gender Difference in Capitalization Processes and the Delinquency of Siblings in Toronto and Berlin', 663.

Female Victimization

Victims of crime were almost wholly neglected by criminologists and sociologists of crime and deviance until the mid-1970s when the women's campaigning groups began to focus on the victim of rape and domestic violence as one of the icons of the plight of females under patriarchy.[71] The first women's refuge to be acknowledged in feminist accounts[72] was Chiswick Family Rescue, founded in 1971 by Erin Pizzey.[73] The first rape crisis centre was founded in Washington at much the same time,[74] and some 750 more centres were to open in the United States within only ten years.[75] Scholarly work followed and it was at first set largely within the frame established by the politics and ideology of the activists: violence against women was represented as a problem hidden in the private recesses of the domestic sphere; it was a mirror of patriarchal oppression—an ineluctably gendered phenomenon centred on male power and female subordination that could not be compared with the victimization of men; and attempts to introduce it into the public domain were met by parallel patriarchal and oppressive responses that brought about the 'secondary victimization' of the woman complainant by the criminal justice system.[76] At its loosest, the word 'victim' was stretched to embrace the female offender who was taken in effect to be a casualty of domination acting protectively against repeated male abuse.[77] The outcome has been that there is now a copious body of research about the experiences of women victims as they confront both their victimization and the criminal justice system.[78]

The introduction of female victims was to have important repercussions for policy and analysis. As we have shown, it galvanized radical criminology and laid part of the foundations for the emergence of left realism. But there was always a strain between criminology and the feminism that had sponsored the rediscovery of the female victim, a strain born not only of the more general tension between the practical engagement of the activist who talked of 'survivors' and the more distant stance of the academic who tended to talk of 'victims', but also of the moralization of the subject which made it difficult to examine the role played by female victims in criminal transactions.[79] 'Victim-precipitation' was called 'victim-blaming', for instance, by Clarke and Lewis, who claimed that 'victim blaming has become institutionalized within the academic world under the guise of victimology.'[80] When women criminals were themselves

---

[71] J. Freeman; 'The Origins of the Women's Liberation Movement'.

[72] There were, for instance, refuges for battered women run by nuns in Quebec in the 1930s and no doubt other examples could be given, but they have not been given a place in the orthodox histories of the movement.

[73] E. Pizzey, *Scream Quietly or the Neighbours will Hear*.

[74] M. Wasserman, 'Rape: Breaking the Silence'.

[75] V. Jaycox, *Creating a Senior Victim/Witness Volunteer Corps*.   [76] Z. Adler, *Rape on Trial*.

[77] J. Nadel, *Sara Thornton: The Story of a Woman who Killed*.

[78] S. Edwards, *Policing 'Domestic' Violence: Women, the Law and the State*; J. Gregory and S. Lees, *Policing Sexual Assault*; and J. Temkin, *Rape and the Criminal Justice System*; B. Krahe and J. Temkin, *Sexual Assault and the Justice Gap*

[79] S. Westervelt, *Shifting the Blame: How Victimization Became a Criminal Defense*.

[80] L. Clark and D. Lewis, *Rape: The Price of Coercive Sexuality*, 147–8.

identified as the casualties and victims of patriarchy, it could become even more difficult to analyse the processes and phenomena of female crime with any degree of scholarly disinterest.[81]

More generally, work in feminist criminology and in criminology with an affinity to feminism has now started to evolve in two principal directions, reflecting the fundamental bifurcation in all social science between the 'empirical' and the 'theoretical'. One wing has increasingly moved from declaratory manifestos and 'immanent critiques' towards empirical studies of women, crime, victimization, and criminal justice. To be sure, there have been such studies since the very beginnings of criminology (many having been inexplicably neglected in the formal feminist history of the discipline), but exegesis and criticism are now being supplemented by a wave of original studies that reflect, in part, the growing number of women who have entered the discipline of criminology.[82]

One wing, as much criminology as feminism perhaps, has added descriptively to what is known about women, deviance, and control. Campbell, for instance, has explored the extent and character of female delinquency and found no support for Albert Cohen's view that it is predominantly sexual. Rather, it is manifest across the range of offences, though with much lower prevalence than is the case for males in all but a few offences, such as shoplifting, where gender-role characteristics suggest greater exposure to 'consumer fetishism'.[83] Nor are girls so resistant to becoming gang members as has often been assumed; but within the gang, they can be seen to play roles reflective of the subordinate and supportive female role in the wider society.[84] Miller recounts how, as a matter of course, young women in segments of the black community take to the streets for a time whilst their children are tended by grandmothers who were prostitutes themselves in their day. In due course, Miller remarks, the women will move from the streets back to domesticity, only to look after their prostitute daughters' children in their turn. The pattern is repeated from generation to generation, only interrupted if the women become so addicted to drugs that they cannot return to the more or less conventional world.[85] Frances Heidensohn examines how women in Britain and North America manage the daunting project of 'breaking into' the hostile male world of police officers.[86] Women, she says, are subject to unusual and severe tests before they can prove themselves. Acceptance may turn on passing strategic benchmarks where character and ability are put to the test. The successful woman, like Cinderella, undergoes a 'transformation scene' that confirms her as a deserving insider. Lucia Zedner narrates how moral definitions of female deviance gave way to 'scientific' explanations invoking biology and psychology under the spell of Darwin and the medicalization of social problems. Zedner argues that women were less and less frequently vested with a capacity for reason and rational choice, their

---

[81] A. Mattravers, *Justifying the Unjustifiable*; and S. Hayman, *The Evolution of the New Federal Women's Prisons in Canada*.

[82] P. Rock, 'The Social Organization of British Criminology'.   [83] A. Campbell, *Girl Delinquents*.

[84] A. Campbell, *The Girls in the Gang*.

[85] E. Miller, *Street Woman*; see also R. L. Dalla, *Exposing the 'Pretty Women' Myth*.

[86] There have been other studies on such a theme. See, e.g., S. Martin, *Breaking and Entering*.

crime becoming viewed as pathology, their character being described as mad rather than bad. And Avril Taylor examined the lives of women drug addicts in Glasgow that were organized, in part, around the distinctively feminine problems of managing pregnancy and childrearing.[87]

Feminist criminologists have also begun to move beyond an insistent focus on women alone to ask larger questions about gender, about the crimes and controls of *men*, and about the differential treatment of men and women in the criminal justice system.[88] As Newburn and Stanko observe, 'the most significant fact about crime is that it is almost always committed by men'.[89] Because men often offend and women do not, the links between crime and gender have engaged the criminologist's attention. The differential exercise of control has been the target of one kind of analysis, the social construction of gender another. Of particular influence in some of the newer work has been Connell's conceptions of 'hegemonic' (or accredited) and 'subordinated' (or discredited) masculinities, a conception based loosely on the writings of Gramsci, which stresses how certain models of maleness can attain ideological and cultural ascendancy. Power, wealth, and personal strength are some of the components of the hegemonic pattern. Without very much empirical evidence, but nevertheless with some plausibility, Connell points to movie and sports stars as instances of a version of tough masculinity which lead to 'practices that institutionalize men's dominance over women'.[90] They are authoritative prototypes, embodied scripts, which delineate appropriate actions and relations.

Connell did not write extensively about crime and criminals, but it is evident that an ideal of male physicality has a strong affinity with the patterns of behaviour that are associated with assaults, domestic violence, street crime, and the like. It is reproduced in schools,[91] on the streets, and on and around the sports field;[92] it legitimates the use of violence; and it explains some of the coercive transactions that unfold between men and women.[93] As Kersten argues 'such constructs of "good" or "real" masculinities are subject to both the self-definition of deviant "outlaw" masculinities and the construction of the criminal offender and (even more pronouncedly) to the image of the "gang" as the collective "other"'.[94]

Philippe Bourgois explains the extremes of violence directed by Puerto Rican crack dealers against women in New York City as part of an effort to protect threatened claims to masculine supremacy in an economic environment marked by the rise of female employment and the decline of male employment.[95] It is a matter of defending traditional conceptions of male face, identity, or pride against new attacks and that is a theme much rehearsed in the work centred on crime and gender. Polk, for example,

---

[87] A. Taylor, *Women Drug Users*; and L. Maher, *Sexed Work: Gender, Race, and Resistance in a Brooklyn Drug Market*.   [88] K. Daly and M. Chesney-Lind, 'Feminism and Criminology'.

[89] T. Newburn and E. Stanko (eds.), *Just Boys Doing Business?*, 1; see also R. Collier, *Masculinities, Crime and Criminology*; S. Winlow, *Badfellas: Crime, Tradition and New Masculinities*; A. Elliss, *Men, Masculinities and Violence*.   [90] R. Connell, *Gender and Power*, 185.

[91] P. Willis, *Learning to Labour*.   [92] G. Armstrong, *Football Hooligans: Knowing the Score*.

[93] T. Newburn and E. Stanko (eds.), *Just Boys Doing Business?*, 4.

[94] J. Kersten, 'Culture, Masculinities and Violence Against Women', 383.

[95] P. Bourgois, 'In Search of Masculinity'.

has argued that many instances of working-class men killing other working-class men in Australia must be referred to attempts to uphold a precarious but highly valued masculine honour.[96]

The other wing, more feminist than criminological, would deflect attention away from the criminal woman to urge the ending of what has just begun. Just as an earlier generation did not wish to endanger the politics of race by looking too closely at the links between race, ethnicity, and crime (other than in the context of the unjust racialized criminalization by the criminal justice system), so some feminists have argued that no good purpose can be served by exploring the criminality of women or reducing women's rule-breaking and the stigmatization and punishment of the woman rule-breaker. A feminist criminology, it has been argued, is prone to 'correctionalism' and collusion with patriarchy,[97] being used as an instrument *against* women.

The grand theorists, in some measure like their Marxist[98] or phenomenological[99] forebears, would claim that a preoccupation with the empirical detail of female crime belittles and circumscribes what should be a larger project altogether, the study of women under patriarchy. Crime and the criminal woman are ideologically generated empirical categories that reify, restrict, and essentialize their subject. Feminists, they say, should move beyond such limited entities to their own distinctive terrain,[100] becoming, as Young put it, 'producers of their own discourse, instead of being the mere receivers of a masculinist master discourse'.[101] Like others before them, it would seem, the feminist grand theorists are quitting the empirical and substantive field of criminology to a more elevated plane of systematic reasoning about the social world.[102] The progenitor of feminist criminology, Carol Smart, for instance, has written about how, 'as feminist theory is increasingly engaging with and generating post-modern ideas, the relevance of criminology to feminist thought diminishes. . . . It should be stressed, of course, that this is not exactly a novel exercise. Criminology seems to be *the* enterprise that many scholars desert or reject'.[103]

Critique

Many feminist criminologists have gone much further than theorizing and deploring the neglect of female criminality and defining priorities to remedy past omissions. They have made of the issue a criterion for the validity or invalidity of criminological theory. Box and Harris put the case that 'any causal explanation of crime which does

---

[96] K. Polk, *When Men Kill.*

[97] J. Allen, 'The "Masculinity" of Criminality and Criminology: Interrogating some Impasses'; and C. Smart, 'Feminist Approaches to Criminality, or Postmodern Woman meets Atavistic Man'.

[98] P. Hirst, 'Marx and Engels on Law, Crime and Morality'.

[99] M. Phillipson, 'Thinking Out of Deviance'.

[100] B. Brown, 'Women and Crime: the Dark Figures of Criminology'; and C. Smart, *Feminism and the Power of Law.*   [101] A. Young, 'Feminism and the Body of Criminology', 21.

[102] P. Rock, 'Has Deviance a Future?'.

[103] C. Smart, 'Feminist Approaches to Criminology, or Postmodern Woman meets Atavistic Man', 70.

not include gender-related factors cannot be valid'.[104] Gelsthorpe and Morris[105] argue that 'Theories are weak if they do not apply to half of the potential criminal popula-tion; women, after all, experience the same deprivations, family structures and so on, that men do. Theories of crime should be able to take account of the behaviour of both men and women and to highlight those factors which operate differently on men and women.' And Heidensohn stated: 'Criminology is poorer in all its forms [because it has] not yet fully accepted and integrated the importance of gender, or its interaction with such factors as race and class.'[106]

Central as its role should be in the sociology of crime and deviance, we do not regard the significance of gender in quite such stark terms. The impulses behind theorizing are diverse, but ultimately irrelevant to the criteria that govern the evaluation of its va-lidity. It so happens that criminological theory has been crime-led and that the subjects around whom theorizing has been formed have been predominantly urban, lower-class, and usually adolescent males in advanced industrial capitalist societies. We do not share the view, advanced by Smart, that the focus was chosen primarily because of governmental or State concern: it seemed to successive generations of sociologists—particularly in the post-war context of increasing affluence—that commonsensical and psychogenic explanations were most deficient in explaining the extent and character of delinquency among this sector of the population. In the process, the criminality and/or greater conformity of every other group became marginalized or bracketed away: not only females, but ethnic minorities, the middle-aged and elderly, rural communities, the middle and upper classes, corporations, and both State socialist and developing countries were neglected as subjects. It is a massive catalogue of default, but it is not to be explained by patriarchy or an obeisance to State control. It may well be that the crime-led character of criminology was profoundly mistaken, based on a misconcep-tion of what constituted crime (a revaluation begun systematically only with the emer-gence of labelling theory in the early 1960s); and that the questions posed were too inattentive to the underlying problem of order, including patriarchal order. That was the task consigned to mainstream sociological theory, though the Gluecks and control theorists took it as their point of entry into the field. The possibilities opened up by these approaches have already enlarged the scope of the study of female offending in particular and the significance of gender for deviance and control more generally.

The theories whose character we have sought to convey in preceding chapters have, in our view, more to offer in the pursuit of the concerns of feminist criminologists than they have been prepared to allow.[107] Matza's concept of 'drift' is a priori as applicable to female as to male subjects. The concepts of 'labelling', 'career', 'stigma', and the like should be as fruitful for the understanding of female deviance as that of males. In terms of substantive theories, Albert Cohen did not preclude girls from subcultural formations, though he may have erred in assuming too readily that his formulations of cause and effect did not apply at all to females and that sexual deviancy exhausted

---

[104] F. Heidensohn, *Women and Crime*, 3.
[105] L. Gelsthorpe and A. Morris, 'Feminism and Criminology in Britain', 231.
[106] F. Heidensohn, 'Women and Crime: Questions for Criminology', 27.
[107] E. Leonard, *Women, Crime and Society*.

their repertoire. The manufacture of excitement is as germane to an understanding of female as of male transgression.[108] The risks attached to female risk taking are, however, quite different from those of men. The differentials in crime rates by age and sex remain central to theorizing delinquency, but existing theories as to why that should be so have not been supplanted by our greater awareness of the domination of women: that has tended to reinforce their premises. Much theory is a moveable feast. A number of the older, apparently male-centred theories have a good deal of utility in explaining female crime. Elaine Player, for example, found anomie theory the most satisfactory framework for explaining female burglary and robbery.[109] And, again, papers delivered at a symposium on ethnography in 2003 pointed to the use of violence by young women in Philadelphia that did not seem to be at all distinctively gendered. Young women attacked young women, just as young men attack young men, citing the need to elicit 'respect'.[110] It may well be, in short, that ostensibly male-centred theories work for women, and that it has only been literary convention that has played a part in suggesting otherwise. For instance, although Matza uses the masculine pronoun throughout, his archetypal deviants in *Becoming Deviant* were all women. Consider, too, the difficulties confessed to by Lyn Lofland, writing in 1973 at just about the time when those literary conventions were under challenge:

> as to sex, I have attempted to avoid as much as possible the use of the term 'man' to stand for all human beings. I have also attempted to avoid excessive use of the pronouns 'he', 'his', and 'him' when referring to both men and women. Neither attempt has been particularly successful. Stylistic convention makes 'man', 'he', 'him', and 'his' difficult words to avoid. At one point, I considered substituting 'woman', 'she', 'her', and 'hers' in all the appropriate places, but finally decided that female chauvinism is no improvement over the male variety. In addition, in reading over a sentence or paragraph where I had made such a substitution, I found that, because of the strangeness of the phrasing, the words drew attention to themselves and even I lost track of what was being said.[111]

Lofland and Matza clearly did not intend the masculine pronoun to refer solely and exclusively to men. Women were included in their analysis; however, language may have masked what was said. This raises the question of whether feminist criminologists are right in asserting that criminology has so markedly ignored women. Perversely, it also raises the question of whether the growing literary convention of invariably applying female pronouns to the third person singular should be interpreted as excluding all *males* from analysis. One distinguished exemplar of this practice is Richard Ericson who insists on the feminine pronoun throughout his more recent writing, even referring to an ideal-typical Hell's Angel as a 'she'.[112] Are we, one wonders, to take it that all Hell's Angels are women or that 'masculine' theories of crime and control do not apply to them? Nor is the overt neglect of female criminality and the significance of

---

[108] S. Welsh, 'The Manufacture of Excitement in Police–Juvenile Encounters'.
[109] E. Player, 'Women and Crime in the City'.
[110] The proceedings were subsequently published as the *Annals of the American Academy of Political and Social Science*, September 2004.   [111] L. Lofland, *A World of Strangers*, xii–xiii.
[112] R. Ericson and K. Haggerty, *Policing the Risk Society*.

gender quite as marked as the critiques insist. Heidensohn[113] and Morris[114] in Britain and Mann[115] in the USA, have written texts which omit to mention Paul Cressy's *The Taxi-Dance Hall* and Walter Reckless' *Vice in Chicago*. Pauline Morris' *Prisoners and their Families* somehow escapes attention in what is defined as uncharted territory. Willis' alleged attachment to the glamour of machismo, a general shortcoming of male sociologists, according to Heidensohn, was accompanied by an unrivalled ability to situate the sexism and racism of his subjects.[116] Such persistent defects mar an otherwise powerful case.

Take too arguments about the impact of certain theories of female crime. It is claimed that the neglect of the positivist remainder in the field of female criminality has had untoward consequences in the treatment of female offenders. This may be so, but the proposition is as yet almost wholly unsupported by evidence: and male offenders are not totally exempt from positivist measures. The jump has been made, for example, from turn-of-the-century Lombrosianism to the 'new' therapeutic Holloway prison for women, but the mediating links are not supplied.[117] On the contrary, the significance of gender and the particular plight of women prisoners in Holloway before 1967 actually appears to have been more complex than any straightforward, unilinear history of ideas might suggest. It was mediated, as all policy questions are, by the political problems of how arguments could be deployed to best advantage in a difficult bureaucratic environment. Sometimes gender differences were cited, sometimes they were not—their phrasing turned on how particular audiences could be persuaded to accede to particular objectives at particular times. The pragmatics of policy-making did not require officials and politicians to make a decision about the 'real' character of female offenders. Neither did they demand unanimity. And it is certainly the case that the name Lombroso does not appear at all in any of the papers or arguments underpinning the development of women's prisons in Britain. Beverley Brown argued:

> [The] theme in feminist criminology has been, crudely, that traditional criminology is the theory, Holloway [Prison]—especially its psychiatric wing—the practice. An additionally cohesive force is added by feminist criminology's emphasis on the monotonous repetition of criminology's view of the female offender, a few basic themes reiterated from the opening shots fired in 1895 by Lombroso and Ferrero's *The Female Offender*. . . . To invoke this rhetoric is to invoke that powerful and epiphanous moment in which feminist criminology was announced, a moment of foundation and denunciation, indeed foundation-by-denunciation, when feminist criminology could simply constitute itself as *critique* . . .[118]

Despite these criticisms, feminist criminology, broadly defined as women's perspectives within criminology,[119] has (despite their self-deprecation about their achievement) significantly reoriented the field. All paradigms are anomalies transformed into novel focus. For feminist criminology, the absence of gender, long acknowledged as

---

[113] F. Heidensohn, *Women and Crime*.
[114] A. Morris, *Women, Crime and Criminal Justice.*   [115] C. Mann, *Female Crime and Delinquency.*
[116] P. Willis, *Learning to Labour.*
[117] G. Pailthorpe, *Studies in the Psychology of Delinquency.*
[118] B. Brown, 'Women and Crime: The Dark Figures of Criminology', 359–60.
[119] L. Gelsthorpe and A. Morris, 'Feminism and Criminology in Britain', 225.

regrettable in criminology, but easily lived with, has inspired a fresh insight that theories of male criminality do not fit too readily the 'facts' of female criminality. The sociology of deviance can only benefit from addressing more creatively the question of why the oppression of women has not led to rates of crime as high as those of males. All new paradigms transform the banal into fresh focus: radical criminology retrieved, but then threw away, the failure to address crimes of the powerful; labelling theorists built on the truism that 'deviant behaviour is that which is so labelled'; control theorists that the real question may be 'Why don't we all deviate?'; subcultural theorists sought motives and meaning in that which was considered 'mindless'; functionalists perceived the sources of conformity in deviance; and the Chicagoans saw that deviant traditions were inescapably social and not products of individual pathology. Feminist criminology may not be a new paradigm in this sense: but it has undeniably revitalized the exploration of existing perspectives. It is only to be hoped that feminist politics and grand theory do not abort what feminism has just started.

Conclusion

Although there had been a long and unacknowledged prior tradition of criminology focused on women, a self-conscious feminist criminology emerged in the late 1960s and 1970s along with a feminist politics, a feminist practice, and radical criminology. Pioneered in the UK by Frances Heidensohn and then by Carol Smart, it criticized the apparent criminological neglect of women as victims, offenders, defendants, and prisoners, and championed their reinstatement on the political and practical grounds that the mistreatment of victims of rape, sexual assault, and domestic violence should be rectified and on the intellectual grounds that no criminology that ignored gender could be complete. In the light of the very low rates of female offending, perhaps its major achievement was tacitly to apply the argument of control theory that the interesting question was not why women commit crimes, but why they do not do so. The answer, Pat Carlen and John Hagan were to say, lay in the differential application of formal and informal social control, women being more prone to emotional regulation by intimates in private space, men to impersonal control by officials in public space. Feminist criminology now embraces studies of victims, criminals, defendants, and criminal justice policy-making and practices. It is now part of the canon of criminology, broadening out to investigate gender and masculinity (or masculinities) as much as femininity. In her overview of the state of feminist criminology in the twenty-first century, Francis Heidensohn[120] notes that feminist criminology has had a demonstrable impact in the UK on policy and practice relating to domestic and sexual violence, the penal treatment of women, and equal opportunities for women working in the criminal justice system. On the other hand she expressed concerns about how little innovation there was in theoretical approaches; gaps in the range of emergent research topics, especially relating to intersectionality, and the continual refusal of some male criminologists to

[120] F. Heidensohn, 'The Future of Feminist Criminology',

give more than token acknowledgement to gender in their work. Heidenshohn concluded her review with a list of reality checks for feminist criminology. She expressed particular concern about the global reality of hatred and subordination of women as expressed through physical and sexual violence, sexual exploitation, genital mutilation, and so-called honour killings. In addition, to lack of protection of basic human rights and safety, despite the notable reforms in some Western societies, she noted that there has also been a global upward trend in the penalization of women and girls.

Further Reading

K. DALY and L. Maher, *Criminology at the Crossroads: Feminist Readings in Crime and Justice*, London, 1998.

F. HEIDENSOHN, *Gender and Justice: New Concepts and Approaches*, London, 2006.

N. LOMBARD, *Violence Against Women: Current Theory and Practice in Domestic Abuse, Sexual Violence and Exploitation*, London, 2013.

C. M. RENZETTI, *Feminist Criminology*, London, 2013.

M. SILVESTRI and C. Crowther-Dowey, *Gender & Crime*, London, 2008.

12

Victimology

Introduction

Victims play an increasingly important role in the politics and practice of criminal justice, as an intellectual topic in their own right and as a significant source of challenge to criminology. Victim-centred theories have even been grouped together and awarded their own title, victimology, amounting to a kind of sub-discipline of criminology, although those who practise it usually open with the half-apologetic statement that it is rather thin and underdeveloped, and then speculate why that should be so. There is still no fully coherent victimological theory in that sense, and, at the very outset, it should be said that there is no good reason why so diverse and complex an entity as victims and victimization should or could be covered by a single set of arguments. Helen Reeves, the Chief Executive Officer of Victim Support, once remarked that to search for a single theory or description of victims and victimization would be quite as misconceived as the search for a single theory or description of criminals and crime. But there is more that can be said about the theoretically weak state of victimology, and, in saying it, one learns something interesting about victims themselves.

The Neglect of the Victim

It used to be commonplace to remark that victims were neglected in criminal law and procedure.[1] Victims' activists talked about the 'forgotten person' who appeared only as a witness, an applicant for compensation, or as a complainant or *alleged* victim until the conclusion of a trial. Lois Herrington,[2] the former Assistant Attorney General of the United States and the chairwoman of the 1982 Presidential Task Force on Victims of Crime, claimed that 'The system served the judges, lawyers, and defendants, while ignoring, blaming, and mistreating the victims. Once they survive the initial impact of a crime, the victims are drawn into a system that treats them with indifference at best and abuse at worst.' The prime conflict at law did not touch significantly on victims: it was deemed to be between two parties only, the prosecution and the defendant, and individual victims merely provided evidence of an offence that, for all practical purposes,

---

[1] N. Christie, 'Conflicts as Property'.
[2] L. Herrington, 'Victim Rights and Criminal Justice Reform', 141.

was committed not so much against them but against the collectivity in the form of the Crown, the State, or the community. They figured very little in formal procedure and scant support or attention was offered them. Private wrongs were a matter for tort and civil procedure, not the criminal trial.[3]

Almost without exception, the foundational writings of criminology followed suit and made little to no reference to victims. The crimes they described were curiously intransitive, as if they lacked an object and impact—as if they never harmed anyone. Kenneth Burke once said that a way of seeing is always a way of not seeing, and, focusing on crimes and criminals, many criminologists most emphatically did not see the victim. Even where victims did come into view, they were typically observed only through a highly focused lens. For instance, David Matza summarily introduced an unresearched and abstract conception of the victim, simply to flesh out what he conjectured to be the offender's reasoning in neutralizing guilt. The victim, he said, could figure as one whose 'qualities may be so debased as to disqualify him from [the assumed] right' to press charges.[4] That was all. It was a fleeting appearance.

The explanation of that neglect is not really mysterious. Criminology is a relatively small discipline with few practitioners and many gaps, and it is not remarkable that the victim should have been overlooked. After all, we still know almost nothing about crime, deviance, and justice in many regions of the world; rural crime and policing in Europe and North America; cybercrime[5] and cyber bullying;[6] sexual grooming;[7] or crimes committed against parents.[8] New crimes, criminals and deviants, and forms of crime control are continually being brought into view. Old crimes mutate. Theories, themes, and research topics proliferate. In such an ill-mapped, densely populated, and shifting world, victims could be taken as little more than just another tract of *terra incognita*. But other epistemological and methodological issues have been in play. Each of the major theoretical approaches seemed to have had good reasons to ignore victims and victimization.

The more positivist criminologists looked for the origins and development of crime in the body and mind of the criminal, the principal causal factors being constitutional, genetic, psychiatric, or psychological, and victims appeared not at all because they lay outside the central field of inquiry.[9] Functionalist writers were interested less in the surface appearances of crime and control—appearances, they held, that could be misunderstood by a naïve common-sense reasoning that was anything but scientific. If what was sometimes disparaged as saloon bar criminology pointed at victims, they became all the more discredited. The theorists' trained eye was turned elsewhere, towards what were thought to be the important deep structures of society where crime and control performed unrecognized services for the collectivity: prostitution buttressing marriage and the family; the stigma of illegitimacy buttressing primogeniture;

---

[3] R. Elias, *Victims of the System*, 2; D. Garland, *The Culture of High Crime Societies*, 357.
[4] D. Matza, *Delinquency and Drift*, 174.
[5] M. Fitzgerald, *Crime Sentencing and Justice*.
[6] P. K. Smith and G. Steffgen, *Cyberbullying through the New Media*.
[7] S. Ost, *Child Pornography and Sexual Grooming*.
[8] R. Condry and C. Miles, 'Adolescent to Parent Violence'.   [9] N. Rafter, *The Criminal Brain*.

organized crime introducing order into otherwise chaotic markets and ineffectual or weak political regimes; deviance resolving problems of anomaly and ambiguity in classification schemes;[10] crime reinforcing social cohesion;[11] and, in a later, radical twist, offenders and prisoners deflecting popular discontents from structured inequalities on to mass-produced scapegoats.[12] There was almost no place there for the pathos and pains of individual victimization or the personal and communal costs of everyday crime.

Symbolic interactionism or 'labelling theory', the approach ostensibly wedded to an empathetic description of how people jointly construct lines of action in everyday life, should have accommodated the victim in its analyses of rule-breaking, but it failed to do so because it tended to drift towards crimes *without* victims: the crimes that are 'created when we attempt to ban through criminal legislation the exchange between willing partners of strongly desired goods or services', and their repression was used principally to illustrate the folly and oppressiveness of many rules and much formal control.[13] As was noted in previous chapters, the interactionists' and phenomenologists' was a largely inward-looking focus that, for purposes of appreciation and easy access to research populations, encouraged them to examine the behaviour of themselves and others like themselves, the sexual deviants, political radicals, and drug-users, who may have had no easily identifiable victims.[14] In all this, they seemed to have entertained almost no notion of rule-breaking as hurtful or distressing. Rather it was fun, romantic, and often heroic (and cultural criminologists, talking about 'edgework' and the excitements of transgression, have perpetuated that vision).[15] Lacking a clear vision of the victim, formal control became little more than an incomprehensible aggravating factor that amplified and confirmed deviance, generating so-called 'secondary deviation',[16] and applied, in many cases, to no good purpose other than to convey the inflated moral indignation of the community and provide work for agencies of social control.[17] In that formulation, in a relativized, negotiated, and morally ambiguous world, there was a 'vacillation between the image of the deviant as mismanaged victim and the deviant as cultural hero'.[18] It 'is not easy', said Sagarin,[19] 'to divide the world into victims and offenders. The hunted fugitive is a victim, but so are people upon whom he preys; and, potentially, the hunters—the decision-making, overdog, and putatively oppressive police—may be victims as well'.

Radical criminologists preferred to talk of crimes as the ephemera of the terminal stages of a capitalist society—the outcome of possessive individualism, class resentment, or primitive rebellion[20]—that would not survive the coming of socialism. And, whilst capitalism lasted, it was argued, there were other, far more pressing issues to consider: the problems of class inequalities, institutional racism, colonialism, misogyny,

[10] M. Douglas, *Purity and Danger*.   [11] K. Erikson, *Wayward Puritans*.

[12] M. Foucault, *Discipline and Punish*; J. Reiman, *The Rich get Richer*.

[13] E. Schur, *Crimes without Victims*.   [14] S. Cohen and L. Taylor, *Escape Attempts*, 2.

[15] J. Ferrell et al., *Cultural Criminology*, 18.   [16] E. Lemert, *Social Pathology*.

[17] H. Becker, *Outsiders*; K. Erikson *Wayward Puritans*.   [18] S. Cohen, 'Guilt, Justice and Tolerance', 19.

[19] E. Sagarin, *Deviants and Deviance*, 133.

[20] E. Hobsbawm, *Primitive Rebels*; I. Taylor et al, *The New Criminology*.

structured oppression, and exploitation and human rights violations.[21] In the language of the time, criminology should 'constitute its own object' and occupy itself with a core critical agenda, not with the petty distractions of volume crime that capitalism and its lawmakers placed in its path. *Those* were held to be the drivers and themes appropriate to a critical criminology, not, say, the relatively insignificant problems of street crime, burglary, and anti-social behaviour. A vocabulary of moral crusade and moral entrepreneurship,[22] moral panic,[23] and moral censure[24] could in its turn be deployed, sometimes carelessly, to dismiss popular fears about crime as ideologically manipulated, misdirected, and irrational. The fear of everyday crime became tantamount to a figment of false consciousness. If there *were* real victims to be acknowledged, they were the immiserated proletariat, the racial underclass, the exploited and unheeded victims of corporate crime, and the prisoners and criminals, who were the real casualties of repressive criminal justice practices. So it was that everyday conceptions of crime could readily be dismissed as obfuscation, demagoguery, penal populism, authoritarian populism, or some other dismissive term for the political malaise or unreason that was thought to distract the so-called subaltern classes. Some even took it that Marxism should not deign to busy itself with crime at all.[25]

There was, by extension, something of a distaste in criminology at large, and in radical criminology in particular, about any involvement with the victim and his or her problems. To study victims was in effect to collude with the politics of a reactionary mob and the machinations of the powerful, heeding groups whose world-views subverted the authority and competence of the progressive criminologist. Garland[26] put it that 'The dominant voice of crime policy is no longer the expert or even the practitioner but that of the long-suffering, ill-served people—especially of 'the victim' and the fearful, anxious members of the public.' Elsewhere he states 'The interests and feelings of victims—actual victims, victims' families, potential victims, the projected figure of "the victim" are now routinely invoked in support of measures of punitive segregation.'[27] One wonders why the word 'victim' should have been placed in quotation marks, and conveyed in such a deprecating fashion, as if it were intended to suggest that the victim's status was merely alleged or *soi-disant*, and not really achieved in good faith at all. Victims, in short, were regarded as potentially dangerous and tainted people with a disturbing history and worrying associations and there was something else permeating that unease. Victims do have something of the 'other' about them.

The Concise Oxford English Dictionary defines *victim* as a 'living creature sacrificed to a deity in performance of religious rite; person or thing injured or destroyed in seeking to obtain an object, in gratification of a passion etc., or as a result of event or circumstance; prey, dupe.'[28] It is a word that evokes strong images of pain, loss of control,

---

[21] P. Hillyard and C Pantazis, *Beyond Criminology: Taking Harm Seriously.*

[22] H. Becker, *Outsiders.*   [23] S. Cohen, *Folk Devils and Moral Panics*, 3rd edn.

[24] C. Sumner, *Censure, Politics and Criminal Justice.*

[25] P. Hirst, 'Marx and Engels on Law, Crime and Morality'.

[26] D. Garland, 'The Culture of High Crime Societies', 13.

[27] D. Garland, 'The Limits of the Sovereign State', 445.

[28] *The Concise Oxford English Dictionary*, 1197.

and submissiveness. It is not a role that anyone would willingly assume. Those be-reaved by murder and manslaughter talk about the primitive fear and embarrassment they believe they provoke, how people do not know what to say to them, sometimes crossing the road in an attempt to avoid them lest their bad luck becomes contagious.[29] And it is as if criminologists themselves have also, in effect, often crossed that road.

The Origins of Victimology

Victimology was founded more or less independently in the 1940s by Beniamin Mendelsohn; Hans von Hentig, Stephen Schafer, and Fredric Wertham.[30] Criminology proper lacking much interest in victims, and victims themselves being 'tainted', victi-mology could not but appear with an odd genealogy, late and from the sidelines, pro-moted by idiosyncratic scholars and activists, and it exhibited some peculiar traits. It was probably inevitable that the first victimologists were unconventional scholars, lying on the outer reaches of the academic study of crime, psychology, psychiatry and the law, wedded to doctrines that may now appear somewhat eccentric or *passé*, and later to be described by one unfriendly critic as 'the lunatic fringe of criminology'.[31] One of the fathers of victimology, von Hentig declared, for instance, that he was attached to the Italian school of criminal anthropology (a school associated with Cesare Lombroso) and to ideas of moral imbecility and constitutional immorality. And it was Mendelsohn,[32] also claimed as the father of victimology, who first awarded the sub-discipline a name and declared it his ambition to analyse the victim from the 'the bio-psycho-social point of view', a project that betrayed a certain grandiosity of purpose.

Victim-Precipitation

The principal foundational idea of those first scholars was *victim-precipitation* and, for good or bad reasons, it came to dog the standing of the sub-discipline thereafter. It was Mendelsohn[33] who first propounded a theory of victim-precipitation, and it alludes to the criminally provocative, collusive, or causal impact of the victim in a dyadic rela-tion variously called the 'penal couple'; the 'reciprocal action between perpetrator and victim';[34] the 'duet theory of crime';[35] a 'situated transaction';[36] 'the functional respon-sibility for crime',[37] or, simply, 'the victim-offender relationship'.[38]

---

[29] P. Rock, *After Homicide*.   [30] W. Doerner and S. Lab, *Victimology*; L Zedner, 'Victims'.

[31] C. Becker, *Criminal Theories of Causation*, 4.

[32] B. Mendelsohn, 'The Origin of the Doctrine of Victimology', 239.

[33] B. Mendelsohn, 'The Origin of the Doctrine of Victimology', 241.

[34] H. von Hentig, 'Remarks on the Interaction of Perpetrator and Victim', 303.

[35] H. von Hentig, 'Remarks on the Interaction of Perpetrator and Victim', 397.

[36] D. Luckenbill, 'Criminal Homicide as a Situated Transaction'.

[37] S. Schafer, *The Victim and his Criminal*, 55.

[38] M. Wolfgang, 'Victim-precipitated Criminal Homicide', 1.

At one pole, victim-precipitation can portray crime quite neutrally as an interactive process or evolving relation between victim and offender, in which each influences not only the conduct of the other but also the form and content of any crime that may ensue. Douglas and Waksler[39] argued that 'perpetrator and victim commonly appear to be involved in a social encounter where the acts of each affect those of the other'. Reiss[40] said much the same when he stressed 'the importance of theories about victimization focusing upon the behavior of all parties to crime events rather than resorting to separate theories about victimization and offending or about victims and offenders'. Collins[41] carried the notion forward to effect in his detailed analysis of the choreography of violent encounters in which victim and offender effectively collaborated together in 'interaction ritual chains'. No exception could be taken to those formulations. Of course, not all crime is significantly interactive—some burglaries and thefts are only tangentially so—but the attention of the early victimologists was fixed on the graver instances of law-breaking, on rape, assault, and murder, and it is important to note that it was framed from the start in a very special way that has perhaps been too little appreciated.

Aspects of victims and victimization are indelibly shaped by the assumptions, ambitions, methods, and questions that scholars apply to observe them. In this, victimology's first big idea, 'victimization' was seen through the eyes of Mendelsohn, a practising defence attorney, and his epiphany occurred during the course of a murder trial. Thoughts of victim-precipitation (and victimology) welled up in the construction of a defence case: 'It was while preparing for the trial of Stephan Codreanu[42] arraigned in 1945 for a crime passionel', he recalled, 'that I began to elaborate the doctrine of Victimology. . . . There can be no doubt that, had it not been for the perversity of his former wife, he would never have been guilty of two crimes . . .'. His allegation was that responsibility for Codreanu's offence should, in effect, be attributed to a wife who had effectively invited what had befallen her. The implications are startling.

There are perhaps three principal defences in any murder trial: the defendant was not there at the time of the alleged offence; someone else did it; or the victim provoked the offence or struck the first blow, thereby lessening the charge to one of second-degree murder or manslaughter, on the one hand, or self-defence, on the other. Defence lawyers are not obliged to be disinterested and impartial. They must be fearless in the discharge of their obligations to promote their clients' interests. They must accept instructions, however fanciful they may appear to be. A defence, in other words, is a lop-sided and motivated construction, one of a pair of competing narratives, that is almost invariably balanced by an equal and opposite account offered by the prosecution. In murder cases fought in the adversarial system, not only is the victim silent but there is no one briefed formally to speak on his or her behalf. It was a consequence that what Mendelsohn introduced into victimology from the beginning was but one side of that pair, and it is not remarkable that victim-precipitation could occasionally take

[39] J. Douglas and F. Waksler, *The Sociology of Deviance*, 249.
[40] A. Reiss, 'Towards a Revitalisation of Theory and Research on Victimisation by Crime', 710.
[41] R. Collins, *Violence*.   [42] B. Mendelsohn, 'The Origin of the Doctrine of Victimology', 241.

a peculiar and distorted form. Victims were portrayed just as their perpetrators would have wished, as people who were causally and, indeed, often culpably complicit in their own downfall. They provoked, conspired, or were lulled into becoming a target. They deserved their fate, and it was that suggestion of moral and causal implication that haunted the idea of victim-precipitation ever after.

So it was that Porterfield and Talbert[43]could remark 'It is amazing to note the large number of would-be murderers who become the victim.' So it was that von Hentig,[44] having also taken up the baton of victim-precipitation, produced a curious taxonomy of murder victims which included the *depressive* 'who lacks ordinary prudence and discretion'; the *greedy of gain* 'who lack all normal inhibitions and well-founded suspicions'; the *wanton type*, where 'female foibles play a role'; and the *tormentor-type*, 'the most primitive way of solving a personal conflict [being] to annihilate physically the cause of the trouble . . .'. 'Are we permitted', he continued, 'to say that in some cases criminality is a self-consuming process of anti-social elements in which criminals prey on criminaloids, killers on suicides on other killers, oversexed on oversexed, dishonest individuals on dishonest?'.

Despite its lack of balance, victim-precipitation played an influential part in the development of theories of criminal victimization. Wolfgang[45] acknowledged that 'von Hentig . . . provided the most useful theoretical basis for analysis of the victim-offender relationship' and then proceeded to employ police and other official records to examine patterns of victim involvement in killings in Philadelphia. He was to be followed by Luckenbill, Polk,[46] and others, all of whom leaned heavily on von Hentig, Wolfgang, and the 'duet theory of crime'. Quite typical was Avison,[47] who argued that ' . . . . the role of the victim is not restricted to precipitation of the crime . . . The victim can contribute in many different ways to the interaction preceding the aggressive behavior, and it may be more meaningful to consider such involvement on a continuum . . . culminating in active participation by the victim'.

Feminist Victimology

The second, double-edged strand of ideas injected into victimology was both internally contradictory and quite at odds with the theorizing that has just been described, and it only uncertainly belongs to the body of victimology proper at all. As was discussed in the last chapter, feminist criminology had a radical tinge from the first, and it arose in large measure as a protest against the domain assumptions of radical criminology. Women, it was said, were raped, abused, assaulted, and harassed, and their wholesale neglect by male criminologists constituted not only a political and sexist affront but an analytic and empirical gap. Victimizations were indisputably real and immediate, and they required exposure, analysis, and redress. Smart[48] lambasted the way in which

---

[43] A. Porterfield and R. Talbert, *Mid-Century Crime in our Culture*, 48.

[44] von Hentig, 'Remarks on the Interaction of Perpetrator and Victim', 304–6, 309.

[45] Wolfgang, 'Victim-precipitated Criminal Homicide', 1.

[46] D. Luckenbill, 'Criminal Homicide as a Situated Transaction'; K. Polk, *When Men Kill*.

[47] N. Avison, 'Victims of Homicide', 58.   [48] C. Smart, *Women, Crime and Criminology*.

women as offenders and victims had been anathematized, and she proposed their re-instatement within an analytic framework emphasizing the workings of patriarchal power and male myopia. Women, her successors[49] came to argue, are kept firmly in their social, spatial, economic, political, and sexual place by the exercise of male coercive control. They are persuaded through fear of male censure and violence to remain submissive within the private, domestic sphere.

Women were, in short, to be thought of as victims generically and individually subjugated by the workings of patriarchy. And looming large, the first stirrings of victimology supplied an appropriate foil not only for contesting the meanings of victimization, gender, and power but also for establishing a countervailing feminist criminology. Early feminist criminology was elaborated through 'immanent critique', a series of running criticisms which amounted to an alternative theory, and one of its prime objects was the failing of criminology and victimology to comprehend female victimization.

Matters escalated when Menachem Amir applied without significant modification of Wolfgang's methodology and even the style of his book title, not to cases of homicide, but to rape. Homicide victims tend not to be available for observation and interview but rape victims might well be so. Yet Amir followed Wolfgang and faithfully relied on official records, talking neither to rape complainants nor to any other participant, and hearing no insider's account of what might have happened. Quoting von Hentig, he said 'We are accustomed to believe that forcible rape is an act which falls upon the victim without her aid or cooperation, but there is often "some reciprocal action between perpetrator and victim" in such cases.'[50] He then proceeded to produce an inventory of victim characteristics that could trigger a sexual assault, and they included meeting an offender in a bar, picnic, or party, possessing a 'bad' reputation, and consuming alcohol. That was a cluster of allegations too far and it was very timely. It became an iconic target for a number of feminists who re-named victim-precipitation misogynist 'victim-blaming'. Lamb[51] protested, 'At the root of all victim-blaming are the perpetrator's own attempts to present the victim as the cause of his violence or abuse . . . Perpetrators will . . . claim that their victims are almost directly responsible for their fates, that the little girl wanted to be fondled, that the raped woman was asking for it, and that the abused wife provoked her beating.' The political and intellectual standing of victim-precipitation plummeted in some quarters and, with it, that of victimology itself. For Meier and Miethe,[52] 'The implication of blame in victim-precipitation analyses has inhibited full development of the concept.' Fattah[53] may have protested at the reaction, describing it as 'unwarranted attacks and unfounded ideological criticism' that revealed no flaws in the integrity of the idea of victim-precipitation itself, only in its execution, but the damage had been done. The very idea that victims, and female victims in particular, can play a role in the formation of criminal events continues to be anathema to some. Nevertheless, once feminism had been established as a solid

---

[49] S. Brownmiller, *Against Our Will*; E. A. Stanko, *Everyday Violence*; P. Bourgois, *In Search of Masculinity*; E. Stark *Coercive Control*; M. P. Johnson, *A Typology of Domestic Violence*.

[50] M. Amir, 'Victim Precipitated Forcible Rape', 493.   [51] L. Lamb, *The Trouble with Blaming*, 78, 79.

[52] R. Meier and T. Miethe, 'Understanding Theories of Criminal Victimization', 463.

[53] E. Fattah, 'Victimology Past, Present and Future', 2.

enterprise in the 1980s and 1990s, it became possible for many women criminologists to move on, distance themselves critically from its early writings, and embark on a flurry of revisions. They remonstrated that, in concentrating on the woman as victim, early feminists had all too frequently colluded in manufacturing an imagery that stressed passivity and submission. An exclusive but indefensible preoccupation with the victimization of women obscured criminal acts committed against men, as if men were never victims and always perpetrators.[54] There were male victims of domestic violence.[55] There were male victims of rape and violence.[56] There were violent female *offenders* and on occasion sexual offenders.[57] There was also a diversity of female victims and offenders differentiated by class, race, ethnicity, and sexuality, not just a single, undifferentiated mass.

Gender began to be interpreted as a binary concept, taking its meaning from the paired contrasts of male and female, and some academic feminists began to progress towards a more balanced consideration of *masculinity* as a counterpoint to their work on femininity.[58] And it then became possible to speak not of a single feminist criminology (or victimology) but of *feminisms* and *criminologies*. Carol Smart[59] even came to question whether it was any longer politically or analytically productive to consider women in a context of crime, victimization, and criminal justice at all. Placing them in such a restricted setting narrowed the analytical focus and invited uncongenial associations.

Feminist criminology had been galvanized in part by a practical and political preoccupation with the injustices experienced by victims of rape, incest, and domestic violence, and by a methodology and epistemology that restored a voice to those whom it studied. There was to be a concomitant strain: those who had founded the early rape crisis centres and women's refuges in the 1970s elevated the importance of victims' experiences and of practical action, and, on occasion, they challenged the right of academics and clinicians to speak about what they had undergone, what they were doing, and who they were. They subordinated academic analysis to testimony, and their evidence lay in narratives of pain and transcendence relayed by the victims themselves.[60] Theirs were stories of suffering and fortitude, and there was an important shift over time away from the alleged quietism and defeat of the language of victimization. They were *survivors*, not victims, casualties of patriarchy, not of crime commonly conceived, and they drew away from the world of crime, deviance, criminal justice, criminology, and victimology.

But they and other activists were also frequently to be found in the same spaces—the conferences, workshops and seminars—as the academic writers with whom they were in uneasy relation and whose legitimacy they questioned. At the beginning, too, they

---

[54] S. Walklate, 'Researching Victims', 189.

[55] Although it should be noted that the frequency and severity of their injuries is less than that of women—see C. Mirrlees-Black, *Domestic Violence*; A. Grady, 'Female-on-male Domestic Abuse', 77.

[56] C. Cohen et al., *Male Rape Is a Feminist Issue.*   [57] M. Matravers, *Justifying the Unjustifiable.*

[58] T. Newburn and E. A. Stanko, *Just Boys Doing Business.*

[59] C. Smart, *Feminism and the Power of Law.*

[60] P. Eastel, *Voices of the Survivors*; K. Plummer, *Telling Sexual Stories.*

were mistrustful of men (the Women's Aid Federation of England would not allow men into their buildings, although the 'independent' refuges did otherwise). To be sure, alignments were not always uniform (members of the Canadian women's movement were always more pragmatic than many of their English counterparts, for example). Neither were they unchanging over time. But a series of political and ontological tensions about definition, authority, hierarchy, and ownership were planted in and around victimology and there they remain.

The feminist challenge made its mark on radical criminology. In tandem with the new instrument of crime surveys, which will be touched on next, it obliged some radical criminologists to concede that not all everyday forms of crime could be lightly dismissed, and that the victimization of women should certainly be taken seriously as a political and social problem. Jones, Maclean, and Young[61] remarked how there had been 'a general tendency in radical thought to idealize [its] historical subject (in this case the working class) and to play down intra-group conflict, blemishes and social disorganization. But the power of the feminist case resulted in a sort of cognitive schizophrenia amongst radicals . . .'. To be sure, shibboleths remained: it proved awkward politically for those three recanting authors to probe too extensively into the background of the high numbers of black women victims they had unearthed in a local crime survey, because that would have dangerously exposed black male *offenders*, but a dent had been made, and it prepared the way for what was to be called 'left realism', the new socialist criminology which could more readily accommodate the brute facts of crime and victimization, and insert victims into a new conceptual contrivance, a quadrilateral of causal forces, that was built on the offender, the victim, informal social control, and the State.[62]

Feminist victimology heralded the emergence of what Haug and Sussman[63] called the 'revolt of the client', a challenge to professional expertise in the name of experiential knowledge. It was accompanied by new, competing claims to authority and the right to speak by victims/survivors and groups of victims/survivors who had attained expertise through their own testimonies of intense personal experience. We know rather little about how victims acquire an understanding of how they should act and who they are in different settings.[64] Many incidents leave little lasting impact. But one moral path is clear. Those who call themselves victims or survivors for any length of time tend to be those whose identity has been irrevocably defined by suffering from a harrowing offence or a succession of linked offences, such as domestic violence or hate crimes that is so harrowing that it marks an existential turning-point. They are, parroting Karl Marx, those who might be called victims *für sich* rather than victims *an sich*, those who are not 'merely' and briefly victims but people who have acquired (and constructed) an enduring 'master status' as victims or survivors, and the way in which they and others choose to describe their condition tends to be couched in the quasi-medical language

---

[61] T. Jones, B. Maclean, and J. Young, *The Islington Crime Survey*, 2–3.
[62] J. Lea and J. Young, *What is to Be Done about Law and Order?*.
[63] M. Haug and S. Sussman, 'Professional Autonomy and the Revolt of the Client'.
[64] P. Rock, 'On Being a Victim'.

of trauma and post-traumatic stress disorder[65]—although that is not necessarily what they mean. They may regard themselves as experts in their own right, entitled to contest the competence and standing of experts and policy-makers. Muir, the president of an Australian victims' organization, the National Association for Loss and Grief, said quite characteristically: 'The telling of individual stories about the human experience of being a victim of crime is an attempt to give voice to an experience which cannot adequately be described through the interpretation of crime statistics'.[66] They are persistent, animated, and organized, and they can command sympathy and support, working increasingly through social media and attracting the attention of the mass media, dominating crime stories, and making an indelible impression on how politicians and others interpret the facts of crime. They have even acquired a power of veto over how public inquiries into victimization should be conducted in England and Wales, effectively serving to dismiss two women who had been nominated to chair a public inquiry into historic child abuse in 2014. So it has come about that more and more frequently, in Anglo-Saxon jurisdictions, victims have come almost exclusively to be represented for analytic, practical, and political purposes as those who have been sexually abused, subject to violent attacks, or bereaved through the murder or manslaughter of family members.[67] Others, the victims of volume crime—theft, robbery, malicious damage, fraud, and so on—have tended to be eclipsed in the process, so that when victims are discussed in many quarters, including the academic world, it is only a small, atypical sub-population who come into view.

The third principal source of victimology was empirical—but no empirical inquiry is ever free of theorizing. Large household surveys of victims were conducted first in the United States, in 1973,[68] and they were designed principally to assist the curtailing of violence by ascertaining what was thought to be the 'real' extent and character of criminal victimization.[69] They were followed by similar surveys in Canada in 1981 (where they were at first opportunistically presented as an exploration of trends in violence succeeding the imminent abolition of capital punishment), and in the United Kingdom in 1982 (where they were at first opportunistically presented within government as a purposive way of responding to the 1981 Brixton riots, and later as a mechanism to improve what was called 'the criminal justice data base'[70]). There would eventually be international crime surveys which compared victimization rates across nations and over time and, within nations, local surveys which looked intensively at crime in neighbourhoods.

Crime surveys chart a population's experience of crime over a given period, and usually of a year. They are plastic instruments, adaptable to different purposes and changing in significance. In the beginning, they were a means of securing a better measure

---

[65] D. Fassin and R. Rechtman, *The Empire of Trauma*; P. Rock, 'Aspects of the Social Construction of Crime Victims in Australia'.

[66] H. Muir, 'Voices of Victims of Crime', 179.   [67] P. Rock, 'Victims Rights'.

[68] Although the British General Household Survey of 1972 (OPCS, 1972) did contain a question about experience of burglary.

[69] A. Biderman and A. Reiss, 'On Exploring the Dark Figure of Crime'.

[70] P. Rock, *A View from the Shadows*; P. Rock, *Helping Victims of Crime*.

of offending, and they concentrated on the victim chiefly as a source of data closest to the so-called dark figure of crime, acting as a check on police records. The authors of the first British Crime Survey reported in 1983 that 'It is one thing to identify the shortcomings of statistics or recorded offences as a measure of crime, quite another to provide an alternative. Only recently has a research technique been developed with this aim in mind—the sample survey of victimization, or "crime survey". The international crime surveys were similarly prompted by the inadequacy of police recording practices for comparing crime in different countries and the absence of alternative standardized measures'.[71]

But it was inevitable that crime surveys also began to yield copious information about other matters: the impact, distribution, incidence, trends, and severity of crime;[72] victims' experiences and perceptions of crime and the criminal justice system; victims' fear of crime and anti-social behaviour; and much else. They mapped crime in ways hitherto conceived methodologically impossible and financially unaffordable, and victimology was flooded with new data. An ever expanding analytic industry was established on their back, showing for example, how crime was massively concentrated spatially in what became known as 'hot spots',[73] socially and temporally.[74] Victimization was not distributed broadly and evenly across society, but in relatively dense pockets where groups and individuals[75] could expect repeatedly to be subject to burglary, theft, robbery, and assault. The best predictor of *who* might be a victim of property crime is recent victimization.[76] The best predictor of *where* a property crime might take place is a home recently burgled and the homes adjacent to it.[77]

Crime is so concentrated that offenders, victims, and witnesses could not but be recruited from very much the same populations (so that, for instance, the young men who assault young men in city centres at night are most likely to have been observed by other young men, because it was they who are abroad at that time and in those places). Jock Young once asked who one's murderer would probably be, and he replied 'If you pick up a mirror and look into it, you will see the image of your most likely attacker.

---

[71] M. Hough and P. Mayhew, *The British Crime Survey*, 1.

[72] Thus crime reported by victims in England and Wales has been steadily decreasing for some twenty years. The survey for July 2015 showed a further drop of 7 per cent, taking figures back to those of 1981, when the first survey was mounted (<http://www.ons.gov.uk/ons/dcp171778_392380.pdf>). It should be noted that the survey does omit certain kinds of crime—those committed against institutions and other kinds of impersonal victim, for instance; and as a household survey, it excludes homeless people. Marian Fitzgerald has also pointed out that it also neglects newer forms of cyber-crime such as online fraud. She comments that 'there seems to have been relatively little interest in some very significant changes in patterns of crime as a result of . . . developments in technology over the last 20 years. Still less attention has been given to the fact that many traditional offences are increasingly being committed in new ways thanks to these developments. Yet these are now conspicuous by their absence from both official measures of trends in crime'. (<http://www.crimeandjustice.org.uk/resources/curious-case-fall-crime>).

[73] L. Sherman, P. Gartin, and M. Buerger, 'Hot Spots of Predatory Crime'.

[74] A. Tseloni and K. Pease, 'Repeat Personal Victimization'.

[75] K. Pease and G. Farrell, *Once Bitten, Twice Shy*; A. Tseloni and K. Pease, 'Area and Individual Differences in Persona; Crime Victimization Incidence'.

[76] G. Farrell and A. Bouloukos, 'A Cross National Comparison of Rates of Repeat Victimization'.

[77] K. Bowers et al., 'Prospective Hot-spotting'.

He will be of the same class as you, of the same ethnic group, probably the same age, a member of your own social circle—dressing like you, with the same accent and habits.'[78] Crime predominantly took place *within*, not across, social strata, the working class attacking the working class, the young the young, males males, minority ethnic groups minority ethnic groups. At the very epicentre, where offending was most rife in the eye of the victimological storm, such social areas could be chaotic and confused indeed. Genn's graphic observations of one 'hot spot', included life in an apartment where fights, verbal abuse, sexual assault and property theft were commonplace, and where the use of violence in the resolution of conflict was virtually automatic'.[79]

Those new maps of crime were to supply the second dent to radical criminology: crime was evidently not centred on the equitable redistribution of property between social classes. It did not serve, as the radicals used to say, to expropriate the expropriators or to exercise class justice, but, in Downes' words, as a regressive tax on the poor.[80]

Smith and Gray[81] reported of a survey in London that 'to a considerable extent the police deal with a limited clientele of people who tend to be in trouble both as victims and as offenders . . . people who tend to be repeatedly victims also have a much higher chance of being arrested'. It became increasingly difficult to conceive of victims and offenders as groups apart, the one wholly innocent and the other wholly guilty, but as members of substantially overlapping groups of people who resemble one another in many particulars, no longer a confrontation between black and white, but of 'grey versus grey'.[82] Elias[83] remarked that it in certain volatile areas, 'it becomes almost a matter of chance as to who will be the victim and who will be the offender for any particular crime, almost a matter of who strikes first. Consequently, it is difficult to clearly attribute guilt . . . '. In certain particularly active areas of society, the hotspots, victims, and offenders may change roles erratically and frequently the moral contours of 'victims' and 'offenders' thereby became a little more blurred in the academy, even though broader political, news media, and activist accounts remained substantially unaffected.

Routine Activities

If victim-precipitation is recognized conventionally as the first victimological theory, a second is routine activities theory, or what some call lifestyle theory victimologically-construed, and it flowed in part out of the crime survey. There is an obvious and strong affinity between hazard-based theories and crime surveys which 'reveal that some persons may be prone to victimization' and risk of victimization.[84] The theory is economy itself: it predicts that crime will occur where there is a convergence in space and time of what are named 'likely offenders, suitable targets and an absence of capable guardians',

---

[78] J. Young, 'Murder Most English', 5.   [79] H. Genn, 'Multiple Victimization', 99.

[80] D. Downes, 'Foreword'.   [81] D. Smith and J. Gray, *Police and People in London*, Vol, 1, 124.

[82] J. Pizarro et al., 'Assessing the Interaction between Offender and Victim Criminal Lifestyles and Homicide Type'.

[83] R. Elias, *Victims of the System*, 253.

[84] M. Gottfredson and M. Hindelang, 'Sociological Aspects of Criminal Victimisation', 123.

and that 'the spatio-temporal organization of society affects patterns of crime . . . Strong variations in specific predatory crime rates from hour to hour, day to day [affect reporting] . . . and these variations appear to correspond to the various tempos of the related legitimate activities upon which they feed'.[85] Crimes, in other words, tend to be moulded by the mundane structures of social life, and they are likely most frequently to occur in areas with the greatest concentrations of people, especially young and single people, and the greatest density of possessions—those self-same hotspots.[86] Convergence in space and time is likely to be enabled by the increased mobility and capacity to re-move goods offered by vehicles; by the building of roads that encourage movement and the geographical dispersal of populations; by shifting patterns of employment that may leave homes unattended; by the demographics of divorce, late marriage, physical longevity, and small families that lead to a proliferation of single person households with their weak guardianship; by new forms of technology which may reduce the size and increase the portability of electrical and electronic goods, and much else.

Victims and Victimization

The rise of victimology and the issues illuminated by crime surveys encouraged schol-ars to ask new and important questions about victims, and they were encouraged by members of government agencies who were becoming ever more anxious about what appeared to be victims' dissatisfaction with the criminal justice system at a time when crime rates were rising inexorably, and police 'clear-up' rates and the numbers of prose-cutions and convictions were falling. The system depended on victims to report crimes and testify in court and it was clear that their experiences were often so disagreeable that they could become intimidated and estranged.

The passage of victims through the criminal justice system became a matter of great practical and academic interest. Shapland et al. was one of the first pieces of research to report a decaying of satisfaction with police responses, a hunger for information and control, an interest in monetary compensation that was far outweighed by a yearning for symbolic recognition, and an experience of their vicissitudes in the criminal justice as, in effect, a form of 'secondary victimization'.[87] The reiterated complaint made by vic-tims after cross-examination in court was that they were made to feel on trial, as if *they* were the wrongdoer. After all, lawyers in the adversarial system do subject witnesses to identical techniques of questioning, irrespective of whether they testify on behalf of the prosecution or defence, in the hope that they will expose (or will be seen *trying* to expose) flaws of memory, inconsistencies of testimony, and defects of character.[88] Morgan and Zedner [89] uncovered the extent of the anguish suffered by child victims at first and second hand, victims who, as witnesses and household members, had often

---

[85] L. Cohen and M. Felson, 'Social Change and Crime Rates Trends', 588, 592.
[86] J. van Kesteren et al., 'The International Crime Victims Surveys', 53.
[87] J. Shapland et al., *Victims in the Criminal Justice System.*
[88] A. Bottoms and J. V. Roberts (eds.), *Hearing the Victim.*   [89] J. Morgan and L. Zedner, *Child Victims.*

been overlooked unless it was as the direct and obvious target of abuse or violence. Children tend to be mute bystanders, all too readily overshadowed, but they could be as discomfited as any by mundane crime such as burglary. Morgan's and Zedner's was one of the first of a number of empirical studies that began to map formerly unexplored victim populations. Running in tandem to their book, there was, for instance, research on racist and 'homophobic' crime, and crimes against the elderly and the disabled, and the population of known victims began to grow ever more crowded, possibly, indeed, over-crowded, as it became swollen with groups newly identified or demanding recognition. It became evident that fresh groups of victims were continually emerging or being invented; that generalization was becoming ever more fraught; and that definitions and boundaries were unstable and ever more eagerly disputed.[90] Although victimization is disagreeable and unwelcome, clearly at stake in an increasingly crowded space were questions of 'respect', recognition, legitimation, compensation, exculpation, and much else. It seemed that there were not only 'primary' victims, the immediate casualties of crime; but 'secondary' victims, who had a family or other intimate connection with those casualties; and others more distant still. Debates about eligibility could become quite heated. Were the police officers, court staff, medical and para-medical staff who witnessed or responded to traumatic incidents to be called 'tertiary victims'? Were they casual spectators? Were soldiers witnessing distressing scenes in battle? Were the families of those killed in homicides or, more contentiously still, in traffic 'accidents'? Who was to count as family? And what of the families of serious offenders, some of whom laid claim to the title of 'the other victims of crime'?[91] Holstein and Miller[92] reflected that "'victim' is a categorization device . . . an interpretive framework . . . that provides a set of instructions for understanding social relations . . . As an act of interpretive reality construction, victimization unobtrusively advises others in how they should understand persons, circumstances, and behaviors under consideration'. And those social relations and that framework are not fixed but emergent and contested, and they may well be anything but progressive or unobtrusive.

Victimology, Human Rights, and Transitional Justice

Victim-precipitation, feminist criminology, routine activities theory and victim case studies are the main home-grown constituents of a full-blown victimology. But victims have also been studied by those working on human rights who might never choose to call themselves victimologists or knowingly contribute to the body of victimological theory. Their writings are necessarily piecemeal but they may also be a valuable resource for the victimologist and criminologist. There is, first, what might be identified as standard scholarly work which alighted on victims, discovering new facts and new patterns of association, but not fully warranting or claiming the title of victimology,

---

[90] J. Jacobs and K. Potter, *Hate Crimes*; M. Pendergast, *Victims of Memory*.
[91] P. Rock, 'Murderers, Victims and "Survivors"'.
[92] J. Holstein and G. Miller, 'Rethinking Victimization', 105, 107.

unless victimology includes *any* piece of academic writing that refers at some point to the victim. Victims will usually materialize here in contingent fashion, rising to the surface as institutions or circumstances evolve. For instance, in a human rights violations context, important questions have emerged about the identity, role, rights, and significance of victims in the new forms of transitional justice, the international criminal tribunals and peace and reconciliation hearings, that have been developed to manage problems of accountability and accommodation in post-conflict societies. Is it better to confront and interrogate or to forget past crimes and injustices? If there is to be a scrutiny of old atrocities, should all parties to conflict be exposed equally, or only those who were, in effect, the losers? Are victims to be given a voice? Are they to be present merely for evidential purposes or for some more substantial end—to educate, expose, purge, or even dictate how proceedings should be conducted? Are they to receive reparation and, if so, what form should it take? Are their demands compatible with the restoration of social harmony and political stability? In return for telling the truth, are those who committed crimes against them to be awarded immunity from prosecution? If so, what might the consequences be for society at large and the victim in particular? Given that transitional justice typically involves multiple objectives, defendants, victims, and legal representatives, given the many conflicting accounts of what may have happened, how is reality to be pieced together and managed for purposes of adjudication, reconciliation, and analysis?[93] Braithwaite's work on restorative justice[94] illuminates the role that can be played by victims and their supporters in mobilizing sentiments of shame and animating rituals of reintegration in confrontations with offenders and their supporters, and it has re-awakened a strong interest in the potential role of the victim in areas of criminology, criminal justice policy, and dispute resolution. But Braithwaite's victim was a minor figure who hardly occupies centre stage and it would be difficult to claim that his research was a piece of *victimology*. Perhaps a better candidate would be the evaluation of RISE, a restorative justice experiment that looked squarely at victims' responses, although it was instigated somewhat as an afterthought and late in the planning of the larger project. Interestingly, it now appears to be the case that what began life as an attempt better to understand and re-integrate offenders has evolved into a scheme whose principal effect has been to make victims less fearful, vengeful, and distressed.[95] It can work through what Rossner[96] has described as a transformative, ritual process in which victims, offenders, and their supporters can become emotionally enmeshed with one another, experiencing a sense of solidarity and a new capacity to take one another's roles, seeing events through the other's eyes. And her work, in its turn, is beginning to open up an examination of the social role of emotions in justice processes. Criminology has made occasional use of victims and victimology to develop points about questions lying more squarely in

---

[93] H. Weinstein, 'Victims, Transitional Justice and Social Reconstruction'; C. McCarthy, *Reparations and Victim Support in the International Court*; S. Buckley-Zistel et al., *Transitional Justice Theories.*

[94] J. Braithwaite, *Crime, Shame and Reintegration.*

[95] L. Sherman and H. Strang, *Restorative Justice: the Evidence*; H. Strang *Repair or Revenge.*

[96] M. Rossner, *Just Emotions.*

its heartland. It was in that sense that victims have been described instrumentally as failures of crime prevention. Block remarked, for example, that 'the study of victims of crime is most importantly the study of the failure of crime prevention by citizenry and by the police and secondarily the study of the active participation and precipitation of criminal events by their victims'.[97] They have been portrayed as checks on the adequacy of official, recorded crime statistics.[98] And they offer, by extension, opportunities to promote the better measurement of vulnerability to crime, propensities to report crime, and trends in crime data over time. Those are all interesting enough areas, but it is not clear that they should be classified as victimology.

A final variation on that theme has been the transposition of criminals and victims in the analysis of familiar criminological questions. There has, for instance, been a modest interest in the growth of victims' movements and campaigns but it has sometimes been lodged in a stock criminological frame that remains wary of the populist punitive potency of victims' rights. Take Boutellier,[99] who represented the new focus simply as part of a demagogic politics of reaction in which victims offer no more than a pretext for class oppression.

Critique

It would be difficult to conclude that victimology amounts to a coherent whole, and attempts to make sense of its history and themes have been as discrepant as any. Fattah, for instance, argued that the discipline progressed from data gathering to legislation to the promotion of victims' rights; thence to state compensation and victim-offender mediation programmes; and finally to the extensive provision of services for victims.[100] His victimology is conceived as a practical project dedicated to achieving recognition and justice for victims and it makes little provision for the academic study of victims and victimization that has been the theme of this chapter. His version is a classic example of the tension between the applied and the theoretical; the committed and the critical; the advocacy and analysis that infuses the discipline. It is no surprise, therefore, that its practitioners should have stumbled over such issues as who should be allowed to speak about or indeed for victims or what is to be made of victim-precipitation. Shapland and Sloan observed that the editors of the first issue of the *International Review of Victimology* asked, 'Is victimology a socio-political movement whose objective is the pursuit of victims' rights, or rather an academic activity concerned "merely" with the pursuit of knowledge?' The question, they imply, remained unanswered twenty years later: 'Victimological research and theory have acquired a distinct identity and operate according to academic research methods and ethics—but they both study and also influence practice and policy.'[101]

---

[97] R. Block, 'Victim-Offender Dynamics in Violent Crime', 76.
[98] M. Gottfredson and M. Hindelang, 'Sociological Aspects of Criminal Victimisation', 118, 119.
[99] H. Boutellier, *Crime and Morality*.   [100] E. Fattah, 'Victimology Past, Present and Future', 18.
[101] J. Shapland and J. Sloan, 'Twenty Volumes of Criminology', 3.

Conclusion

It may well be that victimology is best represented as yet another *rendezvous* sub-discipline where different approaches and ambitions meet around an empirical content and share as a common denominator little more than the word 'victim'. However, victimologists have nevertheless manifestly succeeded in pressing the victim into the centre of criminological analysis, filling a central void; they have promoted the idea that crime is processual, emergent, and interactive, although that is an idea besmirched by the murky origins of victim-precipitation; they have illuminated the negotiated and contested character of claims to victim status, showing that those claims are sometimes resisted; they make it clear that there is no straightforward or transparent connection between victimization and the fear of crime, or between types of crime and their impact on different groups; they show how crime is concentrated in time, space, and society; they have underscored how sharp moral, political, and ontological separations between victim and offender may not always be empirically defensible; they have exposed the hazards of generalizing and imputing traits to victims; and they have demonstrated how engagement with the criminal justice system may produce 'secondary victimization'. In common law jurisdictions, victimologists' support for a victims' rights-centred justice system has had a significant impact on criminal justice thinking and practices. This ranges from the introduction of victim impact statements to restorative justice initiatives. We have, in short, moved far away from simple stereotypes of vulnerability and victimization, away from the little old lady who represented Christie's 'ideal victim', and towards a much more nuanced and expansive appreciation of both the nature of criminal events and their victimization effects.[102]

Further Reading

J. DOAK, *Victims Rights, Human Rights and Criminal Justice*, Oxford, 2008.

C. HOYLE and R. Young, *New Visions of Crime Victims*, Oxford, 2004.

A. KROG, *Conditional Tense: After the South African Truth and Reconciliation Commission*, Cape Town, 2013.

E. MCLAUGHLIN, et al., *Restorative Justice: Critical Issues*, London, 2003.

P. ROCK, *Constructing Victims' Rights*, Oxford, 2004.

---

[102] This is a modified version of a chapter that will be published in S. Walklate, *Handbook of Victims and Victimology*, 2nd edition.

13

Public Criminology: Theory and Policy

Introduction

Many, though by no means all, academics researching crime and deviance would claim some ultimate justification for their activities in the realm of the public good. It is somewhat paradoxical, therefore, that so few of their resources are devoted to political activity in general and the making of public policy in particular. Until recently, their attention to this aspect of their work was usually cursory, often altogether absent. It is accordingly important to enquire why so little has been accomplished.

The answers lie chiefly in the direction of role-definition, translatability, and salience. The first implies a division of labour in which teaching and research take priority. The rigorously academic may simply cancel out the pursuit of competing priorities such as politics, public debate, and policy-making. These activities have their own practitioners in other departments or in other institutions. It is up to them to utilize such materials as academics may furnish. In some ways, the distinction is simply that between 'pure' and 'applied' science. In other respects, issues in role-definition are far more complicated. Sociologists may actively resist the agenda-setting that a concern for 'social problems' implies. 'Sociological problems' do not necessarily coincide with 'social problems' in any but the crudest respects. To force the former into a mould formed by the latter would be as absurd as to yoke astronomy to the tasks of space exploration programmes. Translatability refers to the differences between the 'systems of relevance'[1] of sociology and social policy. The sociologists' mode of discourse, with its employment of what Schutz termed 'second-order constructs', is in principle quite distinct from the mode of discourse of policy-makers, which is framed in terms of 'first-order constructs' embedded in the 'natural attitude' of everyday life. However, sociological theories differ greatly in their receptivity to the constructs of everyday life and the problems of translating theories largely constructed in commonsensical terms into social policy terms are not acute in principle, whatever the practical and political obstacles to their effective implementation may be. In the case of theories which address, for instance, the social functions of crime, or the phenomenological analysis of the meanings of particular forms of deviance, the implications for social policy may

[1] M. Phillipson, *Sociological Aspects of Crime and Delinquency*, ch. 6.

be either non-existent or ineffable. Doing something about anomie is far more problematic than tackling car theft by technical means. In this chapter we shall attempt to assess the relations between theories of deviance and their implications for politics and policy-making with these considerations in mind.

The linkages between theory, policy, and practice are immensely variable and as yet little understood. The extent to which theories are adopted depends only in part on the energy and commitment of the theorist, the degree of empirical support for the theory, or the ease with which the theory can be translated into policy terms. The salience of a theory for policy-makers may have as much to do with the extent and forms of knowledge which officials and politicians have of theory; the consonance between theory and the practical work of government; the scope of the proposals for action; the resources required; the extent to which significant interests are engaged as parties or adversaries; and the likely ratio of costs to benefits. Even these factors are likely to be secondary to the correspondence between the theory and the policy-makers' timetables and rhetoric.

What is evident, however, is the contingent nature of the relationship between theory, research, and policy and it would not do to presume that the sociology of deviance has fixed implications for politics. On the contrary, the influence of ideas will change from State to State, administration to administration, government department to government department, and from one division or branch of a department to another. Very often, what concerns the politician and policy official is not the academic solidity of a theory but its political utility. What is also evident is that the language and emphases of policy documents and political arguments are not constructed as if they were parts of an academic discourse. They are not shaped by questions of methodology, evidence, and intellectual pedigree. On the contrary, their nuances flow from concerns about constituencies and the practicalities of implementation. To be sure, there *will* sometimes be consultation with relevant experts (although how 'expertise' is established is itself a contingent matter). From time to time, theory and research will have the effect of discouraging officials from supporting recommendations that experts consider to be naïve, discredited, or impracticable. (Nonetheless, politicians are not always unprepared to develop policies that are sociologically unreasonable: they heed other kinds of reason as well.) More generally, theory and research findings will tend to be a rhetorical resource to cite when needed: it is always useful to show that proposals are well anchored, even if the demonstration is retroactive. In that process of formulating proposals, the role of theory and theorist is frequently transformed into that of a competent authority which may be relied upon *because* it is competent, people and their ideas being judged rather generally in terms of their apparent soundness and trustworthiness. Questions of demonstration and method are typically considered to be the private business of the expert. Policy-makers do not wish continually to scrutinize the academic qualifications of their experts or the logic of their arguments. They take them on trust. In turn, theory may well creep anonymously into politics. Advice will not be tendered or examined because it is a rational extension of phenomenology or control theory. It will enter as the accredited good sense of sound criminologists and researchers whose job it is to brief officials and politicians. Accordingly, it is frequently difficult to discover the precise intellectual provenance of proposals and it is even more difficult to keep track of them as they assume the clothing of political argument. After all, it would look a little absurd to defend a political proposal before one's Cabinet colleagues on the grounds that it is an instance of solid ethnomethodology, survey methodology, or feminist criminology.

A third feature of the connection between theory and policy is that it is pervasive, piecemeal, and incremental. New theories are rarely catapulted like tracts or manifestos into political settings to be accepted or rejected in their entirety. They 'trickle' in from many sources.

Questions will be asked, ideas synthesized, and opinions formed. Quite often, officials will forget quite who was the author and what was the origin of a particular idea. It is never easy to fix when it was that a theory began to influence action or action a theory. Indeed, it would be naïve to attempt to address the problem.

One other property of that contingent relationship is the changing influence of ideas. As political and practical circumstances fluctuate, so there will be a responsive shift in the bearing of theory and research. Circumstances will colour theory and theory circumstances. Many sociologists are quite mindful of the problematic character of the association between academic ideas and political action and there have been a number of accounts of how it can shift over time. Scull, for example, argued that the case for 'decarceration' changed little between its first exposition in the mid-nineteenth and its redeployment in the mid-twentieth centuries. He argued that the reasons for its initial rejection and its later acceptance have to be explained in terms of its relevance to changes in the political economy of capitalism. Economies undergoing a 'fiscal crisis' could no longer afford an ever-growing control apparatus: there had to be retrenchment. To be sure, Scull's case has been challenged, theoretically perhaps most notably by Cohen,[2] and, on one level, empirically, by the renewed growth in prison-building on both sides of the Atlantic (although that is going into reverse), but it does point to the importance of the political and economic frameworks of penological debate and, ironically, it may actually sustain his argument.

Other sociologists have pointed to the manner in which long-established theories can come into their own when the times are propitious; for instance, anomie theory had been formulated for twenty years before its transposition by Cloward and Ohlin into 'opportunity structure theory' and the rapid development of the Mobilization for Youth project. Short has commented that this example:

> illustrates a principle of great importance for the relation of sociological theory to social policy: that sociological theory is typically crescive, developing by slow and often uncertain increments suggested by either an empirical discovery or a conceptual modification. One implication is that those who would leap to specific concrete social engineering proposals on the basis of new developments in sociological theory are likely to find themselves on shaky ground. There is a scarcity of both social policy-oriented theory and replicated studies demonstrating valid and reliable knowledge.[3]

---

[2] S. Cohen, *Visions of Social Control.*

[3] J. Short, jun, 'The Natural History of an Applied Theory: Differential Opportunity and Mobilization for Youth'.

The issues of role-definition, translatability, and salience combine to make it a rare occurrence for a theory of deviance to be the immediate progenitor of action programmes or social policy changes. It is more common to find competing social policies being justified by their adherents in terms of the support they may derive from theory and research. The theories we have discussed offer distinctive explanations for deviance and it is logically to be inferred that they offer distinctive recipes for appropriate responses to deviance in political, policy, and practical terms. The search for such correspondences reveals the strengths and weaknesses of the theories anew: for they are subject to the constraint that they specify with some precision just what should (or should not) be changed before there can be a significant improvement in the social response to deviance. In certain respects, the implementation of policies and practices based upon a theory can provide more exacting opportunities to test that theory more searchingly. The difficulties involved in such evaluation and the generally negative results that have been obtained in the few instances where it has been attempted at all rigorously, will be alluded to as we deal with each perspective in turn.

Theoretical Perspectives

The Chicago 'School' produced one major project based on the characteristic theoretical assumptions of several of its leading members. The Chicago Area Project was inaugurated by Clifford Shaw and Henry McKay in 1934 and has survived in modified form to the present. The Chicagoans' definition of the role of the sociologist was quite compatible with so direct an involvement in practical intervention. Burgess and Thrasher were similarly concerned to develop responses which embodied their insights into the group nature of delinquency. Thrasher, for example, wrote:

> We need a new penology which shall be penetrating in its insights into the subjective aspect of the boy's life and which shall be much broader in scope than institutional care and the present system of probation and parole. . . . He must not be treated as if he existed in a social vacuum, but . . . as a member of all the various groups to which he belongs—not merely to the gang alone, but the family, the neighbourhood, the school, the church, the occupational group and so on.[4]

The theory of 'social disorganization' seemed readily translatable into terms of social practice. If the causes of delinquency were to be found in the attenuation of social controls born of 'social disorganization', then the most effective responses should be the fostering of such potential for social organization as did exist in the areas most affected. Since the approach stressed the inherent capacity of communities to mobilize their own social control resources, the main burden of the projects should be to enhance the capacity of local residents to take the initiative in promoting links with 'disaffiliated' youth and in seeking indigenous sources for the promotion of their welfare. Shaw and McKay were keen to avoid the ossification of social work that they claimed to be so grave a handicap to the effectiveness and credibility of the settlement houses. They

---

[4] F. Thrasher, *The Gang*, 499–500.

argued that problems had arisen from the recruitment of outside professionals who lacked substantial interests in the areas in which they worked. They wished to promote links between local leaders and local youths in terms that were primarily personal and social rather than clinical and individualistic. They improvised a broad range of community-based programmes, the most imaginative of which was the use of ex-offenders to act as youth workers with gangs. Their aim was to redirect rather than repress or break up the gang. At times, their enthusiasm for such redirection seemed naïve. For example, a certain innocence characterized Thrasher's advocacy of the Scout movement and the YMCA as suitable outlets for the ganging process. But the reformist zeal of such policies received support in their time and lent a salience to strategies which still clings to their modern counterparts. The strategies of redirection, detached youth work with 'unreached', 'disaffiliated', 'unattached', or 'unclubbable' youth (the labels changing with time and place), and the co-optation of indigenous workers, remained in whole or in part basic to the work of the New York City Youth Board in the post-war period,[5] as well as influencing the programmes of Mobilization for Youth and other youth-related programmes in the American 'War on Poverty' in the 1960s. Such strategies tended to be regarded in Britain as 'experimental' well into the post-war period.[6]

The problems of assessing the work of the Chicago Area Project have been shared by all delinquency prevention programmes.

> At the bottom the difficulty rests on the fact that such programs . . . cannot by their very nature constitute more than a subsidiary element in changing the fundamental and sweeping forces which create the problems of groups and of persons or which shape human personality. Declines in rates of delinquency—the only conclusive way to evaluate delinquency prevention—may reflect influences unconnected with those of organized programs and are difficult to define and measure.[7]

Kobrin's own assessment therefore rests on 'logical and analytic grounds', which somewhat weakens the force of his conclusion that 'in all probability these achievements (of the CAP) have reduced delinquency in the program areas, as any substantial improvement in the social climate of an area must'.[8] The circularity of this conclusion reflects the circularity of the parent theory: if delinquency is both symptom and consequence of 'social disorganization', then social programmes to reduce such disorganization must have reduced delinquency.

Finestone challenges Kobrin's view by taking as a basis for evaluation the sheer variety of the projects generated by the CAP. He addresses the problem of assessing the variable strength or weakness of the projects as organizations by adopting certain indicators of their performance. *Inter alia*, their degree of success in fundraising and their degree of autonomy from State-appointed staff workers, are taken as indicators of project success. On these purely organizational terms, the most successful projects

---

[5] New York City Youth Board, *Reaching the Fighting Gang*.
[6] M. Morse, *The Unattached*; and G. Goetschius and M. Tash, *Working with Unattached Youth*. The use of ex-offenders as social workers resurfaced as 'new careers': see D. Briggs, *Dealing with Deviants*; and C. Covington, 'The Hammersmith Teenage Project'.
[7] S. Kobrin, 'The Chicago Area Project', 323.   [8] S. Kobrin, 'The Chicago Area Project', 330.

correlated conversely with the seriousness of the delinquency problem in the areas. 'The Chicago Area Project has not provided a method of coping with the problem of delinquency in its most serious form in the areas of the city with the highest rates.'[9] Finestone's own assessment is limited by the absence of time-series data which alone would warrant so strong a conclusion. However, it does much to confirm the severe limitations of so exclusive an emphasis on community controls and activities alone. Such an emphasis precludes any attempt to deal with the social and economic processes, such as the relatively unchecked expansion of industrial and commercial land-use in the inner city, which arguably erode and 'disorganize' the community from without and which can only be tackled by more comprehensive social and economic policies.[10] Such criticisms have force rather than weight, since we have yet to establish that more fundamental changes would actually promote the reduction of crime and delinquency, or that we have the understanding to implement such changes intelligently.

Functionalist theories would seem to offer the basis for policies that are at least comprehensive in their scope. After all, the analytical aim of functionalism is nothing short of the 'total interconnectedness' of social institutions. However, as Gouldner notes:

> one of Functionalism's basic methodological precepts is that there are no 'causes'. Functionalism thinks of systems as mutually interacting variables rather than in terms of cause and effect. Functionalism's elementary domain assumption has always come down to this: everything influences everything else. But Functionalism has had no theory about the weighting to be assigned to different variables in the system. It has had no theory about which variables are more and which are less important in determining the state of the system as a whole.[11]

Above all, the functionalists sought to discern hidden order in apparent disharmony, to suggest that 'when problems arise in a group, there spontaneously emerge *natural* "defense" or adaptive mechanisms that serve to restore order and equilibrium'.[12] As a result, translating functionalism into policy options was a contradiction in terms. If what appear to be problems are—at the level of 'second-order constructs'—re-transcribed as solutions, then State intervention is only likely, if anything, to make matters worse. From Spencer through Durkheim to Parsons' early and middle phases, functionalists argued that the power of the State was to be kept at a minimum to allow deep evolutionary processes to hold sway. Since the State could only acquire power from interventionist policies, such policies were best avoided. Their consequences would be likely to proliferate in ways that would be difficult to foresee and control. 'Hands off' would be the major functionalist recommendation.

In Gouldner's view, the seeming irrelevance of functionalism to social policy (and of social policy to functionalism) began to change as the Welfare State in America began to assume growing importance, both as an instrument of conflict-resolution

---

[9] H. Finestone, *Victims of Change: Juvenile Delinquents in American Society*, 144. A similar conclusion was reached by J. Mays in his analysis of an allied, smaller-scale Liverpool project in *On the Threshold of Delinquency*.

[10] J. Snodgrass, 'Clifford R. Shaw and Henry D. McKay', and also P. Townsend, 'Area Deprivation Policies'.

[11] A. Gouldner, *The Coming Crisis*, 346–7.   [12] A. Gouldner, *The Coming Crisis*, 346.

and resource-allocation in the American economy and as a major source of finance for social science research. In this changing context, Gouldner somewhat cynically argues, functionalists could not maintain their attitude of pure detachment from political and policy issues. Even Parsons began to adjust his scheme to take account of 'input deficits' suffered by certain socially deprived groups.[13] And in the cases of Smelser and Moore, leading functionalists undertook an attempted convergence with Marxism in the rush to accommodate social change and policy relevance to their theoretical work. In the process, however, the tensions between the parent theory and its new-found applications in the policy realm became all too apparent. Functionalism lost credibility and the 1960s witnessed the pursuit of alternative sociologies, in particular symbolic interactionism, phenomenology, and Marxism.

Ironically, Gouldner ignored the one major respect in which functionalism indirectly led to the development of one theoretical model of great relevance to the realm of policy. *Anomie theory*, in the version formulated by Merton, did indeed share with functionalism a certain opaqueness in relation to policy. It also shared a problem of translating its 'second-order constructs'—culture, deviant 'adaptations'—into the accomplishment of social organization and meaning in everyday life. But its central tenet, that the consequences for high rates of deviance of the disjunction between goals and means would be grave, *was* a causal statement of considerable scope. The strain towards deviance induced by the gap between goals and means should in principle be reducible by the narrowing of that gap. Despite his own leanings towards the political left, Merton did not spell out this clear, implicit directive towards more egalitarian policies in other than parenthetical terms. It did, however, provide a basis for Cloward and Ohlin to define anomie theory afresh as opportunity structure theory some twenty years later. The crucial modification was their linkage of the emergence of delinquent subcultures to the experience of the closure of both legitimate and illegitimate opportunities in adolescence.[14] This change provided a rationale for the Mobilization for Youth (MFY) project, whose main purpose was cast in terms of opportunity expansion. In its turn, MFY became a major influence on the American 'War on Poverty' that dominated US domestic policy in the 1960s.

The immediate origins of MFY lay in the theoretical synthesis offered by Cloward and Ohlin in *Delinquency and Opportunity*. But its salience was partly due to their original undertaking of that task at the request of a settlement house in the Lower East Side, the Henry Street Settlement. As sociologists, they evidently embarked on the process of theorizing with the requirements of policy initiatives in mind. To some extent, the shape of their formulation accounts for the ready translatability of the theory into the language of social intervention. Its coincidence with the demand for initiatives from the new reforming administration of the Kennedys lent it a salience few projects have possessed before or since in either Britain or the USA. The 'new Frontier' was underfoot. 'In summary, it is our belief that most delinquent behaviour is engendered because opportunities for conformity are limited. Delinquency therefore represents

---

[13] A. Gouldner, *The Coming Crisis*, 346–7, 358.

[14] J. Short, jun., 'The Natural History of an Applied Theory', 199–200, discusses this issue.

not a lack of motivation to conform but quite the opposite: the desire to meet social expectations itself becomes the source of delinquency if the possibility of doing so is limited or non-existent.'[15] Clearly aware that translating these tenets into practice would be far from easy, they also stated that 'an appropriate program of action is not necessarily self-evident once a theory of causation has been evolved; it cannot simply be assumed that once we know what the trouble is, we will have little difficulty remedying it.'[16] The difficulties that MFY came to encounter were not foreshadowed in the planning document, mainly because the theory dealt only very indirectly with the issue of power and vested interest with which the project came to engage. The core of these problems may be presented as lying in the inconsistency of tackling at the local, community level inequalities that were theorized as rooted in the wider social structure. 'In both their employment and their education programmes, the projects were cramped by their inability to supersede the limits of local action and tackle the national problems that underlay their frustrations.'[17]

It was a major irony that theory based on a comprehensive analysis of the links between delinquency and social structure should have been translated into a project which intervened at the community level. Yet the realities of American politics ruled out more sweeping reforms and community action programmes could be justified in terms of their efficiency as 'demonstration projects'. 'Demonstration', however, hinged on the effectiveness of research monitoring the results of the projects and on this count the project evidently could not cope with the sheer complexity of the evaluation involved. MFY launched enriched educational programmes, job training schemes, vocational guidance; even, on occasion, actual job provision from the resources of the project itself; and it embraced diverse forms of community protest. As the decade wore on, however, changes of direction multiplied and the job of monitoring the results, already flawed by the absence of a comparative basis, tended to become routinized into administrative book-keeping.[18] Moreover, the politics of the project proved contentious almost from the outset. As Cloward and Piven stated in retrospect: 'The Great Society programs were promulgated by federal leaders in order to deal with the problems created by a new and unstable electoral constituency—namely, blacks—and to deal with this new constituency not simply by responding to its expressed interests, but by shaping and directing its political future.'[19] This view of Great Society politics corresponds with Gouldner's assertion that some sociological backing is actively sought by governments to help legitimate their commitment to limited social reforms. The State must actively promote some reforms, or the massive subventions required for its support are vulnerable to retraction; but the reforms must not be too radical, or the State risks conflict with dominant (capitalist) interests. 'The upper apparatus of the Welfare

---

[15] Mobilization for Youth, *A Proposal for the Prevention and Control of Delinquency by the Expansion of Opportunities*, 44–5.

[16] Mobilization for Youth, *A Proposal for the Prevention and Control of Delinquency by the Expansion of Opportunities*, ix–x.

[17] P. Marris and M. Rein, *Dilemmas of Social Reform: Poverty and Community Action in the United States*, 124.

[18] P. Marris and M. Rein, *Dilemmas of Social Reform: Poverty and Community Action in the United States*, 122–3 and *passim*.   [19] F. Piven and R. Cloward, *Regulating the Poor*, 279.

State, then, needs social research that will "unmask" its competitors; it needs a kind of limitedly "critical" research.'[20] As the history of MFY shows, however, it is difficult to keep the 'critical' component of such research within bounds.

The potential for more radical action was explored early in the life of the MFY and as a result that project drew the fire of local authorities and media. 'Community protest', never more than a minor aspect of MFY, took the form of embracing causes relevant to the aims of the project, while 'expanding opportunities' came to be defined as entailing 'decreasing the sense of powerlessness' among poor people.[21] Organizing a voter registration drive, aiding a local contingent of the March on Washington, encouraging rent strikes, and supporting a local group of Puerto Rican mothers in their campaign to oust a local school principal led to the pillorying of MFY by the New York *Daily News*. The project was accused of employing Communist sympathizers, of financial irregularities, and of inspiring riots in Harlem! The charges, none of which was substantiated on investigation, are evidence of the severe limits within which such projects are politically constrained.

The ultimate constraint upon MFY, the 'War on Poverty' and allied projects in Britain, was the impossibility of meeting the commitment to expand opportunities with the means available. Even for such generously funded projects as MFY, the limitations on creating all but the most temporary jobs were severe. Hence, the project came to focus increasingly on elaborate job-training schemes and placement programmes in relation to existing jobs. Some of these schemes, such as simulated work-situation training, were genuinely imaginative attempts to align job preparation with the kinds of jobs available and the lack of sophistication of the recruits: but there was little to offer trainees at the end of the process, leading Moynihan to conclude that more would have been gained if government had centred its activities directly and simply on the stimulation of employment.[22] Marris and Rein note the difficulties of establishing with any precision just what impact the projects made, but conclude: 'While the projects could claim many individual successes and may well have increased somewhat the range of opportunities, they did so at great cost and without benefit to perhaps two-thirds of those who sought their help.'[23] What remains even more problematic is whether or not these activities made any impact on delinquency in the area. No definitive assessment has emerged, but one study reports that most lower East-side gangs 'ignored MFY and at times were openly hostile to the organization through vandalism'.[24] In one central respect, however, the project's principal assumption does seem borne out by experience.

> As soon as the projects offered an opportunity that seemed genuine, they encouraged more response than they could handle. . . . The children of the slums responded to the projects, because they recognized the sincerity of the intentions; they became discouraged only as it became clear that the promise could not be fulfilled. Disillusionment is not apathy and to confuse them only complacently displaces the responsibility for failure.[25]

[20] A. Gouldner, *The Coming Crisis*, 350.
[21] G. Brager, 1964, quoted in P. Marris and M. Rein, *Dilemmas of Social Reform*, 77.
[22] D. Moynihan, *Maximum Feasible Misunderstanding*, 26.
[23] P. Marris and M. Rein, *Dilemmas of Social Reform*, 77.
[24] J. Short, jun., 'The Natural History of an Applied Theory', 199 n.
[25] P. Marris and M. Rein, *Dilemmas of Social Reform*, 124–5.

In the end, the aims of the project could only be achieved within 'a framework of national redistribution of resources, which deliberately redressed the balance of opportunities between rich and poor communities'.[26] If we have learned anything about the large-scale social and economic correlates of criminality, it is that countries with the greatest internal inequalities are also marked by the highest rates of crime.[27]

The experiences of the 'War on Poverty' were not unique to the United States. In Britain between 1968 and 1978, minuscule versions of similar projects were created by the Community Development Projects (CDP) programme. The CDP programme represented a break with tradition in one respect, as British policy had tended to be shaped by the ideal of effecting social change through national reforms of fiscal, employment, and educational systems. The convergence with American practice was due in part to economic constraints reducing the scope for such reforms, at least within the political terms of the 1960s.[28] Despite some interchange between American and British policy-makers, in which the Americans took pains to spell out the deficiencies of the community-level approach, the government continued to back the projects.[29] It was presumably assumed that the explicit linkage between the British local projects and central government would ensure greater co-operation and enhanced effectiveness. But in the event, despite occasional successes, the projects foundered on much the same rock as the US programmes: a chronic shortage of resources to meet well-documented needs utterly beyond the reach of the community itself. In some cases, project members arrived at much the same analysis as Marris and Rein: the need for national policy to reallocate resources from rich to poor. It must by now be clear that perhaps the major appeal of such projects for governments is that by their adoption, the thorny political issues involved in such reallocation can be, for a time, finessed. The price to be paid is that, with each successive failure, the limits of Social Democratic reformism are cruelly exposed. It was in the wake of such failures that *radical theorists* argued that capitalism was so crisis-ridden that reformism had become untenable and revolutionary praxis offered the only hope of attaining egalitarian ends.

Marxist theorists have never, in principle, had to face problems of role-definition that have so naggingly permeated sociology. 'Philosophers have long sought to understand the world: the point, however, is to change it.' The epitaph on Marx's tomb rams home the need for theory and practice to be related to each other in an urgent dialectic. Praxis represents their ideal unity, theoretically informed practice feeding back into practically informed theory, in a dynamic and self-critical process. Salience depends heavily, however, on the interpretations that are drawn from praxis. Until recently the sheer force of the underlying theory had a truncating effect on revolutionary

---

[26] P. Marris and M. Rein, *Dilemmas of Social Reform*, 126. Those strictures about 'genuine' opportunities should be noted. A number of criminologists and Currie in particular, have argued that employment will act as an alternative to crime only if it is not work that is badly paid and devalued. E. Currie, *Confronting Crime: An American Challenge.*

[27] J. Braithwaite, *Inequality, Crime and Public Policy.*

[28] The policy background is well analysed in Marris and Rein's preface to *Dilemmas of Social Reform.*

[29] Home Office (UK), *Experiments in Social Policy and their Explanation.* For a fuller account, see M. Loney, *Community Against Government.*

practice in Western academic Marxism. The more orthodox interpretations seemed to offer every reason *not* to act until the right conjuncture of revolutionary possibilities had materialized. Moreover, activism in sectors of society not directly connected with production seemed irrelevant. Least relevant of all were the realms of deviance and control. Crime and deviance were in general defined as the inevitable by-products of the state of the *lumpenproletariat* under capitalism: little could be done about these phenomena until capitalism had been eliminated. Only with the redefinition of the potential of deviant groups for revolutionary struggle could criminologists engage at all in more salient activity. It was the achievement of the 'new' criminologists to discern in the upsurge of political consciousness among certain deviant and minority groupings the basis for a different strategy to traditional class action. Participation in injustice based protest movements and campaigns continues to afford important possibilities for their alignment to social justice conflicts, the promotion of alliances between them, and the internationalizing of joint experience and expertise.[30]

Beyond the point of immediate struggle, however, the guidelines for action are thin. Suggestions for the control of policing and the administration of criminal justice to be taken over by working-class communities have made little progress in addressing issues of representativeness, responsibility, and safeguards.[31] The problems of translating radical theory into practice remain formidable, not simply because the obstacles to such practice are in themselves so strong, but also because the theories do not offer criteria for discriminating between the myriad possibilities for action that exist.

There are two major exceptions which are instructive in their provision of polar answers to a radical dilemma. There is the accommodation proposed by radicals who became conscious of the need to take criminal victimization seriously. They are reluctant either to remove themselves from political engagement or to exacerbate what is an already doleful condition. The beginnings of a programme of pragmatic reform were drafted by 'left realist' criminologists who sought to radicalize radical criminology. As was noted in Chapter 10, the realists are concerned with the criminal victimization of the vulnerable and powerless and, in some respects, their 'real world' solutions are not so very different from mainstream liberal proposals. They do have an interest in propounding remedies for the institutionalized victimization experienced by poor, vulnerable, and ill-serviced working-class communities. There is a demand for more responsive and efficient policing and, in particular, for policing that is directed at crime priorities which working-class communities themselves would choose, for policing which eschews aggressive patrol tactics, and for policing that is directed by a more intelligent system of targeting. There is a cautious welcome for neighbourhood watch programmes: 'left realists' are wary about the displacement of crime from target-hardened middle-class to unprotected working-class neighbourhoods. There is limited support for a 'multi-agency' approach to crime, orchestrating the activities of shelters

[30] e.g., the work of the European Deviancy Group.
[31] J. Young, 'Working Class Criminology' and 'Left Idealism, Reformism and Beyond' and, for a discussion of the issues raised, S. Cohen, 'Guilt, Justice and Tolerance: Some Old Concepts for a New Criminology'.

for victims of domestic and sexual violence, social services, local authority crime pre-vention and target-hardening programmes, and the police.[32] There is a recommenda-tion that prison should be used much more sparingly, to be replaced by schemes that integrate rather than further 'marginalize' the already alienated. All these proposals display a marked affinity with those of other theoretical positions and contribute to the construction of a new professional consensus which possesses considerable authority.

Perhaps the most significant manifestation of a realist sensibility is evidenced by the impact of feminist criminology. It exhibits one of the strongest connections between theory, activism, policy, and practice. As was discussed in Chapter 11, there is of course no one feminist criminology but what unites the different perspectives is the campaigning work across issues connected to women as offenders and women as vic-tims. Campaigns have produced some truly remarkable changes in government poli-cies, professional practices, and public attitudes, across numerous jurisdictions, most notably on the policing and prosecution of domestic violence and sexual violence.[33] Activists have also continued to work for the abolition of imprisonment for most cat-egories of female offenders.[34] More recently the research agenda has been broadened to include the experience of women working in the criminal justice system.[35] In addi-tion to a transformative policy-practice orientation, feminist criminologists have also, through utilizing a gendered understanding of crime, fear of crime, victimization, so-cial control, and criminal justice, expanded the conceptual and empirical parameters of the sociology of crime and deviance.

One direction which 'left realists' and others may take has been prepared by John Braithwaite. Recall Jock Young's parallelogram of forces which pointed to the im-portance of 'society' or the community as a source of informal social control. It was Braithwaite's contention that this informal social control operates most powerfully when it deploys techniques of shaming directed by significant others, others who are valued and respected members of the offender's immediate environment, against of-fences which flout 'core consensus values'.[36] Shaming includes the making of apologies and it operates most powerfully when it is conducted in public and so orchestrated that it does not lead to permanent outcasting but permits, indeed encourages, the even-tual moral and social return of the one who has been shamed, 'avoiding stigmatiza-tion'.[37] The conventional criminal justice system fails in both areas, Braithwaite argues. Judges, magistrates, and police officers may lack authority and immediacy in the world of the offender, particularly in the world of the young, working-class offender. Their moral pronouncements may have only a limited effect. The punishments they impose

---

[32] Although it is becoming increasingly clear that multi-agency approaches have their problems; that the police tend to be the agency that dominates agendas and decisions; and that different agencies often disagree about the nature of the problems they are confronting and the methods that should be used to tackle them. A. Sampson et al., 'Crime, Localities and the Multi-Agency Approach'.

[33] E. Stark, *Coercive Control: The Entrapment of Women in Personal Life*.

[34] Baroness Corston, *A Review of Women with Particular Vulnerabilities in the Criminal Justice System*.

[35] K. van Wormer and C. Bartollas, *Women and the Criminal Justice System*.

[36] J. Braithwaite, *Crime, Shame and Reintegration*, 185.

[37] J. Braithwaite, 'Shame and Modernity', 1.

are not calculated to bring about the reintegration of the criminal. Braithwaite's argument is redolent of the earlier work of the anthropologists Llewellyn and Hoebel[38] and of Durkheim and Hirschi and sociologists within the labelling tradition. It prompts reflections about the proper management of the shaming process in informal communities. What Braithwaite said also invited criticism from lawyers such as Andrew Ashworth who see in it a worrying erosion of the safeguards of due process and the importance of the wider public interest in the disposal of cases[39] and the proper relations between offenders, victims, the State, and community. Yet it is by far the most successful instance of the synthesis of a practical programme and an academic argument leading to material change, uniting labelling theory, social anthropology, and the empirical findings of criminology. It has constructed a credible restorative justice alternative to conventional criminal procedure.[40]

Another major exception remains the work of Thomas Mathiesen in the field of penal reform and it embraces none of the pragmatism of the left realists.[41] Instead, Mathiesen veers towards an uncompromising policy of resistance to co-optation. His work addresses the perennial dilemma for radicals of whether to pursue short-term reforms or long-term revolutionary aims. To pursue either exclusively entails severe costs. Reformism is held to risk strengthening the system, so undermining more radical change; and its advocates tend to become 'incorporated' into the system by endless compromise and the acceptance of system terms for the evaluation of reforms. To opt for purely revolutionary ends, however, means isolation from the system, assignment to an 'irresponsible' role, and the loss of credibility in relations with the subordinate groups most affected: in this case, prisoners. Mathiesen proposes a means for resolving this dilemma which would enable radicals to pursue reforms in the short term which would not compromise their long-term aim of radical transformation and which would protect them from incorporation. It is crucial, he argues, to differentiate reforms which are 'system-strengthening' from those which are 'system-weakening'. The latter can be supported and the former resisted, as a means to long-term aims. An example of the former is the 'medicalization' of crime and deviance, superficially a progressive measure (rehabilitation), but fundamentally one which individualizes the causes of crime and deviance and therefore defuses its political aspects. It also dehumanizes offenders by reducing their problems to those of a sickness from which, with appropriate treatment, the State will enable them to recover. Examples of 'system-weakening' reforms would be any concessions wrung from the State which would give greater rights to offenders in their relations with the system, which by definition weaken State power. Prisoners' rights to certain standards of work, education, and freedom from censorship and, *inter alia*, to legal procedures in a prison context, are in this sense system-weakening. Principally, however, the main strategy to be employed is the abolition of repressive laws and of coercive institutions that represent State power. As a corollary,

[38] K. Llewellyn and E. Hoebel, *The Cheyenne Way: Conflict and Case Law in Primitive Jurisprudence*.

[39] A. Ashworth, 'Victims' Rights, Defendants' Rights and Criminal Procedure'.

[40] J. Dignan, *Understanding Victims and Restorative Justice*; and H. Strang, *Repair or Revenge: Victims and Restorative Justice*.

[41] T. Mathiesen, *The Politics of Abolition*.

Mathiesen argues that the ultimate trap for reformers is the insistence by authorities that 'alternatives' be specified in the advocacy of reforms and of targets for abolition. It is necessary to avoid the specification of alternatives, he proposes and instead to pursue a strategy which he terms the 'Unfinished': an open-ended commitment for future initiatives to be derived from praxis which otherwise would be ruled out as 'impractical'.

Mathiesen's strategy clearly has great appeal, particularly in the seemingly intractable field of penal reform. It enables participation in reformist campaigns for the abolition of coercive practices prisons.[42] The aim of abolitionist practice is, however, to provide the basis for a more systematic assault on the power of the State than ad hoc reformist pragmatism allows.

Within the penal field, an examination of particular cases shows the immense complexity of interpretation involved in assessing the potential of reforms for system strength or weakness. The view that the 'medicalization' of crime and deviance is automatically system-strengthening seems questionable in the case of drug dependence, where the right to treatment within the health service is one which many States are reluctant to concede.[43] Moreover, the concern with system-strengthening hardly seems the main point, which is whether or not 'medicalization' works for the offender. The main grounds for opposing it ought to be its appropriateness, rather than its implications for the 'system'. Another problem is the extent to which 'treatment' ideologies may favour greater autonomy rather than the reverse. For example, the late Barlinnie Special Unit was initiated along broad therapeutic lines, but evolved in the direction of the prisoners gaining important concessions in terms of autonomy and joint decision-making, a practical exemplification, in many respects, of the 'Unfinished', but one that would arguably have been wrecked at the outset by an insistence on abolitionism, a refusal to specify alternatives, or a marked hostility to broad therapeutic aims.[44] Similarly, research by Elaine Genders and Elaine Player on the therapeutic community-based prison at Grendon Underwood in Buckinghamshire suggests that that institution, too, works rather well.[45] There *does* seem to be a general tendency to neglect what might work. Indeed, McMahon has written about the manner in which critical penological arguments have directed 'attention away from any moderation of penal control which might have taken place and from the superseding of some previous forms of penal control by preferable ones. Ability to recognize any reduction of penal control is limited'.[46] It may be the case that the granting of rights to prisoners lessens the hold of the State in a repressive sense over certain aspects of their lives. Yet it does not take much sophistication to see such a policy as system-strengthening. The 'State' gains in legitimacy from such enlightened reforms. Indeed, the burden of much Marxist 'critical' theory is to 'unmask' the authoritarian reality of State power

---

[42] J. Sim, *Punishment and Prisons: Power and the Carceral State.*

[43] E. Schur, *Narcotic Addiction in Britain and America.*

[44] D. Cooke, 'Containing Violent Prisoners: An Analysis of the Barlinnie Special Unit' and the inside accounts of former inmates such as J. Boyle, *A Sense of Freedom* and *The Pains of Confinement.*

[45] E. Genders and E. Player, *Grendon: A Study of a Therapeutic Prison*; A. Stevens, *Offender Rehabilitation and Therapeutic Communities.*

[46] M. McMahon, 'Net-Widening', 144. See, too, her *The Persistent Prison?*

behind the façade of 'repressive tolerance' created by the progressive extension of citizenship rights to formerly dispossessed groups within capitalist societies over the past two centuries. In the United States and in Britain, periods of quite significant reductions have occurred in the relative use of prison and mental hospitals.[47] In neither case have discernible system-weakening effects resulted, though the impact on certain families and communities may have been burdensome. In sum, the rationale for praxis offered by Mathiesen seems appropriate only in a very limited number of cases, where the State adopts purely repressive measures. Most reforms, however, have both positive and negative aspects in relation to State power. In the great majority of cases, we would suggest, the dilemma is not so much resolved as reconstituted in different and ultimately ambiguous terms by the abolitionist strategy.

Moreover, this complication of the issue is bought at the price of an over-simplified view of the nature of the 'State', capitalism, and class society. The problem of whether one might not actually *wish* to strengthen the system in certain respects, on the grounds that the 'not-too-bad' society is better than any alternatives so far accomplished, is not even addressed. An unfalsifiable postulate of functional unity between the three phenomena runs through Mathiesen's analysis, much as it does through the work of more structuralist Marxists. 'His position provides for only one role for the state under the capitalist mode of production: it is basically repressive. In his quasi-functionalist analysis, everything from publishing (including the publishers of his book?) to the family (even those of "revolutionary intellectuals"?) are part of the State's repressive apparatus.'[48] Pahl's reference is to Poulantzas, but although Mathiesen is more selective in his analysis of State power, much the same could be said of his class analysis. Prisons are seen as the quintessential mode of repression under capitalism and, as the crisis in capitalism deepens, so will its resort to the penalization of working-class offenders. Indeed, Nils Christie would argue that the growth of the crime control industry, of prisons and security systems, is one of the major marketing successes of capitalism towards the end of the twentieth century.[49]

Mathiesen's analysis makes little sense of the immense variations in imprisonment that obtain between different capitalist societies; nor does it address the problem of the persistence and even extension of penal powers in the State socialist societies such as the PRC. The point at issue is the insistence that all attempts at reform are doomed to 'correctionalism' save those that align with strategies to eliminate capitalism. This entails a drastic foreshortening of perspectives on deviance and control to 'a single-cause theory of conflict (class antagonism)'.[50]

It is possible to give a variety of readings to Mathiesen's concept of the 'Unfinished'. It is indeed absurd to expect reformers to provide, in advance of any actualization of their ideas, the proverbial blueprint for their eventual shape. Such a constraint would rule out even the mildest reform, since it would be logically impossible to argue that

---

[47] A. Scull, *Decarceration*.

[48] R. Pahl, 'Stratification: The Relation Between States and Urban and Regional Development', 9. The reference is to N. Poulantzas, *Classes in Contemporary Capitalism*.

[49] N. Christie, *Crime Control as Industry: Towards Gulags Western Style*.

[50] E. Gellner, 'A Social Contract in Search of an Idiom', 141.

no unintended adjustments to the change would occur. At the other extreme, how-ever, the mirror-image of the above constraint is the insistence that alternatives should never be theorized at all. Quite how it would be possible to square this position with anything resembling democratic debate remains a mystery. The philosophical grounds for this strategy of accomplishing socialism reside in the dialectical method, which postulates the emergence of socialism from the final transcendence of the negation (the dictatorship of the proletariat) of the capitalist thesis. By definition, true socialism is not only unknowable in advance of its actualization: it is theoretically virtuous to avoid the very attempt to specify the central properties which would constitute a truly socialist society. The stubborn tendency of the realities of power, stratification, uneven development, and the division of labour to persist in State socialist societies need not be addressed.[51] This makes of praxis something that looks disturbingly like blind faith and leaves the revolutionaries *carte blanche*: yet the historical precedents for revolution (which we are asked to regard as irrelevant) provide no warrant for the abdication of distrust about its likely aftermath. Experience after 1989 and the death of Western State socialism leads one to enquire how viable the revolutionary project, conventionally conceived, ever was.

Symbolic interactionism as a source of policy remained largely untapped until the 1960s. Interactionists had never much preoccupied themselves with the policy impli-cations of their work. It is possible to read the work of Goffman, for example, without finding any systematic policy inferences. What came to be termed *labelling theory* was more precisely foreshadowed in the work of Tannenbaum and Lemert, neither of whom was typical of interactionism.[52] Only with the publication of Becker's *Outsiders* in 1963 were these separate strands fused and implications for policy quickly spelt out. Becker's own 'whose side are we on?' definition of the sociologists' role, whatever its limitations, made it clear at least that their sympathies should lie with the underdogs and no great difficulty was envisaged in bringing theory to bear upon the task of improving their lot. Translating labelling theory into practice consisted of variations on the theme of 'de-labelling': decriminalization, destigmatization, and decarceration.[53] The salience of such themes grew as the costs of institutional care and custody increased sharply in the 1960s, though the trend towards the reduction of inmate populations had begun in the 1950s, in the case of the mentally ill. The salience of labelling theory was enhanced by the fact that attacks on institutionalization came from other quarters.[54]

The fact that these proposals found a ready audience did not mean that they were easy to formulate in practice. 'De-criminalization' has been linked by Schur in particu-lar to 'crimes without victims', such as drug use, gambling, homosexuality, and abor-tion. The criminal sanction is applied to such forms of deviance more extensively in the United States than in Britain, but since in both societies the great majority of of-fences are crimes *with* victims, the scope for applying this principle much further soon

---

[51] R. Pahl, '"Collective Consumption" and the State in Capitalist and State Socialist Societies'; F. Parkin, *Marxism*; D. Downes, 'Praxis Makes Perfect' and 'Abolition: Possibilities and Pitfalls'.

[52] F. Tannenbaum, *Crime and the Community*; E. Lemert, *Social Pathology*.

[53] E. Schur, *Crimes Without Victims* and *Radical Non-Intervention*.

[54] P. Townsend, *The Last Refuge*; T. and P. Morris, *Pentonville*.

runs into difficulties. There is agreement amongst some[55] that what Miller has called 'criminogenic interventions'[56] by the State are mischievous, tending only to aggravate the propensity to offend, but what then follows is not clear. Schur argued that a policy of 'radical non-intervention' should be adopted towards delinquency. His slogan 'leave the kids alone wherever possible' begs the question of how to interpret the bounds of possibility. 'Status offenders', those whose offences would not be law-violations if committed by an adult, are the primary candidates for this policy. In the United States between 1965 and 1974, 'half of all juveniles arrested for a status offence were placed in secure detention for periods ranging from several days to several months. One-third of all juveniles in correctional institutions (training schools, group homes, half-way houses) were committed as adjudicated status offenders'.[57] Such 'offenders' should ideally be dealt with, if at all, within the community rather than in institutions, but Schur is vague about how its members should respond to runaways, truants, under-age drinkers, and 'ungovernables'. 'Non-intervention can become a euphemism for benign neglect, which in turn is another euphemism for simply doing nothing.'[58] De-labelling does not dispense with the problems the labels addressed, however maladroitly. In California, re-labelling was accomplished by several devices after a Bill was passed in 1976 ending secure detention for status offences. Arrests for status offences dropped by 50 per cent, but more offenders were re-labelled delinquent or neglected in order to achieve secure detention, or were held to require mental health commitments.[59]

'De-stigmatization' turned out to be fraught with similar problems. Schemes to 'divert' the young offender from the stigmatizing processes of the juvenile court have 'now become a national fad: non-serious offenders are diverted to hundreds of agencies in lieu of being sent to court. Meanwhile, those who end up in court are being processed by prosecutors, sworn witnesses, and defense attorneys as well as by judges and probation officers. The benevolent assumption that the juvenile court should be society's superparent has been discredited and is being discarded'.[60] Paradoxically, diversion has not reduced the number being sent to court, nor did it evidently reduce stigmas or the exposure of children to bureaucratic processing.[61] It created a supplementary rather than an alternative means of disposal for juvenile offenders. Those who are 'diverted' to specialized agencies are the younger, less serious offenders whom the police used to caution and release. Evidence on the British projects along these lines is scant, but one study discerns the same tendency for a prestigious demonstration project to redefine its target population from the relatively serious to the less serious offenders and to those 'at risk' of delinquency.[62] 'Re-stigmatization' and its extension to hitherto unaffected groups are predictable consequences of rerouting strategies. Indeed, Cohen

[55] J. Hagan and A. Palloni, 'The Social Reproduction of a Criminal Class in Working-Class London circa 1950–1980'.   [56] J. Miller, *Search and Destroy.*

[57] S. Kobrin et al., 'Offense Patterns of Status Offenders', 233, n. 1.

[58] S. Cohen, review of E. Schur, *Crimes Without Victims.*

[59] K. Teilmann and M. Klein, 'Juvenile Justice Legislation: A Framework for Evaluation', 423.

[60] L. Empey, 'Revolution and Counter-revolution: Current Trends in Juvenile Justice'.

[61] L. Empey, 'Revolution and Counter-revolution: Current Trends in Juvenile Justice', 172.

[62] C. Covington, 'The Hammersmith Teenage Project'.

delineated a new vision of the carceral society in which the State, pretending to with-draw from formal social control, actually intruded ever more invasively into the lives of its subject population. There was a dialectic at work, he argues, in which new classifica-tions and remedies were propounded for the control of deviant groups, the exceptions and the failures presented new problems of management and new institutions were formed to regulate them. In a series of 'iatrogenic feedback loops', social control is pushed ever further outwards.[63]

It was Cohen's vision that the State control apparatus had never receded but had merely thrown out webs of new, formally diversionary programmes and projects, called 'community corrections', that had had the practical consequence of enlarging its sphere and increasing the number of effective entry-points to the carceral institutions at its core. Each time offenders were 'breached' on probation or community service, each time they disobeyed a reparation order or failed to pay a fine, they could be penalized by confinement. Indeed, he said, they might thereby be imprisoned for offences that would never originally have warranted prison. The penal estate grows inexorably and voraciously, Cohen argued. Bottoms, in his turn, challenged Cohen by demonstrating how the proportion of prison sentences steadily declined during the period under de-bate. McMahon, in a most telling piece of analysis, has pointed to a number of funda-mental confusions and misconceptions in the 'net-widening argument'. There are, she argued, many reasons other than net-widening why the absolute numbers of prisoners should have increased.[64] Perhaps Braithwaite's strategy of making offenders ashamed without shaming them, of allowing ritual reintegration into society, and of 'healing' the rift with their victims, is the first major theoretically informed and practically effective resolution of the dilemma. Restorative justice may prove on balance to be inclusionary rather than exclusionary, and not prone to significant net-widening at all.

'Decarceration' was perhaps the strongest and best attested policy that labelling theo-rists stressed in past decades. A combination of supportive theory, empirical evidence on high recidivism rates, and the soaring costs of institutional control swayed governments in a sympathetic direction. However, the dangers of offending the judiciary and alarm-ing 'public opinion' meant that indirect means were usually chosen to reduce the prison population. Such methods tended to backfire or make only negligible impact; parole, suspended sentences, and diversion tended either to encourage 'compensatory' sentenc-ing or widen the population at risk. A confusion of aims led to policy compromises that in some respects proved counter-productive. Only in the Netherlands did the trend to-wards shorter sentences prove sustainable, for two decades at least, in the face of rising crime rates.[65] In one case, however, a more radical decarceration was accomplished. In 1972, all juvenile reformatories in Massachusetts were closed down overnight. A number of community care alternatives have since then been adopted with varying success. The authors of the change in policy claim that, while mistakes have been made, 'there was no indication of an increase in crime by juveniles who knew they would not be incarcerated

---

[63] S. Cohen, *Visions of Social Control*.

[64] M. McMahon, '"Net-Widening": Vagaries in the Use of a Concept'.

[65] D. Downes, *Contrasts in Tolerance*.

in a training school if they engaged in crime and were caught.[66] Moreover, 'since 1972, the State of Massachusetts has not had more than 60 to 85 youngsters in a locked setting on any given day—that for a population of 7 million.'[67] It is claimed that Ohlin's investigation of the reforms showed that recidivism rates are roughly the same in the community-based programmes as in the State training schools and that 'certain programs and combinations of programs work very well indeed'. Group-home programmes turned out badly, but specialized foster-care programmes 'do very well'.[68]

Less optimism is evident in Scull's evaluation of decarceration and community care policies.[69] Scull managed to offend both liberals and radicals with his argument that capitalist societies are actively encouraging decarceration (instead of the reverse), but for fiscal reasons and with generally distressing results. He was particularly scathing about the data on Massachusetts, which he lambasts as so sloppy as to be useless for policy evaluation purposes. Not even crime and recidivism figures are presented in such a way as to make before and after comparison feasible; costs are selectively given only for the period after the change; no attempt is made to assess how well families coped with the responsibility for young offenders when alternatives were not available. The later report by Bakal and Polsky made no attempt to meet these criticisms. Scull's main argument is that the rhetoric of community care and decarceration masked a trend in which the State sloughs off responsibility for the 'mad' and the 'bad' on to cut-price private agencies, whose standards of provision were ineffectively monitored. Moreover, in many cases, the real costs were regressively heaped on to the deviants' own families and on those communities least able to mobilize to screen the deviants out. Hence, they gravitate downwards to form 'deviant ghettoes' in already deprived neighbourhoods. Scull's own evidence on this issue is a little inadequate, but several rigorous studies are cited in support of this argument. Rates of mortality and morbidity deteriorated among groups of psycho-geriatric patients released for various forms of 'community care' by comparison with hospitalized groups; and families of schizophrenics struggled to cope with negligible aid from 'the community'.[70] Scull's evidence is selective and does not meet the counter-criticism that adequate community care might resolve such problems and may not be needed for large numbers of less seriously handicapped institutionalized people than psychogeriatric patients. It is all too clear that, as Titmuss warned decades ago, community care can too easily slide into no care at all.[71] The major alternative, which is to improve institutions, is conveniently buried, largely on the grounds of cost.

The premise that major savings are made by such policies is, however, considerably dented by Lerman's re-analysis of data produced by the California Youth Authority on their Probation Subsidy Scheme and Community Training Program in the 1960s, programmes which proved influential in leading other States to adopt similar measures.[72]

[66] J. Miller, 'Systems of Control and the Serious Youth Offender', 144.

[67] J. Miller, 'Systems of Control and the Serious Youth Offender', 142.

[68] J. Miller, 'Systems of Control and the Serious Youth Offender', 143.   [69] A. Scull, *Decarceration*.

[70] A. Scull, *Decarceration*, 99–103, 141 ff., esp. 156, n. 46.

[71] R. Titmuss, *Commitment to Welfare*, ch. 9: 'Community Care: Fact or Fiction?'

[72] P. Lerman, *Community Treatment and Social Control: A Critical Analysis of Juvenile Correctional Policy*, esp. 58–69 and ch. 8.

The costs of the CTP group exceeded those of the matched group of young prisoners, largely due to a change in the project's design which offered intensive services to the former group for far longer than originally planned. The larger claim of the CTP project was, however, to have achieved a much lower rate of recommittals by comparison with the young prisoner group. Yet when actual offences, as distinct from parole violations, were considered, recidivism was markedly higher among the CTP group, whose lower rate of recommittals is attributed by Lerman to greater organizational tolerance of parole violations. The Probation Subsidy Scheme made larger claims for cost-cutting which, on re-analysis, are convincingly shown to stem from faulty methods of computing hypothetical savings. Lerman's study testifies to the formidable complexities involved in monitoring such projects, not least the dangers of confounding that arise from members' stake in organizational survival. The public availability of the fiscal, behavioural, and research data was crucial to this reappraisal and the Californian correctional authorities have clearly set an exemplary standard in this respect. That no other projects have been the subject of so searching a scrutiny should make for a certain wariness in assessing their claims.

Too great a wariness also carries dangers. All too often, the period of time allotted to evaluation is very brief and it is impossible to make an intelligent assessment of its effects. Programmes are likely to change direction and practice in mid-stream. Political imperatives to deliver may well conflict with research imperatives to suspend judgement. Judgement may be disregarded by officials and politicians.[73] And there has also been an indefensible and irrational tendency to dismiss a whole line of theoretical reasoning after the purported failure of a single demonstration project or experiment. In most other areas of enquiry, the consequence of negative or inconclusive findings would be to modify the original programme in order to change the outcome. Yet unusually hard criteria are applied quite precipitately in social reform experiments. It is not surprising that there have been difficulties in demonstrating any 'payoff' from liberal reforms.

Apparent failure, coupled with the longer-standing disillusionment with rehabilitative policies,[74] helped to encourage a revival of more conservative crime control policies. Irrespective of ideological orientation, governments on both sides of the Atlantic have become 'tough on crime' opting for deterrence, punishment, and incapacitation. The incapacitation argument of James Q. Wilson is only the most extreme of a wide range of demands for a return to retributivism of the 'just deserts' model and the desire to return to the strict legality of due process in the juvenile justice field, generally chime with the tenets of *control theories*. Yet control theories are not necessarily reducible to the demand for control of a more traditional kind. As Heidensohn has pointed out, the extraordinary success with which females are socialized into conformity logically suggests—if we are serious about crime control—the feminization of

---

[73] For an invaluable collection of papers assessing the interplay between research, practice, and policy in the British Government's 'evidence-led' crime reduction initiative of the late 1990s, see the special issue of *Criminal Justice*, August 2004, and especially M. Hough, 'Modernization, Scientific Rationalism and the Crime Reduction Programme'.

[74] R. Martinson, 'What Works? Questions and Answers about Penal Reform', 22–54.

male role-playing and a greater emphasis on informal rather than formal social controls. Instead of which, we currently sentence young male offenders to regimes which are in effect promoting macho hardness. Nor are the theories necessarily opposed to redistributive policies. 'Stake-in-conformity' and 'culture of poverty' theories basically imply much the same set of policies as strain theories: a better deal in terms of jobs, housing, and education for those relatively deprived of such bonds with the social order. The major differences between the two kinds of theories concern the causal priorities of the appropriate means to this end. Strain theories stress the need to equalize and expand opportunities and take motivation for granted. Control theories see motivation as weak or absent and argue that tackling the 'cultural deprivation' of the poor and most-discriminated against minority groups is a precondition for improvement.

The 'situational' version of control theory has the most obvious salience for policy. Again, policy proposals do not necessarily coincide with traditionalist calls for zero tolerance policing and harsher sentencing, measures which are vulnerable on the empirical grounds that they produce no more success in controlling crime than community policing and milder sentencing.[75] The controls that are successful tend to be preventive rather than punitive. There is obvious scope for a wide array of practical situational, routine activity and technical controls to be experimented with along carefully monitored and relatively economical lines. In a few cases, such as the reduction in motorcycle thefts consequent on the compulsion to wear crash helmets, whole classes of crime can be dramatically diminished.[76] In others, notably the inferences drawn from the 'defensible space' hypothesis and the installation of non-toxic gas, initially promising causal links now seem more modest or largely spurious.[77] Overall, the main criticism remains that excessive reliance on such policies may lead to a 'double displacement' effect: that crime takes a more regressive form in relation to the more vulnerable groups in the population and that attention is deflected from more complicated 'dispositional' variables of a social and economic character. What does remain in this area are important initiatives on the rehabilitation of disorganized or vulnerable communities. The physical remodelling of estates may both do something towards the restoration of informal social control.[78] The mere presence of concerned people, visible consultation with affected agencies, the expenditure of money, and a new responsiveness to residents' problems may be enough to bring about some change. At the very least, community leaders may arise and acquire influence in the process of consultation and their new influence may inject organization into what had once been disordered. Let us examine one family of initiatives in a little detail.

The Priorities Estates Project was developed by the Department of the Environment, not the Home Office, and it was not intended explicitly to reduce crime. It was supposed to reverse the decline of problem estates and to ensure that empty, unwanted

---

[75] M. Zander, 'What is the Evidence on Law and Order?', 591–4.

[76] R. Clarke, 'Situational Crime Prevention', 141; M. J. Smith and D. B. Cornish, *Theory for Practice in Situational Crime Prevention*.

[77] R. Mawby, 'Kiosk Vandalism', 30–46; R. Clarke and P. Mayhew (eds.), *Designing Out Crime*; and P. Sainsbury, *Suicide Trends in Europe*.

[78] R. Armitage, *Crime Prevention through Housing Design: Policy and Practice*.

property was once again occupied. Nonetheless, it seems to have had quite real consequences for deviance. Tricia Zipfel, one of its consultants, claimed that there was evidence of burglary rates decreasing on all but one of the Project's estates. The most conspicuous change was observed on the Broadwater Farm Estate in north London: between 1982 and 1984 the burglary rate dropped by 62 per cent.[79] On what Zipfel described as a 'nightmare estate', 'burglaries have virtually been eliminated . . . and the crime rate generally has plummeted'.[80]

The Priority Estates Project explains such changes as an indirect consequence of delegating services, management, and lettings. An elaborate process of negotiation with tenants, local authority departments, police, and local agencies invariably accompanies major intervention and the result is that a great deal of practical control is returned to people living and working on a housing estate. One major example is the introduction of a devolved system of lettings which allows local people to obtain tenancies on hard-to-let estates without undue fuss. It allows networks of friends, acquaintances, and families to enter once-fragmented communities. More, these new tenants often *want* to live on the estates. Their coming reduces the numbers of vacant and squatted properties that damage 'local morale' and are 'a public announcement of trouble'. It helps to construct and restore community and it serves to 'strengthen local ties'.[81] It instals tenants who are prepared to act as the willing, unpaid, and unofficial custodians of space that was formerly unprotected: 'housing would be guarded free of charge by the new occupants'.[82] It imports those who no longer resent living on a 'problem' estate, reversing processes that alienate residents from councils. It increases the homogeneity of a community. It removes squatters and others who have been defined as a source of anti-social behaviour. Similarly, the decentralization of maintenance work seems to improve the quality and rate of repairs, transforming the physical appearance and symbolic character of an estate. Such a decrease in visible public damage can eventually become self-propelling, reducing the number of cues that invite vandalism. Resident caretakers can act as peripatetic guardians of property and channels of information about deviance.

What complicates any discussion of such policy initiatives are the difficulties of establishing their precise effects. In practice, the impact of the work undertaken by the Priority Estates Projects and similar organizations can easily become lost and muddled, confused with all the other social, economic, and political changes that may simultaneously be affecting a community.

The devolution of practical control may be accompanied by a remodelling of the physical environment. When boundaries are installed, there may be a decline in the amount of confused, impersonal public space and an increase in the area of private, defended space.[83] Consultation with the police and other agencies can demystify relations which were once wary or distant, enabling groups to reassess one another,

---

[79] T. Zipfel, 'Broadwater Farm Estate, Haringey: Background and Information Relating to the Riot on Sunday, 6th October 1985', unpublished.   [80] T. Zipfel, 'Hard Work Transforms a Nightmare Estate'.

[81] Department of the Environment, *Local Housing Management*.

[82] A. Power, 'How to Rescue Council Housing'.

[83] Department of the Environment, *Reducing Vandalism on Public Housing Estates*.

respond sympathetically, and then collaborate: 'a commonly reported situation is one where, as a result of beat policing allied to better management of the estate, the tenants are more willing to report damage or challenge anti-social behaviour.'[84] Above all, the very business of implicating tenants in plans and programmes can soften relations between suspicious neighbours and imbue them with a novel sense of organization, purpose, and effectiveness. It gives an opportunity to reassert control.

To be sure, there is some anxiety about the displacement effect of such policies, but there does seem to be an absolute decline in the volume of victimization. As our discussion of Mayhew's analysis of displacement effects may have shown, crime does not always travel when initiatives are introduced. Some simply stops. Since 1995 crime rates have fallen back to 1981 levels, at least as measured by official crime and victim surveys, a trend apparent across most of Europe and North America. Why that should have happened is not apparent. Zimring[85] certainly failed to find any convincing explanation that covered more than one country. Yet situational crime prevention may help to account for some part of those trends, though it should be noted that in Canada and Scotland crime rates were relatively stable throughout the post-1980 period:[86] hence it is far from being the whole story.

Some communities, of course, have become too anomic, too heterogeneous, and too fragmented properly to be called 'communities'. They cannot readily be resuscitated. In Newman's language, they have 'tipped' and have slid into a state of disorder from which there cannot always be a return.[87] Like Rainwater's Pruitt–Igoe project, the only recourse may be physically to destroy the estate and begin again. It was certainly the case that an attempt to introduce 'cocooning neighbourhood watch' (rechristened 'care watch') on a London housing estate collapsed because, like the anomic residents of Pruitt–Igoe, neighbours did not trust one another enough to erect a defensive shield. Neighbours knew one another too little (or perhaps too well) to co-operate; it was feared that the cocooning neighbours might actually be the very people who had burgled the property in the past; and there were anxieties that formal reports to the police and informal personal intervention might lead to retaliation.[88]

There may be other difficulties. Housing estates, projects, and inner-city areas are never neat instances of the uncontaminated laboratory experiment that demands *ceteris paribus*, other things being left equal. Other things are rarely equal. There is so much and such continual intervention from so many bodies, from the police, probation, social services, local and central government, that the impact of any single (and typically modest) crime-prevention initiative is almost always impossible to establish. It was certainly the case that efforts to discern the specific impact on crime of a Priority Estates Programme project in London's Tower Hamlets were confounded by the simultaneous workings of changes in local government housing policy, the initiation of 'right

[84] M. Burbidge, 'British Public Housing and Crime: A Review'.
[85] F. Zimring, *The Great American Crime Decline*.
[86] D. Smith, 'Less Crime without more Punishment'.   [87] Newman, *Community of Interest*.
[88] A. Sampson, *Lessons from a Victim Support Crime Prevention Project*.

to buy' legislation (permitting tenants to purchase their homes), attempts to initiate a HAT (a housing action trust), and the pervasive impact of social change wrought by the Docklands scheme.[89]

Such studies also show the difficulties of distinguishing the impact of the social from the situational aspects of crime prevention programmes. In principle, the two approaches are very different. Social crime prevention, in so far as it tackles the root causes of crime successfully, harbours no risk of its displacement. For example, if the search for excitement is met by sports projects, the displacement effect is nil. Situational measures, such as steering locks and car alarms on high-value vehicles, surveillance systems, and security guards may raise the excitement and risk-taking stakes and/or deflect crime elsewhere. In practice, there are social aspects to situational measures and situational to social. For example, situational measures may carry socially exclusionary effects, as in the barring of shopping precincts to known troublemakers, which risks generating more crime elsewhere. But highly visible situational measures may enhance feelings of security to the point where community life is revived, reducing the drive for exclusion in the longer term. Foster describes how the removal of an experienced home beat officer from a priority estate led to an increase both in crime and the fear of crime, upsetting the 'delicate balance between containing crime and an atmosphere which positively encourages crime'.[90] Even well-conceived social measures on one part of a multiply deprived estate backfired by inadvertently drawing in a far wider population starved of adequate housing and leisure resources: a kind of reverse displacement. No scheme is an island and if welfare provision in general is unduly depleted, a 'mecca' effect is all too likely, swamping project resources by default.[91] It is not easy to strike the optimum balance between social and situational measures, especially when scarce resources encourage practitioners to opt for the short-term, tangible, purely situational response, such as target-hardening.

Just how hard it is in practice to orchestrate an array of policy changes based on a mix of social (usually long-term) and situational (usually short-term) measures is well exemplified by New Labour's 'Third Way' reforms. In the crime control field, policy-making was heavily shaped by the assertion that New Labour would be 'tough on crime, tough on the causes of crime'. Policies were ushered in designed to break with 'Old Labour's allegedly "soft on crime" image'[92] whilst retaining a social reformist agenda. The latter was recognizably rooted in priorities relevant to strain and social control theories and to those of left realism: tackling poverty, social exclusion, and unemployment, inequalities of educational opportunity and health care, and the regeneration of the most deprived communities.

The dissonances between the short-and long-term agendas and cultivating new electoral constituencies in the business and corporate worlds whilst retaining traditional

---

[89] J. Foster and T. Hope, *Housing, Community and Crime.*
[90] J. Foster, 'Informal Social Control and Community Crime Prevention'.
[91] J. Foster and T. Hope, *Housing, Community and Crime.*
[92] D. Downes and R. Morgan, 'Dumping the Hostages to Fortune: The Politics of Law and Order in Postwar Britain'.

working-class support, led New Labour in practice to under-emphasize rampant and growing economic inequality and to over-emphasize assuaging populist punitiveness.[93] A panoply of liberal measures, 'New Deals' on youth unemployment and training and on community regeneration, Sure Start (a UK version of the USA Head Start programme), and on restorative justice, was accompanied and over-shadowed by a string of punitive measures heavily influenced by the American examples of 'zero tolerance' policing and penal incapacitation. 'Final warnings', anti-social behaviour orders (popularly known as ASBOs), minimum mandatory sentencing for burglary, drug dealing, and violence, tighter penalties for breaching community sanctions, lowering the age of criminal responsibility to ten, parenting orders,[94] and a host of other measures tilted the social service and criminal justice systems towards the disciplinary end of the welfare spectrum. A new 'culture of control'[95] has arguably been evolved, partly in response to rising crime rates over the long period from 1955 to 1993, but also in response to changing conceptions of responsibility. The fallacy of conflating explanations of crime (the subject of this book) with excuses for its commission is palpably part of this process.

The intermediatized politics of crime control are now entrenched not only in market societies such as Britain and the USA but also, arguably, in The Netherlands, a country long associated with minimal resort to penal measures.[96] Their defining criterion is the acceptance by all major political parties of what Jonathan Simon[97] termed 'governing through crime', that is, the exploitation for electoral ends of public concern about crime as the overriding condition for governmental legitimacy. This entails a ceaseless 'raising of consciousness' about crime and punishment as *the* issue which above all else constitutes grounds for political credibility. It has greatly extended, over the past decade in Britain, the trend towards the 'criminalization of social policy',[98] the danger that 'fundamental public issues may become marginalized, except in so far as they are defined in terms of their criminogenic consequences . . . As a consequence, we may come to view poor housing, unemployment, racism, failed educational facilities, the lack of youth leisure opportunities, and so on, as no longer important public issues in themselves. Rather, their importance may be seen to derive from the belief that they lead to crime and disorder. The fact that they may do exactly that is no reason not to assert their importance in their own right.'[99] The new fiscal crisis of the State, and the austerity agenda induced by the economic collapse of 2008, may affect the size of the prison estate. There are signs now that Andrew Scull's prophecy may be coming true, though it would take a monumental fall in the American prison population for it to return from its current mass incarceration level of 2.3 million to its 1975 level of under 400,000. The situation in England and Wales, though far less draconian, would still mean a halving of its current level to re-attain its scale in the early 1990s.

---

[93] A. Bottoms, 'The Philosophy and Politics of Punishment and Sentencing'.
[94] Compulsory parenting classes for parents of juvenile offenders.
[95] D. Garland, *The Culture of Control: Crime and Social Order in Contemporary Society*.
[96] D. Downes and R. van Swaaningen, 'The Road to Dystopia? Changes in the Penal Climate of the Netherlands'.   [97] J. Simon, *Governing through Crime*.
[98] A. Crawford, *The Local Governance of Crime: Appeals to Community and Partnerships*, 228–32.
[99] A. Crawford, *The Local Governance of Crime: Appeals to Community and Partnerships*, 229–30.

A related trend is towards the 'criminalization of criminal justice policy'. Skolnick[100] and Packer[101] respectively distinguished the tension between 'law' and 'order', and between due process and crime control as fundamental antinomies in the criminal justice framework. In contemporary Britain, that tension is steadily becoming weighted in favour of order and crime control, rather than law and due process, in the recent governance of crime. Anti-Social Behaviour Orders introduced the less exacting canons of civil rather than criminal law in the determination of guilt, despite the fact that criminal penalties of up to five years' imprisonment could be activated for any breach of the order. Justified as needed to ensure rapid case settlement for 'nuisance value' misconduct, they were used to complement sentencing in criminal cases, logically negating their original purpose.[102] Parenting orders are invoked to coerce parents of young offenders to learn better parenting skills, despite the fact that offenders over the age of nine are now deemed fully responsible for their own offending behaviour. The very concept of individual responsibility for the offence is thereby eroded. The welfare principle in youth justice has been progressively marginalized. Most recently a rapidly unfolding counter–terrorism agenda has reinforced the drift to the normalization of exceptional forms of criminalization.

These examples are far from alone in testifying to the determination of successive governments to drag the criminal justice system into the twenty-first century. Nor, however, has it proved reversible as yet in any society that has adopted it as a key electoral strategy, It is by no means an unalloyed asset. It has led to hyper-active policy-making and incoherent administration, as initiative follows initiative often in response to the latest high-profile crime.

The marked rise of populist politics has encouraged politicians to construct an administrative system beset by institutional amnesia, whereby they forget their own past commitments and dismantle the precautionary safeguards that used to be installed administratively. Having raised the crime control stakes so high, they are then puzzled by their failure to persuade the electorate that crime rates are falling, looking instead for new spectacular initiatives to allay popular discontents. In the process, they have allowed activist victims, some of whose demands for punishment and control are virtually insatiable, to play a much more prominent political role.[103] As a result, the constant harping on the 'war against crime' in its many rhetorical guises constantly abraded citizens' sense of security. The 'fear of crime' thus stubbornly remains largely unchanged. It is arguably the case that, although as yet the 'governing through crime' strategy has proved irreversible in any society that has adopted it, it is actually unsustainable, for good Durkheimian and fiscal reasons. A crime-free society is a contradiction in terms, as the very processes that drive an ever-heightened consciousness of crime prevention lead ineluctably to the demonization of 'normal' deviance, and beyond. An 'infinite aspiration' to the elimination of crime logically leads, in Durkheimian terms, to the paradox of anomie.

---

[100] J. Skolnick, *Justice without Trial.*
[101] H. Packer, *The Limits of the Criminal Sanction.*   [102] E. Burney, *Making People Behave.*
[103] P. Rock, 'The Politics of Victimhood'.

Finally, *phenomenological* approaches favour a more austere set of relations between sociology and social policy than those that are sought by most sociologists. In some respects they adhere to the methodological principles of Weber. Weber had argued that whilst sociologists' own values are inevitably implicated in their choice of subject-matter and definition of a problem ('value relevance'), once they proceed with their investigations their methods and analytical procedures should be as objective as possible ('value freedom'). Moreover, the claims of scientific integrity preclude the use of sociological or scientific work for partisan or political ends in which, as citizens, they are quite properly engaged. Schutz's phenomenology proposed a more radical version of the separation of 'scientific' and 'natural' roles, in which the choice of problem for sociologists should properly be derived from sociological, and not lay or political, definitions of the problems at hand.

> Sociological typifications of action and meaning, Schutz's 'second order constructs', by definition are removed from the common-sense, practical activities of members of society; these typifications are a product of certain kinds of reflection by sociologists on the common-sense world. This would suggest that the main relationship between sociological reflection about the world and practical activity in the world lies . . . in sociology's ability to clarify these practical activities . . . The contribution of sociology, then, . . . is that it can help the members of a society pose their own dilemmas more acutely and clearly.[104]

Worthwhile as this aim is, it disregards the potential of sociological work, for whatever reason, to enter into public and political discourse as a resource and 'stock of knowledge' in its own right. It becomes extremely difficult, if not impossible, under such circumstances for sociologists to claim that they are disseminating knowledge solely as citizens and not in any way as scientists. The distinction between the two roles is, however, an important one and clearly holds implications for scientists in general, not sociologists alone.

These issues have achieved renewed prominence. Triggered by the much vaunted proclamation of Michael Burawoy, in 2004,[105] the idea of a public social science has become pivotal to current reflections about the state of the discipline. In the era of mass incarceration and para-military policing in the USA, such matters have attained intense urgency. What is now distinguished as 'public criminology' has been self-consciously designed to encourage scholars to talk to communities, policy-makers, and other constituencies about matters of practical criminological interest, steering, informing, and responding to lay preoccupations and problems. Its place within the larger body of criminology has been analysed by Ian Loader and Richard Sparks[106] in the guise of a typology of ideal-typical, professional roles. Theirs is not a prescriptive or critical account but a description of varying stances and justifications, veering from the engaged activist, at the one pole, to the detached scientific adviser, at the other. What they omit, for reasons that are not clear, is the position of the disinterested

---

[104] M. Phillipson, *Sociological Aspects of Crime and Deviance*, 16–89 and ch. 6, 'Criminology, Sociology, Crime and Social Policy'.

[105] M. Burawoy, 'For Public Sociology: Contradictions, Dilemmas and Possibilities'.

[106] I. Loader and R. Sparks, *Public Criminology?*

academic who is not bent on making his or her mark on politics or policy but on re-searching intellectual puzzles and problems. The maxim of such a scholar might be to reverse Marx's epitaph and claim that 'criminologists have only sought to change the world, the point is to interpret it'. Crime, criminals, deviants, social control and crimi-nal justice in this formulation are intriguing phenomena to research. This position is clearly in decline as pressures emanating from government and the universities direct scholars more and more towards 'crime control' policy-relevance and verifiable im-pact on crime. In important respects, increasingly, government departments and the criminal justice agencies are setting a 'what works' agenda for researchers and defin-ing what constitutes appropriate methodological approaches. The result is contracted research for criminal justice agencies rather than independent research on criminal justice agencies. It is evident that there is a mounting debate about the proper calling and the nature of the public responsibilities and obligations of the professional crimi-nologist as well as the public implications of the on-going narrowing of the research agenda and therefore the criminological imagination.[107]

Conclusion

The policy implications of theories of deviance are not mere inferences that may be ex-trapolated from them but may also be regarded as an opportunity for their evaluation. If one theme has emerged, it is that, like facts, though for different reasons, theories do not speak for themselves. Social scientists have not, on the whole, taken very seri-ously Kant's assertion that 'nothing is so practical as a good theory'. There is usually no simple or automatic set of usable policy prescriptions to be drawn from theories or indeed research findings. A variety of interpretations are possible and ideally the theo-rist should attempt to clarify their character. Translating theories into practice entails complex deliberations in which the implications for action (or inaction) may be speci-fied, proposals for monitoring and evaluation made, and likely side-effects anticipated. A theory of public problems must be complemented by an understanding of the rap-idly changing policy environment and process. Otherwise, the casting of a theory into the policy world is naïve. The obstacles to these aspirations are great, both intellectu-ally and practically, so that no great mystery surrounds the relative infrequency with which they are even attempted. It remains difficult for most academic researchers to produce clearly defined 'what works' policy recommendations. There are also difficul-ties in communicating research findings in an accessible manner for policy-makers, the news media, and indeed the public. Nevertheless, it is vitally important for crimi-nologists to continue to engage in public debates and to undertake rigorous analysis of policy development and implementation. They cannot just subordinate themselves, in the name of 'impact', to the 'what works' agendas of the various components of the criminal justice system.

---

[107] See the special issues of *Theoretical Criminology* (2007) and *Criminology and Public Policy* (2010) for papers exploring these matters.

Further Reading

L. CHANCER and E. McLaughlin, 'Public Criminologies: Diverse Perspectives on Academia and Policy', *Theoretical Criminology*, 11:2, 2007.

T. CLEAR, 'Policy and Evidence: The Challenge to the American Society of Criminology: 2009 Presidential Address to the American Society of Criminology', *Criminology*, 48:1, 2010.

I. LOADER and R. Sparks, *Public Criminology?*, London, 2010.

M. J. SMITH and D. B. Cornish, *Theory for Practice in Situational Crime Prevention*, Monsey, NJ, 2003.

C. UGGEN and M. Inderbitzin, 'Public Criminologies', *Criminology & Public Policy*, 9:4, 2010.

14

The Metamorphosis of the Sociology of Crime and Deviance

Introduction

From its decisive moment of re-emergence in the mid-1960s, the sociology of crime and deviance has encountered waves of criticism. One critique has projected the view that it is intellectually and practically exhausted.[1] Intellectual exhaustion is evidenced by the claim that the sociology of crime and deviance has been unable to connect with new perspectives in social theory.[2] Practical exhaustion is evidenced by the claim that it is unable to address new trends in crime and crime control[3] and has been replaced by different forms of realist criminologies. This reduces the sociological study of crime and deviance to the status of a chapter in the textbook history of criminology.

The questions that arise from these developments are, naturally enough, how far they indicate a fundamental change of direction in the field and whether or not that spells the effective end of the sociology of crime and deviance as a recognizable subject. Would it now be better termed 'Sociological Criminology' or some other variant on that theme? We would argue that little is gained by hyperactive nominalism. Important battles were won in the 1960s, with the shift from positivist based administrative criminology to the interactionist based sociology of crime and deviance, implying the contestation by sociology of a field largely framed by psychological-legal precepts, and with the acceptance of the premise that crime and deviance were problematic, not immanent, properties of social conduct. Since then the fields have become increasingly meshed, with frequent interchange and borrowings of concepts, methods, and theories. We are not so wedded to theories of 'crime' and 'deviance' that we would resist the abandonment of the concepts in the face of superior alternatives. To do so, however, we would need to be persuaded that such theories had been seriously outpaced by events, fresh theories, or new ideas: this does not seem to be the case.

---

[1] C. Sumner, *The Sociology of Deviance: An Obituary*.
[2] D. Nelken (ed.), *The Futures of Criminology*; D. Garland and R. Sparks (eds.), *Criminology and Social Theory*.
[3] W. Morrison, *Theoretical Criminology: From Modernity to Postmodernism*.

The first set of critiques tend to devalue sociological theories of crime and deviance as lacking purchase on the radical transformations and complexities of the post-modern world, seeing them as 'master narratives' or indeed 'sustaining illusions' that fitted modernist but not post-modern conditions. However, there is no more reason to accept post-modernist eschatology as a foundational narrative or critique than any of the other narratives or critiques which post-modernism rejects.[4]

But perhaps more significantly, there is a sense, as Stan Cohen has noted, in which interactionist based sociological analysis of crime and deviance was/is already post-modernist, that is, in the radical post-positivistic emphasis it gives to the importance of accounts, hierarchies of credibility, regimes of truth, signification processes, the fiction and mediatized drama of public realities, and vocabularies of motive. In the highly unequal division of labour that goes into the social construction of reality, sociologists of crime and deviance have long aimed to reveal the balance between those in and those outside power. The point, however, is to mediate between differentially empowered accounts, rather than to grant them equal validity.

In tune with the 'post' turn, Maureen Cain[5] developed the case for a 'transgressive' post-colonial criminology by reference to the difficulties of applying mainstream Western theories of crime, deviance, and control to non-Western and developing societies. Criminology is entrapped either by orientalism—the assumption that non-Western societies are ineluctably different—or by occidentalism—the assumption that a 'Western' template can be applied in blanket fashion to *all* societies.[6] Post-colonial criminologists are undoubtedly right to criticize superficial and ethnocentric comparative work and to challenge such notions as that the criminological 'facts' that appear to prevail in North America and Western Europe hold globally. But to take these shortcomings, and those that have occurred in the history of crime as grounds for rejecting all previous theorizing, is far too dismissive of its strengths.

The condition of post-modernity may be readily imaginable (science-fiction writers have been doing little else for a century); but it is far from being the unproblematic state of affairs, despite tangible, but uneven, signs of its emergence. For that reason, Giddens' use of the term late modernity seems preferable, though even that raises the question, 'How late is late?' or 'Late in relation to what?' The condition of 'late' modernity has seemed to incubate trends which have created changes for crime, deviance, and control against which to assess the validity and relevance of theory.

The conception of the risk society articulated by Ulrich Beck and Anthony Giddens is, for example, often held to mark an epochal break with modernity and what are defined as simplistic modernist forms of risk thinking, risk consciousness, and risk management, including crime control. In the new 'reflexive modernity' capitalist exploitation of resources and new technologies is seen as increasingly out of or even

---

[4] T. Eagleton, *The Illusions of Postmodernism*.

[5] M. Cain, 'Orientalism, Occidentalism and the Sociology of Crime'; M. Cain and A. Howe, *Women, Crime and Social Harm: Towards a Criminology for the Global Age*.

[6] K. Franko Aas, *Globalization and Crime*; N. Larsen and R. Smandych, *Global Criminology and Criminal Justice*; C. Cuneen, 'Postcolonial Perspectives for Criminology'; M. Lee and K. J. Laidler, 'Doing Criminology from the Periphery'.

beyond control. As if to compensate for the global immensity of the risks and hazards that have been uncontrollably unleashed, notably climate change, governments crack down ever more harshly on forms of risk-taking they feel they *can* control: cigarette smokers are demonized, criminals more harshly sentenced, 'health and safety' elevated to ever more stringent regulation. Yet, as O'Malley[7] notes, 'little or no evidence is produced to indicate that risk consciousness is as generalized or as novel as is claimed.' It is central to the methodology of medical science, on the one hand, and the insurance industry, on the other: hardly new phenomena. 'The idea of criminals as conscious risk-takers, as opposed to simply evil-doers, owes its modern origins to the classical criminology of Bentham and Beccaria.'[8] O'Malley is receptive to the new stress on risk as an element in studies of the creative 'edgework' of certain crimes such as shoplifting. And he is concerned to rescue the concept of risk from a punitive reading to more humane possibilities, both in sentencing and in criminology. But his analysis counters the view that the 'risk society' thesis amounts to a sea-change in theories of crime and deviance.

The second critique views the discipline as unable to address the contemporary realities of crime. The dominance of different forms of realist criminologies, including feminist criminologies, relegates the sociology of crime and deviance to the sidelines. This critique is far more in line with earlier modernist attempts to synthesize diverse theories into a criminological 'master narrative'. 'Left realist' explanations of crime and deviance attempt to combine key elements from anomie and strain, interactionist, control, and radical theories into one. While this synthesis (as suggested in Chapter 10) has done much to reanimate such theories as anomie and subculture, it skates too readily over fundamental problems of analysis and 'root' causes. Left realism encounters exactly the same problems (posed by Matza) as the earlier 'parent' theories on which it depends—for example, over-prediction (its core cause—relative deprivation—accounts for far more crime than exists, even now, especially among women). Such problems are compounded for left realists by the synthesis of competing 'causes' which entails a multiplier effect: over-prediction cubed.

In its most recent incarnation, a left realist based version of cultural criminology, describes the social-psychological turmoil associated with a vertiginous hyper-anomic world spiralling out of control, This world is riddled with the ontological insecurities and risks associated with outrageous inequalities, rampant individualism, fractured identities, xenophobic resentments and hatreds, over-identification with a rampant consumerism and saturated by the mass mediatization, and is marked by ever-increasing globalized strains to deviance, criminality, and violence.[9] What it fails to address, as Lynn McDonald pointed out in her own telling critique of the earlier jeremiads of Marx and Durkheim in the nineteenth century,[10] is that overall crime rates in the consumer societies that it refers to have actually been *falling* from the mid-1990s onwards. Unless official crime rates are simply dismissed out of hand as a form of postmodern

---

[7] P. O'Malley, *Crime and Risk*, 12.   [8] P. O'Malley, *Crime and Risk*, 53.
[9] J. Young, *The Vertigo of Late Modernity*.
[10] L. McDonald, 'Theory and Evidence of Rising Crime in the Nineteenth Century'.

fiction, cultural criminologists and others would, presumably, have to consider Stephen Pinker's thesis that we may be living in the most peaceable and secure era in human existence due to the impact of on-going pacification and civilization processes; humanitarianism and the recognition of human rights; and the decline of inter-state war and crimes against humanity.[11] They have failed to address the remarkable criminological phenomenon.

In contrast, neo-classical criminologists have taken the opposite approach—anti-synthesis. Having stripped away all theoretical positions bar one, that rational choice causes crime and, as a consequence, a multitude of straightforward deterrent means can be deployed,[12] they face the difficult problem of accounting for immense differences in comparative crime problems without convincing reference to social, economic, or cultural variables. Because it lends itself so directly to common-sense and an applied 'what works' focus with positivist scientific methods, neo-classical criminology has been by far the most influential policy prescription. On a similar note, feminist criminologists work on gendered victimization is not just intended to challenge and revitalize the criminological agenda but also to transform criminal justice policy and practice.

Where does this leave the other sociologically grounded theories of crime and deviance that we have discussed? All the theories have had things to say that illuminate the twenty-first century in ways which show their likely continuing potential for development and applications. In a field where continuities and changes are often difficult to differentiate, the following issues seem to have been usefully presaged by the major theories.

Challenge and Renewal

Continuities and change in strain theory offer one of the clearest instances of prescience in the sphere of crime and deviance. The fundamental propositions of the anomie and subcultural traditions of theory from the 1930s on were that inequality, whether persistent or growing, combined with rising expectations fuelled by consumer capitalism, would produce relative deprivation and lead to increasing rates of crime and the emergence or growth of more serious forms of deviance. Early subcultural theory was replete with warnings that automation would lead to mass working-class unemployment unless radical changes in training, education, and job creation were made.[13] Little was done and, in the wake of widespread de-industrialization and 'marketization', massive job losses coincided with rampant consumerism to produce a much-analysed and well-documented widening of inequalities and increase in poverty.[14] Left realism is the main current vehicle for these concerns.

[11] S. Pinker, *The Better Angels of Our Nature*.

[12] J. Wilson and R. Herrnstein, *Crime and Human Nature*; M. Felson and R. V. Clarke, *Opportunity Makes the Thief*; M. Felson, *Crime and Everyday Life*; M. A. Andersen and G. Farrell, *The Criminal Act: The Role and Influence of Routine Activity Theory*.

[13] D. Downes, 'Back to the Future: The Predictive Value of Social Theories of Delinquency'.

[14] W. Hutton, *The State We're In*; and O. James, *Juvenile Violence in a Winner–Loser Culture*.

In many respects the predicted increase in crime rates and changes in the character of crime occurred on cue. In Europe, especially Britain and in North America, property crime and rates of drug-related crime rose sharply. New forms of inequality and social exclusion generated a series of riots unprecedented in modern Britain, which in the 1980s was associated with policing issues and in the 1990s with florid forms of crime such as 'steaming' and 'hotting'.[15] Crime rates then fell. They fell in England and Wales where there have been exceptionally low rates of unemployment. They fell in the USA, and there is no agreement about why they should have done so,[16] but one likely reason was the combined effect of an extraordinarily high prison population, which served to 'take out' some 6 per cent of the group most 'at risk' of crime—young black males—and reduced male unemployment by 2 per cent by the simple process of removing some two million people from the labour market.[17] Even so, according to calculations by Richard Freeman,[18] once allowances are made for this effect, the crime rate of the unincarcerated has still risen—a damning finding for proponents of deterrence, if not incapacitation.

Against this view, several critical notes have been registered. One is that falling inequality and full employment in the 1960s did not lead to falling crime (quite the reverse) and that mass unemployment and huge inequality in the 1930s did not lead to far steeper rises in crime.[19] A second is that 'deficit' theories of crime do not account for its growth among elites.[20] While both objections are powerful reminders that no simple relationship obtains between crime and inequality, the essential accompaniment to such links is the context of market-driven rising expectations. Some of the complexities of this relationship were captured by Simon Field's authoritative study[21] demonstrating short-term cyclical fluctuations correlating property crime and the rate of consumption. This pattern amounts to anomie in action: when times are bad, people are more likely to buy from the 'black market', when times are good, people buy from the more accountable High Street or internet.[22] What remains unclear is how such short-term resolutions to the strain to anomie exhibit a 'ratchet effect' over the longer term,[23] whereby net rises in crime acquire a degree of permanence. The most likely result is that an instrumental moral expediency becomes steadily more acceptable, a process which is challengeable only by punitive means or the closer attainment of that Durkheimian ideal: a just society based on a moral framework acceptable by all.

The limits to prescience are well exemplified by the failure of theorists who correctly predicted a huge increase in the volume and seriousness of crime to deduce where that

---

[15] A. Power and R. Tunstall, *Dangerous Disorder: Riots and Violent Disturbances in Thirteen Areas of Britain, 1991–92.*

[16] F. Zimring, *The Great American Crime Decline*; O. Roeder et al., *What Caused the Crime Decline?*

[17] B. Western and K. Beckett, *How Unregulated is the USA Labor Market? The Penal System as a Labor Market Institution.*

[18] R. Freeman, 'Who Becomes a Criminal?'   [19] D. Smith, 'Youth Crime and Conduct Disorders'.

[20] M. B. Clinard and P. C. Yaeger, *Corporate Crime.*

[21] S. Field, *Trends in Crime and their Interpretation.*

[22] M. Sutton, 'Supply by Theft: Does the Market for Second-Hand Goods Play a Role in Keeping Crime Figures High?'

[23] J. Pitts and T. Hope, 'The Local Politics of Inclusion—The State and Community Safety'.

could lead in the realm of punishment and control. Even the most lynx-eyed radical criminologists seemed bound by the liberal paradigm that no democratic government would countenance so steep a step-change in the character and scale of the prison population as that which occurred in the USA since the mid-1970s, though some, such as Stuart Hall,[24] came close. Nor did the proponents of penal incapacitation, such as James Q. Wilson and John DeIulio, predict so marked a move to mass imprisonment, much as they may have welcomed it. The political ramifications of this shift to a *macho* penal economy include another unpredicted phenomenon, though one which might have occurred to those Democrats who sought to out-tough Republicans in the law-and-order stakes: the unexpected success, at a time of economic prosperity, of the Republican George W. Bush over the Democrat Al Gore in the 2000 Presidential election. Bush's heavily disputed and razor-thin majority turned, *inter alia*, on the penal disenfranchisement of some four million Americans, either held in prisons or denied the vote as felons in key states. As they were and are mostly men of Afro-American or Hispanic minorities, who vote overwhelmingly for the Democratic candidate, not only the 2000 presidency but also many State elections have arguably pivoted on their disenfranchisement. Penal policy has never before had so profound an impact on US and, given the international situation, world politics. The links between politics, crime, and control have not, since the rise of Fascism, had so potent an effect on the shaping of Western democracies.[25]

Two interlocking problems that remain unresolved are, first, why crime rates have fallen rather than risen over the past two decades in the context of increasing inequality in the UK and the USA; and, second, why the fear of crime and criminal victimization has remained relatively unchanged despite that fall. On the first question, it is not enough to point to rising imprisonment in Britain and mass imprisonment in the USA as the answer. Canada, for example, has experienced much the same rise and fall in homicide rates over the past forty years as the USA, but at one-third of the American level and without the resort to mass incarceration.[26] Indeed, Canada has experienced a notable stability in both crime and punishment rates over the past two decades. In the cases of Britain and the USA, it may well be that, despite leaving *some* causes of crime, such as inequality and a rampant winner/loser culture, unaddressed and even worsening, the crime rate can be forced down by more effective policing and punitive and situational crime prevention measures, such as relentless target-hardening, surveillance technologies, sophisticated alarm systems, gentrification dynamics and the proliferation of 'gated' communities, and the refusal of access to 'security bubbles' to all but privileged ID card holders. A securitization culture[27] helps account for both falling crime rates and the persistently high rates of 'fear of crime'. A state of constant,

---

[24] S. Hall, *Drifting into a Law and Order Society*.

[25] D. Garland (ed.), *Mass Imprisonment: Social Causes and Consequences*; and C. Uggen and J. Manza, 'Democratic Contraction? The Political, Consequences of Felon Disenfranchisement in the United States'.

[26] A. Doob and C. Webster, 'Countering Punitiveness: Understanding Stability in Canada's Imprisonment Rate'.

[27] D. Garland, *The Culture of Control*; K. D. Haggerty and R. V. Ericson, *The New Politics of Surveillance and Visibility*.

full-on terrorist 'Red Alert', a heightened sense of threat and vulnerability, and high-profile crimes is not conducive to ontological security, especially when it is given daily reinforcement by governmental and tabloid *imprimaturs*. As Reiner argues:[28]

> There may . . . be a rational kernel to the stubborn refusal of public anxiety to decline with the crime rate . . . Within the decline in overall crime, the most worrying serious violent crimes (especially robbery) have tended to rise . . . Perhaps even more significant is what can be called the paradox of insecurity. An increasing obsession with security practices and paraphernalia, even if successful in reducing risk, can exacerbate the sense of insecurity by acting as reminders of danger . . . What is required is reassurance not about crime but about the causes of crime. The root causes of crime have not diminished appreciably in the 1990s.

Indeed, if those 'root causes' are seen as the growth of extremes of inequality and the winner/loser culture that it has generated, they have markedly increased. Remarkably, the harsh austerity measures taken to shore up the economies of the UK and the USA following the financial catastrophe of 2008–9, have not driven the crime rate upwards despite such levels of securitization. This has led James Q. Wilson to conclude:

> At the deepest level, many of these shifts, taken together, suggest that crime in the United States is falling—even through the greatest economic downturn since the Great Depression—because of a big improvement in the culture. The cultural argument may strike some as vague, but writers have relied on it in the past to explain both the Great Depression's fall in crime and the explosion of crime during the sixties. In the first period, on this view, people took self-control seriously; in the second, self-expression—at society's cost—became more prevalent. It is a plausible case. Culture creates a problem for social scientists like me, however. We do not know how to study it in a way that produces hard numbers and testable theories. Culture is the realm of novelists and biographers, not of data-driven social scientists. But we can take some comfort, perhaps, in reflecting that identifying the likely causes of the crime decline is even more important than precisely measuring it.[29]

These trends also raise problems for labelling theory which, broadly conceived, offered the first major step towards dealing with criminal justice and formal control processes as variables rather than constants in the creation and transformation of deviant and criminal behaviour. The initial excitement of applying the concepts of Becker, Goffman, and Lemert to crime, deviance, and control tended to give way to premature disillusionment when the most obvious means of de-labelling and de-institutionalization failed to lead to crime reduction. Such reactions, however understandable, have tended to obscure the real and continuing impact of labelling theory on social theory and reform movements.

First of all, many of its key insights have been normalized. Generations of students in the social sciences and their applied fields, such as social work and probation work, have now been exposed to the approach and—though its history has not been charted—have deployed its insights as a lexicon for the reappraisal of deviant naming.

---

[28] R. Reiner, *Law and Order: An Honest Citizen's Guide to Crime and Control*, 115–16.
[29] J. Q. Wilson, 'Hard Times, Fewer Crimes'.

The new-found significance of the politics of naming has derived at least in part from the vocabulary and theories of labelling and has had some appreciable effect in the partial emancipation of women, ethnic minorities, the disabled, and gays. Stan Cohen's conceptualization of 'folk devils and moral panic' has worked its way into the English language, a sign of acceptance that the over-interpretation of extreme instances of deviance can be counter-productive. The downside often attributed to this development, political correctness and the 'culture of complaint',[30] has undoubtedly led to excesses in its turn; but net gains in tolerance and heightened understanding have arguably resulted from the re-defining of *some* forms of deviance as diversity.

Second, labelling theory has been given a second wind by the work of Michel Foucault and its critical development by Stan Cohen and others.[31] Cohen's *Visions of Social Control* provides a rich vein of concepts—net-widening, mesh thinning, blurring, penetration, and the proliferation of community controls—which presaged such invasive developments as surveillance cameras, electronic tagging, urine testing, and new 'vocabularies of motive' for States violating human rights and constricting civil liberties. Such invasive, pervasive, and exclusionary devices have the powerful legitimation, often shared by communities as well as 'the State', that they are essential to global wars against crime and terrorism discourses which brook no alternatives to punitive measures unless they are of a rarely achieved, demonstrable effectiveness. Yet the criteria of effectiveness commonly used in the criminological field are far more stringent than those in the world of medicine and the physical sciences.[32]

Third, trends strikingly in line with labelling theorists' premonitions about the future of social control in late modernity have occurred in the realm of social exclusion, a field far wider than crime and necessitating the use of 'deviance' to capture its reach.[33] For example, school exclusions in Britain have risen even more rapidly than crime rates or penal measures, and combined long-term effects with lack of substantive rights regarding due process. Perhaps the most formidable example has been the use to which the term 'underclass' has been put in the work of Charles Murray.[34] As MacNicol predicted,[35] the term 'underclass' has been deployed to attribute blame for poverty to the poor themselves and the 'culture of dependency' which allegedly stems from welfare provision. There are three important strands to the underclass story. The first is the social construction of the concept which, especially in the work of Murray, hinges heavily on the conflation of illegitimate single parenthood, self-induced unemployment, and crime. 'Underclass', even more than its progenitor, the 'culture of poverty', is a set of attributes ascribed to social groups which entrap them into dependence on the State. In contrast, 'social exclusion' implies a set of tendencies, the 'downsizing' of the workforce, the destabilization of work, and the consequent erosion of family and community structures, which exclude certain groups from secure, well-paid employment and viable social networks. Second, the empirical evidence for the 'welfare

[30] R. Hughes, *Culture of Complaint*.   [31] S. Cohen, *Visions of Social Control*.
[32] F. Lösel, 'The Efficacy of Correctional Treatment: A Review and Synthesis of Meta-Evaluations'.
[33] J. Young, *The Exclusive Society*.
[34] C. Murray, *Losing Ground*, *The Emerging British Underclass* and *Underclass: The Crisis Deepens*.
[35] J. MacNicol, 'In Pursuit of the Underclass'.

causes underclass' thesis is comparatively weak. Both within the USA[36] and Europe,[37] comparisons between levels of welfare support, single parenthood, and crime rates fail to match the theory—quite strikingly so in the European case. The converse theory, that joblessness and poor job quality are the root causes of both the need for welfare and the increased resort to crime, has powerful backing in detailed study.[38] Third, the adverse definition and effective abandonment of the excluded as authors of their own misfortune have helped to justify their ghettoization, in the sense of spatial exclusion from shopping malls, designated streets, and public parks,[39] and has greatly increased incarceration[40] and technologically driven surveillance and resettlement.[41] The potency of labelling process is well exemplified in these seemingly disparate trends and stigmatization processes.

It should not be forgotten that labelling theory was always more than a theory of labelling. It centred on the self and the negotiation of social action and has proved robust as a way of looking at very diverse settings in which crime and deviance are enacted. It provides a crucial component in Giddens' theory of structuration,[42] the most ambitious recent attempt to resolve the 'problem of sociology': how society, a human creation, may be experienced as beyond human control. Giddens' resolution of the structure–agency problem by viewing human agency as essential to the production and reproduction of social order and of the self, does not, however, yield immediate gains for the understanding of deviance. Knowledge of crime and deviance cannot be directly inferred from concepts such as globalization, late modernity, neo-liberalism, and the sequestration of experience[43] any more than from notions of class and conflict. But at least it is not interred by them, as in much of functionalism and Marxism. It is all too easy to forget the most obvious and lasting example of the relevance of labelling theory that lies within the sphere in which its rise to prominence began—with the modest-seeming propositions of Howard Becker about marijuana use. Since then, the reach of drugs control, in the form of the 'war on drugs', has expanded vastly in significance, not least due to its impact on the American prison population and its grotesquely disproportionate ethnic composition,[44] but also due to the exponential growth of illicit drug use globally. The 'Great Prohibition'[45] differs from that of 1920s America in extending globally; in being applied to a wide array of drugs rather than one alone—alcohol; in a duration which already greatly exceeds that of the 'old' Prohibition which served, lest we forget, to fuel the take-off of organized crime in America; and

---

[36] C. Jencks and R. Peterson (eds.), *The Urban Underclass*.

[37] NACRO, *Crime and Social Policy*.

[38] W. Wilson, *The Truly Disadvantaged*; R. Freeman, 'Employment and Earnings of Disadvantaged Young Men in A Labor Shortage Economy'; and M. Sullivan, *'Getting Paid': Youth Crime and Work in the Inner City*.

[39] K. Beckett and S. Herbert, *Banished: The New Social Control in Urban America*; A. Bottoms and P. Wiles, 'Crime and Insecurity in the City'.

[40] R. King, 'Prisons'; and F. Zimring and G. Hawkins, 'The Growth of Imprisonment in California'.

[41] M. Davis, 'Beyond Blade Runner'.   [42] A. Giddens, *The Constitution of Society*.

[43] A. Giddens, *Modernity and Self-Identity*.

[44] M. Tonry, *Malign Neglect: Race, Crime, and Punishment in America*; M. Mauer, *The Changing Racial Dynamics of the War on Drugs*.

[45] D. Matza and P. Morgan, 'Controlling Drug Use: The Great Prohibition'.

which generates profits that constitute perverse incentives for drug-related crime, the corruption of officialdom, the exploitation of the miseries of a criminalized underclass, the 'drug mules' of the addictive economy, and the economic deformations of money-laundering and drug production. The most dramatic unintended outcome has been the emergence of narco-terrorism and narco-states. These unwanted side-effects of prohibition, rather than the drugs themselves, have been exhaustively chronicled and analysed.[46] The case for alternative and, on the balance of the evidence, more effective and harm-reducing regulation has been endlessly put. The main counter-argument, that our inability to stem all burglary, theft, and robbery hardly makes the case for their decriminalization, consistently avoids the primacy of the key difference between crimes of victimization and those termed, perhaps too readily, 'crimes without victims'. As Simon and Burns[47] vividly demonstrated crack cocaine and heroin take a brutal toll on users, neighbourhoods, and communities. But the fact remains that householders do not welcome burglars onto their property; car owners do not hand their keys to car thieves; and those who are robbed do not willingly part with their wallets or phones. Drug users in their millions emphatically do collude with their sources of supply and only the labelling perspective can illuminate the refusal of governments, with notable exceptions, to take account of so elementary a fact in their making of policy, and of the consequent mass production of secondary deviance and secondary controls.

Control theories are based on concerns which overlap markedly with those of strain and labelling theories, but which differ profoundly in explaining deviance primarily by the weakening or absence of effective links that bind individuals to key social institutions. Over the past two decades the condition of late modernity has increasingly been defined as systematically damaging to such bonds. The increased scope for financial and physical mobility is seen as fuelling an increasingly hedonistic individualism which holds collective well-being in scant regard. The change from full, stable employment to a flexible labour market is viewed as fragmenting communities and families. Turbo-capitalism affords the many what was once the preserve of the few—an unprecedented scope for movement, choice, the search for individual self-gratification by consuming the fruits of economic growth. To strain theories, the emphasis lies in the gap between expectations and reality as a motor of endless dissatisfaction and relative deprivation which may promote crime. To control theorists, it is the progressive erosion of social cohesion which is the primary cause of increasing rates of offending.

Against this background, social cohesion is seen as needing resuscitation if it is to survive. The 'communitarianism' of Amitai Etzioni[48] is one model for its recovery. But even so civic-minded a reformer as Etzioni accepts 'gated' communities as the price to be paid for their enhancement. Shaming punishments, including electronic tagging, are needed to provide reassurance about security and risk. This drift to a revival of neo-medieval sanctions in the electronic age is seen as the only possible antidote to the

---

[46] D. R. Mares, *Drug Wars and Coffeehouses: The Political Economy of the International Drug Trade*; D. M. Paley, *Drug War Capitalism*; P. Mallea, *The War on Drugs: A Failed Experiment*; R. Saviano, *Zero Zero Zero*.

[47] D. Simon and E. Burns, *The Corner*.

[48] A. Etzioni, *The Moral Dimension* and *The Spirit of Community: Rights, Responsibilities and the Communitarian Agenda*.

centrifugal tendencies of late modernity. It is ironic that, after an unrelenting period of rampant market individualism, even a neo-conservative such as Francis Fukayama acknowledged the need to reassess the claims of the social against the economic. He prefaced his book *Trust* (1995)—a celebration of that precept as a factor in business success—with a quotation from Durkheim (1895).[49] Ormerod reminds his readers that Adam Smith, the proclaimed saint of free enterprise, accepted that society rested on a 'moral economy' which should set limits to economic exploitation. Sampson's work on 'collective efficacy'[50] and Skogan's[51] on neighbourhood cohesion are clear pointers to what might be done.

It is perhaps necessary to disentangle the properties of late modernity from those of the political economy of capitalism which has fashioned their development in particular ways. BBC News is not the same as Fox News, for example, though the unparalleled commercialization of the mass media exerts endless pressures for it to move in a similar direction. John Braithwaite[52] proposes a reading of late modernity, and its impact on community, somewhat different from that of Etzioni. First, he argues that, even in a fairly literal sense, the 'storm centres' of late modernity are tightly knit communities: 'One of the mythologies of late modernity is that capitalism runs on formal controls to the exclusion of the informal. The fact is that at the very centre of capitalism what you have on Wall Street, in Toyko, and in the City of London is a surprisingly communitarian culture of capitalism.'[53] Nor does capitalism necessarily fragment communities more generally: witness Japan and 'Japanese, Chinese, and Jewish communities in the most violent of American cities'.[54] However, he does not stress that, outside these communities, some of which have been exposed as fundamentally criminogenic, capitalism has artificially wreaked havoc in Hispanic and black minorities, as it has in traditional working-class communities in Britain.[55]

Braithwaite's second point is that shaming, in its reintegrative form, largely arose *with* modernity, especially in the family, and is associated historically with reductions in crime, domestic violence, and stigmatizing punishments. And third, while stigmatizing, exclusionary punishment has staged a comeback, the potential for reintegrative shaming, and thus for 'restorative justice', is in some ways greater in modern urban societies than in close rural communities. The very process of growing interdependencies and role segregation increase the scope for shaming in communities of interest (global shaming?).

---

[49] The quote is from *The Division of Labor in Society*: 'A Society composed of an infinite number of unorganized individuals, that a hypertrophied State is formed to oppress and contain, constitutes a veritable sociological monstrosity. . . .A nation can be maintained only if, between the State and the individual, there is interlaced a whole series of secondary groups real enough to the individual to attract them strongly in their sphere of action and drag them, in this way, into the general torrent of social life. . . .Occupational groups are suited to fill this role and this is their destiny.'

[50] R. Sampson, S. Raudenbush, and F. Earls, 'Neighborhoods and Violent Crime: A Multilevel Study of Collective Efficacy'.

[51] W. Skogan, *Disorder and Decline*.   [52] J. Braithwaite, 'Shame and Modernity'.

[53] J. Braithwaite, 'Shame and Modernity', 13.   [54] J. Braithwaite, 'Shame and Modernity', 15.

[55] B. Campbell, *Goliath: Britain's Dangerous Places*; and W. Wilson, *The Truly Disadvantaged* and *When Work Disappears*.

> The segmented self is a double-edged sword. It affords us day-to-day protection from shame as we move around groups with different values; but it leaves us very vulnerable when an act of wrongdoing becomes so public as to become known to all these groups. The latter vulnerability has maximum force with the shaming of crime, because this is the most public institutionalisation of shaming that we have.[56]

However, stigmatizing shaming seems to drive the criminal and the deviant into protective subcultures hardened against shame and replete with symbolic defences against it. Inclusionary shaming holds out the prospect of genuine reintegration. Again, however, Braithwaite relies heavily on examples of groups with a strong 'stake in conformity'—the argument is less easily sustained where the only segmented roles people inhabit are those associated with the underclass.

Situational control theories, as was noted above, more than any other criminological approach, have helped to fashion the character of late modernity. While lacking any interest in theorizing root causes, its principal focus is very much to analyse the temporal, spatial, and technical aspects of crime prevention in a rapidly changing world, to wrong-foot the offender by identifying and reducing opportunities and enhancing detection and capture. Every target hardened, every space rendered defensible, every criminal deterred is a criminological gain. Motivation is stripped down to its operative core. The 'rational criminal', has, as Stan Cohen put it,[57] 'nothing *but* choice'—he is devoid of biographical or symbolic substance, social background, or culture. He is a hedonistic predator, motivated only by gain and defeated only by fear. Guilt, shame, frustration, desperation, and boredom do not figure in the equation. It is a particularly post-modernist conception for a world whose economy is increasingly driven by the impersonal and unfettered money market on a global scale.[58] It harks back to the most modernist theory of all, the utilitarian 'felicific calculus' of Jeremy Bentham. And in Bentham's 'Panopticon' can be found its ideal, a system of total surveillance, control and accountability.

In some respects, however, situational control theorists have moved beyond the purely preventative and controlling objectives to a wider concern with citizenship rights: Pease has argued that situational measures are vindicated even if, because of displacement or crime deflected elsewhere, the volume of crime does not fall. If it is spread more evenly among potential victims, that is a beneficial result, as the overburdening of multiple victims by repeat offending is at least reduced. Foster and Hope argued for the optimum combination of social and situational policies. Out of both can be derived a conspectus for the transformation of deviance from a blight which falls like a plague of locusts on some communities and groups rather than others, to a manageable set of risks which can be insured against in policy as well as security terms. However, the immediate pains of victimization—and the impact that makes on the politics of law and order[59]—gives the purely situational and punitive a built-in

---

[56] J. Braithwaite, 'Shame and Modernity', 15.   [57] S. Cohen, 'Crime and Politics: Spot the Difference'.
[58] O. Engdahl, 'The Role of Money in Economic Crime'.
[59] D. Downes and R. Morgan, 'Dumping the Hostages to Fortune? The Politics of Law and Order in Postwar Britain'.

edge over longer term and more diffuse, but arguably more effective, policies of crime reduction. In an unjust, highly unequal society, the claims of 'restorative' justice are always secondary to those of retribution.

Radical criminology has its lasting role in the elaboration of just this basic point. Having suffered, at least in Britain and in the USA, a number of damaging rebuffs in the late 1970s, it metamorphosed into 'left realism' and 'left idealism'. In its European version, it continued to develop in a less sectarian, more pragmatic way.[60] The conflicts in the USA and Britain either did not happen in European criminology or were far more muted. The feminist critique,[61] the Social Democratic critique,[62] and the internal schism[63] did not register with such force in Dutch, Scandinavian, Italian, or German critical criminology. They rolled on, though the tenor of the 'law-and-order' politics was far more hostile to radical reform and, in particular, abolitionist ideas in penal policy. The result was a criminology more 'critical' than left realism, but more pragmatic than 'left idealism'.[64]

There is an obvious reason why radical criminology is far more vigorous in the twenty-first century. That is, Marxism, at least of a libertarian kind rather than a monolithic orthodoxy, is held to be back on track after about a century of 'guilt by association' with State socialism, a brand of political economy it never upheld but which it found exceptionally difficult to criticize in the context of the Cold War, and to theorize in terms of central canons of Marxism. As Parkin pointed out,[65] Marxism was at a loss to explain Fascism: the State was meant to be the committee for the management of the affairs of the bourgeoisie, not the means for its domination. With Fascism, Stalinism, and Maoism largely consigned to the past, it is said, the true course of history has been resumed. The very fact of capitalist triumphalism is in line with Marxist tenets, for it was only on the basis of the contradictions of a mature capitalism that socialism was to be truly born. Far from being over, the argument with Marxism is only just about to begin all over again, this time in the context of a turbo-capitalism careering out of control and without the counterpoint of socialism exerting a counter-pressure for egalitarian policies in welfare, income, and wealth distribution and the equivalent in international terms of the controls exercised by nation states over business and finance before the 'big bang' of global capitalism in the 1980s.

In criminological terms, elites have also, for the past two decades, been behaving extraordinarily badly. A host of highly criminogenic trends have been set in motion, at times almost perversely—financial deregulation, de-industrialization, financialization, rising inequality, and the force-feeding of the 'new individualism' by consumerist pressures.

The resultant rise in crime, in the 1980s and part of the 1990s, was met by increasingly punitive methods of policing and punishment. In Nils Christie's nightmare,[66] the

---

[60] R. van Swaaningen, *Critical Criminologies: Visions from Europe*.
[61] C. Smart, *Women, Crime and Criminology*.
[62] D. Downes and P. Rock (eds.), *Deviant Interpretations: Problems in Criminological Theory*.
[63] J. Lea and J. Young, *What is to be Done about Law and Order?*
[64] R. van Swaaningen, *Critical Criminologies: Visions from Europe*.
[65] F. Parkin, *Marxism and Class Theory: A Bourgeois Critique*.
[66] N. Christie, *Crime Control as Industry: Towards Gulags Western Style*.

whole cycle resembles a scenario of left functionalism: capitalist contradictions produce rising crime, which is used to justify vastly increased resort to privatized prisons, probation, and policing, which create fresh profits to plough back into yet more of the same: a self-justifying vicious circle of instrumental criminalization. Scaling up, Misha Glenny in his study of globalized arms-trading, money laundering, and corporate crime[67] discerns a growing accommodation between corporate crime and so-called 'organized crime'—and a resultant 'mafiaization' of economic transactions on a global scale. These criminal activities stand outside of the much lauded official drop in crime. There is enough truth in their accounts to ensure a great deal of mileage for radical criminology in the post-millennial era.

Conclusion

Images of future crime and deviance and its control, implicit or explicit in the various approaches discussed in this book, provide one way of assessing their validity. Their fundamentally distinct character, and far-from-perfect fit with the facts, in so far as we have a reasonable grasp of reality, make any such overall assessment highly problematic. Strain theory predicted the increasing rates in both the seriousness and volume of street crime in the wake of de-industrialization. What it failed to predict was the scale of the penal upturn in Britain and the USA in particular; and the concomitant rise in crime among the powerful, a problem of imperfect application rather than theoretical defect. Anomie theory in its Durkheimian form was well-equipped to do so. Radical criminology explicitly attacked the under-prediction of elites' criminality[68] in all previous work, but on grounds which practically ruled out any probability of being an honest capitalist or a dishonest non-capitalist. Labelling theory was pregnant with forebodings about the future shape and functioning of systems of control. Though those were not explicitly cast as predictions of the revival of fear of an 'underclass', the electronic tagging of offenders, or the explosion of imprisonment in the USA, their concerns presaged such developments. Control theories likewise heralded the shift from informal to formal controls as the predictable response of governments to rising crime in the wake of changes in family structure and the erosion of communities in the context of rapid economic change and de-industrialization.

It is possible, though in our view premature, to synthesize all these diverse approaches into one master theory which situates the growing strain to crime and deviance and the consequent over-control of some groups rather than others, in the context of the destructive aspects of neo-liberalism. When taken all together, rather than apart, the weakness of the theories—the tendency to gross over-prediction or under-prediction; the vulnerability to reification; and the risks of theoretical fetishism and over-interpretation—tend to be multiplied rather than reduced. The opposite

---

[67] M. Glenny, *McMafia: Seriously Organised Crime.*
[68] I. Taylor, P. Walton, and J. Young (eds.), *The New Criminology.*

tendency—to argue that because no theory works, no theory can ever work—is equally unwise and reduces criminology to administrative empiricism. It is best to soldier on, but with a more sophisticated use of tried and tested grounded methods: analysing socio-economic trends and cultural shifts; integrating a comparative perspective; observational research and case studies; and a constant openness to other disciplines. The transforming nature of crime and deviance remains a vital indicator of significant sociological transformations.

In any field where knowledge is imperfect and incomplete the need to start afresh recurs and does, at times, amount to the semblance of a paradigmatic revolution—a seismic shift in theorizing from a new set of first principles. Such a shift arguably did occur in this field in the 1960s, drawing on sociological work from Durkheim onwards, but reassembling it in fundamentally new analytical and empirical directions. As yet there do not seem to be the grounds for establishing a comparable shift in perspective. As Keynes remarked, regarding economics, 'No theory is ever dead.' Theories are reworked and different theories are reassembled in novel vein; some which were prematurely abandoned are rediscovered and reanimated in changed times and cultures. Such seems to have been the case of late with the sociology of crime and deviance. Far from being overthrown or eclipsed, it is in the process of metamorphosis. Key questions are not only how the theories might compare in accounting for crime and deviance (both as metatheories and as sources for applied theories relevant to different types and cases), but also how usefully did they predict and handle the trends in crime and its changing context. For the context has undeniably changed. Whether we term it 'high-', 'late-', 'post-', or 'liquid' modernity, the neo-liberal transformation of economies and labour markets in the wake of automation have led to profound changes in family and social structures, life chances and life styles, governing mentalities, and formal systems of crime control. At best, such changes have constituted the conditions for affluent lifestyles and new forms of freedom, of gender, ethnicity, and sexuality.[69] At least, on the cost side, they have engendered new forms and scales of inequality and exclusion once thought incompatible with comprehensive welfare provision. At worst, they presage, as an emergent Green Criminology has emphasized, global havoc, schism, and mass self-extinction by pollution, deforestation, global warming, crises in financial institutions, and other assorted unwanted side-effects of high population and high-consumption rates of growth.[70] The emergent trends are fundamental properties of globalization rather than simply aspects of criminal or deviant misconduct. In stark contrast to Steven Pinker's analysis, Christian Parenti argues that the violent adaptations being produced by a 'catastrophic combination' of environmental crisis, economic neo-liberalization and a combination of super-power and warlord conflict will define the twenty-first century.[71] These violent adaptations in the Global South

---

[69] A. Giddens, *The Consequences of Modernity*; and D. Harvey, *The Condition of Postmodernity*.

[70] P. Kennedy, *Preparing for the Twenty-First Century*; N. Klein, *This Changes Everything: Capitalism vs. the Climate*; A. Giddens, *The Politics of Climate Change*; A. Brisman and N. South, *Green Cultural Criminology: Constructions of Environmental Harm, Consumerism, and Resistance to Ecocide*.

[71] C. Parenti, *Tropic of Chaos: Climate Change and the New Geography of Violence*; see also S. Sassen, *Expulsions: Brutality and Complexity in the Global Economy*.

'take the forms of: ethnic irredentism, religious fanaticism, rebellion banditry, narcotics trafficking, and the small scale resource wars. In the North the multilayered crisis appears as the politics of the armed lifeboat; the preparations for open ended counter-insurgency, militarized borders, aggressive anti-immigrant policing, and a mainstream proliferation of rightwing xenophobia'[72] However much we might want to argue about the evidential basis for such portents they do require of us to place 'local' conceptualizations of crime, deviance, victimization, and control within a rapidly changing global context.

[72] C. Parenti, *Tropic of Chaos*, 226.

Bibliography

Abbott, A., *Department and Discipline: Chicago Sociology at One Hundred*, Chicago, 1999.

Adler, F., *Sisters in Crime*, New York, 1975.

Adler, F. and Simon, R. (eds.), *The Criminology of Deviant Women*, Boston, 1979.

Adler, Z., *Rape on Trial*, London, 1987.

Agnew, R., *Pressured to Crime*, New York, 2010.

Akers, R., 'Problems in the Sociology of Deviance', *Social Forces*, 46.4 (1968).

Albini, J., *The American Mafia: Genesis of a Legend*, New York, 1971.

Aldana-Pindell, R., 'In Vindication of Justiciable Victims' Rights to Truth and Justice for State-Sponsored Crimes', *Vanderbilt Journal of Transnational Law*, 35 (2002).

Alexander, C., *The Asian Gang: Ethnicity, Identity, Masculinity*, London, 2000.

Alihan, M., *Social Ecology*, New York, 1938.

Allan, E. and Steffensmeier, D., 'Youth, Underemployment and Property Crime: Differential Effects of Job Availability and Job Quality on Juvenile and Young Adult Arrest Rates', *American Sociological Review*, 54 (1989).

Allen, J., 'The "Masculinity" of Criminality and Criminology: Interrogating Some Impasses', in M. Findlay and R. Hogg (eds.), *Understanding Crime and Criminal Justice*, Sydney, 1988.

Alvarez, A., *Genocidal Crimes*, London, 2009.

American Friends Service Committee, *Struggle for Justice: A Report on Crime and Punishment in America*, New York, 1971.

Amir, M., 'Victim Precipitated Forcible Rape', *The Journal of Criminal Law, Criminology, and Police Science*, 58:4 (1967).

Amir, M., *Patterns in Forcible Rape*, Chicago, 1971.

Anderson, E., *A Place on the Corner*, Chicago, 1976.

Anderson, E., *Streetwise*, Chicago, 1990.

Anderson, E., *Code of the Street: Decency, Violence, and the Moral Life of the Inner City*, New York, 1999.

Andersen, M. A. and Farrell, G. (eds.), *The Criminal Act: The Role and Influence of Routine Activity Theory*, Basingstoke, 2015

Anderson, N., *The Hobo*, Chicago, 1923.

Angwin, J., *Dragnet Nation: A Quest for Privacy, Security, and Freedom in a World of Relentless Surveillance*, London, 2015.

Anon., 'The Life Histories of W. I. Thomas and Robert E. Park', *American Journal of Sociology*, 79 (1973).

Archard, P., *Vagrancy Alcoholism and Social Control*, London, 1979.

Arendt, H., *Eichman in Jerusalem A Report on the Banality of Evil*, Harmondsworth, 1997.

Armstrong, G., *Football Hooligans: Knowing the Score*, London, 1998.

Armstrong, G. and Wilson, M., 'City Politics and Deviancy Amplification', in I. Taylor and L. Taylor (eds.), *Politics and Deviance*, Harmondsworth, 1973.

Aron, R., 'Max Weber and Power Politics', in O. Stammer (ed.), *Max Weber and Sociology Today*, Oxford, 1971.

Asbury, H., *The Gangs of New York*, New York, 1928.

ASHWORTH, A., 'Victims' Rights, Defendants' Rights and Criminal Procedure', in A. Crawford and J. Goodey (ed.), *Integrating a Victim Perspective within Criminal Justice*, Aldershot, 2000.

ATHENS, L., *Violent Criminal Acts and Actors*, Boston, 1980.

ATKINSON, M., *Discovering Suicide*, London, 1979.

ATKINSON, M., 'Societal Reactions to Suicide', in S. Cohen, (ed.), *Images of Deviance*, Harmondsworth, 1971.

ATKINSON, M. and Drew, P., *Order in Court*, London, 1979.

AVISON, N., 'Victims of Homicide', in I. Drapkin and E. Viano (eds.), *Victimology: A New Focus*, Lexington, Mass, 1973.

BAKAL, Y. and Polsky, H. (eds.), *Reforming Corrections for Juvenile Offenders*, Lexington, Mass., 1979.

BALDWIN, J. and McConville, M., *Negotiated Justice*, London, 1977.

BALDWIN, R., 'Why Rules Don't Work', *Modern Law Review*, 53 (1990).

BALL, D., 'An Abortion Clinic Ethnography', *Social Problems*, 14 (1967).

BANFIELD, E., *The Moral Basis of a Backward Society*, Glencoe, 1958.

BANTING, K., *Poverty, Politics and Policy*, London, 1979.

BARZUN, J. (tr.), *Flaubert's Dictionary of Accepted Ideas*, London, 1954.

BAUMAN, Z., *Modernity and the Holocaust*, Cambridge, 1989.

BAUMGARTNER, M., *The Moral Order of a Suburb*, New York, 1988.

BAYART, J-F., Ellis, S., and Hibou, B., *The Criminalization of the State in Africa*, Indiana, 1999.

BEAMES, T., *The Rookeries of London*, London, 1850.

BEATTIE, J., 'Judicial Records and the Measurement of Crime in Eighteenth Century England', in L. Knafla (ed.), *Crime and Criminal Justice in Europe and Canada*, Waterloo, Ont., 1981.

BEATTIE, J., 'Violence and Society in Early Modern England', in A. Doob and E. Greenspan (eds.), *Perspectives in Criminal Law*, Aurora, 1984.

BECK, U., *Risk Society*, London, 1992.

BECKER, C. *Criminal Theories of Causation and Victims' Contributions to the Etiology of Crime, PhD*, University of Cambridge, 1981.

BECKER, G., 'Crime and Punishment: An Economic Approach', *The Journal of Political Economy*, 76:2 (1968).

BECKER, H., 'The Culture of a Deviant Group', *American Journal of Sociology*, 51 (1961).

BECKER, H., *Outsiders*, New York, 1963.

BECKER, H., 'Marihuana Use and Social Control', in *Outsiders*, New York, 1963.

BECKER, H. (ed.), *The Other Side: Perspectives on Deviance*, New York, 1964.

BECKER, H., 'The Self and Adult Socialization', in E. Norbeck et al. (eds.), *The Study of Personality*, New York, 1968.

BECKER, H., 'The Life History and the Scientific Mosaic', in *Sociological Work*, London, 1971.

BECKER, H. (ed.), *Culture and Civility in San Francisco*, Chicago, 1971.

BECKER, H., Labelling Theory Reconsidered', in P. Rock and M. McIntosh (eds.), *Deviance and Social Control*, London, 1974.

BECKER, H., *Tricks of the Trade: How to Think about Your Research While You're Doing It*, Chicago, 1998.

BECKER, H. and Horowitz, I., 'The Culture of Civility', in H. Becker (ed.), *Culture and Civility in San Francisco*, Chicago, 1971.

BECKER, J., *Hitler's Children*, London, 1978.

BECKETT, K., *Making Crime Pay: Law and Order in Contemporary American Politics*, Oxford, 1997.

BECKETT, K. and Herbert, S., *Banished: The New Social Control in Urban America*, New York, 2009.

BEIRNE, P. and Hill, J., *Comparative Criminology: An Annotated Bibliography*, Westport, 1991.

BELL, D., 'Crime as an American Way of Life', *The Antioch Review*, 13 (1953).

BELL, D., *The End of Ideology*, New York, 1960.

BELLESILES, M., *Arming America: The Origins of a National Gun Culture*, New York, 2000.

BELSON, W., *Juvenile Theft*, London, 1975.

BENNET, T. C. and Wright, R., *Burglars on Burglary*, Aldershot, 1984.

BENNETT, W. and Feldman, M., *Reconstructing Reality in the Courtroom*, New Brunswick, NJ, 1981.

BERGER, P., *The Social Reality of Religion*, Harmondsworth, 1973.

BERGER, P. and Luckmann, T., *The Social Construction of Reality*, London, 1967.

BERGER, R. and Searles, P., 'Victim-Offender Interaction in Rape: Victimological, Situational, and Feminist Perspectives', *Women's Studies Quarterly*, 13:3/4 (1985).

BIANCHI, H. and van Swaaningen, R. (eds.), *Abolitionism: Towards a Non-Repressive Approach to Crime*, Amsterdam, 1986.

BIDERMAN, A. and Reiss, A., 'On Exploring the 'Dark Figure' of Crime', *American Academy of Political Science*, 374 (1967).

BITTNER, E., 'Radicalism and the Organization of Radical Movements', *American Sociological Review*, 28 (1963).

BITTNER, E., 'The Police on Skid Row', *American Sociological Review*, 32:5 (1967).

BITTNER, E., *The Functions of the Police in Modern Society*, Rockville, 1970.

BLACKMAN, S., *Youth: Positions and Oppositions*, Aldershot, 1995.

BLACKMAN, S., *Chilling Out: The Cultural Politics of Substance Consumption, Youth and Drug Policy*, Buckingham, 2004.

BLAU, P., *The Dynamics of Bureaucracy*, Chicago, 1955.

BLAU, P., *Exchange and Power in Social Life*, New York, 1964.

BLEE, K. M., *Inside Organised Racism*, Los Angeles, 2013.

BLOCK, R., 'Victim-Offender Dynamics in Violent Crime', *Journal of Criminal Law and Criminology*, 72:2 (1981).

BLUMER, H., 'Suggestions for the Study of Mass Media Effects', in *Symbolic Interactionism*, Englewood Cliffs, NJ, 1969.

BLUMER, H., 'What is Wrong with Social Theory?', in *Symbolic Interactionism*, Englewood Cliffs, NJ, 1969.

BLUMER, H., *Symbolic Interactionism: Perspective and Method*, Englewood Cliffs, NJ, 1969.

BLUMSTEIN, A. and Hsieh, P., *The Duration of Adult Criminal Careers*, Washington DC, 1982.

BONGER, W., *Criminality and Economic Conditions*, Boston, Mass., 1916.

BORDUA, D., (ed.), *The Police: Six Sociological Essays*, New York, 1967.

BOSWORTH, M. and Hoyle, C., (eds.), *What is Criminology?*, Oxford, 2013.

BOTTOMLEY, K. and Pease, K., *Crime and Punishment*, London, 1986.

BOTTOMS, A., review of *Defensible Space*, *British Journal of Criminology*, 14 (1974).

BOTTOMS, A., 'The Philosophy and Politics of Punishment and Sentencing', in C. Clarkson and R. Morgan (eds.), *The Politics of Sentencing Reform*, Oxford, 1995.

BOTTOMS, A., Mawby, R., and Walker, M., 'A Localised Crime Survey in Contrasting Areas of a City', *British Journal of Criminology*, 27 (1987).

BOTTOMS, A. et al., 'A Tale of Two Estates', in D. Downes, (ed.), *Crime and the City*, Basingstoke, 1989.

Bottoms, A. and Wiles, P., 'Crime and Insecurity in the City', in C. Fijnaut, (ed.), *Changes in Society, Crime and Criminal Justice in Europe*, The Hague, 1996.

Bottoms, A. and Roberts, J. V. (eds.), *Hearing the Victim: Adversarial Justice, Crime Victims and the State*, Cullompton, 2010.

Bourdieu, P., 'Forms of Capital', in J. Richardson, (ed.), *Handbook of Theory and Research for the Sociology of Education*, New York, 1983.

Bourgois, P., *In Search of Respect: Selling Crack in El Barrio*, Cambridge, 1995.

Bourgois, P., 'In Search of Masculinity', *British Journal of Criminology*, 36 (1996).

Bourgois, P. and Schonberg, J., *Righteous Dopefiend*, Berkeley, California, 2009.

Boutellier, H., *Crime and Morality: The Significance of Criminal Justice in Post-Modern Culture*, Dordrecht, 2000.

Bowers, K., Johnson, S., and Pease, K., 'Prospective Hot-Spotting: The Future of Crime Mapping?', *British Journal of Criminology*, 44 (2004).

Box, S., *Deviance, Reality and Society*, London, 1971.

Box, S., *Power, Crime and Mystification*, London, 1983.

Boyle, J., *A Sense of Freedom*, London, 1977.

Boyle, J., *The Pains of Confinement: Prison Diaries*, Edinburgh, 1984.

Braithwaite, J., *Inequality, Crime and Public Policy*, London, 1979.

Braithwaite, J., *Crime, Shame and Reintegration*, Cambridge, 1989.

Braithwaite, J., 'Shame and Modernity', *British Journal of Criminology*, 33 (1993).

Brake, M., *The Sociology of Youth Culture and Youth Subcultures*, London, 1980.

Brantingham, P. and Faust, F., 'A Conceptual Model of Crime Prevention', *Crime and Delinquency*, 22 (1976).

Bratton, W. (with Knobler, P.), *Turnaround: How America's Top Cop Reversed the Crime Epidemic*, New York, 1998.

Braude, L., '"Park and Burgess": An Appreciation', *American Journal of Sociology*, 77 (1970).

Briar, S. and Piliavin, I., 'Delinquency, Situational Inducements, and Commitment to Conformity', *Social Problems*, 13 (1965).

Briggs, D., *Dealing with Deviants*, London, 1975.

Brisman, A. and South, N., *Green Cultural Criminology: Constructions of Environmental Harm, Consumerism, and Resistance to Ecocide*, Oxford, 2014.

Britt, C. L. and Gottfredson, M., *Control Theories of Crime and Delinquency*, New Brunswick, 2003.

Brody, S. and Tarling, R., *Taking Offenders out of Circulation*, C Home Office Research Study No. 64, London, 1980.

Brotherton, D., 'Subversive Subcultures: Searching for a Politics of Nationhood on the Streets of New York', paper delivered at the meetings of the American Society of Criminology, Nashville, Tennessee, 19 November 2004.

Brotherton, D. C., *Youth Street Gangs*, New York, 2015.

Brown, B., 'Women and Crime: The Dark Figures of Criminology', *Economy and Society*, 16 (1986).

Browning, C., *Ordinary Men: Reserve Police Battalion 101 and the Final Solution in Poland*, New York, 1992.

Brownmiller, S. *Against Our Will*, New York, 1975.

Buckley-Zistel, S. et al., *Transitional Justice Theories*, New York, 2014.

Budd, T. and Sharp, C., *Offending in England and Wales: First Results from the 2003 Crime and Justice Survey*, London, 2005.

BULMER, M., (ed.), *Social Policy Research*, London, 1978.

BULMER, M., *The Uses of Social Research*, London, 1982.

BULMER, M., *The Chicago School*, Chicago, 1985.

BULMER, M., *Social Science and Social Policy*, London, 1986.

BURAWOY, M., 'For Public Sociology: Contradictions, Dilemmas and Possibilities', *American Sociological Review*, 70 (2005).

BURBIDGE, M., 'British Public Housing and Crime: A Review', in R. Clarke and T. Hope (eds.), *Coping with Crime*, Boston, 1984.

BURGESS, E., 'The Growth of the City', in R. Park and E. Burgess, *The City*, Chicago, 1967.

BURKE, K., *A Grammar of Motives*, New York, 1945.

BURN, G., *Somebody's Husband, Somebody's Son: The Story of Peter Sutcliffe*, London, 1984.

BURNEY, E., *Putting Street Crime in its Place: A Report to the Community/Police Consultative Group for Lambeth*, London (Goldsmiths College, Centre for Inner City Studies), 1990.

BURNEY, E., *Making People Behave: Anti-social Behaviour, Politics and Policy*, Cullompton, Devon, 2005.

BURT, C., *The Young Delinquent*, London, 1924 (1944, 4th rev. edn).

BURUMA, I., 'The Joys and Perils of Victimhood', in A. Lightman and R. Atwan, *The Best American Essays*, Boston, 2000.

BUTTERFIELD, F., *All God's Children: The Bosket Family and the American Tradition of Violence*, New York, 1995.

CAIN, M., *Society and the Policeman's Role*, London, 1974.

CAIN, M., 'Orientalism, Occidentalism and the Sociology of Crime', *British Journal of Criminology*, Special Issue, 40 (2000).

CAIN, M., *Women, Crime and Social Harm: Towards a Criminology for the Global Age*, Oxford, 2008.

CAMERON, M., *The Booster and the Snitch*, New York, 1964.

CAMPBELL, A., *Girl Delinquents*, Oxford, 1981.

CAMPBELL, A., *The Girls in the Gang: A Report from New York City*, Oxford, 1984.

CAMPBELL, A., 'Speaking Volumes: Homicide', *Times Higher Education Supplement*, 17 February 1995.

CAMPBELL, B., *Goliath: Britain's Dangerous Places*, London, 1993.

CAMPBELL, R. and O'Neill, M. (eds.), *Sex Work Now*, London, 2006.

CAPOTE, T., *In Cold Blood: A True Account of a Multiple Murder and Its Consequences*, London, 1965.

CAREY, J., 'Problems of Access and Risk in Observing Drug Scenes', in J. Douglas, (ed.), *Research on Deviance*, New York, 1972.

CAREY, J., *Sociology and Public Affairs: The Chicago School*, Beverly Hills, 1975.

CARLEN, P., *Magistrates' Justice*, London, 1976.

CARLEN, P., review of D. Downes and P. Rock (eds.), *Deviant Interpretations*, *Sociological Review*, 27:4 (1979).

CARLEN, P., *Women's Imprisonment*, London, 1983.

CARLEN, P., *Women, Crime and Poverty*, Milton Keynes, 1988.

CARLEN, P., *Jigsaw: A Political Criminology of Youth Homelessness*, Buckingham, 1996.

CARLEN, P. and Worrall, A., *Gender, Crime and Justice*, Milton Keynes, 1987.

CARR, P. and Napolitano, L., 'What Moms Supply: What Distinguishes Delinquent and Non-Delinquent Girls in Three High Crime Philadelphia Neighborhoods', forthcoming (2010).

CARR-HILL, R. and Stern, N., *Crime, the Police and Criminal Statistics*, London, 1979.

CASBURN, M., *Girls Will be Girls*, London, 1979.

CAVAN, S., *Liquor License*, Chicago, 1966.

CHAIKEN, J., Lawless, M., and Stevenson, K., *Impact of Police Activity on Crime*: *Robberies on the New York City Subway System*, Santa Monica, Cal., 1974.

CHAMBLISS, W., *Box Man*, New York, 1972.

CHAMBLISS, W., *On the Take*: *From Petty Crooks to Presidents*, Bloomington, Ind., 1978.

CHAMBLISS, W., Michalowski, R., and Kramer, R. C. (eds.), *State Crime in the Global Age*, London, 2010.

CHANCER, L. and McLaughlin, E., 'Public Criminologies: Diverse Perspectives on Academia and Policy', *Theoretical Criminology*, 11 (2007).

CHAPMAN, D., *Sociology and the Stereotype of the Criminal*, London, 1967.

CHESNEY-LIND, M., 'The Judicial Enforcement of the Female Sex Role', *Issues in Criminology*, 8 (1973).

CHEVALIER, L., *Labouring Classes and Dangerous Classes*, London, 1973.

CHOONGH, S., *Policing as Social Discipline*, Oxford, 1997.

CHRISTIE, N., 'Conflicts as Property', *British Journal of Criminology*, 17 (1977).

CHRISTIE, N., 'The Ideal Victim', in E. Fattah, (ed.), *From Crime Policy to Victim Policy*, Basingstoke, 1986.

CHRISTIE, N., *Crime Control as Industry*: *Towards Gulags Western Style*, London, 1993.

CHRISTIE, N., *A Suitable Amount of Crime*, London, 2004.

CICOUREL, A., *Method and Measurement in Sociology*, New York, 1964.

CICOUREL, A., *The Social Organization of Juvenile Justice*, New York, 1968.

CICOUREL, A., 'Interpretative Procedures and Normative Rules in the Negotiation of Status and Role', in *Cognitive Sociology*, Harmondsworth, 1973.

CICOUREL, A., *Theory and Method in a Study of Argentine Fertility*, New York, 1974.

CICOUREL, A. et al., *Language Use and School Performance*, New York, 1974.

CICOUREL, A. and Kitsuse, J., *The Educational Decision Makers*, Indianapolis, 1963.

CLARK, L. and Lewis, D., *Rape: The Price of Coercive Sexuality*, Toronto, 1977.

CLARKE, R., (ed.), *Situational Crime Prevention: Successful Case Studies*, Albany, 1997.

CLARKE, R., '"Situational" Crime Prevention: Theory and Practice', *British Journal of Criminology*, 20 (1980).

CLARKE, R., 'Situational Prevention, Criminology, and Social Values', in A. von Hirsch, D. Garland, and A. Wakefield, (eds.), *Ethical and Social Perspectives on Situational Crime Prevention*, Oxford, 2000.

CLARKE, R. and Cornish, D., *Crime Control in Britain*, Albany, 1983.

CLARKE, R. and Cornish, D., 'Modeling Offenders' Decisions: A Framework for Research and Policy', in M. Tonry and N. Morris (eds.), *Crime and Justice*, Chicago, 1985.

CLARKE, R. and Cornish, D., 'Rational Choice', unpublished paper, n.d.

CLARKE, R. and Felson, M. (eds.), *Routine Activity and Rational Choice*, New Brunswick, NJ, 1993.

CLARKE, R. and Mayhew, P. (eds.), *Designing Out Crime*, London, 1980.

CLARKE, R. and Mayhew, P., 'The British Gas Suicide Story and its Criminological Implications', in M. Tonry and N. Morris (eds.), *Crime and Justice*, Chicago, 1988.

CLARKE, R. and Mayhew, P., 'Crime As Opportunity A Note On Domestic Gas Suicide In Britain And The Netherlands', *British Journal of Criminology*, 29:1 (1989).

CLEAR, T., 'Policy and Evidence: The Challenge to the American Society of Criminology: 2009 Presidential Address to the American Society of Criminology', *Criminology*, 48 (2010).

CLEAVER, E., *Soul on Ice*, New York, 1968.

CLEMMER, D., *The Prison Community*, New York, 1940.

CLINARD, M., (ed.), *Anomie and Deviant Behavior: A Discussion and Critique*, New York, 1964.

CLINARD, M., *Cities with Little Crime: The Case of Switzerland*, Cambridge, 1978.

CLINARD, M. and Abbott, D., *Crime in Developing Countries: A Comparative Perspective*, New York, 1973.

CLINARD, M. B. and Yaeger, P. C., *Corporate Crime*, New York, 2014.

CLOWARD, R. and Ohlin, L., *Delinquency and Opportunity: A Theory of Delinquent Gangs*, New York, 1960.

COCHRANE, R., 'Crime and Personality: Theory and Evidence', *Bulletin of the British Psychological Society*, 27 (1974).

COHEN, A., *Delinquent Boys: The Culture of the Gang*, Glencoe, Ill., 1955.

COHEN, A., 'The Sociology of the Deviant Act: Anomie Theory and Beyond', *American Sociological Review*, 30 (1965).

COHEN, A., *Deviance and Control*, Englewood Cliffs, NJ, 1966.

COHEN, A., *The Elasticity of Evil*, Oxford, 1974.

COHEN, A. and Short, J., 'Juvenile Delinquency', in R. Merton and R. Nisbet (eds.), *Contemporary Social Problems*, New York, 1961.

COHEN, C., *Male Rape Is a Feminist Issue: Feminism, Governmentality and Male Rape*, Basingstoke, 2004.

COHEN, L. and Felson, M., 'Social Change and Crime Rate Trends: A Routine Activity Approach', *American Sociological Review*, 44 (1979).

COHEN, P., 'Working Class Youth Cultures in East London', *Working Papers in Cultural Studies* (Birmingham University), 2 (1972), and in J. Clarke et al. (eds.),

Resistance Through Rituals, London, 1976, and in his *Rethinking the Youth Question* London, 1997.

COHEN, P. and Robins, D., *Knuckle Sandwich: Growing up in the Working Class City*, Harmondsworth, 1978.

COHEN, P. S., *Modern Social Theory*, London, 1968.

COHEN, P. S., 'Is Positivism Dead?', *Sociological Review*, 28 (1980).

COHEN, S., 'Directions for Research on Adolescent Group Violence and Vandalism', *British Journal of Criminology*, 11 (1971).

COHEN, S., (ed.), *Images of Deviance*, Harmondsworth 1971.

COHEN, S., 'Criminology and the Sociology of Deviance in Britain', in P. Rock and M. McIntosh (eds.), *Deviance and Social Control*, London, 1974.

COHEN, S., review of Schur, E., *Crimes Without Victims*, *New Society* (21 Nov. 1974).

COHEN, S., 'It's All Right for You to Talk: Political and Sociological Manifestoes for Social Work Action', in R. Bailey and M. Brake (eds.), *Radical Social Work*, London, 1975.

COHEN, S., 'The Punitive City: Notes on the Dispersal of Social Control', *Contemporary Crises*, 3.8 (1979).

COHEN, S., 'Guilt, Justice and Tolerance: Some Old Concepts for a New Criminology', in D. Downes and P. Rock (eds.), *Deviant Interpretations*, Oxford, 1979.

COHEN, S., *Folk Devils and Moral Panics*, 2nd edn, rev., Oxford, 1980.

COHEN, S., *Visions of Social Control*, Cambridge, 1985.

COHEN, S., *Against Criminology*, New Brunswick, NJ, 1988.

COHEN, S., 'Crime and Politics: Spot the Difference', *The British Journal of Sociology*, 47 (1996).

COHEN, S., *States of Denial: Knowing about Atrocities and Suffering*, Cambridge, 2001.

COHEN, S. and Taylor, L., *Psychological Survival*, Harmondsworth, 1972.

COHEN, S. and Taylor, L. *Escape Attempts*, London 1976.

COHEN, S. and Taylor, L. *Prison Secrets*, London, 1976.

COHEN, S. and Young, J. (eds.), *The Manufacture of News*, London, 1973.

COLEMAN, A., *Utopia on Trial*, London, 1985.

COLEMAN, J., 'Social Capital in the Creation of Human Capital', *American Journal of Sociology*, 94 (1988).

COLEMAN, R. and Sim, J., *State, Power, Crime*, London, 2009.

COLLIER, R. *Masculinities, Crime and Criminology*, London, 1998.

COLLINS, P., *Dickens and Crime*, London, 1964.

COLLINS, R., *Violence: A Micro-Sociological Theory*, Princeton, 2008.

COLQUHOUN, P., *A Treatise on the Police of the Metropolis*, London, 1806.

COMFORT, M., 'Home Sweep: The Social and Cultural Consequences of Mass Incarceration for Women with Imprisoned Partners', Ph.D. dissertation, London School of Economics, 2003.

CONDRY, R. and Miles, C., 'Adolescent to Parent Violence: Framing and Mapping a Hidden Problem', *Criminology and Criminal Justice*, 14 (2014).

CONNELL, R., *Gender and Power*, Stanford, Cal., 1987.

CONNOR, W., *Deviance in Soviet Society*, New York, 1972.

COOKE, D., 'Containing Violent Prisoners: An Analysis of the Barlinnie Special Unit', *British Journal of Criminology*, 29 (1989).

CORNISH, D., 'Analyzing Organized Crimes', unpublished typescript, 2000.

CORNISH, D. and Clarke, R., *The Reasoning Criminal*, New York, 1986.

CORRIGAN, P., *Schooling the Smash Street Kids*, London, 1979.

CORRIGAN, P. and Leonard, P., *Social Work Practice Under Capitalism*, London, 1978.

CORSTON Baroness Jean et al, *A Review of Women with Particular Vulnerabilities in the Criminal Justice System*, London, 2014.

COSER, L., *The Functions of Social Conflict*, London, 1956.

COTE, S., (ed.), *Criminological Theories: Bridging the Past to the Future*, Thousand Oaks, Cal. 2002.

COTTERRELL, R., *Émile Durkheim: Law in a Moral Domain*, Stanford, 1999.

COVINGTON, C., 'The Hammersmith Teenage Project: Social Policy and Practice in an Experimental Community-Based Delinquency Project 1975–78', Ph.D. thesis, University of London (LSE), 1980.

COWELL, D., Jones, T., and Young, J. (eds.), *Policing the Riots*, London (1982).

COWIE, J., Cowie, V., and Slater, E., *Delinquency in Girls*, London, 1968.

COX, B. et al., *The Fall of Scotland Yard*, Harmondsworth, 1977.

CRAWFORD, A., *The Local Governance of Crime: Appeals to Community and Partnerships*, Oxford, 1997.

CRESSEY, D., *Other People's Money*, Glencoe, Ill., 1953.

CRESSEY, D., 'Role Theory, Differential Association and Compulsive Crimes', in A. Rose, (ed.), *Human Behavior and Social Processes*, New York, 1962.

CRESSEY, P., *The Taxi-Dance Hall*, Chicago, 1932.

CROW, I. and Semmens, N., *Researching Criminology*, Buckingham, 2007.

CUNEEN, C., 'Postcolonial Perspectives for Criminology' in M. Bosworth and C. Hoyle (eds.) *What is Criminology*, Oxford, 2013.

CURRIE, E., *Confronting Crime: An American Challenge*, New York, 1985.

CUSSON, M., *Why Delinquency?*, Toronto, 1983.

DALLA, R. L., 'Exposing the 'Pretty Women' Myth: A Qualitative Investigation Of Street-level Prostituted Women', *Journal of Marriage and Family*, 69 (2007).

DALY, K. and Chesney-Lind, M., 'Feminism and Criminology', *Justice Quarterly*, 5 (1988).

DALY, K. and Maher, L., (eds.) *Criminology at the Crossroads: Feminist Readings in Crime and Justice*, London, 1998.

DAMER, S., 'Wine Alley: The Sociology of a Dreadful Enclosure', *Sociological Review*, 22 (1974).

DAVIE, M., 'The Pattern of Urban Growth', in G. Murdock, (ed.), *Studies in the Science of Society*, New Haven, 1937.

DAVIES, C., 'Sexual Taboos and Social Boundaries', *American Journal of Sociology*, 87 (1982).

DAVIES, C., 'From the Sacred Hierarchies to Flatland', Canterbury, 1990.

DAVIES, N., *Dark Heart: The Shocking Truth about Hidden Britain*, London, 1998.

DAVIES, P. et al. (eds.), *Doing Criminological Research*, London, 2011.

DAVIS, D., *Homicide in American Fiction*, Ithaca, NY, 1968.

DAVIS, F., 'The Cab-Driver and his Fare', *American Journal of Sociology*, 64 (1959).

DAVIS, F., 'Deviance Disavowal', in H. Becker, (ed.), *The Other Side*, New York, 1964.

DAVIS, K., 'The Sociology of Prostitution', *American Sociological Review*, 2 (1937).

DAVIS, K., 'Illegitimacy and the Social Structure', *American Journal of Sociology*, 44 (1939).

DAVIS, K., 'The Myth of Functional Analysis as a Special Method in Sociology and Anthropology', *American Sociological Review*, 24 (1959). Reprinted in N. Demerath and R. Peterson (eds.), *System, Change and Conflict*, New York (1967).

DAVIS, K., 'Prostitution', in R. Merton and R. Nisbet (eds.), *Contemporary Social Problems*, New York, 1961.

DAVIS, Mike, *City of Quartz: Excavating the Future in Los Angeles*, London, 1990.

DAVIS, Mike, 'Beyond Blade Runner', *Open Magazine Pamphlet*, 23 (Westfield, New Jersey, 1992).

DAVIS, Mike, *Planet of Slums*, London, 2007.

DAVIS, Murray, 'That's Interesting! Towards a Phenomenology of Sociology and a Sociology of Phenomenology', *Philosophy of the Social Sciences*, 1 (1971).

DAVIS, Murray, *Smut: Erotic Reality, Obscene Ideology*, Chicago, 1983.

DAVIS, N., *Sociological Constructions of Deviance*, Dubuque, Ia., 1975.

DAWKINS, R., *The Blind Watchmaker*, London, 1986.

DEAR, M. and Wolch, J., *Landscapes of Despair: From Deinstitutionalization to Homelessness*, Princeton, 1987.

DEBRO, J., 'Dialogue with Howard S. Becker', *Issues in Criminology*, 5.2 (1970).

DEFOE, D., *The True and Genuine Account of the Life and Actions of the Late Jonathan Wild*, London, 1725.

DENNIS, N. and Erdos, G., *Families without Fatherhood*, 2nd edn, London, 1993.

DENTLER, R. and Erikson, K., 'The Functions of Deviance in Groups', *Social Problems*, 7 (1959).

DENZIN, N., 'Crime and the American Liquor Industry', in N. Denzin, (ed.), *Studies in Symbolic Interaction*, I, Greenwich, Conn., 1978.

DEPARTMENT of the Environment, *Local Housing Management: A Priority Estates Project Survey*, London, 1980.

DEPARTMENT of the Environment, *Reducing Vandalism on Public Housing Estates*, London, 1981.

DEWEY, J., 'The Reflex Arc Concept in Social Psychology', *American Journal of Sociology*, 2 (1896).

DEWEY, J., 'Perception and Organic Action', *The Journal of Philosophy, Psychology and Scientific Methods*, 1124 (1912).

DEWEY, J., 'Realism without Monism or Dualism—II', *The Journal of Philosophy*, 1913 (1922).

DICKINSON, D., *Crime and Unemployment* (mimeo), Cambridge, 1994.

DIGNAN, J., *Understanding Victims and Restorative Justice*, Maidenhead, 2005.

DITTON, J., *Part-Time Crime*, London, 1977.

DITTON, J., *Controlology*, London, 1979.

DITTON, J., 'Crime and the City: Public Attitudes towards Open-Street CCTV in Glasgow', *British Journal of Criminology*, 40 (2000).

DOAK, J., *Victims Rights, Human Rights and Criminal Justice*, Oxford, 2008.

DOBASH, R. and Dobash, R., *Violence Against Wives: A Case Against Patriarchy*, London, 1979.

DOBASH, R. and Dobash, R., 'The Nature and Antecedents of Violent Events', *British Journal of Criminology*, 24 (1984).

DOERNER, W. and Lab, S. *Victimology*, Cincinnati, 1995.

DOLLARD, J., *Caste and Class in a Southern Town*, New Haven, 1937.

DOOB, A. and Webster, C., 'Countering Punitiveness: Understanding Stability in Canada's Imprisonment Rate', *Law and Society Review*, 40 (2006).

DOUGLAS, J., *The Social Meanings of Suicide*, Princeton, 1967.

DOUGLAS, J., 'Deviance and Order in a Pluralistic Society', in J. McKinney and E. Tiryakian (eds.), *Theoretical Sociology*, New York, 1970.

DOUGLAS, J., (ed.), *Deviance and Respectability*, New York, 1970.

DOUGLAS, J., *American Social Order: Social Rules in a Pluralistic Society*, New York, 1971.

DOUGLAS, J., 'The Sociological Analysis of Social Meanings of Suicide', in A. Giddens, (ed.), *The Sociology of Suicide*, London, 1971.

DOUGLAS, J. (ed.), *Understanding Everyday Life*, London, 1971.

DOUGLAS, J. (ed.), *Research on Deviance*, New York, 1972.

DOUGLAS, J., 'The Experience of the Absurd and the Problem of Social Order', in R. Scott and J. Douglas (eds.), *Theoretical Perspectives on Deviance*, New York, 1972.

DOUGLAS, J. et al., *The Nude Beach*, Beverly Hills, 1977.

DOUGLAS, J. and Waksler, F., *The Sociology of Deviance: An Introduction*, 1982.

DOUGLAS, M., *Purity and Danger*, London, 1966.

DOUGLAS, M., *Natural Symbols*, London, 1970.

DOUGLAS, M., (ed.), *Rules and Meanings*, Harmondsworth, 1973.

DOUGLAS, M., *Implicit Meanings*, London, 1975.

DOUGLAS, M., *Risk Acceptability According to the Social Sciences*, London, 1985.

DOUGLAS, M., *How Institutions Think*, Syracuse, 1986.

DOWD, L., 'Witnessing of Incidents and Intervention: Informal Social Control in Action', paper presented to the American Society of Criminology, Chicago, 8–12 November 1988.

DOWNES, D., *The Delinquent Solution: A Study in Subcultural Theory*, London, 1966.

DOWNES, D., 'Foreword' to R. Ericson, *Criminal Reactions: The Labelling Perspective*, Farnborough, 1975.

DOWNES, D., 'Praxis Makes Perfect', in D. Downes and P. Rock (eds.), *Deviant Interpretations*, Oxford, 1979.

DOWNES, D., 'Abolition: Possibilities and Pitfalls', in A. Bottoms, (ed.), *The Crisis in the British Penal System*, Edinburgh, 1980.

DOWNES, D., *Contrasts in Tolerance: Postwar Penal Policy in the Netherlands and England and Wales*, Oxford, 1988.

DOWNES, D., 'Back to the Future: The Predictive Value of Social Theories of Delinquency', in S. Holdaway and P. Rock (eds.), *Thinking About Criminology*, London, 1998.

DOWNES, D., review of K. Hayward, *City Limits: Crime, Consumer Culture and the Urban Experience* in *Criminal Justice*, 5:3 (2005).

DOWNES, D. and Hansen, K., 'Welfare and Imprisonment in Comparative Perspective', in S. Armstrong and L. McAra (eds.), *Perspectives on Punishment*, Oxford, 2006.

DOWNES, D. and Morgan, R., 'Dumping the Hostages to Fortune? The Politics of Law and Order in Postwar Britain', in M. Maguire, R. Morgan, and R. Reiner (eds.), *The Oxford Handbook of Criminology*, 2nd edn, 1997, 3rd 1998, 4th 2002, 5th 2006.

DOWNES, D. and Rock, P. (eds.), *Deviant Interpretations: Problems in Criminological Theory*, Oxford, 1979.

DOWNES, D. and van Swaaningen, R., 'The Road to Dystopia? Changes in the Penal Climate of the Netherlands', in M. Tonry, (ed.), *Crime and Justice*, Vol. 35, Chicago, 2006.

DOWNES, D. and Ward, T., *Democratic Policing*, London, 1986.

DRAKE, S. and Cayton, H., *Black Metropolis*, New York, 1945.

DUNEIER, M., *Sidewalk*, New York, 1999.

DURBIN, F., *The Politics of Democratic Socialism*, London, 1940.

DURKHEIM, É., *Suicide*, London, 1952 (orig. published 1897).

DURKHEIM, É., *The Division of Labor in Society*, New York, 1964 (orig. published 1893).

DURKHEIM, É., *The Rules of Sociological Method*, New York, 1964 (orig. published 1895).

DUSTER, T., *The Legislation of Morality*, New York, 1970.

EAGLETON, T., *The Illusions of Postmodernism*, Oxford, 1996.

EASTEL, P., *Voices of the Survivors*, Melbourne, 1994.

EATON, M., 'Mitigating Circumstances: Familiar Rhetoric', *International Journal of Sociological Law*, 11 (1983).

EATON, M., 'Documenting the Defendant: Placing Women in Social Inquiry Report', in J. Brophy and C. Smart (eds.), *Women in Law*, London, 1985.

EATON, M., *Justice for Women?*, Milton Keynes, 1986.

EDELMAN, M., *Politics as Symbolic Action*, Chicago, 1971.

EDGERTON, R., 'Pokot Intersexuality: An East African Example of the Resolution of Sexual Incongruity', *American Anthropologist*, 66 (1964).

EDWARDS, A. and Levi, M., 'Researching the Organization of Serious Crimes', *Criminology and Criminal Justice*, 8.4 (2008).

EDWARDS, S., *Female Sexuality and the Law*, Oxford, 1981.

EDWARDS, S., 'Police Attitudes and Dispositions in Domestic Disputes: The London Study', *Police Journal* (1986).

EDWARDS, S., *Policing 'Domestic' Violence: Women, the Law and the State*, London, 1989.

EHRENREICH, B., *Nickel and Dimed: Undercover in Low-wage USA*, New York, 2001.

EINSTADTER, W., 'The Social Organization of Armed Robbery', *Social Problems*, 17:1 (1969).

EISNER, M., 'Modernization, Self-Control and Lethal Violence. The Long-term

Dynamics of European Homicide Rates in Theoretical Perspective', *The British Journal of Criminology*, 41 (2001).

EKBLOM, P. and Simon, F., *Crime Prevention and Racial Harassment in Asian-run Small Shops: The Scope for Prevention*, London, 1988.

ELIAS, N., *The Civilizing Process (Vol. 2) State Formation and Civilization*, Oxford, 1982.

ELIAS, N., 'Violence and Civilization: The State Monopoly of Physical Violence and its Infringement', in J. Keane, (ed.), *Civil Society and the State*, London, 1988.

ELIAS, N. and Scotson, J., *The Established and the Outsiders*, London, 1965.

ELIAS, R., *Victims of the System*, New Brunswick, 1983.

ELIAS, R., *The Politics of Victimization*, New York, 1986.

ELLIOTT, D. and Voss, H., *Delinquency and Dropouts*, Lexington, Mass., 1974.

ELLISS, A., *Men, Masculinities and Violence*, London, 2015.

EMERSON, R., *Judging Delinquents*, Chicago, 1969.

EMPEY, L., 'Revolution and Counter-Revolution: Current Trends in Juvenile Justice', in D. Shichor and D. Kelly (eds.), *Critical Issues in Juvenile Delinquency*, Lexington, Mass., 1980.

ENGDAHL, O., 'The Role of Money in Economic Crime', *The British Journal of Criminology*, 48 (2008).

ERICSON, R., *Criminal Reactions*, Farnborough, Hants, 1975.

ERICSON, R. et al., *Negotiating Control*, Toronto, 1989.

ERICSON, R. et al., *Visualizing Deviance*, Toronto, 1987.

ERICSON, R. and Haggerty, K., *Policing the Risk Society*, Toronto, 1997.

ERICSON, R. and Doyle, A., *Uncertain Business: Risk, Insurance, and the Limits of Knowledge*, Toronto, 2004.

ERIKSON, K., 'Notes on the Sociology of Deviance', in H. Becker, (ed.), *The Other Side*, New York, 1964.

ERIKSON, K., *Wayward Puritans*, New York, 1966.

ERIKSON, K., 'Disguised Observation in Sociology', *Social Problems*, 14 1967.

ERIKSON, K., *In the Wake of the Flood*, London, 1979.

ERIKSON, K., *A New Species of Trouble*, New York, 1994.

ESPING-ANDERSEN, G., *The Three Worlds of Welfare Capitalism*, Princeton, 1990.

ETZIONI, A., *The Moral Dimension*, New York, 1990.

ETZIONI, A., *The Parenting Deficit*, London, 1993.

EYSENCK, H., *Crime and Personality*, London, 1961 (3rd edn, rev., London, 1977).

EYSENCK, H., 'Crime and Personality Reconsidered', *Bulletin of the British Psychological Society*, 27 (1974).

EZELL, M. and Cohen, L., *Desisting from Crime: Continuity and Change in Long-term Crime Patterns of Serious Chronic Offenders*, Oxford, 2005.

FARBERMAN, H., 'A Criminogenic Market Structure: The Automobile Industry', *The Sociological Quarterly*, 16 (1975).

FARIS, R., *Chicago Sociology, 1920–1932*, San Francisco, 1967.

FARIS, R. and Dunham, H., *Mental Disorders in Urban Areas: An Ecological Study of Schizophrenia and Other Psychoses*, Chicago, 1939.

FARRELL, G. and Bouloukos, A., 'International Overview: A Cross-national Comparison of Rates of Repeat Victimization', in G. Farrell and K. Pease (eds.) *Repeat Victimization: Crime Prevention Studies*, Vol. 12, Monsey, New York, 2001.

FARMER, P., *Aids and Accusation: Haiti and the Geography of Blame*, Los Angeles, 2006.

FARRINGTON, D. and Morris, A., 'Sex, Sentencing and Reconvictions', *British Journal of Criminology*, 23 (1983).

FASSIN, D. and Rechtman, R., *The Empire of Trauma: An Inquiry into the Condition of Victimhood*, Princeton, 2009.

FATTAH, E., (1979) 'Some Recent Theoretical Developments in Victimology', *Victimology*, 4:2 (1979).

FATTAH, E., 'Victimology Past, Present and Future', *Criminologie*, 33:1 (2000).

FAUPEL, C., *Shooting Dope: Career Patterns of Hard-Core Heroin Users*, Gainesville, Fla., 1991.

FEELEY, M., 'The Vanishing Female: The Decline of Women in the Criminal Process, 1687–1912', *Law and Society Review*, 25, (1991).

FEELEY, M., 'The Decline of Women in the Criminal Process: A Comparative History', in *Criminal Justice History: An International Annual*, Westport, Conn., 1994.

FEELEY, M. and Simon, J., 'The New Penology: Notes on the Emerging Strategy of Corrections and its Implications', *Criminology*, 30, (1992).

FELSON, M., *Crime and Nature*, Thousand Oaks, Calif., 2006.

FELSON, M., *The Ecosystem for Organized Crime*, The European Institute for Crime Prevention and Control, Helsinki, 2006.

FELSON, M., *Crime and Everyday Life*, Thousand Oaks, Calif., 2015.

FELSON, M. and Clarke, R., *Opportunity Makes the Thief*, London, 1998.

FERRELL, J., *Crimes of Style: Urban Graffiti and the Politics of Criminality*, New York, 1993.

FERRELL, J. and Saunders, C. (eds.), *Cultural Criminology*, Boston, 1995.

FERRELL, J. et al., 'Fragments of a Manifesto: Introducing Cultural Criminology Unleashed', in J. Ferrell et al. (eds.), *Cultural Criminology Unleashed*, London, 2004.

FERRELL, J., Hayward, K., and Young, J., *Cultural Criminology: An Invitation*, London, 2008.

FEYERABEND, P., *Against Method: Outline for an Anarchistic Theory of Knowledge*, London, 1975.

FIELD, S., *Trends in Crime and their Interpretation*, London, 1990.

FIELDING, N., *The National Front*, London, 1980.

FINE, G., (ed.), *A Second Chicago School? The Development of a Postwar American Sociology*, Chicago, 1995.

FINE, G.A., (ed.), *A Second Chicago School?: The Development of a Postwar American Sociology*, Chicago, 1995.

FINE, S., *Violence in the Modern City: The Cavanagh Administration, Race Relations and the Detroit Riot of 1967*, Ann Arbor, 1989.

FINESTONE, H., *Victims of Change: Juvenile Delinquents in American Society*, Westport, Conn., 1976.

FISHER, C. and Mawby, R., 'Juvenile Delinquency and Police Discretion in an Inner-City Area', *British Journal of Criminology*, 22 (1982).

FISHMAN, M., *Manufacturing the News*, New York, 1980.

FITZGERALD, M., *Prisoners in Revolt*, London, 1977.

FITZGERALD, M., *Crime Sentencing and Justice*, London, 2005.

FITZGERALD, M., '"Gangs"—a UK Perspective', unpubl., 2008.

FITZGERALD, M. and Sim, J., *British Prisons*, Oxford, 1979.

FLETA, London, ca 1290.

FLETCHER, R., 'Evolutionary and Developmental Sociology', in J. Rex, (ed.), *Approaches to Sociology*, London, 1974.

FLOOD-PAGE, C. et al., *Youth Crime: Findings from the 1998/1999 Youth Lifestyles Survey*, London, 2000.

FOSTER, J., *Villains: Crime and Community in the Inner City*, London, 1990.

FOSTER, J., 'Informal Social Control and Community Crime Prevention', *British Journal of Criminology*, 35 (1995).

FOSTER, J. and Hope, T., *Housing, Community and Crime*, London, 1993.

FOUCAULT, M., *Madness and Civilization*, London, 1967.

FOUCAULT, M., *I, Pierre Rivière*, New York, 1975.

FOUCAULT, M., *The Birth of the Clinic*, New York, 1975.

FOUCAULT, M., *Discipline and Punish: The Birth of the Prison*, London, 1977.

FOUCAULT, M., (C. Gordon), *Power/ Knowledge: Selected Interviews and Other Writings, 1972–1977*, New York, 1980.

FRANKO Aas, K., *Globalization and Crime*, London, 2013.

FRASER, N., 'Foucault on Modern Power: Confusions', in N. Fraser, *Unruly Practices*, Minnesota, 1989.

FREEMAN, J., 'The Origins of the Women's Liberation Movement', *American Journal of Sociology*, 78:4 (1973).

FREEMAN, R., 'Employment and Earnings of Disadvantaged Young Men in a Labor Shortage Economy', in C. Jencks and R. Peterson (eds.), *The Urban Underclass*, 1991.

FREEMAN, R., 'Who Becomes A Criminal?' Talk to Mannheim Centre of Criminology, London School of Economics, 1996.

FREIDSON, E., *Profession of Medicine*, New York, 1970.

FUCHS, V., *Who Shall Live? Health Economics and Social Choice*, New York, 1974.

FUKUYAMA, F., *Trust: The Social Virtues and the Creation of Prosperity*, New York, 1995.

FUKUYAMA, F., *State Building*, London, 2004.

GALLAGHER, S. and Zahavi, D. (eds.), *The Phenomenological Mind*, London, 2012.

GALLIHER, J., 'Chicago's Two Worlds of Deviance Research', in G. Fine, (ed.), *A Second Chicago School?*, Chicago, 1995.

GAMBETTA, D., *The Sicilian Mafia*, Cambridge, Mass. 1993.

GANS, H., *The Urban Villagers*, New York, 1962.

GANS, H., *The Levittowners: Ways of Life and Politics in a New Suburban Community*, New York, 1967.

GARFINKEL, H., *Studies in Ethnomethodology*, Englewood Cliffs, NJ, 1967.

GARLAND, D., 'Frameworks of Inquiry in the Sociology of Punishment', *The British Journal of Sociology*, 41 (1990).

GARLAND, D., *Punishment and Modern Society*, Oxford, 1990.

GARLAND, D., 'The Limits of the Sovereign State: Strategies of Crime Control in Contemporary Society', *British Journal of Criminology*, 36:4 (1996).

GARLAND, D., 'The Culture of High Crime Societies', *British Journal of Criminology*, 40:3 (2000).

GARLAND, D., *The Culture of Control: Crime and Social Order in Contemporary Society*, Oxford, 2001.

GARLAND, D., (ed.), *Mass Imprisonment: Social Causes and Consequences*, London, 2001.

GARLAND D. and Sparks, R. (eds), *Criminology and Social Theory*, Oxford, 2000.

GATRELL, V., 'The Decline of Theft and Violence in Victorian and Edwardian England', in V. Gatrell et al. (eds.), *Crime and the Law: The Social History of Crime Since 1500*, London, 1980.

GAVRON, H., *The Captive Wife*, London, 1966.

GEER, C., 'Crime, Media and Community: Grief and Virtual Engagement in Late Modernity', in J. Ferrell et al. (eds.), *Cultural Criminology Unleashed*, London, 2004.

GELLNER, E., 'Concepts and Society', in B. Wilson, (ed.), *Rationality*, Oxford, 1968.

GELLNER, E., *Legitimation of Belief*, Cambridge, 1974.

GELLNER, E., 'A Social Contract in Search of an Idiom: The Demise of the Danegeld State?', *Political Quarterly*, 46 (1975).

GELLNER, E., 'Ethnomethodology: The Re-Enchantment Industr y or The Californian Way of Subjectivity', *Philosophy of the Social Sciences*, 5 (1975).

GELLNER, E., *Postmodernism, Reason and Religion*, New York, 1992.

GELSTHORPE, L., 'The Jack-Roller: Telling a Story?', *Theoretical Criminology*, 11:4 (2007).

GELSTHORPE, L. and Morris, A., 'Feminism and Criminology in Britain', *British Journal of Criminology*, 28 (1988).

GENDERS, E. and Player, E., *Grendon: A Study of A Therapeutic Prison*, Oxford, 1995.

GENN, H., 'Multiple Victimization', in M. Maguire and J. Pointing, *Victims of Crime*, Milton Keynes, 1988.

GIBBS, J., 'Conceptions of Deviant Behavior: The Old and the New', *Pacific Sociological Review*, 8:1 (1966).

GIDDENS, A., (ed.), *The Sociology of Suicide*, London, 1971.

GIDDENS, A., *Émile Durkheim: Selected Writings*, Cambridge, 1972.

GIDDENS, A., *The Class Structure of the Advanced Societies*, London, 1973.

GIDDENS, A., *The Constitution of Society*, Cambridge, 1984.

GIDDENS, A., *The Constitution of Society: Outline of the Theory of Structuration*, London, 1986.

GIDDENS, A., *The Consequences of Modernity*, Cambridge, 1990.

GIDDENS, A., *Modernity and Self-Identity*, Cambridge, 1991.

GIDDENS, A., *In Defence of Sociology*, Cambridge, 1996.

GIDDENS, A., *The Politics of Climate Change*, Cambridge, 2014.

GILL, M. et al., *The Impact of CCTV: Fourteen Case Studies*, London, 2005.

GILL, O., *Luke Street: Housing Policy, Conflict and the Creation of the Delinquent Area*, London, 1977.

GLENNY, M., *McMafia: Seriously Organised Crime*, New York, 2009.

GLUECK, S. and Glueck, E., *Five Hundred Delinquent Women*, New York, 1934.

GLUECK, S. and Glueck, E., *Unravelling Juvenile Delinquency*, Cambridge, Mass. 1950.

GOETSCHIUS, G. and Tash, M., *Working with Unattached Youth*, London, 1967.

GOFFMAN, A., *On the Run: Fugitive Life in an American City*, New York, 2015.

GOFFMAN, E., 'The Moral Career of the Mental Patient', *Psychiatry*, 22:2 (1959).

GOFFMAN, E., *Stigma: Notes on the Management of Spoiled Identity*, Englewood Cliffs, NJ, 1963.

GOFFMAN, E., *Asylums*, Harmondsworth, 1968.

GOFFMAN, E., 'Where the Action Is', in *Interaction Ritual*, London, 1972.

GOFFMAN, E., *Frame Analysis*, Cambridge, Mass. 1974.

GOLD, M., *Delinquent Behavior in an American City*, Belmont, Cal., 1970.

GOLDBLATT, P. and Lewis, C. (eds.), *Reducing Offending: An Assessment of Research Evidence on Ways of Dealing with Offending Behaviour*, London, 1998.

GOLDTHORPE, J., 'The Uses of History', *British Journal of Sociology*, 42:2 (1991).

GOODEY, J., 'Human Trafficking: Sketchy Data and Policy Responses', *Criminology and Criminal Justice*, 8:4 (2008).

GOOLD, B., *CCTV and Policing: Public Area Surveillance and Police Practices in Britain*, Oxford, 2004.

GORDON, C., *The Old Bailey and Newgate*, London, 1902.

GORDON, P., *White Law*, London, 1983.

GOTTFREDSON, M., 'On the Etiology of Criminal Victimization', *The Journal of Criminal Law and Criminology*, 72:2 (1981).

GOTTFREDSON, M. and Hindelang, M., 'Sociological Aspects of Criminal Victimization', *Annual Review of Sociology*, 7 (1981).

GOTTFREDSON, M. and Hirschi, T., *A General Theory of Crime*, Stanford, Calif., 1990.

GOULDNER, A., 'Anti-Minotaur: The Myth of a Value-Free Sociology', *Social Problems*, 10 (1962).

GOULDNER, A., 'The Sociologist as Partisan', *American Sociologist* 3 (1968). Reprinted in Gouldner, A., *For Sociology: Renewal and Critique in Sociology Today*, London, 1973.

GOULDNER, A., *The Coming Crisis in Western Sociology*, New York and London, 1970.

GOVE, W., (ed.), *The Labelling of Deviance*, London, 1975.

GRADY, A., 'Female-on-Male Domestic Abuse: Uncommon or Ignored?', in C. Hoyle and R. Young (eds.), *New Visions of Crime Victims*, Oxford, 2002.

GRAHAM, S., 'Surveillant Simulation and the City', paper delivered at the NCGIA annual conference, Baltimore, 1996.

GRAHAM, S., *Cities Under Siege: the New Military Urbanism*, London, 2011.

GRAHAM, S., Brooks, J., and Heery, D., 'Towns on the Television', *Local Government Studies*, 22:3 (1996).

GRAHAM, S. and Marvin, S., *Telecommunications and the City: Electronic Spaces, Urban Places*, London, 1996.

GRAZIAN, D., *On The Make: The Hustle of Urban Nightlife*, Chicago, 2008.

GREEN, P. and Ward, T. *State Crime: Governments, Violence and Corruption*, London, 2004.

GREGORY, J. and Lees, S., *Policing Sexual Assault*, New York, 1998.

GRIFFITH, J., *The Politics of the Judiciary*, London, 1977.

GRIFFITHS, A., *The Chronicles of Newgate*, London, 1884.

GURR, T., 'Historical Trends in Violent Crime: A Critical Review of the Evidence', in M. Tonry and N. Morris (eds.), *Crime and Justice: An Annual Review of Research: 3*, Chicago, 1981.

GURR, T., Grabosky, P., and Hula, R., *The Politics of Crime and Conflict: A Comparative History of Four Cities*, Beverly Hills, 1977.

GUSFIELD, J., 'Moral Passage', *Social Problems*, 15:2 (1968).

HABERMAS, J., *Legitimation Crisis*, London, 1975.

HACKING, I., *Rewriting the Soul: Multiple Personality and the Sciences of Memory*, Princeton, 1995.

HADFIELD, P., *Bar Wars: Contesting the Night in Contemporary British Cities*, Oxford, 2006.

HAGAN, F., *Political Crime: Ideology and Criminality*, Boston, 1997.

HAGAN, J., *Crime and Disrepute*, Thousand Oaks, Cal., 1994.

HAGAN, J., *The Disreputable Pleasures*, Toronto, 1977.

HAGAN, J. and Leon, J., 'Rediscovering Delinquency: Social History, Political Ideology and the Rule of Law', *American Sociological Review*, 42 (1977).

HAGAN, J. and McCarthy, B., 'Street-life and Delinquency', *British Journal of Sociology*, 43 (1992).

HAGAN, J. and McCarthy, B., *Mean Streets: Youth Crime and Homelessness*, Cambridge, 1998.

HAGAN, J. and Palloni, A., 'The Social Reproduction of a Criminal Class in Working-Class London circa 1950–1980', *American Journal of Sociology*, 96 (1990).

HAGAN, J. and Rymond-Richmond, W., *Darfur and the Crime of Genocide*, Cambridge, 2009.

HAGAN, J., Gillis, A., and Simpson, J., 'The Class Structure of Gender and Delinquency: Toward a Power-Control Theory of Common Delinquent Behavior', *American Journal of Sociology*, 90 (1985).

HAGAN, J., Simpson, J., and Gillis, A., 'The Sexual Stratification of Social Control', *British Journal of Sociology*, 30 (1979).

HAGAN, J. et al., *Structural Criminology*, Cambridge, 1988.

HAGAN, J. et al., 'Gender Difference in Capitalization Processes and the Delinquency of Siblings in Toronto and Berlin', *British Journal of Criminology*, 44 (2004).

HAGGERTY, K. D., 'Displaced Expertise', *Theoretical Criminology*, 8 (2004).

HAGGERTY. K. D. and Ericson, R. V., *The New Politics of Surveillance and Visibility*, Toronto, 2006.

HALL, S., *Drifting into a Law and Order Society*, London, 1980.

HALL, S. et al. (eds.), *Resistance through Rituals*, London, 1976.

HALL, S. et al., *Policing the Crisis: Mugging, the State and Law and Order*, London, 1978.

HALL, S., Winlow, S., and Ancrum, C., *Criminal Identities and Consumer Culture: Crime, Exclusion and the New Culture of Narcissism*, Cullompton, 2008.

HALLORAN, J. et al., *Demonstrations and Communications*, Harmondsworth, 1970.

HALLSWORTH, S., *Street Crime*, Cullompton, 2005.

HALLSWORTH, S. and Silverstone, D., '"That's Life Innit": A British Perspective on Guns, Crime and Social Order', *Criminology and Criminal Justice*, 9 (2009).

HAMMOND, P., (ed.), *Sociologists at Work* New York, 1964.

HANSEN, K., 'Time to Educate the Criminals?', *Centre Piece*, 5:3 (2000).

HARGREAVES, D., *Social Relations in a Secondary School*, London, 1967.

HARGREAVES, D. et al., *Deviance in Classrooms*, London, 1975.

HARVEY, D., *The Condition of Postmodernity*, London, 1993.

HAUG, M. and Sussman, M., 'Professional Autonomy and the Revolt of the Client', *Social Problems*, 17:2 (1969)

HAUG, M., *The Criminal and his Victim*, Hamden, Conn, 1948.

HAWKINS, K., *Environment and Enforcement*, Oxford, 1984.

HAWTHORNE, G., *Enlightenment and Despair*, Cambridge, 1977.

HAY, D. et al. (eds.), *Albion's Fatal Tree: Crime and Society in Eighteenth-century England*, London, 1975.

HAYMAN, S., 'The Evolution of the New Federal Women's Prisons in Canada', Ph.D. dissertation, London School of Economics, 2003.

HAYWARD, A., (ed.), *Lives of the Most Remarkable Criminals*, London, 1927.

HAYWARD, K., *City Limits: Crime, Consumer Culture, and the Urban Experience*, London, 2004.

HEATH, A., *Rational Choice and Social Exchange*, Cambridge, 1976.

HEATH, A. et al. (eds.), *Understanding Social Change*, Oxford, 2005.

HEBDIGE, R., *Subculture: The Meaning of Style*, London, 1979.

HEIDENSOHN, F., 'The Deviance of Women: A Critique and an Enquiry', *British Journal of Sociology*, 19 (1968).

HEIDENSOHN, F., *Women and Crime*, London, 1985.

HEIDENSOHN, F., 'Women and Crime: Questions for Criminology', in P. Carlen and A. Worrall (eds.), *Gender, Crime and Justice*, Milton Keynes, 1987.

HEIDENSOHN, F., *Women in Control: The Role of Women in Law Enforcement*, Oxford, 1992.

HEIDENSOHN, F., *Gender and Justice: New Concepts and Approaches*, London, 2006.

HEIDENSOHN, F., 'The Future of Feminist Criminology', *Crime, Media, Culture*, 8:2 (2012).

HEILAND, H. G. and Shelley, L., 'Civilization, Modernization and the Development of Crime and Control', in H. G. Heiland, L. Shelley, and H. Katch (eds.), *Crime and Control in Comparative Perspective*, Berlin, 1992.

HENDERSON, L., (1985) 'The Wrongs of Victim's Rights', *Stanford Law Review*, 37:4 (1985)

HENRY, J., *Culture Against Man*, London, 1963.

HENRY, S., *The Hidden Economy*, London, 1978.

HENRY, S. and Mars, G., 'Crime at Work', *Sociology*, 12:2 (1978).

HENRY, S. and Milovanovic, D., *Constitutive Criminology: Beyond Postmodernism*, London, 1996.

HERBERT, D., 'Urban Crime: A Geographical Perspective', in D. Herbert and D. Smith (eds.), *Social Problems and the City*, Oxford, 1979.

HERRINGTON, L., 'Victim Rights and Criminal Justice Reform', *Annals of the American Academy of Political Science* 494 1987.

HEUMANN, M., *Plea Bargaining: The Experiences of Prosecutors, Judges, and Defense Attorneys*, Chicago, University of Chicago Press, 1977.

HEYL, B., *The Madam as Entrepreneur*, New Brunswick, NJ, 1979.

HILL, R. and Crittenden, K., *Proceedings of the Purdue Symposium on Ethnomethodology*, West Lafayette, Ind., 1968.

HILLIER, B., 'In Defence of Space', *RIBA Journal* (November 1973).

HILLIER, B., 'City of Alice's Dreams', *Architecture Journal*, 39 (9 July 1986).

HILLS, J., *The Future of Welfare: A Guide to the Debate*, York, 1993.

HILLYARD, P. et al., 'Leaving a "Stain Upon the Silence"', *British Journal of Criminology*, 44:3 (2004).

HILLYARD, P. and Pantazis, C., (eds.) *Beyond Criminology: Taking Harm Seriously*, London, 2004.

HINDELANG, M., 'The Social versus Solitary Nature of Delinquent Involvements', *British Journal of Criminology*, 11:2 (1971).

HINDESS, B., *The Use of Official Statistics in Sociology: A Critique of Positivism and Ethnomethodology*, London, 1973.

HIRSCHFIELD, K., *Gangster States: Organised Crime, Kleptocracy and Political Collapse*, Basingstoke, 2015.

HIRSCHI, T., *Causes of Delinquency*, Berkeley, California, 1969.

HIRSCHI, T., 'Procedural Rules and the Study of Deviant Behavior', *Social Problems*, 21:2 (1973).

HIRST, P., 'Marx and Engels on Law, Crime and Morality', in I. Taylor et al. (eds.), *Critical Criminology*, London, 1975.

HOARE, Q. and Nowell Smith, G. (eds.), *Selections from the Prison Notebooks of Antonio Gramsci*, London, 1971.

HOBBES, T., *Leviathan*, 1651; Oxford, 1957.

HOBBS, D., *Doing the Business: Entrepreneurship, the Working Class and Detectives in East London*, Oxford, 1988.

HOBBS, D., *Bad Business*, Oxford, 1995.

HOBBS, D., *Lush Life: Constructing Organised Crime in the UK*, Oxford, 2013.

HOBBS, D., Hadfield, P., Lister, L., and Winlow, S., *Bouncers: Violence and Governance in the Night-time Economy*, Oxford, 2003.

Hobsbawm, E., *Primitive Rebels*, Manchester, 1959.

Hobsbawm, E., *Bandits*, Harmondsworth, 1969.

Hoffman-Bustamente, D., 'The Nature of Female Criminality', *Issues in Criminology*, 8 (1973).

Hofstadter, R., *Social Darwinism in American Thought*, New York, 1959.

Holdaway, S., *Inside the British Police*, London, 1983.

Holstein, J. and Miller, G., 'Rethinking Victimization: An Interactional Approach to Victimology', *Symbolic Interaction*, 13:1 (1990).

Homans, G., *The Human Group*, London, 1951.

Homans, G., 'Social Behavior as Exchange', *American Journal of Sociology*, 64 (1958).

Homans, G., 'Bringing Men Back In', *American Sociological Review*, 29 (1964).

Home Office Statistical Bulletin 7/85, 'Criminal Careers of those Born in 1953, 1958 and 1963', London, 1985.

Home Office, *Experiments in Social Policy and their Explanation* (Report of an Anglo-American Conference held at Ditchley Park, Oxfordshire, 29–31 October 1969), Community Development Project, 1970, mimeograph.

Home Office, Research Findings No. 2, London, 1992.

Home Office, *Statistics on Women and the Criminal Justice System 2000*, London, 2000.

Home Office, *The 2001 British Crime Survey: First Results, England and Wales*, London (2001).

Home Office, Statistical Bulletin 09/08, 'Young People and Crime: Findings from the 2006 Offending, Crime and Justice Survey', 2008.

Home Office, Online Report 33/05, 'Minority Ethnic Groups and Crime: Findings from the Crime and Justice Survey', 2005.

Home Office, 'Drug Use among Vulnerable Groups of Young People: Findings from the 2003 Crime and Justice Survey', Findings 254, 2005.

Home Office, 'Findings from the 2003 Offending, Crime and Justice Survey: Alcohol-Related Crime and Disorder', Findings 261, 2005.

Hood, R., 'Hermann Mannheim and Max Grünhut: Criminological Pioneers in London and Oxford', *British Journal of Criminology*, 44 (2004).

Hood, R. and Joyce, K., 'Three Generations: Oral Testimonies on Crime and Social Change in London's East End', *British Journal of Criminology*, 39 (1999).

Hood, R. and Sparks, R., *Key Issues in Criminology*, London, 1970.

Hooker, E., 'Male Homosexuality', in N. Farberow, (ed.), *Taboo Topics*, New York, 1963.

Hope, T., *Burglary in Schools*, London, 1982.

Horowitz, I., 'The Politics of Drugs', in P. Rock, (ed.), *Drugs and Politics*, New Brunswick, NJ, 1977.

Horton, J., 'The Dehumanisation of Alienation and Anomie', *British Journal of Sociology*, 15 (1964).

Hough, M., 'Modernization, Scientific Rationalism and the Crime Reduction Programme', *Criminal Justice*, 4 (2004).

Hough, M. and Mayhew, P., *The British Crime Survey*, London, 1983.

Hough, M. and Mayhew, P. *Taking Account of Crime*, London, 1985.

Howard, 1777 Howard, J., *The State of the Prisons*, London, 1777.

Hoyle, C. and Young, R. (eds.), *New Visions of Crime Victims*, Oxford, 2004.

Hoyt, H., *One Hundred Years of Land Values in Chicago: The Relationship of the Growth of Chicago to the Rise in its Land Values, 1830–1933*, Chicago, 1933.

HUBER, J., 'Symbolic Interaction as a Pragmatic Perspective: The Bias of Emergent Theory', *American Sociological Review*, 38:2 (1973).

HUGHES, E., *The Growth of an Institution: The Chicago Real Estate Board*, Chicago, 1931.

HUGHES, E., 'Robert E. Park', in *The Sociological Eye*, Chicago, 1971.

HUGHES, E., 'Good People and Dirty Work', in *The Sociological Eye*, Chicago, 1971.

HUGHES, R., *The Culture of Complaint*, New York, 1993.

HUMPHREYS, L., *Tearoom Trade*, Chicago, 1970.

HUMPHREYS, L., *Out of the Closets*, Englewood Cliffs, NJ, 1972.

HUTTER, B., *The Reasonable Arm of the Law?*, Oxford, 1988.

HUTTON, W., *The State We're In*, London, 1995.

IANNI, F., *A Family Business*, London, 1972.

IGNATIEFF, M., *A Just Measure of Pain*, London, 1979.

INNES, M., *Understanding Social Control*, Maidenhead, 2003.

INTERNATIONAL Study Institute on Victimology, 'Conclusions and Recommendations', in E. Viano (ed); *Victims and Society*, Washington, 1976.

IRWIN, J., *The Felon*, Englewood Cliffs, NJ, 1970.

JACOBS, J., *The Death and Life of Great American Cities*, Harmondsworth, 1965.

JACOBS, J. and Potter, K., *Hate Crimes: Criminal Law and Identity Politics*, New York, 1998.

JACOBS, J. B., *Can Gun Control Work?*, New York, 2002.

JAMES, O., *Juvenile Violence in a Winner-Loser Culture*, London, 1995.

JAMES, O., *Britain on the Couch: Why We are Less Happy Than in 1950, Though Richer*, London, 1997.

JAMES, W., *A Pluralistic Universe*, New York, 1920.

JAMES, W., *Pragmatism*, New York, 1949.

JAYCOX, V., *Creating a Senior Victim/Witness Volunteer Corps*, Washington, 1981.

JENCKS, C. and Peterson, R. (eds.), *The Urban Underclass*, Washington, 1991.

JENKINS, P., 'Failure to Launch: Why Do Some Social Issues Fail to Detonate Moral Panics?', *British Journal of Criminology*, 49:1 (2009).

JOHNSON, E., 'The Function of the Central Business District in the Metropolitan Community', in *Third Year Course in the Study of Contemporary Society*, Chicago, 1942.

JOHNSON, M. P., *A Typology of Domestic Violence: Intimate Terrorism, Violent Resistance, and Situational Couple Violence*, Lebanon, NH, 2008.

JONES, S., 'Partners in Crime: A Study of the Relationship between Female Offenders and their Co-Defendants', *Criminology and Criminal Justice*, 8:2 (2008).

JONES, T., Maclean, B., and Young, J., *The Islington Crime Survey*, Aldershot, 1986.

JONES, T. and Newburn, T., 'Urban Change and Policing: Mass Private Property Reconsidered', *European Journal on Criminal Policy and Research*, 7:2 (1999).

JONES, T. and Newburn, T., 'The Transformation of Policing? Understanding Current Trends in Policing Systems', *British Journal of Criminology*, 42 (2002).

JUBY, H. and Farrington, D., 'Disentangling the Link between Disrupted Families and Delinquency', *British Journal of Criminology*, 41:1 (2001).

JUDGES, A., *The Elizabethan Underworld*, London, 1930.

KAPLAN, R., 'The Coming Anarchy', *The Atlantic Monthly* (February 1994).

KARMEN, A., *The New York Murder Mystery: The True Story Behind the Crime Crash of the 1990s*, New York, 2000.

KATZ, J., *Seductions of Crime*, New York, 1988.

KATZ, J., 'Ethnography's Warrants', *Sociological Methods and Research*, 25:4 (1997).

KATZ, J. and Jackson-Jacobs, C., 'The Criminologists' Gang' in C. Sumner, (ed.), *The Blackwell Companion to Criminology*, Malden, Mass., 2004.

KELLING, G. and Coles, C., *Fixing Broken Windows*, New York, 1996.

KENNEDY, P., *Preparing for the Twenty- First Century*, New York, 1993.

KERSTEN, J., 'Culture, Masculinities and Violence Against Women', *British Journal of Criminology*, 36 (1996).

KEVLES, D. J., *In the Name of Eugenics*: *Genetics and the Uses of Human Heredity*, New York, 1985.

KINCHELOE, S., 'The Behavior Sequence of a Dying Church', *Religious Education* (1929).

KING, R., 'Prisons', in M. Tonry, (ed.), *The Crime and Justice Handbook*, New York, 1998.

KING, R. and Wincup, E. (eds.), *Doing Research on Crime and Justice*, Oxford, 2007.

KITSUSE, J., 'Societal Reaction to Deviant Behavior', in E. Rubington and M. Weinberg (eds.), *Deviance: The Interactionist Perspective*, New York, 1968.

KITSUSE, J. and Cicourel, A., 'A Note on the Uses of Official Statistics', *Social Problems*, 11:2 (1963).

KLAPP, O., *Collective Search for Identity*, New York, 1969.

KLEIN, D., 'The Etiology of Female Crime: A Review of the Literature', *Issues in Criminology*, 8 (1973).

KLEIN, K., *This Changes Everything: Capitalism vs. the Climate*, New York, 2015.

KLOCKARS, C., *The Professional Fence*, London, 1975.

KLOCKARS, C., 'The Contemporary Crises of Marxist Criminology', *Criminology: An Interdisciplinary Journal*, 16:4 (1979).

KNIGHT, S., *Crime Fiction Since 1800: Detection, Death, Diversity*, New York, 2010.

KOBRIN, S., 'The Chicago Area Project', in N. Johnston, et al. (eds.), *The Sociology of Punishment and Correction*, New York, 1962.

KOBRIN, S. et al., 'Offense Patterns of Status Offenders', in D. Shichor and D. Kelly (eds.), *Critical Issues in Juvenile Delinquency*, Lexington, Mass., 1980.

KONOPKA, G., *The Adolescent Girl in Conflict*, Englewood Cliffs, NJ, 1966.

KORN, A., 'Crime and Legal Control: The Israeli Arab population during the Military Government Period (1948–66)', *British Journal of Criminology*, 40 (2000).

KORN, R. and McCorkle, L., 'Social Roles', in C. Bersani, (ed.), *Crime and Delinquency*, New York, 1970.

KORNHAUSER, R., *Social Sources of Delinquency: An Appraisal of Analytic Models*, Chicago, 1978.

KRAHE, B. and Temkin, J., *Sexual Assault and the Justice Gap: A Question of Attitude*, Oxford, 2008.

KROG, A., *Conditional Tense: After the South African Truth and Reconciliation Commission*, Cape Town, 2013.

KUHN, T., *The Structure of Scientific Revolutions*, Chicago, 1961.

KUMAR, R., *The History of Doing: An Illustrated History of Movements for Women's Rights and Feminism in India 1800–1990*, New Delhi, 1993.

LACEY, N., *The Prisoners' Dilemma: Political Economy and Punishment in Contemporary Societies*, Cambridge, 2008.

LAHEY, B. and Moffitt, T. (eds.), *Causes of Conduct Disorder and Juvenile Delinquency*, London, 2003.

LAKATOS, I., 'Falsification and the Methodology of Scientific Research Programmes', in I. Lakatos and A. Musgrave (eds.), *Criticism and the Growth of Knowledge*, Cambridge, 1970.

LAMB, L., *The Trouble with Blaming*, Cambridge, Mass, 1996.

LANDAU, S. and Nathan, G., 'Juveniles and the Police', *British Journal of Criminology*, 23 (1983).

LANDER, B., *Towards an Understanding of Juvenile Delinquency*, New York, 1954.

LANDESCO, J., *Organized Crime in Chicago*, Chicago, 1968.

LARSEN, N. and Smandych, R., *Global Criminology and Criminal Justice*, London, 2007.

LAQUEUR, W., 'Life as a Weapon', *Times Literary Supplement*, 6 September 2002.

LAUB, J. and Sampson, R., 'Understanding Desistance from Crime', in M. Tonry, (ed.), *Crime and Justice: A Review of Research*, Vol. 28, Chicago, 2001.

LAUB, J. and Sampson, R., *Shared Beginnings: Divergent Lives: Delinquent Boys to Age 70*, Cambridge, Mass., 2003.

LAUFER, R., Gallops, M., and Frey-Wouters, E., 'War Stress and Trauma: The Vietnam Veteran', *Journal of Health and Social Behavior*, 25:1 (1984).

LAYCOCK, G., *Reducing Burglary*, London, 1984.

LEA, J., 'Towards Social Prevention', Working Paper, Enfield, Middlesex Polytechnic, 1986.

LEA, J. and Young, J., *What is to be Done about Law and Order?*, London, 1984.

LEE, M. and Laidler, K. J., 'Doing Criminology from the Periphery: Crime and Punishment in Asia', *Theoretical Criminology*, 17:2 (2013).

LEE, N., *The Search for an Abortionist*, Chicago, 1969.

LEMERT, E., *Social Pathology*, New York, 1951.

LEMERT, E., 'Social Structure, Social Control and Deviation', in M. Clinard, (ed.), *Anomie and Deviant Behavior*, New York, 1964.

LEMERT, E., *Human Deviance, Social Problems, and Social Control*, Englewood Cliffs, 1967.

LEMERT, E., 'An Isolation and Closure Theory of Naive Check Forgery', in *Human Deviance, Social Problems, and Social Control*, Englewood Cliffs, 1967.

LEMERT, E., *Social Action and Legal Change*, Chicago, 1970.

LENIN, V., *Materialism and Empirio-Criticism*, London, 1908.

LERMAN, P., *Community Treatment and Social Control: A Critical Analysis of Juvenile Correctional Policy*, Chicago, 1975.

LERNER, M., *The Belief in a Just World: A Fundamental Delusion*, London, 1980.

LEONARD, E., *Women, Crime and Society*, London, 1982.

LEVINE, K., 'Empiricism in Victimological Research', *Victimology*, 3:1–2 (1978).

LEWIS, O., *Five Families: Mexican Case Studies in the Culture of Poverty*, New York, 1959.

LEWIS, O., *The Children of Sanchez*, New York, 1961.

LEWIS, O., *La Vida: A Puerto Rican Family in the Culture of Poverty*, London, 1967.

LEYTON, E., *Men of Blood: Murder in Modern England*, London, 1995.

LEZNOFF, M. and Westley, W., 'The Homosexual Community', *Social Problems*, 3:4 (1956).

LIANOS, M. and Douglas, M., 'Dangerization and the End of Deviance: The Institutional Environment', *British Journal of Criminology*, 40:2 (2000).

LIDNER, R. and Morris, A., *The Reportage of Urban Culture: Robert Park and the Chicago School*, Cambridge, 2006.

LIEBOW, E., *Tally's Corner: Negro Streetcorner Men in Washington*, London, 1967.

LIEBOW, E., *Tell Them Who I am: The Lives of Homeless Women*, New York, 1993.

LIGHT, R., Nee, C., and Ingham, H., *Car Theft: The Offender's Perspective*, London, 1993.

LINDESMITH, A., *Opiate Addiction*, Bloomington, Ind., 1947.

LINDESMITH, A. and Gagnon, J., 'Anomie and Drug Addiction', in M. Clinard, (ed.), *Anomie and Deviant Behavior*, New York, 1964.

LINDESMITH, A. and Levin, Y., 'English Economy and Criminology of the Past Century', *Journal of Criminal Law, Criminology and Police Science*, 27:6 (1937).

LIPPMANN, W., *Public Opinion*, New York, 1965.

LIPSET, S., *Political Man*, London, 1960.

LIVINGSTONE, S., 'On the Continuing Problem of Media Effects', in J. Curran and M. Gurevitch (eds.), *Mass Media and Society*, London, 1996.

LLEWELLYN, K. and Hoebel, A., *The Cheyenne Way: Conflict and Case Law in Primitive Jurisprudence*, Norman, 1941.

LOADER, I. and Sparks, R., *Public Criminology?*, London, 2010.

LOCKWOOD, D., 'Some Remarks on "The Social System"', *British Journal of Sociology*, 7 (1956).

LOFLAND, L., *A World of Strangers*, New York, 1973.

LOMBARD, N., *Violence against Women: Current Theory and Practice in Domestic Abuse, Sexual Violence and Exploitation*, London, 2013.

LOMBROSO, C. and Ferrero, W., *The Female Offender*, London, 1895.

LONEY, M., *Community Against Government: The British Community Development Project, 1968–1978*, London, 1983.

LOPOTA, H., 'The Function of Voluntary Associations', in E. Burgess and D. Bogue (eds.), *Contributions to Urban Sociology*, Chicago, 1964.

LÖSEL, F., 'The Efficacy of Correctional Treatment: A Review and Synthesis of Meta-Evaluations', in J. McGuire, (ed.), *What Works: Reducing Reoffending*, Chichester, 1995.

LOWMAN, J. and MacLean, R. (eds.), *Realist Criminology: Crime Control and Policing in the 1990s*, Toronto, 1992.

LUCKENBILL, D., 'Criminal Homicide as a Situated Transaction', *Social Problems*, 75:2 (1977).

LUCKENBILL, D. and Best, J., 'Careers in Deviance and Respectability: The Analogy's Limitation', *Social Problems*, 29 (1981).

LUKES, S., 'Alienation and Anomie', in P. Laslett and W. Runciman (eds.), *Philosophy, Politics and Society*, Oxford, 1967.

LUKES, S., *Émile Durkheim: His Life and Work*, London, 1973.

LUKES, S. and Scull, A., *Durkheim and the Law*, Oxford, 1983.

LURIE, A., *Imaginary Friends*, London, 1967.

LYON, D., *The Electronic Eye: The Rise of Surveillance Society*, Cambridge, 1994.

LYON, D., *Surveillance After Snowden*, Cambridge, 2014.

MACK, J., '"Professional Crime" and Criminal Organization', *International Journal of Criminology and Penology*, 6:4 (1978).

MACLEOD, J., *Ain't No Makin' It*, Boulder, Colo., 1995.

MACNICOL, J., 'In Pursuit of the Underclass', *Journal of Social Policy* 16 (1987).

MCAULEY, R., 'The Enemy Within: Economic Marginalisation and the Impact of Crime on Young Adults', University of Cambridge, unpubl. Ph. D. thesis, 2000.

McBarnet, D., 'Pre-trial Procedures and Construction of Conviction', in P. Carlen, (ed.), The Sociology of Law, *Sociological Review Monographs* 23 (1976).

McBarnet, D., 'Whiter than White-Collar Crime', *British Journal of Sociology*, 42 (1991).

McCaghy, C., 'Drinking and Deviance Disavowal', *Social Problems*, 16:1 (1968).

McCarthy, C., *Reparations and Victim Support in the International Criminal Court*, Cambridge, 2012.

McClintock, F., *Crimes of Violence*, London, 1963.

McDonald, L., *The Sociology of Law and Order*, London, 1976.

McDonald, L., 'Theory and Evidence of Rising Crime in the Nineteenth Century', *British Journal of Sociology*, 33:3 (1982).

McGahey, R., 'Economic Conditions, Neighborhood Organization and Urban Crime', in A. Reiss and M. Tonry (eds.), *Communities and Crime*, Chicago, 1986.

McHugh, P., 'A Common-Sense Perception of Deviance', in H. Dreitzel, (ed.), *Recent Sociology: No. 2*, New York, 1970.

McIntosh, M., *The Organization of Crime*, London, 1974.

McLaughlin, E., 'Hitting the Panic Button: Policing/"Mugging"/Media/Crisis' *Crime, Media and Culture* 4 (2008).

McLaughlin, E. et al., *Restorative Justice: Critical Issues*, London, 2003.

McLaughlin, E. and Muncie, J. (eds.), *Criminological Perspectives: Essential Readings*, London, 2013.

McMahon, M., '"Net-Widening": Vagaries in the Use of a Concept', *British Journal of Criminology*, 30 (1990).

McMahon, M., *The Persistent Prison? Rethinking Decarceration and Penal Reform*, Toronto, 1992.

McMullan, J. L., 'Aspects of Professional Crime and Criminal Organization in Sixteenth and Seventeenth Century London: A Sociological Analysis', Ph.D. thesis, University of London (LSE), 1980.

McVicar, J., *McVicar by Himself*, London, 1974.

Maguire, M. (1991) 'The Needs and Rights of Victims of Crime', *Crime and Justice*, 14 (1991).

Maher, L., *Sexed Work: Gender, Race, and Resistance in a Brooklyn Drug Market*, Oxford, 1997.

Malinowski, B., *A Scientific Theory of Culture*, London, 1944.

Malinowski, B., *Crime and Custom in Savage Society*, London, 1926.

Mallea, P., *The War on Drugs: A Failed Experiment*, Toronto, 2014.

Mandeville, B., *The Fable of the Bees*, London, 1714.

Mann, C., *Female Crime and Delinquency*, Alabama, 1984.

Mannheim, H., *Social Aspects of Crime Between the Wars*, London, 1940.

Mannheim, K., *Ideology and Utopia*, London, 1936.

Mannheim, K., 'On the Interpretation of "Weltanschauung"', in *Essays on the Sociology of Knowledge*, London, 1952.

Manning, P., 'Deviance and Dogma', *British Journal of Criminology*, 15 (1975).

Manning, P., *Police Work*, Cambridge, Mass., 1977.

Manning, P., *The Narc's Game*, Cambridge, Mass., 1980.

Marcuse, H., *One-Dimensional Man*, London, 1964.

Mares, D. R., *Drug Wars and Coffeehouses: The Political Economy of the International Drug Trade*, Washington, 2005.

Marris, P. and Rein, M., *Dilemmas of Social Reform: Poverty and Community Action in the United States*, Harmondsworth, 1974.

Marsh, P., Rosser, E., and Harré, R., *The Rules of Disorder*, London, 1978.

MARSHALL, I., 'The Criminological Enterprise in Europe and America', *European Journal on Criminal Policy and Research*, 9 (2001).

MARSHALL, T., *Sociology at the Crossroads*, London, 1964.

MARTIN, S., *Breaking and Entering*, Berkeley, California. 1980.

MARTINS, H., 'Time and Theory in Sociology', in J. Rex, (ed.), *Approaches to Sociology*, London, 1974.

MARTINSON, R., 'What Works? Questions and Answers about Penal Reform', *Public Interest*, 35 (1974).

MARUNA, S., *Making Good: How Ex-Convicts Reform and Rebuild their Lives*, Washington DC, 2001.

MARUNA, S. and Immarigeon, R. (eds.), *After Crime and Punishment*, Cullompton, 2004.

MARX, G., 'The New Police Undercover Work', *Urban Life*, 8.4 (1980).

MARX, G., 'Notes on the Discovery, Collection, and Assessment of Hidden and Dirty Data', in J. Schneider and J. Kitsuse (eds.), *Studies in the Sociology of Social Problems*, Norwood, NJ, 1984.

MARX, G., *Under Cover: Police Surveillance in America*, Berkeley, California, 1988.

MATHIESEN, T., *The Politics of Abolition*, London, 1974.

MATTHEWS, R., *Policing Prostitution: A Multi-Agency Approach*, Enfield, Middlesex, 1986.

MATTHEWS, R. and Young, J. (eds.), *Confronting Crime*, London, 1986.

MATTHEWS, R. and Young, J., 'Replacing "Broken Windows": Crime, Incivilities and Urban Change', in R. Matthews and J. Young (eds.), *Issues in Realist Criminology*, London, 1992.

MATTHEWS, R. and Young, J., 'Reflections on Realism', in J. Young and R. Matthews (eds.), *Rethinking Criminology: The Realist Debate*, London, 1992.

MATRAVERS, A., *Justifying the Unjustifiable: Stories of Women Sex Offenders*, Ph.D. dissertation, University of Cambridge, 2000.

MATZA, D., 'Subterranean Traditions of Youth', *Annals of the American Academy of Political and Social Science*, 338 (1961).

MATZA, D., *Delinquency and Drift*, New York, 1964.

MATZA, D., *Becoming Deviant*, Englewood Cliffs, NJ, 1969.

MATZA, D. and Morgan, P., 'Controlling Drug Use: The Great Prohibition', in T. Blomberg and S. Cohen (eds.), *Punishment and Social Control: Essays in Honor of Sheldon L. Messinger*, New York, 1995.

MATZA, D. and Sykes, G., 'Delinquency and Subterranean Values', *American Sociological Review*, 26 (1961).

MAURER, D., *Whiz Mob: A Correlation of the Technical Argot of Pickpockets with their Behaviour Pattern*, New Haven, Conn. 1964.

MAUER, M., *The Changing Racial Dynamics of the War on Drugs*, Washington, 2009.

MAWBY, R., 'Kiosk Vandalism: A Sheffield Study', *British Journal of Criminology*, 17 (1977).

MAWBY, R., 'Crime and Law: Enforcement in Different Residential Areas of the City of Sheffield', Ph.D. thesis, University of Sheffield, 1979.

MAWBY, R. (ed.), *Policing the City*, Brookfield, Vermont, 1979.

MAXFIELD, M., *Fear of Crime in England and Wales*, London, 1984.

MAYHEW, H., *London Labour and the London Poor*, London, 1862.

MAYHEW, P., 'Displacement and Vehicle Theft: An Attempt to Reconcile Some Recent Contradictory Evidence', *Security Journal*, 2 (1991).

MAYHEW, P., *Residential Burglary: A Comparison of the United States, Canada and England and Wales*, Washington DC, n.d.

MAYHEW, P. and Maung, N., *Surveying Crime: Findings from the 1992 British Crime Survey*, Research Findings No. 2, London: Home Office Research and Statistics Dept., 1992.

MAYHEW, P. and Mirrlees-Black, C., *The 1992 British Crime Survey*, London, 1993.

MAYHEW, P., Clarke, R., and Elliott, D., 'Motorcycle Theft, Helmet Legislation and Displacement', *The Howard Journal*, 28 (1989).

MAYHEW, P. et al., *Crime as Opportunity*, Home Office Research Study No. 34, London, 1976.

MAYS, J., *Growing Up in the City*, Liverpool, 1954.

MAYS, J., *On the Threshold of Delinquency*, Liverpool, 1959.

MAYS, J., *Crime and the Social Structure*, London, 1964.

MEAD, G., 'The Psychology of Punitive Justice', *American Journal of Sociology*, 23 (1918).

MEAD, G., 'The Philosophy of John Dewey', *International Journal of Ethics*, 46:1 (1935).

MEAD, G., *Mind, Self and Society*, Chicago, 1934.

MEAD, G., *The Philosophy of the Act*, Chicago, 1938.

MEIER, R. and Miethe, T., 'Understanding Theories of Criminal Victimization', *Crime and Justice*, 17 (1993).

MELLY, G., *Revolt into Style*, London, 1972.

MELTZER, B. et al., *Symbolic Interactionism*, London, 1975.

MENDELSOHN, B., 'The Origin of the Doctrine of Victimology', *Excerpta Criminologica*, 3 (1963).

MERTON, R., *On the Shoulders of Giants*, Chicago, 1993.

MERTON, R., 'Social Structure and Anomie', *American Sociological Review*, 3 (1938). Revised and enlarged in successive editions of his *Social Theory and Social Structure*.

MERTON, R., *Social Theory and Social Structure*, New York, 1949 and 1957.

MERTON, R., 'The Emergence of a Sociological Concept', in F. Adler and W. Laufer (eds.), *The Legacy of Anomie Theory*, New Brunswick, 1995.

MERTON, R. and Nisbet, R. (eds.), *Contemporary Social Problems*, New York, 1961.

MESSNER, S. and Rosenfeld, R., *Crime and the American Dream*, Belmont, Cal., 1993, 3rd edn, 2001, 4th edn, 2007.

MESSNER, S. and Rosenfeld, R., 'Political Restraint of the Market and Levels of Criminal Homicide: A Cross-National Application of Institutional-Anomie Theory', *Social Forces*, 75:4 (1997).

MILLER, D., *George Herbert Mead*, Austin, Texas, 1973.

MILLER, E., *Street Woman*, Philadelphia, 1986.

MILLER, J., 'Systems of Control and the Serious Youth Offender', in Y. Bakal and H. Polsky (eds.), *Reforming Corrections for Juvenile Offenders*, Lexington, Mass., 1979.

MILLER, J., *Search and Destroy: African-American Males in the Criminal Justice System*, Cambridge, 1996.

MILLER, W., *Cops and Bobbies*, Chicago, 1973.

MILLER, W. B., 'Lower Class Culture as a Generating Milieu of Gang Delinquency', *Journal of Social Issues*, 14 (1958).

MILLER, W. B. et al., 'Aggression in a Boys' Street-Corner Group', *Psychiatry*, 24 (1961).

MILLS, C. Wright, 'Situated Actions and Vocabularies of Motive', *American Sociological Review*, 5:4 (1940).

MILLS, C. Wright, *The Power Élite*, New York, 1956.

MILLS, C. Wright, *The Sociological Imagination*, New York, 1959.

MILLS, C. Wright, *Sociology and Pragmatism*, New York, 1964.

MINKES, J. and Minkes, L. (eds.), *Corporate and White-Collar Crime*, Los Angeles, 2008.

MINISTRY of Justice, *Statistics on Women and the Criminal Justice System 2014*, London, 2014.

MIRRLEES-BLACK, C., *Domestic Violence: Findings from a New British Crime Survey Self-Completion Questionnaire*, London, 1999.

MIZRUCHI, F., *Success and Opportunity: A Study of Anomie*, New York, 1964.

MOBILIZATION for Youth, *A Proposal for the Prevention of Delinquency by the Expansion of Opportunities*, New York, 1960.

MOORE, J., *Going Down to the Barrio: Homeboys and Homegirls in Change*. Philadelphia, 1991.

MORGAN, J. and Zedner, L. *Child Victims: Crime, Impact, and Criminal Justice*, Oxford, 1992.

MORGAN, P., *Child Care: Sense and Fable*, London, 1975.

MORGAN, P., *Delinquent Fantasies*, London, 1978.

MORGAN, P. and Henderson, P., *Remand Decisions and Offending on Bail*, London, 1999.

MORRIS, A., *Women, Crime and Criminal Justice*, Oxford, 1987.

MORRIS, N. and Hawkins, G., *The Honest Politician's Guide to Crime Control*, Chicago, 1970.

MORRIS, P., *Prisoners and their Families*, London, 1965.

MORRIS, R., 'Female Delinquency and Relational Problems', *Social Forces*, 43 (1964).

MORRIS, R., 'Attitudes Towards Delinquency by Delinquents, Non-delinquents and Their Friends', *British Journal of Criminology*, 5 (1965).

MORRIS, T., *The Criminal Area*, London, 1957.

MORRIS, T. and Morris, P., *Pentonville*, London, 1963.

MORRISON, W., *Theoretical Criminology: From Modernity to Postmodernism*, London, 1995.

MORSE, M., *The Unattached*, Harmondsworth, 1965.

MORSON, G., *Narrative and Freedom: The Shadows of Time*, New Haven, 1994.

MOYNIHAN, D., *Maximum Feasible Misunderstanding*, New York, 1969.

MUIR, H., 'Voices of Victims of Crime—The Wounded Storytellers', in B. Giuliano, (ed.), *Survival and Beyond*, Curtin, ACT, 1998.

MUNCIE, J., *Youth and Crime: A Critical Introduction*, London, 1999.

MURDOCK, G. and McCron, R., 'Youth and Class: The Career of a Confusion', in G. Mungham and G. Pearson (eds.), *Working Class Youth Cultures*, London, 1976.

MURRAY, C., *Losing Ground: American Social Policy, 1950–80*, New York, 1984.

MURRAY, C., *The Emerging British Underclass*, London, 1990.

MURRAY, C., *Underclass: The Crisis Deepens*, London, 1994.

MURRAY, C., *Does Prison Work?*, London, 1997.

NADEL, J., *Sara Thornton: The Story of a Woman who Killed*, London, 1993.

NAGEL, I., 'Sex Differences in the Processing of Criminal Defendants', in D. Weisberg (ed.), *Women and the Law*, New York, 1980.

NATIONAL Association for the Care and Resettlement of Offenders (NACRO), *Crime and Social Policy*, London, 1995.

NATIONAL Research Council, *Understanding and Preventing Violence*, Washington, 1993.

NELKEN, D. (ed.), *The Futures of Criminology*, London, 1994.

NELKEN, D., 'Comparing Criminal Justice', in M. Maguire, R. Morgan and R. Reiner (eds.), *The Oxford Handbook of Criminology*, 3rd edn, Oxford, 2002.

NELLIS, M., review of R. Reiner and M. Cross (eds.), *Beyond Law and Order*, *Howard Journal*, 31 (1992).

NETTLER, G., 'Antisocial Sentiment and Criminality', *American Sociological Review*, 24 (1959).

NETTLER, G., *Explaining Crime*, New York, 1978.

NEUWIRTH, R., *Stealth of Nations: the Global Rise of the Informal Economy*, New York, 2012.

NEWBURN, T., 'The Long-Term Impact of Criminal Victimization', *Home Office Research and Statistics Department Research Bulletin*, London, 1993.

NEWBURN, T. and Stanko, E., (eds.), *Just Boys Doing Business?: Men, Masculinities and Crime*, London, 1994.

NEWBURN, T. and Hayman, S., *Policing, Surveillance and Social Control*, Cullompton, Devon, 2002.

NEWBURN, T. and Rock, P., 'Urban Homelessness, Crime and Victimisation in England', *International Review of Victimology*, 13:2 (2006).

NEWMAN, G. R. and Clarke, R., *Policing Terrorism: an Executive Guide*, Washington, 2014.

NEWMAN, K., *No Shame in my Game: The Working Poor in the Inner City*, New York, 1999.

NEWMAN, K., *Rampage: The Social Roots of School Shootings*, New York, 2004.

NEWMAN, K., *Chutes and Ladders: Navigating the Low-Wage Labor Market*, Cambridge, Mass., 2006.

NEWMAN, O., *Defensible Space: People and Design in the Violent City*, London, 1972.

NEWMAN, O., *Community of Interest*, Garden City, 1981.

NEWSON, J. and Newson, E., *Seven Years Old in the Home Environment*, London, 1976.

NEW York City Youth Board, *Reaching the Fighting Gang*, New York, 1960.

NORRIS, C. and Armstrong, G., *The Maximum Surveillance Society: The Rise of CCTV*, Oxford, 1999.

NORRIS, C. and McCahill, M., 'CCTV: Beyond Penal Modernism?', *British Journal of Criminology*, 46:1 (2006).

NOURSE, T, *Campania Foelix*, London, 1700.

NYE, F. and Short, J., 'Scaling Delinquent Behavior', *American Sociological Review*, 22 (1957).

O'BRIEN, M., 'What is *Cultural* About Cultural Criminology?', *British Journal of Criminology*, 45 (2005).

OFSHE, R. and Watters, E., *Making Monsters: False Memories, Psychotherapy, and Sexual Hysteria*, New York, 1994.

O'MALLEY, P., 'War and Suicide', *British Journal of Criminology*, 15 (1975).

O'MALLEY, P., 'Risk, Power and Crime Prevention', *Economy and Society*, 21 (1992).

O'MALLEY, P., *Crime and Risk*, London, 2010.

O'MALLEY, P., 'Aspects of the Social Construction of Crime Victims in Australia', *Victims and Offenders*, 1:3 (2006).

O'MALLEY, P., 'The Sociology of Compliance-Based Regulation: An Intellectual History', in A. Brannigan and G. Pavlich (eds.), *Adventures in the Sociology of Law: Essays in Honour of W.G. Carson*, Abingdon, 2007.

O'MALLEY, P., 'Victims' Rights', in I. Vanfraechem, A. Pemberton, and F. Ndahinda (eds.), *Justice for Victims: Perspectives on Rights, Transition and Reconciliation*, Abingdon, 2014.

ORMEROD, P., *The Death of Economics*, London, 1994.

OST, S., *Child Pornography and Sexual Grooming: Legal and Societal Responses*, Cambridge, 2009.

PACKARD, V., *The Hidden Persuaders*, London, 1957.

PACKER, H., *The Limits of the Criminal Sanction*, Stanford, 1968.

PAHL, R., *Whose City?* London, 1970.

PAHL, R., '"Collective Consumption" and the State in Capitalist and State Socialist Societies', in R. Scase, (ed.), *Industrial Society: Class, Cleavage and Control*, London, 1977.

PAHL, R., 'Stratification: The Relation Between States and Urban and Regional Development', *International Journal of Urban and Regional Research*, 1:1 (1977).

PAILTHORPE, G., *Studies in the* Psychology *of Delinquency*, London (HMSO), 1932.

PAINTER, K., *Crime Prevention and Public Lighting with Special Focus on Women and Elderly People*, Enfield, Middlesex, 1989.

PAINTER, K., *Lighting and Crime Prevention for Public Safety*, Enfield, Middlesex, 1989.

PALEY, D. M., *Drug War Capitalism*, Oakland, California, 2014.

PALMER, J., 'Thrillers: The Deviant Behind the Consensus', in I. Taylor and L. Taylor (eds.), *Politics and Deviance*, Harmondsworth, 1973.

PARENTI, C., *Tropic of Chaos: Climate Change and the New Geography of Violence*, New York, 2011.

PARK, R., 'The City: Suggestions for the Investigation of Human Behavior in the City Environment', *American Journal of Sociology*, 20 (1915). Reprinted in R. Park and E. Burgess (eds.), *The City*, Chicago, 1925.

PARK, R., *The Crowd and the Public*, Chicago, 1921.

PARK, R., *The Immigrant Press and its Control*, New York, 1922.

PARK, R., 'Community Organization and Juvenile Delinquency', in R. Park and E. Burgess (eds.), *The City*, Chicago, 1925.

PARK, R., 'The City as a Social Laboratory', in T. Smith and L. White (eds.), *Chicago: An Experiment in Social Science Research*, Chicago, 1929.

PARK, R., Burgess, E. and McKenzie, R. (eds.), *The City*, Chicago, 1925 (reprinted 1968).

PARKER, H., *The View From the Boys*, Newton Abbot, 1974.

PARKER, H., Bakx, K., and Newcombe, R., *Living with Heroin*, Milton Keynes, 1988.

PARKER, T. and Allerton, R., *The Courage of His Convictions*, London, 1964.

PARKIN, F., *Marxism and Class Theory: A Bourgeois Critique*, London, 1979.

PARSONS, T., *The Social System*, New York, 1951.

PATRICK, J., *A Glasgow Gang Observed*, London, 1973.

PAVLICH, G., 'Critical Genres and Radical Criminology in Britain', *The British Journal of Criminology*, 41 (2001).

PAXTON, P., 'Is Social Capital Declining in the United States? A Multiple Indicator Assessment', *American Journal of Sociology*, 105 (1999).

PEARCE, F., *Crimes of the Powerful: Marxism, Crime and Deviance*, London, 1976.

PEARSON, G., *The Deviant Imagination*, London, 1975.

PEARSON, G., '"Paki-Bashing" in a North East Lancashire Cotton Town: A Case Study and its History', in G. Mungham and G. Pearson (eds.), *Working Class Youth Culture*, London, 1976.

PEARSON, G., *Hooligan: A History of Respectable Fears*, London, 1983.

PEARSON, G., *The New Heroin Users*, Oxford, 1987.

PEASE, K. and Farrell, G. *Once Bitten, Twice Shy: Repeat Victimisation and its Implications for Crime Prevention*, Home Office Crime Prevention Unit 46, London, 1993.

PEASE, K., Forrester, D., and Chatterton, M., 'Lightning Strikes Twice for the Burglary Victim', *Police Review*, 1998.

PENDERGAST, M., *Victims of Memory: Sex Abuse Accusations and Shattered Lives*, Hinesburg, Vt., 1996.

PETERSILIA, J. et al., *Criminal Careers of Habitual Felons*, Washington, 1978.

PHILLIPSON, M., *Sociological Aspects of Crime and Delinquency*, London, 1971.

PHILLIPSON, M., 'Thinking Out of Deviance', unpublished paper, 1974.

PHILLIPSON, M. and Roche, M., 'Phenomenology, Sociology and the Study of Deviance', in P. Rock and M. McIntosh (eds.), *Deviance and Social Control*, London, 1974.

PIKE, L., *A History of Crime in England*, London, 1876.

PILIAVIN, I. and Briar, S., 'Police Encounters with Juveniles', *American Journal of Sociology*, 70 (1964).

PINKER, S., *The Better Angels of Our Nature*, New York, 2014.

PITTS, J., *Reluctant Gangsters: The Changing Face of Youth Crime*, Cullompton, 2008.

PITTS, J. and Hope, T., 'The Local Politics of Inclusion—The State and Community Safety', *Social Policy and Administration*, 31:5 (1997).

PIVEN, F. and Cloward, R., *Regulating the Poor*, New York, 1971.

PIZARRO, J., Zgoba, K., and Jennings, W., 'Assessing the Interaction between Offender and Victim Criminal Lifestyles and Homicide Type', *Journal of Criminal Justice*, 39:5 (2011).

PIZZEY, E., *Scream Quietly or the Neighbours Will Hear*, Harmondsworth, 1974.

PLATT, A., *The Child Savers: The Invention of Delinquency*, Chicago, 1969 and 1975.

PLATT, A., review of *The New Criminology*, *Sociological Quarterly*, 14 (1973).

PLATT, A., '"Street Crime": A View From the Left', *Crime and Social Justice*, 9 (1978).

PLAYER, E., 'Women and Crime in the City', in D. Downes, (ed.), *Crime and the City*, London, 1989.

PLUMMER, K., *Sexual Stigma: An Interactionist Account*, London, 1975.

PLUMMER, K., 'Misunderstanding Labelling Perspectives', in D. Downes and P. Rock (eds.), *Deviant Interpretations*, Oxford, 1979.

PLUMMER, K., *Documents of Life*, London, 1983.

PLUMMER, K., (ed.), *Modern Homosexualities: Fragments of Lesbian and Gay Experience*, London, 1992.

PLUMMER, K., *Telling Sexual Stories: Power, Change and Social Worlds*, London, 1994.

POLICE Review, 3 August 1963.

POLLAK, O., *The Criminality of Women*, New York, 1950.

POLK, K., *When Men Kill: Scenarios of Masculine Violence*, Cambridge, 1994.

POLSKY, N., *Hustlers, Beats and Others*, Chicago, 1967.

POPPER, K., *The Logic of Scientific Discovery*, London, 1959 (1934).

POPPER, K., *Conjectures and Refutations*, London, 1963.

PORTERFIELD, A., *Youth in Trouble*, Fort Worth, Texas, 1946.

PORTERFIELD, A. and Talbert, R., *Mid-Century Crime in Our Culture*, New York, 1954.

POULANTZAS, N., *Classes in Contemporary Capitalism*, London, 1975.

POWER, A., 'How to Rescue Council Housing', *New Society*, 4 June 1981.

POWER, A., *Estates on the Edge: The Social Consequences of Mass Housing in Northern Europe*, New York, 1997.

POWER, A. and Tunstall, R., *Dangerous Disorder: Riots and Violent Disturbances in Thirteen Areas of Britain, 1991–92*, York, 1997.

POYNER, B., *Design Against Crime*, London, 1983.

POYNER, B., Helson, P., and Webb, B., *Layout of Residential Areas and its Influence on Crime*, London, 1985.

PRATT, M., *Mugging as a Social Problem*, London, 1981.

PRESDEE, M., *Cultural Criminology and the Carnival of Crime*, London, 2000.

PRESIDENT'S Commission on Law Enforcement and Administration of Justice, *Crime and Its Impact: An Assessment*, Washington, DC, 1967.

PROBYN, W., *Angel Face*, London, 1977.

PROVINE, D., *Unequal under Law: Race in the War on Drugs*, Chicago, 2007.

PRYCE, K., *Endless Pressure: A Study of West Indian Life-Styles in Bristol*, Harmondsworth, 1979.

PUNCH, M., *Policing the Inner City*, London, 1979.

PUNCH, M., 'Officers and Men: Occupational Culture, Interrank Antagonism and the Investigation of Corruption', unpublished paper, 1980.

PUNCH, M., *Dirty Business: Exploring Corporate Misconduct*, London, 1996.

PUTNAM, R., 'Bowling Alone: America's Declining Social Capital', *Journal of Democracy*, 6:1 (1995).

PUTNAM, R., *Bowling Alone: The Collapse and Revival of American Community*, New York, 2000.

QUETELET, A., *Essai de Physique Sociale*, Brussels, 1869.

QUINNEY, R., 'Crime Control in Capitalist Society', in I. Taylor, P. Walton, and J. Young (eds.), *Critical Criminology*, London, 1975.

QUINNEY, R., *The Social Reality of Crime*, Boston, Mass., 1970.

RAFORD, N. and Trabulsi, A., *Warlords Inc*, Berkeley, 2015.

RAFTER, N., *The Criminal Brain: Understanding Biological Theories Of Crime*, New York, 2008.

RAFTER, N., (ed.), *The Origins of Criminology*, New York, 2009.

RAGIN, C. and Becker, H. (eds.), *What is a Case?: Exploring the Foundations of Social Inquiry*, Cambridge, 1992.

RAINS, P., *Becoming an Unwed Mother*, Chicago, 1971.

RAINWATER, L., *Behind Ghetto Walls*, Chicago, 1970.

RALPHS, R., Medina, J., and Aldridge, J., 'Who Needs Enemies with Friends Like These? The Importance of Place for Young People Living in Known Gang Areas', *Journal of Youth Studies* 12 (2009).

RAUSHENBUSH, W., *Robert Park: Biography of a Sociologist*, Durham, NC, 1979.

RAW, C., Hodgson, G., and Page, B., *Do You Sincerely Want to be Rich? Bernard Cornfield and IOS: An International Swindle*, London, 1971.

RAWLINSON, P., 'Russian Organised Crime: A Brief History', in P. Williams, (ed.), *Russian Organized Crime: The New Threat*, London, 1997.

RAWSTHORNE, T., 'The Objectives and Content of Policy-Oriented Research', *Home Office Research Unit Research Bulletin*, 6 (1978).

RECKLESS, W., 'The Distribution of Commercialized Vice in the City', in E. Burgess, (ed.), *The Urban Community*, Chicago, 1926.

RECKLESS, W., *Vice in Chicago*, Chicago, 1933.

RECKLESS, W., 'The Good Boy in a High Delinquency Area', *Journal of Criminal Law, Criminology and Police Science*, 48:1 (1957).

RECKLESS, W., *The Crime Problem*, New York, 1967.

RECKLESS, W., Dinitz, S., and Murray, E., 'Self-Concept as an Insulator against Delinquency', *American Sociological Review*, 21 (1956).

REIMAN, J., *The Rich Get Richer and the Poor Get Prison: Ideology, Class, and Criminal Justice*, New York, 2003.

REINER, R., *Law and Order: An Honest Citizen's Guide to Crime and Control*, Cambridge, 2007.

REINER, R., 'Citizenship, Crime, Criminalization: Marshalling a Social Democratic Perspective', *New Criminal Law Review*, 13 (2010).

REINER, R. and Cross, M. (eds.), *Beyond Law and Order: Criminal Justice Policy and Politics into the 1990s*, London, 1991.

REISS, A., *The Police and the Public*, New Haven, 1971.

REISS, A., 'The Social Integration of Queers and Peers', *Social Problems*, 9 (1961).

REISS, A., 'Inappropriate Theories and Inadequate Methods as Policy Plagues: Self-Reported Delinquency and the Law', in N. Demerath et al., *Social Policy and Sociology*, New York, 1975.

REISS, A., 'Foreword: Towards a Revitalization of Theory and Research on Victimization by Crime', *Journal of Criminal Law and Criminology*, 72:2 (1981).

REISS, A. and Rhodes, A., 'The Distribution of Juvenile Delinquency in the Social Class Structure', *American Sociological Review*, 26 (1961).

REISS, A. and Tonry, M. (eds.), *Communities and Crime*, Chicago, 1986.

RENZETTI, C. M., *Feminist Criminology*, London, 2013.

REUTER, P., *Disorganized Crime*, Cambridge, Mass. 1983.

REVIEW Symposium, *British Journal of Criminology*, 24 (1984).

REX, J., *Key Problems of Sociological Theory*, London, 1961.

REX, J., *Discovering Sociology*, London, 1973.

REX, J. and Moore, R., *Race, Community and Conflict*, London, 1967.

REYNOLDS, F., *The Problem Housing Estate*, Hants, 1986.

RHODES, L, *Total Confinement: Madness and Reason in the Maximum Security Prison*, California, 2004.

RIESMAN, D., *The Lonely Crowd*, Yale, 1950.

RILEY, D. and Shaw, M., *Parental Supervision and Juvenile Delinquency*, London, 1985.

ROBERTSON, R. and Taylor, L., *Deviance, Crime and Socio-Legal Control*, Oxford, 1973.

ROBINS, D., *We Hate Humans*, London, 1984.

ROBINS, D., *Tarnished Vision*, Oxford, 1992.

ROCK, P., *Making People Pay*, London, 1973.

ROCK, P., 'Review of Smart, C., *Women, Crime and Criminology*', *British Journal of Criminology*, 17 (1977).

ROCK, P., (ed.), *Drugs and Politics*, New Brunswick, NJ, 1977.

ROCK, P., *The Making of Symbolic Interactionism*, London, 1979.

ROCK, P., 'Has Deviance a Future?', in H. Blalock, (ed.), *Sociological Theory and Research*, New York, 1981.

ROCK, P., *A View From the Shadows*, Oxford, 1986.

ROCK, P., *A History of British Criminology*, Oxford, 1988.

ROCK, P., *Helping Victims of Crime: The Home Office and the Rise of Victim Support in England and Wales*, Oxford, 1990.

ROCK, P., foreword to J. Lowman, and B. MacLean (eds.), *Realist Criminology: Crime Control and Policing in the 1990s*, Toronto, 1993.

ROCK, P., 'Rules, Boundaries and the Courts', *British Journal of Sociology*, 49 (1998).

ROCK, P., 'The Social Organization of British Criminology', in M. Maguire, et al. (eds.), *The Oxford Handbook of Criminology*, Oxford, 1994.

ROCK, P., *Reconstructing a Women's Prison*, Oxford, 1996.

ROCK, P., *After Homicide: Practical and Political Responses to Bereavement*, Oxford, 1998.

ROCK, P., 'Murderers, Victims and "Survivors": The Social Construction of Deviance', *British Journal of Criminology*, 38 (1998).

ROCK, P., 'Holloway' in N. Rafter, (ed.), *Encyclopedia of Women and Crime*, Phoenix, 2000.

ROCK, P., 'On Becoming a Victim', in C. Hoyle and R. Wilson (eds.), *New Visions of Crime Victims*, Oxford, 2002.

ROCK, P., *Constructing Victims' Rights: the Home Office, New Labour and Victims*, Oxford, 2004.

ROCK, P., 'Chronocentrism and British Criminology', *British Journal of Sociology*, 56 (2005).

ROCK, P., 'The Politics of Victimhood', *Safer Society*, 11 July 2006.

ROCK, P. and Cohen, S., 'The Teddy Boy', in V. Bogdanor and R. Skidelsky (eds.), *The Age of Affluence*, London, 1970.

ROCK, P. and McIntosh, M. (eds.), *Deviance and Social Control*, London, 1974.

ROEDER, O. et al., *What Caused the Crime Decline?*, New York, 2013.

RORTY, R., *Objectivity, Relativism and Truth*, Cambridge, 1991.

ROSE, A., (ed.), *Human Behavior and Social Processes*, New York, 1962.

ROSENHAN, D., 'On Being Sane in Insane Places', *Science*, 179 (1973).

ROSENHAN, K., 'Female Deviance and the Female Sex Role', *British Journal of Sociology*, 26 (1973).

ROSSNER, M., *Just Emotions: Rituals of Restorative Justice*, Oxford, 2013.

ROTH, J. and Eddy, E., *Rehabilitation for the Unwanted*, New York, 1967.

ROYAL Academy of Engineering, *Dilemmas of Privacy and Surveillance: Challenges of Technological Change*, London, 2007.

RUBINGTON, E. and Weinberg, M. (eds.), *Deviance: The Interactionist Perspective*, New York, 1968.

RUBINSTEIN, J., *City Police*, New York, 1973.

RUDÉ, G., *The Crowd in History*, New York, 1964.

RUNCIMAN, W., *Relative Deprivation and Social Justice*, London, 1966.

RUSCHE, G. and Kirchheimer, O., *Punishment and Social Structure*, New York, 1939.

RUSSELL, D. and Van de Ven, N. (eds.), *Crimes Against Women: Proceedings of the International Tribunal*, Millbrae, California, 1976.

RUTTER, M., *Maternal Deprivation Reassessed*, 2nd edn, Harmondsworth, 1981.

RUTTER, M. and Smith, D., *Psychosocial Disorders in Young People*, Chichester, 1995.

SACKS, H., 'Notes on Police Assessment of Moral Character', in D. Sudnow, (ed.), *Studies in Social Interaction*, New York, 1972.

SAGARIN, E., *Deviants and Deviance: An Introduction to the Study of Disvalued People*, New York, 1975.

SAINSBURY, P., 'The Epidemiology of Suicide', in A. Roy, (ed.), *Suicide*, Baltimore, Williams and Wilkins 1986.

SAINSBURY, P., *Suicide Trends in Europe: An International Epidemiological Study*, unpublished.

SAMPSON, A., *Lessons from a Victim Support Crime Prevention Project*, London, 1991.

SAMPSON, A. et al., 'Crime, Localities and the Multi-Agency Approach', *British Journal of Criminology*, 28 (1988).

SAMPSON, R., 'Race and Criminal Violence: A Demographically Disaggregated Analysis of Urban Homicide', *Crime and Delinquency*, 31 (1985).

SAMPSON, R., 'Effects of Inequality, Heterogeneity, and Urbanization on Intergroup Victimization', *Social Science Quarterly*, 67 (1986).

SAMPSON, R. and Laub, J., *Crime in the Making: Pathways and Turning Points Through Life*, Cambridge, Mass. 1993.

SAMPSON, R. and Raudenbush, S., 'Systematic Social Observation of Public Spaces: A New Look at Disorder in Urban Neighborhoods', *American Journal of Sociology*, 105 (1999).

SAMPSON, R. and Woolredge, J., 'Linking the Micro and Macro Levels of Lifestyle-Routine Activity and Opportunity Models of Predatory Victimization', *Journal of Quantitative Criminology*, 3 (1987).

SAMPSON, R., Morenoff, J., and Gannon-Rowley, T., 'Assessing "Neighborhood Effects": Social Processes and New Directions in Research', *Annual Review of Sociology*, 28 (2002).

SAMPSON, R., Raudenbush, S., and Earls, F., 'Neighborhoods and Violent Crime: A Multilevel Study of Collective Efficacy', *Science* 277 (1997).

SAMUEL, R., (ed.), *Ruskin College, History Workshop Pamphlets*, Oxford, 1970.

SASSEN, S., *Expulsions: Brutality and Complexity in the Global Economy*, New York, 2014.

SAVIANO, R., *Zero Zero Zero*, New York, 2015.

SCHAFER, S., *The Victim and his Criminal: A Study in Functional Responsibility*, New York, 1968.

SCHEFF, T., *Being Mentally Ill*, London, 1966.

SCHEFF, T., (ed.), *Mental Illness and Social Processes*, New York, 1967.

SCHEFF, T., 'Negotiating Reality: Notes on Power in the Assessment of Responsibility', *Social Problems*, 16:1 (1968).

SCHICHOR, D., 'Crime Patterns and Socio-economic Development: A Cross-National Analysis', *Criminal Justice Review*, 15 (1990).

SCHNEIDER, E., *Vampires, Dragons, and Egyptian Kings: Youth Gangs in Postwar New York*, Princeton, NJ, 1999.

SCHUR, E., *Narcotic Addiction in Britain and America*, London, 1963.

SCHUR, E., *Crimes without Victims: Deviant Behavior and Public Policy*, Englewood Cliffs, NJ, 1965.

SCHUR, E., *Radical Non-Intervention: Rethinking the Delinquency Problem*, Englewood Cliffs, NJ, 1973.

SCHUTZ, A., 'Common-Sense and Scientific Interpretation of Human Action', in *Collected Papers*, I, The Hague, 1964.

SCHUTZ, A., 'The Social World and the Theory of Social Action', in *Collected Papers*, II, The Hague, 1964.

SCHUTZ, A., *The Structures of the Life-World*, London, 1974.

SCHWENDINGER, H. and Schwendinger, J., 'Defenders of Order or Guardians of Human Rights', in I. Taylor et al. (eds.), *Critical Criminology*, London, 1975.

SCOTT, M. and Lyman, S., 'Accounts, Deviance and Social Order', in J. Douglas, (ed.), *Deviance and Respectability*, New York, 1970.

SCOTT, R., *The Making of Blind Men*, New York, 1969.

SCOTT, R., 'A Proposed Framework for Analyzing Deviance as a Property of Social Order', in R. Scott and J. Douglas (eds.), *Theoretical Perspectives on Deviance*, New York, 1972.

SCOTT, R., *Why Sociology Does Not Apply*, New York, 1979.

SCOTT, R. and Douglas, J. (eds.), *Theoretical Perspectives on Deviance*, New York, 1972.

SCOTTISH Office Central Research Unit, *The Effect of Closed Circuit Television on Recorded Crime Rates and Public Concern about Crime in Glasgow*, Edinburgh, 1999.

SCULL, A., 'Mad-Doctors and Magistrates', *Archives of European Sociology*, 15 (1976).

SCULL, A., *Decarceration: Community Treatment and the Deviant: A Radical View*, Englewood Cliffs, NJ, 1977.

SERGEANT, H., *Among the Hoods: Exposing the Truth about Britain's Gangs*, London, 2013

SELLIN, T., *Culture Conflict and Crime*, New York, 1938. Selected in M. Wolfgang et al. (eds.), *The Sociology of Crime and Delinquency*, New York, 1962.

SELLIN, T., 'The Basis of a Crime Index', *Journal of the American Institute of Criminal Law and Criminology*, 22 (1931).

SELLIN, T., 'The Significance of Records of Crime', in M. Wolfgang et al. (eds.), *The Sociology of Crime and Delinquency*, New York, 1962.

SEMPLE, J., *Bentham's Prison: A Study of the Panopticon Penitentiary*, Oxford, 1993.

SENNETT, R., *The Corrosion of Character: The Personal Consequences of Work in the New Capitalism*, New York, 1998.

SENNETT, R., *The Culture of the New Capitalism*, New Haven, 2006.

SERENY, G., *Albert Speer: His Battle with Truth*, Basingstoke, 1995.

SHAPLAND, J. and Vagg, J., *Policing by the Public*, Oxford, 1988.

SHAPLAND, J., Willmore, J., and Duff, P., *Victims in the Criminal Justice System*, Aldershot, 1985.

SHAPLAND, J, Atkinson, A., Atkinson, H., Dignan, J., Edwards, L., Hibbert, J., Howes, M., Johnstone, J., Robinson, G., and Sorsby, A., *Does Restorative Justice Affect Reconviction?: The Fourth Report From the Evaluation of Three Schemes*, London, 2008.

SHAPLAND, J. and Sloan, J., 'Twenty Volumes of Victimology: The Special Issue', *International Review of Victimology*, 20:1 (2014).

SHARROCK, W., 'Ethnomethodology and British Sociology: Some Problems of Incorporation', unpublished paper, delivered to the British Sociological Association Conference, Lancaster University, 1980.

SHAW, C., *The Jack-Roller*, Chicago, 1930.

SHAW, C., *The Natural History of a Delinquent Career*, Chicago, 1931.

SHAW, C., 'Male Juvenile Delinquency and Group Behavior', in J. Short, (ed.), *The Social Fabric of the Metropolis*, Chicago, 1971.

SHAW, C. and McKay, H., *Juvenile Delinquency and Urban Areas: A Study of Rates of Delinquents in Relation to Differential Characteristics of Local Communities in American Cities*, Chicago, 1942.

SHEARING, C. and Stenning, P., 'From the Panopticon to Disney World', in A. Doob and E. Greenspan (eds.), *Perspectives in Criminal Law*, Aurora, Ontario, 1985.

SHELLEY, L., *Crime and Modernization*, Carbondale, Ill., 1981.

SHELLEY, L. I., *Dirty Entanglements: Corruption, Crime, And Terrorism*, Cambridge, 2014.

SHERMAN, L. and Berk, R., *The Minneapolis Domestic Violence Experiment*, Washington, 1984.

SHERMAN, L. and Berk, R., 'Hot Spots of Predatory Crime: Routine Activities and the Criminology of Place', *Criminology*, 27:1 (1989).

SHERMAN, L. and Weisburd, D., 'General Deterrent Effects of Police Patrol in Crime 'Hot Spots': A Randomized, Controlled Trial', *Justice Quarterly*, 12:4 (1995).

SHERMAN, L. and Strang, H., *Restorative Justice: The Evidence*, London, 2007.

SHERMAN, L., Gartin, P., and Buerger, M., 'Hot Spots of Predatory Crime: Routine Activities and the Criminology of Place', *Criminology*, 27 (1989).

SHIBUTANI, T., *The Derelicts of Company K*, Berkeley, California, 1978.

SHILS, E., *The Present State of American Sociology*, Glencoe, Ill., 1948.

SHILS, E., 'Tradition, Ecology and Institution in the History of Sociology', *Daedalus*, 9 (1970).

SHINER, M., *Drug Use and Social Change*, Basingstoke, 2009.

SHOHAM, S., *The Mark of Cain*, Jerusalem, 1970.

SHORT, E. and Ditton, J., 'Seen and Now Heard: Talking to the Targets of Open Street CCTV', *British Journal of Criminology*, 38 (1998).

SHORT, J., (ed.), *The Social Fabric of the Metropolis: Contributions of the Chicago School of Urban Sociology*, Chicago, 1971.

SHORT, J., 'The Natural History of an Applied Theory: Differential Opportunity and Mobilization for Youth', in N. Demerath et al. (eds.), *Social Policy and Sociology*, New York, 1975.

SHORT, J. and Strodtbeck, F., *Group Process and Gang Delinquency*, Chicago, 1967.

SHOVER, N., *Aging Criminals*, California, 1985.

SILVERSTONE, D., *Night Clubbing: Drugs, Clubs and Regulation*, Abingdon, forthcoming.

SILVESTRI, M. and Crowther-Dowey, C., *Gender and Crime*, London, 2008.

SIMMEL, G., *Conflict and the Web of Group Affiliations*, New York, 1955.

SIM, J., *Punishment and Prisons: Power and the Carceral State*, London, 2009.

SIMON, D. and Burns, E., *The Corner: A Year in the Life of an Inner-City Neighborhood*, New York, 1997 (1st UK edn, Edinburgh, 2009).

SIMON, J., 'The Emergence of a Risk Society: Insurance, Law, and the State', *Socialist Review* 95 (1987).

SIMON, J., 'The Ideological Effects of Actuarial Practices', *Law and Society Review*, 22 (1988).

SIMON, J., 'Governing through Crime', in L. M. Friedman and G. Fisher (eds.), *The Crime Conundrum: Essays in Criminal Justice*, Boulder, Co., 1997.

SIMON, J., *Governing Through Crime: How the War on Crime Transformed American Democracy and Created a Culture of Fear*, Oxford, 2007.

SIMON, R., *Women and Crime*, Lexington, 1975.

SIMPKIN, M., *Trapped Within Welfare: Surviving Social Work*, London, 1979.

SKLAIR, L., 'The Fate of the "Functional Requisites" in Parsonian Sociology', *British Journal of Sociology*, 21 (1970).

SKOGAN, W., *Disorder and Decline: Crime and the Spiral of Decay in American Neighborhoods*, New York, 1990.

SKOLNICK, J., *Justice without Trial*, New York, 1966.

SMALL, A., 'Fifty Years of Sociology in the United States', *American Journal of Sociology*, 21 (1916).

SMART, C., *Women, Crime and Criminology*, London, 1977.

SMART, C., *Feminism and the Power of Law*, London, 1989.

SMART, C., 'Feminist Approaches to Criminology, or Postmodern Woman Meets Atavistic Man', in L. Gelsthorpe and A. Morris (eds.), *Feminist Perspectives in Criminology*, London, 1990.

SMIGEL, E. and Ross, H., *Crimes Against Bureaucracy*, New York, 1970.

SMITH, D., 'Youth Crime and Conduct Disorders', in M. Rutter and D. Smith, *Psychosocial Disorders in Young People: Time Trends and their Causes*, Chichester, 1995.

SMITH, D., 'Less Crime Without More Punishment', *Edinburgh Law Review*, 3 (1999).

SMITH, D., 'Changing Situations and Changing People', in A. von Hirsch, D. Garland, and A. Wakefield (eds.), *Ethical and Social Perspectives on Situational Crime Prevention*, Oxford, 2000.

SMITH, D. and Gray, J., *Police and People in London*, London, 1983.

SMITH, M. J. and Cornish, D. B. (eds.), *Theory for Practice in Situational Crime Prevention*, Monsey, NY, 2003.

SMITH, P. K. and Steffgen, G., 'Cyberbullying through the New Media', *Social Work with Groups*, 37 (2014).

SMITH, S., *Crime, Space and Society*, London, 1987.

SMITH, S. and Razzell, P., *The Pools Winners*, London, 1975.

SNODGRASS, J., 'Clifford R. Shaw and Henry D. McKay: Chicago Criminologists', *British Journal of Criminology*, 16:1 (1976).

SOLOMON, P., *Soviet Criminologists and Criminal Policy*, London, 1978.

SOOTHILL, K. and Walby, S., *Sex Crime in the News*, London, 1991.

SOOTHILL, K. and Peelo, M., 'Constructing British Criminology', *Howard Journal*, 46:5 (2007).

SOUTH, N., 'Drugs, Alcohol and Crime', in M. Maguire, R. Morgan, and R. Reiner (eds.), *The Oxford Handbook of Criminology*, Oxford, 2002.

SPARKS, R. et al., *Surveying Victims*, Chichester, 1977.

SPERGEL, I., *Racketville, Slumtown, Haulburg*, Chicago, 1964.

SPIEGEL, J., 'Problems of Access to Target Populations', in R. Conant and M. Levin (eds.), *Problems in Research on Community Violence*, New York, 1969.

SPIERENBURG, P., *The Spectacle of Suffering: Executions and the Evolution of Repression*, Cambridge, 1984.

SPIERENBURG, P., *A History of Murder: Personal Violence in Europe from the Middle Ages to the Present*, Cambridge, 2008.

SROLE, L., 'Social Integration and Certain Corollaries: An Exploratory Study', *American Sociological Review* 21 (1956).

STANDER, J. et al., 'Markov Chain Analysis and Specialization in Criminal Careers', *British Journal of Criminology*, 29 (1989).

STANKO, E., *Everyday Violence: How Women and Men Experience Sexual and Physical Danger*, London, 1990.

STANKO, E., 'Typical Violence, Normal Precaution: Men, Women, and Interpersonal Violence in England, Wales, Scotland and the USA', in J. Hanmer and M. Maynard (eds.), *Women, Violence and Social Control*, London, 1987.

STARK, E., *Coercive Control: The Entrapment of Women in Personal Life*, Oxford, 2009.

STRANG, H., *Repair or Revenge: Victims and Restorative Justice*, Oxford, 2002.

STEINER, G., *Language and Silence: Essays and Notes 1958–1966*, London, 1967.

STENSON, K. and Brearley, N., 'Left Realism in Criminology and the Return to Consensus Theory', in R. Reiner and M. Cross, *Beyond Law and Order: Criminal Justice Policy and Politics into the 1990s*, London, 1991.

STEPHENS, J., *Loners, Losers and Lovers*, Seattle, 1976.

STEVENS, A., *Offender Rehabilitation and Therapeutic Communities*, London, 2014.

STINCHCOMBE, A., 'Institutions of Privacy in the Determination of Police Administrative Practice', *American Journal of Sociology*, 69 (1963).

STINCHCOMBE, A., *Rebellion in a High School*, Chicago, 1964.

STINCHCOMBE, A., *Constructing Social Theories*, New York, 1968.

STONE, L., *The Family, Sex and Marriage in England, 1500–1800*, Harmondsworth, 1979.

STRANG, H., *Repair or Revenge: Victims and Restorative Justice*, Oxford, 2002.

STRAUSS, A., *Mirrors and Masks: The Search for Identity*, Glencoe, Illinois, 1959.

SUDNOW, D., 'Normal Crimes: Sociological Features of the Penal Code', *Social Problems*, 12 (1965).

SULLIVAN, M., '*Getting Paid*': Youth Crime and Work in the Inner City, Ithaca, NY, 1989.

SUMNER, C., *Reading Ideologies: An Investigation into the Marxist Theory of Ideology and Law*, London, 1979.

SUMNER, C., 'Marxism and Deviancy Theory', in P. Wiles, (ed.), *The Sociology of Crime and Delinquency in Britain*, ii. *The New Criminologies*, London, 1976.

SUMNER, C., 'Race, Crime and Hegemony: A Review Essay', *Contemporary Crises*, 5 (1981).

SUMNER, C. (ed.), *Crime, Justice and Underdevelopment*, London, 1982.

SUMNER, C., *Censure, Politics and Criminal Justice*, Buckingham, 1990.

SUMNER, C., *The Sociology of Deviance: An Obituary*, Buckingham, 1994.

SUMNER, C., (ed.), *The Blackwell Companion to Criminology*, Oxford, 2004.

SUMNER, M., *Prostitution and Images of Women*, unpublished MSc. (economics), University of Wales, 1980.

SUNDHOLM, C., 'The Pornographic Arcade', *Urban Life and Culture*, 2:1 (1974).

SUTHERLAND, E., *Principles of Criminology*, Chicago, 1924. Extensively revised as Sutherland, E. and Cressey, D., *Criminology*, New York, 1979.

SUTHERLAND, E., *White Collar Crime*, New York, 1949.

SUTHERLAND, E., *The Professional Thief*, Chicago, 1956.

SUTHERLAND, E. and Cressey, D., *Principles of Criminology*, 5th edn, Chicago and New York, 1955.

SUTTLES, G., *The Social Order of the Slum*, Chicago, 1968.

SUTTLES, G., *The Social Construction of Communities*, Chicago, 1972.

SUTTON, M., 'Supply by Theft: Does the Market for Second-Hand Goods Play a Role in Keeping Crime Figures High?', *British Journal of Criminology*, 35:3 (Summer 1995).

SYKES, G., *The Society of Captives*, Princeton, 1958.

SYKES, G. and Matza, D., 'Techniques of Neutralization', *American Sociological Review*, 22 (1957).

SZASZ, T., *The Manufacture of Madness*, New York, 1970.

TANNENBAUM, F., *Crime and the Community*, New York, 1938.

TANNER, D., *The Lesbian Couple*, Lexington, Mass., 1978.

TAYLOR, A., *Women Drug Users*, Oxford, 1993.

TAYLOR, H., 'Forging the Job: A Crisis of "Modernization" or Redundancy for the Police in England and Wales, 1900–39', *British Journal of Criminology*, 39 (1999).

TAYLOR, I., 'Client Refusal', *Case Conference*, 7 (1972).

TAYLOR, I., 'Left Realist Criminology and the Free Market Experiment in Britain', in J. Young and R. Matthews (eds.), *Rethinking Criminology: The Realist Debate*, London, 1992.

TAYLOR, I., *Crime in Context: A Critical Criminology of Market Societies*, Cambridge, 1999.

TAYLOR, I. and Taylor, L. (eds.), *Politics and Deviance*, Harmondsworth, 1973.

TAYLOR, I., Walton, P., and Young, J., *The New Criminology: For a Social Theory of Deviance*, London, 1973.

TAYLOR, I. et al. (eds.), *Critical Criminology*, London, 1975.

TAYLOR, L., *Deviance and Society*, London, 1971.

TAYLOR, L., 'The Significance and Interpretation of Replies to Motivational Questions', *Sociology*, 6:1 (1972).

TEH, Y., *The Mak Nyahs: Female Transsexuals*, Singapore, 2002.

TEILMANN, K. and Klein, M., 'Juvenile Justice Legislation: A Framework for Evaluation', in D. Shichor and D. Kelly (eds.), *Critical Issues in Juvenile Delinquency*, Lexington, Mass., 1980.

TEMKIN, J., *Rape and the Criminal Justice System*, Aldershot, 1995.

TIERNEY, J. and O'Neill, M., *Criminology: Theory and Context*, London, 2009.

TSELONI, A. and Pease, K., 'Repeat Personal Victimization', *British Journal of Criminology*, 43 (2003).

TSELONI, A. and Pease, K., 'Area and Individual Differences in Personal Crime Victimization Incidence', *International Review of Victimology*, 20:1 (2014).

TETT, G., *Fool's Gold: How Unrestrained Greed Corrupted a Dream, Shattered Global Markets and Unleashed a Catastrophe*, London, 2009.

THOMAS, K., *Man and the Natural World: Changing Attitudes in England 1500–1800*, Harmondsworth, 1984.

THOMAS, W. I., *The Unadjusted Girl*, Boston, 1923.

THOMAS, W. I. and Znaniecki, F., *The Polish Peasant in Europe and America*, New York, 1927.

THOMPSON, E., 'The Moral Economy of the English Crowd in the Eighteenth Century', *Past and Present*, 50 (1971).

THOMPSON, E., *Whigs and Hunters: The Origin of the Black Act*, London, 1975.

THOMPSON, H., *Hell's Angels*, New York, 1966.

THRASHER, F., *The Gang: A Study of 1,313 Gangs in Chicago*, Chicago, 1927.

TIERNEY, J., *Criminology: Theory and Context*, 1st edn, Hemel Hempstead, 1996; 2nd edn, Harlow, 2006.

TILLEY, N., *Understanding Car Parks, Crime and CCTV: Evaluation Lessons from Safer Cities*, London, 1993.

TIRADO, L., *Hand to Mouth: Living in Bootstrap America*, New York, 2014.

TITMUSS, R., *Commitment to Welfare*, London, 1968.

TOBY, J., 'Social Disorganization and Stake in Conformity: Complementary Factors in the Predatory Behaviour of Hoodlums', *Journal of Criminal Law, Criminology and Police Science*, 48 (1957).

TOBY, J., 'An Evaluation of Early Identification and Intensive Treatment Programs for Pre-Delinquents', *Social Problems*, 13 (1965).

TOMBS, S. and Whyte, D. (eds.), *Unmasking the Crimes of the Powerful*, New York, 2003.

TONRY, M., *Malign Neglect: Race, Crime and Punishment in America*, New York, 1995.

TOWNSEND, P., *The Last Refuge*, London, 1963.

TOWNSEND, P., 'Area Deprivation Policies', *New Statesman*, 6 August 1976.

TOYNBEE, P., *Hard Work: Life in Low-Pay Britain*, London, 2003.

TRASLER, G., *The Explanation of Criminality*, London, 1962.

TRASLER, G., 'Situational Crime Control and Rational Choice: A Critique', in K. Heal and G. Laycock (eds.) *Situational Crime Prevention*, London: HMSO, 1986.

TRAVER, H., 'Crime Trends', in H. Traver and J. Vagg (eds.), *Crime and Justice in Hong Kong*, Hong Kong, 1991.

TUCHMAN, B., *A Distant Mirror: The Calamitous Fourteenth Century*, London, 1979.

TUNSTALL, J., *Media Sociology*, London, 1970.

TURK, A., *Criminality and the Legal Order*, Chicago, 1969.

TURNBULL, C., *The Mountain People*, London, 1973.

TURNER, R., 'Role-Taking: Process versus Conformity', in A. Rose, (ed.), *Human Behavior and Social Processes*, New York, 1962.

TYLER, G., 'The Great Electrical Conspiracy', in M. Wolfgang et al. (eds.), *The Sociology of Crime and Delinquency*, New York, 1962.

UGGEN, C. and Manza, J., 'Democratic Contraction? The Political Consequences of Felon Disenfranchisement in the United States', *American Sociological Review* 68 (2003).

UGGEN, C. and Inderbitzin, M., 'Public Criminologies', *Criminology & Public Policy*, 9 (2010).

VALENTINE, C., *Culture and Poverty*, Chicago, 1968.

VALVERDE, M., 'Feminist Perspectives on Criminology', in J. Gladstone, R. Ericson, and C. Shearing (eds.), *Criminology: A Reader's Guide*, Toronto, 1991.

VAN Buitenen, P., *Blowing the Whistle: One Man's Fight Against Fraud in the European Commission*, London, 2000.

VAN Creveld, M., *The Transformation of War*, New York, 1991.

VAN Kesteren, J., van Dijk, J., and Mayhew, P., 'The International Crime Victims Surveys: a Retrospective', *International Review of Victimology*, 20:1, 5 (2014).

VAN Kesteren, J., van Dijk, J., and Mayhew, P., 'Researching Victims', in R. King and E. Wincup (eds.) *Doing Research on Crime and Justice*, Oxford, 2000.

VAN Swaaningen, R., *Critical Criminology: Visions from Europe*, London, 1997.

VAN Wormer, K. and Bartollas, C., *Women and the Criminal Justice System*, 4th edn, New York, 2014.

VENKATESH, S., *Gang Leader for a Day*, New York, 2009.

VON Hentig, H., 'Remarks on the Interaction of Perpetrator and Victim', *Journal of Criminal Law and Criminology*, 31 (1940).

VON Hirsch, A., (ed.), *Doing Justice*, New York, 1976.

WACQUANT, L., 'Deadly Symbiosis: When Ghetto and Prison Meet and Mesh', in D. Garland (ed.), *Mass Imprisonment: Social Causes and Consequences*, London, 2001.

WACQUANT, L., 'Scrutinizing the Street: Poverty, Morality, and the Pitfalls of

Urban Ethnography', *American Journal of Sociology*, 107:6 (2002).

WADDINGTON, P., *Calling the Police: The Interpretation of, and Response to, Calls for Assistance from the Public*, Aldershot, 1993.

WADDINGTON, P., 'Mugging as a Moral Panic', *British Journal of Sociology*, 37 (1986).

WADSWORTH, M., *Roots of Delinquency: Infancy, Adolescence and Crime*, London, 1979.

WALKER, N., *Behaviour and Misbehaviour: Explanations and Non-explanations*, Oxford, 1977.

WALKLATE, S., 'Researching Victims', in R. King and E. Wincup (eds.), *Doing Research on Crime and Justice*, Oxford, 2007.

WALKLATE, S. and Evans, K., *Zero Tolerance or Community Tolerance*, Aldershot, 1999.

WALLERSTEIN, J. and Wyle, C., 'Our Law-Abiding Law-Breakers', *Federal Probation*, 25 (1947).

WALSH, D., *Break-Ins*, London, 1980.

WALSH, D., *Heavy Business*, London, 1985.

WARD, D. and Kassebaum, G., *Women's Prison*, London, 1966.

WASSERMAN, M., 'Rape: Breaking the Silence', *The Progressive*, November 1973.

WEINSTEIN, H., 'Victims, Transitional Justice and Social Reconstruction: Who is Setting the Agenda?', in I. Vanfraechem, A. Pemberton, and F. Ndahinda (eds.), *Justice for Victims: Perspectives on Rights, Transition and Reconciliation*, Abingdon, 2014.

WEIS, J., 'Dialogue with Matza', *Issues in Criminology*, 6:1 (1971).

WEIS, K. and Borges, S., 'Victimology and Rape: The Case of the Legitimate Victim', *Issues in Criminology*, 8:2 (1973)

WELLS, J., 'Crime and Unemployment', in K. Coates, (ed.), *The Right to Work*, Nottingham, 1995.

WELSH, B. C. and Farrington, D. P., *Making Public Places Safer: Surveillance and Crime Prevention*, Oxford, 2009

WELSH, S., 'The Manufacture of Excitement in Police-Juvenile Encounters', *British Journal of Criminology*, 21 (1981).

WENDER, J., *Policing and the Poetics of Everyday Life*, Champagne Urbana, 2009.

WERTHMAN, C. and Piliavin, I., 'Gang Members and the Police', in D. Bordau, (ed.), *The Police: Six Sociological Essays*, New York, 1967.

WERTHAM, F., *The Show of Violence*, New York, 1949.

WEST, D., *Present Conduct and Future Delinquency*, London, 1969.

WEST, D., *Delinquency: Its Roots, Careers and Prospects*, London, 1982.

WEST, D. and Farrington, D., *Who Becomes Delinquent?*, London, 1973.

WEST, D. and Farrington, D., *The Delinquent Way of Life*, London, 1977.

WESTERGAARD, J., 'The Withering Away of Class: A Contemporary Myth', in P. Anderson and R. Blackburn (eds.), *Towards Socialism*, London, 1965.

WESTERN, B., *Punishment and Inequality in America*, New York, 2006.

WESTERN, B. and Beckett, K., 'How Unregulated is the U. S. Labor Market? The Penal System as a Labor Market Institution', *American Journal of Sociology*, 104 (1999).

WESTERVELT, S., *Shifting the Blame: How Victimization Became a Criminal Defense*, New Brunswick, 1998.

WESTLEY, W., 'Violence and the Police', *American Journal of Sociology*, 59 (1953).

WESTMARLAND, L., *Researching Crime and Justice*, London, 2011.

WHYTE, W. F., *Street Corner Society*, Chicago, 1965.

WHYTE, W. H., Jr., *The Organization Man*, New York, 1956.

WIKSTRÖM, P-O., 'The Social Ecology of Crime: The Role of the Environment in Crime Causation', in H. Schneider, (ed.), *Internationales Handbuch der Kriminologie*, Berlin, 2007.

WILKINS, L., *Social Deviance*, London, 1964.

WILKINSON, R., *Mind the Gap: Hierarchies, Health and Human Evolution*, Yale, 2001.

WILKINSON, R. and Pickett, K., *The Spirit Level: Why More Equal Societies Almost Always Do Better*, London, 2010.

WILLIS, P., *Learning to Labour: How Working Class Kids Get Working Class Jobs*, Farnborough, Hants, 1977.

WILLIS, P., *Profane Culture*, London, 1978.

WILMOTT, P., *Adolescent Boys in East London*, London, 1966.

WILSON, A., *Northern Soul: Music, Drugs and Subcultural Identity*, Cullompton, 2007.

WILSON, H., 'Parental Supervision: A Neglected Aspect of Delinquency', *British Journal of Criminology*, 20 (1980).

WILSON, H. and Herbert, G., *Parents and Children in the Inner City*, London, 1978.

WILSON, J. Q., *Varieties of Police Behavior*, Cambridge, Mass. 1968.

WILSON, J. Q., *Thinking About Crime*, New York, 1975.

WILSON, J. Q. and Herrnstein, R., *Crime and Human Nature*, New York, 1985.

WILSON, J. Q. and Kelling, G., '"Broken Windows": The Police and Neighborhood Safety', *The Atlantic Monthly* (March 1982).

WILSON, J. Q., 'Hard Times, Fewer Crimes', *Wall Street Journal*, 28 May 2011.

WILSON, W., *The Truly Disadvantaged: The Inner City, The Underclass and Public Policy*, Chicago, 1987.

WILSON, W., *When Work Disappears: The World of the New Urban Poor*, New York, 1996.

WINLOW, S., *Badfellas: Crime, Tradition and New Masculinities*, Oxford, 2001.

WINLOW, S. and Hall, S., *Violent Night: Urban Leisure and Contemporary Culture*, Oxford, 2006.

WINLOW, S. et al., *Riots and Political Protest: Notes from the Post-Political Present*, London, 2014.

WING LO, T., *Corruption and Politics in Hong Kong and China*, Buckingham, 1993.

WIRTH, L., *The Ghetto*, Chicago, 1928.

WIRTH, L., 'Culture Conflict and Misconduct', in *On Cities and Social Life*, Chicago, 1964.

WIRTH, L., 'Human Ecology', in *On Cities and Social Life*, Chicago, 1964.

WIRTH, L., 'Ideological Aspects of Social Disorganization', in *On Cities and Social Life*, Chicago, 1964.

WITT, S., *How Music Got Free: The End of an Industry, the Turn of the Century, and the Patient Zero of Piracy*, New York, 2015.

WITZER, R., *Legalising Prostitution*, New York, 2012.

WOLFE, T., *Radical Chic and Mau-Mauing the Flak-Catchers*, London, 1971.

WOLFGANG, M., 'Victim-Precipitated Criminal Homicide', *Journal of Criminal Law, Criminology and Police Science*, 48:1 (1957).

WOLFGANG, M., *Patterns in Criminal Homicide*, Philadelphia, 1958.

WOLFGANG, M. and Ferracutti, F., *The Subculture of Violence*, London, 1964.

WOLFGANG, M. et al. (eds.), *The Sociology of Crime and Delinquency*, New York, 1962.

WOLFGANG, M. et al., *Delinquency in a Birth Cohort*, Chicago, 1972.

WOLFGANG, M. et al., *Evaluating Criminology*, New York, 1978.

WOOTTON, B., *Social Science and Social Pathology*, London, 1959.

WORSLEY, P., *The Trumpet Shall Sound*, London, 1957.

WRIGHT, R., 'Women as "Victims" and as "Resisters": Depictions of the Oppression of Women in Criminology Textbooks', *Teaching Sociology*, 23:2 (1995).

WRIGHT, R. and Decker, S., *Armed Robbers in Action: Stickups and Street Culture*, Boston, 1997.

WRIGHT, R., Brookman, F., and Bennett, T., 'The Foreground Dynamics of Street Robbery in Britain', *British Journal of Criminology*, 46 (2006).

WRONG, D., 'The Oversocialized Conception of Man in Modern Sociology', *American Sociological Review*, 26 (1961).

YARROW, M. et al., 'The Psychological Meaning of Mental Illness in the Family', in E. Rubington and M. Weinberg (eds.), *Deviance*, New York, 1968.

YOUNG, A., 'Feminism and the Body of Criminology', unpub. paper, 1991.

YOUNG, J., *The Drugtakers*, London, 1971.

YOUNG, J., 'The Role of the Police as Amplifiers of Deviancy', in S. Cohen, (ed.), *Images of Deviance*, Harmondsworth, 1971.

YOUNG, J., 'Working Class Criminology', in I. Taylor, P. Walton, and J. Young (eds.), *Critical Criminology*, London, 1975.

YOUNG, J., 'Mass Media, Drugs and Deviance', in P. Rock and M. McIntosh (eds.), *Deviance and Social Control*, London, 1974.

YOUNG, J., 'Left Idealism, Reformism and Beyond', in R. Fine et al. (eds.), *Capitalism and the Rule of Law*, London, 1979.

YOUNG, J., 'Murder Most English', *Time Out*, 14-21 January, 856, (1987).

YOUNG, J., 'Incessant Chatter: Recent Paradigms in Criminology', in M. Maguire, R. Morgan, and R. Reiner (eds.), *Oxford Handbook of Criminology*, Oxford, 1994.

YOUNG, J., 'Left Realist Criminology', in M. Maguire, et al. (eds.), *The Oxford Handbook of Criminology*, Oxford, 1997.

YOUNG, J., 'From Inclusive to Exclusive Society', in V. Ruggiero, et al. (eds.), *The New European Criminology*, London, 1998.

YOUNG, J., *The Exclusive Society*, London, 1999.

YOUNG, J., 'Crime and the Dialectics of Inclusion/Exclusion', *The British Journal of Criminology*, 44 (2004).

YOUNG, J., *The Vertigo of Late Modernity*, Thousand Oaks, Calif., 2007.

YOUNG, J., 'Moral Panic: Its Origins in Resistance, Ressentiment and the Translation of Fantasy into Reality', British Journal of Criminology, 49 (2009).

YOUNG, J., *The Criminological Imagination*, Cambridge, 2011.

YOUNG, P., *The Pilgrims of Russian Town*, Chicago, 1932.

YOUSAF, K. et al., *Young Teenagers and Crime*, Glasgow, 1991.

ZANDER, M., 'What is the Evidence on Law and Order?', *New Society*, 3 December 1979.

ZEDNER, L., *Women, Crime and Custody in Victorian England*, Oxford, 1991.

ZEDNER, L., 'Victims', in M. Maguire et al. (eds.), *The Oxford Handbook* of *Criminology*, Oxford, 2002.

ZIMRING, F., *The Great American Crime Decline*, New York, 2007.

ZIMRING, F. and Hawkins, G., 'The Growth of Imprisonment in California', *British Journal of Criminology*, Special Issue 34 (1994).

ZIPFEL T., 'Broadwater Farm Estate, Haringey: Background and Information Relating to the Riot on Sunday, 6th October 1985', unpub.

ZIPFEL T., 'Hard Work Transforms a Nightmare Estate', *Peptalk*, 2 (1985).

ZORBAUGH, H., *The Gold Coast and the Slum*, Chicago, 1929.

Index

Printed and bound by CPI Group (UK) Ltd, Croydon, CR0 4YY